Turning Point

Other Titles by Dick B.

Dr. Bob's Library: Books for Twelve Step Growth

Anne Smith's Journal, 1933-1939: A.A.'s Principles of Success

Design for Living: The Oxford Group's Contribution to Early A.A.

The Akron Genesis of Alcoholics Anonymous

New Light on Alcoholism: The A.A. Legacy from Sam Shoemaker

The Books Early AAs Read for Spiritual Growth

Courage to Change (with Bill Pittman)

The Good Book and The Big Book: A.A.'s Roots in the Bible

That Amazing Grace: The Role of Clarence and Grace S. in Alcoholics Anonymous

Good Morning! Quiet Time, Morning Watch, Meditation and Early A.A.

Turning Point

A History of Early A.A.'s Spiritual Roots and Successes

Dick B.

With a Foreword by Paul Wood, Ph.D.

Paradise Research Publications
San Rafael, California

Paradise Research Publications, 247 Bret Harte Rd., San Rafael, CA 94901

Published 1997
Printed in the United States of America
This Paradise Research Publications Edition is published by arrangement with Good Book Publishing Company, P.O. Box 959, Kihei, Maui, HI 96753-0959

Cover Design by Richard Rose, Sun Lithographic Arts

Publisher's Cataloging in Publication

B., Dick
    Turning point : a history of early A.A.'s spiritual roots and successes / Dick B.
    with a foreword by Paul Wood, Ph.D., President, National Council on Alcoholism and Drug Dependence, Inc.
        p. cm.
        Includes bibliographical references, index, and appendices.
        Preassigned LCCN: 96-92645
        ISBN: 1-885803-07-9

    1. Alcoholics Anonymous--History. 2. Oxford Group--Influence. 3. Bible--Influence. 4. Shoemaker, Samuel M. (Samuel Moor), 1893-1963. 5. Smith, Anne, 1891-1949. I. Title

HV5278.B34 1996   362.29'286

Self-surrender has been and always must be regarded as the vital turning-point of the religious life, so far as the religious life is spiritual and no affair of outer works and ritual and sacraments.

William James, *The Varieties of Religious Experience*

What you want is simply a vital religious experience. You need to find God. You need Jesus Christ. . . . Conversion is the only means by which a radically bad person can be changed into a radically good person. It is thus a breach, a breaking off, a turning, a change. . . . William James speaks with great emphasis upon this crisis of self-surrender. He says . . . "Self-surrender has always been and always must be regarded as the vital turning point. . . ."

Rev. Samuel M. Shoemaker, Jr., *Realizing Religion*

But there is One who has all power—That One is God. May you find Him now! Half measures availed us nothing. We stood at the turning point. We asked His protection and care with complete abandon. Here are the steps we took, which are suggested as a Program of Recovery.

Alcoholics Anonymous, First Edition

Contents

Foreword

Bill W. once told an audience, "We alcoholics were looking for the spirit, but we went to the wrong address." The premise of Dick B.'s massive body of work is that many alcoholics are still going to the wrong address, misinformed on the true spiritual nature of Alcoholics Anonymous. Dick has worked patiently and thoroughly, for over six years, to restore the street signs and roadmarkers so that these pilgrims may find their way to the spiritual homestead of their great movement.

Dick first contacted me when he was working on one of his earliest titles. During our meeting, he took me down the street from our office to Calvary Episcopal Church where the Reverend Sam Shoemaker held forth in A.A.'s formative years. It was there that Rowland Hazard, Ebby Thacher, and Bill Wilson spent some of the earliest months of their sobriety. Because of that trip to the Calvary Episcopal Church, I read the biography of Dr. Frank Buchman, founder of the Oxford Group, and began to study the roots of recovery—beginning with Dr. Carl Jung's historic suggestion to Rowland Hazard that Hazard attempt to overcome his alcoholism via a spiritual experience. My own spiritual life has been deepened and broadened by reading Dick B.'s books and other works that they suggest.

Carl Jung wrote to Bill W. that he [Jung] had come to feel that alcoholism was the result of a void in a person's life where the spirit was intended to dwell. If that can be true of organizations as well as people—and I believe it can—Dick B. is doing a great service by filling a spiritual void with sound scholarship and dedicated devotion to the principle that "God as I understand Him" means giving as much of myself to as much of God as I understand.

PAUL WOOD, Ph.D., President
National Council on Alcoholism and Drug Dependence, Inc.

Preface

This title marks the consummation of six years of travel, interviews, and research. It puts in one place, augments, and updates materials presented in somewhat more detail in my ten, previously published titles. Its objective is to present accurate, detailed, historical evidence. Evidence that demonstrates what early AAs borrowed from the Bible, Christianity, and religion. Principles and practices that enabled them to fashion a *spiritual program of recovery* from alcoholism *and* a *design for living* in harmony with the will of God. The work draws heavily on the Big Book's First Edition (published in 1939) *and* on earlier manuscripts and papers written by Bill W. himself. The latter are located at Bill's home at Stepping Stones and are virtually unknown to AAs today.

Our introductory chapter illustrates how little research and writing has been done by others in this spiritual history area and what the consequences of that historical gap have been. Part One of the work (titled *A Spiritual Program for Drunks*) covers two aspects of A.A.'s spiritual roots: Chapter Two points to the nature of A First Century Christian Fellowship (later also known as the Oxford Group) which provided A.A. with the recovery *structure* for its program. Chapter Three details A.A.'s *dual beginnings* (in Switzerland and in Akron) that actually produced the A.A. Fellowship and its spiritual program of recovery.

Part Two (titled *The Good Book Source*) treats the specific principles early AAs borrowed for their program from the Bible. A.A.'s co-founders Dr. Robert Smith and Bill Wilson both stated A.A. was based on the philosophy in Jesus's Sermon on the

Mount. Dr. Bob said A.A. got its basic ideas from its study of the Bible—which Dr. Bob and Bill called the "Good Book." Several of our chapters therefore cover the precise biblical ideas on which A.A. is founded—ideas about God; major ideas taken from the Sermon on the Mount, 1 Corinthians 13, and the Book of James; quotes and paraphrases from the Bible; and the impact of these and other biblical segments on A.A.'s Twelve Steps, basic text, and fellowship.

Bill Wilson declared that the principles underlying A.A.'s Twelve Steps were borrowed primarily from the Oxford Group. Hence Part Three (titled *The Oxford Group's Contribution*) details twenty-eight major Oxford Group ideas that impacted upon A.A.— and where they can be found in A.A.'s Big Book, Steps, and Fellowship. Bill Wilson always tried to tie A.A.'s Oxford Group debt the teachings of the Reverend Sam Shoemaker, rector of Calvary Episcopal Church in New York; and Shoemaker *was* a major Oxford Group leader in America. Plenty will therefore be found in our work as to the precise teachings of Sam Shoemaker that contributed to A.A. ideas.

Other sources of A.A.'s spiritual ideas have been given short historical shrift. For example, Bill Wilson called Dr. Bob's wife, Anne Smith, the "Mother of A.A." and a "Founder of A.A." Yet her enormous contribution has been virtually ignored. But not by this title! Part Four (titled *Other Spiritual Sources*) presents much on Anne Smith and the spiritual journal she wrote and shared with early AAs. There is also a chapter on the immense number of religious books Dr. Bob studied and recommended to early AAs for their spiritual recovery and growth. Until the author's research, these materials had never really been the subject of study. Finally, "Quiet Time" (and the Bible study, spiritual reading, prayer, and "listening" it involved) are thoroughly covered in a chapter on this additional A.A. spiritual source.

Part Five (titled *History to the Rescue*) was written to provide a helpful tool for many individuals and groups. It will be of value to AAs, Al-Anons, their families, and other Twelve Step programs. To church and clergy. To therapists and counselors. To the medical and psychological professions. To scholars and historians. And to government agencies concerned with problems of alcoholism and addiction. For Chapter Fourteen assembles and summarizes A.A.'s diverse spiritual roots. It abstracts where they are found exemplified in the Twelve Steps and A.A. writings. Chapter Fifteen indicates ways to fill the large, existing, historical void—in part through the author's previous research and publications, in part through this comprehensive historical work, and in part through further work by those who dare to pick up the ball and run with it hereafter.

There is a critical need for details on the history of early A.A.'s spiritual roots and successes. These specifics can give hope to those presently in Twelve Step programs. They can provide understanding of language and ideas even AAs themselves do not fully comprehend today. They can enlighten professionals in the same area. They can offer a bridge to A.A. to those in the religious community who wonder where A.A. came from, and why it seems so distant from church doors and Bible stores. They can help those who deal with the many who seem lost in Twelve Step programs and can't seem to connect those programs with their own beliefs in God, the Bible, and Christianity.

Acknowledgements

So many have contributed to our research and writing that we refer the reader to our other titles for detailed acknowledgements. Here we will mention: (1) Those who read this manuscript for accuracy and detail. (2) Those who provided major historical evidence pertinent to specific components of A.A.'s spiritual roots.

My son Ken heads the list because of the time he has spent researching, editing, traveling, and handling computer aspects. Mrs. Walter Shipley and Steve F. reviewed several chapters. Oxford Group authority K. D. Belden reviewed the second chapter on the Oxford Group. A.A. historian Mel B. commented on details in chapter three. Previously, biblical comment and review were contributed by my son Ken; by Clarence S.'s widow, Grace; and by several of Clarence and Grace's sponsees (Steve F., Mitch K., Carol M., Dale M., John S., and Danny W.). Frank Buchman's biographer Garth Lean and Lean's colleague Michael Hutchinson (both deceased) reviewed the Oxford Group material drawn from our title *Design for Living*. So did Oxford Group activists James Houck, T. Willard Hunter, Jim and Ellie Newton, L. Parks Shipley, Sr., and George Vondermuhll, Jr. The Akron evidence could not have been presented without the early help of the Seiberling children (John, Dorothy, and Mary). The material on Dr. Bob and Anne would not have been available without help from their family (Sue Smith Windows and Bob and Betty Smith). And the Quiet Time material was enhanced by a host of Oxford Group survivors who answered questionnaires and contributed resources. Our title *Good Morning!: Quiet Time, Morning Watch, Meditation, and Early A.A.* contains their names.

1

The Lacuna

A Critical Historical Void

Webster's tells us a *lacuna* is "a blank space or a missing part: GAP." And recently, a scholarly Roman Catholic priest endorsed one of our titles on early A.A.'s spiritual roots, saying:

> Though there have been excellent histories of A.A.'s beginning years, each and corporately, have left one major lacuna—the precise origins of A.A.'s spiritual principles.[1]

---

[1] The priest was Father Paul B., M.A., Ph.D., Roman Catholic Diocese of Kansas City, Missouri. Among the more important histories are A.A.'s "Conference Approved" *Alcoholics Anonymous Comes of Age: A Brief History of A.A.* (New York: Alcoholics Anonymous World Services, Inc., 1957); *Alcoholics Anonymous: The Story of How More than One Hundred Men Have Recovered from Alcoholism (New York City: Works Publishing Company, 1939); Alcoholics Anonymous, 3rd ed. (New York: Alcoholics Anonymous World Services, 1976); DR. BOB and the Good Oldtimers: A Biography, with Recollections of Early A.A. in the Midwest* (New York: Alcoholics Anonymous World Services, Inc., 1980); *Pass It On: The Story of Bill Wilson and How the A.A. Message Reached the World* (New York: Alcoholics Anonymous World Services, 1984). Non-conference approved histories include Robert Thomsen, *Bill W.* (New York: Harper & Row Publishers, 1975); *Lois Remembers: Memoirs of the Co-founder of Al-Anon and Wife of the Co-founder of Alcoholics Anonymous* (New York: Al-Anon Family Group Headquarters, Inc., 1979); Ernest Kurtz, *Not-God: A History of Alcoholics Anonymous*, exp. ed. (Center City, MN: Hazelden, 1991); Mel B., *New Wine, The Spiritual Roots of the Twelve Step Miracle* (Center City, MN: Hazelden, 1991; Nell Wing, *Grateful to Have Been There: My 42 Years with Bill and Lois, and the Evolution of Alcoholics*

(continued...)

1

Many have come to believe this gap has resulted in unfortunate consequences for today's A.A. fellowship and recovery program.

For one thing, historians today often characterize A.A. as "spiritual rather than religious."[2] Much of A.A.'s own literature today contains similar phrases.[3] And these descriptions have sometimes caused A.A.'s spiritual program to be described in new and totally different ways. One recent commentary, for example, defines A.A.'s *spirituality* as the spirituality of *imperfection*—"a spirituality aware first of *its own* imperfection."[4]

Yet that is not the way A.A.'s co-founder Bill Wilson spoke of spirituality as he penned the First Edition of A.A.'s basic text—the *Big Book*—in 1938.[5] For Bill wrote:

> We never apologize to anyone for depending upon our Creator. We can laugh at those who think spirituality the way of weakness. Paradoxically, it is the way of strength. . . . All men of faith have courage. They trust their God. We never apologize for God (p. 81).

In the foregoing phrases, Bill defined spirituality as having to do with dependence upon our Creator; trust in our God; and reliance upon that God (rather than self) for power, strength, and courage. Bill's focus then was not on *imperfection*. It was on the fact that *real alcoholics* are beyond human aid and, without a doubt, "100%

---

[1] (...continued)
Anonymous (Illinois: Parkside Publishing Corporation, 1992); and Bob Smith and Sue Smith Windows, *Children of the Healer: The Story of Dr. Bob's Kids* (Illinois: Parkside Publishing Corporation, 1992).

[2] See, for example, Kurtz, *Not-God*, pp. 175-78; Ernest Kurtz and Kathryn Ketcham, *The Spirituality of Imperfection: Modern Wisdom from Classic Stories* (New York: Bantam Books, 1992), pp. 24-25; Mel B., *New Wine*, p. 5.

[3] See, for example, *Questions & Answers on Sponsorship* (New York: Alcoholics Anonymous World Services, 1983), p. 23.

[4] Kurtz and Ketcham, *The Spirituality of Imperfection*, p. 25.

[5] "Big Book" is the name AAs have affectionately given to their basic text *Alcoholics Anonymous*. *Big Book*˙ is a registered trademark of Alcoholics Anonymous World Services, Inc. It is used here to refer to all editions of A.A.'s basic text.

hopeless, apart from Divine help."[6] In the Big Book's First Edition, Bill said:

> For we are now on a different basis; the basis of trusting and relying upon God. We trust infinite God rather than our finite selves (p. 80).

In a subsequent letter, Bill added:

> For myself, of late years, I am finding it much easier to believe that God made man, than that man made God.[7]

In researching early A.A.'s spiritual thinking, the author has concluded that the farther one travels toward early A.A., the less confusion he or she finds as to the meaning of words like *God*, *Spirit*, *religion*, and *spiritual*. The greater the abyss between yesterday and today, the greater has been the AA's inclination to fashion his or her own *god* and *spirituality*, instead of letting *God* tell man about God and things spiritual. And this has led inexorably to a confusion of which God is not the author.[8] To make the point, a distinguished A.A. historian—still active in the Fellowship, and with many years of sobriety—said of today's A.A.:

> If pressed for what the program's actual definition of *spiritual* is, however, it's doubtful that many A.A. members could explain.[9]

Contrast with this present-day dilemma the kind of understanding of A.A. and religion that seemed quite clear to one of early A.A.'s most ardently sought-after endorsers. In his 1939 book review of

---

[6] Big Book, First Edition, p. 55; and, as to real alcoholics, see pp. 41-42,

[7] *As Bill Sees It: The A.A. Way of Life...Selected Writings of A.A.'s Co-founder* (New York: Alcoholics Anonymous World Services, 1967), p. 73.

[8] See 1 Corinthians 14:33: "For God is not *the author* of confusion . . ."

[9] Mel B., *New Wine*, p. 5.

Alcoholics Anonymous, the famous preacher and writer Dr. Harry Emerson Fosdick said:

> The core of their whole procedure is religious. [And, later, in his autobiography, Dr. Fosdick added:] Moreover, these testimonies [in the *Grapevine*, A.A.'s official journal] bear witness to religion's reality, for Alcoholics Anonymous is deeply religious.[10]

And the author is convinced that today's confusion over A.A.'s spirituality is due largely to a lack of specific information about A.A.'s own spiritual roots. A void that has meant that neither AAs nor commentators on A.A. can agree on what A.A. *is* from a theological standpoint.

But the real spiritual problem in today's A. A. Fellowship is not just a concern over whether A.A. is spiritual or religious or with present-day definitions of *spirituality*. The real problem has to do with the nature and ingredients of A.A.'s *spiritual solution* to alcoholism, as it has come to be viewed. Words and phrases common in A.A. terminology—words and phrases which originally referred to God Almighty, the Creator (Who had the power needed for a spiritual solution)—have taken on new Twelve Step meanings. Phrases such as "Higher Power," "Power greater than ourselves," and "God as we understood Him" have opened the door to totally confusing and sometimes completely absurd names for the "power." Some AAs today, and many well-wishers outside of A.A., have sought help from some peculiar, and supposed deity, which one writer proclaimed could simply be "that which keeps me sober." But such a "power" could then even include both paraldehyde and antabuse, deterrents which—though common at various times in the treatment of alcoholism—have nothing to do with the design for living, the spiritual experience, recovered

---

[10] *A.A. Comes of Age*, pp. 323-24. Note that both quotes are from an A.A. Conference Approved title.

spiritual life which A.A. originally offerred its adherents through the power of God on which it relied.

The lack of understanding of words which originally pertained to the God of the Bible in early A.A. has led to all kinds of unusual ideas in recovery center, therapy, and Twelve Step jargon today. You can often hear or read about an "any god" that is supposed to exist in what have unfortunately come to be described today as "self-help" programs.[11] AAs, historians, and recovery literature frequently refer to today's "higher power" as "Him, Her, or It." As a "lightbulb," a "rock," a "chair," a "doorknob," a "tree," or a "bulldozer." As the "Group," a "Group Of Drunks," "Good Orderly Direction," "Good," the "Big Dipper," the "man upstairs." And even as "Ralph." The author has personally heard and/or read all these appellations. So have many other AAs and writers. And the names and phrases can quickly be found in today's "recovery" literature.[12]

For now, let's look at the following quotes from some current A.A. Conference Approved pamphlets:

> While some members [of A.A.] prefer to call this Power "God," we were told that this was purely a matter of personal interpretation; we could conceive of the Power in any terms we thought fit.

> Some choose the A.A. group as their "Higher Power;" some look to God—*as they understand Him*; and others rely upon entirely different concepts.

> Some alcoholics choose to consider the A.A. group itself as the power greater than themselves; for many others, this power is

---

[11] Compare *Alcoholics Anonymous*, pp. 43, 45, 46: "As to two of you men, whose stories I have heard, there is no doubt in my mind that you were 100% hopeless apart from *divine help* [italics added]. . . . We had to find a power by which we could live, and it had to be a *Power greater than ourselves*. . . . And it means, of course, that we are going to talk about God. . . . even though it was impossible for any of us to fully define or comprehend that Power, which is God."

[12] In Chapter Four, we document specific examples of these many usages.

God—*as they individually understand Him*; still others rely upon entirely different concepts of a Higher Power.

However, everyone defines this power as he or she wishes. Many people call *it* God, others think *it* is the A.A. group, still others don't believe in *it* at all (italics added).

Most men and women who have been in A.A. for more than a few months recognize that its program is based on spiritual principles. At the same time, they appreciate that some alcoholics have been able to achieve and maintain sobriety without any belief in a personal Higher Power.

Some sponsors talk about the program in a more spiritual way than others do. But nearly all call attention to the source of strength to be found in "a Power greater than ourselves." Again, the sponsor points out, it is up to the newcomer to determine what that A.A. phrase means. It expresses an idea that people of many faiths—or of no particular faith—can and do accept with complete harmony.[13]

It is the author's own experience that many of us who come into A.A. are very sick—physically, mentally, emotionally, and spiritually. The First Edition of A.A.'s basic text, *Alcoholics Anonymous* (which most of us affectionately call the "Big Book"), states in the Foreword: "Many do not comprehend that the alcoholic is a very sick person" (p. vii).

To which the author would add: "Sick—desperate, searching, gullible; yet not devoid of all reasoning power." Upon hearing in an A.A. meeting that one's "higher power" could be a *rock*, one of the author's A.A. sponsees remarked the he needed *divine help,*

---

[13] The quotes are all from pamphlets published (or, in one instance, approved) by Alcoholics Anonymous World Services. In the order quoted, and with date of publication and page quoted, they are: (1) *This is AA: An Introduction to the AA Recovery Program,* 1984, p. 15; (2) *Members of the Clergy Ask About Alcoholics Anonymous,* Revised, 1992, p. 13; (3) *44 Questions,* 1952, p. 19; (4) *A Newcomer Asks,* England, n.d., p. 4; (5) *Questions & Answers on Sponsorship,* 1976, pp. 23, 17.

not geological help. Another, commenting on the statement that "god" could be a *tree*, said that he too needed *divine help*, not the help of a *stump*. And many times, when a person has said to the author that an "higher power" could be a chair, the author has invited that person to get down off his or her chair, get on his or her knees, and pray to the chair. And that settles the matter for that particular person on the spot, usually with no further comment.

However, the problem in the historical void is not disposed of that easily. For the newcomer *is* usually very sick and confused. He or she *is* often seizing whatever concept is offered; and he or she *does* very often appropriate the simple, and sometimes ridiculous, appellations handed out so liberally by well-meaning, but historically uninformed, elders and counselors. For days, months, and years, an AA may remain in what A.A. co-founder Bill Wilson often called "a spiritual kindergarten."[14] The Reverend Sam Shoemaker (from whom Bill Wilson said A.A. got most of its spiritual ideas)—rector of the Calvary Episcopal Church in New York—frequently decried self-made religion, half-baked prayers, and absurd names for God. These, Shoemaker pointed out, led to spiritual *misery*; not to the vital religious or conversion *experience* upon which A.A.'s Twelve Step recovery program is grounded.

There is much more to the gap. Biblical descriptions of God—which are liberally sprinkled through A.A.'s Big Book—often go unrecognized for what they are. Examples are *Creator*, *Maker*, *Father*, and *Spirit*. Biblical quotes in the Big Book such as "Thy will be done," "faith without works is dead," and "love thy neighbor as thyself" go unexplained as to source and meaning. This gives rise to all manner of private and personal interpretation which cannot be termed helpful.[15] A.A.'s founders borrowed

---

[14] As an example, *As Bill Sees It* states: "We are only operating a spiritual kindergarten . . ." (p. 95).

[15] Compare 2 Peter 1:20: "Knowing this first, that no prophecy of the scripture is of any private interpretation."

some 200 words and phrases from Sam Shoemaker and the Oxford Group (originally known as "A First Century Christian Fellowship").[16] Yet this language is used without source attribution and today has often been given new, special, often diverse, and unintended meanings when examined out of context and without reference to the Oxford Group's "practical program of action" upon which the Twelve Steps are based.

We will see more. But the most important historical void in A.A. has to do with the Bible itself. Many in today's A.A. are scared to death to mention the Bible. The author has personally seen instances of attempts to ban the bringing of a Bible into an A.A. meeting, of demands that the name Jesus Christ never be mentioned in a meeting, and of statements that A.A. left the Bible behind in Akron over fifty years ago. In fact, one oldtimer just recently said at a meeting the author attended that AAs no longer refer to the Bible because "the Bible didn't work."

One historian wrote:

> Yet A.A.'s total omission of "Jesus," its toning down of even "God" to "a Higher Power" which could be the group itself, and its changing of the *verbal* first message into hopeless helplessness rather than salvation: these ideas and practices, adopted to avoid any "religious" association, were profound changes.[17]

Indeed they were!

The *profound changes* have left A.A., some sixty years later, with an almost total historical vacuum concerning its religious, Christian, and Bible roots. Many AAs today simply do not know the basic deliverance ideas their founders took from the Bible and upon which their recovery program is based. The *changes* have meant that countless AAs today are devoid of conviction as to the accuracy and integrity of the recovery ideas their successful forebears borrowed *from* the Bible. You can hear such opinions

---

[16] See Appendix 2.

[17] Kurtz, *Not-God*, p. 50.

quite often in today's meetings. The *changes* have also offered today's AAs complete license to tailor to their own liking jerry-built theological ideas. Ideas which were an almost predictable outcome of what Bill Wilson's wife Lois styled "a universal spiritual program, not a specific religious one, since all drunks were not Christian."[18]

The author questions both the practicality and existence of the "universal" program of which Lois Wilson spoke. More important, such a program, if it ever existed, defies the spiritual learning and experience of centuries. It invites atheists, agnostics, critics, and skeptics to do their own thing, both personally and at the publication level, in the A.A. literature of today. All of which leads to A.A. co-founder Dr. Bob's personal story in the First Edition of A.A.'s Big Book:

> If you think you are an atheist, an agnostic, a skeptic, or have any other form of intellectual pride which keeps you from accepting what is in this book, I feel sorry for you. . . . Your Heavenly Father will never let you down (p. 193)!

And Dr. Bob was not speaking of a lightbulb, a tree, or a group when he referred to "Your Heavenly Father."

Before we move on, however, there is a *caveat*. We will mention it here and discuss it in detail in our concluding chapters. The caveat is this: There certainly are AAs today who have remained abstinent for many years without following either Dr. Bob's suggestion or the path to a relationship with God which is the subject of the Big Book's recovery program.

First of all, the only requirement for "membership" in today's A.A. is a "desire to stop drinking"—*not* a belief in God. Also, there *are* people in A.A. today who are atheists, agnostics, former church members, or believers in some non-Christian religion. Further, there are many who *do* talk about an "higher power" which is most assuredly not the Almighty God of the Bible. Many

---

[18] *Lois Remembers*, p. 113.

do assert that A.A. is "spiritual" and not "religious." Finally, in today's A.A. meetings one will often hear an oldtimer tell the newcomer: Just "don't drink, and go to meetings." Or, "just put the plug in the jug." Or, "Your higher power can be the 'group' or 'Good Orderly Direction,' 'Group of Drunks,' or 'anything that is more powerful than yourself.'"

Second, there is a school of thinking which takes its cue from the Reverend Sam Shoemaker and Professor Williams James—both called "founders of A.A." by Bill Wilson. The school might be called the "act-as-if" group. Or certainly the "experiment-of-faith" adherents. Paraphrasing Immanuel Kant, Professor Williams James wrote:

> We can act *as if* there were a God; feel *as if* we were free; consider Nature *as if* she were full of special designs; lay plans *as if* we were to be immortal; and we find then that these words do make a genuine difference in our moral life. . . . So we have the strange phenomenon, as Kant assures us, of a mind believing with all its strength in the real presence of a set of things of no one of which it can form any notion whatever.[19]

Shoemaker put the "act as if" experiment this way:

> How did this man "get religion?" *By acting as if he had faith*—until, indeed, there was an opening for God to come through. Faith is primarily a kind of expectant loyalty toward God, life and the universe, and only secondarily an intellectual conviction. It is much more like falling in love than like adopting a philosophy. In its earlier stages, the finding of faith may be much like a scientific experiment. . . . Some will say, "But isn't it hypocrisy to 'act as if' when you really don't believe at all?" My answer is that it is not hypocrisy for a scientist to regard a hypothesis as true long enough to prove that it is or is not. A real

---

[19] James, *The Varieties of Religious Experience*, p. 56.

experiment, entered into with an honest and open mind, is an avenue to truth.[20]

Undeniably, some AAs adopt this approach. Some are still traversing that "avenue of truth" *and* have not had a drink in years. Some attend scads of meetings. As Bill Wilson saw it, many may be on the path *to* believing, and may yet come to believe *in God*. But we write with the firm conviction that the program of recovery developed by Bill W. and Dr. Bob in the 1930's was based on the premise stated in the "a,b,c's" of the Big Book—"that probably no human power could relieve us of our alcoholism;" and that "God could and would if He were sought."

Note also that the "God" reference in the "a,b,c's" is not merely to God as the Power that can relieve the alcoholic from his or her obsession to drink. The reference is to alcohol*ism*—the underlying malady from which alcoholics must be delivered if they are to recover. And if any "power" other than God could have accomplished that deliverance, Bill Wilson would not have commenced the Big Book with the endorsement of Bill's friend and physician Dr. William Duncan Silkworth—"the benign little doctor who loved drunks." For it was Dr. Silkworth's opinion, based on his own experience in working with some 50,000 real alcoholics (and confirmed, then, by the opinion of most of the medical profession), that medicine alone was not the answer to alcoholism.

The Generalities and Credits

Bill Wilson's Credits to the Oxford Group and Sam Shoemaker

A.A.'s own commentaries are *not lacking in applause* for A.A.'s spiritual mentors. The commentaries are *lacking in specifics*. To

---

[20] Samuel M. Shoemaker, "'Act As If—': The First Step toward Faith," A *Reader's Digest* Reprint, condensed from *Christian Herald* (October, 1954), p. 155. See also S. M. Shoemaker, *How to Find God* (New York, Faith at Work, n.d.), p. 6; *Sam Shoemaker at His Best* (New York: Faith at Work, 1964), pp. 25, 77.

see that AAs did not fall short in attributing spiritual success to spiritual sources, let's start with various statements Bill Wilson made at one time or another about A.A.'s origins:

A.A. was not invented![21]

Nobody invented Alcoholics Anonymous.[22]

As a society we must never become so vain as to suppose that we have been the authors and inventors of a new religion. We will humbly reflect that each of A.A.'s principles, *every one of them*, has been borrowed from ancient sources [italics in original].[23]

Having now accounted for AA's Steps One and Twelve, it is natural that we should ask, "Where did the early AAs find the material for the remaining ten Steps? Where did we learn about moral inventory, amends for harms done, turning our wills and lives over to God? Where did we learn about meditation and prayer and all the rest of it?" The spiritual substance of our remaining ten Steps came straight from Dr. Bob's and my own earlier association with the Oxford Groups, as they were then led in America by that Episcopal rector, Dr. Samuel Shoemaker.[24]

Every river has a wellspring at its source. AA is like that too. In the beginning, there was a spring which poured out of a clergyman, Dr. Samuel Shoemaker. 'Way back in 1934 he began to teach us the principles and attitudes that afterward came to full flower in AA's Twelve Steps for recovery.[25]

The early A.A. got its ideas of self-examination, acknowledgment of character defects, restitution for harm done, and working with others straight from the Oxford Groups and directly from Sam

---

[21] *As Bill Sees It*, p. 67.
[22] *The Language of the Heart: Bill W.'s Grapevine Writings* (New York: The AA Grapevine, Inc., 1988), p. 202.
[23] *A.A. Comes of Age*, p. 231.
[24] *The Language of the Heart*, p. 298.
[25] *The Language of the Heart*, p. 177.

Shoemaker, their former leader in America, and from nowhere else.[26]

I recalled that preacher Sam [Shoemaker] probably had a lot to do with the vital spiritual experience that was my first gift of faith. He had also taught me principles by which I could survive and carry on.[27]

Though I [Bill] wish the "co-founder" tag had never been hitched to any of us, I have no hesitancy in adding your [Sam Shoemaker's] name to the list.[28]

I am always glad to say privately that some of the Oxford Group presentation and emphasis on the Christian message saved my life.[29]

The basic principles which the Oxford Groupers had taught were ancient and universal ones, the common property of mankind.[30]

Now that Frank Buchman [the founder of the Oxford Group] is gone and I realize more than ever what we owe to him, I wish I had sought him out in recent years to tell him of our appreciation.[31]

To these statements, A.A.'s Conference Approved biography of Bill Wilson (*Pass It On*) added:

Criticism and rejection notwithstanding, Lois and Bill [Wilson] did not become immediately disillusioned with the Oxford Group or with its principles, from which Bill borrowed freely (p. 169).

---

[26] *A.A. Comes of Age*, p. 39.

[27] *The Language of the Heart*, p. 178.

[28] Dick B., *New Light on Alcoholism: The A.A. Legacy from Sam Shoemaker* (Corte Madera, CA: Good Book Publishing Company, 1994), p. 3.

[29] *Pass It On*, p. 171.

[30] *A.A. Comes of Age*, p. 39.

[31] *Pass It On*, p. 387.

"I [Bill Wilson] had to ask myself which was the more important: that the O.G. [Oxford Group] receive credit and that I have the pleasure of so discharging my debt of gratitude, or that alcoholics everywhere have the best possible chance to stay alive regardless of who gets the credit" (p. 173).

Bill's first three steps were culled from his reading of James [Professor William James], the teachings of Sam Shoemaker, and those of the Oxford Group (p. 199).

Bill was about to write the famous fifth chapter [of the Big Book], "How It Works." The basic material for the chapter was the word-of-mouth program that Bill had been talking ever since his own recovery. It was heavy with Oxford Group principles (pp. 196-97).

While Bill was always generous in recognizing A.A.'s debt to the Oxford Group, he would always tie the Oxford Group connection to Dr. Shoemaker (p. 174).

A.A.'s Conference Approved biography of Dr. Bob (*DR. BOB and the Good Oldtimers*) said the following:

This was the beginning of A.A.'s "flying-blind period." They had the Bible, and they had the precepts of the Oxford Group. They also had their own instincts. They were working, or working out, the A.A. program—the Twelve Steps—without quite knowing how they were doing it (p. 96).

In *Bill W.*, Wilson's own biographer, Robert Thomsen, summed up as follows:

They [Bill and Bob] had both wound up trying to give shape and meaning to their lives by adhering to the excruciatingly high standards of the Oxford Group (p. 239).

Indeed, all the principles, all the foundation stones of the structure he [Bill] and Bob were trying to shape, had come directly from Sam Shoemaker's Oxford Group (p. 161).

By the time she [Lois Wilson] returned to Brooklyn [from Akron where Bill had been living with Dr. Bob and Anne Smith all the summer of 1935] all four of them [Bill and his wife Lois and Bob and his wife Anne] were agreed that their efforts to find a practical program of recovery must be given top priority. They were agreed, but it was not an easy project (p. 249).

But fortunately again—or so Bill and Bob believed at the time—there was the Oxford Group with its dynamic course of action all mapped out. They tried to base everything they did, every step they took toward formulating their program, on Oxford Group principles (p. 249).

Emphasis on the Bible by Dr. Bob and A.A.'s Akron Pioneers

A.A.'s co-founder, Dr. Bob, always emphasized the importance of the Bible to A.A.'s program. And, but for the fact that *all* of A.A.'s spiritual sources emphasized the Bible as the source of their principles and practices, you might conclude from the following statements by A.A. co-founder Dr. Bob that Dr. Bob was talking about entirely different A.A. origins than those of which Bill spoke. For Dr. Bob made it crystal clear that A.A.'s roots were planted firmly in what Dr. Bob and Bill *both* called the *Good Book*.

Here are some of Dr. Bob's remarks about the Good Book, as they are set forth in A.A.'s Conference Approved literature:

When we [Bill and Dr. Bob] started in on Bill D. [A.A.# 3], we had no Twelve Steps, either; we had no Traditions. But we were convinced that the answer to our problems was in the Good Book. To some of us older ones, the parts that we found absolutely

essential were the Sermon on the Mount, the thirteenth chapter of
First Corinthians, and the Book of James.[32]

It wasn't until 1938 that the teachings and efforts and studies that
had been going on were crystallized in the form of the Twelve
Steps. . . . We already had the basic ideas, though not in terse
and tangible form. We got them, as I said, as a result of our study
of the Good Book.[33]

In a rare record of Dr. Bob's remarks at a Youngstown, Ohio,
luncheon, Bob is quoted as stating:

Members of Alcoholics Anonymous begin the day with a prayer
for strength and a short period of Bible reading. They find the
basic messages they need in the *Sermon on the Mount*, in
Corinthians and the Book of James.[34]

A pamphlet published by "AA of Akron" and commissioned by
Dr. Bob as a guide for beginners and sponsors said this:

There is the Bible that you haven't opened for years. Get
acquainted with it. Read it with an open mind. You will find
things that will amaze you. You will be convinced that certain
passages were written with you in mind. Read the Sermon on the
Mount (Matthew V, VI, and VII). Read St. Paul's inspired essay
on love (I Corinthians XIII). Read the Book of James. Read the
Twenty-third and Ninety-first Psalms. These readings are brief but
so important.[35]

---

[32] *The Co-founders of Alcoholics Anonymous: Biographical Sketches Their last Major
Talks* (New York: Alcoholics Anonymous World Services, 1972, 1975), p. 13.

[33] *Co-Founders*, p. 14.

[34] Wally P., *But, For the Grace of God...How Intergroups & Central Offices Carried
the Message of Alcoholics Anonymous in the 1940's* (Wheeling, WV: The Bishop of
Books, 1995), p. 45.

[35] *A Manual for Alcoholics Anonymous*, 6th ed. (Akron: AA of Akron, 1993), p. 8.

DR. BOB and the Good Oldtimers reported:

Each morning [Bill recalled of the period when he lived with Dr. Bob and Anne Smith in their Akron home in the summer of 1935], there was a devotion. . . . After a long silence, in which they [we] awaited inspiration and guidance, Anne would read from the Bible. James was our favorite. . . . Reading from her chair in the corner, she would softly conclude, "Faith without works is dead" (p. 71).

This [verse] was a favorite quotation of Anne's, much as the Book of James was a favorite of early A.A.'s—so much so that "The James Club" was favored by some as a name for the Fellowship. Sue [Dr. Bob's daughter, Sue Smith Windows] also remembered the quiet time in the mornings—how they sat around reading from the Bible (p. 71).

We had much prayer together in those days and began quietly to read Scripture and discuss a practical approach in its application in our lives (p. 111)

The Bible was stressed as reading material, of course (p. 151).

Hospitalization was another must in the early days. . . . The advantage of having the alcoholic alone in a room as a captive audience also had something to do with it. These patients were allowed only a Bible as reading material (p. 102).

Dr. Bob was the first group leader I heard refer simply and without ostentation to God. He cited the Sermon on the Mount as containing the underlying spiritual philosophy of A.A. (p. 228).

Dr. Bob was a prominent man in Akron. Everybody knew him. When he stopped drinking, people asked, "What's this not-drinking-liquor-club you've got over there?" "A Christian fellowship," he'd reply (p. 118).

Dr. Bob was always positive about his faith, Clarence said. If someone asked him a question about the program, his usual response was: "What does it say in the Good Book?" Suppose he was asked, "What's all this 'First Things First?'" Dr. Bob would be ready with an appropriate quotation: "Seek ye first the kingdom of God and His righteousness, and all these things shall be added unto you" (p. 144).[36]

As to the Bible and the early A.A. days in Akron, Bill Wilson said:

We much favored the Apostle James. The definition of love in Corinthians also played a great part in our discussions.[37]

I learned a great deal from you people [T. Henry Williams and his wife Clarace], from the Smiths themselves, and from Henrietta [Seiberling]. I hadn't looked in the Bible, up to this time, at all.[38]

For a great many of us have taken to reading the Bible. It could not have been presented at first, but sooner or later in his second, third, or fourth year, the A.A. will be found reading the Bible quite as often—or more—as he will a standard psychological work.[39]

Wilson's secretary, Nell Wing, said in *Grateful to Have Been There*:

Members gathered there informally [at the home of Dr. Bob and Anne in the early days] as well as attending the Oxford Group meetings at the home of T. Henry and Clarace Williams. Early members described how, at their meeting, Bob liked to sit with an open Bible on his lap, out of which a passage would be selected

---

[36] See the account as recalled by Clarence S. in Dick B., *That Amazing Grace: The Role of Clarence and Grace S. in Alcoholics Anonymous* (San Rafael, CA: Paradise Research Publications, 1996), p. 30.

[37] Kurtz, *Not-God*, p. 320, n. 11.

[38] Dick B., *The Good Book and the Big Book: A.A.'s Roots in the Bible* (San Rafael, CA: Paradise Research Publications, 1995), p. 18.

[39] W. W., Lecture 29, *The Fellowship of Alcoholics Anonymous* (Yale Summer School of Alcohol Studies: Quarterly Journal of Studies on Alcohol, 1945), p. 467 (italics added).

at random and read. A discussion would then follow on its relevance to the personal problems of those present (p. 81).

And Dr. Bob was not the only one to lead meetings with Bible reading. Dick S., an early AA, opened meetings with prayer and a passage from the Bible.[40] So did A.A. No. 3, Bill D. of Akron.[41]

Dr. Bob's wife, Anne, kept a spiritual journal from 1933 to 1939 in which she recorded her studies in the Bible, the teachings of the Oxford Group, Christian literature to read, and the life-changing principles of the early A.A. program. AAs and their families would come to the Smith home for what many joshingly called "spiritual pablum." John R., an Akron pioneer, recalled:

> Before one of these meetings [in Dr. Bob's home], Anne used to pull out a little book [her spiritual journal] and quote from it. We would discuss it. Then we would see what Anne would suggest from it for our discussion.[42]

As to the Bible, Anne wrote and shared:

> Let all of your reading be guided. . . . Of course the Bible ought to be the main Source Book of all. No day ought to pass without reading it.[43]

Robert R. Smith, son of Dr. Bob and Anne, wrote in the Foreword to *The Good Book and The Big Book*:

> Before there was a Big Book—in the period of "flying blind"—God's Big Book was the reference used in our home. The

---

[40] Dick B., *The Akron Genesis of Alcoholics Anonymous* (Corte Madera, CA: Good Book Publishing Company, 1994), p. 189.

[41] Dick B., *The Akron Genesis*, p. 190.

[42] Dick B., *Anne Smith's Journal, 1933-1939: A.A.'s Principles of Success* (San Rafael, CA: Paradise Research Publications, 1994), p. 9.

[43] Dick B., *Anne Smith's Journal*, p. 60.

summer of 1935, when Bill lived with us, Dr. Bob had read the Bible completely three times. And the references that seemed consistent with the program goals were the Sermon on the Mount, 1 Corinthians 13, and the Book of James. At Anne's "Quiet Time"—a daily period held with the alcoholics in our home—the Bible was used (p. ix).

Clarence S., one of the original A.A. pioneers and a sponsee of Dr. Bob's, frequently made the following statements:

Everything in this [A.A.'s] program came from the Bible.[44]

A.A. was grounded in the Bible.[45]

A.A.'s basic ideas came from Matthew chapters 5-7 [Jesus's Sermon on the Mount], 1 Corinthians 13 [the so-called "love" chapter], and the Book of James.[46]

Clarence told his A.A. sponsees to read those three segments; and they did just that. The reading (his widow Grace recalled) was not recommended reading; it was required. When asked by an AA, "Where did that come from in the Bible?" Clarence would reply, "Do you own a Bible?" If the person did not, Clarence would give the AA a Bible. He would then say, "That's a textbook. Not a novel. Not something to spot read here and there. It's a study. Read the Word. Get the Word in your heart. 'Thy word have I hid in mine heart that I might not sin against thee'" [Psalm 119:11].[47]

When Clarence was hospitalized and achieving sobriety in February of 1938, the only piece of literature allowed and present in his hospital room was the Holy Bible. And, after Clarence had left the hospital and gone that very evening to the home of T. Henry Williams for Clarence's first Oxford Group meeting, Dr.

---

[44] Dick B., *That Amazing Grace*, p. 43.
[45] Dick B., *That Amazing Grace*, p. 33.
[46] Dick B., *That Amazing Grace*, p. 34.
[47] Dick B., *That Amazing Grace*, pp. 87-88.

Bob then sent him on his way to Cleveland with a Bible, stating it "would help me fix drunks."

As a dramatic illustration of the importance of the Bible to early A.A., Dr. Bob's Bible was inscribed by him and donated to A.A.'s first group, Akron No. 1 (the King School Group). To this very day, the Bible is brought the podium at the beginning of each meeting and remains there until the meeting is closed. One A.A. historian reports, "Many A.A. pioneers fondly referred to the Holy Bible as the 'Big, Big Book.'"[48]

A.A. Trustee-to-be Frank Amos Documents the Akron Emphasis

John D. Rockefeller, Jr., had been asked to support early A.A. financially; and he sent his agent, Frank Amos, to Akron to determine the nature and reasons for the success of the early A.A. program in Akron. Among other things, Amos said (as documented in *DR. BOB and the Good Oldtimers*):

> He [an alcoholic] must have devotions every morning—a "quiet time" of prayer and some reading from the Bible and other religious literature. Unless this is faithfully followed, there is grave danger of backsliding (p. 131).

> In many respects, their meetings have taken on the form of the meetings described in the Gospels [sic] of the early Christians during the first century (pp. 135-36).

> The A.A. members of that time did not consider meetings necessary to maintain sobriety. They were simply "desirable." Morning devotion and "quiet time," however, were musts (p. 136).

---

[48] Wally P., *But for the Grace of God*, p. 225.

The Missing Details

With all the foregoing references to borrowed principles, Oxford Group ideas, Sam Shoemaker's teachings, and the importance of the Bible, you would expect voluminous and precise details in A.A. itself concerning the specifics in its spiritual roots. But you will find virtually nothing, even in non-A.A. commentaries about A.A. And, in such materials, there is no consistent picture of all the spiritual segments and how they fit together. We therefore need to take a look at the lacuna—*the huge gap*—before we begin.

First of all, Bill Wilson never really specified for posterity *what was borrowed* from *what*, from *where*, or from *whom*. Dr. Bob never really specified for succeeding members *what* basic ideas came from the Sermon on the Mount, 1 Corinthians 13, or the Book of James. Furthermore neither Bill nor Bob provided any significant details about the Oxford Group's famed Four Absolutes. The Oxford Group's Five C's (which provided the heart of A.A.'s borrowed recovery structure) were seldom, if ever, reported in writing as part of the vocabulary of either co-founder—despite the fact that Dr. Bob's wife discussed them at length.

The early Sam Shoemaker's teachings, as to which Bill Wilson spoke in such laudatory terms, are never specified or even adequately summarized, analyzed, or discussed within A.A. Bible devotionals were part of the daily life of early AAs; but the *contents* of such devotionals as *The Upper Room* and *My Utmost for His Highest* (which were read almost daily in early A.A.) have been left to collectors and bookstores. They simply cannot be found, from a discussion standpoint, in any A.A. Conference Approved history. God—the Almighty God of the Bible, the Oxford Group, Sam Shoemaker, the Bible devotionals, and early A.A. literature—has often been converted into some unknown or vague "god of one's own understanding," a "higher power" of nebulous strength, or a "power greater than oneself" which could be a doorknob or a bulldozer.

Before one can appreciate the importance of learning about the history of early A.A.'s spiritual principles, one must know what has been—and still is—missing from A.A.'s own Conference Approved materials and from other scholarly histories of A.A.

And, as we've just summarized, the following *details* are missing: (1) The specific ideas, verses, chapters, and segments of the Bible upon which early AAs so successfully relied for their very lives. (2) The Oxford Group's life-changing program of action and its relationship to A.A.'s own life-changing Steps which are patterned so closely on the Oxford Group program. (3) The hundreds of words, phrases, and ideas in the books, sermons, writings, and teachings of the Reverend Sam Shoemaker which earned him the title of "co-founder" of A.A. (4) The clear feed-in to A.A.'s recovery ideas from Bible devotionals, Christian literature early AAs read, and even the new thought ideas to which they were exposed in the formative days. (5) The specific language from the Bible and from Oxford Group/Shoemaker writings which was virtually copied into the Big Book and the Twelve Steps and which, if identified and explained, can aid materially in understanding A.A. language and ideas. (6) The caveats by Wilson, Shoemaker, and others admonishing against reliance upon A.A. as a religion, and upon self-made religion, half-baked prayers, and absurd names for God Almighty. (7) A comprehensive piecing together of material from all these sources to learn how they interrelate and form the simple whole which constitutes the Twelve-Step recovery program that achieved so much success in A.A.'s earliest years.

The Good News

The Evidence is Available

Prior to A.A.'s International Convention in Seattle, Washington, in 1990, the author had heard from a young AA (now dead of alcoholism) that A.A. was based on the Bible. When the author asked this young man where he had gotten his idea, the young man suggested that the author read *DR. BOB and the Good Oldtimers*. This the author did; and he was astonished to see the countless references in that Conference Approved A.A. history to the Bible's use in early A.A. Yet there *were no specifics*. So a trip to A.A.'s convention in Seattle seemed important to enable historical data to be gathered. But alas! The data simply were not there.

Nonetheless, an oldtimer from Oklahoma (whom the author met at the 1990 convention's archives panel) began sending the author Oxford Group books of the 1930's. And the relevance of the contents to A.A. principles and practices was overwhelming. Also, A.A.'s archivist at General Services in New York sent the author a very short list of books early AAs read and a very short list of books by an American Oxford Group leader, the Reverend Sam Shoemaker.

And the hunt was on!

Near the author's residence in Marin County, California, was a Presbyterian Seminary Library, loaded with aging Oxford Group and other Christian titles read by the AAs in the 1930's. There were a limited number of Shoemaker titles as well. Also nearby was the Golden Gate Baptist Seminary in Tiburon, California; and some of the Oxford Group/Shoemaker books were available there. Moreover, the religious seminaries of many denominations have teamed together in Berkeley, California, on "holy hill" to provide combined library resources at the Graduate Theological Union. And still more of the priceless materials were available there.

It therefore soon became possible—through the helpfulness of other AAs, A.A. scholars and historians, and used bookstores—to gather and study not only the Oxford Group/Shoemaker books, but also books about Oxford Group mentors. The latter included Professors Horace Bushnell and Henry B. Wright of Yale, Evangelists Dwight Moody and F. B. Meyer, Dr. Robert E. Speer of Princeton, Professor Henry Drummond of Edinburgh, Professor William James of Harvard, Dr. Carl Jung of Switzerland, and Dr. John Mott of world-wide YMCA fame. And all of these progenitors of the Oxford Group had contributed substantially to the life-changing thinking, writings, and programs developed by Frank Buchman and Sam Shoemaker. But the specifics and relevance of their writings to the A.A. program simply had not been substantially reported or analyzed.

There was much more to be learned. The author discovered from Dr. Bob's children that much of Dr. Bob's religious library was still in their possession. The author personally examined it and compared it with what he had found in seminaries, libraries, and bookstores. Also, Dr. Bob's wife Anne had listed, in the spiritual journal she kept throughout much of the 1930's, many of the books that were recommended to early AAs and their families for spiritual ideas and growth. And the author read these.

Other information was gleaned from interviewing the three children of Henrietta Seiberling who, though not an alcoholic, was a well-educated woman, an Oxford Group adherent, and a person dedicated to helping Dr. Bob and (later) many other alcoholics and their families. She taught them about, and to rely upon, the Bible, Oxford Group principles, and other Christian writings and ideas of the day. Still more information about Christian literature relevant to early A.A., and even many copies of books, were gained from more than a dozen Oxford Group survivors in the United States, Canada, and abroad. Also, from the daughter of T. Henry Williams, the Oxford Group activist in whose home the earliest A.A. meetings were held. And later from several Oxford Group centres in the United States and abroad, and from close associates of the Reverend Sam Shoemaker such as Mrs. W. Irving Harris, widow of Shoemaker's assistant minister in the 1930's.

In fact, Mrs. Harris donated to the author most of Irving Harris's library and supplied information as to the recommended Oxford Group/Shoemaker books of the 1930's. She sent the author lists of the books as they had been published in Shoemaker's parish publication (*The Calvary Evangel*) and stocked in the Oxford Group bookstall located in Calvary House, the Oxford Group headquarters adjacent to Shoemaker's Calvary Episcopal Church in New York. Early Oxford Group literature from Great Britain (which came the author's way) also frequently listed the principal Oxford Group books suggested for reading.

And lest it appear that the author has conducted his quest alone, one should realize how many AAs, Oxford Group people, scholars, historians, and collectors now (and at last) are focusing on the spiritual origins of A.A. Some are moving into cyberspace. And many have shared their findings with the author.

At A. A. Big Book Seminars conducted all over the world today, A.A.'s Oxford Group origins and the Oxford Group's practical program of action are usually mentioned. One A.A. historian has been investigating A.A.'s spiritual origins, writing for official A.A. publications, and also writing on his own and from his own perspective for many years. He shared his findings liberally with the author. A number of individual AAs have directed their attention to particular early Oxford Group and A.A. personalities. Two, for example, have done their best to get facts on Bill Wilson's friend and Oxford Group mentor Rowland Hazard. Another has assembled a great deal of material on Shoemaker and A.A. Several in Maryland have investigated early East Coast A.A. pioneers John Henry Fitzhugh M. and Jim B. One writer (who was given custody of almost all the papers of pioneer Clarence S.) has spent more than a decade preparing a book and speaking on Clarence's A.A. role. A number of oldtimers have frequented used bookstores looking for out-of-print religious literature read in early A.A.; and the author knows of at least half a dozen significant collections around the United States that have been the result.

Manuscripts, memos, correspondence, and pamphlets concerning all these matters are very much available. They are scattered from the Hartford Seminary Archives in Connecticut to the personal materials of Oxford Group activist T. Willard Hunter in Claremont, California. From Oxford Group collections in Tirley Garth, England; Washington, D.C.; Allentown, Pennsylvania; and Fort Myers Beach, Florida, to pertinent collections at Dr. Bob's Home. They can also be found in the Akron Founders Day Archives; the Bill Wilson home at Stepping Stones in New York; the Episcopal Archives in Austin, Texas; the Calvary Episcopal Church archives in New York and Pittsburgh; and the literature of

Faith at Work and the Pittsburgh Experiment in Virginia and Pittsburgh, respectively. They also exist in public and private libraries in Baltimore, Maryland; Akron, Ohio; Washington, D.C.; Princeton, New Jersey; Peace Dale and Providence, Rhode Island; New Haven, Connecticut; and several other locations.

Tapes and videos of Bill W., Dr. Bob, Lois Wilson, the early Akron scene, Sam Shoemaker, Clarence S., Ed. A., Clancy U., Dr. Bob's children, and Congressman John F. Seiberling can be found and heard. And recent titles by Bill Wilson's secretary Nell Wing and by Dr. Bob's children (Sue Smith Windows and Robert R. Smith) make many more background specifics available.

The Facts Have Been Recovered

The reward for the author has been the accessibility of the evidence; and one wonders why it took some fifty-five years for AAs and others to begin examining it.

The author has met several times with Dr. Bob's children. He was shown almost all of Dr. Bob's library and provided with full lists of Dr. Bob's books. Dr. Bob's children were very open and generous in answering questions about early A.A. and the Bible, the Oxford Group, quiet time, and so on. The author met personally with former Congressman John F. Seiberling and his sister Dorothy Seiberling Steinberg. Both provided lists of their mother's (Henrietta's) books as did Henrietta's other daughter, Mary Seiberling Huhn. The author was shown Henrietta Seiberling's Bible and the markings and memos in it. All of Henrietta's children answered questions about their mother's beliefs, Bible reading, Oxford Group participation, and comments.

Dorothy Williams Culver (daughter of Oxford Group enthusiast T. Henry Williams, who did so much for Bill and Bob in Akron) opened her memoirs and materials to the author. So did the daughters of Dr. Sam Shoemaker—Sally Shoemaker Robinson and Nickie Shoemaker Haggart. The latter enabled the author to inspect Shoemaker's personal journals for the 1930's, and to copy pages containing both positive and possible references to A.A. and to Bill Wilson.

More than a dozen Oxford Group people around the world reviewed the author's manuscripts and sent Oxford Group books, pamphlets, and memos. They provided specific recollections and pictures of Frank Buchman; Sam Shoemaker; Shoemaker's businessmen's team (to which Wilson belonged); and of Oxford Group houseparties, programs, invitations, and news articles. Shoemaker's good friend (Mrs. W. Irving Harris) provided the author with personal memos about Shoemaker and Wilson, and specific details about Oxford Group events, personalities, and materials with which and with whom early AAs in New York were involved.

Of perhaps major importance were four historical finds—one of which seems to have been unknown, one of which seems to have been ignored, and two of which have simply remained untapped.

Lois Wilson's Oxford Group Notes and Other Stepping Stones Items

On his second visit to the home of Bill and Lois Wilson in Bedford Hills, New York, the author was shown and allowed to copy Lois Wilson's "Oxford Group Notes." These (incorporated in a tiny ringed notepad) named events, ideas, and personalities Bill and Lois Wilson encountered while attending Oxford Group meetings and activities. To the author's knowledge, no one had written on these notes. Previously, at the Wilson home, the author was allowed to inspect and copy many Shoemaker/Wilson, Dr. Bob/Bill, and other letters as well as several pre-Big Book manuscripts written by Bill which put an entirely new light on Bill Wilson's earliest days and religious convictions at that time.

Anne Smith's Spiritual Journal

The next find concerned the spiritual journal kept by Dr. Bob's wife Anne Ripley Smith from 1933 to 1939. We will cover the specifics later. Suffice it to say here, that Dr. Bob's daughter requested and the author was allowed to obtain from A.A.'s General Services Archives copies of Anne's sixty-four page journal. This journal is gem! It showed what the early AAs were hearing at Oxford Group meetings, what the Oxford Group program was, what the significant Bible ideas were, and what religious reading was recommended. As time went on, the author more and more saw the true significance of this work.

Anne had shared the contents of the journal with early AAs and their families; and those contents contained every single Oxford Group concept and every single Twelve Step concept that later wound up in the A.A. program of recovery. However, the journal has been ignored. One staff member at A.A. General Services commented to the author about the journal: "Oh, that's just Annie." The contents of her journal were unreported, and their significance was unrecognized. However, if the reader were to read the journal's contents, he or she would not be surprised to learn that Bill Wilson called Anne "a founder of A.A." and the "Mother of A.A."

The Roles of Henrietta Seiberling, and T. Henry and Clarace Williams

Bill Wilson and his tiny group of New York AAs broke away from the Oxford Group in August of 1937. Then Clarence S. and his Cleveland AAs broke from Akron's self-styled "alcoholic squad of the Oxford Group" in May of 1939. Before long, the Akron AAs began holding their regular meetings in Dr. Bob's home and finally at the King School; and the Oxford Group link was severed. Though all of this was not without objections, the severance also brought an historical chasm that left the specific spiritual contributions of Henrietta Seiberling, of Mr. and Mrs. T. Henry Williams, virtually unreported and certainly unknown.

Again, Bill Wilson was generous in his praise of these non-alcoholic founders of A.A.; but he said virtually nothing of what they taught. We have covered the details in one of our earlier works.[49] And we will not repeat them here, except where they fit into the specific segments in this title.

However, the reader should know the following facts. T. Henry Williams (a descendent of the American colonist, Roger Williams) was raised in Connecticut in the Baptist denomination. He served for several years at a city mission in Connecticut as part of his church work. He studied Bible at Woodstock, Connecticut, under a well-known Bible teacher, L. Ammidown. After moving to Akron, Williams became famous for his invention of a "watch-case" mold for manufacturing tires. And he continued his church affiliation in a Methodist Church where he taught Sunday School and regularly attended church for the rest of his life.

T. Henry became an ardent Oxford Group member shortly after his second wife, Clarace, joined the Group in 1932. The Williams house became dedicated to God (as T. Henry might have put it); and shortly it was the place where early AAs regularly met as part of the Oxford Group. Clarace Williams had, prior to her marriage to T. Henry, trained to be a Baptist missionary. And the couple worked tirelessly to teach the early AAs about God, the Bible, Guidance, and prayer.

Some facts about the Williams pair's spiritual contributions have been reported. For example, it was known that T. Henry was much involved in early A.A. surrenders to God, in teaching AAs about the Four Absolutes of the Oxford Group, and in observing Quiet Time. What has not been known, however, is the amount of Oxford Group literature that was available to early AAs at every meeting and gathering held at the Williams home. And this fact perhaps accounts for the widespread knowledge of Oxford Group principles and practices among the early Akron AAs.

Henrietta Seiberling has often been cast, in A.A. historical presentations, as the person who introduced Dr. Bob and Bill and who, with Anne Smith, infused spirituality into Bob and Bill in the early days. However, the author had an opportunity to see in detail

---

[49] See Dick B., *The Akron Genesis of Alcoholics Anonymous* (Corte Madera, CA: Good Book Publishing Company, 1994), pp. 65-105.

the spiritual literature, the biblical materials, and the specific notes that Henrietta made on all of these. The upshot is that Henrietta not only worked with, and taught, early AAs a great deal about the Bible, Christian literature, and the Oxford Group; she was a staunch advocate in A.A. for the power of God, the guidance of God, and the love of God in all matters.

As with the Williams couple, we will not separately detail the matters Henrietta taught because there is little direct evidence of what that was. But we can confirm that Henrietta appears to have read the same materials in the Bible, the Bible devotionals, the Christian literature of the day, and the Oxford Group writings that were read by Dr. Bob, by his wife Anne, and by the Williams's. And, keeping in mind the accolades to Henrietta by A.A.'s founders, the degree of her participation in early A.A. activities, and the frequency of her contacts with the founders, it is safe to assume that much of the material we cover in this title can be related directly to the   contributions of Henrietta Buckler Seiberling to A.A. throughout the 1930's and into the 1940's.

The Historical Facts from Pioneer Clarence S.

Finally and most recently, the author interviewed and wrote a title about the widow of A.A.'s venerable pioneer Clarence S. The author found that the earliest Bible, Oxford Group, and recovery program ideas had been transmitted by Clarence to his A.A. sponsees. He had explained and detailed them to his widow Grace; and these early A.A. principles had been put into practice to the date of Clarence's death. Moreover, they are practiced in A.A. today by his widow, by his and her sponsees, and by the spiritual retreats they conducted and which their sponsees continue to conduct. While Clarence's practices may or may not be in vogue in today's A.A., they certainly show "how it worked" in early A.A.

The Sources Are Reliable

In his last five years of research and writing, the author has been asked by many if he were trying to wed A.A. to the Oxford Group, or to return A.A. to the Bible, or to make A.A. a Christian Fellowship as it was in the 1930's. While the questions may seem flattering, there is, in the author's opinion, no person or group in A.A. today that would have either the support or the power to be successful in such a venture.

However, the immediate answer is that none of the three proposals forms any part of the author's very clear mission. The author's effort has been to *report* history, *not make it*. If some in today's A.A. can utilize that early spiritual history for study, understanding, support, or growth, all the better. However, the author has been focused on the integrity of the data. And, though some certainly quarrel with the idea of telling today's AAs about their roots in the Bible, Christianity, and the teachings of the Oxford Group and Sam Shoemaker, no one, to the author's knowledge, has entered a significant evidentiary objection to the historical data as reported.

It is one thing to point emphatically to A.A.'s supposed "universality" today in an attempt to refute or ignore the early program's tenets. But it is quite another to argue with the testimony of the children of Dr. Bob and Anne; the children of Henrietta Seiberling, Sam Shoemaker, and T. Henry Williams; the Oxford Group people (Jim H. of Maryland and Parks Shipley of New Jersey, for example) who went to early meetings with Bill Wilson; and with the multitudes of books, pamphlets, diaries, journals, articles, letters, memos, and pamphlets the author has cited in countless footnotes, and had the privilege of reading and examining.

Moreover, the quest is far from over.

Almost the entire Shoemaker/Wilson correspondence for the critical period of 1934 to 1939 has seemingly disappeared from the Episcopal Church Archives in Texas. Copies of some of this material are known to exist, but have not surfaced or been made the subject of research and publication. The same can be said of information about several important Shoemaker/Wilson friends such as Rowland Hazard, F. Shepard Cornell, Victor Kitchen, Cebra Graves, Charles Clapp, Jr., Professor Philip Marshall Brown, Ebby Thacher, John Henry Fitzhugh M., Rev. Garrett Stearly, and others.

Nonetheless, it is possible this very day to present a virtually complete structure of A.A.'s biblical roots upon which present evidence and future finds can be hung. The author hopes to be a part of the continuing quest for spiritual facts and hopes this present title can be a major catalyst for criticism, analysis, and further research. The evidence is there; and it is reliable. We trust that *Turning Point* will substantially fill the historical void.

Part 1

A Spiritual Program for Drunks

"A beacon had been lighted. God had shown alcoholics how it might be passed from hand to hand."[1]

---

[1] "RHS," *The A.A. Grapevine* (New York: A.A. Grapevine, Inc., 1951), p. 8.

35

2

The Oxford Group Roots

Contrary to what many have thought to be the case, A.A. really had *two* beginnings, not one.

Bill Wilson almost always recounted the story of A.A.'s beginnings by telling of the treatments of an alcoholic American businessman (Rowland Hazard) by the famous Swiss psychiatrist (Dr. Carl Jung) in Switzerland during a period from 1930 to 1931. The Hazard/Jung episode eventually led to Bill's conversion and recovery, and will be discussed in the next chapter.

The other equally significant yet seldom discussed A.A. starting point—which ultimately led to Dr. Bob's conversion and recovery—occurred in Akron, Ohio. Also, in 1931.

Both events involved separate religious experiences in "A First Century Christian Fellowship" (later known as the Oxford Group) by each of A.A.'s founders.

The two separate series of events converged in Akron, Ohio, in 1935, and resulted in the founding of Alcoholics Anonymous on June 10, 1935. Even then, the founding and subsequent development of A.A.'s recovery program centered around the Oxford Group's ideas. Therefore, before studying A.A.'s beginnings and the specifics of what it derived *from* the Bible, the Oxford Group, Sam Shoemaker, the Bible devotionals and other root segments, we need to take a look at the origin and nature of the Oxford Group itself.

The author and many others have written extensively on the Oxford Group; and there now are ample resources available for learning details about the Oxford Group's origins, principles, and practices.[1] But we need here to present at least an overview so that years of shunting aside materials on the Oxford Group and its ideas within A.A.'s rooms do not becloud the origins, nature, and substantial relationship between Oxford Group ideas and practices and A.A.'s Twelve Steps, Big Book, Fellowship, slogans, and practices.

Oxford Group Founder, Frank Buchman

We begin with the Oxford Group's founder, Dr. Frank Nathan Daniel Buchman.

Buchman was born in Pennsburg, Pennsylvania, on June 4, 1878. He died on August 7, 1961, at Freudenstadt in the Black Forest of Germany. He was laid to rest in Allentown, Pennsylvania, the location of his family home.

---

[1] See Dick B., *Design for Living: The Oxford Group's Contribution to Early A.A.*, rev. ed (San Rafael, CA: Paradise Research Publications, 1995); *New Light on Alcoholism: The A.A. Legacy from Sam Shoemaker* (Corte Madera, CA: Good Book Publishing Company, 1994); *Anne Smith's Journal, 1933-1939: A.A.'s Principles of Success*, rev. ed (San Rafael, CA: Paradise Research Publications, 1994); *Good Morning!: Quiet Time, Morning Watch, Meditation, and Early A.A.* (San Rafael, CA: Paradise Research Publications, 1996); H. A. Walter, *Soul Surgery: Some Thoughts on Incisive Personal Work*, 6th ed. (London: Blandford Press, n.d.); Harold Begbie, *Life Changers: Narratives of a Recent Movement in the Spirit of Personal Religion* (London: Mills & Boon Ltd, 1923); A. J. Russell, *For Sinners Only* (London: Hodder and Stoughton, Ltd., 1932); The Layman with a Notebook, *What is the Oxford Group?* (New York: Oxford University Press, 1933); Leslie D. Weatherhead, *Discipleship* (London: Student Christian Movement Press, Ltd., 1934); R. H. S. Crossman, *Oxford and the Groups* (Oxford: Basil Blackwell & Mott, Ltd., 1934); Robert H. Murray, *Group Movements Throughout the Ages* (London: Hodder and Stoughton, Ltd., 1935); Walter Houston Clark, *The Oxford Group: Its History and Significance* (New York: Bookman Associates, 1951); Theophil Spoerri, *Dynamic Out of Silence: Frank Buchman's Relevance Today* (London: Grosvenor Books, 1976); Garth Lean, *On the Tail of a Comet: The Life of Frank Buchman* (Colorado Springs: Helmers & Howard, 1988).

When Buchman was eight, his parents sent him to Perkiomen Seminary (later Perkiomen School) in Pennsburg, Pennsylvania. The seminary was run by a liberal German sect that favored Bible study and the concept of "the inner light" which they considered came through the direct inspiration and rule of the Holy Spirit. The sect, known as the Schwenkfelders, may well have had an impact on Buchman's life. One scholar wrote (relevant to this probable influence on Buchman) of Schwenkfelder beliefs: That their religion was primarily an interior matter between the individual and the Holy Spirit; that the church and sacraments were of secondary importance; and that the Spirit could rule congregations as well as individuals.[2] In fact, the archivist at Buchman's home in Allentown believed this school may also have implanted in Buchman the idea of "world-changing through life-changing" as part of their view of life.[3]

The Buchman family moved to Allentown, Pennsylvania, when Buchman was sixteen. Buchman attended Allentown High School and then duly entered Muhlenberg College—run by the Lutheran Ministerium. The college was designed to provide the Lutheran Church with a steady flow of ministers. Graduating with honorable mention from Muhlenberg in the summer of 1899, Buchman went on to Mount Airy (Lutheran) Theological Seminary, at Mount Airy in Germantown, Pennsylvania.

In 1901, Buchman attended a meeting of the Lutheran Church's Inner Mission Society and became interested in missionary social work. In the summer of 1901, he also attended the Northfield Student Conference in Massachusetts. Buchman believed this conference "completely changed" his life. He graduated from Mt. Airy in the summer of 1902. Later, he studied abroad at Westminster College at Cambridge. On September 10, 1902, he was ordained to the Gospel Ministry at St. John's Lutheran Church

---

[2] See David C. Belden, "The Origins and Development of the Oxford Group (Moral Re-Armament)," St. Edmund Hall, Oxford, Submission for D.Phil. Thesis, January, 1976, pp. 86-87.

[3] Letter from K. D. Belden to the author dated 7/27/96.

in Allentown; and he was immediately asked to start a new church in Philadelphia. As his biographer (Garth Lean) put it, Buchman then began to "discover" his spiritual principles as he went along. For example, in his first parish, there was the principle that God was reliable and that, in a life of "faith and prayer," practical needs were met.

The Keswick Experience

In 1908, Frank Buchman had a spiritual transformation experience during his attendance at a conference at Keswick in the Lake Country of North England.[4] Almost every account of Buchman's life calls this his "Keswick Experience." It was this experience that Buchman called the "turning point" of his life. For he found he could be effective in the lives of other individuals and came to believe that winning people to Christ must be his main objective.

Prior to going to Keswick, Buchman had formed a Lutheran Hospice for Young Men under the authority of his church's Home Mission Board. But he got in a dispute with the Board in Philadelphia because he felt they were too parsimonious for him to be able to feed the boys properly—something he always believed in doing. Buchman therefore resigned. He went to England nursing a grudge against the Board. During the Keswick conference, Buchman heard a woman preach a sermon on the "Cross" at a nearby church. Buchman was overwhelmed. He saw that, to retain his consciousness of God, his heart must be empty of all sin and free from the angry past. He then surrendered his life to Christ and wrote letters of apology to those he hated. He received immediate relief; and he learned there can be no living and transforming sense of unity with the divine will—no "God Consciousness"—while the heart nurses bitterness.

On his letters of apology, Buchman wrote words from an old hymn:

---

[4] R. C. Mowat, *The Message of Frank Buchman: A Study of "Remaking the World"* (London, Blandford Press, 1951), p. 53.

When I survey the wondrous Cross
On Which the Prince of Glory died,
My richest gain I count but loss
And pour contempt on all my pride.

Then he told each board member: "I have nursed ill-will against you. I am sorry. Forgive me?"[5] From his release, Buchman received important ideas on the Cross, elimination of resentment, restitution, and forgiveness. Buchman remarked:

With an experience of the Cross, you will shrink from nothing. I learned at Keswick that I was as wrong as anybody else. I was most in need of change. I was the one to begin.

That same day, Buchman walked around the lake with another man at the same lodgings in Keswick. The walk ended in the man's giving his life to Christ. "No wonder," said one Oxford Group historian, "Frank believed that basic change could lead to miracles in other people."[6] And this whole experience was to weave its way into basic A.A. thinking many years later. One Oxford Group writer analyzed Buchman's experience as follows:

1. He [Buchman] caught a vision of the Cross.
2. He had been convicted of sin in his life [a concept to have an effect on A.A.'s Fourth Step resentment list and its Sixth Step involving willingness to change].
3. He had made an unreserved surrender to Jesus Christ [a concept that formed a vital part of *early A.A.* "surrenders" and later influenced its Steps Three and Seven].
4. He had made frank confession and restitution [concepts that are part and parcel of Steps Five, Eight, Nine, Ten, and Eleven].

---

[5] Frank Buchman, *Remaking the World: The Speeches of Frank N. D. Buchman* (London: Blandford Press, 1961), p. 315.

[6] Letter from K. D. Belden to the author dated 7/27/96.

5. He had witnessed to the renewing power of Christ [the original
   essence of A.A.'s Twelfth Step "pass it on" idea].[7]

Moral Principles

On his return from Keswick to America, Buchman became aligned
with, and later became the full-time secretary of, the Penn State
YMCA for seven years. During this period, Buchman had the
clear conviction, "Christianity has a moral backbone," and that it
was the lack of this that made many ineffective. He felt those who
professed faith but lived filth denied before men the power of God
as a force in their nature. He later pointed to segments of the Book
of James, Chapter Three, on careless and hurtful speaking. He
quoted James 3:8: "But the tongue can no man tame; *it is* an
unruly evil, full of deadly poison." And these concepts were to
become watchwords for A.A.'s Dr. Bob and his wife Anne, and
were even mentioned in Dr. Bob's farewell address to AAs just
before his death.

As to morality issues, Buchman was to develop one of many
phrases that succinctly explained his ideas from the Bible.
Buchman believed that humanity is in rebellion against universally
accepted moral standards (and against God), that the Bible offers
a cure in the person of Jesus of Nazareth, and that the Bible gives
promises and illustrations of the satisfaction and miracles that flow
out of the decision to cooperate with God's plan. Buchman was
soon to term his life-changing concepts the "Cure of Souls."

The biblical foundations, according to Buchman, consisted of
three parts: Sin, Christ, and a miracle. Or (as Buchman often
phrased the three essential facts in a conversion): "Sin is the
disease. Jesus Christ is the cure. The result is a miracle."[8]

---

[7] Clarence I. Benson, *The Eight Points of the Oxford Group: An Exposition for
Pagans and Christians* (London: Oxford University Press, 1936), p. xii.

[8] See Buchman, *Remaking the World*, p. 142; Walter, *Soul Surgery*, p. 86; Miles G.
W. Phillimore, *Just for Today* (Lake Tahoe, California, privately printed booklet, 1940),
p. 63; Harry J. Almond, *Foundations for Faith*, 2d ed. (London: Grosvenor Books,
1980), pp. 9-29.

Quiet Time Roots

During his Penn State tenure, Buchman received a visit at the college from the famous Congregational preacher, Dr. F. B. Meyer. Meyer told Buchman that he [Buchman] needed to make personal, man-to-man interviews; and Buchman began thinking in terms of people rather than numbers. And there was another important outcome of the Meyer/Buchman visit. The following colloquy ensued:

> Meyer . . . asked, "Do you let the Holy Spirit guide you in all you are doing?" Buchman replied that he did indeed pray and read the Bible in the morning and sometimes received inspirations then and at other times in the day. "But," persisted Meyer, "do you give God enough uninterrupted time really to tell you what to do?"

The conversation motivated Buchman to change dramatically his morning devotions. He made a decision to give at least an hour each day in the early morning to listening to God, a period which he came to refer to as a "quiet time." Buchman's successor Peter Howard believed Buchman, at that time, "learned the secret of full obedience to the voice of God." And Buchman later became well-known for the expression:

> When man listens, God speaks.
> When man obeys, God acts.[9]

Buchman also received quiet time inspiration from Professor Henry B. Wright of Yale University. One Oxford Group writer and long-time Buchman associate wrote: "The Yale professor [Wright] was probably the most influential single individual in Frank's entire life, outside his mother."[10] At the time of his early

---

[9] Buchman, *Remaking the World*, pp. 35, 42, 46; Cecil Rose, *When Man Listens*, rev. ed (London: Blandford Press, 1936).

[10] T. Willard Hunter, *World Changing Through Life Changing*. Thesis, Newton Center, Mass; Andover-Newton Theological School, 1977, pp. 15-16.

acquaintance with Buchman, Wright was Assistant Professor of Latin History and Literature at Yale. Buchman had been much encouraged by contact with Wright and by studying Wright's book, *The Will of God and a Man's Lifework.*[11] Wright was later appointed to a special chair in Christian Methods at Yale Divinity School; and Wright visited Buchman each year to aid Buchman in his work with students at Penn State.

Of Wright's book, Buchman's biographer (Lean) concluded:

> The central theme of Wright's book [*The Will of God*] was that an individual could, through "two-way prayer"—listening for guidance as well as talking—find God's will for his life and for the ordinary events of the day. Wright himself set aside half an hour for such listening prayer first thing every morning. At such times—and indeed at any time in the day—he declared that what he [Wright] called "luminous thoughts" came from God, provided only that the human receiver was clean enough to pick them up. These thoughts Wright wrote down in a notebook and always tried to carry out.

The Four Absolutes

Wright's book was also vitally important to Buchman for its study of the "perfect" standards of Jesus which Dr. Robert E. Speer had earlier extracted from the Gospels.[12] Jesus said in his Sermon on the Mount (Matthew 5:48): "Be ye therefore perfect, even as your Father which is in heaven is perfect." In his book, *The Principles of Jesus*, Speer had spelled out from the Gospels four standards of perfection which he believed Jesus had set. Speer called these "absolute" standards—honesty, purity, unselfishness, and love. These "Absolutes"—which Professor Henry Wright later termed Absolute Honesty, Absolute Purity, Absolute Unselfishness, and

---

[11] Henry B. Wright, *The Will of God and a Man's Lifework* (New York: The Young Men's Christian Association Press, 1909).

[12] Robert E. Speer, *The Principles of Jesus: Applied to Some Questions of To-day* (New York: Association Press, 1902), pp. 33-36.

Absolute Love—were analyzed in detail in Wright's book. They were further confirmed by Wright from the church epistles in the New Testament; and they became vividly impressed upon the mind of Frank Buchman.[13]

The "Four Absolutes" became hallmarks of the goals for which Oxford Group people strove in their lives. The Four Absolutes also became the "yardsticks" by which early AAs took their moral inventories and then endeavored to practice as the principles of their recovery program. Buchman once wrote Wright from China: "Much in my message is due to you."

Three additional points in the Frank Buchman story need to be examined before we return to other Oxford Group matters.

The Five C's

The first point involved events occurring in 1917 when Frank Buchman developed a life-changing program called the Five C's. The program was described as an "art."[14] The following is an account in Harold Begbie's *Life Changers*—a book about Frank Buchman—in which, among other things, Begbie told how the life-changing "C's" received their name:

> It was a youthful fellow-passenger across the Pacific in 1917 who was the means of crystallizing certain principles of action which since have formed the basis of his [Buchman's] work. She had heard him refer to normal Christianity as enabling the ordinary person to do the extraordinary thing, and asked one evening how an ordinary person like herself could win others to Christ. "But," she cautioned, "if you tell me, you must tell me very simply." In his "quiet time" next morning these five words came, and he wrote them down—Confidence, Confession, Conviction, Conversion, Continuance.[15]

---

[13] See Buchman, *Remaking the World*, pp. 31, 36, 40, 96.

[14] Letter from Buchman's biographer Garth Lean to author.

[15] Harold Begbie, *Life Changers*, 12th. ed (London: Mills & Boon, Ltd, 1932), p. 169.

This art, which enabled ordinary people to win others to Christ, earned Buchman the title "soul-surgeon"—a name Begbie bestowed upon him in a chapter in *Life Changers*.[16] The five principles themselves had previously been the subject of *Soul Surgery* (a book written in 1919) which was probably the first real Oxford Group handbook. It dealt with evangelistic personal work ideas; and it was designed to enable life-changing through the transforming power of Jesus Christ. Frank Buchman collaborated on *Soul Surgery* with Professor Henry B. Wright (of whom we have previously spoken) and with a scholar named Howard A. Walter, who had been Literary Secretary for the Young Men's Christian Associations of India, Burma, and Ceylon. Walter published the book in a series of articles in *The Indian Witness* with special reference to the Evangelistic Campaign then in progress in the Indian Church.

Walter completed the manuscript, but he died before it was published. Wright died not long thereafter. But the old soul-surgeon, Frank Buchman, long utilized the Five C's as a vital part of his life-changing art; and we will discuss these in a subsequent chapter and illustrate how they became the heart of A.A.'s Twelve Step, life-changing practical program of action.

Buchman and Sam Shoemaker

The second point involved Buchman's long association with his chief American lieutenant-to-be, the man whom Buchman profoundly influenced in China in 1918 and for many years thereafter. This man was Samuel Moor Shoemaker, Jr.—later to become rector for over twenty-five years of Calvary Protestant Episcopal Church in New York City.

Sam had attended Princeton University and then, during World War I, had answered calls to serve the Y.M.C.A. in the camps of troops training in Texas, and later in camps at Kent, England. Dr. Sherwood Eddy persuaded Shoemaker to go to China with him to

---

[16] Begbie, *Life Changers*, 12th ed, pp. 24-41.

work for the Princeton-in-Peking project, and Princeton alumni staffed the center there. Shoemaker arrived in Peking on October 29, 1917. He spent two years in China teaching English, Bible, and a business course.

On January 19, 1918, Frank Buchman and his group came to Peking for a personal work campaign. Shoemaker had met Frank Buchman and known about his work as YMCA secretary at Penn State. On his first meeting with Shoemaker, Buchman was urging the application of the Four Absolutes. Shoemaker felt himself to be in a spiritual crisis. He asked Buchman what was the matter with his (Sam's) life. Buchman suggested it might be sin which was excluding Shoemaker from vital consciousness of God and which was making him spiritually impotent. Buchman suggested Sam take an inventory of his life, measuring it against the Four Absolutes; and this Shoemaker did—finding himself wanting.

Shoemaker then knew he had to surrender. Next—as he often mentioned in his personal journals—on January 19, 1918, he made his "great decision to surrender all to God." Shoemaker referred to that decision and that date on the 19th day of January of each year in every personal journal he kept thereafter. As to his January, 1918, decision, Shoemaker recounted that he had first walked to his room and then had begun reflecting:

My sins rose up before me straight as tombstones. If I took this plunge it meant a clearing up all along the line. It meant confession. It meant a break with all that had gone before—a new life. . . . Was I willing to do this thing, or was I not willing? . . . Without a scrap of emotion, but with what I can only call a great heave of my will, I knelt down to make my submission, to give myself, without reservation, to God. . . . I was sensible only of calm, of a feeling that something needful and right had been done. I felt very little at the time. I simply realized that I had jumped a fence at which I had long balked. There was no breaking in of light upon me, nor anything unusual. After the prayer, which tore away a wall of my own erection—the wall of unwillingness to face God's Will fully—I prayed again, but without ecstasy. I rose from that prayer hoping that I might be used to help others, and feeling I had done what was required of me. . . . As I lay in bed there came to me a distinct

Voice, and that Voice said, "There is no work of Mine to do for him who is not wholly Mine." They were no words of mine. . . . And they revealed to me what I believe to be the central truth of religion.[17]

Shoemaker immediately launched out from this experience by leading a young Chinese business friend to a decision which enabled the man to find Christ. And in his Peking days, Sam's greatest excitement was passing on to the young people around him his own new-found spiritual experience.

Sam returned to America and, in 1920, was ordained a deacon in the Protestant Episcopal Church—with Frank Buchman present. Shoemaker attended General Theological Seminary in Chelsea Square in New York City. He was ordained a priest in 1921 and began serving as assistant minister at Grace Church, in New York. It was also in 1921 that Shoemaker wrote his first significant book (one of over thirty). The title was *Realizing Religion*; and it was copyrighted by the International Committee of Young Men's Christian Association.[18] In that very first book, Sam used phrases about sin, self-will, the turning point, conversion, surrender, finding God, the Sermon on the Mount, and 1 Corinthians 13 that seem to have become a part of the working knowledge and language of Bill Wilson many years later.

Subsequent Shoemaker books, up to the time of A.A.'s publication of the Big Book, all contained endless ideas that wound up in A.A. But it must be added that the materials could also be found in Oxford Group books by others; for Shoemaker was ever writing on the principles and practices he had learned from, shared with, and expounded upon for, Frank Buchman.

An example of Shoemaker's fealty to Buchman can be found in the frequency with which Shoemaker spoke of "A First Century Christian Fellowship" in Shoemaker's 1929 title—*Twice-Born*

---

[17] See Dick B., *New Light on Alcoholism*, pp. 41-42.

[18] Samuel M. Shoemaker, Jr., *Realizing Religion* (New York: Association Press, 1923).

Ministers.[19] The book is dedicated "To Frank N. D. Buchman, Minister of Jesus Christ in Grateful Fellowship." Shoemaker said in his Foreword:

> I should also like to say that I do not consider this book to be the outcome alone of our work at Calvary Church. The First Century Christian Fellowship is now a movement of international proportions, and we at Calvary are a part of it. With the experiences of some of the men in this book I personally had nothing to do. They came about by means of other members of the Fellowship, some in other lands. I am glad to be able through this book to pay a little of my debt to the First Century Christian Fellowship, and to record again my wholehearted and unconditional identification with it (p. 23).

Later, in 1932, Shoemaker wrote the following to the Parishioners of Calvary Church:

> We must all realize that the work which has been characteristic of Calvary Parish for the past few years is part of a much larger movement which is making a tremendous spiritual contribution in many countries today. A First Century Christian Fellowship, or the Oxford Group, has been called by the Archbishop of York "one of the main movements of the Spirit in our time.". . . The message and power of the Oxford Group managed to interest a great many typical modern people in religion when times were good. What may it not do in a time when men are coming to feel their need for God! . . . The evident need of our country and the world for spiritual awakening, and the manifest effectiveness of the Oxford Group to meet that need with the message of Christ, lays a special obligation upon us all at Calvary to share with others what has helped us.[20]

---

[19] Samuel M. Shoemaker, Jr., *Twice-Born Ministers* (New York: Fleming H. Revell Company, 1929).

[20] Samuel M. Shoemaker, Jr., *Calvary Church Yesterday and Today: A Centennial History* (New York: Fleming H. Revell, 1936), pp. 270-71.

But we must return to our report on the Buchman/Shoemaker odyssey.

For at least twenty years—from 1918 to 1938—Buchman and Shoemaker were very close friends and associates. In 1925, Shoemaker accepted a call to be rector of Calvary in New York City. He remained there for the next twenty-six years. Much of this time, Shoemaker was (with Ray Purdy, Kenaston Twitchell, and Garrett Stearly) one of Buchman's principal American leaders.

It was during his tenure as rector of Calvary in New York (1925 through 1951) that Shoemaker had the responsibility for Calvary Rescue Mission where Bill Wilson was to make his decision for Christ. In the autumn of 1928, Shoemaker's Calvary Church opened Calvary House, a tall facility immediately adjacent to Calvary Church.

Shoemaker, many of his associates, and their families lived at Calvary House. It was there that Frank Buchman also lived when he was in America. Calvary House was the site of many Oxford Group meetings (meetings frequently attended by Bill and Lois Wilson at a later date). Calvary House was a major center of Oxford Group work in America. In fact, it was virtually the American Headquarters for the Oxford Group. It housed the Oxford Group bookstore and offices. It was the location of the Oxford Group's major outreach publication—*The Calvary Evangel* (which was also Shoemaker's parish publication). Of *The Evangel* (during Calvary Church's Oxford Group affiliation), Shoemaker's assistant minister, Rev. W. Irving Harris, said the parish journal "included so much Moral Re-Armament [Oxford Group] material that it became very much like an American house organ for the Oxford Group."

For almost twenty years, Shoemaker wrote the greatest number of materials which could really be termed Oxford Group books. He participated widely in Oxford Group team activities around the world; and he was a principal leader at many Oxford Group houseparties (a few of which were attended by Bill and Lois Wilson)—particularly at houseparties held on the East Coast of the United States.

Shoemaker was also the sparkplug of an Oxford Group businessmen's team to which Bill Wilson belonged for a while. That team numbered among its members such Oxford Group adherents as Rowland Hazard, F. Shepard Cornell, Victor Kitchen, Hanford Twitchell, Charles Clapp, Jr., Parks Shipley, and others with whom Bill Wilson fellowshipped and shared so many of the Oxford Group principles in A.A.'s earliest days.

In November of 1935, as an Oxford Group team member, Bill Wilson participated with his business friends in several large gatherings in the United States in which Frank Buchman and Sam Shoemaker were host to Carl Hambro—President of the Norwegian Parliament and of the League of Nations at that time; and (in his personal journal entries for that period) Shoemaker specifically mentioned Wilson's role.

World Changing through Life Changing

The third point concerns Buchman's major focus on *world-changing* through life-changing.[21] This focus began as early as 1921 and may well have resulted some years later in the basic name-change of Buchman's fellowship from the Oxford Group to Moral Re-Armament. Also, this concentration by Buchman on helping "drunken nations" rather than "drunken people," as Buchman put it, probably played a large role in the eventual break with Buchman's world-changing movement by Bill Wilson and his alcoholics in New York and later by Shoemaker and some of his colleagues at Calvary Church.

---

[21] For some personal reflections on the world-changing period, other than those of Sam Shoemaker and of Garth Lean (Buchman's biographer), see *A Journalist for God: The Memoirs of Reginald Holme* (Surrey, England: A Bridge Builders Publication, 1995); Howard C. Blake, *Way to Go: Adventures in Search of God's Will* (Merrifield, VA: Pooh Stix Press, 1992); K. D. Belden, *The Hour of the Helicopter* (Surrey, England: Linden Hall, 1992); Eleanor Forde Newton, *I Always Wanted Adventure* (London: Grosvenor Books, 1992); H. W. "Bunny" Austin, *Frank Buchman as I Knew Him* (London: Grosvenor Books, 1975); Alan Thornhill, *One Fight More* (London: Frederick Muller Ltd, 1943).

In May of 1921, Buchman was in Cambridge. He got the sense that God was calling him to a wider task. One night, during a bicycle ride, he was struck with the thought: "You will be used to remake the world." It seemed so preposterous that Buchman was reluctant to acknowledge it. But he gained a new sense of specific mission. Later, at Oxford, while attending a meeting, Buchman was asked to speak. He said that: "any real change in the world had to start with a change in people."

Buchman had been working at Hartford Seminary for a number of years. He sailed for America in November of 1921. Colonel David Forster, whom he had gotten to know in England, was a member of the British delegation to the Peace Conference in Washington, and had written Frank urging him to come down to Washington to see what they could do at the Peace Conference. Buchman felt he needed to part company with Hartford. On his return, one night, while traveling by train, he got the thought "Resign, resign, resign"—which may well have been in his mind before. He jotted down, "Resign on principle. Don't worry about finances. You must make an untried experiment. Step out alone." The thought was given decisive force at this moment, and proved a major turning point in his life. Buchman resigned from his post as a lecturer at Hartford; and never again did he hold a paid position. Within a few months, he was back in England; and the Oxford Group was getting under way.

In 1922, Buchman and a few friends formed "A First Century Christian Fellowship." Buchman said the Fellowship was "a voice of protest against the organized, committeeised and lifeless Christian work" and "an attempt to get back to the beliefs and methods of the Apostles."

By 1924, Buchman found himself in a good deal of hot water at Princeton University. He decided to take what he called "an apostolic group" of younger people with him on a prolonged expedition through Europe, the Middle East, India, China, and Australia. And he invited Sherwood ("Sherry") Day, Sam Shoemaker, Loudon Hamilton, Eustace Wade, Godfrey Webb-Peploe, and Van Dusen Rickert to join him for the journey.

It was during this trip that Shoemaker returned to accept the rectorship call at Calvary Church; but Sherry Day was to continue as Buchman's close associate for many years thereafter. And it was Day who soon wrote a statement (which we will discuss in a moment) defining what the Group's basic beliefs were.

As the years rolled by, Buchman was twice nominated for the Nobel Peace prize. He was decorated by the governments of Greece, Japan, the Republic of China, Thailand, and the Philippines—in addition to France (Legion of Honour) and Germany (Grand Cross of Merit). An adviser to Chancellor Konrad Adenauer of Germany outlined five reasons why Buchman might have qualified for the Nobel nominations: (1) foundations for a new trust between Germany and France; (2) unity between Japan and her neighbors; (3) interracial unity and moral basis of self-government in Africa; (4) moves helping the Islamic World to build a bridge between East and West; and (5) racial teamwork in the United States.

Franz Cardinal Konig, Archbishop of Vienna (considered by many as the general choice for Pope at one point during the Conclave of October, 1978—and who declined) wrote of Buchman:

In the last century, there was a feeling among intellectuals that we could build a better world without God. Then came the First World War, and many felt that many things had gone wrong. Buchman was among them, and he began to think what could be done. His great idea was to show that the teaching of Jesus Christ is not just a private affair but has the great force to change the whole structure of the social orders of economics, of political ideas, if we combine the changing of structures with a change of heart. In that sense he opened a completely new approach to religion, to the teachings of Jesus Christ, and to the life of modern man.

What Was the Oxford Group?

There are several approaches to defining Oxford Group principles and practices.

The first is to look at the story of Frank Buchman, as we just have done. The second is to obtain the broadest possible description of Buchman's ideas; and we shall do this first by quoting what the British journalist, A. J. Russell, said in his widely popular book *For Sinners Only*. Russell's book changed countless lives among the people who read it.[22] Next, we shall glance briefly at the statement of the Oxford Groups's principles, which was prepared by long-time Buchman/Shoemaker associate Sherwood Sunderland Day in the 1920's. Then we will quote what one of the many Oxford Group "handbooks" had to say about the Group itself. We will follow with some of the Oxford Group's unique ideas. And finally, we will review Hallen Viney's *How Do I Begin?*—which served as a "tract" that explained, in illustrated and sketch form, how one began his or her practice of Oxford Group principles.

The Summary in For Sinners Only

In the early 1930's, A. J. Russell wrote *For Sinners Only*. The book at once became immensely popular among Oxford Group adherents and others. It was frequently used by Dr. Bob and the early Akron AAs to learn about the Oxford Group program. And Russell had this to say:

> God had a plan. They [the Oxford Group] were trying to fit in with it. Knowledge of that plan, God's guidance and God's power were available for all who chose to work in with that plan. This guidance and power transcended every form of self-determination. God-guidance in God's strength could be the normal experience of everybody at all times (p. 23). . . .
>
> Not only has God a plan for every life . . . but when, through sin we spoil that plan, God is always ready with another.

---

[22] K. D. Belden wrote the author on 7/27/96: "At one house party, I heard that the question was asked, 'How many people are here because they read a book?' And 200 put their hands up, nearly all because of *For Sinners Only*."

Unfortunately, most of us refused to follow the plan when we saw it, or, if unaware of it, to pray for the plan to be revealed. Our sin of sins, embodying all other sins, was independence towards God; doubting God's interest in us, that He had a plan for us, that He would show us the plan, and that He would help us to carry out the plan which was the only satisfactory plan for our lives (p. 27). . . .

[T]hose who attempted to live without God's plan, as revealed by the Holy Spirit, were as certain to encounter disaster as those living under God's daily direction were certain of success. . . . My objection to this argument was human nature's chronic inability to know when it was being guided. To that the Three [Troubadours] offered the answer of two-way prayer; petitions and quiet listening for the reply, especially in the morning when preparing for the day's work.[23] They called this early morning listening to God "Quiet Times." The Oxford Group believed God spoke to them when they needed His guidance. . . . They emphasized that the condition of clear guidance was complete surrender of everything—will, time, possessions, family, ambitions—all to God. . . . It meant a handing over of our little in return for God's All-Sufficiency. . . . Accepting completely the discipline of God brought not bondage, but the fullest freedom to do what we wished—and that was always the Will of God. . . . I learned that it was a practice of the Group to keep a guidance-book and record in it those thoughts which came in periods of quiet listening to God. . . . Reaching back into the first century for their standards of Christian fellowship, they were ready to scrap any later practices they believed redundant or old-fashioned, and to substitute the earliest customs for something that met modern needs. They did much of their work through house-parties, where visitors shared their religious experiences and drew close to God (pp. 28-29).

---

[23] The three "troubadours" were the subject of the second chapter of Russell's book; and they had all stood with Buchman for many years. They were the reverends Garrett Stearly and John Roots (both clergymen of the Anglican Communion and sons of bishops), and Charles Haines (of whom Lois Wilson spoke in her notes).

. . . They were even so orthodox as to believe that everyone, parson as well as prodigal, must at some time come to himself, must experience the forgiveness of God through Jesus Christ. In short, the Cross was central in their teaching. At the Cross, man reached a turning-point when he decided to live as God directed and guided instead of according to his own human standards. Old-fashioned evangelicals called it conversion, but through misuse that word had for many minds lost its original potency, and so they preferred the simpler word "Change." . . . Those who sought to change others were called "Life-Changers" instead of evangelists (p. 30). . . .

They challenged the world to turn back to God, to cut out sin, to make restitution for past sins, and to let God take full command of every area of life, just as the early disciples challenged the world. . . . While the Group practiced social service, they felt man's deepest need was not money, but God, for those who truly sought first the Kingdom of Heaven had all other things added unto them. That was their own experience. Men and women who were keenly hungry for the true God, who was more ready to manifest Himself to them than they were to seek Him. The work of life-changing was never more necessary than now. . . . There was no joy in life so great as leading a prodigal home to his Heavenly Father, always half-way down the road to meet him. . . . Life-changing was contagious. . . . But How? . . . The best answer to the How of both sinner and potential Life-Changer was the Group custom of Sharing. Changed men might go wrong in trying to change others by argument, but they were on safe ground in recounting their own experiences as Apostles recounted theirs. . . . Not emotional decisions, as witnessed in some of the old fashioned mass-revivals, but decisions taken in quiet heart-to-heart talks . . . telling their own experience of their indwelling Master (pp. 31-33).

I was certainly getting the hang of what the Oxford Group were after. First, there was absolute Surrender, including Faith in the Cross of Christ, bringing Guidance by the Holy Spirit; then there was Sharing, bringing true Fellowship and shining faces; then Life-Changing, bringing God's Kingdom and Joy, in Heaven in the Sinner, and in the Life-Changer; then Faith and Prayer, bringing all things needful and helping forward God's plan to provide for everybody; also those four standards of Love, Honesty, Purity and Unselfishness on which Christ never compromised; and, of course, Restitution. Later I was to understand perhaps the strongest principle of all—Fearless Dealing with Sin. Meanwhile, there were two other principles easier to swallow—Teamwork and Loyalty. Jesus practiced team-work. . . . Truth is presented more adequately through a team than through one individual. . . . Then there was the principle of Loyalty. First, there must be supreme loyalty to Jesus Christ [and] . . . to those trying to live in loyalty to Christ. Above all, the Group was a Fellowship—a first-century Christian Fellowship controlled by the Holy Spirit (pp. 42-43).[24]

Reverend Sherry Day's Principles of the Group

Early on, the Oxford Group published a pamphlet by Sherwood Sunderland Day—whom we have mentioned above. Shoemaker's daughter Nickie Shoemaker Haggart told the author that Day was one of her father (Sam Shoemaker's) closest friends. Day's pamphlet was titled *The Principles of the Group*.[25] It began:

The principles of "The Oxford Group" are the principles of the Bible. The Group is not an organization, not a sect, not even a new method. The Group is a life—that life which is hid with Christ in God. It is well to bear in mind at the very start that the principles of the New Testament are not a set of rulings by the careful observance of which one finds eternal life, but that they are rather revelations, pictures, if you will, of what is bound to take place in any life that is surrendered to the Will of God. The

---

[24] On interviewing Dr. Bob's children, the author found *For Sinners Only* in Dr. Bob's library. See Dick B., *Dr. Bob's Library: Books for Twelve Step Growth* (San Rafael, CA: Paradise Research Publications, 1994), pp. 2, 6, 14, 23, 43, 77. In reviewing the spiritual journal kept and shared with early AAs by Dr. Bob's wife (Anne), the author again found *For Sinners Only* highly recommended. See Dick B., *Anne Smith's Journal*, p. 81. A.A.'s *DR. BOB and the Good Oldtimers* also spoke of the importance of Russell's book (see p. 310).

[25] Sherwood Sunderland Day, *The Principles of the Group* (Great Britain, The Oxford Group, n.d.).

principles of the "Group" are as old as the experiences recorded
in the Bible, and should be to-day, as they were in the early
Church, the normal and constant practice of Christians. It is also
well to remember that it is never possible to find Life—peace with
God—victory—power—whatever names you may use, by merely
trying to follow out principle. That Life comes to one as a
possession through but one gateway—a personal experience of
Jesus Christ and Him crucified.

Day then set forth what he said were "some of these principles
. . . which have been all but lost from our Christian message and
which need reaffirming today":

1. **God-Guidance**. "By 'guidance' is meant communion--
   communion with our Father, the Living God. 'Listening to
   God,' 'two-way prayer,' 'thinking God's thoughts after Him,'
   are all phrases often used in speaking of this experience."[26]

2. **Fearless Dealing with Sin**. "While the first great fact of history is
   Jesus Christ, the second is the presence of sin. What is it? The
   Bible calls it Sin and the 'Group' has no better word. 'Anything that
   separates me from God or from another person is for me sin' is the
   simplest and most thorough definition I know. The Bible frankly
   faces the fact of sin, but does not end there. It offers a cure."[27]

3. **Sharing**. "A sharing Christian is a propagating Christian. . . . The
   word 'sharing' as used by the Group covers two distinct things,
   further described as confession and witness. The facts about
   sharing are these: (a) It is necessary for the one who shares.
   'Confess your faults one to another' is the admonition of St.
   James. . . . (b) It is necessary in helping others. It immediately
   establishes confidence. The person confessed to knows that the
   confessor 'has been through a like experience.'"[28]

---

[26] See also the foundational Oxford Group pamphlet—Eleanor Napier Forde's *The Guidance of God* (Great Britain: The Oxford Group, 1930).

[27] See Walter, *Soul Surgery*, p. 86.

[28] See also the foundational Oxford Group pamphlet—J. P. Thornton-Duesbury's *Sharing* (Great Britain: The Oxford Group, n.d.).

4. **The Necessity for Adequate Intelligent Expressional Activity.** "'There is no vital sustained experience of Jesus Christ where there is not adequate expressional activity.' Every word in that sentence counts. It means that no high level of contagious life can be maintained without trying to pass that life on to others."[29]

5. **Stewardship.** "The message of the New Testament is that life is a whole—that it cannot be divided up into any such compartments as 'sacred' or 'secular'. . . . when we surrender to Jesus Christ it is merely the acknowledgement that He who bought us with a price owns us and all that He has entrusted to us. On such a basis houses, lands, money, things, relationships, gifts, all that we are and have make up a trust which we are to administer."[30]

6. **Teamwork.** "Jesus Christ believed in teamwork. He gathered a small group about Him and set the example for all His followers in that respect. He believed that the highest life for the individual is to be found in association with others—in the group—in His Church. When His followers were of one mind, with one accord, in one place, the Spirit came."[31]

---

[29] As to the expression *pass it on*, see Buchman, *Remaking the World*, p. x: "The best way to keep an experience of Christ is to pass it on;" *Pass It On* (New York: Alcoholics Anonymous World Services, Inc., 1984), the title and p. 7; Samuel M. Shoemaker, Jr., *They're on the Way* (New York: E. P. Dutton, 1951), p. 159.

[30] See 1 Corinthians 6:20: "For ye are bought with a price. . . ." Acts 2:36: ". . . God hath made that same Jesus, whom ye have crucified, both Lord and Christ;" and Acts 2:44-45: "And all that believed were together, and had all things common; And sold their possessions and goods, and parted them to all *men*, as every man had need. And they, continuing daily with one accord in the temple, and breaking bread from house to house, did eat their meat with gladness and singleness of heart."

[31] See Garth Lean, *Cast out Your Nets: Sharing Your Faith with Others* (London: Grosvenor, 1990)—Chapter Fourteen is titled "Building a Team," pp. 121-28; K. D. Belden: *Reflections on Moral Re-Armament* (London: Grosvenor, 1983)—Chapter 6 is titled "Teamwork: God in community," pp. 62-72. See Matthew 18:20: "For where two or three are gathered together in my name, there am I in the midst of them."

7. **Loyalty**. "The supreme loyalty in life should be to Jesus
Christ, but that loyalty involves lesser loyalties, and it often
happens that one is disloyal to Christ because he has failed in
these 'lesser loyalties.' The person or group of persons that
have been used to reveal Jesus Christ to us, are persons and
groups which demand our loyalty."[32]

A Summary of Oxford Group "Structure"

Several long-time Oxford Group activists have informed the author
that the following title was not written by an Oxford Group
adherent. However, *What is The Oxford Group?* was owned by
Dr. Frank Buchman and circulated by him.[33] Several copies were
owned and circulated by Dr. Bob among early AAs. And the book
has this to say:

> You cannot belong to the Oxford Group. It has no membership
> list, subscriptions, badge, rules, or definite location. It is a name
> for a group of people who, from every rank, profession, and
> trade, in many countries, have surrendered their lives to God and
> who are endeavoring to lead a spiritual quality of life under the
> guidance of the Holy Spirit. The Oxford Group is not a religion;
> it has no hierarchy, no temples, now endowments; its workers
> have no salaries, no plans but God's Plan; every country is their
> country, every man their brother. They are Holy Crusaders in
> modern dress, wearing spiritual armour. Their aim is "A New
> World Order for Christ, the King.". . . The Oxford Group works
> within churches of all denominations, planning to bring those
> outside back into their folds and to re-awaken those within to their
> responsibilities as Christians. It advocates nothing that is not the

---

[32] See Irving Harris: *The Breeze of the Spirit: Sam Shoemaker and the Story of Faith-at-Work* (New York: The Seabury Press, 1978). Harris was Shoemaker's assistant minister and pointed out that Shoemaker had asked Sherry Day to sum up their mutual convictions. The summary was very similar to that in The Oxford Group's pamphlet and appeared in one of the 1926 issues of *The Calvary Evangel*. Harris quoted Day's seven principles at pp. 18-21; Then, on page 21, Harris quoted Day: "It was said of the first Christians, 'See how they love one another.'"

[33] See Dick B., *Design for Living*, pp. 31-32.

fundamental basis of all Christian Faith, and takes no side in sectarian disputes (pp. 3-4).

Some Unique Oxford Group Ideas

Several ideas in the Oxford Group were unusual for their time. They influenced A.A. And we call attention to the following:

1. **Oxford Group names**. As we've said, in 1922, Buchman formed "A First Century Christian Fellowship." His biographer wrote that this Fellowship was never much more than a name. But that does not appear to have been the case in the United States. For Shoemaker and his American entourage often referred to the Group as "A First Century Christian Fellowship" through the early 1930's. And well into the 1930's, Oxford Group invitations and programs commonly included *both* the Oxford Group name and the First Century Christian Fellowship name. A.A.'s *Pass It On* said that Dr. Bob and the other Akron AAs continued to refer to the group, through the late 1930's, as "A First Century Christian Fellowship;" and Dr. Bob frequently referred to A.A.'s own early Akron meetings as "a Christian fellowship."

In the 1920's, some referred to Buchman's fellowship as the "Groups." However, in 1928, a "team" was touring South Africa by train. The team sometimes booked a compartment; and on one occasion, the compartment was labeled by the railway, "the Oxford Group;" and the press thereafter described the team as the Oxford Group and may well have picked up the name from the compartment label. The name merely described the composition of the team of seven, six of whom were from Oxford. But the Oxford Group name met with favor among participants in A First Century Christian Fellowship; and by the early 1930's, the name "Oxford Group" was in common usage. In passing, one can note how frequently the words *fellowship* and *group* are used in A.A.

By 1938, Frank Buchman took a new turn. According to one of Buchman's colleagues, it was becoming increasingly plain to Buchman that the world, so massively rearming, was moving inexorably towards war. Buchman felt something needed to be done to avert the war or, if nothing could be done, then to rebuild afterwards. On a holiday in the Black Forest, Buchman received compelling guidance that, "the next great movement in the world would be a movement of moral and spiritual rearmament."[34] He felt many who had found a rich personal experience of faith through the Oxford Group were hugging it to themselves. Buchman wanted them to enter the struggle to answer the problems of the wider world. So Buchman launched his world outreach under the name "Moral Re-Armament." In Great Britain today, the name *Oxford Group* remains the legal name of the incorporated entity. The legal entity in the United States is called *Moral Re-Armament, Inc.* Buchman's biographer (Lean) suggested to the author that the idea of *The Oxford Group and Its Work of Moral Re-Armament* perhaps best expresses where the movement is today.

2. **Houseparties**. The Oxford Group often held what it called houseparties—in Great Britain, the United States, and elsewhere. Bill and Lois Wilson attended several during their Oxford Group affiliation in early A.A. These functions were preceded by invitations with the names of leading adherents, often including both Buchman and Shoemaker, as well as some who were Bill Wilson's team friends. Conclaves were frequently held at a country inn, a hotel, or a private residence. They usually had choir time; then meetings in small groups; and then a big time period in the Bible each morning. Bible studies, lasting one and a half hours, were often led by Cleve Hicks (who was mentioned in Lois Wilson's Oxford Group Notes). In fact, about 1933, these Bible studies formed a disciplined forty-five or sixty minutes part of each

---

[34] Buchman's colleague was K. D. Belden who wrote the author on July 27, 1996, "This is a vital point and really lies behind the defection of Sam Shoemaker and Frank's very old friend Sherry Day." Belden believes there was a mentality which did not wish to move beyond the confines of personal religion and reacted strongly against being called on to rethink their attitudes and move into the wider field. Buchman's convictions and efforts did bear fruit in the years after the war with France and Germany, Japan, and the colonial worlds of Africa and Asia, said Belden.

morning meeting. Then there would be reading, with individuals questioning and sharing. There was a quiet time for each individual; and each morning opened with group quiet time.

The following invitation exemplifies the agenda: Miss Mary Angevine, of a Bible seminary in New York, was to conduct Bible classes during the conference. The dates extended from May 2 to May 12, 1930. Topics included: (a) spiritual diagnosis; (b) the place of the guidance of God in human lives; (c) the principles of sharing Christian experiences; (d) the methods of helping those in difficulties; (e) the place of possessions; and (f) the principles involved in developing a national and international fellowship. A prominent editor called these meetings the "church in the house."

3. **Teams**. Frank Buchman would persuade varied categories of key people to accompany him on his evangelical trips. Members might include a docker from the Clyde, or a worker from London's East End, or a young man or woman with a vital experience. These varied types assured that audiences could not say, "That speaker is not like me." Buchman usually remained in the background at meetings as much as possible, calling on team members and others to do the talking. Buchman felt a *team*, of whatever size, was more effective and gave a wider picture of God's action than any individual could give. As we have said, Bill Wilson belonged to a businessmen's team in New York and participated in some major team events on the East Coast of America in late 1935.

As we will show in a moment, A.A.'s own beginnings in Akron involved the presence of an Oxford Group *team* of thirty who came, with Buchman, to witness in churches and meetings to the effectiveness of Oxford Group principles and practices. Adopting this team idea, early AAs in Akron called themselves "the alcoholic *squad* of the Oxford Group" (emphasis added); and they visited drunks in hospitals as a team, sharing their experience, and witnessing to the effectiveness of that early program.

4. Story-telling; sharing experience—"News, not views". If there was one Oxford Group practice that had more influence on *today's* A.A. meetings and message-carrying ideas than any other, it was the practice of *sharing*. Sharing meant sharing for confession (the foundation of A.A.'s Fifth Step); and sharing for witness (the foundation for a major portion of A.A.'s Twelfth Step).

Oxford Group houseparties, meetings, and teams the world over focused on the sharing of experience. Oxford Group adherents commonly told what God had done for them in changing their lives.[35] This was the message Bill Wilson's "sponsor" Ebby Thacher carried to Bill when "he [Ebby] made the point blank declaration to Bill [who was still drunk] that God had done for him what he could not do for himself."[36] Ebby's declaration persists to this day in the Big Book's "promises" and elsewhere.[37]

And, though the A.A. meetings of today are far different from those when A.A. was an integral part of the Oxford Group, they still focus on *stories*—the sharing of experience, strength, and hope. The original outline for A.A.'s basic text (*Alcoholics Anonymous*) intended for that title to consist entirely of personal stories of recovered alcoholics.[38] The sharing of personal stories about deliverance was what the most successful Shoemaker/Oxford Group books and meetings had done.[39] Even so, the plan for the

---

[35] See Thornton-Duesbery, Sharing; James 5:16: "Confess your faults one to another . . . ;" 1 John 1:3: "That which we have seen and heard declare we unto you, the ye also may have fellowship with us: and truly our fellowship is with the Father, and with his Son, Jesus Christ."

[36] *Alcoholics Anonymous*, 3rd ed., p. 11.

[37] *Alcoholics Anonymous*, 3rd ed., p. 84: "We will suddenly realize that God is doing for us what we could not do for ourselves."

[38] Bill Wilson's publishing partner, Henry P., prepared what amounted to a sales brochure for the proposed book. It included a long list of the types of individuals (i.e. a barber, an attorney, a doctor, etc.) whose stories were to tell how those persons had recovered. The author discovered and was allowed to copy Henry P.'s proposal during one of the author's visits to the Wilson Home at Stepping Stones in New York.

[39] See Begbie, *Life Changers*; Russell, *For Sinners Only*; Shoemaker, *Twice-Born Ministers* and *Children of the Second Birth* (New York: Fleming H. Revell, 1927).

A.A. text was changed; and a basic "textbook" of 164 pages eventually resulted. But the idea of including stories was retained, and they were set forth at length immediately following the text.

Thus the Multilith draft of A.A.'s proposed basic text said this:

> There is a group of personal narratives. Then clear-cut directions are given showing how an alcoholic may recover. These are followed by more than a score of personal experiences. Each individual, in the personal stories, describes in his own language and from his own point of view the way he found or rediscovered God (p. 13).

The First Edition of *Alcoholics Anonymous* was edited to say:

> Each individual, in the personal stories [in the back of the book] describes in his own language, and from his own point of view the way he established his relationship with God (p. 39).

Many stories in the First Edition (several mentioning the Bible and Christianity) have been eliminated; but the foregoing language can still be found on page twenty-nine of the Third Edition.

The Oxford Group believed their stories should be about *facts*, not opinions. They coined the phrase "News, not views." The evangelist D. L. Moody who influenced Buchman's ideas taught: "You do not share one inch beyond your experience." Buchman thus taught: "Don't go beyond your own experience. You may win your argument and lose the man." Early AAs often urged the sharing of *news, not views*. Even today, they frequently caution that one should not share beyond his or her own experience. To which *Alcoholics Anonymous* adds at page 164: ". . . [O]bviously you cannot transmit something you haven't got."

How Do I Begin?

Even at this late historical date, the author receives phone calls and letters from AAs asking if it is still possible to "do" the Oxford Group program. And, at an earlier time, it was to answer such questions that a well-known Oxford Group adherent, the Reverend Hallen Viney, wrote his little tract *How Do I Begin?*[40]

Viney commenced: "It's a matter of being in touch with God."[41] He continued:

> First of all I believe that God wants to talk to you. It is just as simple as that. . . . It's an experiment. . . . Remember, there are one or two conditions attached to this [experiment of] listening. It's rather like telephoning; God can't talk through a dirty contact. If you want to hear what He has to say, you must first find out, as I had to, whether you've got a good connection."

Elaborating on this *good connection* illustration, Viney said there might be things blocking the listening process; and he suggested Four Tests for determining blocks to God:

> . . . [If] you really want to listen to God . . . [you have] got to find the fault in the telephone and then to put it right. . . . [T]here are four pretty good tests to help you be definite in finding these faults. They are absolute honesty, absolute purity, absolute unselfishness, absolute love. . . . [Therefore,] if I thought about absolute honesty, purity, unselfishness and love, I might find a few things about myself which stop this listening business. . . .

---

[40] Hallen Viney, *How Do I Begin?* (New York: The Oxford Group, n. d.). The following listing for Viney, as a prominent Oxford Group associate, appears in the announcement of The Oxford Group Luncheon for Editors of the Daily Press, on April 13, 1932: The Rev. Hallen Viney, Downing College, Cambridge, Chaplain, R.N.V.R. K. D. Belden expresses, from the British viewpoint, that they never gave the pamphlet the weight it receives in our title. Belden adds, "Still, it was all sound stuff. Halen was an electrical engineer working in the States, and I think was probably gathered in by Calvary Church. He came back to Britain and went to a theological college (Wycliffe Hall, Oxford) and was ordained. After working in a London parish, he finally became full time." Letter to author from Belden, 7/27/96.

[41] A.A.'s today use the expression *conscious contact with God*.

Next, said Viney, you "write them down":

> And a good way I found to make it more definite was to take four
> pieces of paper and head each one with one of those absolutes.
> Ask yourself the question, "Where am I not being absolutely
> honest?" . . . As answers begin to form in your mind don't argue
> with them, just write them down whatever they are. . . . Then go
> on to the next absolute. . . . I began to wonder if the paper would
> hold out!

Then you set things right. But there must be power behind it.
Viney explained:

> If you make this list honestly, you find you cannot put things in
> order yourself. . . . A man can't live up to these absolute standards
> on his own strength. You need something more than your own
> strength . . . that something more is the power of Christ, as an
> experience in your own life. . . . Now we can have the same
> power ourselves because of what he did, because of His death and
> resurrection. . . . Don't worry about the theory now . . . a lot of
> people get into first-hand touch with God without knowing all the
> theory at first. They understand more later, as they gain more
> experience.

Viney concluded with a concept that became the heart of A.A.'s
Third Step. There must be a "decision for life," and he added:

> It means carrying out God's will seven days a week and twenty-four
> hours a day. . . . For one thing it means getting up earlier to listen
> to God. . . . Some people sit up in bed with a pencil and note-book.
> . . . God normally talks to people through their thoughts. . . .
> Think over the problems of the day against the background
> question, "What does God want?" rather than "What do I want?"
> You will find convictions forming in your mind as to the right thing
> to do. Write these convictions down. . . . You can test them [the
> thoughts that come] by those four standards: Absolute Honesty,
> Purity, Unselfishness, and Love. They'll naturally be in line with
> the New Testament. If in doubt you can check them with other
> people who listen to God. . . . Why don't you try it?

Note that, in his last major address to AAs in Detroit,
Michigan, in December of 1948, Dr. Bob said:

> The four absolutes, as we called them, were the only yardsticks
> we had in the early days, before the Steps. I think the absolutes
> still hold good and can be extremely helpful. I have found at
> times that a question arises, and I want to do the right thing, but
> the answer is not obvious. Almost always, if I measure my
> decision carefully by the yardsticks of absolute honesty, absolute
> unselfishness, absolute purity, and absolute love, and it checks up
> pretty well with those four, then my answer can't be very far out
> of the way. If, however, I do that and I'm still not too satisfied
> with the answer, I usually consult with some friend whose
> judgment, in this particular case, would be very much better than
> mine. But usually the absolutes can help you to reach your own
> personal decision without bothering your friends.

Oxford Group Mentors

The author has previously written at some length on the contributions to Oxford Group thinking by some famous writers and
speakers of the late 1800's and early 1900's.[42] The discussion
here will therefore be confined to a summary of the names and
some of the most cogent ideas that were passed along by these
mentors to Frank Buchman, and that eventually influenced A.A.

Dr. Horace Bushnell

Horace Bushnell was a professor of divinity at Yale University. In
1868, his title *The New Life* was published.[43]

---

[42] See Dick B., *Design for Living*, pp. 39-72.

[43] Horace Bushnell, *The New Life* (London: Strahan & Co., 1868). See also Mary
B. Cheney, *Life and Letters of Horace Bushnell* (New York: Harper & Brothers, 1890);
and Robert L. Edwards, *Of Singular Genius of Singular Grace: A Biography of Horace
Bushnell* (Cleveland: Pilgrim Press, 1992).

A most important concept was that God has a plan. Bushnell devoted a whole chapter to that subject. He called it "Every Man's Life a Plan of God." Oxford Group writers and their mentors quoted Bushnell for this. Bushnell also discussed conviction, conversion, surrender of self, being born again, obedience, getting rid of self-will, and selfishness. Also, the concept of "willingness" he found in John 7:17.

Oxford Group people credited Bushnell with being one of the sources of these ideas in which they believed. And the ideas can be found in Buchman's teachings, and in A.A. literature and principles.

Evangelist D. L. Moody

Dwight L. Moody was born February 5, 1837, and died December 22, 1899. One of his biographers claimed he was the most widely heralded representative of evangelical Protestantism after 1870—a "professional revivalist."[44]

Moody has been hailed as one of those who heavily influenced Frank Buchman; and traces of Moody ideas can be found in Buchman's speeches and in Oxford Group writings.

Moody and Buchman both believed the Bible was the inspired Word of God. Moody urged: "Take the Bible; study it . . . feed on the Word . . . pass on the message."[45] As to Bible study, Buchman often said: "Read accurately, interpret honestly, apply drastically."[46] Also: "Read it through. Pray it in. Write it down. Work it out. Pass it on."[47] As mentioned, the "pass it on" message was to become virtually an A.A. motto.

---

[44] See James Findlay, Jr., *Dwight L. Moody American Evangelist* (Chicago: University of Chicago Press, 1969).

[45] William R. Moody, *The Life of D. L. Moody* (New York: Fleming H. Revell, 1900), pp. 497, 19.

[46] Lean, *On the Tail of a Comet*, p. 157; Harry J. Almond, *Foundations for Faith*, 2d ed. (London: Grosvenor, 1980), p. 31.

[47] Almond, *Foundations for Faith*, p. 31.

Moody was said to be "saturated" with Scripture. Similarly, one of Buchman's close friends described Buchman as "soaked in the Bible." Both Moody and Buchman held the Word to be totally reliable. Moody was well known for the phrase "Crucify the great 'I.'" And this same thought can be found in many of Buchman's speeches and also in Oxford Group books. The concept is strongly embedded in the instructions for taking A.A.'s Third Step.

Moody presented the 32nd Psalm as seven words: Conviction, Confession, Forgiveness, Prayer, Protection, Guidance, and Joy. Such words certainly have counterparts in Buchman's Five C's, and in other Buchman and A.A. ideas. The Oxford Group and A.A. also have strong ties to the tenets of rigorous honesty and restitution. Compare these words by Moody:

> If you have ever taken money dishonestly, you need not pray God to forgive you and fill you with the Holy Ghost until you make restitution. Confession and restitution are the steps that lead to forgiveness.[48]

There was a powerful indirect influence on Frank Buchman and the Oxford Group by Moody through Professors Henry B. Wright and Henry Drummond, whom we will discuss in a moment. Perhaps the most significant, in A.A. terms, were these words of Moody's:

> The world has yet to see what God can do in, for, by and through a man whose will is wholly given up to Him.

The words were on the wall of Wright's lecture room at Yale; and Buchman saw them many times. Wright would begin all lectures with two minutes of silent consideration of Moody's words. Then Wright would say, "Will you be that man? Will you be that man?" Wright linked Moody's challenge with the Bible verse, "I, if I be

---

[48] Emma Moody Fitt, *Day by Day with D. L. Moody* (Chicago: Moody Press, n.d.), p. 93.

lifted up, will draw all men unto me" [See John 12:32]. Buchman said he yielded himself to that principle; and Sam Shoemaker later titled one of his own books, *If I Be Lifted Up*. This Shoemaker book was very popular in early A.A.

Evangelist F. B. Meyer

Many in the Oxford Group wrote of the influence on Frank Buchman of the noted evangelist and Congregational minister F. B. Meyer. Buchman first met Meyer at a Northfield Student Conference in Massachusetts. In 1907, while Buchman was working at the Lutheran youth hospice, Meyer had sent and inscribed to Buchman a copy of his book, *Reveries and Realities, or Life and Work in London*. As we previously wrote, Meyer visited Penn State while Buchman was YMCA secretary there. Meyer had told Buchman he should work on man-to-man interviews.

Meyer also persuaded Buchman to greater communion with God in the morning. Meyer's book *The Secret of Guidance* suggests the importance Meyer placed on the guidance of God—a major Oxford Group stress.[49] Buchman cited this latter book as one which helped him.[50]

In *The Secret of Guidance*, Meyer dealt with the necessity for surrender of the will to God. Meyer stated that Jesus was constantly insisting on a surrendered will as the key to perfect knowledge. The Oxford Group was to emphasize Jesus's words in John 7:17 as a key to its so-called experiment of faith based on believing, *doing* God's known will, and then *knowing*.

---

[49] F. B. Meyer, *The Secret of Guidance* (New York: Fleming H. Revell, 1896).

[50] K. D. Belden wrote the author on 7/27/96: "Meyer's influence was decisive for Frank, especially that direction to give the first hour of the day to listening to God before the phones start ringing. Buchman was always a tremendous worker, but now he had clear direction from day to day which led him into people's lives with far-reaching results, and which remained with him for the rest of his life. It was at the heart of his effectiveness."

Meyer espoused Bible study, prayer, and waiting on God. And he included in his Guidance book a chapter titled, "Where am I wrong?" Whether this particular chapter influenced Buchman's self-examination ideas, we do not know. But the idea of looking for one's own part in a resentment situation was fundamental to Buchman's thinking and later to A.A.'s own Fourth Step.

Professor Henry Drummond

Henry Drummond was born August 17, 1851, and died on March 11, 1897. He became Professor of Natural Science at Free Church College, Glasgow, Scotland. Dwight Moody brought Drummond to Moody's second student summer conference at Northfield, Massachusetts, in 1887; and it was then and there that Drummond delivered his talk *The Greatest Thing in the World.*[51]

The subject was 1 Corinthians 13—the famous "love" chapter of the Bible. Essays, booklets, and pamphlets containing Drummond's address sold over a million copies. Frank Buchman widely recommended *The Greatest Thing in the World* for study and absorption.

Buchman's enthusiasm seems to have been shared by Dr. Bob. For Dr. Bob said early AAs considered 1 Corinthians 13 "absolutely essential" to their recovery program. In fact, Dr. Bob's great interest in Drummond's book is dramatized by the following remarks of Dorothy S. M.:

> Once, when I was working on a woman in Cleveland, I called and asked him [Dr. Bob], "What do I do for somebody who is going into D.T.'s?" He told me to give her the medication, and he said, "When she comes out of it and she decides she wants to be a different woman, get her Drummond's 'The Greatest Thing in the World.' Tell her to read it through every day for 30 days, and she'll be a different woman."[52]

---

[51] See Henry Drummond, *Essays and Addresses* (New York: James Potts and Company, 1903).

[52] *DR. BOB*, p. 310.

Interestingly, Henry Drummond himself had made a similar suggestion at the close of the lecture in which he delivered his "greatest thing in the world" address, which later became incorporated in his best-selling book. Drummond said:

> Now I have all but finished. How many of you will join me in reading this chapter [1 Corinthians 13] once a week for the next three months? A man did that once and it changed his whole life. Will you do it? It is for the greatest thing in the world. You might begin by reading it every day, especially the verses which describe the perfect character. "Love suffereth long, and is kind; loveth envieth not; love vaunteth not itself." Get these ingredients into your life.[53]

Drummond believed that the Scriptures of the Old and New Testaments were the Word of God and the only rule of faith and manners. He wrote a number of books which became a part of Dr. Bob's library and were loaned out to early AAs.

The author believes, along with several other commentators, that Drummond's book *The Changed Life* has a title indicating its probable influence on Oxford Group life-change, life-changers, and changed life phraseology. In another book, *Natural Law in the Spiritual World* (owned by Dr. Bob), Drummond stressed the importance of conversion. Though they sometimes used different terminology, the Oxford Group, Shoemaker, and early AAs all focused on the importance of conversion and the new birth.

In *The Ideal Life*, Drummond held forth in detail that the Universal Will of God was to be learned from the Bible, and that the particular will of God could be received through divine Guidance. Henry Wright quoted Drummond for these concepts; and they became a part of Buchman's thinking.

John 7:17 and the idea of willingness to obey and do God's Universal Will as a condition to knowing His particular will were articulated by Drummond in *The Ideal Life*. F. W. Robertson had

---

[53] Henry Drummond, *The Greatest Thing in the World and other addresses* (World Bible Publishers, Inc.), p. 53.

delivered a sermon on John 7:17 under the title "Obedience the Organ of Spiritual Knowledge." This sermon deeply influenced Drummond and Moody, and later Professor Henry Wright.

Drummond also seems to have inspired Buchman's ideas on "spiritual diagnosis, soul-surgery, and personal evangelism." Drummond's *The New Evangelism* is much quoted in Howard Walter's *Soul Surgery* which, as we previously discussed, was written in collaboration with Buchman and Henry B. Wright.

Dr. Robert E. Speer

We have already discussed Speer's Four Absolute Standards—honesty, purity, unselfishness, and love. We've also mentioned how Professor Wright renamed these the Four Absolutes which became so vitally important in the Oxford Group and in early A.A. As to the standards, Oxford Group writers still often refer to Wright's "Absolutes" as the "Standards." As the speech of Dr. Bob's shows, Dr. Bob called them the "yardsticks."

While all writers agree that Speer and his *Principles of Jesus* were the source of the Four Absolutes, most have erroneously claimed Speer abstracted the standards from Jesus's Sermon on the Mount. Sam Shoemaker and other Oxford Group activists and commentators have so stated.[54]

However, Speer reconstructed the principles from several Gospels. And Wright found the four standards in many Church Epistles. Eventually, some writers simply pointed out that the principles could be found *in* the Sermon on the Mount.[55]

---

[54] K. D. Belden wrote on 7/27/96: "I'm glad you make the point that the Four Standards are not a summary of the Sermon on the Mount as people sometimes unthinkingly assume, but are a distillation of Christ's moral teaching in a form which everyone can grasp and apply."

[55] See, for example, Harry J. Almond, *Foundations for Faith*, rev. ed. (London: Grosvenor, 1980), pp. 11-12.

Professor William James

Professor William James of Harvard University wrote *The Varieties of Religious Experience*.[56] We have personally heard a number of old-time Oxford Group adherents state that they had never heard of James's influence on Frank Buchman. However, William James and his book are frequently quoted in Walter's *Soul Surgery*. Harold Begbie dedicated his first title, *Twice-Born Men*, to James; and *Twice-Born Men* (though written in 1909 and before the Oxford Group existed) was much read by Oxford Group people and by early AAs. Furthermore, Sam Shoemaker frequently quoted William James and James's book.

Bill Wilson received a copy of James's book in the earliest days of his sobriety, either from Ebby Thacher or from Rowland Hazard (both of whom were Oxford Group adherents). Bill cited James's book by name in *Alcoholics Anonymous* and later proclaimed James the father of modern psychology and a "founder" of Alcoholics Anonymous—though James was long dead at the time. Both Dr. Bob and Anne Smith read the William James book and referred to it in their discussions.

We will see as we go along that William James's language often popped up—in one form or another—in Oxford Group writings, in Sam Shoemaker's books, in Anne Smith's Journal, and in A.A.'s own literature. Bill Wilson thought he had obtained A.A.'s First Step requirement of "deflation at depth" or "defeat" or "hitting bottom" from James's book. A distinguished A.A. historian took issue with Bill's contention. But our own view is that James's definition of conversion (which was quoted in Sam Shoemaker's first significant title) necessarily involved starting with surrender of a "self, hitherto divided and consciously wrong, inferior, and unhappy." To us, this sounds a lot like "deflation-at-depth."

---

[56] William James, *The Varieties of Religious Experience* (New York: Vintage Books/The Library of America, 1990).

In any event, Oxford Group people commonly referred to James's definitions of conversion, self-surrender, change, religious experience, the "turning point," and discovering God.

Dr. John R. Mott

John R. Mott was engaged in a crusade to "evangelise the world in this generation;" and that was his central theme among the Christians with whom he worked most closely. In 1888, he became Student Secretary of the International Committee of the YMCA. In 1895, he was General Secretary of the World Student Christian Federation, which he largely created. By the First World War, he was General Secretary of the American YMCA. Buchman's biographer said Mott was "perhaps the dominant figure in the student evangelical movement" and that Mott was Buchman's "old friend and mentor." In fact, it was John Mott who sent Buchman to Penn State with the attendant far-reaching consequences.

Buchman first met Mott in the summer of 1901 while he was at the Northfield Student Conference in Massachusetts, founded by D. L. Moody, and then led by Mott and Robert E. Speer. Around 1909, Mott's office arranged for Buchman's appointment as YMCA Secretary at Penn State College where he was to be in charge of religious work at the college. Buchman picked up a good many of Mott's ideas for carrying the Christian message to individual people. Mott's books and pamphlets were often referred to in *Soul Surgery*. Mott was an effective advocate of world outreach, and embodied evangelical ideas of enthusiasm, dedication, Bible study, the life of prayer, and full commitment to Christ.

At every opportunity, Mott promoted the concept of the "Morning Watch" which Buchman and Shoemaker both advocated. Later, Buchman and Shoemaker both called this devotional period "Quiet Time." But they cut their teeth on Mott's principle as discussed by the following Oxford Group writer:

> But, amid much else that has been forgotten, one sentence spoken by Mott proved revolutionary. He said something of this kind: "If

you wish to make your life effective and useful for God and your fellow-men, it is essential that you should put aside unhurried time every day for a morning watch with God."[57]

Of Mott's influence, Buchman's biographer observed:

Mott's strategy depended on the peace and freedom of movement and communications which preceded the First World War, and during that war its thrust slackened. . . . The American YMCA . . . became more and more involved, after 1917, in providing amenities for the troops. Its Secretaries in the mission fields of India and China were inadequate to their primary task, and no match for a Communist missionary like Borodin. Buchman, on his return home after the war, found that the old modes of working—through the YMCA, Northfield and so on—no longer possessed the power which they had previously. He felt that something less organizational, much more dependent upon the kind of transparent fellowship which he and his friends had established through total honesty in Tientsin, was necessary [but] . . . he had absorbed and retained much of the optimism and many of the tactics of Mott's great design.

Professor Henry B. Wright

Much has been written of the influence of Henry B. Wright on Frank Buchman; and certainly Wright's *The Will of God and a Man's Lifework* is heavy with materials on God's Plan, the Will of God, God's Universal and Particular Will for Man, the experiment of faith, John 7:17, and the Four Absolutes. Wright's book talked much of "two-way prayer"—the practice of setting aside a time each day for "listening," prayer, then receiving "that arresting tick," and then writing down thoughts received. Wright certainly challenged all men, including Buchman, to give up their will to God.

---

[57] See, for example, Jack C. Winslow, *When I Awake* (London: Hodder & Stoughton, 1938), pp. 5, 9-11; Harry Emerson Fosdick, *The Meaning of Prayer* (New York: Association Press, 1915), p. xi—containing an introduction by Mott; and Samuel M. Shoemaker, Jr., *Realizing Religion*, pp. 60-66.

As we have said in *Design for Living*, however, it is only fair to point out that most of the ideas from Wright that influenced Frank Buchman were ideas Wright derived from others.[58] Wright frequently referred to Horace Bushnell, Dwight L. Moody, Henry Drummond, F. B. Meyer, Henry Drummond, John Mott, Robert E. Speer, and others as Wright organized the ideas he discussed at such length in *The Will of God*. We believe, therefore, that Wright's influence on Buchman should be attributed more to his status as teacher, colleague, and collaborator, than as to any role as the originator of the ideas. Buchman's colleague, K. D. Belden, adds: "Whatever influences the men who were cited on your preceding pages had on Frank, there was a quality in him [Frank] which went further in understanding the battle that needed to be fought for the modern world and how to set about it."[59]

The Buchman and Shoemaker Split

Before we leave this survey of the Oxford Group itself, we should point out how its influence on Bill Wilson, through Sam Shoemaker, came to an end shortly after A.A.'s recovery program was published in the Spring of 1939 in its basic text, the Big Book.

There is little profit in going into details. But there definitely was a complete break between Sam Shoemaker and Frank Buchman in late 1941. Despite frequent discussions of the matter, the reasons for the break are not fully known.

In 1941, Sam Shoemaker announced to the American and British press that he had decided to end his association with Buchman. Shoemaker asked Buchman to remove all personal and Oxford Group material and personnel from Calvary House. In *Design for Living*, we set forth in full the November 1, 1941,

---

[58] Dick B., *Design for Living*, pp. 67-72.

[59] Letter to the author from Belden dated 7/27/96. See also R. C. Mowat, *Modern Prophetic Voices from Kierkegaard to Buchman* (Oxford: New Cherwell Press, 1994).

letter from Shoemaker and his associate rector J. Herbert Smith which was sent to all Calvary Church parishioners.[60]

Shoemaker pointed to the years of close association between his parish and the work of the Oxford Group and Moral Re-Armament. He expressed gratitude to Buchman and other group leaders. But Shoemaker pointed to a change in the Oxford Group. He said it was, *at first,* "a movement of vital personal religion working within the churches to make the principles of the New Testament practical as a working force today."

Without defining the change, he said there were *new* policies and points of view about which he had misgivings; and he closed by expressing the hope that parishioners and friends would adhere to the spiritual truths enunciated by the Oxford Group, which were fundamental Christian truths, which transformed lives, and helped equip people to meet the needs of others.

One of Shoemaker's daughters told the author the real dispute was over Buchman's request that Shoemaker leave his church and devote himself to Moral Re-Armament objectives—a proposal to which she said her father would not agree. At an earlier point, in our title *The Oxford Group & Alcoholics Anonymous*, we had written that we believed the reasons of the break could be attributed to Shoemaker's desired focus on vital personal religion (working within the churches), and Buchman's desired focus on national and supernational change to save the world; and Buchman's biographer concurred in this analysis.

Whatever the problem between Buchman and Shoemaker, there is no denying that *both* gave A.A. almost its entire spiritual recovery program structure. Now, therefore, we are ready to review the *beginnings* of *early* A.A. to see what the pioneer AAs inherited and fashioned in those developmental days into their highly successful program that was then published in their basic text, *Alcoholics Anonymous*.

---

[60] Dick B., *Design for Living*, pp. 146-47.

3

A.A.'s Spiritual Beginnings

A.A. had two points of commencement. Both involved the Oxford Group. Both were much related to the influence of the Reverend Samuel M. Shoemaker, Jr. Yet only one has, until recently, received any significant historical attention. Even that one (the New York origin) has had substantial facts omitted, deleted, and edited from historical accounts. The New York story begins with Rowland Hazard and Dr. Carl G. Jung.

It centers around Bill Wilson (who lived in New York) and Sam Shoemaker's Calvary Church, Calvary House, and Calvary Mission (which were located in New York). And we have called this beginning "The New York Genesis of A.A."

The New York Genesis of A.A.

According to Bill Wilson, A.A. had its origins in Switzerland about 1930. The details involve an American businessman from Rhode Island who had been plagued for years by alcoholism. The man was Rowland Hazard.[1]

---

[1] Primary references for the New York story are *Pass It On* (New York: Alcoholics Anonymous World Services, Inc., 1984); *Alcoholics Anonymous Comes of Age: A Brief History of A.A.* (New York: Alcoholics Anonymous World Services, Inc., 1957); Robert
(continued...)

Rowland Hazard and Dr. Carl Gustav Jung

Rowland Hazard was born in Peace Dale, Rhode Island, on October 29, 1881. He died on December 20, 1945. He was of the tenth generation of a famous Rhode Island family whose lineage began in America when Thomas Hazard came to Boston in 1635. In 1639, Thomas became one of the nine founders of Newport, Rhode Island. Rowland's great grandfather founded the Peace Dale woolen mills; and his grandfather helped found the Peace Dale Congregational Church. Rowland attended Yale and graduated in 1903. He served in the Rhode Island Senate and was a captain in the United States Army in World War I.

Though the history of Rowland's alcoholism seems clouded, his disease possibly commenced during World War I. The Third Edition of A.A.'s Big Book records: "For years he [Rowland] had floundered from one sanitarium to another. He had consulted the best known American psychiatrists" (p. 26). As Bill Wilson wrote Carl Jung many years later: "Having exhausted other means of recovery from his alcoholism, it was about 1931 that he [Rowland] became your [Dr. Carl G. Jung's] patient . . . [and] remained

---

¹ (...continued)

Thomsen, *Bill W.* (New York: Harper & Row, 1975); *Alcoholics Anonymous*, 1st ed. (New Jersey, Works Publishing Company, 1939); *Alcoholics Anonymous*, 3rd ed. (New York: Alcoholics Anonymous World Services, Inc., 1976); *Lois Remembers: Memoirs of the co-founder of Al-Anon and wife of the co-founder of Alcoholics Anonymous* (New York: Al-Anon Family Group Headquarters, 1979); Bill Wilson, *How the Big Book Was Put Together* (New York: A.A. General Services Archives. Transcript of Bill Wilson Speech delivered in Fort Worth, Texas, 1954); Bill Wilson, *Bill Wilson's Original Story* (Bedford Hills, New York: Stepping Stones Archives, n.d.)—a manuscript whose individual lines are numbered 1 to 1180; Bill Wilson, *Main Events: Alcoholics Anonymous Fact Sheet by Bill* (Bedford Hills, New York: Stepping Stones Archives, November 1, 1954); Bill Wilson, *W. G. Wilson Recollections* (Bedford Hills, New York: Stepping Stones Archives, September 1, 1954)—a transcript of Bill's dictations to Ed B.; Dick B., *New Light on Alcoholism: The A.A. Legacy from Sam Shoemaker* (Corte Madera, CA: Good Book Publishing Company, 1994); *The Akron Genesis of Alcoholics Anonymous* (Corte Madera, CA: Good Book Publishing Company, 1994).

under your care for perhaps a year."[2] In 1954, Bill related: "At the end of twelve months' treatment, he [Rowland] left the doctor to face the world. Thoroughly understanding himself and thoroughly on guard, he could hardly fail, he thought. Yet, in a matter of weeks, he got drunk, unaccountably drunk. Frightened, he tried to fight off the compulsion, but alcohol soon had his old way with him."[3]

Considering Jung his "court of last resort," Rowland returned to Jung for more care. Jung said: "I must be frank, I never saw one alcoholic of your kind recover under my care, and I can do nothing for you." Rowland asked: "Is there then nothing I can do?" And Jung said: "Occasionally, Rowland, alcoholics have recovered through spiritual experiences, better known as religious conversions." Brightening a little, Rowland said: "But doctor, you know I am a religious man. I used to be a vestryman of the Episcopal Church." Jung replied:

No, Rowland, that isn't enough. Faith and good works are good, very good, but by themselves they almost never budge an alcoholic compulsion like yours. I'm talking about the kind of religious experience that reaches into the depths of a man, that changes his whole motivation and outlook and so transforms his life that the impossible becomes possible.[4]

Rowland asked: "If I must have such an experience, where and how do I find it?" Jung answered:

That's something I can't tell you. All you can do is place yourself in a religious atmosphere of your own choosing, admit your personal powerlessness to go on living. If under such conditions you seek with all your might, you may then find, but the

---

[2] Letter from Bill Wilson to Professor Dr. C. G. Jung, dated January 23, 1961, Wilson's home in Bedford Hills, New York. Earlier accounts by Bill placed Rowland's first Jung visit in 1930. See, for example, Wilson, *W. G. Wilson Recollections*, p. 109.

[3] Quotes in footnotes 3, 4, and 5 from Wilson, *W. G. Wilson Recollections*, p. 110.

[4] *W. G. Wilson Recollections*, p. 111.

experience you need is only occasional; here and there, now and then, alcoholics have recovered through them. You can only try.[5]

Piecing together further facts from Wilson's January 23, 1961, letter to Jung, and Jung's reply to Wilson on January 30, 1961, the following is an elaboration on what occurred between Hazard and Jung:

[Wilson to Jung:] You frankly told him [Rowland] of his hopelessness, so far as any further medical or psychiatric treatment might be concerned. This candid and humble statement of yours was beyond doubt the first foundation stone upon which our society has since been built.

[Jung to Wilson:] His craving for alcohol was the equivalent on a low level of the spiritual thirst of our being for wholeness, expressed in medieval language: the union with God. . . .[6] The only right and legitimate way to such an experience is, that it happens to you in reality and it can only happen to you when you walk on a path which leads to higher understanding. . . . I am strongly convinced that the evil principle prevailing in this world, leads the unrecognized spiritual need into perdition, if it is not counteracted either by a real religious insight or by the protective wall of human community. An ordinary man, not protected by an action from above and isolated in society, cannot resist the power of evil, which is called very aptly the Devil. . . . You see, Alcohol in Latin is "spiritus" and you use the same word for the highest religious experience as well as for the most depraving poison. The helpful formula therefore is *spiritus contra spiritum*.

[Wilson to Jung:] When he [Rowland] then asked you if there was any other hope, you told him that there might be, provided he

---

[5] Wilson, *W. G. Wilson Recollections*, p. 112.

[6] Letter from C. G. Jung to Wilson, dated January 30, 1961, a copy of which was provided to the author by the archivist at Wilson's home. At the above point in his letter, Jung footnoted the following: "As the hart panteth after the water brooks, so panteth my soul after thee, O God. (Psalm 42,1)."

could become the subject of a spiritual or religious experience—in short, a genuine conversion. You pointed out how such an experience, if brought about, might re-motivate him, when nothing else could. But you did caution, though, that while such experiences had sometimes brought about recovery to alcoholics, they were, nevertheless, comparatively rare. You recommended that he place himself in a religious atmosphere and hope for the best. . . . Shortly thereafter, Mr. Hazard joined the Oxford Groups, an evangelical movement then at the height of its success in Europe, and one with which you are doubtless familiar. You will remember their large emphasis on the principles of self-survey, confession, restitution and the giving of oneself in service to others. They strongly stressed meditation and prayer. In these surroundings Roland [sic] Hazard did find a conversion experience that released him for the time being from his compulsion to drink. Returning to New York, he became very active with the "O.G." here, then led by an Episcopal clergyman, Dr. Samuel Shoemaker. . . . At this time (1932-1934), the Oxford Groups had already sobered a number of alcoholics, and Roland [sic] addressed himself to the help of still others.

[Wilson continued, after first having recounted the chain of events that led from Rowland Hazard to Ebby Thacher and then to Wilson's own "spiritual experience":] In the wake of my spiritual experience, there came a vision of a society of alcoholics, each identifying with, and transmitting his experience to the next—chain style. If each sufferer were to carry the news of the scientific hopelessness of alcoholism to each new prospect, he might be able to lay every newcomer wide open to a transforming spiritual experience. This concept proved to be the foundation of such success as Alcoholics Anonymous has since achieved. This has made conversion experiences—in nearly every variety reported by James [Professor William James]—available on an almost wholesale basis.

Several diligent historians have tried to determine when and how Rowland Hazard "became active" with the Oxford Group. To the author's knowledge, none has thus far been successful.[7] But the author has seen (in the Reverend Sam Shoemaker's personal journals), and heard (from Oxford Group activists of the early 1930's), that all these people were working with, and knew, Rowland in that period. And the best answer as to date seems to be that Rowland probably "joined" the Oxford Group in New England somewhere between 1932 and 1934—more probably the earlier year. Rowland then became, as Wilson put it in A.A.'s Big Book (and elsewhere), a free man *and* free from the compulsion to drink.

From Sam Shoemaker's personal journals, from Shoemaker correspondence in the Archives of the Episcopal Church in Austin, Texas, and from an address by Bill Wilson on November 9, 1954, the following facts have been established:

1. Hazard was (in correspondence found in Shoemaker's files) listed as a member of the Oxford Group's Metropolitan Team, as of January 14, 1935. Hazard's name appeared with the names of Bill Wilson's other Oxford Group businessmen's team friends—Charles E. Clapp, Jr., F. Shepard Cornell, Reverend John P. Cuyler, Rev. Irving Harris, Victor Kitchen, L. Parks Shipley, Sr., and Hanford Twitchell.[8]

2. Hazard's name was also frequently mentioned in Shoemaker's personal journals (for the period 1934 through 1936) in company with the names of many of the foregoing Metropolitan Team members.[9]

3. Hazard made the statement to Bill Wilson [concerning Hazard's early exposure to the Oxford Group] ". . . reading *For Sinners*

---

[7] Two AAs have devoted much time to the subject and shared generously with the author their findings. They are Mel B. of Toledo, Ohio, and Ron R. of Bowling Green, Kentucky.

[8] List in Shoemaker files at Episcopal Church Archives.

[9] The author personally inspected and copied a number of Sam Shoemaker's handwritten journal entries from mid-1934 to January of 1936. The journals were provided by Shoemaker's two daughters.

Only was a profound influence." Bill added that he [Rowland] took it with him on the train from New York to Detroit and it changed his life.[10]

4. Bill Wilson was not clear in his memory, but it was either Rowland Hazard or Ebby Thacher who brought Wilson a copy of Williams James's *The Varieties of Religious Experience*. Bill first read the book while he was getting sober in Towns Hospital in December, 1935. The book became a foundation for one or two of Bill's concepts regarding the Twelve Step program; and Bill later called William James a "founder" of A.A.[11]

5. For the period, 1935 to 1938, Shoemaker's files contain substantial correspondence between Shoemaker and Hazard concerning Oxford Group events and matters.[12]

6. Ten days after he was released from Towns Hospital in New York City, and had begun his sustained sobriety, Bill Wilson began meeting with a handful of ex-drunks, who were sticking together and meeting at Stewart's Cafeteria after regular Oxford Group meetings. These ex-drunks included Rowland Hazard, Ebby Thacher, and Grace McC.[13]

7. Calvary Church archives in New York reveal that Hazard served on the Vestry of Sam Shoemaker's Calvary Church for at least three years, beginning in 1938.[14]

---

[10] From a speech by Bill Wilson on November 9, 1954, a copy of which the author obtained from the Episcopal Church Archives in Texas.

[11] Thomsen, *Bill W.*, p. 230.

[12] Episcopal Church Archives, Texas.

[13] Thomsen, *Bill W.*, p. 230.

[14] When the author visited Calvary Church in New York, he inspected the Church's archives. He was then also guided by the Vicar, the Rev. Steve Garmey, to a stained glass window dedicated to Rowland Hazard. Pointing to the importance of Hazard's role in the early A.A. picture, Shoemaker also commented on this memorial window in an address to an A.A. International Convention.

8. According to Bill Wilson's wife Lois, Rowland "joined the Oxford Group and stayed sober . . . he [Rowland] remained an ardent Oxford Grouper until his death in 1945."[15]

While the evidence of Hazard's continued sobriety has not been thoroughly documented, the widow of one of Hazard's children believed that Hazard did die sober.[16] Lois Wilson's comments (as quoted above) tend to corroborate this belief. Newspaper accounts state that Rowland was stricken at his desk in the offices of the Bristol Manufacturing Company of which he was vice-president and general manager.[17]

Why such an extended discussion of Rowland? The answer lies in the many statements by both Bill Wilson and by Bill's "sponsor" Ebby Thacher that Rowland was thoroughly versed in Oxford Group principles and practices. Also that much had been learned by Ebby *and* Bill from Rowland. Hence Rowland stands as a major funnel of Oxford Group spiritual thinking to early A.A. in New York. We will also see, in a moment, how much Ebby himself *did* assimilate from the Oxford Group and pass on to Bill.

Some A.A. commentators have looked on Rowland as a mere Oxford Group *link* to Bill Wilson. But Bill was exposed, through Hazard, to some of the major Oxford Group principles that Hazard had learned. Hazard was a highly educated man. He absorbed his Oxford Group information from his extensive participation in Group activities, from reading Oxford Group/Shoemaker literature, from his personal association with Sam Shoemaker, and from regular meetings and conversations Rowland had with Professor Philip Marshall Brown—a close friend of Shoemaker's and the author of an important Oxford Group handbook, *The Venture of Belief*.[18]

Now to the next major Oxford Group root that inspired Bill Wilson in New York's early spiritual "program."

---

[15] *Lois Remembers*, p. 93.

[16] Report to author of phone conversation of Mrs. Charles Hazard with Mel B.

[17] *Evening Bulletin*, Providence, Rhode Island, December 21, 1945

[18] Philip Marshall Brown, *The Venture of Belief* (New York: Fleming H. Revell, 1935). Shoemaker wrote the introduction to this title by Brown.

Ebby Thacher, Shep Cornell, and Rowland Hazard

We have omitted one name from the foregoing triumvirate—the name of Cebra Graves. Cebra was part of the Oxford Group team that indirectly brought Ebby Thacher to Bill Wilson; but the author has found virtually nothing about how much Oxford Group information, if any, Cebra Graves himself imparted to Ebby. Therefore, the following discussion does not rule out the possibility; it simply tells Cebra's role in the chain of events.

Edwin Throckmorton Thacher hailed from a wealthy family in Albany, New York. Bill had met him during Bill's school days at Burr and Burton Academy in Manchester, Vermont. But "Ebby," as Bill called him, was an alcoholic. Ebby had been thrown out of bars and hotels and even been asked not to return to certain cities.

In 1929, Bill and Ebby chartered a plane with a young, alcoholic pilot. All were equipped with flasks which were passed among the three. In front of a large crowd, their plane dipped, circled, and landed near an open ditch. Ebby had often been involved in such capers. And the last episode, as Bill had heard the story, had Ebby driving off the road and plowing into the parlor and kitchen of a farmhouse.

Things had not gone well for Ebby in the drinking realm. In about July of 1934, several Oxford Group people, including F. Shepard ("Shep") Cornell, Rowland Hazard, and Cebra Graves, visited Ebby. Shep and Cebra (Ebby's former drinking companions) told him "they had run into the Oxford Group and had gotten some pretty sensible things out of it based on the life of Christ, Biblical times."[19] Of the three visitors, Rowland impressed Ebby the most because of Rowland's drinking career and the fact that Rowland was, as Ebby put it, "a good guy." Also, because Rowland stuck by Ebby as the days went by.

Ebby himself commented that Rowland had been given a thorough indoctrination in Oxford Group teachings and that Rowland had passed them on to him. Ebby said:

---

[19] *Pass It On*, p. 113.

He [Rowland] passed as much of this on to me as he could. We would sit down and try to rid ourselves of any thoughts of the material world and see if we couldn't find out the best plan for our lives for that day and to follow whatever guidelines came to us. [Rowland, said Ebby, impressed upon him] the four principles of the Oxford Group [the Four Absolutes—honesty, purity, unselfishness, and love]. He [Rowland] was particularly strong in advocating absolute honesty. . . . Honesty with yourself, honesty with your fellowman, honesty with God.[20]

Despite Rowland's teachings, Ebby went back to the bottle. He was arrested and became a strong prospect for imprisonment. But Rowland and Cebra Graves appeared before Cebra's father (who was the judge about to sentence Ebby to six months in Windsor Prison for repeated intoxication). Rowland told the judge he would be responsible for Ebby. Ebby was released to Rowland's care and stayed with Rowland in Shafstsbury, Vermont, for a while. Then Cebra Graves and Shep Cornell brought Ebby to New York City. And, since Ebby did not have a cent, they lodged him in Calvary's Mission on the East Side.

At and prior to that time, F. Shepherd Cornell (an ex-alcoholic) was extremely active in Oxford Group meetings, houseparties, and teams.[21] Bill rightly or wrongly said Cornell was then "near the top echelon on the Oxford Groups."[22] Shep, as Lois Wilson described him, "not only was a fellow grouper but also worked in Wall Street and summered in Manchester."[23] Cornell frequently helped drunks recover, working in company with Sam Shoemaker.[24] Lois Wilson was later to record in her Oxford

---

[20] *Pass It On*, p. 114.

[21] In November of 1996, A.A. historian Mel B. wrote the author: "Shep wasn't an ex-alcoholic. He abstained during this period, but drank moderately later on."

[22] Wilson, *W. G. Wilson Reflections*, p. 120.

[23] *Lois Remembers*, p. 91.

[24] See Samuel M. Shoemaker, *Courage to Change: The Christian Roots of the 12-Step Movement*, compiled by Bill Pittman and Dick B., (Grand Rapids, MI: Fleming H. Revell, 1994), pp. 135-50; Charles Clapp, Jr., *The Big Bender* (New York: Harper & Brothers, 1938).

Group Notes that Shep had led a meeting at a houseparty she and Bill attended. Lois also reported in her memoirs that, in Bill's early months of sobriety, she, Bill, Ebby, and Shep C. "constantly went to Oxford Group meetings."[25] Lois said, of a later period, that Shep Cornell joined the Wilsons a few times at the weekly meetings in the Wilson home, where several were endeavoring to help drunks.[26] Here again, therefore, was an Oxford Group heavy-weight who was contributing to Wilson's spiritual ideas.

(Returning to the story of Ebby, Rowland, and Shep)—Ebby began staying in New York City with one of the "brotherhood" who ran Calvary Episcopal Mission on 23rd Street. Ebby said he was trying to stay honest, make restitution, and pursue Oxford Group practices and principles. Ebby soon realized he was no longer fighting alcohol; he was released from it. As Bill put it, Ebby "felt mighty grateful for what he had received. Then he [Ebby] thought of me."[27] One of the Oxford Group principles, as Ebby put it, was: "there was no price tag on giving—if it's just giving yourself." Inspired by that thought, Ebby phoned his old drinking buddy, Bill Wilson, to do a little message carrying free of charge; and we will see in a moment what a tremendously successful message Ebby truly carried.

Ebby himself had apparently made a decision for Christ on November 1, 1934. He soon phoned Bill. Following Ebby's phone call and a visit by Ebby with Bill, Bill trundled himself down to Calvary Mission to accomplish what Ebby had accomplished. As Billy Du Val, the Assistant Superintendent at Calvary Mission, recalled it:

> Bill [Wilson] told us he had been at Calvary Church the previous Sunday night and saw Abbe Thacher [sic] get up in the pulpit and

---

[25] *Lois Remembers*, p. 91.

[26] *Lois Remembers*, p. 102.

[27] Wilson, *W. G. Wilson Reflections*, p. 117.

give witness to the fact that with the help of God he had been
sober for a number of months.[28]

And there was much more, most of it unreported in either A.A.'s
Big Book or its histories. In fact, as one distinguished A.A.
historian—an oldtimer with over forty years of sobriety—put it,
Ebby has been short-changed as far as A.A. spiritual history is
concerned.[29]

Ebby Thacher and Bill Wilson

Ebby had apparently been a practicing alcoholic most of his adult
life, both before and after he joined the Oxford Group, both before
and after he became a born again Christian, and both before and
long after he met Bill Wilson. In fact, Bill has rightly been
credited with great loyalty to Ebby. Bill always called Ebby his
"sponsor." Bill took great pains to see that Ebby was taken care
of during Ebby's many subsequent years of drinking after A.A.
was founded. And this often resulted in derision.

Yet Ebby had been sober but a short period of time when he
became aligned with the Oxford Group, met with Bill, and then substantially indoctrinated Bill in Oxford Group practices. And, if one
examines Bill's Story in the Big Book and then examines the pre-
Big Book manuscripts, it emerges that Ebby's impact on Bill was
enormous. Ebby both directly and indirectly persuaded Bill (who,
several times in writing, proclaimed himself to have been an atheist)
to make a decision for Christ, find God, and—in a very definite
way—respect both clergy and religion. These were things Bill was
hardly likely to have done without Ebby Thacher's influence.

Let's consider some absolutely new religious ideas Ebby "sold"
his drunken friend Bill. The *preliminary* part of the story is
adequately reported in the Big Book of A.A. as follows:

---

[28] The author was permitted to inspect and copy the Du Val letter located at the
Stepping Stones Archives.

[29] Phone conversation between Mel B. and the author in 1995.

1. Ebby visited Bill in Bill's cups, and Bill wanted to know why Ebby looked so "fresh-skinned and glowing [and] . . . inexplicably different." And, we should add, sober! Ebby replied: "I've got religion." This expression was very common in the Oxford Group but was one which—except for the occasion—could hardly have won Bill to *any* cause—certainly not that of religion. Yet, it soon was to challenge Bill to (what for Bill were) incredible acts of decision, piety, and witnessing.[30]

2. When Bill chose to argue with Ebby and make objections to ideas about God, religion, and faith, Ebby [in Bill's words] "made the point-blank declaration that 'God had done for him what he [Ebby] could not do for himself.' His human will had failed. Doctors had pronounced him incurable. Society was about to lock him up. . . . Then he had, in effect, been raised from the dead. . . . That floored me. It began to look as though religious people were right after all."[31] An admission that was hardly a part of Bill's former thinking.[32]

3. According to Bill, Ebby then persuaded Bill to make what the Oxford Group described as an "experiment of faith." For Bill to make his *beginning* as a believer, said Ebby, Bill needed only to "choose your [his] own conception of God" building upon a foundation of willingness to believe.[33] Starting with that simple religious idea, said Ebby, Bill then needed to take the "program of action" outlined by the Oxford Group.[34] If Bill needed and

---

[30] The quotes are from the First Edition of the Big Book, pp. 18-19.

[31] Big Book, First Edition, pp. 20-21. The expression as to God's doing for someone what he could not do for himself was a common one in the Oxford Group. See Dick B., *Design for Living: The Oxford Group's Contribution to Early A.A.* (San Rafael, CA: Paradise Research Publications, 1995), pp, 341, 358.

[32] See Big Book, First Edition, pp. 19-21. In fact, in one of his earlier manuscripts, Bill said: "At any rate I thought I understood as well as anyone what good morals were and with the exceptions of my drinking I felt superior to most Christians I knew. I might be weak in some respects but at least I was not hypocritical. So my interest in Christianity other than its teaching of moral principles and the good I hoped it did on balance was slight" (See Wilson, *Bill Wilson's Original Story*, lines 908-915).

[33] Big Book, First Edition, p. 22.

[34] See Big Book, First Edition, p. 54.

wanted God enough, said Ebby, God would come. Bill declared
he had then humbly become *willing*. And, said Bill, "He [God]
came."[35] Thus had many Oxford Group adherents "found" God.
And they had done so by commencing with *willingness* to take
action in what Shoemaker and other Oxford Group people called
an "experiment of faith."[36]

Considering the short length of Ebby's Oxford Group experience
and sobriety, Ebby had fostered a miracle in Bill, and Bill seemed
to know it. But there was much more—most of it inadequately
reported.

Bill oiled himself liberally with liquor and wound his way to
Calvary Rescue Mission to accomplish that to which he had
previously seen Ebby give testimony at Shoemaker's Calvary
Church. Here also, historians have short-changed the significance
of what Bill Wilson did at Calvary Rescue Mission. The following
are the facts, culled from the author's interview with Mrs. Sam
Shoemaker, records as to what regularly occurred at the Mission,
Billy Du Val's eye-witness statement, and statements Bill made in
manuscripts now located at the Wilson archives at Stepping Stones.

1. J. Geroldsek, one of the "brotherhood" who lived outside the
Mission, was in charge of the meeting which Bill attended.

---

[35] See Big Book, First Edition, p. 22.

[36] While this part of the story is quite consistent with Oxford Group ideas, the author
has found it in *none* of Bill's early manuscripts he examined at Stepping Stones. Nor
does it exist in the earliest full draft of the Big Book. It remains for other historians to
determine whether Bill added these ideas to enable A.A. to appeal to atheists and
agnostics or whether the presentation was actually the one Ebby gave Bill. The matter
is further clouded by the fact that Bill was inebriated during most of this period and
frankly stated he could remember nothing of certain events. Ebby, in just a few months,
was in a similar condition. The question therefore remains: Did Bill simply surrender
himself to God, believing God existed—as most Oxford Group people did; or did he go
through the intellectual process of becoming "willing to believe," then "choosing his own
conception of God for a beginning," and then making the surrender that enabled him to
find God through a religious "conversion."

2. Geroldsek had just finished his Bible lesson. Hymns *usually* followed, and they probably followed on the evening of Bill's appearance at the Mission.

3. Geroldsek began his testimonial. Bill was very drunk. Bill interrupted, but was allowed to speak. In addition to what was quoted above, Bill said that if Ebby Thacher could get help there, he was sure he needed help and could get it at the Mission also.

4. Bill said he remembered: "There were hymns and prayers. Tex, the leader, exhorted us. Only Jesus could save, he said. Certain men got up and made testimonials. Numb as I was, I felt interest and excitement rising. Then came the call. Penitents started marching forward to the rail. Unaccountably impelled, I started too. . . . Soon I knelt among the sweating, stinking penitents. . . . Something touched me. I guess it was more than that. I was hit. . . . Jumping to my feet I began. Afterward, I could never remember what I said. I only know that I was in earnest and people seemed to pay attention."[37] [Some historical accounts have said that Ebby was present on that occasion, but Billy Du Val stated emphatically that *neither* Tex Francisco *nor* Ebby Thacher was there].

5. Both Mrs. Samuel Shoemaker and Sam Shoemaker's Assistant Minister, the Reverend W. Irving Harris, made clear that Bill Wilson then and there made a "decision for Christ" at the rail at Calvary Mission. Mrs. Shoemaker specifically so stated in a telephone interview with the author from her home in October of 1991. She said she was *present* when Bill made his decision. Reverend Harris said, in a personally typed memorandum, presently in the author's possession: "and it was at a meeting at Calvary Mission that Bill himself was moved to declare that he had decided to launch out as a follower of Jesus Christ."[38]

---

[37] Wilson, *W. G. Wilson Reflections*, p. 121.

[38] One historian wrote the author that he doubted the material in this paragraph. However, we show elsewhere that both Bill Wilson and his wife, Lois, made comments about Bill's being sure he was "born again." The author finds no particular reason to doubt the words of Mrs. Shoemaker and of Shoemaker's assistant minister, Irving Harris.

6. Sam Shoemaker put the purpose of Calvary Mission in the simplest form. Writing to his friends in Calvary Church, on November 25, 1932, Shoemaker said about "Calvary Mission" that it was "where God reclaims men who choose to be reborn."

7. Bill said: "I drank on for another two or three days. But I kept pondering that Mission experience. Sometimes it seemed real. Then again I would brush it away, charge it off to an alcohol-fired imagination. . . . Yes, if there was any great Physician that could cure the alcohol sickness, I'd better seek Him now, at once. I'd better find what my friend [Ebby] had found. . . . If getting well required me to pray at high noon in the public square with the other sufferers, would I swallow my pride and do that? . . . Perhaps I wouldn't need an emotional conversion. After all, a *conservative atheist* like me ought to be able to get on without anything like that. Anyhow, I'd better start for the hospital and right now" (italics added).[39]

8. Bill then checked in to Towns Hospital where Dr. William D. Silkworth met him in the hall. Waving a bottle around, Bill said to Silkworth, "At last, Doc, I've found something."[40] We leave it to the reader to conclude what Bill had *found* prior to admission to Towns. An A.A. Conference Approved history has stated, "Silkworth remembered that Bill was carrying two books on philosophy, from which he hoped to get a new inspiration."[41] But this addendum does not appear in the early Wilson manuscripts the author has read. It does not appear in Bill's biography. It does not appear in Lois Wilson's memoirs. And it seems an unlikely statement of what Bill really "found"—considering the Oxford Group's emphasis on "finding God." Also, Bill's own

---

[39] Wilson, *W. G. Wilson Reflections*, pp. 123-24.

[40] In one of his manuscripts, Bill said, at p. 3, "I waved a bottle and told the doctor: 'Well, this time, I've got something.'"

[41] *Pass It On*, p. 120.

decision for Christ at the Mission rail, and the statements he made about being "born again."[42]

9. Shortly, Bill received visits at Towns Hospital from Ebby; and then, after Bill followed the instructions given him by Ebby, Bill had what he called his "hot flash" religious experience. In his *Recollections*, Bill related the "hot flash" story as follows: "I remember saying to myself, 'I'll do anything, anything at all. If there be a Great Physician, I'll call on him.' Then, with neither faith nor hope, I cried out, 'If there be a God, let Him show Himself.' The effect was instant, electric. Suddenly my room blazed with an indescribably white light. I was seized with an ecstasy beyond description. I have no words for this. Every joy I had known was pale by comparison. The light, the ecstasy. I was conscious of nothing else for a time. Then, seen in mind's eye, there was a mountain. I stood upon its summit where a great wind blew. A wind, not of air, but of spirit. In great, clean strength it blew right through me. Then came the blazing thought, 'You are a free man.' I know not at all how long I remained in this state, but finally the light and the ecstasy subsided. I again saw the wall of my room. As I became more quiet, a great peace stole over me and this was accompanied by a sensation difficult to describe. I became acutely conscious of a presence which seemed like a veritable sea of living spirit. I lay on the shores of a new world. 'This,' I thought, 'must be the great reality. The God of the preachers. . . .' No matter how wrong things seemed to be, there could be no question of the ultimate rightness of God's universe. For the first time I felt that I really belonged. I knew that I was loved and could love in return. I thanked my God Who had given me a glimpse of His absolute self. . . . Save a brief hour of doubt next to come, these feelings and convictions, no matter what the vicissitude, have never deserted me since. For a reason I cannot begin to comprehend, this great and sudden gift of sudden grace has always been mine. . . . Out of no faith, faith had suddenly appeared. No blind faith either, for it was fortified

---

[42] Compare also *Lois Remembers*. Lois spoke of Bill's decision at Calvary Mission and his arrival at Towns Hospital—using the expressions "emotional conversions" and Bill's "rebirth" (pp. 88, 98).

by the consciousness of the presence of God. Despair had turned into utter security. Darkness was banished by cosmic light. For sure I'd been *born again*" (italics added).[43] Wilson asked what he needed to do to find and perfect this new relationship with his Creator—the "Father of Lights," as Bill phrased it.[44]

10. Wondering whether he had simply been hallucinating, Bill called Dr. Silkworth. Bill said: "Doctor, is this real? Am I still perfectly sane?" Then came his [Dr. Silkworth's] reply. Words which [in Bill's account] "were to make AA history." Said Silkworth, "Yes, my boy, your were sane, perfectly sane in my judgment. You have been the subject of some great psychic occurrence, something that I don't understand. I've read of these things in books, but I've never seen one myself before. You have had some kind of *conversion experience*"(italics added).[45]

The foregoing is a synopsis of Bill's quest to find God after he had met Ebby. Again, there is much more.

Ebby's Instructions Resembling A.A.'s Later Steps

A.A. history has it that Bill wrote the Twelve Steps in December, 1938; and the author has no reason to doubt that he did. Of far

---

[43] Bill told an almost identical story and used the words *born again* in another early manuscript the author found at Stepping Stones. One writer has opined that Bill Wilson's spiritual experience, or "hot flash," may only have been delusions and hallucinations characteristic of momentary alcoholic toxic psychosis. That writer refers to what he states William James called "anaesthetic revelations." See Bill Pittman, *AA: The Way It Began* (Seattle, WA: Glen Abbey Books, 1988), p. 169. For an extensive discussion as to whether Bill's *hot flash* was attributable to a sudden dramatic spiritual experience or to chemical reaction from the drugs used in the "detox" process, see Mel B., *New Wine: The Spiritual Roots of the Twelve Step Miracle* (Minnesota: Hazelden, 1991), pp. 77-88.

[44] See James 1:17. See also Mel B., *New Wine*, p. 86. In an earlier manuscript, Bill commented as to himself: "'The tragic thing about you [Bill] is that you [Bill] have been playing God.' That was it. Playing God. . . . So then came the question—If I were no longer to be God, then how was I to find and perfect the new relationship with my Creator—with the Father of Lights who presides over all?" (Wilson, *Bill Wilson's Original Story*, Lines 949-969).

[45] Wilson, *W. G. Wilson Reflections*, p. 130-31.

greater importance, however, is the fact that Bill also said many, many times that nobody invented A.A. and that everything in A.A. had been borrowed.

And exactly how much the Twelve Steps were borrowed is apparent from a careful reading of Bill's Story in A.A.'s Big Book. The extent of the borrowed material is also clear to the few of us who have seen Bill's pre-Big Book manuscripts at Stepping Stones and have also studied Anne Smith's Journal. Twelve *concepts* (a structured sequence of principles culled primarily from the Oxford Group, and closely resembling Bill's ultimate Twelve Step language) were very much *in place* when Ebby was explaining those concepts to Bill in Towns Hospital in December of 1934—four years before the Twelve Steps themselves were written.

The author's initial insight into this fact was gained when he first attended the Big Book Seminars conducted by Joe McQ. and Charlie P. in Sacramento, California. Later, he was to find the seminar teachings confirmed as he examined and copied Bill's manuscripts at Stepping Stones and obtained a copy of Anne Smith's Journal from A.A. General Services Archives in New York. One could look particularly at pages 13 to 15 of the Third Edition of A.A.'s Big Book. There, describing the actions he took at Towns Hospital *in 1934* under Ebby's tutelage, Bill set forth almost every principle he later incorporated into the Twelve Steps.

At Stepping Stones, the author found a manuscript titled "Bill Wilson's Original Story." Every line was numbered. The numbers ran from 1 to 1180; and that was all there was. Yet for the student of A.A.'s Big Book, and for those who wonder about the source of the Twelve Steps, the material is so important that we will quote it exactly as written—omitting only those portions which do not seem directly to pertain to the step ideas as Ebby *explained* them to Bill in 1934. Bill began by describing Ebby's approach:

Nevertheless here I was sitting opposite a man who talked about a personal God, who told me how he had found Him, who described to me how I might do the same thing and who convinced me utterly that something had come into his life which had accomplished a miracle. The man was transformed; there was no denying he had been *reborn* (lines 935-942, italics added).

For the man on the street who just wondered about such things, it was a providential approach, for with a small beginning of faith and a very large dose of action along spiritual lines, he could be sure to demonstrate the Power and Love of God as a practical workable twenty four hour a day design for living (lines 984-988).

Then Bill set forth in much detail the steps his friend Ebby suggested he [Bill] take. Bill said:

This is what my friend [Ebby] suggested I do. One: Turn my face to God *as I understand Him* and say to Him with earnestness, complete honesty and abandon, that I henceforth place my life at His Disposal and Direction forever. That I do this in the presence of another person, who should be one in whom I have confidence and if I be a member of a religious organization, then with an appropriate member of that body (lines 989-995, italics added).[46]

TWO: Having taken this first step, I should next prepare myself for God's Company by taking a thorough and ruthless inventory of my moral defects and derelictions. This I should do without any reference to other people, and their real or fancied part in my shortcomings should be rigorously excluded—"Where have I failed"—is the prime question. I was to go over my life from the beginning and ascertain in the light of my own present understanding where I had failed as a completely moral person. Above all things in making this appraisal I must be entirely honest with myself. As an aid to thoroughness and as something to look at when I got through I might use pencil and paper (lines 995-105).[47]

---

[46] A.A.'s Step Three states: Made a decision to turn our will and our lives over to the care of God *as we understood Him.*

[47] A.A.'s Step Four states: Made a searching and fearless moral inventory of ourselves. The First Edition of the Big Book suggests that each of the shortcomings—resentment, fear, selfish sex, and harms—be set "on paper" (pp. 77, 80, 82, and 83).

First take the question of honesty. Where, how and with whom had I ever been dishonest? With respect to anything. What attitudes and actions did I still have which were not completely honest with God with myself or with the other fellow? I was warned that no one can say that he is a completely honest person. That would be superhuman and people aren't that way. Nor should I be misled by the thought of how honest I am in some particulars. I was too [sic] ruthlessly tear out of the past all of my dishonesty and list them in writing (lines 1005-1013).[48]

Next I was to explore another area somewhat related to the first and commonly a very defective one in most people. I was to examine my sex conduct since infancy and rigorously compare it with what I thought that conduct should have been. My friend explained to me that peoples [sic] ideas throughout the world on what constitutes perfect sex conduct vary greatly[.] Consequently, I was not to measure my defects in this particular by adopting any standard of easy virtue as a measuring stick, I was merely to ask God to show me the difference between right and wrong in this regard and ask for help and strength and honesty in cataloguing my defects according to the true dictates of my own conscience (lines 1013-1024).[49]

Then I might take up the related questions of greed and selfishness and thoughtlessness. How far and in what connection had I strayed and was I straying in these particulars? I was assured I could make a good long list if I got honest enough and vigorous enough (lines 1024-1028).[50]

Then there was the question of real love for all of my fellows including my family, my friends and my enemies. Had I been completely loving toward all of these at all times and places. If not, down in the book it must go and of course everyone could put plenty down along that line (lines 1028-1032).[51]

---

[48] Compare the Oxford Group's standard—Absolute Honesty.

[49] Compare the Oxford Group's standard—Absolute Purity.

[50] Compare the Oxford Group's standard—Absolute Unselfishness.

[51] Compare the Oxford Group's standard—Absolute Love.

[M]y friend pointed out that resentment, self-pity, fear, inferiority, pride and egotism, were attitudes which distorted one's perspective and usefulness[.] [T]o entertain such attitudes was to shut oneself off from God and people about us. Therefor[e] it would be necessary for me to examine myself critically in this respect and write down my conclusions (lines 1033-1039).[52]

Step number three required that I carefully go over my personal inventory and definatly [sic] arrive at the conclusion that I was now willing to rid myself of all these defects[.][53] [M]oreover I was to understand that this would not be accomplished by myself alone, therefore I was to humbly ask God that he take these handicaps away (lines 1040-1046).[54]

To make sure that I had become really honest in this desire, I should sit down with whatever person I chose and reveal to him without any reservations whatever the result of my self appraisal. From this point out I was to stop living alone in every particular. Thus was I to keep myself free in the future of those things which shut out God's power. It was explained that I had been standing in my own light, my spiritual interior had been like a room darkened by very dirty windows and this was an undertaking to wipe them off and keep them clean. Thus was my housekeeping to be accomplished, it would be difficult to be really honest with myself and God and perhaps to be completely honest with another person[.] [B]y telling another the truth, I could however be

---

[52] See Dick B., *The Good Book and The Big Book: A.A.'s Roots in the Bible* (San Rafael, CA: Paradise Research Publications, 1995), pp. 140-43. Compare the Oxford Group's discussions of resentment, selfishness and self-centeredness, dishonesty and fear; also its definition of sin as anything which blocks us from God and from another human being. When Bill finally wrote the Big Book some four years later, he dropped the Standards of the Oxford Group—the Four Absolutes. Instead, Bill utilized the Oxford Group's suggestions as to such shortcomings as resentment, fear, selfish sex, and harms as the basis for the Fourth Step's suggested written inventory. See Dick B., *Design for Living*, pp. 184-89; and Frank N. D. Buchman, *Remaking the World* (London: Blandford Press, 1961), p. 38.

[53] A.A.'s Step Six states: Were entirely ready to have God remove all these defects of character.

[54] A.A.'s Step Seven states: Humbly asked Him to remove our shortcomings.

absolutely sure that my self searching had been honest and effective. Moreover I would be taking my first spiritual step towards my fellows for something I might say could be helpful in leading the person to whom I talked [to] a better understanding of himself. In this fashion I would commence to break down the barriers which my many forms of self will had erected. Warning was given me that I should select a person who would be in no way injured or offended by what I had to say, for I could not expect to commence my spiritual growth at the expense of another (lines 1046-1067).[55]

Step number four demanded that I frankly admit that my deviations from right thought and action had injured other people[.] [T]herefore I must set about undoing the damage to the best of my ability. It would be advisable to make a list of all the persons I had hurt or with whom I had bad relations (lines 1071-1075).[56]

People I disliked and those who had injured me should have prefered [sic] attention, provided I had done them injury or still entertained any feeling of resentment towards them. Under no circumstances was I to consider their defects or wrong doing[.] [T]hen I was to approach these people telling them I had commenced a way of life which required that I be on friendly and helpful terms with every body; that I recognized I had been at fault in this particular[;] that I was sorry for what I had done or said and had come to set matters right insofar as I possibly could. Under no circumstances was I to engage in argument or controversy. My own wrong doing was to be admitted and set right and that was all. Assurance was to be given that I was prepared to go to any length to do the right thing. Again I was warned that obviously I could not make amends at the expense of

---

[55] A.A.'s Step Five states: Admitted to God, to ourselves, and to another human being the exact nature of our wrongs. Note that the sequence of Steps as described in Bill's story at p. 22 of the First Edition of the Big Book is different from the sequence set forth above. But there is a close resemblance of the discussion above to that in the First Edition's *Fifth* Step language at pp. 84-88.

[56] A.A.'s Step Eight states: Made a list of all persons we had harmed, and became willing to make amends to them all.

other people, that judgement [sic] and discretion should be used lest others should be hurt. This sort of situation could be postponed until such conditions became such that the job could be done without harm to anyone. One could be contented in the meanwhile by discussing such a matter frankly with a third party who would not be involved and of course on a strictly confidential basis. Great [sic, care?] was to be taken that one did not avoid situations difficult or dangerous to oneself on such a pretext. The willingness to go the limit as fast as possible had to be at all times present (lines 1075-1098).[57]

This principle of making amends was to be continued in the future for only by keeping myself free of bad relationships with others could I expect to receive the Power and direction so indispensable [sic] to my new and larger usefulness.[58] This sort of discipline would help me to see others as they really are; to recognize that every one is plagued by various [sic] of self will; that every one is in a sense actually sick with some form of self; that when men behave badly they are only displaying symptoms of spiritual ill health (lines 1098-1106).[59]

Did Edwin Throckmorton Thacher really say all these things to Bill Wilson? While Bill was *detoxing* in Towns Hospital? When Ebby was a *mere* two or three months sober? Either Bill's memory was faulty or Ebby received a remarkable grasp of Oxford Group ideas. Ideas taught to him by such friends as Rowland Hazard, Shep Cornell, Cebra Graves, and the brothers at Sam Shoemaker's Calvary Mission.

Bill certainly said Ebby traversed this territory. Bill made the same claim in several of the early manuscripts the author found at Stepping Stones. Bill made similar remarks in the tape Bill made

---

[57] A.A.'s Ninth Step states: Made direct amends to such people wherever possible, except when to do so would injure them or others. Compare Big Book, First Edition, pp. 89-96.

[58] A.A.'s Step Ten states: Continued to take personal inventory and when we were wrong promptly admitted it.

[59] Compare First Edition, pp. 78-80.

in 1954. And Bill covered the substance of these remarks at pages 22 and 23 of the First Edition of the Big Book *and elsewhere.* Other researchers and historians can determine, perhaps, just what Rowland and Cebra and Shep and the people at the rescue mission taught Ebby and what Ebby taught Bill if the material differed from the above. But it is certain that Rowland and the others were fully qualified to pass that kind of program to others such as Ebby *and* Bill.

What of Eleventh Step ideas?[60] Bill says little of prayer and meditation in the early manuscripts. In 1954, Bill said of one of Ebby's Towns Hospital visits:

> He was just paying a friendly visit, asking for nothing. He wasn't going to try any evangelism on my [sic] after all. This obliged me to start asking questions myself. When he began to repeat his pat little formula for getting over drinking? [sic] Briefly and without ado he did so. Again he told how he found he couldn't run his own life, how he got honest with himself as never before. How he'd been making amends to the people he'd damaged. How he'd been trying to give of himself without putting a price tag on his efforts, and finally how he'd tried prayer just as an experiment and had found to his surprise that it worked.[61]

In the First Edition of the Big Book, Bill had written of Ebby's teachings:

> I was to test my thinking by the new God-consciousness within. Common sense would thus become uncommon sense. I was to sit quietly when in doubt, asking only for direction and strength to meet my problems as He would have me. Never was I to pray for myself, except as my requests bore on my usefulness to others. Then only might I expect to receive. But that would be in great measure. . . . Simple, but not easy; a price had to be paid. It

---

[60] A.A.'s Step Eleven states: Sought through prayer and meditation to improve our conscious contact with God *as we understood Him,* praying only for knowledge of His will for us and the power to carry that out.

[61] Wilson, *W. G. Wilson Recollections,* pp. 125-26.

meant destruction of self-centeredness. I must turn in all things to
the Father of Lights who presides over us all (p. 23).[62]

The author has found little indication, other than that which can
be inferred from the quote above and another reference to "faith
without works," that either Ebby or Bill discussed the Bible, the
Book of James, the Sermon on the Mount, or 1 Corinthians 13, or
very much about prayer and meditation. Did they? At this point,
we know only that Shoemaker had mentioned the Sermon and
Corinthians in his first book.[63] And Shoemaker kept mentioning
them. Oxford Group writings also mentioned James, Corinthians,
and the Sermon.[64]

But Bill's subsequent remarks about the Bible may be quite
revealing concerning what he did *not* hear from Ebby or did not
care about or did not *grasp* in those earliest days in New York.
And perhaps the same might have been true for Ebby. Bill later
said:

1. [After Bill and Dr. Bob had worked with their first newcomer
prospect in Akron and failed:] Then came a lull on the Twelfth
Step front. In this time, Anne and Henrietta [Dr. Bob's wife and
Henrietta Seiberling] infused much needed spirituality into Bob
and me.[65]

2. [Interviewing Oxford Group/A.A. pioneers T. Henry and
Clarace Williams:] I learned a great deal from you people, from
the Smiths themselves, and from Henrietta [Seiberling]. I hadn't
looked in the Bible, up to this time, at all. You see, I had the

---

[62] Compare James 1:17.

[63] Samuel M. Shoemaker, *Realizing Religion* (New York: Association Press, 1923),
pp. 42-43, 46, 50-51, 75.

[64] See, for example, H. A. Walter, *Soul Surgery: Some Thoughts on Incisive
Personal Work*, 6th ed. (London: Blandford Press, n. d.), pp. 29, 62; The Layman with
a Notebook, *What Is the Oxford Group?* (New York: Oxford University Press, 1933),
pp. 29, 31, 36, 48-49, 106.

[65] Dick B., *The Akron Genesis*, p. 80; *The Language of the Heart: Bill W.'s
Grapevine Writings* (New York: The A.A. Grapevine, Inc., 1988), p. 357.

[conversion] experience first, and then this rushing around to help drunks, and nothing happened.[66]

3. [Commenting on his three month sojourn with Dr. Bob and his wife Anne in Akron in the summer of 1935:] "For the next three months, I lived with these two wonderful people. I shall always believe they gave me more than I ever brought them." Each morning there was a devotion, he [Bill Wilson] recalled. After a long silence, in which they awaited inspiration and guidance, Anne would read from the Bible. "James was our favorite," he [Bill] said. "Reading from her chair in the corner, she would softly conclude, 'Faith without works is dead.'"[67]

4. [Remarking about prayer and meditation in early Akron A.A., Bill said:] I sort of always felt that something was lost from A. A. when we stopped emphasizing the morning meditation.[68]

Back now to the steps Ebby Thacher passed on to Bill Wilson during Bill's final stay at Towns Hospital in December of 1934. As we have seen, little seems to have been said about prayer and meditation. It appears virtually nothing was said about the spiritual principles in the Book of James, the Sermon on the Mount, and 1 Corinthians 13. But it *is* clear that Ebby Thacher covered the Oxford Group's Four Absolutes—honesty, purity, unselfishness, and love. As we will see, Ebby also mentioned a *verse* from the Book of James.

Twelfth Step material *was* presented by Ebby.[69] Bill had had his "hot flash" conversion experience. Bill said Ebby returned to the hospital on the third day with William James's *The Varieties*

---

[66] Dick B., *The Akron Genesis*, p. 64.

[67] *DR. BOB and the Good Oldtimers* (New York: Alcoholics Anonymous World Services, Inc., 1980), p. 71. Unless otherwise indicated, future references to this title will use the name *DR. BOB*. See also, Dick B., *The Akron Genesis*, pp. 132-33.

[68] *DR. BOB*, p. 178.

[69] A.A.'s Twelfth Step states: Having had a spiritual awakening as the result of these steps, we tried to carry this message to alcoholics, and to practice these principles in all our affairs.

of Religious Experience in his hand. As we said, Bill was later
uncertain whether this book was given to him by Ebby or
Rowland. But Bill said of his conversion experience:

> As I gave an account [to Ebby] of my crashing experience, he
> seemed a little nonplussed. He'd seen no bright lights, nor had he
> stood on a high mountain. Yet, as we compared notes, it became
> evident that the end products of his experience were the same. He
> felt he'd found a new dimension of life and he carried the same
> feeling of being free and released. The only difference was that
> I'd been hit hard and suddenly. What had happened to him in
> weeks, had happened to me in minutes.[70]

The last two parts of A.A.'s Twelfth Step have to do with carrying
the message and practicing the principles of the Steps. As to these
matters, Bill had written of Ebby:

> One alcoholic had been talking to another as none others could.
> He had made me ready for the gift of release. He had then held
> his own gift up for me to see. He was the living proof of all he
> claimed. Nothing theoretical or second hand about this. When my
> rebellion was done I saw, I believed, and I followed it. That had
> been the missing link: one alcoholic talking to another, bearing
> hopelessness in one hand and hope in the other. I could make my
> own choice, and that I had done. As these realizations burst in
> upon me I became wildly excited. It was now daylight clear why
> the clergymen's advice, "You can do it, but only with God's
> help," hadn't worked. By contrast, Roland [sic], Ebby and I had
> admitted that we of ourselves couldn't do anything at all. Nearly
> all the cases cited by Professor James had made the same
> admission. They, of themselves, couldn't do a thing about their
> several dilemmas. Before they could receive the gift[,] their self-
> confidence had to be destroyed—absolutely destroyed. Ego
> deflation at great depth was the key to the riddle. The sociologists

---

[70] Wilson, *W. G. Wilson Recollections*, p. 132.

and psychologists who would restore self-confidence had been mistaken. God-confidence was the thing, not self-confidence.[71]

Bill wrote the following of the advice Ebby had given him:

> My friend had emphasized the absolute necessity of demonstrating these principles in all my affairs. Particularly was it imperative to work with others as he had worked with me. Faith without works was dead, he said.[72] And how appallingly true for the alcoholic! For if an alcoholic failed to perfect and enlarge his spiritual life through work and self sacrifice for others, he could not survive the certain trials and low spots ahead. If he did not work, he would surely drink again, and if he drank, he would surely die. Then faith would be dead indeed. With us it is just like that.[73]

The New York Outreach Fails

Bill Wilson cannot be accused of lack of zeal in acting upon Ebby's advice. In fact, Bill seemed to produce a spark in the Reverend Sam Shoemaker even *before* Bill got sober and left Towns Hospital. Sally Shoemaker Robinson (Sam's older daughter) reported the following:

> In his journal for November 1934 Sam Shoemaker wrote "A significant thing today . . . met Bill Wilson."[74]

And Bill's wife Lois came charging to declare Bill's works. As late as June of 1985, Lois Wilson wrote to a Brooklyn A.A. newsletter and said:

---

[71] Wilson, W. G. *Wilson Reflections*, pp. 134-35.

[72] See James 2:20: "But wilt thou know, O vain man, that faith without works is dead?"

[73] Big Book First Edition, p. 23.

[74] Foreword by Sally Shoemaker Robinson to Terry Webb, *Tree of Renewed Life: Spiritual Renewal of the Church through the Twelve-Step Program* (New York: The Crossroad Publishing Company, 1992), p. 7.

As far as I am concerned, A.A. began in 1934 in my father's old
house on Brooklyn Heights where Bill and I were living. When
Bill came home to 182 Clinton St. from Towns Hospital in New
York after his spiritual awakening, he began immediately bringing
drunks to the house.[75]

In a fact sheet the author located at Stepping Stones (covering
the period 1934 to 1941, and dated November 2, 1954), Bill made
two significant remarks:

1. For balance of 1934, continued working among alcoholics at
Towns Hospital, Calvary Mission, and among the few in the
Oxford Groups.

2. [Having described a number of the drunks with whom he and
Lois had worked unsuccessfully at Clinton Street, Bill added:]
"This is a fair sampling of the sort of people that we had on
Clinton Street for the ensuing three years, until 1939 to be exact.
Not a single one of them made a recovery in our house but we
learned a lot about drunks" (italics added).

In her memoirs, Lois said of this early New York period:

It was an ecstatic time for us both. With Ebby and another
alcoholic, Shep C., as our companions, we constantly went to
Oxford Group meetings at Calvary Episcopal Church on Fourth
Avenue. . . . Bill went back to Towns constantly to work on
alcoholics there and often visited the Calvary Mission where Alec,
the fisherman, had taken residence. . . . Although *he had not
permanently sobered up anyone in New York*, simply trying to
help others had kept him from even thinking of drinking (italics
added).[76]

---

[75] See Dick B., *The Akron Genesis*, pp. 3-4.
[76] *Lois Remembers*, pp. 91, 95.

A.A.'s own biography of Bill said:

> In those early months of 1935, Bill Wilson preached the Oxford
> Group message to anybody who would listen. He spent long hours
> at Calvary Mission and at Towns, where Dr. Silkworth, at the
> risk of his professional reputation, gave Bill permission to talk
> with some of the patients. "Burning with confidence and
> enthusiasm, I pursued alcoholics morning, noon, and night," Bill
> recalled.[77]

Even during his first ten days out of the Towns Hospital, Bill met
a chemistry professor named Fred B. at an Oxford Group meeting.
Bill invited Fred B. to join the small group of alcoholics who met
at Stewart's Cafeteria in the neighborhood after Oxford Group
meetings. And though he was less than sixty days sober, Bill
received a congratulatory letter from the Reverend Sam Shoemaker
as to his work with the professor.[78] Bill, as godfather, soon
sponsored this man (Fred B.) at Fred's baptism at Calvary Church
on March 14, 1935.[79]

Yet Bill had *no* success in bringing anyone to recovery. In his
memo, titled "Fact Sheet by Bill - November 2, 1954," Bill said:

> Drunks could not seem to accept the rigor of the Oxford Groups
> program. They'd stay sober only briefly and then flop. *No success
> at all* (italics added).

On page 4 of a memo concerning his experiences during his first
six months and just prior to meeting Dr. Bob in Akron for the first
time, Bill wrote:

> So I began. At first nothing much happened. But somehow I
> stayed sober, though my first friend [Ebby], alas, fell by the
> wayside. After months people began to say, "Is Lois still working

---

[77] *Pass it On*, p. 131.

[78] See Dick B., *The Akron Genesis*, p. 162.

[79] See Dick B., *New Light on Alcoholism*, pp. 246, 348.

in that department store? When is that guy Bill going to quit being a missionary and go to work?" After some months of such pressure, I wormed my way in a business deal that took me to Akron, Ohio. Getting out there, the deal fell flat. Subject as I often was to waves of self-pity and resentment, this was really tough. Burned up and discouraged, I was in mortal danger of getting drunk. Then came still another vital realization. *In working with other alcoholics for six months past, there had been no success.* But now I knew that this labor had done something for me; now I realized I must find another alcoholic to work with or fall myself (italics added).[80]

Most writers, including Bill, have ascribed Bill's total lack of success in sobering up drunks in New York's early days to Bill's "preaching." The story goes that Bill consulted Dr. Silkworth concerning his [Bill's] failures; and Silkworth told Bill to tell the drunks *first* about the hopelessness of their disease. *And* to hit them hard with that information. Then, said Silkworth, Bill could go on with his preaching. But apparently that was not enough.

Bill's wife Lois is recorded as giving this explanation:

While Lois later admitted that their success rate was low during the 1935-1936 period at Clinton Street, she pointed out that many of the alcoholics Bill worked with during that time did recover later on. In other words, Lois said, the seeds of sobriety were being planted, to take root slowly.[81]

Consider these facts, however: Bill had been an atheist to begin with.[82] To T. Henry and Clarace Williams, Bill confided that he had never studied the Bible until he came to Akron. In his endless

---

[80] Page four of a five-page memorandum by Bill which the author found and was permitted to copy at Stepping Stones, Bedford Hills, New York.

[81] *Pass It On*, p. 166.

[82] One of the many places in which Bill described himself as an atheist can be found in Wilson, *Original Story*, p. 98: "Perhaps I wouldn't need an emotional conversion. After all, a conservative atheist like me ought to be able to get on without anything like that."

writings and talks, Bill never said much about the books of the Bible Dr. Bob considered absolutely essential to the early program and the A.A. successes in Akron. Bill spoke very little about quiet time, prayer, and meditation—which were considered "musts" in the Akron program.[83] And he himself proclaimed he was in awe of Dr. Bob's spiritual knowledge and prayer abilities. In fact, said Bill, he relied on Dr. Bob in these areas.

Thus, we believe the reader should—as we approach A.A.'s Akron Genesis—ask whether Bill really had developed any well-shaped *spiritual message* in his pre-Akron days. In a letter designed to help Dr. Bob with his finances, Bill wrote:

At Akron, Ohio, there is a physician, Dr. Robert H. Smith, who has been responsible during the past four years for the recovery of at least 100 chronic alcoholics of types hitherto regarded by the medical profession as hopeless. . . . For more than four years, without charge to sufferers, without fanfare and almost without funds, Dr. Smith has carried on work among alcoholics in the Akron-Cleveland area. In this human laboratory, he has proved that any alcoholic, not too mentally defective, can recover if he so desires. The possible recovery among such cases has suddenly been lifted from almost nil to at least 50 percent, which, quite aside from its social implications, is a medical result of the first magnitude. Though, as a means of recovery, we all engage in the work, Dr. Smith has had more experience and has obtained better results than anyone else.[84]

Years later, Bill said:

. . . [Dr. Bob] has treated 5,000 drunks at St. Thomas Hospital in Akron. His spiritual example was a powerful influence, and he never charged a cent for his medical care. So Dr. Bob became the

---

[83] See *DR. BOB*, p. 136.

[84] Dick B., *The Akron Genesis*, p. 221.

prince of all twelfth-steppers. Perhaps nobody will ever do such a job again (italics added).[85]

A.A.'s Conference Approved history stated:

> "He [Dr. Bob] prayed, not only for his own understanding, but for different groups of people who requested him to pray for them," said Bill Wilson. "I was always glad to think that I was included in those prayers," *said Bill.* . . . "Bob was far ahead of me in that sort of activity. *I was always* rushing around talking and organizing and *'teaching kindergarten.'* I never grew up myself" (italics added).[86]

To be sure, Bill *must have had the mechanics* of the Oxford Group's life-changing program in his mind. He was, for years, obsessed with the importance of telling about his "hot flash" conversion experience. But Bill seems never (even in later years) to have gone much beyond the A.A. *"spiritual kindergarten"*—a phrase which (in terms of his own spiritual growth) Bill *often used.*[87] Bill spoke rarely, if ever, about such fundamental Christian ideas as the new birth (John 3:3-7; Romans 10:9; and 2 Corinthians 5:17) and the renewed mind (Romans 12:1-2) which were a vital part of Akron's thinking.[88]

Nonetheless, some vital points about Bill Wilson's New York "ministry" and failures must certainly be made. Whether they be considered a part of A.A.'s *spiritual* heritage or not—Bill brought

---

[85] Dick B., *Dr. Bob's Library: Books for Twelve Step Growth* (San Rafael, CA: Paradise Research Publications, 1994), p. 102.

[86] *DR. BOB*, p. 315.

[87] See for citations Dick B., *The Good Book and the Big Book*, p. 188.

[88] See Dick B., *Anne Smith's Journal: A.A.'s Principles of Success* (San Rafael, CA: Paradise Research Publications, 1994), pp. 46-47, 77, 132-33, 142-43; *That Amazing Grace: The Role of Clarence and Grace S. in Alcoholics Anonymous* (San Rafael, CA: Paradise Research Publications, 1996), pp. 34, 52, 89, 92.

with him from his earliest days some vital parts of A.A.'s early thinking that stuck.[89]

First, Bill inculcated in A.A. the entirety of Dr. William D. Silkworth's diagnosis that alcoholics suffer from a two-part, progressive disease—an obsession of the mind that drives them to drink, and an allergy of the body that compels them to drink to the point of death or insanity. *Second*, Bill proposed four ideas essential to establishing the alcoholics' powerlessness over alcohol: (1) Willpower will not help them.[90] (2) Self-knowledge will not help them.[91] (3) Fear will not help them.[92] (4) Probably no human power can help them (or, to put it as the Big Book puts it: They are 100% hopeless apart from divine help).[93] *Third*, the first condition for recovery is (and, according to Bill, should be) ego-deflation in depth.[94] *Finally*, each alcoholic must help another alcoholic or he or she will surely drink and then surely die. As the Oxford Group and Sam Shoemaker put it, you must "give it away to keep it."[95]

Not everyone would agree, but it appears these four critical portions of the A.A. program probably came from Professor William James of Harvard; Richard R. Peabody and his title, *The Common Sense of Drinking*; and the Oxford Group's important

---

[89] Note too that such differing views as those of Clarence S. and Dr. Ernest Kurtz would perhaps proclaim that *all* A.A.'s Twelve Step ideas are spiritual. See Dick B., *That Amazing Grace: The Role of Clarence and Grace S. in Alcoholics Anonymous* (San Rafael, CA: Paradise Research Publications, 1996), p. 92; Ernest Kurtz and Katherine Ketcham, *The Spirituality of Imperfection: Modern Wisdom From Classic Stories* (New York: Bantam Books, 1992), pp. 102-03, 109-10.

[90] Big Book, First Edition, p. 15.

[91] Big Book, First Edition, p. 16.

[92] Big Book, First Edition, pp. 17-18.

[93] Big Book, First Edition, pp. 21, 35-37, 54-55, 72.

[94] See Ernest Kurtz, *Not-God: A History of Alcoholics Anonymous*, exp. ed. (Minnesota: Hazelden, 1991), p. 21.

[95] See Dick B., *The Good Book and The Big Book*, pp. 161-62.

principle: "sharing for witness."[96] Undoubtedly, it was Bill Wilson's incessant search for drunks to help that fashioned A.A.'s cardinal principle that one drunk must help another and share experience, strength, and hope.

But it was to be in Akron that the spiritual studies and truths, the spiritual experiments, and the spiritual transformations were developed from the Bible and the Oxford Group program into a recovery program that worked for others than Bill Wilson alone.

The Akron Genesis of A.A.

A.A.'s Akron beginnings present an entirely different picture from that in New York.[97] Most assuredly, the Reverend Sam Shoemaker played an important role. So did the Oxford Group. But from the very first, the concern in Akron was with helping

---

[96] See William James, *The Varieties of Religious Experience* (New York: Vintage Books, 1990); Richard R. Peabody, *The Common Sense of Drinking* (Boston: Little, Brown, And Company, 1935); Frank N. D. Buchman, *Remaking the World* (London: Blandford Press, 1961), p. x: "The best way to keep an experience of Christ is to pass it on;" Mel B., *New Wine*, pp. 16, 24-25, 81, 117-19; *Pass It On*, pp. 124, 197.

[97] Primary source materials for this segment are: The personal journal of Samuel Shoemaker for 1931; the personal diaries of James D. Newton for 1931, 1933 to 1936; the Shoemaker files at the Episcopal Church Archives in Texas; James D. Newton, *Uncommon Friends: Life with Thomas Edison, Henry Ford, Harvey Firestone, Alexis Carrel, & Charles Lindbergh* (New York: Harcourt Brace Jovanovich, Publishers, 1987); T. Willard Hunter, *"It Started Right There": Behind the Twelve Steps and the Self-help Movement* (Washington, D.C.: Moral Re-Armament, n.d.); Bob E., Handwritten Memo to Lois Wilson on pamphlet entitled "Four Absolutes;" Bob E. Letter to Nell Wing, Stepping Stones Archives; Record of Bob E. of Akron Ohio Dictated to Bill Wilson on 6-18-1954; *DR. BOB and the Good Oldtimers*; *RHS* (New York: The A.A. Grapevine, January, 1951); *The Co-Founders of Alcoholics Anonymous: Biographical sketches Their last major talks* (New York: Alcoholics Anonymous World Services, Inc., 1972, 1975); Bob Smith and Sue Smith Windows, *Children of the Healer* (Illinois: Parkside Publishing Corporation, 1992); Dick B., *Dr. Bob's Library; Anne Smith's Journal, 1933-1939; The Akron Genesis; Design for Living: The Oxford Group Contribution to Early A.A.; That Amazing Grace: The Role of Clarence and Grace S. in Alcoholics Anonymous* (San Rafael, CA: Paradise Research Publications, 1996); *Good Morning! Quiet Time, Morning Watch, Meditation, and Early A.A.* (San Rafael, CA: Paradise Research Publications, 1996).

drunks to recover by effective spiritual means. And the story begins with the very severe and well-known drinking problem of Harvey Firestone, Sr.'s son Russell—also known as "Bud."

Jim Newton, The Firestones, and Sam Shoemaker

In 1924, the Florida real estate boom was at its height. James D. Newton, an enterprising young luggage salesman, arrived in Fort Myers at age 20. With the help of his father, Newton acquired fifty-five acres of raw land in Fort Myers. The tract was adjacent to the homes of the famous inventor, Thomas Alva Edison, and the auto manufacturer, Henry Ford. On April 7, 1926, Jim Newton officially opened the residential real estate development in Fort Myers known as Edison Park. In the interim between his arrival in Florida and the opening of Edison Park, Newton had become well acquainted with Thomas Edison. He became almost a second son to Edison and his wife, Mina. Edison, in turn, had two younger friends—well known in American business. One was Edison's neighbor, Henry Ford; and the other was Edison's frequent visitor from the Miami winter scene, Harvey Firestone, Sr.

During the last decade of Edison's life, the press began making something of the inventor's birthday, which occurred on February 11th. By that time, Edison had become extremely deaf. With many well-wishers coming to town for the birthday event, Mrs. Edison asked Jim Newton if he would take charge of the Edison birthdays. Newton became the greeter, introduced guests to each other, and arranged accommodations at the Royal Palm Hotel. A good many of the rich and famous, including President Herbert Hoover, Henry Ford, and Harvey Firestone, Sr., were there. Following one of these occasions in 1928, Newton was approached and befriended by an admiring Firestone. Firestone asked Newton to leave Florida and come to Akron as "Secretary to the President" of Firestone Tire and Rubber Company. Newton accepted, moved to Akron, and later became President of Firestone Realty. Subsequently he was moved into the sales field and was told he was being groomed for the presidency of Firestone.

In 1923, Newton had become connected with the Oxford Group through a meeting in Massachusetts. Oxford Group adherents were finding a sense of direction during quiet times and were finding it by experiment. Newton heard from one young man that Group people were using Jesus's Sermon on the Mount as a guide for their actions and motives. The man told Newton that the guide had been reduced to four absolute standards—honesty, purity, unselfishness, and love. He told Newton his own [the man's] life had not measured up. Then he asked Newton, in terms of "purity," how Newton would feel if his thoughts were flashed on a screen. Newton understood the significance of the question, admired the man's honesty, and could relate to the man's shortcomings.

Newton asked how he himself could conduct the life-changing experiment. The young man suggested, as Newton put it, that "I . . . turn over as much of my will as I understood to as much of God as I comprehend."[98] Newton asked what he would have to do the next morning. The man replied *he* didn't know, but *Newton* would know the next morning *if* he made *the* decision. Jim then, for the first time in his life, got on his knees with another man and said: "I have my ideals, but I can't live up to them. I don't have what it takes. Okay, I've loused things up—If you're there and can call the shots, here's my will and my life. You run it, you fly it."[99]

Following instructions, Newton got up the next morning five minutes earlier. He listened to see what thoughts came into his mind. Two thoughts were there: (1) Give back the money he'd gotten "mixed up with mine" in a cash register. (2) Tell his customers in New England that he hadn't been entirely honest with them. He wrote the thoughts down. He asked his young friend: "Is

---

[98] Newton, *Uncommon Friends*, p. 154. As we've seen from Ebby's instructions to Bill, this idea of surrendering as much of one's self as one knew or understood to as much of God as he or she knew or understood was common in the Oxford Group. See Dick B., *The Good Book and the Big Book*, pp. 53-62.

[99] Newton, *Uncommon Friends*, p. 155.

this direction, or guidance from God?" The friend asked what Newton thought. Newton decided to act on the thoughts; and the experiment worked. Newton said:

> I noticed a new sureness and straightness, especially in my dealings with people. I started off each day by being quiet and giving God a chance to show me through my thoughts how he wanted me to live. That way, I began to experience a sense of direction I'd never had before.[100]

Newton explained all this in later years to his friend Charles Lindbergh. He likened his experiment to the time he asked to be a candidate for the school swimming squad, but couldn't swim. Newton joined the squad. The swim coach told him to go to the edge of the pool, kick his legs, move his arms, and then find that the water held him up. Newton said:

> Finally I pushed away and found I *did* stay up. I had moved from *believing* to *knowing*. That's what happened to me when I made the experiment of asking God to direct my life.[101]

To Lindbergh's wife Anne, Newton elaborated further at another time:

> [Anne asked regarding those who *didn't* believe. Newton replied:] If you don't believe in God—and my own belief at that time was pretty vague—then you can make an experiment. . . . I asked God, if there was a God, to make clear to me what I should do. God did exactly that. He showed me the first steps I must take. . . . An inner voice . . . tells you not only what you may have done wrong, but an intuition about what you need to do, a direction in which to go, a feeling or illumination about some part of your life. . . . I consciously try to let God's presence soak in. It gives me a perspective on myself, on work, friends, life. . . . [T]here's

---

[100] Newton, *Uncommon Friends*, p. 156.
[101] Newton, *Uncommon Friends*, pp. 156-57.

nothing vague about it. It's all in the New Testament. Be willing and obedient, and you will experience a new power and a new direction in your daily life.[102]

From 1923 on, and to the date of this writing, James Draper Newton has been an Oxford Group activist and an ardent practitioner of Oxford Group principles. He became a good friend of Dr. Frank N. D. Buchman, of the Reverend Samuel M. Shoemaker, and of one of their closest co-workers, Eleanor Napier Forde (who later became Newton's wife).

The Bud Firestone Recovery on the Train

Back now to Newton's arrival at Firestone Tire and Rubber in Akron. At that time, Newton became and was, for many years to remain, a close friend of one of Firestone's sons, Bud. However, Newton soon became aware of Bud's drinking problem. In fact, he learned it from Bud himself when Bud told him that he had been in and out of institutions to "dry out." Newton set out to help Bud and even, with the elder Firestone's permission, joined Bud at yet another institution where Bud tried still another cure.

There is no question that Newton introduced Bud to the meat of Oxford Group ideas. Newton had learned the principles and practices from the Group's top articulators. He was not, and was never to become an alcoholic. Yet Newton could see that Bud's capers were the talk of Akron. And Bud—who, according to Newton, was a keen businessman with his father's capabilities for negotiation—was breaking his father's heart. Firestone Senior had come to believe that the situation with Bud was hopeless.

After Bud returned with Newton from an institution on the Hudson River, Newton invited Bud to go with him to a conference in Denver where Bud would meet people Newton knew in the

---

[102] Newton, *Uncommon Friends*, pp. 168-69. See John 7:17 and Samuel M. Shoemaker, *Religion That Works* (New York: Fleming H. Revell, 1928), pp. 14-15, 36, 46.

Oxford Group. Newton's personal diaries for the period reveal the
following:

9/19/31	Lunch with Harvey, Betty, Bud. Later long talk and prayer with Bud.
9/20/31	Bud in pretty bad shape when we met the Firestones Sr. who arrived on Leviathan at 1:30. . . . Mr. F. would talk only of the visit in Switzerland with Frank (Buchman) and Marion and Ken (Twitchell). Intrigued with it. Mr. F. invited Sam [Sam Shoemaker] to ride to Akron with us. Bud and Sam talked until late.
9/21/31	Arrived Akron. Bud made an initial decision [to surrender to God]. We--Bud, Dorothy [Bud's wife] and Sam--started for Denver after quiet time with Mr. F. [Other source information discloses that Shoemaker met with Firestone Senior, Bud Firestone, Leonard Firestone, and Newton.] Firestone plane to Toledo--got train there. Bud fairly well behaved. [In *Uncommon Friends*, Newton said "On the train to Denver we agreed I would carry his liquor for him. He had been drinking a fifth of whiskey or more each day. That arrangement we made put a small barrier between himself and the alcohol, and it slowed down the consumption some, but it wasn't enough" (p. 84)].
9/22/31	Enroute Denver. Bud stays in drawing room. Comes out for supper with the team. Philip Marshall Brown [the professor who wrote *Venture of Belief*]. . . Dr. Irene Gates. . . Olive Jones [Superintendent of Education at Calvary Church and author of *Inspired Children*] and Sam [Shoemaker].
9/23/31	Arrive Denver. Irene (Dr. Gates) takes hold. Bud and Dorothy great. Bishop Perry (presiding Episcopal Bishop) received me. Real chat together. Wholeheartedly for the fellowship (Oxford Group).
9/23/31 to 9/26/31	[Entries simply refer to Denver]

9/27/31   Dinner for Bishops Freeman, Spencer, Stearly, Wood, Page, Atwood. Talked with Mr. F. on the phone. Later he talked with Bud.

9/28/31
to
9/29/31   [Entries basically refer to Denver area]

9/30/31   Denver. Left for NY 4 p.m. Group has meeting in pullman tonight. Great talk with Mr. F. before left (Group including Sam) want Bud to go to NY instead of Akron but he doesn't want to).

10/1/31   Enroute to Chicago. Quiet time in pullman. 40 there including Bishop Freeman and Page. Sam and Bud talk. Bud changed--miraculously--Christ (JDN) left group at Chicago, went to Akron. [Other source information indicates Shoemaker took Bud Firestone into a compartment on the train and led Bud to a decision for Christ. In *Uncommon Friends*, Newton wrote: "Finally I [Newton] was able to get him [Bud] together with a friend of mine, Sam Shoemaker, a skilled counselor, who helped him make a decision to let God deal with the stresses that had driven him [Bud] to alcohol. . . . Bud's decision. . . had an extraordinary effect. His whole life changed. It was visible right away; his face relaxed, some of the lines were gone. He had come to terms not just with the drinking, but with the underlying cause that was making him drink" (pp. 84-85)]. About these events, Bud said: (1) "I gave my life to Jesus Christ." (2) "I let God guide my life now."[103]

10/2/31   [Entries on this date and for the ensuing period refer to Newton's return to Akron where he dined with Firestone Senior, Firestone's wife, and Leonard Firestone. They talked about Bud. Newton and the senior Firestone departed for New York. Then follows:] "Mr. F. awed by change Christ has made in Bud." . . . Group quiet time on lawn. Mr. F. read

---

[103] Mel B., *New Wine*, p. 67.

Bible, shared and prayed. . . . Leonard F. at Calvary. Mr. F., Bud and Dorothy there. . . . Quiet time with Mr. F. Lunch with others. . . . Dorothy, Bud and I to Tuesday night group at Calvary (Sam's regular Tuesday night meetings). Dinner with Firestone family. . . . Sam and Mr. F. had great talk alone."

10/8/31 Meeting at Calvary. Spoke. Bud's witness was marvelous.

10/9/31 Calvary Church. Lunch with Sam and Helen [Shoemaker's wife]. Dinner with Charles and Carolyn Edison [The elder Edison had died, and these were Edison's family]. Much interested in Bud's change.

10/11/31 NY lunch with Harvey, Bud and Prince Charles of Belgium at new Waldorf Astoria.

10/12/31 Dinner at Calvary. Long talk on train with Mr. F. and Bud.

10/13/31 Arrive Akron. Bud and his dad had great talk. Bud looking fine.

This, then, describes the deliverance of Bud Firestone through the help and support of the Firestone family, of Jim Newton, of Sam Shoemaker—and through the miraculous power of God. Newton said: "The family doctor called the transformation a medical miracle. He had thought withdrawal would take much longer."[104]

The 1933 Oxford Group Events in Akron

The Bud Firestone-Jim Newton-Sam Shoemaker story does not end with October, 1931. In a telephone interview with the author in March of 1992, Newton elaborated on what Bud had done thereafter with the Oxford Group. Bud had not merely made a decision to surrender. He had followed through with the Oxford Group's life-changing program that later found its way into A.A.'s Twelve Steps. Firestone made restitution. He studied the Bible and

---

[104] Newton, *Uncommon Friends*, p. 86.

observed Quiet Time with Newton for many years. He witnessed to others. He met with the New York businessmen's team of which Bill Wilson, Newton, and others were a part. He attended house-parties. In fact, when the author visited the Episcopal Church Archives in Texas, he found a number of letter exchanges between Sam Shoemaker and Bud Firestone.

In December of 1933, Bud sent Sam Shoemaker a letter concerning the witnessing trip Bud and Jim Newton had taken to England on behalf of the Oxford Group. Bud enclosed copies of Newton's diary. It showed that the pair had met with Oxford Group leaders Frank Buchman, Ken Twitchell, John Roots, Garrett Stearly, and others. They attended a "leader's quiet time" and then went to a "team quiet time" where forty were present. Accompanied by Frank Buchman, they went to a Business Men's meeting at a Church where two hundred were present, and the team witnessed. Similar later events were recorded including talks with Oxford Group leaders Ray and Elsa Purdy and "Bunny" Austin (the famous British tennis star). Newton and Bud often witnessed together at events both large and small.

Regrettably, however, a large amount of relevant Shoemaker-Firestone correspondence is missing. A small note was placed in the front of a file at the Episcopal Church Archives—a file which contained correspondence between Bud Firestone and Sam Shoe-maker. The handwritten note states: "This is only a portion of correspondence—representative—have discarded some very personal & confidential data." There is no point in speculating about the nature of the concealed data. The archivist's note [not the note of any person on the present staff] does establish, however, that there was an even closer link between Shoemaker and the Firestones. In fact, one letter from Shoemaker to Frank Buchman discusses the Bud Firestone miracle and the importance to the Oxford Group cause of the Firestone family.

The next Akron landmark concerns the famous events which occurred in January of 1933. The author will not here reproduce the voluminous newspaper reports from Akron's two major newspapers in that period. But he did examine every one of the daily Oxford Group articles in the *Akron Times-Press* and the *Akron Beacon Journal* from January 16 to January 23, 1933. Details from the articles can be found quoted at pages 37 to 47 of the author's *The Akron Genesis of Alcoholics Anonymous*.

The veritable blitzkrieg of news covered everything from testimonials at large meetings, sharing in the church pulpits, small meetings, Oxford Group principles, statements by Oxford Group leaders, comments by Akron clergy, tidbits on society dinners and teas accompanying the events, feature articles on particular Oxford Group members, and personal comments by members of the Firestone family. And what was the occasion?

A grateful Harvey Firestone, Sr., his pastor (Dr. Walter Tunks, rector of St. Paul's Episcopal church), Jim Newton, and Mr. and Mrs. Bud Firestone invited Dr. Frank N. D. Buchman and a "team" to come to Akron and tell of the life-changing power of Christ. Bud Firestone had his religious experience to share. He was to tell of his experience of Christ, his deliverance from alcoholism, and his life-change. And his grateful father's prestige brought the city to attention.

The newspapers told of the coming of Dr. Buchman and his group of 30 brokers, bankers, business and professional men who—in the words of Bud Firestone—would conduct evangelistic appearances amounting to "a revival of old-time religion." A huge meeting was set for the Mayflower Hotel ballroom. The papers announced that though Bud Firestone had been "converted" more than a year previously and had traveled throughout the country speaking at Oxford Group meetings, "the Akron sessions will introduce the Oxford Group teaching to Ohio for the first time."

And introduce it they did. More than a score of Akron church pulpits were thrown open to Buchman and his disciples. Front page news articles quoted Firestone Senior as saying "Need 'Rebirth.'" They told of Sherry Day's seven principles of the Group. They told of "two-way" prayer and "listening to God." They told of daily Bible study, the Oxford Group definition of sin, and the injunction in the Book of James: "Confess your faults one to another." They quoted Dr. Buchman: "Life changing on a colossal basis is the only hope left in the world today." They contained critiques by the local clergy. They quoted Bud Firestone's wife as saying: "I had grown weary of the task of running my own life and I was willing to let God run it." They contained testimonials adjuring listeners to reject "selfishness, self-centeredness." In short, six years before A.A.'s Big Book was published, Akron people were hearing specific Oxford Group language that later became coin of the realm in A.A.

The huge revival might have gone to naught as far as A.A. is concerned; but it was attended by several people who felt they needed to hear the message. Henrietta Seiberling (a non-alcoholic) was present and became a major player in the early A.A. scene. Anne Ripley Smith (Dr. Bob's wife) was there for spiritual uplift. Two other friends, Delphine Weber (whose husband was the principal of King School where A.A. meetings were later held) and Clarace Williams (whose home was later used for the earliest A.A. meetings), were there with Henrietta and Anne.

The Prayers for Dr. Bob's Recovery

The story of events thereafter has often been told. But, from the spiritual side, it is vital to know that Oxford Group activity continued in Akron from January of 1933 to June of 1935 (when A.A. was founded). Dr. Bob and Anne became church goers. The Oxford Group people introduced Dr. Bob to all their literature. Dr. Bob and Anne became thoroughly familiar with the Oxford Group principles we have previously outlined. They prayed and had quiet times in and out of meetings. They read almost everything the Oxford Group had to offer. They met in Oxford Group fellowship meetings. Dr. Bob began an intense study of the Bible and Christian literature, including the Oxford Group books. Anne Smith faithfully recorded in the spiritual journal she began keeping in 1933 the Oxford Group's teachings, the Bible ideas, the Christian literature that was read, and the Group's life-changing program. *And Dr. Bob stayed drunk.*

Drunk, that is, until a turning point was reached several weeks before Bill Wilson arrived in Akron. Though Henrietta Seiberling knew virtually nothing of alcoholism, she and the Oxford Group people were relentless in their plans to help Dr. Bob. Suddenly—though she knew nothing of the principle that an alcoholic cannot take even one drink—Henrietta received specific guidance. She received the guided thought that Dr. Bob should not touch one drink. She convened an Oxford Group meeting at T. Henry Williams' home at 676 Palisades Drive in Akron, where all were prepared to "share something costly." This technique epitomized the Oxford Group's art of getting others to share their "sins." The meeting was held. The plan worked. And Dr. Bob made the "startling" disclosure: "This may cost me my profession, but I am a silent drinker [most accounts say "a secret drinker"], and I can't stop." Secret in Dr. Bob's mind, but hardly a secret to anyone else in the Akron scene.

In any event, Henrietta asked whether Dr. Bob would like the group to pray. Bob agreed; and there, in the Williams' living room, *the group went down on their knees*. T. Henry told this story:

> Years later a visitor in that home asked, "T. Henry, you know something about Alcoholics Anonymous, don't you?" "Sure do," he replied, and pointing to a section of his living room carpet, said, "It started right there." It was the spot where Dr. Bob had knelt that night.

Two weeks later Bill Wilson arrived.[105]

Prayers for Dr. Bob Answered; A.A. Founded

There is more to this miraculous story; and most of the events have frequently been told in much detail. Wilson arrived in Akron. He was staying at the Mayflower Hotel. He was tempted to drink.

---

[105] The foregoing paragraph and quote are taken largely from Hunter, *"It started right there"*, p. 8.

On the wall at the opposite end of the lobby was a church directory. Wilson had learned that, to stay sober, he must work with another drunk. He looked at the church directory and selected the name of Dr. Walter Tunks, rector of St. Paul's Episcopal Church. This was the same Dr. Tunks who had been pastor to the Firestone family, who knew of Bud Firestone's deliverance, and who had helped host the Oxford Group testimonials of 1933 in Akron. After phoning many numbers recommended by Tunks, Bill reached Henrietta Seiberling—the very person who had been at the Oxford Group events in 1933 with Anne Smith and the very person who had persuaded Dr. Bob and others to pray for Bob's deliverance. Wilson announced to Mrs. Seiberling: "I'm from the Oxford Group in New York, and I'm a rum hound from New York." As AAs today often say: "Was this odd, or was it God?"

Pass It On reported:

> Her [Henrietta's] silent reaction, she said, was *"This is really manna from heaven."* Aloud, she said, "You come right out here." It may seem remarkable that a woman alone with three teenage children would be so quick to invite a strange man into her home. But there was a strong bond of trust among Oxford Group members. Henrietta Seiberling relied on God's guidance in her life. She was certain that the telephone call was the help she and other Oxford Group members had been seeking for one of their members. Only a few weeks earlier, the man [Dr. Bob] had finally admitted to the group that he was a secret drinker, and Henrietta believed that as a result of his honesty, help would come for him in some form, some way. This visitor from New York might be that very help. When Bill arrived, she made the telephone call to the man she had in mind. The man's name was Dr. Robert Smith. He was a physician. He was an alcoholic. And he was in desperate straits (p. 137, italics added).

Little more needs to be added here because the history is available in great detail in the books we cited at the beginning of this segment. The important basic facts are these: (1) Bill carried no new spiritual message to Dr. Bob, and Bob so stated. Bob remarked that he had heard it all before. He had spent two and a half years in the Bible, in the Oxford Group, in prayer and meditation, in religious services at church, and in Christian literature. (2) Bill's impact lay in the fact that he was willing to spend and did spend six hours talking to the reluctant Dr. Bob. Dr. Bob had read much about alcoholism and had heard the opinions of fellow professionals who had treated alcoholics. But Bill was the first person he had talked with who knew *from his own experience* what alcoholism was. Bob said:

> In other words, he talked my language. He knew all the answers, and certainly not because he had picked them up in his reading.[106]

After one brief drinking episode at a medical convention he may not even have attended, Dr. Bob decided to go through with the Oxford Group program. The date, according to present accounts, was June 10, 1935—the date Dr. Bob had his last drink. AAs agree today that this date marks the founding of Alcoholics Anonymous at its birthplace in Akron, Ohio.[107]

The Midwest Experiment Succeeds

There is a good deal of historical material on the Akron days from the date of Dr. Bob's last drink to the date A.A.'s Big Book was published in the Spring of 1939. There is very little on the specifics borrowed from the spiritual materials and ideas that inspired the recovery program and the high success rate it achieved. This segment will therefore focus on what was used, done, and achieved in the spiritual arena from June 10, 1935 to the date of the Big Book's publication in 1939.

---

[106] *Pass It On*, p. 143.
[107] Dick B., *The Akron Genesis*, pp. 2-5.

Bill W., Dr. Bob, and the Basics

Bill Wilson certainly brought with him to Akron six months of intense exposure to the Oxford Group. He had listened to Ebby, Rowland, and Shep. He had constantly and regularly attended Oxford Group meetings. He had held his extra meetings-after-the-meetings at Stewart's Cafeteria with such people as Rowland. He had certainly heard Sam Shoemaker in the pulpit and leading meetings and had met with him personally on more than one occasion, as Shoemaker's personal journals disclose. Bill may or may not have read Oxford Group literature. But he certainly heard lots of Oxford Group talk from such fellow business team members as Victor Kitchen (author of *I Was a Pagan*), Loudon Hamilton (author of *MRA: How It All Began*), Philip Marshall Brown (author of *The Venture of Belief*), and Charles Clapp, Jr. (author of *The Big Bender*).

Bill also was in the company of a good many clergymen who were either living at Calvary House, on Shoemaker's staff, or leaders in the Oxford Group. These men of the cloth were not only team members; they frequently led meetings attended by Bill. They included the Reverends J. Herbert Smith, W. Irving Harris, John Potter Cuyler, Jr., Garrett Stearly, Ray Purdy, and Cleve Hicks. Whatever Bill really learned from all this, he certainly *preached* about it. He preached at Towns Hospital. He preached at Calvary Rescue Mission; and he preached to alcoholics at Oxford Group meetings when he could find them. As with so much of the rest of the spiritual details, however, Bill has left us no information as to *what* he preached.

Dr. Bob had engaged in his spiritual quest for two and a half years. The Oxford Group in Akron had become a major interest for him. The names of his Oxford Group companions were not stellar, but Dr. Bob's actual study of Oxford Group literature and ideas was intense. Dr. Bob seems to have read every Oxford Group book that was suggested to, or placed before him. He regularly attended meetings. He learned from such highly intelligent, sober activists as T. Henry and Clarace Williams, Henrietta Seiberling, and his own wife Anne.

The Oxford Group itself continued its outreach in Akron, sending a "continuance" team there in 1934 to help adherents grow spiritually. As we will soon see in some detail and have covered in much detail in *Anne Smith's Journal, 1933-1939*, Anne was faithfully writing down, analyzing, and sharing the ideas she was hearing and studying from the Bible, from Oxford Group speakers, from Oxford Group books, and from other Christian literature. T. Henry had studied the Bible, assembled Oxford Group literature, and was a regular church-goer. His wife Clarace had studied to be a missionary and was equally well-versed in Christian principles. Henrietta Seiberling was an Oxford Group enthusiast, a Bible student, and a prolific reader of the Christian literature of the day.

This was the setting when Dr. Bob and Bill began comparing notes and building their program. For the three months that Bill lived with the Smiths in the summer of 1935, Bill and Bob daily stayed up into the wee morning hours discussing the Bible, Oxford Group principles, and alcoholism. They regularly attended Oxford Group meetings. They had Quiet Time each day with Anne. Henrietta Seiberling frequently spoke with Bob and with Bill and taught them what she could of her knowledge of the Bible, the Oxford Group, and Christian ideas. Each day Anne read the Scriptures with Bob and Bill and discussed Christian literature with them. Bill made it clear that the Book of James and Corinthians (from the Bible) were much discussed.

Dr. Bob often said that the Sermon on the Mount contained the underlying philosophy of A.A.; and in light of other remarks he made about the basic sources of A.A. ideas in the Bible, it seems most probable that the Sermon was also much discussed. Certainly language from the Sermon underlay several of the ultimate Twelve Step ideas—language such as "Thy will be done" and "love thy neighbor as thyself." So did the "confession" and "faith without works" ideas in James. So did the "believing" idea in Hebrews 11:6. So did the "love" principles in 1 Corinthians

13—particularly as they were analyzed in Drummond's *The Greatest Thing in the World.*

Oxford Group/Bible ideas on trust in God, guidance, self-examination, restitution, daily housecleaning, prayer, meditation, spiritual experiences, witnessing, practicing the Four Absolutes and other spiritual principles simply had to have been part of the daily fare. These ideas appeared fairly soon in the "six steps" early AAs developed and used for their remarkable successes.[108]

Proof that Anne Smith shared the contents of her spiritual journal with Bill Wilson has never been brought to the author's attention. Yet we know Anne often shared at length with Bill in the summer of 1935, particularly when Dr. Bob was away at the office. We know that Anne daily read to Bob and Bill from the Scriptures and from Christian literature. We know that Bill once said:

> For the next three months [in the summer of 1935], I lived with these two wonderful people. I shall always believe they gave me more than I ever brought them.[109]

It has also been established that Anne read from the Scriptures, Christian literature, devotionals, and Oxford Group materials to the many AAs and their families at the Smith home in subsequent months. She used her journal as part of this practice during the daily quiet times Anne held at the Smith home each morning.

---

[108] Many in A.A. have come to believe that the Oxford Group had "six steps" which early AAs appropriated. But that may not be the case. *Pass It On* states: "There is no evidence that the Oxford Group had such a specific program" (p. 197). In a footnote on page 206, *Pass It On* documents its statement with the remarks of the Reverend T. Willard Hunter, who spent eighteen years in full-time staff positions for the Oxford Group and M.R.A.; and the author has found no precise Oxford Group counterpart for A.A.'s original six Steps. A.A.s original first Step focused on an admission that the alcoholic was "licked," or (as Bill put it) that there had been deflation at depth. However, the author's own research has turned up many examples in the writings of the Oxford Group, Shoemaker, and Anne Smith, of the "Manage me" prayer. Indirectly, therefore, there *was* an admission of defeat when the Oxford Group person got down on his or her knees to surrender and said, "O, God, manage me because I can't manage myself."

[109] *DR. BOB*, p. 71.

The author therefore finds it difficult not to believe that Anne used her spiritual journal in the same way and for the same purposes when she was talking to Bill and Bob during the earliest three months of A.A.; for Anne had begun keeping her journal from 1933 forward. Recall Bill's statement that Anne had infused much needed spirituality into Bob and himself.

After Anne died on June 1, 1949, Bill wrote:

> Anne was the wife of Dr. Bob, co-founder of Alcoholics Anonymous. She was, quite literally, the mother of our first group, Akron Number One. Her wise and beautiful counsel to all, her insistence that the spiritual come before anything else, her unwavering support of Dr. Bob in all his works; all these were virtues which watered the uncertain seed that was to become A.A. Who but God could assess such a contribution? We can only say that it was priceless and magnificent. In the full sense of the word, she was one of the founders of Alcoholics Anonymous.[110]

DR. BOB and the Good Oldtimers said:

> Dr. Bob, noting that there were no Twelve Steps at the time and that "our stories didn't amount to anything to speak of," later said they were convinced that the answer to their problems was in the Good Book. . . . This was the beginning of A.A.'s "flying-blind period." They had the Bible, and they had the precepts of the Oxford Group. They also had their own instincts. They were working, or working out, the A.A. program—the Twelve Steps—without quite knowing they were doing it (p. 96).

DR. BOB and the Good Oldtimers also said:

> With the last drink under his belt and the idea of service in his heart, Dr. Bob was eager to join Bill in finding another drunk to "fix," as they put it in those days. . . . [Dr. Bob's pastor, the Reverend J. C. Wright, sent them a prospect, Eddie R. Then Bill

---

[110] *The Language of the Heart*, pp. 353-54.

and Bob] tore over to Cleveland in the middle of the night, got him here [Akron] and to the hospital and commenced to give him the Towns (Hospital) treatment. That, plus more oxidizing, has been magical. . . and is creating a great stir at the City hospital, where the doctors are all agog, being unable to do anything with these cases. ("Oxidizing" was probably short for "Oxfordizing" . . .) (p. 78).

Though Bob and Bill were unsuccessful, in the earliest days, with this particular drunk, they did score in their next effort which involved A.A. Number 3—Bill D. And the point of all this is that Bill and Bob were not only studying, discussing, and analyzing the basic ideas from the Bible and the Oxford Group; they were immediately at work putting them into practice to *help drunks*. Bill wrote his wife in May of 1935 stating events in such a way as to indicate he and Bob had started carrying the message together at least within two weeks or so of their first meeting on Mother's Day of 1935.[111]

Hospitalizations

Early AAs much favored hospitalization of the newcomer. He was often too jittery and befogged to be anyplace else. Dr. Bob was able to hospitalize the drunks in Akron City Hospital and monitor their condition. The newcomer was a "captive" to the procedure; and the recovered AAs could reach him personally with their own stories—stories designed to help him identify his own plight and the hope and help that were available. This process was typical of the Oxford Group technique of "sharing as witness."[112]

A story, as told by A.A. pioneer Clarence S., will serve to highlight the hospitalization picture:

---

[111] *DR. BOB*, p. 70.

[112] See J. P. Thornton-Duesbury, *Sharing* (Great Britain, The Oxford Group, n.d.), pp. 6-10.

Clarence walked from the bus depot in Akron in snow three feet deep to Akron City Hospital—the place to which Dr. Bob had directed him. Upon arrival, Clarence fainted. He woke up in a hospital room in which the only literature was a Bible. Clarence managed to make it through the night without a drink; and the next day (February 11, 1938) marked the beginning of Clarence's first day of sobriety—a sobriety he maintained for forty-six years until the date of his death. He remained in Akron City Hospital for a total of six days.

Soon, two men visited Clarence in his hospital room. They introduced themselves, and said to him, "We have an answer to your problem." They told him the stories of their lives. They told him what had happened to them. And they showed him they were now sober. They said Clarence could have what they had if he wanted it. Dr. Bob visited Clarence that afternoon (and every afternoon of Clarence's hospitalization). Two more drunks appeared and told Clarence they too had an answer to his problem. They told their stories and departed. On the last day of Clarence's hospitalization, Dr. Bob sat on Clarence's bed; and the "answer" was provided.[113]

Dr. Bob minced no words on this point. *DR. BOB and the Good Oldtimers* recorded this typical colloquy:

[Dr. Bob:] "Do you believe in God, young fella?" . . .

[Clarence:] "What does that have to do with it?"

[Dr. Bob:] "Everything."

[Clarence:] "I guess I do."

[Dr. Bob:] "Guess, nothing! Either you do or you don't."

[Clarence:] "Yes, I do."

---

[113] The two paragraphs are essentially from Dick B., *That Amazing Grace*, pp. 25-26.

[Dr. Bob:] That's fine. Now we're getting someplace. All right, get out of bed and on your knees. We're going to pray."

[Clarence:] "I don't know how to pray."

[Dr. Bob:] "I guess you don't, but that's all right. Just follow what I say, and that will do for now."

[Clarence, later:] "I did what I was ordered to do. There was no suggestion."[114]

Clarence was then taken to his first Oxford Group meeting at T. Henry Williams' house. *Dr. Bob gave him a Bible* and told Clarence to "go out and fix drunks as an avocation."[115]

Meetings

The early A.A. meetings in Akron were Oxford Group meetings. They were attended by alcoholics, their wives, and family members, as well as by Oxford Group people. Bill V. H., who got sober in early 1937, estimated the proportion of Oxford Group to non-Oxford Group people at about 50-50. Oxford Group literature was set out on tables in the furnace room of T. Henry's house adjacent to the meeting room. Bill V. H. said this Oxford Group literature was passed around, and he remembered well "how we all challenged ourselves on the Four Absolutes of the Oxford Movement."[116] Wally G., who got sober in late 1938, said: "T. Henry's meetings ran more or less along Oxford Group lines. . . . Early meetings used Oxford Group terminology—witnessing, stories, restitutions, shared confessions."[117]

The regulars were Dr. Bob and Anne Smith. Both "Smitty" and "Sue," their children, came to a few meetings. Henrietta

---

[114] Essentially from *DR. BOB*, p. 144 and Dick B., *That Amazing Grace*, p. 26.

[115] Dick B., *That Amazing Grace*, p. 26.

[116] Dick B., *The Akron Genesis*, p. 187.

[117] Dick B., *The Akron Genesis*, p. 187.

Seiberling was there, and her children all attended meetings. Of course, there were T. Henry and Clarace. And Dr. Bob called all of these meetings "a Christian Fellowship."[118] Working as a team, the drunks called themselves "the alcoholic squad of the Oxford Group."[119] Some Oxford Group people in Akron may have looked down on the Williams meeting and its alcoholics. Hence one member commented that the T. Henry meetings were "sort of a clandestine lodge of the Oxford Group."[120]

One historian commented: "It would appear in hindsight that most of their waking lives was a continuous A.A. meeting."[121] Viewed broadly, this statement was true. Dr. Bob's children put it this way in their memoirs:

> Slowly Bill and Bob developed a little group of recovering people who formally met at Oxford Group meetings but kept in constant communication with each other at get-to-gethers in their homes. The Smith's house on Ardmore Avenue was the hub of the Akron group.[122]

And there was a structure to it all. The structure was patterned on Oxford Group life-changing ideas: Quiet Time in the homes and at meetings. Preparation meetings, the guidance of God, meetings in the homes, breaking bread together, and larger meetings, such as the one at T. Henry's home (later at Dr. Bob's and thereafter at King School).

Quiet Times involved Bible study, the reading of Bible devotionals and Christian literature, as well as two-way prayer—praying to God and listening for thoughts from God.[123] These Quiet Times were commonplace each day at the Smith home

---

[118] Dick B., *The Akron Genesis*, pp. 219-20.

[119] *DR. BOB*, pp. 137, 128, 100.

[120] *DR. BOB*, p. 121.

[121] Kurtz, *Not-God*, p. 42.

[122] Smith and Windows, *Children of the Healer*, pp. 5-6.

[123] See Dick B., *Good Morning: Quiet Time, The Morning Watch, Meditation, and Early A.A.*

and later at the homes of others such as Wally and Annabelle G.

On Mondays, the pioneers would hold what they called a "set-up" meeting. They got those together who felt they had a part and felt responsibility for it. They would try to plan who would be the best one to lead the meeting. They would sit down and ask God's guidance and direction as to what to put together for the meeting. If necessary, they would call people and ask them to prepare to take a certain part and be willing to give, keeping the new person in mind.

On Wednesday, the regular meetings were held. We will speak in a moment about surrenders, for they were frequently claimed to be a condition precedent to participation. Several summarized the content of the regular meetings. Bob E., an Akron oldtimer whom Dr. Bob had sponsored, wrote the following to A.A.'s archivist, Nell Wing, describing a typical Akron meeting:

> The general set up [of] a meeting was done by Dr. Smith & a few others in an upstairs bed room just before the regular 8:30 meeting & it usually followed a page of *The Upper Room* which was supplied to us by Ernie G.'s mother (@ 5 cents a piece) & we all carried them. They fit in our side pocket, they were the size of a Reader's Digest only not so thick. Each page was called a "thought for the day." 1st there was a short quote of scripture, next a short prayer, next the short story for the day was read. Next if the group was still small enough we would hold hands in a circle and have a short quiet time during which we silently asked God for guidance. Then we shared or witnessed whatever we felt guided to talk about, a problem or an experience with a point worth sharing. If it didn't help anybody it helped you. Then came instructions from Dr. Smith & announcements and asking for help or suggestions in handling a new man.[124]

There are a variety of descriptions indicating that meetings did not always follow an identical format. But several items seem very clear.

---

[124] Dick B., *The Akron Genesis*, pp. 197-98.

Meetings opened with prayer and with reading from the Bible (or Scripture in the Bible devotionals such as *The Upper Room* and *My Utmost for His Highest*). Sometimes the meeting topic would be on a Bible subject, sometimes on a matter in the Bible devotionals, and occasionally on some other topic vital to the lives of those present. Drinking stories ("drunkalogs" as they are often called in today's A.A.) were apparently *not a significant part* of the Akron meetings.[125] There was Quiet Time, prayer, and listening for guidance. Literature of the Oxford Group and other literature, such as the devotionals, was discussed and passed out to those present. Sometimes it was swapped. Clarace Williams remembered that *As a Man Thinketh* by James Allen was occasionally used. Dr. Bob kept the meeting focused on the need of a newcomer, usually making an announcement on that topic. The meeting closed with the Lord's Prayer. Names, phone numbers, and addresses were often exchanged. And a social time followed. In the later days, members went to Kistler's Donut Shop for sociality.[126]

Clarace Williams pointed out: They always planned for having something on Saturday night—the night that people needed it (as she put it). She said they had a party, sometimes at the Williams home or someplace else, with plenty of food and lots of coffee.

The Surrenders to Jesus as Lord

AAs today are fond of saying that the only requirement for A.A. membership is a desire to stop drinking.[127] The fact is that A.A., like the Oxford Group, really has no membership. No rosters or rolls or membership lists exist; there are no dues or fees; there is no sergeant-at-arms to enforce rules; and there is no membership application, questionnaire to be completed, or sponsorship into A.A. of new members. But that was not the case in early A.A.

---

[125] Dick B., *The Akron Genesis*, p. 192.

[126] Dick B., *The Akron Genesis*, pp. 187-92, 197-99, 72-74.

[127] Big Book, p. 564.

There are countless statements by oldtimers that no one got into early A.A. without "surrendering." In Akron, this meant surrender on your knees. It meant giving your life to Jesus Christ as Lord and Master. And it meant being "born again." Many in today's A.A. may doubt this; but let's have the pioneers speak for themselves.

In a phone call to Danny W. in Lancaster, California, from Lorain, Ohio, on January 9, 1994, pioneer Ed A. said:

> They would not let you in unless you surrendered to Jesus Christ on your knees.

One oldtimer, Larry B. of Cleveland, Ohio, wrote the author on September 18, 1992, stating he was in and out of A.A. between 1939 and 1944. Of his own surrender, Larry said:

> They took me and that man upstairs to be a born again human being and be God's helper to alcoholics.

One day, Clarence S. came to an Oxford Group meeting at the T. Henry Williams home in Akron. Clarence had gotten sober on February 11, 1938. Dr. Bob was his sponsor. And Dr. Bob had sent Clarence off to Cleveland with a Bible and told him to fix drunks as an avocation. But Clarence had not been successful. He came to the Oxford Group meeting in a state of despair over his inability to convert drunks.

Dr. Bob said to him, "Young fella, it's about time you made your surrender." Clarence was bewildered. He said, "What is *that*, Doc?" Dr. Bob said, "You'll see when this meeting is over." Clarence said he went upstairs to T. Henry's master bedroom with Dr. Bob, T. Henry, and an Oxford Group member who was not an alcoholic. These men told Clarence to get on his knees, and they joined him on their knees around T. Henry's bed. These three men then led Clarence through a "Sinner's Prayer."

As Clarence's wife Grace recalled her husband's words, Clarence described that prayer as follows:

Father, I come to you in Jesus's name. Lord, Jesus, I am sorry for my sins. Please forgive me for every wrong thing I've ever done. I thank you for dying on the cross in my place. I ask you to come into my heart. Be the Lord of my life. And I will love you and serve you till you take me home.

Clarence said it was at this time that he was born again; and he often informed his sponsees that this surrender prayer was the very one Dr. Bob had used from the beginning of the A.A. surrenders in Akron.[128]

The early surrenders, accompanied by "a prayer," were often mentioned by others.[129] Bob E. commented: "You had to be on your knees with another person, praying and sharing out loud. You know, in the first draft of the Twelve Steps, people were to be on their knees when they surrendered. But the other drunks made Bill take it out."[130] The kneeling, praying, and surrendering procedures were certainly Oxford Group practices; but there is a strong suggestion that the group idea in Akron was based on the Book of James, so very popular in early A.A.

James 5:13-16 state:

Is any among you afflicted? let him pray. Is any merry? let him sing psalms. Is any sick among you? let him call for the elders of the church; and let them pray over him, anointing him with oil in the name of the Lord: And the prayer of faith shall save the sick, and the Lord shall raise him up; and if he have committed sins, they shall be forgiven him. Confess your faults one to another, and pray for one another, that ye may be healed. The effectual fervent prayer of a righteous man availeth much.

---

[128] The foregoing material and quote are from Dick B., *That Amazing Grace*, p. 27. For a somewhat different version set forth in earlier titles (and which data the author *now* considers may be *erroneous*), see Dick B., *The Akron Genesis*, pp. 194-97; see also the Third and Seventh Step prayers in Clarence S., *Going through the Steps*, 2d ed. (Altamonte Springs, FL: Stephen Foreman, 1985).

[129] *DR. BOB*, pp. 77, 83, 85, 88-89, 92, 100-01, 104, 110.

[130] *DR. BOB*, p. 118.

Though he seems to stand alone in his belief, one of Clarence S.'s sponsees staunchly declares that the afore-quoted procedure from the Book of James was the basis for the surrenders in Akron.[131] Certainly the Book of James was highly read and favored in early A.A.; and many wanted to call the A.A. fellowship *The James Club*.[132]

Many other sponsees of Clarence have never heard that early surrenders involved anointing-with-oil prayers. Nor has Clarence's widow. But this procedure is observed *after* the close of every one of the spiritual retreats for AAs and their families which were founded either by Clarence, Clarence and his wife Grace, or by Grace S.[133] The author has personally been present at several of these retreats; and all purport to be based on the original spiritual ideas of early A.A. as reported and passed on by Clarence.

The Books and Pamphlets They Read

We will have much more to say about the literature and devotionals in a later chapter. But no one can understand the spiritual nature of the early program without understanding the amount and kind of reading and study that occurred.

There can be no doubt the Bible was paramount. Dr. Bob had read it through three times and quoted it quite often. Oxford Group principles were based on the Bible, and Oxford Group people frequently quoted the Bible in their meetings and literature. Bible study was a *must* in the Oxford Group. And it was a must for Shoemaker and his adherents. Anne Smith called it the "main source book." Henrietta Seiberling was an avid Bible student. Early A.A. meetings very frequently opened with Scripture reading.[134]

Early AAs studied devotionals which were totally Bible oriented. *The Upper Room, My Utmost for His Highest, The Runner's Bible,*

---

[131] See Dick B., *The Akron Genesis*, pp. 194-97.

[132] *Pass It On*, p. 147; *DR. BOB*, p. 71.

[133] See Dick B., *That Amazing Grace*, pp. 86-87, 101.

[134] Dick B., *The Akron Genesis*, pp. 189-90, 207.

Daily Strength for Daily Living, and *Victorious Living* were—one or another—in daily use. Early meeting topics were often drawn from them; and most contained a Bible verse, a relevant comment, verses for study, a prayer, and a daily thought.

Other Christian literature was in wide use. The author has seen many of Dr. Bob's own books with Bob's name, address, and "please return" written in Bob's own hand. The books were recommended by Anne, Bob, and Henrietta; and they were either purchased, swapped, or circulated. In fact, Dr. Bob kept a log of the books he loaned, required their return, and often then quizzed the borrowers on the subject matter to make sure the person had read the material.[135]

Many early AAs commented on the importance of the Methodist quarterly called *The Upper Room*. A number of A.A. pioneers said it was their first reading item (i.e., first after the Bible in the hospital). They received it almost the moment they "joined."[136]

The Homes

AAs today like to say: "Stick with the winners." Sam Shoemaker wrote often and eloquently of the importance of *fellowship*. In an early book, Shoemaker said:

---

[135] Dick B., *That Amazing Grace*, p. 31.

[136] Clancy U. of Hawaii (who had been sponsored by Dr. Bob and Clarence S.) said: "I was handed 'The Upper Room' at one of my first meetings." See Dick B., *The Good Book and The Big Book*, p. 42, n. 21. Bob E. said of Paul S. ". . . the last two days I was in the hospital, he brought me an 'Upper Room' or something to read" (Bob E. transcript, p. 4). Wally G. (whose story "Fired Again" appears at pages 325-31 of the Big Book, First Edition) said: "Anyway we followed this *Upper Room* which . . . consisted of a verse or story in support of the verse from the Bible for each day, and a thought for the day, together with a suggestion as to our reading." See Dick B., *The Books Early AAs Read for Spiritual Growth*, 4th ed (San Rafael, CA: Paradise Research Publications, 1996), p. 33. William V. H. (whose story "A Ward of the Probate Court" appeared at pages 296-302 of the First Edition) said: "This *Upper Room* was a little daily reading booklet that I've used ever since. . . . [E]ach member was furnished with a copy which was good for three months of daily readings." See Dick B., *The Books Early AAs Read*, p. 34. For further indications of the importance of this devotional, see *DR. BOB*, pp. 71, 139, 151, 178, 220, 311.

Suppose some church began by being friendly and welcoming, and went on to train a group of people who could actually meet the needs of individuals, who knew how to carry unconvinced people into a genuine experience of Christ—so that a congregation became, not a lot of disjointed individuals, but a brotherhood shot through with human links—what might not that church do in a great city?[137]

The Book of Acts told of "First Century Christianity" in these terms:

Then they that gladly received his word were baptized; and the same day there were added *unto them* about three thousand souls. And they continued steadfastly in the apostles' doctrine and fellowship, and in breaking of bread, and in prayers. And fear [reverence] came upon every soul: and many wonders and signs were done by the apostles. And all that believed were together, and had all things common; And sold their possessions and goods, and parted them to all *men*, as every man had need. And they, continuing daily with one accord in the temple, and breaking bread from house to house, did eat their meat with gladness and singleness of heart. Praising God, and having favour with all the people. And the Lord added to the church daily such as should be saved (Acts 2:41-47).

This principle of fellowshipping with like-minded *believers* was not only biblical; it was Akron A.A. in the 1930's.

Frank Amos felt he saw that kind of picture when he came to Akron to assess the early "program." Speaking of this program, Amos specified the need for admitting defeat at the hands of alcohol, the need for an absolute surrender to God "realizing that in himself there is no hope;" the need for removal of sins; the necessity for a "quiet time" of prayer and some reading of the Bible and other religious literature; the necessity for helping other alcoholics; the importance of frequent meetings "with other

---

[137] Shoemaker, *Religion That Works*, p. 85.

reformed alcoholics" and the formation of "both a social and a religious comradeship;" and the importance of attending some religious service at least once weekly. Amos said the Akronites were doing these things.

Amos then mentioned a doctor thirty-five years of age who had "been an alcoholic and had been cured by Smith and his friends' activities and the Christian technique prescribed." He said the alcoholic group [in 1938] comprised "some 50 men and, I believe, two women former alcoholics—all considered practically incurable by physicians—who have been reformed and so far have remained teetotalers." Amos said he heard varying stories "many of them almost miraculous." In a later report, Amos said "Of the 110 members then in the program, 70 were in the Akron-Cleveland area [and] in many respects, their meetings have taken on the form of the meetings described in the Gospels [sic] of the early Christians during the first century."[138]

The kinship was not merely in the meetings, then. Drunks in Akron broke bread with each other, constantly met with each other, and were often housed together in the Smith home (and later other homes) for months at a time. They had the Quiet Times, Bible study, reading, and prayer there that we have previously mentioned. They truly fellowshipped together daily and searched for a better way of life. And many—such as Earl T., Clarence S., and Arch T. (all "soundly indoctrinated by Dr. Bob and the Akronites," as Bill once put it)—went on to found or spark A.A. in major cities such as Cleveland, Chicago, Detroit, and Houston. And it all started successfully at 855 Ardmore Avenue in Akron (the Smith home) where people were given love, kindness, solid Bible education, Christian principles and examples, job assistance, lodging, *and food* at great personal sacrifice by the Smiths, their family, and by Henrietta, and Mr. and Mrs. T. Henry Williams. Bill himself frequently participated when he visited Akron.

---

[138] The material is from *DR. BOB*, pp. 128-36. The author was provided with complete copies of the Amos reports on his visit to the Stepping Stones Archives.

Was the Akron Program "Spiritual" and "Successful?"

What a variety of ideas about "spirituality" one finds in A.A. meetings today! The word "spirituality" does not appear in the Twelve Steps. It is used only twice in the basic text of *Alcoholics Anonymous* (the first 164 pages).[139] In neither case can its meaning be easily comprehended either in the sentence, the context, or from a prior use. *Merriam Webster's Collegiate Dictionary*, 10th ed., defines the adjective "spiritual" as "of, relating to, consisting of, or affecting the spirit." The noun refers to "things of a spiritual, ecclesiastical, or religious nature." "Spirituality" is defined as "something that in ecclesiastical law belongs to the church or to a cleric as such." Also, "sensitivity or attachment to religious values."[140] These ideas are hardly what is referred to when certain AAs say today that A.A. is "spiritual and not religious."[141] But the honest historian who takes Dr. Bob at his word must concede that A.A.'s basic ideas came from the Bible. Bob's sponsee Clarence S. echoed Bob's words.[142] So did the early Akron AA pamphlets prepared at Dr. Bob's behest. And Bill Wilson never disputed the point.

The New Bible Dictionary, 2d ed., points out: "Thus in the NT [New Testament] *pneuma* [the underlying Greek word for 'spirit']

---

[139] See *A Concordance to Alcoholics Anonymous* (Reno, Nevada: Purple Salamander Press, 1990), p. 721.

[140] Joseph F. Eagan, S.J., S.T.D., wrote: "The foundation and basis of all Christian spirituality remains the person of the risen Christ as we come to know him in the Christian Scriptures and encounter him in the liturgical and sacramental life of the church, especially in the eucharistic celebration. The constants in Christian spirituality remain *faith*, *hope* and *love* of God and others, *prayer*, *avoidance of sin*, *asceticism*." See chapter on "Spirituality" in Joseph F. Eagan, *Restoration and Renewal: The Church in the Third Millennium* (Kansas City: Sheed & Ward, 1995), pp. 112-31.

[141] Mel B. wrote: "Spirituality. . . . In the Twelve Step program, we learned about contacting a spiritual Power that makes startling and wonderful changes in our lives. People see a new spirit in our lives and a new spirit as we go about our business. This spirited way of life comes from returning to what must be the Source of our being." Mel B., *Walk in Dry Places* (Center City, MN: Hazelden, 1996), note for September 25.

[142] Dick B., *That Amazing Grace*, p. 34.

is used nearly 40 times to denote that dimension of the human personality whereby relationship with God is possible" (p. 1137a). It adds: "Likewise in John [the Gospel of John] the Spirit from above is the power effecting new birth . . . , for the Spirit is the life-giver . . . , like a river of living water flowing from the Christ bringing life to him who comes and believes" (p. 1139b).

Placed in the context of early A.A.'s Christian roots, one who defines "spiritual" or A.A. "spirituality" without reference to the Bible is missing the boat as far as early A.A. history is concerned. One can say to those who take such a position, much as Jesus said to the Sadducees: "Ye do err, not knowing the scriptures, nor the power of God" (Matthew 22:29). When the early AAs were talking about "Spirit" and "God," they were talking about their "Father in heaven"—the God Almighty of the Scriptures, the "Father" in the Lord's Prayer, and the God of the Bible who described Himself as Creator.[143]

Can we therefore say that the Akron program was "spiritual?" We believe it so qualifies. It was based on the Bible. The founders were referring to the God of the Bible. They surrendered to Jesus as Lord. Dr. Bob cited Jesus's Sermon on the Mount [Matthew 5, 6, and 7] as containing the underlying spiritual philosophy of A.A.[144] In keeping with 1 John 4:8 and 4:16, Dr. Bob presented God to the earliest AAs as a God of love who was interested in their individual lives.[145] His wife Anne frequently quoted the phrase "God is love."[146] And the First Edition of the Big Book made clear it was "going to talk about God" (p. 57). And that the "Power" to which it referred "is God" (p. 58).

---

[143] See, for example, the Big Book First Edition story of John Henry Fitzhugh M. ("Our Southern Friend), pp. 240-41. See also the last sentence of Dr. Bob's personal story on p. 193: "Your Heavenly Father will never let you down!" And Bill's reference to the "God of our fathers;" Compare Bill's phrase with the language in Exodus 3:13; Deuteronomy 1:11; Joshua 18:3; 1 Chronicles 12:17; Acts 3:13; 5:30; 7:32; 22:14; 24:14.

[144] *DR. BOB*, p. 228; also stated to author Mel B. by Bill W.

[145] *DR. BOB*, p. 110.

[146] Dick B., *Anne Smith's Journal*, pp. 4, 15.

Was this early program an astonishing success? By all accounts, it was *from the beginning*. J. Carroll Wright was the Minister of The West Side Branch of the First Presbyterian Church in Akron. Dr. Bob and Anne were charter members of this church and remained connected with that church throughout A.A.'s formative years. In a letter the author discovered in the Episcopal Church Archives in 1996, Wright wrote Sam Shoemaker a long letter on November 6, 1935. Wright told Shoemaker of his interest in the success of the Oxford Group. And then he said to Sam:

> There has been a gradual shift of opinion in the whole church and I feel now if such a project [approaching the business community] is carried through there will be definite results. People are being changed here. We have an alcoholic section at work since Bill Wilson was here in the summer and alcoholics are being changed.

Early A.A. claimed *at least* a seventy-five percent success rate among those who really tried. Early AAs actually *recovered* from their seemingly hopeless disease at that very high percentage rate.[147] Bill Wilson claimed 80%; Cleveland A.A. reported a 93% success rate; and Jack Alexander wrote in his famous 1941 *Saturday Evening Post* article of a "One hundred-percent effectiveness with non-psychotic drinkers who sincerely want to quit . . ."[148]

What About Early New York A.A.?

When the author first started researching the spiritual history of early A.A., he focused on Bill Wilson and the New York area. Assuming, as many might, that since A.A. "headquarters" had always been located in New York, the author thought that the

---

[147] See Big Book Third Edition pp. xiii, xv, xvii, xxiii, 17, 20, 29, 45, 90, 96, 113, 132, 133, 146, 165, 309, 310. For corroboration by others, see Dick B., *The Good Book and The Big Book*, p. 7, n 17.

[148] For discussion and documentation, see Dick B., *Design for Living*, pp. 3-8. *DR. BOB* states at page 261: "Records in Cleveland show that 93 percent of those who came to us never had a drink again."

spiritual elements must have centered there. But he was soon to find that there was very little sobriety in early New York A.A.; that there was a strong leaning toward atheism among members there; and that Bill Wilson himself had pointed to Akron as the spiritual powerhouse.

Not-God records of Bill's first three weeks of living with Dr. Bob and Anne Smith:

> Bill Wilson found himself in awe of Dr. Bob's "spiritual knowledge" and cherished the guidance of Anne Smith as each morning her pleasant voice read and interpreted the Christian Scriptures and the Oxford Group devotional books (p. 32).[149]

Speaking of his first six-hour meeting with Dr. Bob, Bill reported in *Alcoholics Anonymous Comes of Age*:

> Always better versed in spiritual matters than I, he [Dr. Bob] had paid little attention to that aspect of my story [the part pertaining to "spiritual matters"]. Even though he could not make them work, he already knew what the spiritual answers were (pp. 69-70).

Bill commented on his own early, stubborn resistance to God. Bill said that AAs could predetermine their own demise by such an attitude:

> Mine was exactly the kind of deep-seated block we so often see today in new people who say they are atheistic or agnostic. Their will to disbelieve is so powerful that apparently they prefer a date with the undertaker to an open-minded and experimental quest for God.[150]

---

[149] This latter part of the quote is not accurate. Anne frequently read and quoted from the entire Bible—not just the "Christian Scriptures." Furthermore, the devotional books were *not* Oxford Group books although one (*My Utmost for His Highest*) was in wide use among Oxford Group people. Finally, the literature that Anne read and recommended, as recorded in her journal, included much more Christian literature than just that of the Oxford Group.

[150] *The Language of the Heart*, pp. 245-46.

In his recent trip to the Episcopal Archives in Austin, Texas, the author found a letter from Bill Wilson to Sam Shoemaker on the letterhead of The Alcoholic Foundation in New York. The letter was dated January 15, 1945. It stated in part:

> Saving some of our Catholic members and a few others, we are, as a group, pretty deficient on the prayer and meditation side. Quite a number of older AAs run into a period of seeming spiritual bankruptcy, indeed, one might guess, by excessive activity not balanced by sufficient intake. Apparently it is possible to get very bad indigestion on a straight diet of "good works."

The author began searching for the names of those in New York who—like such *Ohio* pioneers as Bill D., Earl T., Arch T., and Clarence S.—stayed sober for many years. And reached out successfully to other areas. We also researched other Ohio A.A. oldtimers such as Bob E., Ed A., and John R. who stayed sober for years. Yet, when the author examined the early New York roster, he encountered the names of Ebby T., Hank P., and "Fitz." Ebby (whom Bill called his sponsor) stayed drunk for most of his later years. On March 22, 1946, Bill wrote his old Oxford Group friend Shep Cornell (then living in Wisconsin):

> About Charlie Clapp: after having done a swell job in the Army he began to flounder heavily after his discharge. Some months ago he became an ardent A.A. and his situation looks far better. You will remember Herb D. . . . and Ernest McK. . . . Herb has been all right for a good many years and, saving a couple of misadventures, so has Mac. But poor old Hank Parkhurst after four years on the rocks, began having more trouble which has continued.[151]

"Fitz" was the son of an Episcopal Minister. Fitz was the one who argued unsuccessfully that the Big Book should contain the Biblical

---

[151] Episcopal Archives, Texas.

and Christian material on which A.A. had been founded. Although Fitz did not live long into the 1940's, he did stay sober.

Bill's biographer tells part of the early A.A. story in New York this way:

> Ever since his night at Towns [when Bill had his spiritual experience], Bill had had no argument with God. . . . He was also convinced that alcoholism was a three-pronged illness, mental, physical and spiritual, and that this was something no man could handle on his own, but that as soon as an alcoholic could recognize the spiritual side of his illness, begin tending it, and the spiritual malady was overcome, then the physical and the mental aspects straightened out. Bill never questioned this. The others, however, had not had his night at Towns. There were agnostics in the Tuesday-night group, and several hard-core atheists who objected to any mention of God. . . . At some time each of them had been totally unable to stop drinking on his own, yet when two of them had worked at it together, somehow they had become more powerful and they had finally been able to stop.[152]

Piecing together the facts as Bill and Lois recounted them in various places, there was no success in New York during Bill's first six months of sobriety. There was no success with anyone the Wilsons kept in their home from 1934 to 1939. There was much focus by Bill and his partner Hank on raising funds, on writing the Big Book, and on financing it through stock subscriptions and other means. And there appears to have been very little success by the time Bill began putting the basic textbook together in the Spring of 1938.

Perhaps the following remarks explain the reason. In January of 1940, Wilson wrote Dorothy S.M. and said:

> During the past 12 months we have had quite a number who felt that the fellowship, the helpful attitude toward others, the warming of the heart at social gatherings, was going to be sufficient to

---

[152] Thomsen, *Bill W.*, p. 255.

overcome the alcoholic's obsession. Taking stock at the year's end, we find that this school of thought has few survivors, for the bottled heat treatment has persuaded them that we must find some sort of spiritual basis for living, else we die. A few, who have worked ardently with other alcoholics on the philosophical, rather than the spiritual plane, now say of themselves: "We believed that Faith without works was dead, but we have now conclusively proved that works without Faith is dead also."[153]

A few months later, Bill wrote to an alcoholic who was trying to get A.A. started in a new city. Explaining the importance of the "spiritual angle," Bill said:

I explain this at some length because I want you to be successful with yourself and the people with whom you work. We used to pussyfoot on this spiritual business a great deal more out here [New York City] and the result was bad, for our record falls quite a lot short of the performance of Akron and Cleveland, where there are now about 350 alcoholics, many of them sober 2 or 3 years, with less than 20% ever having had any relapse. Out there they have always emphasized the spiritual way of life as the core of our procedure and we have begun to follow suit in New York for the simple reason that our record was only half as good, most of the difficulties being directly attributable to temporizing over what it really takes to fix the drunks, *i.e., the spiritual* (italics in original).[154]

Henrietta Seiberling frequently nagged the co-founders about neglect of faith and the power of God. She once said a Hollywood actor had been looking all over the country but found something in the Akron A.A. King School Group that wasn't in any other group. She explained:

---

[153] From Wilson correspondence quoted in Ernest Kurtz and Katherine Ketcham, *The Spirituality of Imperfection: Modern Wisdom from Classic Stories* (New York: Bantam Books, 1992), p. 109.

[154] From Wilson's private correspondence quoted in Kurtz and Ketcham, *The Spirituality of Imperfection*, pp. 109-10.

I think it was our great stress and reliance on guidance and quiet times. [Of her work with AAs, she said:] And I tried to give to the people something of my experience and faith. What I was most concerned with is that we always go back to faith. [When Dr. Bob and Bill suggested to Henrietta that they should not talk too much about religion or God, Henrietta said:] Well, we're not out to please the alcoholics. They have been pleasing themselves all these years. We are out to please God. And if you don't talk about what God does, and your faith, and your guidance, then you might as well be the Rotary Club or something like that. Because God is your only source of power. [She said Bill and Dr. Bob agreed with her on that point.][155]

Henrietta always adjured AAs to give "news, not views" about what God had done for them. At the last A.A. dinner she attended, she complained about the speakers. She said:

And I spoke to Bill afterwards and I said there was no spirituality there or talk of what God had done in their lives. They were giving views, not news of what God had done [*DR. BOB* points out that "Give news, not views" was an Oxford Group slogan.].[156]

Bill said very little of the people he worked with in those earliest years in New York. And, when the author began inquiring about the earliest A.A. in New York, Earl H.—an A.A. oldtimer in Oklahoma who is still an active A.A. and collector of A.A. historical items—informed the author that he was on the wrong track in trying to document the spiritual roots in early New York A.A. Earl essentially said in a phone call to the author: "There was no significant sobriety there."[157]

---

[155] Dick B., *The Akron Genesis*, pp. 97-98.

[156] Dick B., *The Akron Genesis*, pp. 237-38.

[157] The period to which we believe Earl H. had reference would, the author believes, be at that point where there were forty pioneers. This was the time when Bill and Bob felt they had significant proof that God had shown how the message of recovery could successfully be passed by one alcoholic to another.

There is a half-truth, half-joke story one hears after he or she stays sober long enough in A.A. to get to know early A.A. and the respective focuses of Bill W. and of Dr. Bob. The saying goes that if only Dr. Bob had been the founder, A.A. would never have left Akron; and that if only Bill had been the founder, A.A. would have consisted of franchised operations the world over. To be sure, Dr. Bob focused his efforts, after the founding days, on Akron; and he, working with Sister Ignatia at St. Thomas Hospital in Akron, personally helped over five-thousand alcoholics without pay. Bill began, in 1938, to focus his efforts on hospitals, missions, and a book. Bill was outvoted on the first two but then spent much of the next few years promoting the Big Book, seeking *big* financial support, and working to enlarge A.A.'s outreach around the world. The result is a world-wide fellowship with over two million members at any given time. Yet the two men worked closely together in A.A.'s formative years. They seemed to balance each other in viewpoint. Bill said: ". . . my partnership with Dr. Bob was a perfect one. We never had a hard word between us."[158] This, then, was the setting of A.A.'s spiritual beginnings.

Now we shall turn to the specific segments of early A.A.'s spiritual history that contributed to the ideas Bill and Bob adopted as they developed their spiritual program of recovery.

---

[158] *Co-Founders*, p. 34 (where Bill also said all the credit was due to Dr. Bob). And perhaps rightly so. For Dr. Bob's last major address showed he never shared Bill's distaste for the Oxford Group Four Absolutes (*Co-Founders*, pp. 17-18, Dr. Bob stating: "I think the absolutes still hold good and can be extremely helpful"). Nor did Dr. Bob want to see the adoption of Bill's "Twelve Traditions," which Dr. Bob reluctantly accepted on his death bed. See Dick B., *That Amazing Grace*, pp. 18, 61-62.

Part 2

The Good Book Source

"If someone asked him [Dr. Bob] a question about the program, his usual response was: 'What does it say in the Good Book?'"[1]

---

[1] *DR. BOB and the Good Oldtimers* (New York: Alcoholics Anonymous World Services, Inc., 1980), p. 144. Unless otherwise indicated, this title will be referred to hereafter as *"DR. BOB."*

4

God

Did A.A. ideas about, and descriptions of, God and His characteristics—as A.A. has embodied those ideas and descriptions in its
basic textbook—come from the Good Book?[1] Let's answer the

---

[1] Primary reference sources for this chapter are *DR. BOB and the Good Oldtimers*
(New York: Alcoholics Anonymous World Services, Inc., 1980); Dick B., *The Good
Book and the Big Book: A.A.'s Roots in the Bible* (San Rafael, CA: Paradise Research
Publications, 1995); *Good Morning!: Quiet Time, Morning Watch, Meditation and Early
A.A.* (San Rafael, CA: Paradise Research Publications, 1996): *Anne Smith's Journal,
1933-1939: A.A.'s Principles of Success* (San Rafael, CA: Paradise Research
Publications, 1994); *Dr. Bob's Library: Books for Twelve Step Growth* (San Rafael, CA:
Paradise Research Publications, 1994); *The Akron Genesis of Alcoholics Anonymous*
(Corte Madera, CA: Good Book Publishing Company, 1994); *That Amazing Grace: The
Role of Clarence and Grace S. in Alcoholics Anonymous* (San Rafael, CA: Paradise
Research Publications, 1996); *The Books Early AAs Read for Spiritual Growth*, 4th ed.
(San Rafael, CA: Paradise Research Publications, 1996): *Design for Living: The Oxford
Group's Contribution to Early A.A.* (San Rafael, CA: Paradise Research Publications,
1995); *New Light on Alcoholism: The A.A. Legacy from Sam Shoemaker* (Corte Madera,
CA: Good Book Publishing Company, 1994); Sherwood Sunderland Day, *The Principles
of the Group* (Oxford: University Press, n.d.); Harry J. Almond, *Foundations for Faith*,
2d ed. (London: Grosvenor Books, 1980); Miles Phillimore, *Just for Today* (Privately
published pamphlet, 1940). Other primary references are the Bible devotionals early
A.A.'s used, and which will be specified at a later point. Unless otherwise indicated,
DR. BOB and the Good Oldtimers will hereinafter be referred to as *DR. BOB.* A.A.'s
basic textbook—*Alcoholics Anonymous* (New York: Alcoholics Anonymous World
Services, 1976)—will, except where otherwise noted, be called by the affectionate name
AAs use—the Big Book.

157

question by comparing the present-day language in A.A.'s Big Book with some language in the Bible.[2]

The Frequency of Biblical Names for God

"God" is mentioned 277 times by name, *with* a capital "G," in the third edition of A.A.'s Big Book.[3] The Big Book also contains 107 specific pronouns—he, him, his, and himself—which are capitalized and clearly refer to "God."[4] Adding to these the Big Book's use of Biblical names for God (such as "Creator," "Maker" and as specified below), the God of the Bible is mentioned over 400 times.[5]

The Bible, of course, *begins* with "God."[6]

Genesis 1:1 speaks of God in relation to *creation*. And the Bible frequently calls God the *Creator*. For example, Isaiah 40:28 says: "Hast thou not known? hast thou not heard, *that* the everlasting God, the Lord, the Creator of the ends of the earth, fainteth not, neither is weary?"[7] A.A.'s Big Book refers to God

---

[2] Unless otherwise indicated, we will be referring to the Big Book, 3rd ed.

[3] Several writers have counted the usage of "God" in the Big Book's Third Edition. We have accepted the count by A.A. historian George T. of Illinois, who informed us by phone on April 25, 1995, that he had counted the use of the word "God" and compared and confirmed his count with the number of appearances of the word "God" listed in Stephen E. and Frances E. Poe's *A Concordance to Alcoholics Anonymous* (Nevada: Purple Salamander Press, 1990)—a reference work we have found to be definitive and very helpful on such points. See also Stewart C., *A Reference Guide to the Big Book of Alcoholics Anonymous* (Seattle, WA: Recovery Press Inc., 1986), pp. 115-16.

[4] Count by George T., *supra*.

[5] The total count is for all references is: 277 references to "God;" 107 references to God by pronouns used as substitutes for the name "God;" and at least 17 references to Biblical names for God; which add up to more than 400 references to the God of the Bible.

[6] Genesis 1:1 states: "In the beginning God created the heaven and the earth."

[7] See also Ecclesiastes 12:1 ("Remember now thy Creator in the days of thy youth . . ."). Also Isaiah 43:15; Romans 1:25; 1 Peter 4:19.

as "Creator" twelve times.[8] The Big Book addresses a prayer to "My Creator," in what AAs call their "Seventh Step Prayer."[9]

Other Biblical names for God are often used in the Big Book and other A.A. literature. The Big Book uses the Biblical expressions "Maker,"[10] "Father,"[11] "Father of Lights,"[12] and "Spirit."[13] Bill Wilson and Dr. Bob both described God as their "Heavenly Father," just as Jesus Christ did in his Sermon on the Mount.[14] In an early draft of the Big Book, Bill Wilson spoke of "the way in which he happened to find the *living God*" (italics added).[15] And the Bible often referred to God as "the living God."[16] Wilson had also remarked that alcoholics had "a form of lunacy which only *God Almighty* could cure" (italics added).[17] And Bill wrote of "*God, our Father*, who very simply says, 'I am waiting for you to do my will'" (italics added).[18]

There are two other important ideas *about* God which A.A. took directly from the Bible.

---

[8] Big Book, pp. 13, 25, 28, 56, 68, 72, 75, 76, 80, 83, 158, 161.

[9] Big Book, p. 76.

[10] Psalm 95:6; Big Book, pp. 57, 63.

[11] Matthew 5:45; Big Book, p. 62.

[12] The Big Book uses the expression "Father of Light" (p. 14). James 1:17 (from which the phrase came) renders it "Father of lights." Bill corrected the expression in *Alcoholics Anonymous Comes of Age* (New York: Alcoholics Anonymous World Services, 1957) where Bill spoke of God as "the Father of Lights, who presides over all men" (p. 225).

[13] John 4:24; Big Book, p. 84.

[14] Matthew 6:32; *A. A. Comes of Age*, p. 234; Big Book, p. 181.

[15] Dick B., *Design for Living*, p. 155, n. 18.

[16] Matthew 16:16; Acts 14:15; Romans 9:26; 2 Corinthians 3:3, 6:16; 1 Timothy 3:15, 4:10; Hebrews 9:14; 10:31; and Revelation 7:2. Acts 14:15 speaks of "the living God, which made heaven and earth." Isaiah 37:17 calls God "the living God;" and *The Companion Bible* discusses, at page 1614, the frequent use of the phrase "the living God" in both the Old and New Testaments.

[17] Dick B., *The Akron Genesis*, pp. 12-13. For "Almighty God" in the Bible, see Genesis 17:1; 35:11; Exodus 6:3; Ezekiel 10:5; Revelation 15:3.

[18] *A.A. Comes of Age*, p. 105. For "God our Father" in the Bible, see Romans 1:7; 1 Corinthians 1:3; 2 Corinthians 1:2; Ephesians 1:2; Philippians 1:2; Colossians 1:2; 1 Thessalonians 1:1; 2 Thessalonians 1:1.

God is

The first has to do with the belief that "God is." Hebrews 11:6 states:

> But without faith *it is* impossible to please *him*: for he that cometh to God must believe that he is, and *that* he is a rewarder of them that diligently seek him.

Oxford Group writers, including Dr. Sam Shoemaker, frequently cited Hebrews 11:6 for the proposition that one must start his or her experiment of faith by believing that God is.[19] Shoemaker wrote:

> Security lies in a faith in God which includes an experiment. It lies in believing that God is. . . .[20]

Earlier, Shoemaker had written, in a title owned and circulated by Dr. Bob among early AAs: "God is, or He isn't. You leap one way or the other."[21] Dr. Bob frequently insisted that a newcomer profess his belief in God.[22] And Bill Wilson pursued the same path when he used the following language in A.A.'s Big Book (which language closely parallels the foregoing quote of Shoemaker's language):

> Either God is everything or else He is nothing. God either is, or He isn't. What was our choice to be? (Big Book, p. 53).

---

[19] Dick B., *Design for Living*, p. 165. See also Leslie D. Weatherhead, *How Can I Find God?* (London: Hodder & Stoughton, 1933), p. 72. Weatherhead was a distinguished British clergyman who frequently wrote about the Oxford Group. Two of his titles were owned by A.A. co-founder, Bill Wilson.

[20] Samuel M. Shoemaker, Jr., *National Awakening* (New York: Harper & Brothers, 1936), pp. 40-41.

[21] Samuel M. Shoemaker, Jr., *Confident Faith* (New York: Fleming H. Revell, 1932), p. 187. For the importance of this Shoemaker book to Dr. Bob, see Dick B., *Dr. Bob's Library*, pp. 47-48.

[22] *DR. BOB*, p. 144.

A Loving God

The second important A.A. concept from the Bible describes "God" as a loving God. The idea almost certainly has origins in 1 John 4:8 and 4:16 where the Bible twice declares, "God is love." Dr. Bob's wife, Anne Smith, frequently used the verse "God is love" to help downhearted, confused, and frustrated alcoholics with whom she worked.[23] Dr. Bob emphasized God as a God of love who was interested in individual lives.[24] Bill Wilson embodied the idea of a loving God in A.A.'s Tradition Two, which states, "For our group purpose there is but one ultimate authority—a loving God as He may express Himself in our group conscience."[25] And A.A. language is rich with descriptions of God as love.[26]

A Special "god" for A.A.?

What about the "god" in A.A.'s *later* years? What of the elaborations on a "power greater than yourself" that one hears in today's recovery center talk, hears in A.A. meetings, and even

---

[23] Dick B., *Anne Smith's Journal: 1933-1939* (San Rafael, CA: Paradise Research Publications, 1994), pp. 4, 15; *The Akron Genesis*, p. 121; Ernest Kurtz, *Not-God: A History of Alcoholics Anonymous*. Exp. ed. (Minnesota: Hazelden, 1991), p. 55. See also *The Upper Room: Daily Devotions for Family and Individual Use* for 5/24/36; 5/4/37; 8/27/37. *The Upper Room* is a quarterly daily Bible devotional, which commenced publication in April, 1935, and was published by the General Committee on Evangelism through the Department of Home Missions, Evangelism, Hospitals Board of Missions, Methodist Episcopal Church, South, Nashville, Tennessee. The author was able to obtain copies of the quarterly for almost the entire formative period of early A.A. from 1935 to 1939. In some cases, we were unable to determine whether the issue was for 1936 or 1939 and have listed both as possible dates. In the beginning, copies were in the hands and homes of almost every AA. We therefore cite it frequently for verses that were brought to their attention individually or in meetings where the devotional was also used and discussed.

[24] *DR. BOB*, p. 110.

[25] Big Book, pp. 564-65.

[26] *DR. BOB*, pp. 110, 117; *Pass It On*, p. 121; Big Book, p. 63; *Twelve Steps and Twelve Traditions* (New York: Alcoholics Anonymous World Services, 1953), p. 9.

reads in A.A.'s own *later* literature? About some "god" who has been called a "lightbulb," a "chair," a "bulldozer," a "stone," a "tree," "Santa Claus," "the Big Dipper," "Good," "Good Orderly Direction," the "group," "Group Of Drunks," the "man upstairs," *and* "Ralph!" Are we exaggerating? The answer is that the author has personally heard in hundreds of A.A. meetings, and read in A.A. literature, almost every one of these appellations; and many others actively involved in, or who are observers of today's A.A., have heard one or more of the expressions.[27]

We certainly know that the foregoing names, some just plain ridiculous, did not come from the Bible. And we have not found any in the basic text of A.A.'s Big Book.

But what about A.A.'s *own* "Higher Power?" "A Power greater than ourselves?" And "God *as we understood Him?*" Phrases which AAs frequently use today. Phrases which some present-day commentators and even some A.A. Conference Approved literature seem to have codified into a special A.A. deity which some "choose to call God." Could these concepts, which appear to have given rise to strange ideas about "a" god, possibly have had their origins in the Bible or have come from A.A.'s Biblical roots?

---

[27] See Dick B., *Design for Living*, p. 158, n. 35. Refer also to *Daily Reflections* (New York: Alcoholics Anonymous World Services, 1990): pp. 79 ("Good Orderly Direction"), 175 ("a table, a tree, then my A.A. group"), 334 ("Him, or Her, or It"). Clarence often referred to the frequency and absurdity of the use by some AAs of the phrase "lightbulb" to describe "God." See Dick B., *That Amazing Grace*, pp. 46-50—referring particularly to Clarence's famous pamphlet: *My Higher Power—The Lightbulb*. See also Barnaby Conrad, *Time Is All We Have* (New York: Dell Publishing, 1986), p. 21; Nan Robertson, *Getting Better: Inside Alcoholics Anonymous* (New York: Fawcett Crest, 1988), pp. 124, 129; Jan R. Wilson and Judith A. Wilson, *Addictionary: A Primer of Recovery Terms and Concepts from Abstinence to Withdrawal* (New York: Simon and Schuster, 1992), pp. 181-83. For other usages of a similar nature in A.A.'s *own* literature, see *Twelve Steps and Twelve Traditions*, p. 27; Big Book, p. 248; *Members of the Clergy Ask about Alcoholics Anonymous* (New York: Alcoholics Anonymous World Services, 1961, revised 1992), p. 13.

Whence Came "Higher Power?"

First, what about "Higher Power?"

You will not find this expression in the Authorized (King James) Version of the Bible which was in such widespread use in early A.A.[28]

In the fourteen Shoemaker books and many pamphlets the Reverend Sam Shoemaker wrote *prior* to the Big Book's publication in 1939, we have not located any instance of Shoemaker's using the phrase "higher power." In later years, however (after Shoemaker's close friend, Bill Wilson, himself had begun using the phrase with some frequency), Shoemaker did write of an higher power.[29]

In an interview with the author in the summer of 1991, the Reverend T. Willard Hunter (a long-time Oxford Group activist and writer) informed the author that he (Hunter) had never heard the expression "Higher Power" used in the Oxford Group.[30] And, in reviewing thousands of pages of early Oxford Group writings, the author himself has seen the expression used by an Oxford Group writer only once. Bill Wilson's Oxford Group team cohort and friend, Victor C. Kitchen, wrote:

> I concluded that there must be some Higher Power to account for all the things taking place in space much as scientists concluded that there must be an atom to account for all the things taking place in physics.[31]

---

[28] See Robert Young, *Young's Analytical Concordance*. Newly Revised and Corrected (Nashville, TN: Thomas Nelson Publishers, 1982), pp. 481-82, 765-66. Compare Romans 13:1 which uses the expression "higher powers" and is speaking of "rulers" and the "powers that be."

[29] Samuel M. Shoemaker, Jr., *How to Become a Christian* (New York: Harper & Brothers, 1953), p. 143. But note Shoemaker's criticism of the idea of "Higher Power" as "God."

[30] Dick B., *Design for Living*, p. 157, n. 33.

[31] Victor C. Kitchen, *I Was a Pagan* (New York: Harper & Brothers, 1934), p. 85.

Kitchen's statement is contained in a paragraph in which Kitchen writes of "God" by name, with a capital "G." Furthermore, the paragraph is describing the way in which Kitchen came to "know" God. Kitchen's title is liberally sprinkled with references to the Bible, Jesus Christ, and Christianity, as well as specific references to God, His Power, and His Guidance.

The author has found only one other early reference to "Higher Power" in A.A. root literature. That reference is contained in a title owned and read by Dr. Bob.[32] This was Ralph Waldo Trine's *In Tune with the Infinite*.[33] It could possibly be argued that Trine was referring to "God" as He is described in the Bible, for Trine uses many Biblical references and verses in his book. However, Trine had his own brand of "new thought" and hence cannot be said specifically to have referred to God as He was, in Trine's book, or in later A.A., understood in terms of the Bible's own descriptions of God.

Now let's go to A.A.'s Big Book and "Higher Power." In the Big Book's basic text (the first 164 pages), the expression "Higher Power" (capitalized) is used only twice. Does this phrase refer to God as He is described in the Bible? Most AAs today might answer with an emphatic "no." But we believe that is because so few know just where the expression came from. And because the expression has been taken out of context in A.A.'s later years.

The phrase "Higher Power" is used on Big Book page 43, which states that the alcoholic's defense against the first drink "must come from a Higher Power." The two words are capitalized. They follow a paragraph which states that the "average alcoholic" has a generally hopeless plight and is in fact "100% hopeless, apart from *divine help*" (Big Book, p. 43, italics added). The "Higher Power" phrase is followed, two *and* three pages

---

[32] Dick B., *Dr. Bob's Library*, pp. 18, 67, 68, 82. See also Mel B., *New Wine: The Spiritual Roots of the Twelve Step Miracle* (Minnesota: Hazelden, 1991), pp. 105-06, 111.

[33] Ralph Waldo Trine, *In Tune with the Infinite*, 1933 ed. (Indianapolis: Bobbs-Merrill, 1897), p. 199.

later, by statements that the Big Book is "going to talk about God" (p. 45), and that "we commenced to get results, even though it was impossible for any of us to fully define or comprehend that Power, which is God" (p. 46).

Given the frequency with which the Big Book mentions God by name and describes Him as Creator, Maker, and so on, we believe the reference on page 43 is to the same God Almighty of the Bible, to whom more than 400 specific references were made in the Big Book. This even though the Big Book's chapter to agnostics encourages them to effect their "first conscious relation with God" as they understood Him by *starting* with their "own conception of God, however limited it was" (p. 47, italics added).

A similar case can be made for the only other occurrence of "Higher Power" in the basic text of the Big Book. On page 100, the Big Book suggests, "Follow the dictates of a Higher Power and you will presently live in a new and wonderful world, no matter what your present circumstances!" Does this phrase imply Wilson was creating some new kind of universal deity? Not if we consider the *preceding sentence* which says:

> When we look back, we realize that the things which came to us when we put ourselves in God's hands were better than anything we could have planned.[34]

There are many instances of Oxford Group Biblical references, and references in the Bible itself, to trust in Almighty God by placing

---

[34] The phrase "Higher Power" on page 100 should also be considered in the context of the following specific, unqualified references to God in other portions of the chapter: (1) relying upon human assistance "rather than upon God" (p. 98); (2) placing "dependence upon other people ahead of dependence on God" (p. 98); (3) burning into the consciousness of every man that he must "trust in God and clean house" (p. 98); stressing that "his recovery is not dependent upon people. It is dependent upon his relationship with God" (pp. 99-100); and saying to the reader: "Keep on the firing line of life with these motives and God will keep you unharmed" (p. 102).

things "in God's hands" and awaiting His direction.[35] And Dr. Norman Vincent Peale, who knew Bill Wilson quite well, personally informed the author in an interview at Pawling, New York, in August of 1992, that he (Peale) had never talked to anyone familiar with the expression "Higher Power" who did not believe that the expression referred to God. Peale wrote to the same effect in his book, *The Power of Positive Thinking.*[36] Sam Shoemaker wrote:

> You must go yourself to an "open" meeting [of A.A.] and listen to what recovered men and women say of . . . what life is like, now that they look to the Higher Power, which AA calls God so as to include all in their program. . . . AA often calls God or Christ a "power greater than ourselves." . . .[37]

Bill Wilson's Higher Power

Bill Wilson set a different course in *Twelve Steps and Twelve Traditions*—published after Dr. Bob's death in 1951. Wilson there

---

[35] See Kitchen, *I Was a Pagan*, p. 108; Geoffrey Allen, *He That Cometh* (New York: The Macmillan Company, 1933), p. 161—"He will come with the promise of new health, if we give ourselves entirely into His Hands;" Samuel M. Shoemaker, Jr., *The Experiment of Faith: A Handbook for Beginners* (New York: Harper & Brothers, 1957), p. 63—"They all prayed together and put themselves in God's hands, and a change began;" *The Church Alive* (New York: E. P. Dutton & Co., 1950), p. 145—"The results of our efforts are not in our hands but His." See also Psalm 31:5: "Into thine hand I commit my spirit;" and comment in Mary W. Tileston, *Daily Strength for Daily Needs* (New York: Grosset & Dunlap, 1928), p. 110.

[36] See discussion of Dr. Peale's interview and Peale's opinion in Dick B., *New Light on Alcoholism*, p. 87, n. 17. See also Norman Vincent Peale, *The Power of Positive Thinking*, Special Peale Center Edition (New York: Peale Center for Christian Living, 1990), pp. 262-75, where Peale wrote an entire chapter, titled "How to Draw upon That Higher Power." Peale specifically referred to Alcoholics Anonymous and many times called the Higher Power God. Thus at page 268, Peale said: "When he [the alcoholic] accepts this point of view [of Alcoholics Anonymous] he is in a position to receive help from other alcoholics and from the Higher Power—God."

[37] Samuel M. Shoemaker, Jr., *The Twelve Steps of AA: What They Can Mean to the Rest of Us* (New York: The Evangel, n.d.), pp. 1-2.

referred several times to a "Higher Power" (pp. 25, 28, 34, 38, 39, 107). Wilson did refer to "God" in that title with much more frequency than he did to a "higher power." But he said:

> You can, if you wish, make A.A. itself your 'higher power'" (p. 27). He added: "You will find many members who have crossed the threshold just this way. . . . Relieved of the alcohol problem, their lives unaccountably transformed, they came to believe in a Higher Power, and most of them began to talk of God" (pp. 27-28).

This statement entreating A.A.'s "to look to an 'Higher Power'—namely their own group"— was an idea that Wilson pursued in his later writings.[38]

Wilson's unique, later suggestion that "the group" could be one's "higher power" seemed to open the door for many to call the A.A. "group" their substitute for God—the God of the Bible whom Wilson had defined as Creator. In fact, Wilson virtually invited some to make a "substitute" god when he wrote: "Many a man like you has begun to solve the problem by the method of substitution."[39] Such reasoning, however, was something Dr. Bob's wife, Anne Ripley Smith, had criticized at a much earlier point in time. She called a similar characterization of the group a "funk hole."[40]

Apparently Anne's views got lost in a shuffle to shelve the "God of our fathers," to whom Bill still sometimes referred even in his later writings.[41] And when Bill used the expression "God of our fathers," he was utilizing solid Biblical terminology for God— both God as He is described in the Old Testament and God

---

[38] *As Bill Sees It: The A.A. Way of Life . . . selected writings of A.A.'s co-founder* (New York: Alcoholics Anonymous World Services, 1967), pp. 276, 310.

[39] *Twelve Steps and Twelve Traditions*, p. 27.

[40] Dick B., *Anne Smith's Journal*, pp. 89-90.

[41] See, for example, *Twelve Steps and Twelve Traditions*, p. 29.

as He is described in the New.[42] But a different kind of thinking seems to have been brewing. And if her remarks represented Bill Wilson's views, Bill's wife, Lois, explained this thought process as follows:

> Finally [speaking about the language of the Big Book which was being readied for publication] it was *agreed* that the book should present a universal spiritual program, not a specific religious one, since all drunks were not Christian (italics added).[43]

We are not aware that any such "agreement" occurred *prior* to publication of the Big Book in the Spring of 1939, *or even after* that time. But Lois's *assumption* about universality may have applied to the way Bill Wilson *later* viewed, and tried to shape the fellowship's thinking. The Foreword to the Big Book's *Second* Edition, describing the Fellowship "as it was in 1955," does assert that "By personal religious affiliation, we include Catholics, Protestants, Jews, Hindus, and a sprinkling of Moslems and Buddhists."[44] The Big Books's *Third* Edition, published in 1976, declares:

> [T]he Realm of Spirit is broad, roomy, all inclusive; never exclusive or forbidding to those who earnestly seek. It is open, we believe, to all men.[45]

Yet this "broad, roomy, all inclusive" language can also be found in the Big Book's *first* edition; and the phrase is used in the context of choosing "your own conception of God."[46] The First

---

[42] See Exodus 3:13; Deuteronomy 1:11; Joshua 18:3; 1 Chronicles 12:17; Daniel 2:23; Acts 3:13; 5:30; 7:32; 22:14; 24:14.

[43] *Lois Remembers: Memoirs of the Co-founder of Al-Anon and Wife of the Co-founder of Alcoholics Anonymous* (New York: Al-Anon Family Group Headquarters, 1987), p. 113.

[44] Big Book, p. xx.

[45] Big Book, p. 46.

[46] Big Book, First Edition, p. 59.

Edition context did *not* refer to an "Higher Power," but rather to "a higher Power."[47] As we've shown, this First Edition reference to God as a "Power" simply followed Oxford Group descriptions of God. And the First Edition certainly did not refer to the "Group," or to a "Lightbulb" in connection with God. Nor even to some "universal" spiritual idea. For the foregoing "higher Power" usage is found in the First Edition's chapter to agnostics which stated it was "going to talk about God."[48]

That First Edition chapter also stated "we had to stop doubting the power of God."[49] It then related the story of a minister's son who had found and established a relationship with God, "his Creator."[50] As a punch line in the story, the First Edition stated, in capital letters, as to the man's "great thought" (the message the man had received): "WHO ARE YOU TO SAY THERE IS NO GOD."[51] And it concluded, as to God, "Even so has God restored us all to our right minds."[52] Interestingly, in his 1939 book review of *Alcoholics Anonymous*, Dr. Harry Emerson Fosdick quoted the foregoing passage—WHO ARE YOU TO SAY THAT THERE IS NO GOD; and Fosdick concluded—as to AAs and their basic text of 1939—"of God Himself they are utterly sure."[53]

The author reviewed the correspondence between Dr. Bob and Bill at the time Bill was sending the Big Book's proposed chapters to Akron for review. And there seemed to be nothing but acceptance on Dr. Bob's part. Very little, if any, discussion of Bill's drafts. No apparent disagreement. And this is not surprising considering Dr. Bob's firm belief in God and the frequency with which Bill had written of God the Creator, God the Maker, and

---

[47] Big Book, First Edition, p. 55.

[48] Big Book, First Edition, p. 57.

[49] Big Book, First Edition, p. 65.

[50] Big Book, First Edition, pp. 68-69. This minister's son was "Fitz" whose story "Our Southern Friend" appears in the personal stories and who plumped for the Big Book to contain the Biblical and Christian material on which the program was based.

[51] Big Book, First Edition, p. 69.

[52] Big Book, First Edition, p. 69.

[53] *A. A. Comes of Age*, p. 323.

God the Father in the Big Book that was being fashioned. The co-founders may have expressly or tacitly concurred that the Big Book's references to God were sufficient without detailed elaboration of God's characteristics; but in six years of researching this topic, the author has found nothing that establishes that Bill and Dr. Bob *ever* agreed on a "universal spiritual program," though that may well be what many AAs believe is representative of the A.A. fellowship as it exists today.

Today, understandably, there are varied opinions as to what A.A., as such, believes about God and A.A.'s own "Higher Power." One thing is certain: present-day A.A. literature is saturated with references to *some* "Higher Power."[54] We think the appropriate view of today's A.A. would be that there probably is not and cannot be any definition acceptable to all AAs, other than the definition the Big Book itself suggests. That suggestion is that the newcomer *commence* spiritual growth by choosing his or her own conception of *God*.[55]

Two historians of A.A., Dr. Ernest Kurtz and Katherine Ketcham, concluded, however:

> The use of the phrase *Higher Power*—his, hers, yours, or mine—rather than the word *God*, reminds members of A.A.'s tolerance of individual differences in religious belief and spiritual inclination. The most basic understanding of the concept "Higher Power" within Alcoholics Anonymous is that it is *that which keeps me sober*.[56]

The problem with such a conclusion is that the "lightbulbs," "chairs," and "trees" (which have become higher powers for many present-day AAs) can hardly be said to keep anyone sober. At least

---

[54] As examples, see *Twelve Steps and Twelve Traditions*, pp. 24, 25, 28, 34; *As Bill Sees It*, pp. 73, 116, 200, 276; *Came to Believe* (New York: Alcoholics Anonymous World Services, 1973), pp. 5, 30, 81, 95; *Daily Reflections*, pp. 79, 175, 334, 335.

[55] Big Book, pp. 12, 46-47.

[56] Ernest Kurtz and Katherine Ketcham, *The Spirituality of Imperfection: Modern Wisdom from Classic Stories* (New York: Bantam Books, 1992), p. 208. *Cf.* pp. 109-10.

the author has seen no instances of sustained "lightbulb sobriety" among the thousands of people he has met in A.A.

Our own attendance at A.A. meetings, together with our sponsorship of many men in A.A., causes us to doubt the accuracy of the foregoing quote. We do not believe there is any clarity of understanding among the members of Alcoholics Anonymous about the meaning of "higher power." In fact, we have often felt, in hearing the "higher power" expression at meetings in the United States, that the phrase has no meaningful understanding *at all* to most of its users except when they *do* refer to God as they *have* formulated an understanding of Him.

We believe our observation is corroborated by that of Mel B., an A.A. with almost half a century of sobriety, who still actively attends meetings and writes and speaks extensively on A.A. history and ideas. Mel wrote:

> But AA went no further than this [referring to the existence of Creative Intelligence, a Spirit of the Universe underlying the totality of things] in defining what it meant by "Spirit," and never insisted that even this was the end of the matter. This open-minded, conciliatory approach headed off arguments before they ever started. AA members have always issued disclaimers when discussing God: Typical is, "Our program is spiritual, not religious." If pressed for what the program's actual definition of *spiritual* is, however, it is doubtful that many AA members could explain.[57]

We definitely agree with Mel B.'s conclusion as to confusion among AAs over the meaning of "spiritual." But we do not believe that AAs "have always issued disclaimers when discussing God." At best, Mel B.'s statement can only apply to A.A. Conference Approved literature of *today*; for neither Dr. Bob nor Bill, nor many of those who wrote stories for A.A.'s First Edition of the Big Book, had any hesitancy about mentioning *God*. And most

---

[57] Mel B., *New Wine: The Spiritual Roots of the Twelve Step Miracle* (Center City, MN: Hazelden, 1991), pp. 4-5.

early AAs spoke frequently of their studies about God in the Bible
and in the Bible devotionals in such wide use in early A.A.

"God As We Understood Him"

What then of A.A.'s use of the phrase "God as we understood
Him."[58] Was this "God" some new "god" fabricated by Bill
Wilson to suppress controversy and which ignored the "God
Almighty" and "Creator" (so named in the Bible) to which Wilson
often referred in his Big Book text and other early statements and
writings?

The answer lies with history.

Bill Wilson said his friend and "sponsor" Ebby Thacher had
suggested to him (Bill) before Bill got sober, *"Why don't you
choose your own conception of God?"* (Big Book, p. 12; italics in
original).[59] And it is important to remember the context of Ebby's
suggestion. When Ebby first witnessed to Bill, Bill had begun
ruminating about his childhood antipathy toward ministers, the
world's religions, and God. (And though it is not well known, Bill
had characterized himself as an atheist).[60] Hence Ebby suggested
that Bill start with the Oxford Group concept from John 7:17 of
"willingness to believe."[61] Echoing Ebby's teaching, Bill said,

---

[58] See the specific language of A.A.'s Third Step and Eleventh Step which use the
phrase "God *as we understood Him*" (Big Book, pp. 59-60; italics in original).

[59] Please note the earlier discussion that this material from Ebby does not seem to be
in any of the earlier manuscripts.

[60] See Bill's statement in *As Bill Sees It*, p. 276, speaking of "A Higher Power for
Atheists," and stating: "I was once that way myself." Also our discussion elsewhere of
Lois Wilson's statement to T. Willard Hunter that Bill had been an atheist. And finally,
Bill's references to himself in earlier manuscripts as a "conservative atheist."

[61] John 7:17: "If any man will do his [God's] will, he shall know of the doctrine,
whether it be of God, or *whether* I speak of myself," said Jesus. Sam Shoemaker and the
Oxford Group utilized this concept for their so-called "experiment of faith." A person
could begin his quest for God, they said, by obeying what he or she had heard from
Scripture about God's will. Then, by obeying that known word of God, he or she would
quickly see that the doctrine was of God and would therefore confirm the initial belief

(continued...)

"Nothing more was required of me to make my beginning" (p. 12, italics in original).

So obeying the known precepts of God (*as one conceived of Him* at the *beginning* of surrender) was how the unbeliever or doubter could *start*. The famous Bible scholar, theologian, and philosopher B. H. Streeter, of Oxford University, had been teaching the Oxford Group people from the Bible:

> "Straight is the gate, and narrow is the way."[62] Those who have
> entered in thereby tell us that we may expect another prize—a new
> conviction that God exists and a new understanding of His will,
> as well as new strength and happiness in His free service. "If any
> man willeth to do his will, he shall know of the teaching, whether
> it be of God (John vii. 17)." The truth of this is a thing which can
> be tested by experiment; and it can be tested in no other way. It
> is by getting into water that you prove the practicability of
> swimming—and its joy.[63]

Unfortunately, Bill left material out of the Big Book which he had used in his earlier pre-Big Book manuscripts and which showed that *Ebby* had given him specific instructions on commencing an experiment via the "God as you understand Him" idea. Ebby delivered this message when he told Bill how to begin Bill's quest for "faith." For, said Bill, in two early accounts of his first visit with Ebby Thacher—accounts not included in A.A.'s Big Book—Ebby had suggested to him in 1934 that he (Bill) should

---

[61] (...continued)
in God and know more about God. Quoting John 7:17, Shoemaker put it this way in *Religion That Works* (New York: Fleming H. Revell, 1928), p. 36: "If any man will begin by living up to as much as he understands of the moral requisites of God, he will later, in the light of his experience, come to see straight intellectually. . . . A moral experiment is worth ten times an intellectual investigation in apprehending spiritual truth. Obedience is as much the organ of spiritual understanding as reason."

[62] See Matthew 7:14.

[63] B. H. Streeter, *The God Who Speaks* (London: Macmillan & Co., 1943), p. 126.

surrender himself to God *as Bill understood God.*[64] Ebby's
suggestion certainly did not counter the information that Ebby had
been giving Bill as to "God" from the Oxford Group. In fact,
Ebby's suggestion followed Oxford Group practice rather well. For
Oxford Group people had long suggested that one begin his or her
experiment of faith through "surrender as much of himself as he
understands to as much of God as he understands" or that he or
she "surrender as much of himself as he knows to as much of God
as he knows."

And let's look at this history.

The American Oxford Group leader Sam Shoemaker had
frequently taught of surrender to God *as you understand Him.*[65]
Shoemaker wrote, for example: "So they prayed together, opening
their minds to as much of God as he understood . . ."[66] Other
Oxford Group people *and* Dr. Bob's wife, Anne Smith, spoke of
"a surrender of all that I know of self, to all that I knew of
God."[67] In no sense were these writers speaking about any deity

---

[64] See Bill Wilson, *Original Story*. On page 30, Bill stated: "This is what my friend
[Ebby Thacher] suggested I do: Turn my face to God as I understand Him and say to
Him with earnestness—complete honesty and abandon—that I henceforth place my life
at His disposal and direction forever" (lines 989-92). See also W.W., "The Fellowship
of Alcoholics Anonymous," *Quarterly Journal of Studies on Alcohol* (Yale University,
1945), pp. 461-73, in which Bill is quoted on page 463 as saying that Ebby Thacher had
told him, "So, call on God as you understand God. Try prayer."

[65] See Dick B., *Design for Living*, p. 306.

[66] Samuel M. Shoemaker, Jr., *Children of the Second Birth* (New York: Fleming H.
Revell, 1927), p. 47. See also page 25, where Shoemaker wrote: "So he said that he
would "surrender as much of himself as he could, to as much of Christ as he
understood." Later, Shoemaker also wrote: (1) "We begin the actual Christian experience
when we surrender as much of ourselves as we can to as much of Christ as we
understand. . . . Commit yourself to Him in an act of dedication." See *How to Become
a Christian*, p. 72. (2) "Begin honestly where you are. Horace Bushnell once said, 'Pray
to the dim God, confessing the dimness for honesty's sake.'" See *How to Find God*, p.
6 (New York: Reprint from Faith at Work Magazine, n.d.). For other examples of such
Shoemaker language, see Dick B., *Design for Living*, p. 306, n. 21.

[67] See Stephen Foot, *Life Began Yesterday* (New York: Harper & Brothers, 1935),
pp. 12-13, 175; James D. Newton, *Uncommon Friends: Life with Thomas Edison, Henry
Ford, Harvey Firestone, Alexis Carrel, & Charles Lindbergh* (New York: Harcourt
Brace, 1987), p. 154; Dick B., *Anne Smith's Journal*, pp. 25, 95.

but God Almighty—the God of the Bible. For Anne Smith and most of the Oxford Group people were devoted and daily Bible students who had a firm belief in God as He is described *in* the Bible.[68]

We believe the understanding of God held by Ebby Thacher, Bill Wilson, Dr. Bob, and Anne Smith during A.A.'s development years is *not* the "God as we understood Him" which sometimes sweeps through the meetings of A.A. today. For we have observed that phrases such as "Higher Power," "God as we understood Him," and a "Power greater than ourselves" have often become vehicles for describing an object—animate or inanimate, powerful or powerless, great or small—that an AA or a professional therapist or counselor may or may not choose to call "god." This without regard to what the Big Book said or meant and despite what A.A.'s founders understood by that expression in the 1930's. But the fact remains that Sam Shoemaker, Oxford Group writers such as Stephen Foot, and Anne Smith all were writing about the God of the Bible and suggesting surrender to as much of that *God* as one understands or knows. And they made those suggestions before Bill Wilson ever discussed the matter with Ebby Thacher and well before Wilson wrote the Twelve Steps.

When Ebby suggested to Bill in 1934 that Bill surrender to God as Bill then understood God, Bill reported in the First and Third Editions of the Big Book that he (Bill) did just that. Bill said that, at Towns Hospital:

> I humbly offered myself to God, as I *then* understood Him, to do with me as He would. I placed myself unreservedly under His care and direction.[69]

Bill's reference to God as Bill *then* understood God should be considered in light of Bill's own starting point as either an atheist or an agnostic—someone who does not believe in or is still in doubt

---

[68] See Dick B., *Design for Living*, pp. 152-58, 163-66, 249-53, 302-04; *New Light on Alcoholism*, pp. 63-64, 67, 311-12, 316.

[69] Big Book, First Edition, p. 22; Third Edition, p. 13 (italics added).

about God.[70] Bill's reference to God as Bill *then* understood Him should be taken in light of his statement to T. Henry and Clarace Williams in 1954 that he (Bill) really knew little (in 1935) about the Bible *until* he came to Akron and learned from the Smiths, Mr. and Mrs. Williams, and Henrietta Seiberling.[71]

In contrast to Dr. Bob, who—when Bob and Bill met—believed in God Almighty and insisted upon such belief as a condition to beginning recovery, Bill had started his recovery six months earlier in New York without such belief. And Bill was therefore advised, in accordance with John 7:17, to surrender to God as Bill then understood God and to follow the moral precepts of God which would produce an experience of God and convince Bill of God's existence and the validity of God's moral doctrine. Which surrender must, with those very ideas, have been made by Bill!

For, when Bill took the Oxford Group "steps" at Towns Hospital, and underwent his "hot flash" experience, he announced almost triumphantly:

This . . . must be the great reality. The God of the preachers.[72]

Note that Bill had begun an experiment of faith as an atheist *or* an agnostic. He had admitted alcohol had become his master.[73]

---

[70] As we've said, Bill stated on one occasion that he was an atheist. His wife, Lois, informed T. Willard Hunter in an interview that Bill had been an atheist (Tape of the Hunter/Lois Wilson interview in the author's possession). In the Big Book itself, Bill made two statements on the subject: (1) "I was not an atheist" (p. 10), though it is not clear from the statement that Bill had not *previously* been an atheist. (2) "But cheer up, something like half of *us* thought we were atheists or agnostics" (p. 44, italics added).

[71] See Dick B., *The Akron Genesis*, p. 64; and page 69 contains the following remarks by T. Henry Williams (which probably represent what Williams taught Bill Wilson): "Our conception of God makes all the difference in the world as to our attitude toward others. Either we accept the fact that there is a God and put Him on the throne in our lives and community or we deny His existence and climb up and usurp the throne for ourself . . ."

[72] *Pass It On*, pp. 120-21; Big Book, pp. 13-14.

[73] From Bill's Story, Big Book, p. 8: "I had met my match. I had been overwhelmed. Alcohol was my master."

After some self-wrangling, Bill surrendered and found himself "in the sunlight at last;" he had become *willing to believe* and concluded, "Nothing more was required for me *to make my beginning.*"[74] Then, he humbly surrendered, took an inventory, and sought to change his life.[75] When he had done that, he had his famous conversion experience and claimed *knowledge* of the "great reality"—the "God of the preachers."[76] These latter expressions seem very likely to have been expressions Bill had been hearing from Ebby Thacher and Oxford Group people.

Oxford Group theologian B. H. Streeter had been saying (about God) to Oxford Group people: "He [God] is the *all-pervading Reality.*"[77] And Sam Shoemaker's teachings to his Oxford Group circle, including Ebby, about the experiment to find faith in God, seem exemplified by this quote:

> Every so often in human history, the Spirit of God comes into the world in fresh manifestation of power. We notice a kind of cycle in the spiritual life of mankind: somewhere a *great Reality is born*, which brings a new discovery of God and new tides of life . . .[78]

Atheists and agnostics in the Oxford Group had, despite their doubts or denials, *begun* their experiment believing that God is.[79] Then they *acted* upon Jesus's challenge in John 7:17 by following God's known moral precepts as set forth in the Bible. They believed this action would leave them with faith *in*, a "conscious contact" *with*, and substantial knowledge *about* God. In other words, they began with such understanding of God *as they had,*

---

[74] Big Book, p. 12 (italics in original).

[75] Big Book, pp. 13-14.

[76] *Pass It On*, pp. 120-21.

[77] Streeter, *The God Who Speaks*, p. 12 (italics in quote were added). See also, p. 1: "a great Unseen Reality to which could be given the name of God."

[78] Shoemaker, *National Awakening*, p. 23. For another reference to "Great Reality," see Glenn Clark, *The Soul's Sincere Desire* (Boston, Little, Brown, 1925) p. 30.

[79] See Hebrews 11:6; Dick B., *Design for Living*, pp. 163-66.

and then *learned* about God and the truth of His doctrine *from the action* they took in obedience to God's known will.[80]

A.A. legend has it that the expression "as we understood Him" was the product of a suggestion by former atheist, Jim B. And Jim B. told it that way in his Big Book story "The Vicious Cycle" and also in a history of early A.A. which Jim compiled.[81] However, Jim B.'s recollection never produced an acknowledgement by Bill Wilson that the "God as we understood Him" language *originated* with Jim B., rather than having arisen out of *Bill's own* earlier Oxford Group exposure.

In fact, in a letter from Wilson to Tom B., dated March 25, 1968, Bill wrote of Jim B.'s history of A.A. and commented that he felt "in some respects his [Jim's] recollections are rather mistaken."[82] Bill also said that:

> Jim, along with Hank Parkhurst and others, brought a strenuous objection to my use of the word God throughout the Steps. [and Bill added] It was out of this discussion, in which Jim participated, that we came on the idea of toning the thing down by the use of "God as we understand Him." [Then Bill referred Tom B. to Bill's own history of early A.A. where Bill had said:] "Who first suggested the actual compromise words I do not know."[83]

In another account concerning the issue, Bill said at Fort Worth, Texas, in 1954, "The idea of 'God as you understand Him' came out of that perfectly ferocious argument and we put that

---

[80] Dick B., *Design for Living*, pp. 50, 54-56, 160-63, 272-75.

[81] See Big Book, p. 248: "so my only contribution to their literary efforts was my firm conviction, being still a theological rebel, that the word God should be qualified with the phrase 'as we understand Him'—for that was the only way I could accept spirituality." In his *Evolution of Alcoholics Anonymous*, Jim B. wrote: "Another thing changed in this last rewriting was qualifying the word 'God' with the phrase 'as we understand him' (This was one of the writer's few contributions to the book)."

[82] Letter furnished to the author by Maryland archivist, Bill R.

[83] *A. A. Comes of Age*, p. 167. See also p. 17.

in."[84] Unfortunately, Bill did not refer to the earlier "God-as-you-understand-Him" expressions in the Oxford Group and in the teachings of Anne Smith. But Bill indicated that, while Hank Parkhurst was *quoting* Jim B. to support Parkhurst's arguments against using "God" in the Big Book text, Jim B. was probably not even present when the compromise language was finalized.[85]

The fact is that "God as we understood Him" seemed to shock no one when that expression was adopted in the office of Bill Wilson's first secretary, Ruth Hock, at the time the Big Book was being put together. Ruth Hock said that adding the phrase "God as we understood Him" to A.A.'s Big Book and Twelve Step language at the formative stage never "had much of a negative reaction anywhere."[86] Her comment seems to hold water as of the date it was made.

As we've shown, Oxford Group adherents and people (such as Dr. Bob's wife) in Akron's Alcoholic Squad of the Oxford Group had been using such an expression or similar phrases for many years prior to the Big Book's writing in 1938.[87] And Bill had told a very revealing story about Jim B. when Bill addressed the Yale Summer School of Alcohol Studies in 1945.

Bill devoted much of his talk to "Jimmy" [Jim B.] "an alcoholic . . . [of] the type that some of us now call the blockbuster variety." Bill pointed to the number of times "Jimmy" objected to "this God business." Jim was staying drunk, and "louder and louder did he get with his anti-God talk." Finally, as Bill said Jim had told the story, Jim thought to himself, "Maybe these fellows have got something with their God-business." For

---

[84] Tape, titled, "How the Big Book Was Put Together, Bill Wilson, 1954, Fort Worth, Texas" (copy supplied to author by A.A. General Services in New York).

[85] Speaking of the battle in Henry Parkhurst's office, Bill said: "Present were Fitz, Henry, our grand little secretary Ruth, and myself. . . . Praying to God on one's knees was still a big affront to Henry. He argued, he begged, he threatened. He quoted Jimmy to back him up. . . . Little by little both Fitz and Ruth came to see the merit in his contentions" (*A. A. Comes of Age*, pp. 166-67).

[86] *Pass It On* (New York: Alcoholics Anonymous World Services, 1984), p. 199.

[87] See discussion in Dick B., *Anne Smith's Journal*, pp. 24-29.

Jim had reached out for a Gideon Bible when he was very sick. He picked it up and read from it; and Bill recounted that "Jimmy has not had a drink to this day, and that was about 5 years ago."[88]

The point is that when Bill was completing the Big Book in late 1938 and early 1939, there was nothing new about "the God-business" or "God as you understand Him." History is clear that a couple of former atheists objected to Bill's *incessant use* of the word "God" in the Big Book. There *was* a dispute in the New York area. There *was* a "compromise" among the New York alcoholics in that Bill inserted "God as we understood Him" in two of the Twelve Steps. But even the 1976 (Third Edition of the) Big Book *retained* over 400 references to God, *without qualification*. And the phrase "as we understood Him" was certainly something Bill had heard from his friend and Oxford Group sponsor, Ebby. Bill specifically so stated. The phrase is something Bill also could hardly have missed in the Oxford Group circles in which he traveled in New York. And the phrase is something he well could have heard from Anne Smith when Bill lived with Dr. Bob and Anne in Akron; for Bill heard Anne teaching daily from the Scriptures, from Oxford Group literature, and from her spiritual notes about surrendering to God *as you know Him*.[89]

Further, such firm believers in God as A.A. co-founder, Dr. Bob, and his Akron AAs, had had the opportunity to review, prior to publication, every page of Wilson's Big Book manuscript—a manuscript containing hundreds of references to God as He *is* described in the Bible. There is no evidence that the Akron people had agreed with Bill or among themselves to a deletion of God from the Big Book; for they saw or had the opportunity to see the Bible's God named and described hundreds of times in the Big Book drafts and stories as they were proposed. And these Akron

---

[88] See W. W., Lecture 29, "The Fellowship of Alcoholics Anonymous" (New Haven: Quarterly Journal of Studies on Alcohol, 1945), pp. 461-473, particularly p. 468.

[89] Dick B., *Anne Smith's Journal*, p. 25. Anne wrote: "Try to bring a person to a *decision* to surrender as much of himself as he knows to as much of God as he knows" (italics added).

people gave the basic text of Bill's Big Book their "warmest support."[90] Warmest support even with the Big Book's very few and very limited references to "Higher Power" and "God as we understood Him" which apparently had produced no negative reaction.[91]

"A Power Greater Than Ourselves"

We've shown that the Oxford Group commonly spoke about opening one's heart, and surrendering, to one's own conception of God. To as much of God as one knows (in other words, to as much of God as one understands *at the time of surrender*). Though at least one Oxford Group writer did call *God* a "Higher Power," Oxford Group-Shoemaker writings (and that Oxford Group author's book) are filled with the mention of *God* as a "Power" to be sought and a "Power" to bring about life-change.

Stephen Foot wrote an immensely popular Oxford Group title in the early 1930's. His *Life Began Yesterday*, contains good examples of the Oxford Group's synonymous references to God and Power—the God of the Bible.[92] Foot spoke much of the "Power that can change human nature" and "this Power by which human nature can be changed."[93] In the next breath, Foot was writing—in language prophetic of that in A.A.'s Third Step—about "a decision to surrender to God."[94] The companion Oxford Group title of the same period, *I Was a Pagan*, spoke *once* of a "Higher Power" but *then* asked "just what this secret or this power

---

[90] Dick B., *The Akron Genesis*, pp. 223-33; *A.A. Comes of Age*, p. 159.

[91] Even in the Third Edition, "Higher Power" was mentioned only twice in the basic text (pp. 43, 100). "God as we understood Him" phraseology was used only seven times in the basic text (pp. 13, 47, 59, 60, 63, 164). But, as we have shown, the *unqualified* language about "God," the use of pronouns specifically referring to Him, and the inclusion of Biblical names for Him occurred over 400 times in the Third Edition.

[92] Foot, *Life Began Yesterday*, pp. 4-5, 13, 15, 22-23, 30, 35, 47, 87, 112.

[93] Foot, *Life Began Yesterday*, p. 22.

[94] Foot, *Life Began Yesterday*, p. 44.

was."[95]   Kitchen's   next   sentence   referred   to   "God-consciousness"—an expression that seems to have found its way to A.A.'s Big Book.[96] Kitchen also wrote of "A power within yet coming from outside myself—a power far stronger than I was."[97] Again, Kitchen was talking about "God."[98]

Dr. Bob's wife, Anne, wrote in her journal about the Apostle Paul's *lack* of adequate power and said:

> A stronger power than his [Paul's] was needed. God provided the power through Christ.[99]

Clearly, Anne was speaking of the power of God. And Bill Wilson's spiritual teacher Sam Shoemaker spoke of God in terms of "A vast Power outside themselves."[100] And "A Force outside himself, greater than himself."[101]

Bill Wilson followed suit in the Big Book when he spoke of the need in recovery for a willingness to believe in a Power greater than ourselves and then made it crystal clear that the Power "is

---

[95] Kitchen, *I Was a Pagan*, p. 28.

[96] Kitchen, *I Was a Pagan*, p. 28. See also Dick B., *Design for Living*, pp. 277, n. 458, and 339-40, for other Oxford Group references to "God-consciousness." Also, see Big Book, pp. 13, 51, 85, 569-70.

[97] Kitchen, *I Was a Pagan*, 63; compare p. 78.

[98] Kitchen, *I Was a Pagan*: (1) "that was what gave them the power to *apply* beliefs and *carry out* the plan of God—a power that I did not have" (p. 56, italics in original); (2) "they said I would have to surrender my will and make it subject to the will of God" (p. 56); (3) "Forming a clean contact with God, however, does no good unless God then chooses to release His power. And God, as I have said before, will not do so unless He knows that He can *trust* you with that power" (pp. 66-67, italics in original); (4) "With my new experience, however, the Holy Ghost or Spirit became a definite force flowing from God to me as electricity flows from a power house" (p. 78).

[99] Dick B., *Anne Smith's Journal*, p. 22; Big Book, p. 45: "Lack of power, that was our dilemma. We had to find a power by which we could live, and it had to be a *Power greater than ourselves*" (italics in original).

[100] Samuel M. Shoemaker, Jr., *A Young Man's View of the Ministry* (New York: Association Press, 1923), p. 42.

[101] Samuel M. Shoemaker, Jr., *If I Be Lifted Up* (New York: Fleming H. Revell, 1931), p. 176.

God."[102] Bill underlined this "God" point many times by pointing out that the aim of the recovery program of Alcoholics Anonymous, at the time of the writing of the Big Book, was the establishment of a "relationship with God."[103]

Again, one can hardly claim that the "power greater than ourselves" in *today's* A.A. is inevitably God Almighty as He is described in the Bible. But we think a strong case can be made that there was *no other understanding* of that phrase when Oxford Group writers, as well as Bill Wilson and Dr. Bob's wife, Anne Smith, first began using it. There can be little doubt that when Sam Shoemaker spoke of a "Power," Shoemaker was speaking of God; for his sermons and writings are filled with references to God and Power.[104] So too the Oxford Group writers mentioned above.[105] So too Anne Smith, in the sentences quoted above, when she spoke of God's providing the power through Christ. As we've shown, Dr. Bob frequently spoke of God and his (Dr. Bob's) Heavenly Father. And so did Bill Wilson.

Based on all our research, we therefore believe that from the time of A.A.'s founding in 1935: (1) Bill Wilson and Dr. Bob believed in, relied upon, and described God as He is described in the Bible.[106] (2) They used Bible terminology to describe God in

---

[102] Big Book, p. 46.

[103] See Big Book, pp. 29, 13, 28, 100, 164. For the historical roots of this "relationship with God" idea, see Dick B., *Design for Living*, pp. 36, 78, 155, 168, 180, 223, 274, 302, 323, 325, 332-33 (and note particularly the citations on p. 332, n. 105).

[104] See, for example, one of Shoemaker's earliest titles, *A Young Man's View of the Ministry*, p. 42, where Shoemaker commented that changed people seemed "propelled by a vast Power outside themselves."

[105] For an example, see Streeter, *The God Who Speaks*, p. 110 (quoting 1 Corinthians 2:4-5, and stating): "Not argument, but fact, says Paul; not persuasion but power from God. It is clear that things happened to people as a result of this experience." Compare also Acts 1:8: "But ye shall receive power . . ." and Streeter, *The God Who Speaks*, p. 111.

[106] Thus, by 1937, when he was speaking of how he and Dr. Bob realized they had developed a successful recovery program out of their period of "flying blind" with the Bible and the Oxford Group precepts, Bill said: "A beacon had been lighted. God had shown alcoholics how it might be passed from hand to hand." *RHS* (New York: AA

(continued...)

their work with others. (3) And—however roomy and inclusive they wished to make early A.A. and later A.A.—they did not endeavor *in their early days* to establish some new theology, religion, or sectarian doctrine about a "god" of their own creation or perception.[107] They were, at most, proposing for those of little or no faith an experiment of faith that would enable them to *begin* their path to a relationship with God and then, for the great majority, to *believe* in God.[108]

Consider, for example, these statements by Bill Wilson as the A.A. years rolled on:

[Speaking in July, 1953, about what Ebby had first told him:] I had to pray to God for guidance and strength, even though I wasn't sure there *was* any God (italics added);[109]

[July, 1953:] Those expressions ["a Higher Power" or "God as we understand Him"] . . . have enabled thousands of us *to make a beginning* . . . (italics added).[110]

[1957:] In Step Two we decided to describe God as a "Power greater than ourselves." In Steps Three and Eleven we inserted

---

[106] (...continued)
Grapevine, Inc., 1951), p. 8. *DR. BOB* stated at p. 96: "This [the period from 1935 on, when there were no Twelve Steps] was the beginning of A.A.'s 'flying-blind' period. They had the Bible, and they had the precepts of the Oxford Group. They also had their own instincts. They were working, or working out, the A.A. program—the Twelve Steps—without quite knowing how they were doing it." And, as Oxford Group spokesman Sherry Day had written in the first page of his Oxford Group pamphlet, *The Principles of the Group*: "The principles of 'The Oxford Group' *are* the principles of the Bible" (italics added).

[107] In *A.A. Comes of Age*, Bill said at page 232: "Speaking for Dr. Bob and myself I would like to say that there never has been the slightest intent, on his part or mine, of trying to found a new religious denomination. Dr. Bob held certain religious convictions, and so do I. This is, of course, the personal privilege of every A.A. member."

[108] See, for example, Bill's comment in *A.A. Comes of Age*, p. 81: "Alcoholics may be led to believe in God, but none can be forced."

[109] *The Language of the Heart: Bill's Grapevine Writings* (New York: The A.A. Grapevine, Inc., 1988), p. 196.

[110] *The Language of the Heart*, p. 201.

the words "God *as we understood Him* . . ." Such were the final concessions to those of little or no faith; this was the great contribution of our atheists and agnostics. They had widened our gateway so that all who suffer might pass through, regardless of their belief or *lack of belief.* God was certainly there in our Steps, but He was now expressed in terms that anybody—*anybody at all*—could accept and try (italics in original).[111]

[January, 1958:] Like any good scientist in his laboratory, our friend can assume a theory and pray to a "higher power" that *may* exist and *may* be willing to help and guide him. He keeps on experimenting—in this case, praying—for a long time. . . . As he goes along with his process of prayer, he begins to add up the results. . . . Even if few of these things happen [serenity, tolerance, less fear, less anger], he will still find himself in possession of great gifts. . . . He can now accept himself and the world around him. He can do this because he now accepts a God who is All—and who loves all. When he now says, "Our Father who art in Heaven, hallowed be thy name," our friend deeply and humbly means it.[112] When in good meditation and thus freed from the clamors of the world, he knows that he is in God's hand . . . (italics in original).[113]

[January, 1958:] Mine was exactly the kind of deep-seated block we so often see today in new people who say they are atheistic or agnostic. Their will to disbelieve is so powerful that apparently they prefer a date with the undertaker to an open-minded and experimental *quest for God* (italics added).[114]

[June, 1961:] Perfect humility would be a full willingness, in all times and places, to find and do the *will of God.* . . . I see that my journey toward God has scarce begun (italics added).[115]

---

[111] *A. A. Comes of Age*, p. 167 (published in 1957).

[112] Bill here virtually quotes verbatim a portion of the Lord's Prayer in Jesus's Sermon on the Mount (Matthew 6:9).

[113] *The Language of the Heart*, pp. 241-42.

[114] *The Language of the Heart*, pp. 245-46.

[115] *The Language of the Heart*, p. 259.

[June, 1966, speaking about his sponsor, Ebby:] he was proposing
the attitudes and principles that I used later in developing AA's
Twelve Steps to recovery. . . . He had pushed ajar that great gate
through which all in AA have since passed to find their freedom
under God (italics added).[116]

Were these the words of a co-founder who believed that "god"
could be a light-bulb, a chair, or the group? We think not. Bill
sometimes said he was an atheist and sometimes said he was an
agnostic. And such self-characterizations seem to refer to Bill's
status *before* he had his conversion experiences at Calvary Rescue
Mission and at Towns Hospital. But, at *those* places, he was
surrendering to God—"the God of the preachers." God, as Ebby
had explained God to Bill from Oxford Group precepts and as Bill
had heard God spoken of at the Calvary Mission and later at
Shoemaker's Oxford Group meetings at Calvary House.

The Oxford Group often spoke of the *experiment of faith* which
began with obeying as much of the will of God as one knew.[117]
And that seemed to be the gateway to God which Bill was
suggesting with his use of the word "Power" and the phrase "as
we understood Him." But the gateway in those early days most
assuredly opened the path to the God of the Bible Bill mentioned
so many times in his pre-publication drafts of the Big Book.

We cannot say Bill's approach appeals to us. Nor do we believe
it was the approach Dr. Bob used when he asked a newcomer if
the newcomer *believed* in God—the God of the Bible.[118] This
God of love Who was the subject of Dr. Bob's daily Bible study.

---

[116] *The Language of the Heart*, p. 368.

[117] John 7:17. See Streeter, *The God Who Speaks*, p. 126: "The truth of this [John
7:17] is a thing which can be tested by experiment; and it can be tested in no other
way;" Shoemaker, *National Awakening*, p. 40: "It [true security] lies in a faith in God
which includes an experiment. It lies in believing that God is, that He has a plan, and
that He will reveal that plan to us. It lies in fitting in with that plan ourselves, and
finding that God will take care of us when we dare to make that experiment."

[118] See the account in *DR. BOB* about Dr. Bob's demanding quiz of Clarence S. as
to whether Clarence believed in God (p. 144). See Also, Dick B., *Design for Living*, p.
166; *That Amazing Grace*, p. 26.

Nor do we think Bill's approach is easy for the Christian AA to take as he or she compares Bill's words with those of Jesus, Peter, and Paul as recorded in John, Acts, and Romans.[119]

Whatever today's AAs might wish to believe or come to believe, we conclude that Bill Wilson's *own* early access to "faith" occurred through his believing basic ideas *from the Good Book* which: (1) He heard from Ebby Thacher when Ebby visited Bill and flatly declared that God had done for him (Ebby) what he could not do for himself.[120] (2) He utilized when he "gave his life to God" at Sam Shoemaker's Calvary Rescue Mission where there had been hymns, Bible reading, and an altar call (All of which, according to Mrs. Samuel Shoemaker, Jr., who said she was present, resulted in Bill's making his "decision for Christ").[121] (3) He further pursued when he checked in at Towns Hospital, followed Ebby Thacher's instructions, and humbly entrusted his life to God's care.[122] Recall again, Dr. Bob's statement, about Bill and himself, that "We got them [the basic ideas] . . . as a result of our study of the Good Book."[123]

Bill's own learning experiences from his visit with Ebby, his surrender at Calvary Rescue Mission, and his "hot flash" conversion at Towns Hospital caused Bill, we believe, to declare

---

[119] John 14:6: "Jesus saith unto him, I am the way, the truth, and the life; no man cometh unto the Father, but by me." Acts 4:7-12: "By what power, or by what name, have ye done this? Then Peter, filled with the Holy Ghost, said unto them. . . . Be it known unto you all, and to all the people of Israel, that by the name of Jesus Christ of Nazareth, whom ye crucified, whom God raised from the dead, *even* by him doth this man stand here before you whole. . . . Neither is there salvation in any other: for there is none other name under heaven given among men, whereby we must be saved." Romans 10:8-9: ". . . that is, the word of faith, which we preach; That if thou shalt confess with thy mouth the Lord Jesus, and shalt believe in thine heart that God hath raised him from the dead, thou shalt be saved."

[120] Big Book, p. 11.

[121] Dick B., *New Light on Alcoholism*, p. 242.

[122] See, for example, Proverbs 3:5-6; Dick B., *Design for Living*, pp. 158-63; Big Book, p. 13.

[123] *DR. BOB*, p. 97.

that he had given his life to God as Bill *then* understood God.[124] We believe those experiences caused Bill to declare, *at least twice*, "For sure I had been born again."[125] And Bill's understanding at that time (of the God of the Bible) permeated and remained in the language of the Big Book he penned some four years later.

Furthermore, the persistence of *Bill's* Biblical understanding of God, whether Bill called Him a "Higher Power" or "God as we understood Him" or "A Power greater than ourselves," is exemplified by the following statement by Bill on A.A.'s Twentieth Anniversary:

> Many people wonder how A.A. can function under such a seeming anarchy. . . . Happily for us, we found we need no human authority whatever. We have two authorities which are far more effective. One is benign, the other malign. There is God, our Father, who very simply says, "I am waiting for you to do my will." The other authority is named John Barleycorn, and he says, "You had better do God's will or I will kill you." . . . So, when all the chips are down, we conform to God's will or perish.[126]

---

[124] Big Book, First Edition, p. 22: "There I humbly offered myself to God, as I then understood Him, to do with me as He would."

[125] See documentation in Dick B., *The Akron Genesis*, pp. 328-31.

[126] *A. A. Comes of Age*, p. 105.

5

The Sections of the Bible
Dr. Bob Found "Essential"

Dr. Bob had said in his last major address to AAs in Detroit that he and the older members of A.A. considered the Book of James, the Sermon on the Mount, and 1 Corinthians 13 to be "absolutely essential" to their successful recovery program.[1] We think those materials so important that they justify a separate item-by-item review at this point.

The Book of James

We think the Book of James was probably the most important source book in the Bible, so far as early AAs were concerned. It was much studied by A.A.'s co-founders.[2] Quotes and ideas from the Apostle James can be found throughout the Big Book and in A.A. literature. And even the most fundamental phrases in A.A., such as "It Works" and Bill Wilson's own "Works Publishing Company," which published the First Edition of the Big Book,

---

[1] *The Co-Founders of Alcoholics Anonymous: Biographical Sketches Their last Major Talks* (New York: Alcoholics Anonymous World Services, Inc., 1972, 1975), p. 13.

[2] *DR. BOB*, pp. 71, 213; Dick B., *Design for Living*, pp. 10-12; *The Akron Genesis* pp. 272-73; *Dr. Bob's Library*, pp. 9, 12, 38, 82, 89, 90; *Anne Smith's Journal*, pp. 36, 38, 40, 76, 99, 122, 129, 131, 138, 144.

may have had their origin in the "Faith without works is dead" language in James.[3]

We will therefore review the Book of James, chapter by chapter. As we do so, we will point to traces of that book which we believe can be found in, or probably influenced, the text of the Big Book.[4]

Our readers will find many references to *The Runner's Bible* in our footnotes on James; for we believe that this little devotional book may have provided Dr. Bob, Anne Smith, and perhaps even Bill Wilson, with much of the fodder that caused them to focus on James and conclude that James was their "favorite" book of the Bible (See *DR. BOB*, p. 71; *Pass It On*, p. 147).

James Chapter 1

1. *Patience.* Chapter One is not the only chapter in the Book of James which mentions patience.[5] Nor is it the only portion of the

---

[3] See, for example, Big Book, p. 88: "It works—it really does. . . . Faith without works is dead;" Nell Wing, *Grateful to Have Been There* (Illinois: Parkside Publishing, 1992), pp. 70-71.

[4] In this segment on the Book of James, we will frequently cite Nora Smith Holm, *The Runner's Bible* (New York: Houghton Mifflin Company, 1915). Early AAs talked much about the Book of James, but we have never been able to find a commentary on that book such as the ones that were in use by Dr. Bob and others in connection with the Sermon on the Mount and 1 Corinthians 13. On the other hand, *The Runner's Bible* is specifically mentioned in A.A.'s memorial issue on Dr. Bob's death—*RHS* (New York: AA Grapevine, Inc., 1951), p. 34. The book was suggested to us by Dr. Bob's son Robert R. Smith as being important. And we now know the Dr. Bob owned, loaned out, and on one occasion actually sent this and another spiritual book to a friend who was having trouble with anger. See also Dick B., *Dr. Bob's Library*, pp. 30-31. As we were writing *The Good Book and The Big Book*, we noticed in *The Runner's Bible* the frequency with which all of Dr. Bob's "absolutely essential" books and chapters of the Bible (Matthew 5, 6, 7; 1 Corinthians 13, and James) were there mentioned. We particularly noted the frequency with which The Runner's Bible mentioned and discussed verses from the Book of James. We therefore believe this may have been a major reference source for the chapters and verses from James that early AAs relied upon.

[5] See also James 5:7-11: "Be *patient*, therefore, brethren, unto the coming of the Lord. . . . Be ye also *patient*; stablish your hearts; for the coming of the Lord draweth

(continued...)

Bible that stresses patience.[6] But James was a favored Biblical source in early A.A., and James 1:3-4 states:

> Knowing *this*, that the trying of your faith worketh patience.
> But let patience have *her* perfect work, that ye may be perfect and entire, wanting nothing.[7]

Patience certainly wound up as one of the most frequently mentioned spiritual principles in the Big Book.[8]

2. *Asking wisdom of God with unwavering believing.* James 1:5-8 states:

> If any of you lack wisdom, let him ask of God, that giveth to all *men* liberally, and upbraideth not; and it shall be given him.
> But let him ask in faith, nothing wavering. For he that wavereth is like a wave of the sea driven with the wind and tossed.
> For let not that man think that he shall receive anything of the Lord.
> A double minded man *is* unstable in all his ways.[9]

---

[5] (...continued)
nigh . . . ; Take, my brethren, the prophets, who have spoken in the name of the Lord, for example of suffering affliction, and of *patience*. Behold, we count them happy which endure. Ye have heard of the *patience* of Job, and have seen the end of the Lord; that the Lord is very pitiful, and of tender mercy" (italics added).

[6] See, for example, Hebrews 10:36: "For ye have need of *patience*, that, after ye have done the will of God, ye might receive the promise" (italics added). In addition to *The Upper Room* and *The Runner's Bible*, we will also frequently be citing Mary W. Tileston, *Daily Strength for Daily Needs* (Boston: Roberts Brothers, 1893). This highly popular daily devotional was a part of Dr. Bob's library and is still being sold at the date of our publication. As to Hebrews 10:36, see Tileston, *Daily Strength for Daily Needs*, p. 325.

[7] See Tileston, *Daily Strength for Daily Needs*, pp. 32, 48; *The Upper Room* for 4/24/36 or 4/24/39.

[8] Big Book, pp. 67, 70, 83, 111, 118, 163.

[9] These verses were discussed in Holm, *The Runner's Bible*, pp. 51, 60, 62; and in other favorites of Dr. Bob and Henrietta Seiberling such as Glenn Clark, *The Soul's Sincere Desire*, p. 59; *I Will Lift Up Mine Eyes* (New York: Harper & Brothers, 1937), (continued...)

Asking for God's direction and strength and receiving "Guidance" from Him, are major themes in both the Old and New Testaments. They were vital Oxford Group ideas as well. We discussed them at length in our titles on Quiet Time, the Oxford Group, and Anne Smith's spiritual journal.[10] And the Big Book, including the Eleventh Step itself, is *filled* with such Guidance concepts.[11]

3. *Every good and perfect gift comes from God, the Father of lights.* James 1:17 states:

Every good gift and every perfect gift is from above, and cometh down from the Father of lights, with whom is no variableness, neither shadow of turning.

Bill seemed to be referring to this verse when he wrote on page 14 of the Big Book:

I must turn in all things to the Father of Light [*sic*] who presides over us all.[12]

---

[9] (...continued)
pp. 136-37; and Harry Emerson Fosdick, *The Meaning of Prayer* (New York: Association Press, 1915), p. 118. All were part of Dr. Bob's library.

[10] Dick B., *Good Morning!* (the entire book); *Design for Living*, pp. 246-69, 319-22, 337-38; *New Light on Alcoholism*, pp. 66-67; *Anne Smith's Journal*, pp. 53-64, 107-116. See also Holm, *The Runner's Bible*, pp. 126-30; Oswald Chambers, *My Utmost for His Highest* (New Jersey: Barbour and Company, 1963), pp. 155, 319. Chambers' book was another highly popular book in early A.A. *and* in the Oxford Group. It is still on sale. And it too will be frequently cited in this segment on "essential books;" for early AAs used it a great deal in their meetings and Quiet Times.

[11] Big Book, pp. 13, 46, 49, 62-63, 69-70, 76, 79-80, 83, 84-88, 100, 117, 120, 124, 158, 164.

[12] At the conclusion of the "Long Form" Twelve Traditions in Appendix One of the Big Book, Bill wrote: "To the end that our great blessings may never spoil us; that we shall forever live in thankful contemplation of Him who presides over us all" (Big Book, p. 568). See Holm, *The Runner's Bible*, p. 9, quoting: "The Father of lights, with whom is no variableness, neither shadow of turning."

The Big Book often describes God as a loving and providing God.[13]

4. *Let every man be slow to speak, slow to wrath.* James 1:19-20 states:

Wherefore, my beloved brethren, let every man be swift to hear, slow to speak, slow to wrath: For the wrath of man worketh not the righteousness of God.

The verse is quoted in *The Runner's Bible* and seems quite relevant to the Big Book's injunction, "If we were to live, we had to be free of anger. . . . God save me from being angry."[14]

5. *Be ye doers of the word, and not hearers only.* James 1:21-22 states:

Wherefore lay apart all filthiness and superfluity of naughtiness, and receive with meekness the engrafted word, which is able to save your souls.
But be ye doers of the word, and not hearers only, deceiving your own selves.

Shoemaker devoted an entire chapter in one of his titles to this verse, stating:

I think St. James' meaning is made much clearer in Dr. Moffatt's translation, "Act on the Word, instead of merely listening to it." Try it out in experiment, and prove it by its results—otherwise you only fool yourself into believing that you have the heart of religion when you haven't.[15]

---

[13] Big Book, pp. 10-11, 13, 25, 28, 49, 52, 56-57, 59, 63, 68, 76, 83, 85, 100, 117, 120, 124, 130, 133, 158, 161, 164. See also Holm, *The Runner's Bible*, pp. 65, 140.

[14] Holm, *The Runner's Bible*, pp. 31, 49; Big Book, pp. 66-67.

[15] Samuel M. Shoemaker, *The Gospel According to You* (New York: Fleming H. Revell, 1934), pp. 45-55; Holm, *The Runner's Bible*, pp. 47, 135, 148; Tileston, *Daily Strength for Daily Needs*, p. 272. For the full text, see James 1:21-25.

In the same chapter, Shoemaker also pointed out that prayer is often more a struggle to find God than the enjoyment of Him and cooperation with His will.

We cannot find a specific reference to James 1:21-22 in the Big Book; but A.A. stresses over and over that A.A. is a program of *action*.[16] A.A.'s program emphasizes action in the experiment of faith it adopted from John 7:17—*seeking* God by *following* the path that leads to a relationship with God.[17] James 1:22 stresses *doing* God's will as expressed in His Word—not merely listening to it. Thus it seems possible that A.A.'s stress on *action* might have derived in part from James 1:21-22.

6. *Pure religion and undefiled before God . . . to visit the fatherless and widows in their affliction.* James 1:27 states:

> Pure religion and undefiled before God and the Father is this, To visit the fatherless and widows in their affliction, *and* to keep oneself unspotted from the world.[18]

At the very least, this verse bespeaks unselfishness and helpfulness to others which are cardinal A.A. principles.[19]

James Chapter 2

Chapter Two of the Book of James may have made two direct and major contributions to the language of the Big Book and also to A.A.'s philosophy. The concepts were "Love thy neighbor as thyself" and "Faith without works is dead."

---

[16] Big Book, pp. 14-15, 19, 25, 57, 59-60, 63-64, 72, 75-77, 85, 87-88, 89-103.

[17] As to relationship with God, see Big Book, pp. 13, 28-29, 72, 100, 164; compare p. 452. As to the path, see Big Book, pp. xxii, 15, 58, 72, 100, 116; compare p. 349.

[18] AA of Akron's *Spiritual Milestones* quotes this verse and then states: "And all we need to do in the St. James passage is to substitute the word 'Alcoholic' for 'Fatherless and Widows' and we have Step Twelve" (pp. 13-14).

[19] See Holm, *The Runner's Bible*, p. 78; Tileston, *Daily Strength for Daily Needs*, p. 251; Big Book, pp. 14, 20, 89, 159.

1. *Love thy neighbor as thyself.* James 2:8 states:

> If ye fulfill the royal law according to the scripture, Thou shalt
> love thy neighbor as thyself, ye do well.

This commandment, "Love thy neighbor," exists in other parts of
both the Old and New Testaments. Thus, when the Big Book uses
this phrase, we cannot say for sure whether the quote is from
James or from one of the other Bible verses to the same effect.[20]
But the Big Book certainly does state:

> Then you will know what it means to give of yourself that others
> may survive and rediscover life. You will learn the full meaning
> of "Love thy neighbor as thyself" (p. 153).[21]

James seems a very probable source for this Biblical quote since
Dr. Bob favored both the "love" concept *and* the Book of
James.[22]

2. *Faith without works is dead.* Said to be the favorite verse of
Anne Smith and perhaps the origin of many expressions in A.A.
concerning "works," this expression, or variations of it, appear
several times in Chapter Two of the Book of James.[23] For example, James 2:20 states:

> But wilt thou know, O vain man, that faith without works is dead?

---

[20] See Matthew 5:43; 19:19; 22:39; Mark 12:31; 12:33; Luke 10:27; Romans 13:9;
Galatians 5:14; Leviticus 19:18.

[21] See also Big Book, p. 236. And review James 2:14-17, which specifically
discusses helping a brother or sister who is naked and in lack of daily food. See also
Holm, *The Runner's Bible*, pp. 77-78.

[22] *DR. BOB*, pp. 338, 110; and see Holm, *The Runner's Bible*, p. 28; Tileston, *Daily
Strength for Daily Needs*, p. 46.

[23] James 2:14, 17-18, 20, 22, 26. See Wing, *Grateful to Have Been There*, pp. 70-
71.

The "faith without works" phrase and its action concept are quoted or referred to many times in the Big Book.[24] Oxford Group people also put emphasis on these James verses, using them in connection with the importance of witnessing.[25]

James Chapter 3

1. *Taming the tongue.* In his Farewell Address to A.A., Dr. Bob said:

> Let us also remember to guard that erring member the tongue, and if we must use it, let's use it with kindness and consideration and tolerance.[26]

A major portion of James, Chapter Three, is devoted to the trouble that can be caused by an untamed tongue.[27] These are a few of the verses:

> Even so the tongue is a little member and boasteth great things. Behold, how great a matter a little fire kindleth! And the tongue *is* a fire, a world of iniquity; so is the tongue among our members that it defileth the whole body, and setteth on fire the course of nature; and *it is* set on fire of hell. . . . But the tongue can no man tame; it is an unruly evil, full of deadly poison.
> . . . Out of the same mouth proceedeth blessing and cursing. My brethren, these things ought not to be.

These verses do not appear in the Big Book. But Anne Smith referred to them frequently in her journal, as did other A.A. roots

---

[24] Big Book, pp. 14-15, 76, 88, 93, 97.

[25] See The Layman with a Notebook, *What Is The Oxford Group?* (London: Oxford University Press, 1933), pp. 35-38.

[26] *DR. BOB*, p. 338.

[27] James 3:1-13.

sources.[28] But, in paraphrasing the verses, Dr. Bob seemed to be speaking of tolerance, courtesy, consideration, and kindness. James said that good *conversation* should be a focus—conversation, we believe, laced with consideration, kindness, and tolerance.[29] And these latter principles *are* very much emphasized in the Big Book.[30]

2. *Avoidance of envy, strife, and lying*. James 3:14-16 makes clear that a heart filled with envy, strife, and lies is not receiving wisdom from God, but rather from devilish sources. The verses state:

> But if ye have bitter envying and strife in your hearts; glory not, and lie not against the truth.
> This wisdom descendeth not from above, but is earthly, sensual, devilish.
> For where envying and strife is, there is confusion and every evil work.

We do not find "envy" as much decried in the Big Book as jealousy; but a more modern translation of these King James verses equates "envy" *with* "jealousy."[31] And the Big Book most assuredly condemns jealously.[32] In fact, it states as to jealousy *and* envy:

> Keep it always in sight that we are dealing with that most terrible human emotion—jealousy (p. 82).

---

[28] Dick B., *Anne Smith's Journal*, pp. 28, 44, 76, 77; Holm, *The Runner's Bible*, p. 68; Tileston, *Daily Strength for Daily Needs*, p. 324; *The Upper Room* for 9/22/38; Howard A. Walter, *Soul Surgery: Some Thoughts on Incisive Personal Work* ((Oxford: The Oxford Group, 1928), p. 62. See also James 1:26.

[29] See James 3:13.

[30] Big Book, pp. 67, 69-70, 83-84, 97, 118, 125, 135.

[31] *The Revised English Bible* (London: Oxford University Press, 1989), New Testament, p. 208.

[32] Big Book, pp. 37, 69, 82, 100, 119, 145, 161.

The greatest enemies of us alcoholics are resentment, jealousy, envy, frustration, and fear (p. 145).

As to strife, the Big Book states:

After all, our problems were of our own making. Bottles were only a symbol. Besides, we have stopped fighting anybody or anything. We have to (p. 103)![33]

On the lying and dishonesty counts, we point to the Four Absolutes, and suggest the frequency with which the Big Book emphasizes A.A.'s requirement of grasping and developing a manner of living which "demands rigorous honesty" (p. 58).[34] In the case of James 3:14-16, however, we move farther from the level of certainty that these particular verses were an exclusive or even major source for the traits of envy, jealousy, strife, and dishonesty, decried also in many other parts of the Bible.[35]

James Chapter 4

1. *Asking amiss for selfish ends.* We shall have much more to say about selfishness and self-centeredness. But we do point to the following in James 4:3:

Ye ask, and receive not, because ye ask amiss, that ye may consume it upon your lusts.

---

[33] See James 3:17-18: "But the wisdom that is from above is first pure, then peaceable, gentle, *and* easy to be intreated, full of mercy and good fruits, without partiality, and without hypocrisy. And the fruit of righteousness is sown in peace of them that make peace." And see Holm, *The Runner's Bible*, pp. 46, 54.

[34] See also Big Book: (1) p. 58: "Those who do not recover are people who cannot or will not completely give themselves to this simple program, usually men and women who are constitutionally incapable of being honest with themselves." (2) p. 58: "many of them do recover if they have the capacity to be honest." (3) p. 64: "We took stock honestly." (4) p. 65: "Nothing counted but thoroughness and honesty."

[35] See, however, Holm, *The Runner's Bible*, p. 54.

Some Christian sources that were favorites of Dr. Bob's discuss this verse at length.[36] And the Big Book authors may have obtained from James 4:3 their inspiration for the following:

> We ask especially for freedom from self-will, and are careful to make no request for ourselves only. We may ask for ourselves, however, if others will be helped. We are careful never to pray for our own selfish ends. Many of us have wasted a lot of time doing that and it doesn't work (p. 87).

2. *Humility*. The Book of James has no corner on the Biblical injunction to be humble.[37] But the importance of James, and the remarks of Shoemaker under Item 3 immediately below, suggest that the following verses from James may have been a source of the Big Book's humility language quoted below. James 4:7, 10 state:

> Submit yourselves therefore to God. Resist the devil, and he will flee from you.
> Humble yourselves in the sight of the Lord, and he shall lift you up.[38]

The Big Book is filled with discussions of humility, of humbling one's self before God, and of humbly asking for His help. Examples include:

> There I humbly offered myself to God, as I understood Him, to do with me as He would (p. 13).

> He humbly offered himself to his Maker—then he knew (p. 57).

---

[36] See Clark, *The Soul's Sincere Desire*, p. 35; Holm, *The Runner's Bible*, p. 60; *The Upper Room* for 6/17/36.

[37] See Matthew 18:4; 23:12; 1 Peter 5:6; Micah 6:8; 2 Kings 22:19; 2 Chronicles 33:23.

[38] See also, Holm, *The Runner's Bible*, pp. 59, 94, 112.

Just to the extent that we do as we think He would have us, and humbly rely on Him, does He enable us to match calamity with serenity (p. 68).

We constantly remind ourselves we are no longer running the show, humbly saying to ourselves many times each day "Thy will be done" (pp. 87-88).[39]

3. *Trusting God and cleaning house.* James 4:8 states:

Draw nigh to God, and he will draw nigh to you. Cleanse your hands, ye sinners; and purify your hearts, ye double minded.[40]

The Big Book says on page 98:

Burn the idea into the consciousness of every man that he can get well regardless of anyone. The only condition is that he trust in God and clean house.

Pointing out that one can establish conscious companionship with God by simply, honestly, and humbly seeking Him, the Big Book says at page 57:

He has come to all who have honestly sought Him. When we drew near to Him He disclosed Himself to us!

In Step Seven, the Big Book relates "cleaning house" of character defects to "humbly asking" God to remove them. The verses in James, which speak of drawing near to God, cleansing our hearts, humbling ourselves in His sight, and then being "lifted" up by God, seem directly involved in the Big Book's Seventh Step language. In fact, many years after the Big Book was written, Sam Shoemaker wrote about his understanding of the Seventh Step and said in A.A.'s *Grapevine* in 1964:

---

[39] See also Big Book, pp. 59, 63, 73, 76, 85, 164.

[40] See for discussion, Chambers, *My Utmost for His Highest*, p. 309.

Sins get entangled deep within us, as some roots of a tree, and do not easily come loose. We need help, grace, the lift of a kind of divine derrick.[41]

4. *Taking your own inventory.* James 4:11-12 states:

Speak not evil one of another, brethren. He that speaketh evil of *his* brother, and judgeth his brother, speaketh evil of the law, and judgeth the law: but if thou judge the law, thou art not a doer of the law, but a judge. There is one lawgiver, who is able to save and to destroy: who art thou that judgest another?[42]

We will be discussing the Fourth Step idea of taking your own inventory in connection with relevant verses in the Sermon on the Mount which were often quoted by Oxford Group people and by Anne Smith. Yet the Big Book makes much of looking "for our own mistakes," asking "Where were we to blame," and realizing that "The inventory was ours, not the other man's."[43] Since AAs favored the Book of James and its insights, we believe the foregoing James verses also had an impact on the A.A. idea of avoiding judgment of another in favor of examining one's own conduct for wrongdoing.[44]

James Chapter 5

1. *Patience.* In our discussion of James, Chapter One, we covered patience verses also present in James 5:7, 8, 10, 11.

---

[41] Samuel M. Shoemaker, *Those Twelve Steps as I Understand Them*; Volume II, *Best of the Grapevine* (New York: The A.A. Grapevine, Inc., 1986), p. 130.

[42] Holm, *The Runner's Bible*, p. 68; Tileston, *Daily Strength for Daily Needs*, p. 13.

[43] Big Book, p. 67.

[44] See also Big Book, p. 66.

2. *Grudge not one against another.* James 5:9 reads:

> Grudge not one against another, brethren, lest ye be condemned; behold, the judge standeth before the door.

A major portion of the Big Book's Fourth Step discussion is devoted to resentment, about which page 64 says:

> Resentment is the "number one" offender. It destroys more alcoholics than anything else. From it stem all forms of spiritual disease.

The Big Book then suggests putting resentments on paper—making a *"grudge list"* (pp. 64-65). Oxford Group spokesman Ebenezer Macmillan wrote at length on the importance of eliminating resentments, hatred, or the *"grudge"* that "blocks God out effectively."[45] Shoemaker specified "grudges" as one of the "sins" to be examined in an inventory of self.[46] Since the Big Book lists resentments or "grudges" as one of the four major "character defects" which *block us from God*,[47] we think it quite possible that the "grudge" language in the Big Book was influenced by Akron's interest in James, and perhaps specifically in James 5:9.

3. *The "Healing Ministry of James."* James 5:14-15 states in part:

---

[45] Ebenezer Macmillan, *Seeking and Finding* (New York: Harper & Brothers, 1933), pp. 96-98. There is a copy of Macmillan's book in the library of Bill's home at Stepping Stones; and it is one of the very few Oxford Group books to be found anywhere at Stepping Stones until very recent donations were made by an AA to the archives.

[46] Samuel M. Shoemaker, *Twice-Born Ministers* (New York: Fleming H. Revell, 1929), p. 182; *How to Become a Christian*, pp. 56-67.

[47] See Big Book discussions at pages 71-72, 64-65, 84, 86.

Is any sick among you? let him call for the elders of the church; and let them pray over him, anointing him with oil in the name of the Lord: And the prayer of faith shall save the sick, and the Lord shall raise him up . . .

Apparently all early Akron AAs agreed that newcomers had to make surrenders to God, asking him to take alcohol out of their lives.[48] Surrenders were made on the knees, in the presence of others, and with prayers. T. Henry Williams of the Oxford Group was, with Dr. Bob, usually involved. T. Henry said:

After the meeting, we might take the new man upstairs, and a group of men would ask him to surrender his life to God and start in to really live up to the four absolutes and also to go out and help the other men who needed it. This was in the form of a prayer group. Several of the boys would pray together, and the new man would make his own prayer, asking God to take alcohol out of his life, and when he was through, he would say, "Thank you, God, for taking it out of my life." During the prayer, he usually made a declaration of his willingness to turn his life over to God.[49]

As previously stated, there is a strong likelihood that this process represented and included a decision for Christ and even involved anointing with oil. But the surrender prayers appear to have come from foregoing verses of James.[50] The author hopes that more information on the "healing ministry of James" will surface at least from A.A. sources and, if the foregoing verses were used in the Oxford Group, from Oxford Group sources.[51]

---

[48] *DR. BOB*, pp. 92-93, 101-02, 110, 118, 131, 139, 142.

[49] *DR. BOB*, p. 139.

[50] See Dick B., *The Good Book and the Big Book*, pp. 100-01; *That Amazing Grace*, pp. 27, 50-51.

[51] See Holm, *The Runner's Bible*, pp. 62, 114-15.

4. *Asking God's forgiveness for sins.* We repeat James 5:15, partially quoted above. The entire verse says:

> And the prayer of faith shall save the sick, and the Lord shall raise him up; and if he have committed sins, they shall be forgiven him.[52]

The Big Book says this of asking God's forgiveness when we fall short:

> If we are sorry for what we have done, and have the honest desire to let God take us to better things, we believe we will be forgiven and will have learned our lesson (p. 70).

> When we retire at night, we constructively review our day. . . . After making our review, we ask God's forgiveness and inquire what corrective measures should be taken (p. 86).

The foregoing Big Book quotes show that its authors believed they could, after surrender, still gain forgiveness from God for the shortcomings in which they indulged after their initial surrender. Here again, James has no corner on the statement that God makes it possible, through forgiveness, for a believer to regain fellowship with Him. 1 John 1:9 may also have been a source of these Big Book ideas:

> If we confess our sins, he is faithful and just to forgive us *our* sins, and to cleanse us from all unrighteousness.

See also our discussion of forgiveness in connection with the Sermon on the Mount. The Books of James, 1 John, or Matthew could each or all have been the basis for the Big Book forgiveness concepts.

---

[52] Holm, *The Runner's Bible*, p. 114; Fosdick, *The Meaning of Prayer*, pp. 157-58.

5. *Confess your sins one to another.* It has often been noted that *both* the Oxford Group principle of sharing by confession *and* Step Five in the Big Book were derived from James 5:16:

Confess your faults one to another, and pray for one another, that ye may be healed.[53]

6. *Effectual, fervent prayer works.* James 5:16 states:

The effectual fervent prayer of a righteous man availeth much.

The Big Book abounds with prayers.[54] And it states:

Step Eleven suggests prayer and meditation. We shouldn't be shy on this matter of prayer. Better men than we are using it constantly. It works, if we have the proper attitude and work at it.

Because of the popularity of the Book of James, it seems quite possible that the foregoing portion of James 5:16 persuaded early AAs and Bill Wilson as to the effectiveness of prayer.[55]

We believe the foregoing review of a good many verses in the Book of James suggests why Dr. Bob felt this particular book of the Bible was an essential source of the program early AAs were shaping in the 1930's.

---

[53] See Dick B., *Design for Living*, pp. 72, 189-92, 311-12; *New Light on Alcoholism*, pp. 70, 160, 209, 230, 236, 314; *Anne Smith's Journal*, p. 131; *What Is The Oxford Group?*, p. 31; *The Upper Room* for 12/4/35; Fosdick, *The Meaning of Prayer*, pp. 157-58.

[54] See, for example, Big Book, pp. 63, 67, 69, 70, 76, 80, 82-88, 164.

[55] Holm, *The Runner's Bible*, pp. 62, 114; *The Upper Room* for 8/19/35; Macmillan, *Seeking and Finding*, p. 128; Walter, *Soul Surgery*, p. 29; Fosdick, *The Meaning of Prayer*, p. 158.

The Sermon on the Mount

Our discussion here will not deal with this or that commentary on Matthew Chapters 5-7. It will focus on the Sermon on the Mount itself; for this Sermon which Jesus delivered was not the property of some particular writer. The fact that Dr. Bob read the Matthew chapters *themselves* as well as the many interpretations of them seems to verify an A.A. belief that the Sermon itself is one of the principles comprising "the common property of mankind," which Bill Wilson said the AAs had borrowed. And we will now review some major points we believe found their way from the Sermon into the thinking behind the Big Book.

The Lord's Prayer—Matthew 6:9-13

Oxford Group meetings closed with the Lord's Prayer—in New York and in Akron.[56] The author has attended at least two thousand A.A. meetings, and almost every one has closed with the Lord's Prayer. At the 1990 International A.A. Conference in Seattle, which this author attended, some 50,000 members of Alcoholics Anonymous joined in closing their meetings with the Lord's Prayer. The question here concerns what parts, if any, of the Lord's Prayer found their way into the Big Book; and we do point out here that the prayer is *part of the Sermon on the Mount.*

Here are the verses of the Lord's Prayer (King James Version) as found in Matthew 6:9-13. Jesus instructed the Judaeans, "After this manner therefore pray ye":

Our Father which art in heaven, Hallowed be thy name.
Thy kingdom come. Thy will be done in earth, as *it is* in heaven.
Give us this day our daily bread.

---

[56] Telephone interview by the author with Mrs. Julia Harris, October 5, 1991; *DR. BOB*, pp. 137-42.

And forgive us our debts, as we forgive our debtors.[57]
And lead us not into temptation, but deliver us from evil: For
thine is the kingdom, and the power, and the glory, for ever.
Amen.

Dr. Bob studied commentaries on the Sermon by Oswald
Chambers, Glenn Clark, Emmet Fox, and E. Stanley Jones.[58]
And these writers extracted a good many teachings, prayer guides,
and theological ideas from the Lord's Prayer in the Sermon.
There are a few concepts and phrases in the Lord's Prayer which
either epitomize A.A. thinking or can be found in its
language—whether the A.A. traces came from the Lord's Prayer
itself or from other portions of the Bible.

The Big Book uses the capitalized word "Father" when
referring to God; and the context of the usage shows that the name
came from the Bible.[59] The Oxford Group also used the term

---

[57] AAs usually substitute the word "trespasses" for "debts," as do many Christian
denominations.

[58] Dick B., *Dr. Bob's Library*, pp. 38-40; and see Oswald Chambers, *Studies in the
Sermon on the Mount* 4th ed (London: Simpkin, Marshall, Ltd., n.d.); Glenn Clark, *The
Soul's Sincere Desire; The Lord's Prayer and Other Talks on Prayer from The Camps
Farthest Out* (Minnesota: Macalester Publishing, 1932); *I Will Lift Up Mine Eyes*; Emmet
Fox, *The Sermon on the Mount* (New York: Harper & Row, 1934); and E. Stanley
Jones, *The Christ of the Mount: A Working Philosophy of Life* (New York: The Abingdon
Press, 1931). There were other books Dr. Bob and Anne studied; and these too discussed
the Sermon at some length: James Stalker, *The Life of Jesus Christ* (New York: Fleming
H. Revell Company, 1891; T. R. Glover, *The Jesus of History* (New York: Association
Press, 1919); and Robert E. Speer, *Studies of The Man Christ Jesus* (New York: Fleming
H. Revell Company, 1896)

[59] At page 14, the Big Book speaks of "Father" and "God" in the context of "Father
of Light" from James 1:17 [there rendered "Father of Lights"]. At page 62, of "Father"
and "God," stating "He is the Father, and we are His children." See, for example, 1
John 3:2, "Beloved, now are we the sons of God;" and 1 John 5:2, "By this we know
that we love the children of God, when we love God, and keep his commandments." In
A. A. Comes of Age, Bill Wilson wrote: "There is God, our Father, who very simply
says, 'I am waiting for you to do my will'" (p. 105); "We knew that ours was a
fellowship of the Spirit and that the grace of God was there" (p. 44).

"Father," among other names, when referring to God.[60] The concept and expression of God as "Father" is not confined to the Sermon on the Mount. It can be found in many other parts of the New Testament.[61] But AAs have given the "Our Father" prayer a special place in their meetings.[62] So the Lord's Prayer seems the likely source of their use of the word "Father."

The phrase "Thy will be done" is directly quoted in the Big Book and underlies A.A.'s contrast between "self-will" and "God's will."[63] The Oxford Group stressed, as do A.A.'s Third and Seventh Step prayers, that there must be a *decision to do God's will and to surrender to His will.* These ideas were often symbolized in the prayer, "Thy will be done."[64]

Finally, "Forgive us our debts" or "trespasses" clearly implies that God can and will "forgive;" and these concepts can be found in the Big Book, whether they came from the Lord's prayer or from other Biblical sources such as the Book of James.[65]

The Sermon on the Mount—Matthew Chapters 5-7

There is an interesting contrast of views on the Sermon on the Mount among three of the commentators Dr. Bob studied:

---

[60] Dick B., *Design for Living*, pp. 152-55; *New Light on Alcoholism*, pp. 63, 114, 135, 141,

[61] See, for example, Matthew 10:20; 11:25; 12:50; 15:13; 18:35; 26:39; John 10:25; 12:28; 16:27; 17:24; Acts 1:4; 2:33; Romans 1:7; 1 Corinthians 8:6; Ephesians 2:18; Colossians 1:12; 1 Thessalonians 3:13; James 1:27; 1 Peter 1:17; 1 John 2:1.

[62] See comment about this in Mel B., *New Wine*, p. 157.

[63] Big Book, pp. 67, 85, 88. See also p. 63: "May I do Thy will always." And pp. 86-87, "we ask God to direct our thinking. . . . We ask especially for freedom from self-will."

[64] Henry Wright, *The Will of God and a Man's Lifework* (New York: The Young Men's Christian Association Press, 1909), pp. 50-51; Macmillan, *Seeking and Finding*, p. 273; *What Is The Oxford Group?*, pp. 47-49; Shoemaker, *Children of the Second Birth*, pp. 58, 175-87; *If I Be Lifted Up*, p. 93; *The Upper Room* for 12/3/37.

[65] Big Book, pp. 70, 86.

Oswald Chambers wrote in his *Studies in the Sermon on the Mount*:

Beware of placing our Lord as Teacher first instead of as Saviour. That tendency is prevalent today, and it is a dangerous tendency. We must know Him first as Saviour before His teaching has any meaning for us, or before it has any meaning other than an ideal which leads us to despair. . . . If Jesus is only a Teacher, then all He can do is tantalize us by erecting a standard we cannot come anywhere near. But if we know Him first as Saviour, by being born again from above, we know that He did not come to teach us only: *He came to make us what He teaches we should be.* The Sermon on the Mount is a statement of the life we will live when the Holy Spirit is having His way with us (p. i).

Stating that he believed the greatest need of modern Christianity is the rediscovery of the Sermon on the Mount as the only practical way to live, E. Stanley Jones wrote:

Pentecost [when the gift of the holy spirit became available] had the content of the Sermon on the Mount in it and therefore the power manifested was Christian. *Pentecost divorced from the Sermon on the Mount is spiritual pow-wow instead of spiritual power* (italics added).[66]

Emmet Fox seemed to say "A plague on both of your houses." In his *The Sermon on the Mount*, Fox said:

. . . [A] far-fetched and very inconsistent legend was built up concerning original sin, vicarious blood atonement, infinite punishment for finite transgressions; and, in certain cases, an unutterably horrible doctrine of predestination to eternal torment, or eternal bliss was added. Now no such theory as this is taught in the Bible. . . . The "Plan of Salvation: which figured so prominently in the evangelical sermons and divinity books of a

---

[66] Jones, *The Christ of the Mount*, p. 18

past generation is as completely unknown to the Bible as it is to the Koran. There never was any such arrangement in the universe, and the Bible does not teach it at all (pp. 4-5).

We leave it to some other commentary to analyze what Bible Fox was reading, but noone can dispute Fox's popularity in the 1930's and the persistence of his books, even today. Whatever a reader's views, it seems fair to say that Dr. Bob was quite willing to study and learn from a wide variety of Bible views, including perhaps those with whom he might have disagreed. And now, we will review Jesus's Sermon, chapter by chapter, to locate principal thoughts Dr. Bob and Bill may have had in mind when each said A.A. embodied the Sermon on the Mount's philosphy.

Matthew Chapter 5

1. *The Beatitudes.* The *Beatitudes* are found in Matthew 5:3-11. The word "beatitudes" refers to the first word "Blessed" in each of these verses.[67] *Vine's Expository Dictionary of Old and New Testament Words* explains the word "blessed" as follows:

> In the beatitudes the Lord indicates not only the characters that are blessed, but the nature of that which is the highest good.[68]

We have italicized Webster's definitions for the key words in each verse, quoting also the King James Version, which was the version Dr. Bob and early AAs most used.

The Sermon says: "Blessed" are: (v. 3) the poor (*humble*) in spirit: for theirs is the kingdom of heaven; (v. 4) they that mourn

---

[67] Merriam Webster's says "blessed" means "enjoying the bliss of heaven." It defines "bliss" as "complete happiness. The Greek New Testament word from which "blessed" was translated means, according to Ethelbert Bullinger, a Greek Biblical scholar, "happy." Ethelbert W. Bullinger, *A Critical Lexicon and Concordance to the English and Greek New Testament* (Michigan: Zondervan Publishing House, 1981), p. 104.

[68] W. E. Vine, *Vine's Expository Dictionary of Old and New Testament Words.* Vol. I (New York: Fleming H. Revell, 1981), p. 133.

(*feel or express grief or sorrow*): for they shall be comforted; (v. 5) the meek (*enduring injury with patience and without resentment*); for they shall inherit the earth; (v. 6) they which do hunger and thirst after righteousness (*acting in accord with divine or moral law*): for they shall be filled; (v. 7) the merciful (*compassionate*): for they shall obtain mercy; (v. 8) the pure (*spotless, stainless*) in heart: for they shall see God; (v. 9) the peacemakers: for they shall be called the children of God; (v. 10) they which are persecuted for righteousness' sake: for theirs is the kingdom of heaven; (v. 11) ye when men shall revile you, and persecute you, and shall say all manner of evil against you falsely, for my sake (*end or purpose*): for great is your reward in heaven: for so persecuted they the prophets which were before you.

Did Dr. Bob, Anne, Bill, or Henrietta Seiberling study and draw on these Beatitude verses for A.A.'s recovery program purposes?[69] We do not know. However, Anne Smith spoke in her spiritual journal of the Beatitudes in terms of Christ-like virtues to be cultivated.[70] And *we* certainly see some Beatitude ideas that can also be found in A.A.'s spiritual principles. Following are the Bible ideas, footnoted to Big Book pages emphasizing the same thoughts: (1) Humility;[71] (2) Comfort for the suffering;[72] (3) Patience and tolerance to the end of eliminating resentment;[73] (4) Harmonizing actions with God's will;[74] (5) Compassion, which Webster defines as "sympathetic consciousness of others' distress

---

[69] Dr. Bob and his wife, and Bill and his wife, and Henrietta Seiberling often studied Chambers' *My Utmost for His Highest*. Chambers says at page 207, "the Beatitudes contain the dynamite of the Holy Ghost. . . . The Sermon on the Mount is not a set of rules and regulations: it is a statement of the life we will live when the Holy Spirit is getting His way with us." *The Upper Room* did a study of the Beatitudes in its devotionals for 7/17/38, 7/18/38, 7/19/38, 7/20/38, 7/21/38, 7/22/38.

[70] Dick B., *Anne Smith's Journal*, p. 133.

[71] Big Book, pp. 59, 73.

[72] Big Book, pp. 20, 77, 97.

[73] Big Book, pp. 67, 70, 118.

[74] Big Book, p. 164.

together with a desire to alleviate;"[75] (6) "Cleaning house;"[76] (7) Making peace;[77] (8) Standing for and acting upon spiritual principles because they are God's principles, whatever the cost.[78] We see Twelve Step ideas in the Beatitudes; and A.A. founders probably saw them too.

2. *Letting your light shine.* Matthew 5:13-16 suggest glorifying your Heavenly Father by letting others *see* your good works. That is, "Letting your light shine" does not mean glorifying yourself, but rather glorifying God by letting others see the spiritual *walk in action*—letting them *see* the immediate results of surrender to the Master.[79] These ideas may be reflected in the Big Book's statement: "Our real purpose is to fit ourselves to be of maximum service to God . . ." (p. 77).

3. *The Law of Love in action.* In Matthew 5:17-47, Jesus confirms that the Law of Love fulfills the Old Testament Law. He rejects anger without cause, unresolved wrongs to a brother, quibbling with an adversary, lust and impurity, adultery, retaliation, and hatred of an enemy.[80] Our title *Design for Living* discusses

---

[75] Big Book, p. 159.

[76] In *My Utmost for His Highest*, Chambers wrote: "the pure in heart see God. . . . If we are going to retain personal contact with the Lord Jesus Christ, it will mean there are some things we must scorn to do or to think, some legitimate things we must scorn to touch" (p. 86). Dr. Frank Buchman used the verse "blessed are the pure in heart, for they shall see God" in the context of getting people to change—to "hate sin, confess sin, and forsake sin." See A. J. Russell, *For Sinners Only* (London: Hodder & Stoughton, 1932), p. 63. This was part of the 5 C process of life-changing (As to the Five C's, see Dick B., *Design for Living*, pp. 175-79). For an additional reference to the "pure in heart," see *The Runner's Bible*, at page 77: "The pure in heart see only God . . . only Good, hence their conversation is not of evil, of imperfection, destruction, death; but of things that are perfect, that make for peace and happiness and spiritual growth." See Big Book, pp. 64, 98.

[77] Big Book, p. 103.

[78] Big Book, p. 77.

[79] See *The Upper Room* for 5/2/35, 6/10/38; Holm, *The Runner's Bible*, pp. 74, 77.

[80] See AA of Akron's *Spiritual Milestones*, p. 3.

in some detail many of these ideas as roots of A.A. principles.[81]
So does our next Part on the Oxford Group's contributions to early
A.A. And these verses in Chapter Five of the Sermon may well
have influenced A.A. language which suggests the importance of:
(1) Overcoming resentments;[82] (2) Being willing to make peace
quickly;[83] (3) Making restitution;[84] (4) Avoidance of retaliation
for wrongdoing by others;[85] and (5) Making peace even with
enemies.[86]

---

[81] Dick B., *Design for Living*, pp. 149-297.

[82] Matthew 5:21-22. Verse 22 states: But I say unto you, That whosoever is angry
with his brother without a cause shall be in danger of the judgment: and whosoever shall
say to his brother, Raca [calling their brother names such as "good-for-nothing" in their
resentment] shall be in danger of the council: but whosoever shall say, Thou fool, shall
be in danger of hell fire. See Holm, *The Runner's Bible*, p. 82; *The Upper Room* for
10/18/35; Jones, *The Christ of the Mount*, p. 136.

[83] Matthew 5:25 says: "Agree with thine adversary quickly." Both *The Runners Bible*
(at page 67) and *My Utmost for His Highest* (at page 182) stressed Matthew 5:25 in
connection with making amends. And *My Utmost for His Highest* also referred to
Matthew 5:26—paying "the uttermost farthing"—with regard to the amends concept (p.
183).

[84] Matthew 5:23-24 reads: "Therefore if thou bring thy gift to the altar, and there
rememberest that thy brother hath ought against thee; leave there thy gift before the altar,
and go thy way; first be reconciled to thy brother, and then come and offer thy gift."
Oxford Group and other writers commonly cited this verse in connection with their
writings on restitution. See Clarence I. Benson, *The Eight Points of the Oxford Group*
(London: Humphrey Milford, Oxford University Press, 1936), p. 30; Russell, *For
Sinners Only*, p. 120; Weatherhead, *Discipleship*, p. 113; Macmillan, *Seeking and
Finding*, p. 176; Shoemaker, *The Conversion of the Church*, pp. 47-48; *DR. BOB*, p.
308; Clark, *The Soul's Sincere Desire*, p. 57; *My Utmost for His Highest*, p. 46; E.
Stanley Jones, *The Christ of the Mount*, pp. 133, 140.

[85] Matthew 5:38-41; Verses 38 and 39 say: "Ye have heard that it hath been said,
An eye for an eye, and a tooth for a tooth. But I say unto you, That ye resist not evil:
but whosoever shall smite thee on thy right cheek, turn to him the other also." See
Chambers, *My Utmost for His Highest*, p. 196; Big Book, pp. 62, 77-78.

[86] Matthew 5:43-47; Verses 43 and 44 state: "Ye have heard that it hath been said,
Thou shalt love thy neighbor, and hate thine enemy. But I say unto you, Love your
enemies, bless them that curse you, do good to them that hate you, and pray for them
which despitefully use you, and persecute you." See *The Upper Room* for 5/22/35,
9/13/38; Big Book, pp. 77-78, 103, 135.

Matthew Chapter 6

1. *Anonymity*. Matthew 6:1-8, 16-18—dealing with almsgiving "in secret," praying "in secret," fasting "in secret," avoidance of "vain repetitions," and hypocrisy—may, as we discuss later, have played a role in the development of A.A.'s spiritual principle of anonymity. Jesus said, "your Father knoweth what things ye have need of, before ye ask him" and "thy Father, which seeth in secret, shall reward thee openly." The vain practices Jesus condemned focused on inflation of self—something A.A. disdains.[87] The author has located no direct tie between the teachings of Jesus on anonymity and A.A.'s traditions on this spiritual principle. But the concepts are parallel.[88]

2. *Forgiveness*. Matthew 6:14-15 state:

> For if ye forgive men their trespasses, your heavenly Father will also forgive you: But if ye forgive not men their trespasses, neither will your Father forgive your trespasses.[89]

Emmet Fox made the following emphatic statements; and his thinking may well have influenced the A.A. amends process:

> The forgiveness of sins is the central problem of life. . . . It is, of course, rooted in selfishness. . . . We must positively and definitely extend forgiveness to everyone to whom it is possible that we can owe forgiveness, namely, to anyone who we think can have injured us in any way. . . . When you hold resentment

---

[87] Big Book, p. 62; compare p. 292. See Ernest Kurtz, *Not-God*. Expanded ed. (Minnesota: Hazelden, 1991), pp. 20-21.

[88] Holm, *The Runner's Bible* does discuss these "in secret" verses at some length; see pp. 61-62. See also Clark, *The Soul's Sincere Desire*, pp. 38, 53; Fosdick, *The Meaning of Prayer*, p. 57; Jones, *The Christ of the Mount*, pp. 202-07.

[89] Note this was written to the Judaeans in the Gospel period. A different situation existed *after* Jesus had accomplished redemption—becoming the payment for sin, assuring remission of sins past, and enabling forgiveness of future sins by confessing them to God. See Romans 3:19-30; 8:1-4; Ephesians 2:1-8; 1 John 1:8-9; 2:1-2; 2:12; 3:1-9.

against anyone, you are bound to that person by a cosmic link, a real, tough metal chain. You are tied by a cosmic tie to the thing that you hate. The one person perhaps in the whole world whom you most dislike is the very one to whom you are attaching yourself by a hook that is stronger than steel.[90]

Did Fox's writing on this point influence the Big Book's emphasis on forgiveness? We do not know. But at least two writers did claim that Fox's writings influenced Bill Wilson.[91] Other writers, whose works were read by AAs, used language similar to that used by Fox in his discussion of forgiveness of enemies.[92] But the Sermon on the Mount is not the only place in the New Testament where forgiveness is stressed. Thus, after Christ had accomplished remission of past sins, Paul wrote in Colossians 3:13:

Forbearing one another, and forgiving one another, if any man have a quarrel against any: even as Christ forgave you, so also *do ye*.

Henrietta Seiberling taught her children 1 John 4:20:

If a man say I love God, and hateth his brother, he is a liar: for he that loveth not his brother whom he hath seen, how can he love God whom he hath not seen.[93]

---

[90] Fox, *The Sermon on the Mount*, pp. 183-88. Cp. Big Book, page 66: "It is plain that a life which includes deep resentment leads only to futility and unhappiness. . . . We found that it is fatal. . . . If we were to live, we had to be free of anger. The grouch and the brainstorm were not for us. They may be the dubious luxury of normal men, but for alcoholics these things are poison."

[91] See Mel B., *New Wine*, p. 5; Igor Sikorsky, Jr., *A.A.'s Godparents* (Minnesota: CompCare Publishers, 1990). Compare Dick B., *Design for Living*, pp. 22-24.

[92] See, for example, Clark, *I Will Lift Up Mine Eyes*, p. 32: "Your first duty is to forgive others. Turn to all those who have trespassed against you and forgive them. . . . So, first of all, take up these sins that others have committed against you, and forgive them one by one. Forgive them completely and utterly."

[93] Dick B., *The Akron Genesis*, p. 92; Shoemaker, *The Twelve Steps of AA*, p. 4.

In any event, the Big Book states at page 77:

> The question of how to approach the man we hated will arise. It
> may be he has done us more harm than we have done him and,
> though we may have acquired a better attitude toward him, we are
> still not too keen about admitting our faults. Nevertheless, with a
> person we dislike, we take the bit in our teeth. It is harder to go
> to an enemy than to a friend, but we find it more beneficial to us.
> We go to him in a helpful *and forgiving spirit*, confessing our
> former ill feeling and expressing our regret. Under no condition
> do we criticize such a person or argue. Simply we tell him that
> we will never get over drinking until we have done our utmost to
> straighten out the past (italics added).

3. *The "sunlight of the Spirit?"* Speaking of the futility and
unhappiness in a life which includes deep resentment, the Big
Book presents the interesting idea that "when harboring such
feelings we shut ourselves off from the sunlight of the Spirit."[94]
One often hears this idea quoted in A.A. meetings. Yet its origins
seem unreported and undocumented. Anne Smith referred
frequently in her journal to the verses in 1 John which had to do
with fellowship with God.[95] So did A.A.'s Oxford Group
sources.[96] And the following are the most frequently quoted
verses from 1 John having to do with God as "light" and the
importance of *walking in the light* to have fellowship with Him:

> That which we have seen and heard declare we unto you, that ye
> may have fellowship with us: and truly our fellowship *is* with the
> Father, and with his Son, Jesus Christ. And these things write we
> unto you, that your joy may be full. This then is the message
> which we have heard of him, and declare unto you, that God is
> light, and in him is no darkness at all. If we say that we have

---

[94] Big Book, p. 66.

[95] Dick B., *Anne Smith's Journal*, pp. 71, 120, 130, 145.

[96] Dick B., *Design for Living*, pp. 104, 288-89, 329; Phillimore, *Just for Today*, p.
7; Theophil Spoerri, *Dynamic out of Silence: Frank Buchman's Relevance Today*
(London: Grosvenor Books, 1976), p. 204.

fellowship with him, and walk in darkness, we lie, and do not the truth: But if we walk in the light, as he is in the light, we have fellowship one with another, and the blood of Jesus Christ his Son cleanseth us from all sin (1 John 1:3-7).[97]

We are dealing, in this portion, with the Sermon on the Mount. But we also mention the foregoing verses from 1 John 1:3-7 (having to do with walking in God's light as against walking in darkness). We believe the ideas in 1 John, together with the following verses in the Sermon, may possibly have given rise to Bill's references to the alcoholic's being blocked from the "sunlight of the Spirit" when he or she dwells in such dark realms as excessive anger. Matthew 6:22-24 state:

The light of the body is the eye: if therefore thine eye be single, thy whole body shall be full of light. But if thine eye be evil, thy whole body shall be full of darkness. If therefore the light that is in thee be darkness, how great *is* that darkness! No man can serve two masters: for either he will hate the one, and love the other; or else he will hold to the one, and despise the other. Ye cannot serve God and mammon.

4. *Seek ye first the kingdom of God.* Matthew 6:24-34 seem to have had tremendous influence on A.A. Their substance is that man will be taken care of when he seeks first the kingdom of God and His righteousness. Verse 33 says:

But seek ye first the kingdom of God, and his righteousness; and all these things shall be added unto you.

Dr. Bob specifically explained the origin of A.A.'s slogan "First Things First."[98] When asked the meaning of "First Things First," he replied, "Seek ye first the kingdom of God and His

---

[97] See also Tileston, *Daily Strength for Daily Needs*, p. 165; Holm, *The Runner's Bible*, p. 7.

[98] Big Book, p. 135; *DR. BOB*, p. 192.

righteousness, and all these things shall be added unto you."[99] He told his sponsee Clarence S. that "First Things First" came from Matthew 6:33 in the Sermon on the Mount.[100] And this verse was widely quoted in the books that Dr. Bob and the Akron AAs read and recommended.[101]

On page 60, the Big Book states the A.A. solution to obtaining relief from alcoholism: "God could and would if He were sought." We believe the concept of "seeking" results by reliance on God instead of reliance on self is a bedrock idea in the Big Book.[102] And we believe the concept was much influenced by the "seeking the kingdom of God first" idea in Matthew 6:33.

Matthew Chapter 7

1. *Taking your own inventory.* Much of A.A.'s Fourth, Ninth, Tenth, and Eleventh Step procedures involve looking for your own part, for your own fault, in the house-cleaning and life-changing process which, in Appendix II of the Third Edition of the Big Book, became described as "the personality change sufficient to bring about recovery from alcoholism" (Big Book, p. 569).[103] Matthew 7:3-5 states:

---

[99] *DR. BOB*, p. 144.

[100] Dick B., *That Amazing Grace*, pp. 30, 38. See also AA of Akron, *A Manual for Alcoholics Anonymous*, p. 7.

[101] Russell, *For Sinners Only*, p. 36; Clark, *The Soul's Sincere Desire*, pp. 16, 34; Shoemaker, *National Awakening*, p. 41; *A Young Man's View of the Ministry*, p. 80; Chambers, *My Utmost for His Highest*, p. 142; Holm, *The Runner's Bible*, p. 127; Tileston, *Daily Strength for Daily Needs*, p. 327; Jones, *The Christ of the Mount*, pp. 218-19; Glover, *The Jesus of History*, p. 111; Macmillan, *Seeking and Finding*, p. 226; *The Upper Room* for 9/4/35, 11/19/35, 5/20/37, 12/2/38; Chambers, *Studies in the Sermon on the Mount*, pp. 60-61.

[102] Big Book, pp. 11, 14, 25, 28, 43, 52-53, 57, 62, 68. Page 68 states: "Wasn't it because self-reliance failed us? Self-reliance was good as far as it went, but it didn't go far enough . . . we are now on a different basis; the basis of trusting and relying upon God. We trust infinite God rather than our finite selves."

[103] See the inventory procedures described in the Big Book, at pp. 67, 69-70, 76, 84, 86, 98.

And why beholdest thou the mote [speck] that is in thy brother's eye, but considerest not the beam [log] that is in thine own eye? Or how wilt thou say to thy brother, Let me pull the mote [speck] out of thine eye; and, behold, a beam [log] *is* in thine own eye. Thou hypocrite, first cast out the beam [log] out of thine own eye; and then shalt thou see clearly to cast out the mote [speck] out of thy brother's eye.

These verses were frequently cited by A.A.'s spiritual sources as biblical authority for the requirement of self-examination and finding one's own part, one's own erroneous conduct, in a relationship problem.[104]

2. *Ask, seek, knock.* Matthew 7:7-11 states:

Ask, and it shall be given you; seek, and ye shall find; knock, and it shall be opened unto you;
For every one that asketh receiveth; and he that seeketh findeth; and to him that knocketh it shall be opened.
Or what man is there of you, whom if his son ask bread, will he give him a stone?
Or if he ask a fish, will he give him a serpent?
If ye then, being evil, know how to give good gifts unto your children, how much more shall your Father which is in heaven give good things to them that ask him?

Shoemaker wrote:

Our part [in the crisis of self-surrender] is to ask, to seek, to knock. His [God's] part is to answer, to come, to open.[105]

---

[104] Samuel M. Shoemaker, *God's Control* (New York: Fleming H. Revell, 1939), pp. 62-72; Chambers, *My Utmost for His Highest*, pp. 169, 174; Russell, *For Sinners Only*, pp. 309-16; Geoffrey Allen, *He That Cometh* (New York: The Macmillan Company, 1933), p. 139; Kitchen, *I Was a Pagan*, p. 110-11; Chambers, *Studies in the Sermon on the Mount*, p. 68; Clark, *The Soul's Sincere Desire*, p. 61; Jones, *The Christ of the Mount*, p. 244. See Dick B., *Anne Smith's Journal*, pp. 30-31

[105] Shoemaker, *Realizing Religion*, p. 32; Dick B., *That Amazing Grace*, p. 72.

The Runner's Bible has an entire chapter titled, "Ask and Ye shall receive."[106] *My Utmost for His Highest* says about these verses beginning with Matthew 7:7

> The illustration of prayer that Our Lord uses here is that of a good child asking for a good thing. . . . It is no use praying unless we are living as children of God. Then, Jesus says—"Everyone that asketh receiveth."[107]

The foregoing verses indicate the importance of becoming a child of God, establishing a harmonious relationship with Him, and then expecting good results from the Father. We believe those verses influenced the following, similar ideas in the Big Book:

> If what we have learned and felt and seen means anything at all, it means that all of us, whatever our race, creed, or color are the children of a living Creator with whom we may form a relationship upon simple and understandable terms as soon as we are willing and honest enough to try (p. 28).

> God will constantly disclose more to you and to us. Ask Him in your morning meditation what you can do each day for the man who is still sick. The answers will come, *if your own house is in order*. But obviously you cannot transmit something you haven't got.[108] *See to it that your relationship with Him is right*, and great events will come to pass for you and countless others. This is the Great Fact for us (p. 164, italics added).

In this same vein, Dr. Bob's wife, Anne, had written in her workbook:

---

[106] Holm, *The Runner's Bible*, pp. 59-65. See also *The Upper Room* for 4/8/38; Jones, *The Christ of the Mount*, pp. 256-57; Clark, *I Will Lift Up Mine Eyes*, p. 30.

[107] Chambers, *My Utmost for His Highest*, p. 237. Clarence S. used the verse to assure answers to Seventh Step prayers. See Dick B., *That Amazing Grace*, p. 72.

[108] For the teachings by Dr. Bob's wife and others that "we can't give away what we haven't got," see Dick B., *Anne Smith's Journal*, p. 69; *Design for Living*, p. 362.

We can't give away what we haven't got. We must have a genuine contact with God in our present experience. Not an experience of the past, but an experience in the present—actual, genuine.[109]

3. *"Do unto others."* The so-called "Golden Rule" cannot readily be identified in the Big Book though it is a much-quoted portion of the Sermon on the Mount which Dr. Bob and Bill said underlies A.A.'s philosophy. The relevant verse is Matthew 7:12:

Therefore all things whatsoever ye would that men should do to you, do ye even so to them: for this is the law and the prophets.[110]

Perhaps the following two segments from the Big Book bespeak the philosophy:

We have begun to learn tolerance, patience and good will toward all men, even our enemies, for we look on them as sick people. We have listed the people we have hurt by our conduct, and are willing to straighten out the past if we can (p. 70).

Then you will know what it means to give of yourself that others may survive and rediscover life. You will learn the full meaning of "Love thy neighbor as thyself" (p. 153).

4. *He that doeth the will of my Father.* The author believes that the bottom line, in terms of what A.A. might have derived from the Sermon on the Mount, can be found in Matthew 7:21:

---

[109] Dick B., *Anne Smith's Journal*, p. 121.

[110] See discussion in Clark, *I Will Lift Up Mine Eyes*, p. 45; Jones, *The Christ of the Mount*, p. 295.

Not every one that saith unto me, Lord, Lord, shall enter into the kingdom of heaven; but he that doeth the will of my Father which is in heaven.[111]

Bill Wilson made the major point in the Big Book and in his other writings that the key to success in A.A. was doing the will of the Father—the Father Who is the subject of the Lord's Prayer, and the God upon whom early AAs depended. Wilson wrote:

I was to sit quietly when in doubt, asking only for direction and strength to meet my problems as He would have me (Bill's Story, Big Book, p. 13).

He humbly offered himself to his Maker—then he knew (Big Book, p. 57).

. . . praying only for knowledge of His will for us and the power to carry that out (Step Eleven, Big Book, p. 59).

May I do Thy will always (portion of "Third Step Prayer," Big Book, p. 63)!

Thy will be done (Big Book, pp. 67, 88).

Grant me strength, as I go out from here, to do your bidding. Amen (portion of "Seventh Step Prayer," Big Book, p. 76).

There is God, our Father, who very simply says, "I am waiting for you to do my will" (*Alcoholics Anonymous Comes of Age*, p. 105).

---

[111] See Henry Drummond, *The Ideal Life: Addresses Hitherto Unpublished* (New York: Hodder & Stoughton, 1897), p. 232-43; Wright, *The Will of God*, p. 43; Allen, *He That Cometh*, p. 139; Streeter, *The God Who Speaks*, p. 85; Jones, *The Christ of the Mount*, p. 300; Dick B., *Design for Living*, pp. 162, 259-60, 284; *The Upper Room* for 11/2/37; Fox, *The Sermon on the Mount*, pp. 146-48; Chambers, *Studies in the Sermon on the Mount*, p. 93.

The Thirteenth Chapter of First Corinthians

1 Corinthians 13 is often called the Bible's "love" chapter because it focuses on the importance of love in the Christian's life. In the King James Version, the word "charity" is used, but the underlying Greek word is *agapē*, which is more properly translated "love." And the most significant characteristics of love are found in the following verses:

> Charity [love] suffereth long, *and* is kind; charity envieth not; charity vaunteth not itself, is not puffed up, Doth not behave itself unseemly, seeketh not her own, is not easily provoked, thinketh no evil, Rejoiceth not in iniquity, but rejoiceth in the truth (1 Corinthians 13:4-6).

One of the most popular books in early A.A. was Professor Henry Drummond's study of 1 Corinthians 13.[112] The title of the book, *The Greatest Thing in the World*, was taken from the last verse of the Corinthians chapter, which read:

> And now abideth faith, hope, charity, these three; but the greatest of these *is* charity (1 Corinthians 13:13).[113]

Drummond's book was part of Dr. Bob's library, and a copy is still owned by Dr. Bob's family.[114] A.A. oldtimer Bob E. sent a memo to Bill Wilson's wife, Lois, in which Bob E. listed *The*

---

[112] Henry Drummond, *Addresses* (Philadelphia: Henry Altemus, 1892). Drummond's study of 1 Corinthians 13 has been reprinted many times; and we shall use here for our citations the following popular edition: Henry Drummond, *The Greatest Thing in the World and other addresses* with introduction by J. Y. Simpson (World Bible Publishers, Inc., n.d.). The wide use of Drummond's book in early A.A. is discussed in *DR. BOB*, 1980), pp. 151, 310. See also Dick B., *Anne Smith's Journal*, p. 131; *The Books Early AAs Read for Spiritual Growth*, 4th ed, pp. 1, 7, 9, 32; *Dr. Bob's Library*, pp. xi, 12-14, 18, 21, 41, 43, 53, 60, 64, 82, 92.

[113] See Drummond, *The Greatest Thing in the World*, pp.18-19. See also references in *The Upper Room* for 10/8/35; 9/11/38.

[114] Dick B., *Dr. Bob's Library*, pp. 41-42.

Greatest Thing in the World as one of three books Dr. Bob regularly provided to alcoholics with whom he worked.[115]

Drummond's significant influence on A.A. from 1 Corinthians 13 seems readily discernible from Drummond's own simplified description of love's *ingredients*. Drummond listed nine.[116] Here we set out Drummond's words, then the correlative Bible verses, and then (in the correlative footnote) the parallel A.A. principle:

Drummond's Version of Meaning   *Authorized (King James) Version Language*

1. Patience   "Love suffereth long."[117]
2. Kindness   "And is kind."[118]
3. Generosity   "Love envieth not."[119]
4. Humility   "Love vaunteth not itself, is not puffed up."[120]
5. Courtesy   "Doth not behave itself unseemly."[121]
6. Unselfishness   "Seeketh not her own."[122]
7. Good Temper   "Is not easily provoked."[123]

---

[115] Dick B., *Dr. Bob's Library*, pp. 21. The other two books that were mentioned by Bob E. and regularly provided to alcoholics by Dr. Bob were James Allen's *As a Man Thinketh* and Emmet Fox's *The Sermon on the Mount*.

[116] Drummond, *The Greatest Thing in the World*, pp. 26-27.

[117] See our discussion of "patience" in connection with the Book of James where we cite the frequent occurrences of the *patience* principle in the Big Book.

[118] Big Book, pp. 67, 82, 83, 86.

[119] See our discussion of "envy" and "jealousy" in connection with the Book of James, with citations as to the occurrence of these words and ideas in the Big Book.

[120] See our discussion of "humility" in connection with the Book of James, with citations of the occurrences of this principle in the Big Book.

[121] Drummond said, at page 31: "Courtesy is said to be love in little things." He equated it with being "considerate." And the Big Book stresses this latter principle (p. 69).

[122] "Absolute Unselfishness" was one of the four standards embodied in the Oxford Group's Four Absolutes. And the Big Book specifically decries "selfishness" many times (pp. 62, 69, 84, 86).

[123] Drummond wrote at length on the vice of "ill temper," pointing out that it involved want of patience, want of kindness, want of generosity, want of courtesy, and want of unselfishness. Drummond said all are instantly symbolized in one flash of Temper. Certainly one aspect of such Temper is *lack of tolerance*, And the Big Book
(continued...)

8. Guilelessness   "Thinketh no evil."[124]
9. Sincerity   "Rejoiceth not in iniquity, but rejoiceth in truth."[125]

Dr. Bob believed and stated that A.A.'s steps could be simmered down to love and service.[126] He presented God as a God of love.[127] Dr. Bob's wife, Anne, frequently quoted the "God is love" verses in 1 John 4:8; 4:16.[128] Dr. Bob and Anne both studied Kagawa's book on love.[129] Kagawa devoted an entire chapter of his book not only to 1 Corinthians 13, but also to Drummond's analysis of 1 Corinthians 13 in Drummond's *The Greatest Thing in the World*.[130] And the Big Book itself talks repeatedly of the principle of love.[131]

Jesus Christ's greatest message, as stated in Mark 12:30-31, concerned the two great commandments on love:

---

[123] (...continued)
stressed the principle of tolerance and used the slogan, "Live and let live," to symbolize the importance of tolerance (Big Book, pp. 19, 67, 70, 83-84, 125, 118, 135).

[124] Drummond essentially equates this principle with looking on the bright side, looking for the best in others. Perhaps his analysis equates with A.A. stress on unselfishness, tolerance, and certainly on love.

[125] Here Drummond covered a cardinal A.A. spiritual principle—*honesty*. Honesty was one of the Oxford Group's Four Absolutes; and the principle appears throughout the Big Book as a vital spiritual concept (Big Book, pp. xiv, xxvii, 13, 26, 28, 32, 44, 47, 55, 57-58, 63-65, 67, 70, 73, 117, 140, 145).

[126] *DR. BOB*, p. 338.

[127] *DR. BOB*, p. 110.

[128] *DR. BOB*, pp. 116, 117. See also *The Upper Room* for 5/24/36, 5/4/37, 8/22/37; Holm, *The Runner's Bible*, pp. 6, 27, 29, 31-32. In a telephone conversation held May 23, 1995, Dr. Bob's son, Robert R. Smith, confirmed to the author that *both* Dr. Bob and Anne frequently used *The Runner's Bible* for prayer and meditation; and the pages just cited from *The Runner's Bible* quote 1 John 4:16 and the entirety of 1 Corinthians 13.

[129] Toyohiko Kagawa, *Love The Law of Life* (Philadelphia: The John C. Winston Company, 1929). Dick B., *Dr. Bob's Library*, pp. 40-41; *Anne Smith's Journal*, pp. 83-85.

[130] Kagawa, *Love the Law of Life*, pp. 137-44.

[131] Big Book, pp. 83-84, 86, 118, 122, 153.

And thou shalt love the Lord thy God with all thy heart, and with all thy soul, and with all thy mind, and with all thy strength; this is the first commandment. And the second is like, namely this, Thou shalt love thy neighbor as thyself. There is none other commandment greater than these.[132]

The foregoing verses from Mark were cited for the standard of "Absolute Love," as it was discussed in Akron's *A Manual for Alcoholics Anonymous*, from which we have previously quoted. The Old Testament contained the same commandments.[133]

We believe—from examining 1 Corinthians 13; from the frequent mention of "love" in the Big Book; from studying the reading and remarks of Dr. Bob and Anne; from Bill Wilson's mention of Corinthians, and from the repeated mention of 1 Corinthians 13 in A.A.'s religious sources—that the love ingredients summarized by Henry Drummond probably had a direct impact on Twelve Step principles and Big Book language.[134]

The Twenty-third and Ninety-first Psalms

The Twenty-third and sometimes the Ninety-first Psalms surface as parts of the Bible upon which early AAs were urged to

---

[132] See also Luke 10:27 and Holm, *The Runner's Bible*, p. 27; Harry Emerson Fosdick, *The Meaning of Faith* (New York: The Abingdon Press, 1917), p. 104; Tileston, *Daily Strength for Daily Needs*, p. 205; *The Upper Room* for 5/19/37; Glover, *The Jesus of History*, p. 60.

[133] Deuteronomy 6:5; Leviticus 19:18. See also Streeter, *The God Who Speaks*, pp. 48-49.

[134] See also the discussions in Glenn Clark's books which were read by A.A.'s founders and much used by some of the early AAs. Clark, *The Soul's Sincere Desire*, pp. 69-70; Clark, *I Will Lift Up Mine Eyes*, pp. 65-66; also, Clarence I. Benson, *The Eight Points of the Oxford Group: An Exposition for Christians and Pagans* (London: Oxford University Press, 1936), p. 47.

rely.[135] They often were discussed in A.A.'s source books.[136] Both Psalms speak eloquently and emphatically of the loving and delivering qualities of God. Consider, for example, the Twenty-third Psalm:

> The Lord *is* my shepherd; I shall not want. He maketh me to lie down in green pastures: he leadeth me beside the still waters. He restoreth my soul: he leadeth me in the paths of righteousness for His name's sake. Yea, though I walk through the valley of the shadow of death, I will fear no evil: for thou *art* with me; thy rod and thy staff they comfort me. Thou preparest a table before me in the presence of mine enemies: thou anointest my head with oil; my cup runneth over. Surely goodness and mercy shall follow me all the days of my life: and I will dwell in the house of the Lord forever.

The author has yet to locate historical references either to Psalm 23 or to Psalm 91 that specify how early AAs used these Psalms. But the following passages from the First Edition of the Big Book seem indicative of the importance early AAs placed upon trusting God Almighty:

> Sometimes we think fear ought to be classed with stealing. It seems to cause more trouble. We reviewed our fears thoroughly. . . . We asked ourselves why we had them. Wasn't it because self-reliance failed us? . . . Perhaps there is a better way—we think so. For we are now on a different basis; the basis of trusting and relying upon God. We trust infinite God rather than our finite selves. . . . We never apologize to anyone for depending upon our Creator. We can laugh at those who think spirituality the way

---

[135] See *A Manual for Alcoholics Anonymous*, 6th rev. ed. (Akron, OH: A.A. of Akron, 1989), p. 8; Wally P., *But, for the Grace of God . . . How Intergroups and Central Offices Carried the Message of Alcoholics Anonymous in the 1940's* (West Virginia: The Bishop of Books, 1995), p. 44; Dick B., *The Good Book and The Big Book*, p. 16-17; Dick B., *That Amazing Grace*, pp. 23, 40, 41, 96, 97.

[136] Phillimore, *Just for Today*, p. 29; Holm, *The Runner's Bible*, p. 132; *The Upper Room* for 7/1/38.

of weakness.[137] . . . All men of faith have courage. They trust their God (pp. 80-81).[138]

We see in many segments of the Big Book's First Edition, including the phrases quoted above, a very clear call to rely upon God. It seems quite probable that the promises and assurances given in Psalm 23 and Psalm 91 helped arm the seemingly hopeless early AAs with the wherewithal to be delivered from alcoholism and from all of their problems.

---

[137] Note how the Big Book equates "spirituality" with "depending upon our Creator."
[138] See also Big Book, 3rd ed., pp. 110-11, 112, 115.

6

Biblical Impact on Big Book Language

Now to some of the Bible's direct impact on A.A. language in the Big Book and elsewhere.

Direct Quotes from the Bible

Even today's Third Edition of the Big Book contains a number of direct quotes from the King James Version of the Bible early AAs used. The following direct quotes can be found in the basic text portion of the Big Book:

1. Thy will be done.[1]
2. Thy will (not mine) be done.[2]
3. Love thy neighbor as thyself.[3]

---

[1] Big Book, pp. 67, 88; compare p. 443; From a portion of the Lord's Prayer in the Sermon on the Mount—Matthew 6:10.

[2] Big Book, p. 85; and compare "Thy will be done, not mine," pp. 229, 381. As rendered in the King James Version, Luke 22:42: "nevertheless not my will, but thine, be done."

[3] Big Book, p. 153; compare p. 236; Leviticus 19:18; Matthew 19:19; 22:39; Mark 12:31; Romans 13:9; Galatians 5:14; James 2:8. (and compare Luke 10:27; and Matthew 5:43).

4.   Faith without works is dead.[4]
5.   Father of Light.[5]

Recognizable Biblical Words and Concepts

The following words and ideas, though not necessarily verbatim quotes from the Bible, are firmly embedded in A.A. and have specific sources in the Bible and in the books Dr. Bob studied and recommended. In the footnotes, we list a reference to the expression in A.A. literature, then to the biblical source(s), and finally to books in Dr. Bob's library where they are discussed.

1.   God.[6]
2.   God is.[7]
3.   God is love.[8]
4.   God-sufficiency.[9]
5.   Creator.[10]
6.   Maker.[11]

---

[4] Big Book, pp. 76, 88; compare pp. 14, 473; James 2:20, 26 (compare James 2:14, 17).

[5] Big Book, p. 14 [*sic*]; the biblical text reads: "Father of lights". See James 1:17.

[6] Big Book (Over 200 specific, unqualified references to God); Genesis 1:1; Harold Begbie, *Life Changers* (London: Mills and Boon, Ltd., 1923), pp. 47-48.

[7] Big Book, p. 53; Hebrews 11:6; Samuel M. Shoemaker, Jr., *The Gospel According to You* (New York: Fleming H. Revell, 1934), p. 47; *Confident Faith*, p. 187.

[8] Dick B., *The Akron Genesis*, p. 121; Kurtz, *Not-God*, p. 55; 1 John 4:8; 4:16; Holm, *The Runner's Bible*, p. 6; Streeter, *The God Who Speaks*, p. 104; Clark, *I Will Lift Up Mine Eyes*, pp. 79, 89, 93, 132; Tileston, *Daily Strength for Daily Needs*, p. 139; *The Upper Room* for 5/24/36, 5/4/37, 8/27/37.

[9] Big Book, pp. 52-53; 2 Corinthians 3:5; 9:8. 2 Cor. 3:5 states: "Not that we are sufficient of ourselves to think any thing as of ourselves; but our sufficiency *is* of God." Samuel M. Shoemaker, Jr., *If I Be Lifted Up* (New York: Fleming H. Revell, 1931), p. 107; Holm, *The Runner's Bible*, p. 138.

[10] Big Book, pp. 13, 25, 28, 56, 68, 72, 75, 76, 80, 83, 158, 161; Isaiah 40:28; (compare Genesis 1:1); Begbie, *Life Changers*, p. 20.

[11] Big Book, pp. 57, 63; compare p. 525; Psalm 95:6—"O come, let us worship and bow down: let us kneel before the Lord our maker." We found no correlative Oxford Group source; so Bill and Dr. Bob may have taken this directly from the Bible.

7. Father.[12]
8. Spirit.[13]
9. Honesty ("Absolute Honesty").[14]
10. Unselfishness ("Absolute Unselfishness").[15]
11. Love ("Absolute Love").[16]
12. Patience.[17]

---

[12] Big Book, p. 62; Matthew 5:45—"That ye may be the children of your Father which is in heaven: . . ."; Philip Marshall Brown, *The Venture of Belief* (New York: Fleming H. Revell, 1935), p. 25; Clark, *The Soul's Sincere Desire*, p. 8.

[13] Big Book, p. 46 ("the Realm of Spirit"); p. 66 ("the sunlight of the Spirit"); p. 84 ("the world of the Spirit"); p. 85 ("the flow of His Spirit into us"); p. 164 ("the Fellowship of the Spirit"); John 4:24—"God *is* a Spirit: and they that worship him must worship *him* in spirit and in truth."; Holm, *The Runner's Bible*, pp. 16-19; Streeter, *The God Who Speaks*, pp. 109-10.

[14] Big Book, pp. 13, 28, 32, 57-58, 63-65, 67, 70, 73, 83, 145; Matthew 5:33-37; Philippians 4:8; Ephesians 4:25—"Wherefore putting away lying, speak every man truth with his neighbour: for we are members one of another."; *Pass It On*, p. 114; *The Language of the Heart*, p. 200; *The Co-founders of Alcoholics Anonymous*, p. 13; Robert E. Speer, *The Principles of Jesus* (New York: Association Press, 1902), p. 35; Wright, *The Will of God*, p. 187; *What Is The Oxford Group?*, pp. 73-83; Russell, *For Sinners Only*, pp. 320-21; Samuel M. Shoemaker, Jr., *Twice-Born Ministers* (New York: Fleming H. Revell, 1929), p. 150; Clark, *I Will Lift Up Mine Eyes*, pp. 54-60.

[15] Big Book, pp. xxv, 93, 127; Matthew 5:41-42; 16:24-26; Philippians 2:4-8 (verse 4 states: "Look not every man on his own things, but every man also on the things of others."); *Co-Founders*, p. 13; Stephen Foot, *Life Began Yesterday* (New York: Harper & Brothers, 1935), pp. 47, 57, 80; Speer, *The Principles of Jesus*, p. 35; Wright, *The Will of God*, p. 197; Russell, *For Sinners Only*, pp. 324-29.

[16] Big Book, pp. 83-84, 86, 153, 118; 1 Corinthians 13; Matthew 5:43-46 (these verses state: "Ye have heard that it hath been said, Thou shalt love thy neighbour, and hate thine enemy. But I say unto you, Love your enemies, bless them that curse you, do good to them that hate you, and pray for them which despitefully use you, and persecute you; That ye may be the children of your Father which is in heaven: for he maketh his sun to rise on the evil and on the good, and sendeth rain on the just and on the unjust. For if ye love them which love you, what reward have ye? do not even the publicans the same?"); *What is the Oxford Group?*, pp. 107-08; Henry Drummond, *Addresses* (Philadelphia: Henry Altemus, 1892), pp. 11-20, 31-33; Helen Smith Shoemaker, *I Stand by the Door: The Life of Sam Shoemaker* (Texas: Word Books, 1967), p. 24; *Co-Founders*, p. 13; *The Upper Room* for 5/22/35, 9/13/38.

[17] Big Book, pp. 67, 70, 83, 111, 163; 1 Corinthians 13:4; James 1:3-4; Hebrews 10:36; Drummond, *The Greatest Thing in the World*, pp. 28-30; Tileston, *Daily Strength for Daily Needs*, p. 32; *The Upper Room* for 4/24/36 or 4/24/39.

13. Tolerance.[18]
14. Kindness.[19]
15. Forgiveness.[20]
16. Restitution (Amends).[21]
17. Grudges.[22]
18. Self-examination (Step Four).[23]
19. Admission of shortcomings or wrongs (Step Five).[24]
20. Setting things right with your brother (Steps Eight and Nine).[25]

---

[18] Big Book, pp. 19, 67, 70, 83-84, 118, 125; *Co-Founders*, pp. 4-5; 1 Corinthians 13:5; Drummond, *The Greatest Thing in the World*, pp. 28, 39-46.

[19] Big Book, pp. 67, 82, 83, 86; Ephesians 4:32; 1 Corinthians 13:4; Holm, *The Runner's Bible*, p. 66; Drummond, *The Greatest Thing in the World*, pp. 28, 30-33; *The Upper Room* for 12/26/35.

[20] Big Book, pp. 77, 79, 86; Matthew 6:14-15; Luke 17:3-4; Colossians 3:13 (Col. 3:13 states: "Forbearing one another, and forgiving one another, if any man have a quarrel against any: even as Christ forgave you, so also *do* ye."); Fox, *The Sermon on the Mount*, pp. 183-91; Holm, *The Runner's Bible*, pp. 82-83, 88.

[21] Big Book, p. xvi; compare p. 292; see also pp. 76-83; Numbers 5:6-7; Russell, *For Sinners Only*, pp. 119-35; *What is The Oxford Group?* pp. 55-65.

[22] Big Book, p. 65; James 5:9 (Jas. 5:9 states: "Grudge not one against another, brethren, lest ye be condemned: behold, the judge standeth before the door."); Shoemaker, *Twice-Born Ministers*, p. 182; Begbie, *Life Changers*, p. 38; Macmillan, *Seeking and Finding*, pp. 96-98.

[23] Big Book, pp. 64-71, 76, 84, 86, 98; Matt. 7:3-5 (verse 5 says, in part: ". . . [F]irst cast out the beam out of thine own eye: . . ."); Chambers, *My Utmost for His Highest*, pp. 169, 174; Kitchen, *I Was a Pagan*, pp. 110-11; Russell, *For Sinners Only*, pp. 309-16; Allen, *He That Cometh*, p. 140; Samuel M. Shoemaker, Jr., *The Church Can Save the World*, 2d ed. (New York: Harper & Brothers, 1938), pp. 81-121; Dick B., *Anne Smith's Journal*, pp. 30-31.

[24] Big Book, pp. 72-75; James 5:16 (Jas. 5:16 states, in part: "Confess *your* faults one to another, and pray one for another. . . ."); *What Is The Oxford Group?*, p. 29; Samuel M. Shoemaker, Jr., *The Conversion of the Church* (New York: Fleming H. Revell, 1932), pp. 35-39; *The Upper Room* for 12/4/35; Dick B., *Anne Smith's Journal*, pp. 36-41.

[25] Big Book Steps Eight and Nine; Matthew 5:23-26; *DR. BOB*, p. 308; Russell, *For Sinners Only*, p. 120; Leslie D. Weatherhead, *Discipleship* (London: Student Christian Movement, 1934), p. 113; Macmillan, *Seeking and Finding*, p. 176; Shoemaker, *The Conversion of the Church*, pp. 47-48; Holm, *The Runner's Bible*, p. 67; Chambers, *My*

(continued...)

21. Guidance of God (Step Eleven—"prayer and meditation").[26]
22. Witnessing (Step Twelve—"passing it on").[27]
23. Trust in God.[28]
24. Draw near to God, and He will draw near to you.[29]
25. Humble yourself.[30]

---

[25] (...continued)
Utmost for His Highest, pp. 182-83; *The Upper Room* for 1/12/36 or 1/12/39; Jones, *The Christ of the Mount*, p. 140.

[26] There are a host of Bible verses connected with this principle. For a discussion of the Big Book materials, the Bible verses, and the roots sources, see Dick B., *New Light on Alcoholism*, pp. 66-67; *Design for Living*, pp. 221-36, 246-69; *The Akron Genesis*, pp. 274-75; *Anne Smith's Journal*, pp. 53-64, 107-16; *The Good Book and The Big Book*, pp. 151-59; and *Good Morning!*, pp. 59-64.

[27] Again, there are a host of Bible verses connected with the idea of witnessing. Such verses as (1) Matthew 4:19, containing Jesus's suggestion that his disciples become "fishers of men" (See Shoemaker, *Realizing Religion*, p. 82); (2) 2 Corinthians 5:20, containing Paul's writings about being "ambassadors for Christ" (See *The Upper Room* for 8/28/38; *What Is The Oxford Group?*, p. 35); (3) Acts 1:8: "and ye shall be witnesses unto me both in Jerusalem, and in all Judaea, and in Samaria, and unto the uttermost part of the earth" (See Dick B., *Design for Living*, pp. 293-297; *New Light on Alcoholism*, p. 68, for references to A.A. root sources; also *The Upper Room* for 4/11/35). The A.A. expression "pass it on" could well have originated in the following witnessing challenge by Oxford Group founder, Dr. Frank N. D. Buchman, who said: "The best way to keep an experience of Christ is to pass it on" (Frank N. D. Buchman, *Remaking the World: The Speeches of Frank N. D. Buchman*. London: Blandford Press, 1961, p. x).

[28] Big Book, pp. 68, 98; Jeremiah 17:5-8; Proverbs 3:5 (Prov. 3:5 states: "Trust in the Lord with all thine heart; and lean not unto thine own understanding."); Dick B., *Dr. Bob's Library*, pp. 96-97; Holm, *The Runner's Bible*, pp. 41-45, 126; *The Upper Room* for 5/15/35; 10/17/35; Tileston, *Daily Strength for Daily Needs*, p. 31. Shoemaker wrote: "People [who] have 'got something' . . . believe in and trust God. They generally trust God as they have come to know Him in Christ." See Shoemaker, *Religion That Works*, pp. 24-25.

[29] Big Book, p. 57; James 4:8 (James 4:8 states: "Draw nigh to God, and he will draw nigh to you. Cleanse *your* hands, *ye* sinners; and purify *your* hearts, *ye* double minded."); *What Is The Oxford Group?*, p. 17; Chambers, *My Utmost for His Highest*, p. 309.

[30] Big Book, pp. 13, 57, 68; 1 Peter 5:5, 6; James 4:7, 10 (verse 10 states: "Humble yourselves in the sight of the Lord, and he shall lift you up."); Holm, *The Runner's Bible*, pp. 59, 81, 94. Speaking of humility, Dr. Bob said: "I'm talking about the attitude of each and every one of us toward our Heavenly Father. Christ said, 'Of Myself, I am

(continued...)

26.   Seek ye first the Kingdom of God.[31]
27.   Good Samaritan.[32]

A.A. Slogans and Watchwords with Biblical Roots

Either from Dr. Bob's own explanations, from specific religious literature read by early AAs, or from the nature of the language itself, one can readily identify biblical concepts in some well-known A.A. slogans and watchwords:

1.   First Things First.[33]
2.   One day at a time.[34]

---

[30] (...continued)
nothing—My strength cometh from My Father in heaven.' If He had to say that, how about you and me?" *Co-founders*, pp. 14-15. Cp. John 5:19, 30; 8:28—which seem to contain the ideas to which Dr. Bob referred.

[31] Big Book, p. 60; compare p. 135; Matthew 6:33; *DR. BOB*, p. 144; Shoemaker, *National Awakening*, p. 42; *The Upper Room* for 9/4/35; 11/19/35; 5/20/37; 12/2/38; Chambers, *Studies in the Sermon on the Mount*, 4th ed., pp. 60-61; Dick B., *Anne Smith's Journal*, p. 132; *That Amazing Grace*, pp. 30, 38.

[32] Big Book, p. 97; Luke 10:33-37.

[33] Big Book, p. 135; Matthew 6:33. Dr. Bob stated specifically that "First Things First" came from "Seek ye first the Kingdom of God" in the Sermon on the Mount. See *DR. BOB*, pp. 144, 192. The phrase "First Things First" can also be found in Oxford Group writings such as Walter, *Soul Surgery*, 6th ed., p. 25; Macmillan, *Seeking and Finding*, p. 17. See also AA of Akron, *A Manual for Alcoholics Anonymous*, p. 7.

[34] Matthew 6:34: "Take therefore no thought [be not anxious] for the morrow: for the morrow shall take thought for the things of itself. Sufficient unto the day *is* the evil thereof." The popular A.A. idea ("one day at a time") was specifically taught by Dr. Bob's wife, Anne Smith, in her journal. See Dick B., *Anne Smith's Journal*, pp. 50, 53-54, 59, 62-63, 134. Dr. Bob stated that the A.A. expression "Easy Does It" means "you take it a day at a time;" *DR. BOB*, p. 282. And Dr. Bob informed his sponsee, Clarence Snyder, that the concept of "one day at a time" came from Matthew 6:34 in the Sermon on the Mount. Mitch K., Clarence's A.A. sponsee, provided the information about Matthew 6:34 to the author in a personal interview in Charleston, West Virginia, in August, 1992. See also *The Upper Room* for 11/25/35; 8/17/37; 9/26/38; 6/19/36 or 6/19/39; AA of Akron, *A Manual for Alcoholics Anonymous*, p. 18.

3. But for the grace of God.[35]
4. Easy Does It.[36]
5. Let go and let God.[37]

Two Other Biblical Concepts

There are two other important concepts found in A.A. history and traditions that also seem to have biblical roots.

The Erring Tongue

The first concerns the idea of "guarding that erring member, the tongue." James 3:1-13 discusses at some length the trouble that the tongue can cause. In a major A.A. address, Dr. Bob cautioned AAs about the hurtful use of the tongue.[38] Dr. Bob's wife, Anne,

---

[35] Big Book, p. 25; Luke 2:40; Acts 11:23; Romans 5:15; 2 Corinthians 1:12. AAs are very familiar with the Biblical expression—the Grace of God—which connotes that their recovery appears neither to have been deserved nor earned, but rather came to them as a gift because of the love of a gracious God. Anne Smith wrote, for example: "Takes whole power of Christ to help us do the smallest thing. Step that puts man in position to receive Grace of God who alone commands;" Dick B., *Anne Smith's Journal*, p. 24. Bill Wilson wrote: "We knew that ours was a fellowship of the Spirit and that the grace of God was there;" *A.A. Comes of Age*, p. 44. Dr. Bob said: "I don't believe I have any right to get cocky about getting sober. It's only through God's grace that I did it." *Co-founders*, p. 15.

[36] Big Book, p. 135; Matthew 6:34. As discussed above in connection with "one day at a time," Dr. Bob explained to his sponsee, Clarence Snyder, that "Easy Does It" and "One day at a time" were synonymous in their meaning; and that Matthew 6:34 was the source of the expression; see also Dick B., *The Akron Genesis*, p. 118.

[37] That "let go and let God" is an expression commonly heard in A.A. is beyond doubt. The author has personally heard it many times in A.A. meetings. See also Bill Wilson's use of the expression in *A. A. Comes of Age*, p. 48. But the biblical origins, if any, are less clear. The expression was common among A.A.'s religious sources. See Benson, *The Eight Points of the Oxford Group*, p. 68; Clark, *The Soul's Sincere Desire*, p. 60. The expression's closest biblical relative can perhaps be found in Shoemaker's *National Awakening* where Shoemaker utilized the Moffatt translation of Psalm 46:10. Shoemaker said we need to "give in," and admit that God is God, and self is not God (pp. 45-51).

[38] *Co-Founders*, p. 5; *DR. BOB*, p. 338.

was also concerned about the hurtfulness of the loose tongue; for she spoke of the problem several times in her spiritual journal.[39] And the admonitions in the Book of James were noticed by other A.A. roots sources.[40]

The Principle of Anonymity

We have located no A.A. writings which credit the all important anonymity principle of Alcoholics Anonymous to the Bible. Yet Dr. Bob and Bill W. certainly felt A.A. embodied the philosophy of the Sermon on the Mount; and Bill Wilson claimed anonymity to be a vital A.A. a spiritual principle.

A.A.'s Eleventh and Twelfth Traditions in the "long form" state in part:

> Our relations with the general public should be characterized by personal anonymity. We think A.A. ought to avoid sensational advertising. . . . There is never need to praise ourselves. We feel it better to let our friends recommend us. And finally, we of Alcoholics Anonymous believe that the principle of anonymity has an immense spiritual significance.[41]

In his Sermon on the Mount, Jesus repeatedly proclaimed a principle of anonymity, and in several ways. In Matthew 6:1, Jesus said:

> Take heed that ye do not your alms before men, to be seen of them; otherwise ye have no reward of your Father which is in heaven.

Jesus then denounced as hypocrites those who did their alms in public and who "sound a trumpet before thee . . . that they may

---

[39] Dick B., *Anne Smith's Journal*, pp. 28, 44, 76, 77.

[40] Tileston, *Daily Strength for Daily Needs*, p. 324; Walter, *Soul Surgery*, p. 62.

[41] Big Book, pp. 567-68.

have the glory of men." He said alms should be given in secret and that God, who sees in secret, will reward openly.[42]

Jesus took the same position as to prayer, denouncing those who "love to pray standing in the synagogues and in the corners of the streets, that they may be seen of men." He told his followers to enter into a closet and pray to the Father in secret.[43] He also cautioned against "vain repetitions" [as to prayers], saying "your Father knoweth what things ye have need of, before ye ask him."[44] Then Jesus taught his followers the Lord's Prayer (Matthew 6:9-13).

Jesus concluded his anonymity teaching by declaring that "fasting" should also be done in secret to avoid hypocrisy.[45] In other words, Jesus devoted a large segment of his Sermon on the Mount to the proposition that people should not be showing off before men in their almsgiving, prayers, and fasting, but rather should address themselves to God for such purpose as God may have for such actions. And many of A.A.'s root sources discuss these biblical principles at some length.[46]

Bill Wilson said of the anonymity principles in A.A.'s Traditions Eleven and Twelve:

So the Eleventh Tradition stands sentinel over the lifelines, announcing that there is no need for self-praise . . . no press agents, no promotional devices, no big names. . . . One may say that anonymity is the spiritual base, the sure key to all the rest of our Traditions. It has come to stand for prudence and, most importantly, for self-effacement. . . . In it we see the cornerstone of our security as a movement; at a deeper spiritual level it points

---

[42] Matthew 6:1-4.

[43] Matthew 6:5-6.

[44] Matthew 6:7-8. See Dick B., *Anne Smith's Journal*, p. 57 [the verse is erroneously cited as Matthew 6:33 in that title].

[45] Matthew 6:16-18.

[46] *The Upper Room* for 5/11/35; 8/22/35; 10/21/35; 7/25/37; 6/26/38; Holm, *The Runner's Bible*, pp. 61-62; E. Stanley Jones, *The Christ of the Mount*, pp. 200, 203, 206; Fosdick, *The Meaning of Prayer*, p. 57; Clark, *The Soul's Sincere Desire*, pp. 38-39, 54-54.

us to still greater self-renunciation. . . . Our AA Traditions are, we trust, securely anchored in those wise precepts: charity, gratitude, and humility. Nor have we forgotten *prudence*. May these virtues ever stand clear before us in our meditations; may Alcoholics Anonymous serve God in happy unison for so long as he may need us.[47]

While Bill did not, in these phrases, tie self-effacement and self-renunciation to worship of God, he did speak of the end of serving God; and Bill's Twelve Steps and Twelve Traditions certainly do rest on the idea of surrender of self to God. We believe, therefore, that the principles of anonymity Jesus taught were probably a cornerstone of the self-effacement ideas in A.A.'s Traditions— considering A.A.'s own emphasis on the Sermon on the Mount as embodying its spiritual philosophy.

---

[47] *The Language of the Heart*, pp. 91-94.

7

The Good Book and the Twelve Steps

Both Bill Wilson and Dr. Bob pointed to sources outside of A.A. for the roots of its spiritual ideas.

As we have said, Bill stated many times and in many ways: Nobody invented Alcoholics Anonymous. . . . Everything in A.A. is borrowed from somewhere else. . . . every one of them [A.A.'s principles] has been borrowed from ancient sources. Dr. Bob was equally clear that A.A.'s basic ideas came from the AAs' study of the Bible. Yet neither Bill nor Dr. Bob gave specifics as to the verses, commentaries, or teachers (other than Shoemaker) from which or from whom their biblical ideas had been taken.

At this point in our research, however, we believe it possible to review all the sources that were read, listened to, and discussed by Dr. Bob, Bill, and the others in early A.A. and have a fairly good picture of what they took from the Bible. Our previous titles have already covered in great depth the biblical A.A. ideas that seem to have originated with Sam Shoemaker, the Oxford Group, Henrietta Seiberling, and Dr. Bob's wife, Anne.[1]

---

[1] Details on other A.A. sources are covered in Dick B., *New Light on Alcoholism: The A.A. Legacy from Sam Shoemaker*; *The Akron Genesis of Alcoholics Anonymous*; *Anne Smith's Journal: A.A.'s Principles of Success*; *Design for Living: The Oxford Group's Contribution to A.A.*; *Dr. Bob's Library: Books for Twelve Step Growth*; *The Books Early AAs Read for Spiritual Growth*, 4th ed; *That Amazing Grace: The Role of*
(continued...)

But the major problem in trying to *pinpoint* A.A.'s biblical roots has to do with the difference between parallel language and borrowed language. Several writers and publishers have presented parallels between A.A. language and language found in the Bible.[2] But our concern is historical. We wish to pinpoint parallels between A.A. language and biblical language *only* where the A.A. language appears actually to have been borrowed from the Bible. To do this, we frequently refer to the daily Bible devotionals, the general Christian literature of early A.A. days, Sam Shoemaker's teachings, and the Oxford Group writings to which early AAs were regularly exposed. We cannot always be sure that early AAs took a specific idea from a specifically quoted source; but we can say that AAs frequently used the named source and that the source relied on the biblical segments to which we refer.

We are concerned with what early AAs used that worked, not with what some writer or publisher believes AAs *should have* taken from the Bible. Nor with what they *can take*. For A.A.'s own successful approach was to describe steps that were *taken* and the experiences that *occurred* by following the recovery program AAs borrowed from medicine, religion, and their own experience.

---

[1] (...continued)
Clarence and Grace S. in Alcoholics Anonymous; and *Good Morning!: Quiet Time, Morning Watch, Meditation, and early A.A.* Publishing data on these titles will be found in our bibliography.

[2] See, for example, Dr. Robert Hemfelt and Dr. Richard Fowler, *Serenity: A Companion for Twelve Step Recovery* (Nashville, Thomas Nelson Publishers, 1990); Paul Barton Doyle, *In Step with God: A Scriptural Guide for Practicing 12 Step Programs* (Tennessee: New Directions, 1989). Typical also of this approach are letters which came the author's way in 1995 in which two different correspondents likened the Steps to: (1) "a 5,000 year old Hebrew prayer called 'A Psalm for Serenity,' based on Psalm XIX;" and (2) "John Wesley's Decisions of Wholeness." See also Dr. Cal Chambers, *Two Tracks-One Goal: How Alcoholics Anonymous Relates to Christianity* (Langley, B.C.: Credo Publishing Corporation, 1992); Martin M. Davis, *The Gospel and the Twelve Steps: Developing a Closer Relationship with Jesus* (Sam Diego, CA: RPI Publishing, 1993).

Then to let others decide for themselves what they, as individuals, wish to do in furthering their own religious growth.[3]

We will now discuss each of the Twelve Steps AAs took to recover; and we will examine each Step in terms of relevant Bible verses AAs studied and/or the Biblical sources to which they were exposed as they put the Steps together.

Step One and Deflation at Depth

[Step One: We admitted we were powerless over alcohol—that our lives had become unmanageable.][4]

A.A.'s medical mentor, Dr. William D. Silkworth, chief psychiatrist at Towns Hospital in New York, and the man who treated Bill Wilson as Bill sought and attained recovery, said:

Men and women drink essentially because they like the effect produced by alcohol. The sensation is so elusive that, while they admit it is injurious, they cannot after a time differentiate the true from the false. To them, their alcoholic life seems the only normal one. They are *restless, irritable and discontented*, unless they can again experience the sense of ease and comfort which comes at once by taking a few drinks—drinks which they see others taking with impunity.

Sam Shoemaker often wrote of a much deeper, spiritual problem causing irritability and discontent in most people of that day. Shoemaker's first title said:

---

[3] Big Book, p. 28: "We think it no concern of ours what religious bodies our members identify themselves with as individuals. This should be an entirely personal affair which each one decides for himself in light of past associations or his present choice."

[4] In this chapter and elsewhere in our book, *The Twelve Steps of Alcoholics Anonymous* are reprinted with permission of Alcoholics Anonymous World Services, Inc.

The modern mind is restless and easily bored. It is also intensely individualistic. . . . There has always been a large amount of unhappiness in the world, but it seems as if our modern America had got more than its share. Look at the sheer irritability you can find in any city you know! Can you count off half a dozen really happy, really peaceful people whom you know? So many "problems," so many "complex situations." Now the thing which is striking about much of the misery one sees is that it is *spiritual misery.*[5]

Bill Wilson seemed to cover this same religious territory when he wrote the following in A.A.'s Big Book:

[W]e have been not only mentally and physically ill, we have been *spiritually sick.* When the *spiritual malady* is overcome, we straighten out mentally and physically.[6]

There was, felt A.A.'s founders, a spiritual problem underlying the alcohol problem.[7] Bill wrote in 1960:

Of course, we have since found that these awful conditions of mind and body invariably bring on the third phase of our malady. This is the sickness of the spirit; a sickness for which there must necessarily be a spiritual remedy. We AAs recognize this in the first five words of Step Twelve of the recovery program. Those words are: "Having had a spiritual awakening. . . ." Here we name the remedy for our threefold sickness of body, mind and soul. Here we declare the necessity for that all-important spiritual awakening.[8]

The spiritual problem, as Shoemaker characterized it, was estrangement from, and lack of contact with, God through Christ.[9]

---

[5] Shoemaker, *Realizing Religion*, pp. 2-9.

[6] Big Book, p. 64 (italics added).

[7] Kurtz, *Not-God*, pp. 45, 199, 204, 381-82.

[8] *The Language of the Heart*, p. 297.

[9] See footnote 5.

Our question concerns the biblical roots, if any, from which A.A.'s sources identified the spiritual problem—a problem epitomized by the Big Book's cry that there was a need for the seemingly hopeless alcoholic to find God. And to find Him *now*.[10]

Some of the early AAs (including Dr. Bob), and a good many religious writers of that day, read and quoted *The Confessions of St. Augustine*.[11] Augustine wrote, "Thou madest us for Thyself, and our heart is restless, until it repose in Thee."[12] This idea struck several of A.A.'s root source writers as the real spiritual problem, for they frequently quoted the foregoing statement by Augustine.[13] Sam Shoemaker added—in connection with this Augustine quote: "The emptiness, loneliness, homesickness, wistfulness, wonderment which all men feel at some time is a hollow place in the human soul that God is meant to fill."[14]

Dr. Leslie D. Weatherhead—whose titles were read by many early AAs, including Henrietta Seiberling and Bill Wilson—quoted Job 23:2-3 to describe man's despairing need to find God:

Even to day *is* my complaint bitter: my stroke is heavier than my groaning. Oh that I knew where I might find him! *that* I might come *even* to his seat![15]

In a book read by many early AAs, Dr. Harry Emerson Fosdick quoted Psalm 55:1-5 in describing man's plight without God's listening ear:

---

[10] See the comment by Fosdick in *The Meaning of Faith*, p. 36: "*Men never really find God until they need him*; and some men never feel the need of him until life plunges them into a shattering experience (italics in original)."

[11] See Dick B., *Dr. Bob's Library*, p. 25; and *The Confessions of St. Augustine*, trans. by E. B. Pusey (New York: A Cardinal Edition, Pocket Books, 1952).

[12] *The Confessions*, p. 1.

[13] See Harold Begbie, *Twice-Born Men* (New York: Fleming H. Revell, 1909), p. 263; Shoemaker, *National Awakening*, p. 46; Glover, *The Jesus of History*, pp. 97, 121; compare Fox, *The Sermon on the Mount*, pp. 111, 175.

[14] Shoemaker, *National Awakening*, p. 46.

[15] Leslie D. Weatherhead, *How Can I Find God?* (London: Hodder & Stoughton, 1933), p. 1. See also *The Upper Room* for 7/2/35.

Give ear to my prayer, O God; and hide not thyself from my supplication. Attend unto me, and hear me: I mourn in my complaint, and make a noise. Because of the voice of the enemy, because of the oppression of the wicked: for they cast iniquity upon me, and in wrath they hate me. My heart is sore pained within me: and the terrors of death are fallen upon me. Fearfulness and trembling are come upon me, and horror hath overwhelmed me.[16]

The Reverend Sam Shoemaker quoted the Apostle Paul's description of man's spiritual problem *and* its solution:

O wretched man that I am! who shall deliver me from the body of this death? I thank God through Jesus Christ our Lord . . . (Romans 7:24-25).[17]

And one of the early A.A. pioneer stories in the Big Book's first edition quoted from the foregoing chapter of Romans and indicated that the quoted verses marked the turning point toward recovery. *Smile With Me, At Me* states:

One morning, after a sleepless night worrying over what I could do to straighten myself out, I went to my room alone—took my Bible in hand and asked Him, the One Power, that I might open to a good place to read—and I read. "For I delight in the law of God after the inward man. But I see a different law in my members, warring against the law of my mind and bringing me into captivity under the law of sin which is in my members. Wretched man that I am! Who shall deliver me out of the body of this death?" That was enough for me—I started to understand. Here were the words of Paul a great teacher. When, then if I had slipped? Now, I could understand. From that day I gave and still give and always will, time everyday to read the word of God and

---

[16] Fosdick, *The Meaning of Faith*, p. 184.

[17] Shoemaker, *National Awakening*, p. 48; Shoemaker, *Religion That Works*, p. 45. See also Glover, *The Jesus of History*, p. 149. This latter book was read and recommended by Dr. Bob and Anne Smith.

let Him do all the caring. Who am I to try to run myself or anyone else.[18]

Dr. Carl G. Jung eventually gave AAs an even more specific biblical picture of their spiritual problem and the necessary spiritual solution. As we have said, years after Bill Wilson had written the Big Book and the Twelve Steps, Jung responded to a letter from Bill. He explained to Bill that he (Jung) had told one of Bill's Oxford Group mentors, Rowland Hazard, the solution to the alcoholic's spiritual problem. To Rowland's spiritual restlessness and discontent. And to his estrangement from God. Jung wrote:

His [the alcoholic's] craving for alcohol was the equivalent on a low level of the spiritual thirst of our being for wholeness, expressed in medieval language: the union with God.[19]

Jung then referred Bill to Psalm 42:1:

As the hart panteth after the water brooks, so panteth my soul after thee, O God.[20]

Viewed from a spiritual standpoint, the core of A.A.'s First Step powerlessness and unmanageability could possibly be said to rest on biblical grounds. Citing biblical authority, Clarence S. often said that alcoholics needed a new *Manager*.[21] AAs certainly needed to recognize the deadly physical and mental disease that medicine had revealed to them.[22] The alcoholic needed to know he or she was powerless over alcohol because of a mental

---

[18] Big Book, First Edition, p. 347.

[19] *Pass It On*, p. 384.

[20] *Pass It On*, p. 384-85.

[21] Dick B., *That Amazing Grace*, p. 67.

[22] Bill wrote: "[Dr. Silkworth] was soon to contribute a very great idea without which AA could never have succeeded. For years he had been proclaiming alcoholism an illness, an obsession of the mind coupled with an allergy of the body. By now I knew this meant me. I also understood what a fatal combination these twin ogres could be." *The Language of the Heart*, p. 197.

obsession, coupled with a physical allergy.[23] And that life had become unmanageable.[24] But the alcoholic would never recover, found Bill and Dr. Bob, without spiritual wholeness, without finding God—without union *with* God, as Carl Jung put it. And the spiritual *problem*, which Jung described, had long before been defined in the Bible by Job, David, and Paul: Man was wretched of and by himself.[25] And man needed to learn and concede that spiritual fact—those Biblical writers said—in order to see his need for God as the solution to his seeming spiritual hopelessness.

Professor William James—whom Bill Wilson regarded as the father of modern psychology, "a founder" of A.A., and the author of the First Step's "deflation at depth" idea—had described the solution to every person's need for union with God via a conversion experience in the following terms:

> To be converted, to be regenerated, to receive grace, to experience religion, to gain an assurance, are so many phrases which denote the process, gradual or sudden, by which a self hitherto divided, and consciously wrong inferior and unhappy, becomes unified and consciously right superior and happy, in consequence of its firmer hold upon religious realities.[26]

Hence many A.A. spiritual sources, including Anne Smith, quoted this James definition as an example of man's divided self—which was consciously wrong, inferior, and unhappy—and which needed regeneration, change and conversion by the grace of God.[27]

---

[23] Big Book, pp. xxiv, 23, 37, 59.

[24] Big Book, p. 60: "That we were alcoholic and could not manage our own lives."

[25] See also Paul's statement in Ephesians 2:12: "That at that time [when Gentiles were called Uncircumcision] ye were without Christ, being aliens from the commonwealth of Israel, and strangers from the covenants of promise, having no hope, and without God in the world."

[26] William James, *The Varieties of Religious Experience* (New York: Vintage Books/The Library of America Edition, 1990), p. 177. For Wilson's views of James as psychology's father, as an A.A. "founder," and as the source of A.A.'s "deflation at depth" idea, see *Pass It On*, pp. 124-25, 197; *A. A. Comes of Age*, p. 64.

[27] Dick B., *Design for Living*, p. 60; *Anne Smith's Journal*, p. 101.

The solution to the divided self problem, said many of A.A.'s sources, was crucifixion of the big "I."[28] Surrender of self.[29] A turning point involving self-surrender of the ego.[30] And at least two of A.A.'s root sources (Sam Shoemaker and Anne Smith) referred to the turning point (which began with a divided, deflated self, requiring such a surrender) as "powerlessness" and loss of power.[31]

Several A.A. spiritual sources also pointed to the unmanageability of a spiritually sick life, focused on self—a life of self-centeredness and ego-centricity, in which self constituted God.[32] A common prayer in use at that stage of the path was "O, God, manage me, because I cannot manage myself."[33] Dr. Bob's wife often recommended such a prayer as a means of connecting with God in the face of powerlessness.[34]

Shoemaker summed up the spiritual problem as follows:

---

[28] Edgar J. Goodspeed, *The Wonderful Career of Moody and Sankey in Great Britain and America* (New York: Henry S. Goodspeed & Co., 1876), p. 46; Peter Howard, *Frank Buchman's Secret* (Garden City, NY: Doubleday & Company, 1961), p. 43; *The World Rebuilt: The True Story of Frank Buchman and the Achievements of Moral Re-Armament* (New York: Duell, Sloan and Pearce, 1951), p. 242; Paul Campbell and Peter Howard, *Remaking Men* (New York: Arrowhead Books, 1954), p. 75; *What is the Oxford Group?*, pp. 23-24; Russell, *For Sinners Only*, p. 60; Bremer Hofmeyr, *How to Change* (New York: Moral Re-Armament, n.d.), p. 3.

[29] Leslie D. Weatherhead, *Discipleship* (London: Student Christian Movement Press, 1934), p. 16. For the many discussions of the self-surrender idea in A.A. roots, see Dick B., *Design for Living*, pp. 170-75.

[30] *What Is the Oxford Group?*, pp. 23-24; Shoemaker, *If I Be Lifted Up* (New York: Fleming H. Revell, 1931), p. 28; Weatherhead, *How Can I Find God?*, p. 84; Dick B., *Design for Living*, pp. 47, 78, 334.

[31] Shoemaker, *If I Be Lifted Up*, pp. 131, 133; *How to Become a Christian*, p. 77; Dick B., *Anne Smith's Journal*, p. 22.

[32] Dick B., *Design for Living*, pp. 77, 79, 183, 299, 300, 347; *New Light on Alcoholism*, pp. 145, 230, 300; *Anne Smith's Journal*, pp. 19-21. See also Big Book, pp. 52, 53, 60-64, 71, 87-88.

[33] Dick B., *Design for Living*, pp. 77, 79, 182-83; *New Light on Alcoholism*, pp. 145, 230, 300.

[34] Dick B., *Anne Smith's Journal*, pp. 20-22.

God is God, and self is not God—that is the heart of it. It is an actual fact that we become God to ourselves unless we have God to believe in: the final reference becomes ourselves.[35]

My principles "listened" well but they worked like the devil's own. . . . I realized the horror I was passing through, and suddenly gave up that path because I saw it ending in a blank wall or worse. One is reminded of a very old verse: "There is a way which seemeth right unto a man, but the end thereof are the ways of death."[36]

The Big Book said:

So our troubles, we think, are basically of our own making. . . . Neither could we reduce our self-centeredness much by wishing or trying on our own power. We had to have God's help. This is the how and why of it. First of all, we had to quit playing God. It didn't work (p. 62).

Jesus taught:

Ye do err, not knowing the scriptures, nor the power of God.[37]

And we believe the early AAs were following the path Jesus suggested.[38] They studied the Good Book; and they sought the power of God for the solution to their spiritual misery and despair.[39]

---

[35] Shoemaker, *National Awakening*, p. 48.

[36] Shoemaker, *Realizing Religion*, p. 7, quoting Proverbs 16:25.

[37] Matthew 22:29; see Holm, *The Runner's Bible*, p. 51.

[38] Note that the Big Book declared that probably no human power could relieve AAs of their alcoholism, but that "God could and would if He were sought" (p. 60).

[39] Big Book, pp. 56-57, state: "For the first time, he lived in conscious companionship with his Creator. . . . God had restored his sanity." Illustrating the means, Big Book, p. 64, states: "When the spiritual malady is overcome, we straighten out mentally and physically."

Step Two, Willingness, Belief, and Seeking

[Step Two: Came to believe that a Power greater than ourselves could restore us to sanity.]

Reduced to its essence, and as described in A.A.'s Big Book, the Second Step required (1) "*willingness* to believe," (2) *belief* in a "Power, which is God," and (3) "*seeking*" the power of God for relief from alcoholism. Some might disagree with our description of the Second Step requirements, but Bill Wilson put those ideas very explicitly in the following Big Book phrases:

> *It was only a matter of being willing to believe in a Power greater than myself. Nothing more was required of me to make my beginning.* I saw that growth could start from that point. Upon a foundation of complete willingness I might build what I saw in my friend [Bill's "sponsor," Ebby Thacher] (p. 12; italics in original).

> Its [the Big Book's] main object is to enable you to find a Power greater than yourself which will solve your problem . . . it means, of course, that *we are going to talk about God* . . . even though it was impossible for any of us to fully define or comprehend that *Power, which is God* (pp. 45-46; italics added).

> We needed to ask ourselves but one short question. "Do I now *believe, or am I even willing to believe,* that there is a Power greater than myself?" As soon as a man can say that he does believe, or is willing to believe, we emphatically assure him that he is on his way (p. 47; italics added).

> Circumstances made him willing to believe. He humbly offered himself to his Maker—then he knew. Even so has God restored us all to our right minds. . . . He has come to all who have honestly *sought* Him (p. 57; italics added).

[P]robably no human power could have relieved our alcoholism.
. . . God could and would *if He were sought* (p. 60; italics
added).

All three A.A. concepts—willingness, belief, and seeking—were
borrowed by AAs from Bible verses A.A.'s sources had frequently
quoted.

Concerning *willingness*, the Reverend Sam Shoemaker was
A.A.'s most articulate Bible teacher.[40] Shoemaker said that if one
wished to "come to believe," he or she should follow the
injunction of Jesus in John 7:17. The essence of Jesus's teaching
was, that if one obeyed the known commandments and doctrines
of God by acting upon them, he or she would learn about, believe
in, and know more about, God and His will. This, because God
would then reveal *more*.[41] A.A.'s religious sources taught that
obedience to God's will is the organ of spiritual *knowledge*.[42] For
the *willingness* idea, these A.A. sources quoted John 7:17:

If any man will do his will, he shall know of the doctrine,
whether it be of God, or *whether* I speak of myself.

Concerning *belief,* many of A.A. religious sources quoted
Hebrews 11:6. Oxford Group people and other A.A. sources, as

---

[40] See also the discussion by Shoemaker's Oxford Group friend, Professor Philip
Marshall Brown. See Brown, *The Venture of Belief*, pp. 29, 36.

[41] See, for example, Shoemaker, *Religion That Works*, p. 36; Russell, *For Sinners
Only*, p. 211; Brown, *The Venture of Belief*, pp. 29, 36; Dick B., *Design for Living*, pp.
41, 50, 54-56, 70, 149, 164, 190, 217, 272-74, 313, 315-16, 333; *The Upper Room* for
4/26/35, 6/28/37, 12/1/37; Fosdick, *The Meaning of Prayer*, p. 59; *The Meaning of
Faith*, pp. 216-17; Clark, *I Will Lift Up Mine Eyes*, p. 27; Chambers, *Studies in the
Sermon on the Mount*, p. 37.

[42] See Henry Drummond, *The Ideal Life* (New York: Hodder & Stoughton, 1897),
pp. 227-320; F. B. Meyer, *The Secret of Guidance* (New York: Fleming H. Revell,
1896), p. 11; Wright, *The Will of God*, pp. 102-279; Benson, *The Eight Points*, pp. 134-
42.

well as *early* AAs, subscribed to the idea that they could not come to God without believing that God is.[43] Hebrews 11:6 states:

> But without faith *it is* impossible to please *him*: for he that cometh to God must believe that He is, and *that* he is a rewarder of them that diligently seek him.

Concerning the *seeking*, early AAs took their cue from the Sermon on the Mount and religion's countless references to seeking *first* the Kingdom of God.[44] As we've mentioned, Dr. Bob was very emphatic that A.A.'s well-known "First Things First" slogan came from Matthew 6:33.[45] The verse declares:

> But seek ye first the kingdom of God, and his righteousness; and all these things [earthly needs for food, drink, clothing] shall be added unto you.

Step Three and the Decision to Surrender

[Step Three: Made a decision to turn our will and our lives over to the care of God *as we understood Him*.]

We have not located, among A.A.'s religious sources, any *direct* biblical references to the "decision" that is the heart of Step Three. However, we have shown, in Chapter 3, that a decision to make Jesus Lord was a part of the early A.A. surrender. Such a

---

[43] Weatherhead, *How Can I Find God?*, p. 72; Shoemaker, *The Gospel According to You*, p. 47; Shoemaker, *National Awakening*, pp. 40-41; Shoemaker, *Religion That Works*, p. 55; Shoemaker, *Confident Faith*, p. 187; Chambers, *My Utmost for His Highest*, p. 304; Fosdick, *The Meaning of Faith*, pp. 8, 92; Dick B., *Design for Living*, pp. 165, 331; *New Light on Alcoholism*, p. 126; *DR. BOB*, p. 144.

[44] Shoemaker, *National Awakening*, p. 41; *The Upper Room* for 9/4/35; 11/19/35; 6/20/37; 12/2/38; Holm, *The Runner's Bible*, p. 127; Chambers, *My Utmost for His Highest*, p. 142; *Studies in the Sermon on the Mount*, pp. 60-61; Fosdick, *The Meaning of Faith*, pp. 192-93; Dick B., *Design for Living*, p. 284; *Anne Smith's Journal*, pp. 132, 140; *Dr. Bob's Library*, p. 93.

[45] *DR. BOB*, p. 144.

decision is mandated in the following Bible verse discussed by two of A.A.'s sources:

> That if thou shalt confess with thy mouth the Lord Jesus, and shalt believe in thine heart that God hath raised him from the dead, thou shalt be saved (Romans 10:9).[46]

And there are ample Bible verses, adopted by AAs from their root sources, which served as guides for *making* the decision to surrender to God and to *entrust* their lives to His care. The *decision* in early A.A.—and today, in some cases—involved a surrender made on the knees.[47] Sometimes, the A.A. surrender language came from the Lord's Prayer—a part of the Sermon on the Mount. That *decision language* declared simply, "Thy will be done."[48] A variant involved Jesus's similar expression, "Not my will, but thine, be done."[49]

As we have shown, Clarence S. said the decision and accompanying prayer involved the "Sinner's Prayer."[50] Clarence said that you have to make a choice as to the God you choose. He added, "I would prefer to choose a *living* God, not a dead God" and referred to 1 Thessalonians 1:9: "How ye turned to God from

---

[46] Shoemaker, *If I Be Lifted Up*, p. 83; Glenn Clark, *Touchdowns For The Lord: The Story of "Dad" A. J. Elliott* (Minnesota: Macalester Park Publishing Company, 1947), pp. 55-56.

[47] For the history of the A.A. surrender "on the knees," see *Pass It On*, pp. 198-99.

[48] Matthew 6:10; Big Book, pp. 67, 88; compare p. 443; Matthew 6:10; *What Is The Oxford Group?*, p. 48; Samuel M. Shoemaker, Jr., *Children of the Second Birth*, pp. 175-87; *The Upper Room* for 12/3/37; Dick B., *Design for Living*, p. 181; *The Akron Genesis*, p. 96.

[49] Luke 22:42; Big Book, p. 85; compare pp. 229, 381; Mary Wilder Tileston, *Daily Strength for Daily Needs*, 1977 Printing, pp. 296, 146; *The Upper Room* for 6/21/38; *What is the Oxford Group?*, p. 48; Shoemaker, *Children of the Second Birth*, pp. 58, 182; Glenn Clark, *The Soul's Sincere Desire*, p. 40; *I Will Lift Up Mine Eyes*, p. 27.

[50] See Chapter 3 and Dick B., *That Amazing Grace*, p. 27.

idols to serve the living and true God."[51] Clarence also quoted
Ephesians 4:22-24 as to the Third Step process:

> That ye *put off* concerning the former conversation the old man,
> which is corrupt according to the deceitful lusts;
> And *be renewed* in the spirit of your mind;
> And that ye *put on* the new man, which after God is created in
> righteousness and true holiness (italics added).[52]

Sam Shoemaker cited Psalm 46:10 as to the *need* for surrendering and finding God. Shoemaker quoted Dr. Moffatt's
translation of Psalm 46:10 as follows:

> "Give in," he cries, "admit that I am God, high over nations,
> high over the world."[53]

Both the Big Book and Sam Shoemaker spoke of "abandoning
yourself to God," and such language indicated the total surrender
of the will that was expected.[54] The Third Step's actual surrender
phraseology can be found in A.A. sources which used such
language as "turned over to Him her life for His direction" and a
"decision to cast my will and my life on God."[55]

Additional Bible verses which A.A.'s sources associated with
a decision to surrender were:

---

[51] See Dick B., *That Amazing Grace*, p. 68. Cp. Big Book, p. 28: ". . . All of us,
whatever our race, creed, our color, are children of a *living* Creator with whom we may
form a relationship upon simple and understandable terms" (italics added).

[52] Dick B., *That Amazing Grace*, p. 68.

[53] Shoemaker, *National Awakening*, pp. 45-54. The better known King James Version
of Psalm 46:10 reads: "Be still, and know that I am God: I will be exalted among the
heathen, I will be exalted in the earth."

[54] Big Book, pp. 164, 59, 63; Shoemaker, *Religion That Works*, p. 19.

[55] Samuel M. Shoemaker, Jr., *Children of the Second Birth*, p. 82; *Twice-Born
Ministers*, p. 134.

I can of mine own self do nothing: as I hear, I judge: and my judgment is just; because I seek not mine own will, but the will of the Father which hath sent me (John 5:30).[56]

Know ye not, that to whom ye yield yourselves servants to obey, his servants ye are to whom ye obey; whether of sin unto death, or of obedience unto righteousness (Romans 6:16).[57]

Know ye not that ye are the temple of God, and *that* the Spirit of God dwelleth in you? (1 Corinthians 3:16).[58]

God *is* a Spirit: and they that worship him must worship *him* in spirit and in truth (John 4:24).[59]

For in him we live, and move, and have our being; as certain also of your own poets have said, For we are also his offspring (Acts 17:28).[60]

Repent ye therefore, and be converted, that your sins may be blotted out, when the times of refreshing shall come from the presence of the Lord (Acts 3:19).[61]

Step Four and Self-examination

[Step Four: Made a searching and fearless moral inventory of ourselves.]

---

[56] Meyer, *The Secret of Guidance*, p. 11.

[57] Wright, *The Will of God*, p. 31; Chambers, *My Utmost for His Highest*, p. 283.

[58] Holm, *The Runner's Bible*, p. 17; *What Is The Oxford Group?*, p. 39; Clark, *I Will Lift Up Mine Eyes*, p. 30.

[59] Fosdick, *The Meaning of Faith*, p. 85; *What Is the Oxford Group?*, p. 41; *The Upper Room* for 5/1/35; Holm, *The Runner's Bible*, p. 4.

[60] Fosdick, *The Meaning of Faith*, pp. 86-87; *What Is the Oxford Group?*, p. 42; R. C. Mowat, *Modern Prophetic Voices from Kierkegaard to Buchman* (Great Britain, New Cherwell Press, 1994), pp. 72-73; B. H. Streeter, *The God Who Speaks*, p. 12.

[61] Holm, *The Runner's Bible*, p. 88; *What Is The Oxford Group?*, p. 43. On repentance, see discussion in Benson, *The Eight Points*, pp. 7-9; *The Upper Room* for 6/1/37.

A.A.'s root sources were concerned with taking a *moral* inventory. By this, they meant examining one's life in terms of how it measured up to the Oxford Group's "Four Absolutes"—honesty, purity, unselfishness and love. More importantly, they wished to learn those "sins" or "shortcomings" which were blocking them from God and from others.[62]

The basic idea that self-examination is required to establish a satisfactory relationship with God came from several verses in the Sermon on the Mount. These verses state that one should look for his own faults, his own part in difficulties, before looking at the faults of another. A.A. sources quoted Matthew 7:3-5:

> And why beholdest thou the mote [speck] that is in thy brother's eye, but considerest not the beam [log] that is in thine own eye? Or wilt thou say to thy brother, "Let me pull out the mote out of thine eye;" and, behold, a beam is in thine own eye? Thou hypocrite, first cast out the beam out of thine own eye; and then shalt thou see clearly to cast out the mote out of thy brother's eye.[63]

The Oxford Group's self-examination "yardsticks" were *positive*. The self-examination was to be in the context of how well a person was living up to the "absolute" moral standards taught by Jesus. The Oxford Group's standards were taken from Dr. Robert E. Speer's reconstruction of Jesus's uncompromising teachings on perfection.[64] Speer believed he had identified Jesus's four "absolute" moral standards in the following verses:

---

[62] See Dick B., *Design for Living*, pp. 166-70, for the varying Oxford Group definitions of sin, all of which characterized "sin" as that which blocks us from God and from others.

[63] Allen, *He That Cometh*, pp. 81, 140; Kitchen, *I Was a Pagan*, p. 111; Shoemaker, *The Church Can Save the World*, pp. 88-121; Shoemaker, *God's Control*, pp. 62-72; Dick B., *Anne Smith's Journal*, pp. 30-31.

[64] Robert E. Speer, *The Principles of Jesus* (New York: Association Press, 1902). Speer discussed Jesus's standard of perfection at page 34 and quoted Matthew 5:48 from the Sermon on the Mount: "Be ye therefore perfect, even as your Father which is in heaven is perfect."

Honesty (which Speer spoke of as "an absolute standard of truth"). Speer urged, if Satan is the father of lies, how can any lie be justifiable? Speer's unmistakable reference is to John 8:44: "Ye are of *your* father the devil, and the lusts of your father ye will do. He was a murderer from the beginning, and abode not in the truth, because there is no truth in him. When he speaketh a lie, he speaketh of his own: for he is a liar, and the father of it."[65]

Unselfishness. Speer cited: (1) Mark 10:45: "For even the Son of man came not to be ministered unto, but to minister, and to give his life a ransom for many." (2) Luke 22:27: "For whether *is* greater, he that sitteth at meat, or he that serveth? *is* not he that sitteth at meat? but I am among you as he that serveth." (3) Luke 14:33: "So likewise, whosoever he be of you that forsaketh not all that he hath, he cannot be my disciple."[66]

Purity. Speer cited: (1) Mark 7:15: "There is nothing from without a man, that entering into him can defile him: but the things which come out of him, those are they that defile the man." (2) Matthew 5:29-30: "And if thy right eye offend thee, pluck it out, and cast *it* from thee: for it is profitable for thee that one of thy members should perish, and not *that* thy whole body should be cast into hell. And if thy right hand offend thee, cut it off, and cast *it* from thee: for it is profitable for thee that one of thy members should perish, and not *that* thy whole body should be cast into hell."[67]

Love. Speer basically cited (1) John 13:34: "A new commandment I give unto you, That ye love one another; as I have loved you, that ye also love one another." (2) John 13:1: "Now before the feast of the passover, when Jesus knew that his hour was come that he should depart out of this world unto the Father, having

---

[65] Speer, *The Principles of Jesus*, p. 35.

[66] Speer, *The Principles of Jesus*, p. 35. See also Streeter, *The God Who Speaks*, p. 84.

[67] Speer, *The Principles of Jesus*, p. 35.

loved his own which were in the world, he loved them unto the end."[68]

Later writers, including Dr. Sam Shoemaker, thought Speer's four standards actually *came* from Jesus's teachings in the Sermon on the Mount.[69] And the standards did, in the sense that they were founded on the standard of perfection Jesus enunciated in the Sermon. But the verses which Speer himself cited as authority were not all from the Sermon on the Mount though they *were* taught by Jesus and were consistent *with* his Sermon on the Mount teachings.

Professor Henry B. Wright, who was a major influence on the thinking of Oxford Group Founder Frank Buchman, examined Speer's four absolute standards in light of the following Gospel verses.[70] (Wright termed the principles in the verses the "Four Absolutes.")[71]:

Honesty. Luke 16:10-11: "He that is faithful in that which is least is faithful also in much: and he that is unjust in the least is unjust also in much. If therefore ye have not been faithful in the unrighteous mammon, who will commit to your trust the true *riches?*"[72]

Unselfishness. Luke 9:23-24: "And he said to *them* all, If any man will come after me, let him deny himself, and take up his cross daily, and follow me. For whosoever will save his life shall lose it: but whosoever will lose his life for my sake, the same shall save it."[73]

---

[68] Speer, *The Principles of Jesus*, p. 35.

[69] Dick B., *Design for Living*, pp. 237-38.

[70] For a discussion of Wright's immense influence on Frank Buchman, see Dick B., *Design for Living*, pp. 67-72.

[71] Wright, *The Will of God*, pp. 167-218:

[72] Wright, *The Will of God*, p. 187.

[73] Wright, *The Will of God*, p. 197.

Purity. Matthew 5:8: "Blessed *are* the pure in heart: for they shall see God."[74]

Love. Matthew 25:41-43, 45: ". . . Depart from me, ye cursed, into everlasting fire, prepared for the devil and his angels; For I was an hungered, and ye gave me no meat: I was thirsty, and ye gave me no drink: I was a stranger, and ye took me not in: naked, and ye clothed me not: sick, and in prison, and ye visited me not. . . . Then shall he answer them, saying, Verily I say unto you, Inasmuch as ye did *it* not to one of the least of these, ye did *it* not to me."[75]

Not surprisingly, A.A.'s other progenitors in the Oxford Group, including Wright himself, found the same four absolute moral principles in a good many other New Testament verses including the following: Mark 10:19-21; 1 Corinthians 13; Ephesians 4:15-16; Colossians 3:5-14; 1 Thessalonians 4:3-12; and James 3:17.[76]

A recent Oxford Group writer and leader, the Reverend Harry J. Almond, pointed to portions of the Sermon on the Mount he believed *did* embody the Four Absolutes. Almond cited:

Honesty. Matthew 5:33-37: "Again, ye have heard that it hath been said by them of old time, Thou shalt not forswear thyself, but shalt perform unto the Lord thine oaths: But I say unto you, Swear not at all; neither by heaven; for it is God's throne: Nor by the earth; for it is his footstool . . . ; neither by Jerusalem; for it is the city of the great King. . . . But let your communications be, Yea, yea; Nay, nay: for whatsoever is more than these cometh of evil."

Unselfishness. Matthew 5:38-42: "Ye have heard that it hath been said, An eye for an eye, and a tooth for a tooth: But I say unto

---

[74] Wright, *The Will of God*, p. 179. See also Russell, *For Sinners Only*, p. 63.

[75] Wright, *The Will of God*, p. 207.

[76] Wright, *The Will of God*, p. 167; *What is the Oxford Group?*, p. 109; Harry J. Almond, *Foundations for Faith*. 2d ed (London: Grosvenor Books, 1980), p. 12; Benson, *The Eight Points*, pp. 44-57.

you, That ye resist not evil: but whosoever shall smite thee on thy right cheek, turn to him the other also. And if any man will sue thee at the law, and take away thy coat, let him have *thy* cloak also. And whosoever shall compel thee to go a mile, go with him twain. Give to him that asketh thee, and from him that would borrow of thee turn not thou away."

Purity. Matthew 5:27-28: "Ye have heard that it was said by them of old time, Thou shalt not commit adultery: But I say unto you, That whosoever looketh on a woman to lust after her hath committed adultery with her already in his heart."

Love. Matthew 5:43-47: "Ye have heard that it hath been said, Thou shalt love thy neighbor, and hate thine enemy. But I say unto you, Love your enemies, bless them that curse you, do good to them that hate you, and pray for them which despitefully use you and persecute you, That ye may be the children of your Father which is in heaven: for he maketh his sun to rise on the evil and on the good, and sendeth rain on the just and on the unjust. For if ye love them which love you, what reward have ye? do not even the publicans the same? And if ye salute your brethren only, what do ye more *than others?* do not even the publicans so?"[77]

In his last major address to AAs, Dr. Bob still spoke highly of the Oxford Group's "Four Absolutes" and said they were the "yardsticks" by which AAs could measure their conduct and, in effect, "take their inventory."[78] Dr. Bob's wife, Anne, frequently urged the Four Absolutes as moral standards for conduct.[79] Clarence S. took a much broader position on the Fourth Step inventory. Clarence said his sponsees were to look for the

---

[77] For these four renditions, see Almond, *Foundations for Faith*, pp. 11-13. In a letter to the author in 1994, Dr. Morris Martin, who had been Frank Buchman's personal secretary for many years, informed the author that Almond's writings would correctly reflect Buchman's biblical teachings. See also Streeter, *The God Who Speaks*, pp. 83-84.

[78] *The Co-Founders of Alcoholics Anonymous: Biographical sketches Their last major talks* (New York: Alcoholics Anonymous World Services, 1972, 1975), pp. 12-14.

[79] Dick B., *Anne Smith's Journal*, pp. 31-34, 59-60, 104-06, 108, 115-20.

characteristics that *caused* them to take the actions they did. He had them review some twenty "defects" and check whether those defects were problems for them. Clarence said when you had found the *nature* of your defects, you didn't need to know the exact wrong itself. He frequently cited Mark 7:18-23 and Galatians 5:16-26 for the *nature* of defiling things man nurtures within himself and which need to be purged.[80]

In later years, A.A.'s co-founder Bill Wilson became quite critical of the Four Absolutes, claiming they were too "absolute" for alcoholics to follow.[81] And perhaps in consequence, Wilson framed the Big Book's moral inventory in terms of *negatives*. AAs were enjoined to examine their lives for: (1) Resentments and grudges; (2) Fears; (3) Selfishness and self-seeking, particularly in the sex area; (4) Dishonesty; and (5) "Harms" they had caused others by their conduct.[82]

The biblical *roots* which defined A.A.'s "negative" yardsticks were not as concisely or precisely defined in A.A.'s religious sources as were the four "positive" absolutes. But we believe those negative moral yardsticks do pop out rather clearly from the Bible verses early AAs studied or to which they were exposed. The verses to which Clarence S. referred in Mark 7:18-23 and Galatians 5:16-26 cover these negative items.

In their search for objectionable conduct that blocked them from God, AAs were, in their Fourth Step, to *put on paper* their resentments, fears, selfish sex conduct, and harms to others.[83] And the underlying requirement was that they apply rigorous honesty in their inventory.[84]

We believe the following biblical teachings by A.A.'s sources had a major influence in defining the negatives AAs were to search

---

[80] See Dick B., *That Amazing Grace*, pp. 69-71.

[81] *A. A. Comes of Age*, pp. 74-75; *Pass It On*, pp. 171-74.

[82] See Big Book, pp. 64-70, 84, 86.

[83] Big Book p. 64 (resentments); p. 68 (fears); p. 69 (selfish sex conduct); p. 70 (people hurt by the conduct).

[84] Big Book, pp. 58, 65, 67, 69. See also pp. 84, 86.

for, list in writing, and root out. We believe this because of the pervasive A.A. source teachings *about* these spiritual problems, and the similarity between A.A. language and the biblical root teachings:

Resentments and grudges: "Grudge not one against another, brethren, lest ye be condemned: behold, the judge standeth before the door" (James 5:9). "But I say unto you, That whosoever is angry with his brother without a cause shall be in danger of the judgment: and whosoever shall say to his brother, Raca, shall be in danger of the council: but whosoever shall say, Thou fool, shall be in danger of hell fire" (Matthew 5:22—in the Sermon on the Mount).[85]

Fears: "The Lord *is* my light and my salvation; whom shall I fear? the Lord *is* the strength of my life; of whom shall I be afraid?" (Psalm 27:1) "Yea, though I walk through the valley of the shadow of death, I will fear no evil: for thou *art* with me; thy rod and thy staff they comfort me" (Psalm 23:4); "Fear not: for I *am* with thee" (Isaiah 43:5); "Be not afraid, only believe" (Mark 5:36); "For God hath not given us the spirit of fear; but of power, and of love, and of a sound mind" (2 Timothy 1:7); "There is no fear in love; but perfect love casteth out fear: because fear hath torment" (1 John 4:18).[86]

Selfishness. "Charity . . . seeketh not her own" (1 Corinthians 13:4, 5).[87]

---

[85] See *The Upper Room* for 10/18/35; Holm, *The Runner's Bible*, p. 82; Shoemaker, *Twice-Born Ministers*, p. 182; *How to Become a Christian*, pp. 55-64; Begbie, *Life Changers*, p. 38; Macmillan, *Seeking and Finding*, pp. 96-98; Jones, *The Christ of the Mount*, p. 136; Dick B., *Anne Smith's Journal*, pp. 34-36.

[86] Holm, *The Runner's Bible*, pp. 41-44, 132; *The Upper Room* for 7/11/35, 8/22/35, 5/2/37, 8/2/37, 8/6/37, 7/1/38; Tileston, *Daily Strength for Daily Needs*, p. 228; Fosdick, *The Meaning of Faith*, pp. 191-92, 240; Clark, *The Soul's Sincere Desire*, pp. 8-9, 14; *What is the Oxford Group?*, p. 2; Streeter, *The God Who Speaks*, p. 68; Foot, *Life Began Yesterday*, p. 35; Dick B., *The Akron Genesis*, p. 94.

[87] Henry Drummond, *The Greatest Thing in the World*, 2d ed (World Bible Publishers), pp. 26, 32, 33; *DR. BOB*, pp. 96, 310; Dick B., *Anne Smith's Journal*, p. 131.

Dishonesty. "Charity . . . rejoiceth not in iniquity, but rejoiceth in the truth" (1 Corinthians 13:4, 6); "Finally, brethren, whatsoever things are true, whatsoever things *are* honest, whatsoever things *are* just . . . if *there be* any virtue, and if *there be* any praise, think on these things" (Philippians 4:8).[88]

Harms caused. Oxford Group writer Olive M. Jones succinctly defined "restitution" from the Oxford Group viewpoint as follows: "*Restitution*, by which we make amends, restore, so far as human power permits, for the wrong done."[89] The four principal sets of Bible verses from which came the A.A. suggestions as to amends for harm done were: Numbers 5:6-7; Matthew 5:23-24; and Luke, Chapter 15, and 19:1-10. We will quote and discuss these verses at a later point in connection with Step Nine.[90]

Step Five and Confession

[Step Five: Admitted to God, to ourselves, and to another human being the exact nature of our wrongs.]

Except for scattered mention of a few other verses, AAs and their sources consistently referred to James 5:16 as the root of their "confession" step.[91] James 5:16 states:

---

[88] Drummond, *The Greatest Thing in the World*, pp. 27, 39; *DR. BOB*, pp. 96, 310; Clark, *I Will Lift Up Mine Eyes*, pp. 54, 93; *The Upper Room* for 9/12/35, 5/14/36, 7/20/37; Tileston, *Daily Strength for Daily Needs*, p. 364; Holm, *The Runner's Bible*, p. 116; Fosdick, *The Meaning of Prayer*, p. 72.

[89] Olive M. Jones, *Inspired Children* (New York: Harper & Brothers, 1933), p. 136.

[90] See also Weatherhead, *Discipleship*, pp. 114-23; Benson, *The Eight Points*, pp. 30-43.

[91] J. P. Thornton-Duesbury, *Sharing* (Pamphlet of The Oxford Group, published at Oxford University Press, no date), p. 5; Sherwood Sunderland Day, *The Principles of the Group* (Oxford: University Press, n.d.), p. 6; *What is the Oxford Group?*, pp. 29, 31; Streeter, *The God Who Speaks*, p. 125; Weatherhead, *Discipleship*, p. 32; Almond, *Foundations for Faith*, p. 13; Garth Lean, *Cast Out Your Nets* (London: Grosvenor, 1990), p. 48; Shoemaker, *The Conversion of the Church*, p. 35; Fosdick, *The Meaning of Faith*, p. 190; *The Meaning of Prayer*, pp. 157-58; *The Upper Room* for 12/4/35; *Pass*

(continued...)

Confess *your* faults one to another, and pray for one another, that ye may be healed. The effectual fervent prayer of a righteous man availeth much.

Step Six, Conviction, and Readiness to Change

[Step Six: Were entirely ready to have God remove all these defects of character.]

It is difficult to pinpoint the Sixth's Step's biblical link to A.A. The link, if any, was never discussed by Bill Wilson; and apparently it was not discussed either by Dr. Bob or his wife, Anne. However, A.A.'s link to the Oxford Group's "Five C's" and their "soul-surgery" art is very clear.[92] And the third "C" in the Oxford Group formula for life-change was "Conviction."[93] "Conviction" was mentioned *by name and by concept* by Bill Wilson's wife, Lois, in Lois's "Oxford Group Notes" and subsequent 1937 diary entries.[94] Dr. Bob's wife, Anne Smith, addressed the "conviction" subject quite frequently in the spiritual journal she kept between 1933 and 1939.[95]

Shoemaker's Oxford Group colleague Olive M. Jones defined "conviction" as follows: "*Conviction*, by which we come to a conscious realization of our sins which shut God away from us."[96]

---

[91] (...continued)
It On, p. 128; Dick B., *Anne Smith's Journal*, pp. 36, 38, 40, 99, 129, 131-32, 142, 144; Dick B., *That Amazing Grace*, p. 71.

[92] See Dick B., *Design for Living*, pp. 175-79; *New Light on Alcoholism*, p. 64; *Anne Smith's Journal*, pp. 96-97; and see also *DR. BOB*, p. 54.

[93] Dick B., *Design for Living*, pp. 192-97; Walter, *Soul Surgery*, 6th ed., pp. 64-78.

[94] Dick B., *New Light on Alcoholism*, pp. 337-41; *The Akron Genesis*, p. 155. For example, during one of his two visits to Stepping Stones Archives at Bedford Hills, New York, the author was allowed by the archivist to inspect and copy entries from Lois Wilson's diary for 1937. That diary contained an entry for February 8, 1937, which stated, "Convicted of trying to be a fixer . . ." For February 13, 1937, Lois wrote, "Convicted of being put out when my personal things have been mishandled . . ."

[95] Dick B., *Anne Smith's Journal*, pp. 41-45, 100-01.

[96] Olive Jones, *Inspired Children*, pp. 135-36.

Understood from the vantage point of its Oxford Group roots in the Five C's, the Step Six "conviction" idea could have come from several biblical roots. Repentance or dying to self, is the way Glenn Clark summarized the conviction concept.[97] And note that the biblical source verses progress from the idea that one must convict himself or herself of sin to the idea that *God* brings people to conviction:

> "Against thee, thee only, have I sinned, and done *this* evil in thy sight . . ." (Psalm 51:4); "Iniquities prevail against me: as *for* our transgressions, thou shalt purge them away" (Psalm 65:3); "And the son said unto him, Father, I have sinned against heaven, and in thy sight, and am no more worthy to be called thy son" (Luke 15:21); "For we know that the law is spiritual: but I am carnal, sold under sin" (Romans 7:14); "Who is weak, and I am not weak? who is offended, and I burn not?" (2 Corinthians 11:29); "And when he [the Comforter] is come, he will reprove [convict] the world of sin, and of righteousness, and of judgment" (John 16:8). "But God commendeth his love toward us, in that, while we were yet sinners, Christ died for us" (Romans 5:8).[98]

Clarence S. referred to the following Bible verses as to the power of God available to those who *are* convicted and ready to change.[99]

Matthew 21:22:
And all things, whatsoever ye shall ask in prayer, believing, ye shall receive.

1 John 5:14:
And this is the confidence that we have in him, that, if we ask anything according to his will, he heareth us.

---

[97] Clark, *I Will Lift Up Mine Eyes*, p. 77.

[98] Walter, *Soul Surgery*, pp. 64-78; Fosdick, *The Meaning of Faith*, pp. 54, 146; *The Upper Room* for 6/2/37; Chambers, *My Utmost for His Highest*, p. 324; Glover, *The Jesus of History*, p. 149.

[99] The verses were provided the author by several of Clarence's sponsees.

Step Seven, Humble Submission, and Rebirth

[Step Seven: Humbly asked Him to remove our shortcomings.]

Early AAs believed God was willing and able to change them. They expected the change to occur if they asked Him for it. In his correspondence with Dr. Carl Jung, Bill Wilson made it clear that he [Bill] had written the great psychiatrist concerning the subject of "conversion" and "conversion experiences." Bill said the conversion experience concept proved to be the foundation of the successes A.A. had achieved.[100] As we have shown, a *conversion experience* certainly meant, among other things, to Bill and to Bill's spiritual teachers, that one had been "born again of the spirit."[101]

This early A.A. idea that one needed to be "converted" and "born again" by the power of God seemed to vanish in later A.A. language. Yet the early A.A. concept that one achieves freedom from sin by the grace of God was firmly rooted in John 3 and the new birth principle. Hence even the third edition of the Big Book—seemingly almost by oversight—proclaimed, "as we became conscious of His presence, we began to lose our fear of today, tomorrow or the hereafter. We were reborn" (p. 63).

The following were the verses most frequently cited by A.A. sources in connection with the conversion experiences to which AAs had been led in their early days:

Jesus answered and said unto him, Verily, verily, I say unto thee, Except a man be born again, he cannot see the kingdom of God. . . . Jesus answered, Verily, verily, I say unto thee, Except a man be born of water and of the Spirit, he cannot enter the kingdom

---

[100] *Pass It On*, p. 383.

[101] Shoemaker, *Realizing Religion*, pp. 21, 35; *Children of the Second Birth*, p. 32; *Religion That Works*, p. 14; *Twice-Born Ministers*, pp. 10, 56; *Confident Faith*, pp. 137, 140; *National Awakening*, pp. 55-66; Allen, *He That Cometh*, pp. 19, 32, 48-49; Jones, *Inspired Children*, p. 136; Drummond, *The Ideal Life*, pp. 212-26; Frank Buchman, *Remaking the World* (London: Blandford, 1961), p. 23; Begbie, *Life Changers*, p. 117.

of God. . . . Marvel not that I said unto thee, Ye must be born again (John 3:3, 3:5, 3:7).[102]

Submit yourselves therefore to God. Resist the devil, and he will flee from you (James 4:7).[103]

Humble yourselves in the sight of the Lord, and he shall lift you up (James 4:10).[104]

See also 2 Corinthians 5:17—which was the favorite verse of Clarence S. and will be discussed in connection with the Twelfth Step.[105] More important to Clarence S., in terms of Seventh Step language, were Matthew 7:7-11 from the Sermon on the Mount; Psalm 103; and James 5:13-16.

Clarence pointed out that the assurance of God's help was given in the Sermon on the Mount:

Ask, and it shall be given you; seek, and ye shall find; knock, and it shall be opened unto you: for everyone that asketh receiveth; and he that seeketh findeth; and to him that knocketh it shall be opened. Or what man is there of you, whom if his son ask bread will he give him a stone? Or if he ask a fish, will he give him a serpent? If ye then, being evil, know how to give good gifts unto your children, how much more shall your Father which is in heaven give good things to them that ask him (Matthew 7:7-11)?[106]

---

[102] See Olive Jones, *Inspired Children*, which states at page 136: "*Conversion*, which means simply a changed life. 'Ye must be born again,' said Christ." See also Shoemaker, *Twice-Born Ministers*, pp. 56, 10; *National Awakening*, pp. 55, 57, 58; Buchman, *Remaking the World*, p. 23; Begbie, *Life Changers*, p. 117; Allen, *He That Cometh*, pp. 19-43; Chambers, *My Utmost for His Highest*, pp. 228, 333; *Studies in the Sermon on the Mount*, pp. 16, 31; *The Upper Room* for 6/8/37, 5/22/38.

[103] Holm, *The Runner's Bible*, pp. 59, 94, 112, 115.

[104] Samuel M. Shoemaker, *Those Twelve Steps as I Understand Them*; Volume II, *Best of the Grapevine* (New York: The A.A. Grapevine, Inc., 1986), p. 130.

[105] Dick B., *That Amazing Grace*, pp. 33-34.

[106] Dick B., *That Amazing Grace*, p. 72.

Clarence pointed to Psalm 103 to show the fullness of God's forgiveness—of God's simply "forgetting" and "erasing" the defects the Steps uncovered:

> Bless the Lord, O my soul, and forget not all his benefits: Who forgiveth all thine iniquities . . . (Psalm 103:2-3).

> For as the heaven is high above the earth, *so* great is his mercy toward them that fear [respect] him. As far as the east is from the west, *so* far hath he removed our transgressions from us (Psalm 103:11-12).[107]

As we have discussed, there were group prayers in the early surrenders by which God's help was sought, when believers prayed together, for taking of alcohol from the newcomer's life and the removal of his transgressions when believers prayed together. Clarence S. said he learned from Dr. Bob and the Book of James the following:

> Is any among you afflicted? let him pray. Is any merry? let him sing psalms. Is any sick among you? let him call for the elders of the church; and let them pray over him, anointing him with oil in the name of the Lord: and the prayer of faith shall save the sick, and the Lord shall raise him up; and if he have committed sins, they shall be forgiven him, confess your faults one to another, and pray one for another that ye may be healed. The effectual fervent prayer of a righteousness man availeth much (James 5:13-16).[108]

Clarence never doubted that the slate was wiped clean of defects in the Seventh Step. But he pointed to the fact that though sins have been cast out, they will return. He cited the following:

> When the unclean spirit is gone out of a man, he [the unclean spirit] walketh through dry places, seeking rest, and findeth none.

---

[107] Dick B., *That Amazing Grace*, p. 73.
[108] Dick B., *That Amazing Grace*, p. 73.

Then he saith, I will return into my house from whence I came out; and when he [the unclean spirit] is come, he findeth *it* empty, swept, and garnished. Then goeth he, and taketh with himself, seven other spirits, more wicked than himself, and they enter in and dwell there: and the last *state* of that man is worse than the first. Even so shall it be also unto this wicked generation (Matthew 12:43-45).[109]

Clarence said that, after the Seventh Step cleanout, the character defects will come back, and the effort to keep them at bay is a life-time task. This life-time task, said Clarence, is the basis for the Tenth Step.

Step Eight, Willingness to Make Amends

[Step Eight: Made a list of all persons we had harmed, and became willing to make amends to them all.]

The Big Book states:

We have made a list of all persons we have harmed and to whom we are willing to make amends. . . . Now we go out to our fellows and repair the damage done in the past. We attempt to sweep away the debris which has accumulated out of our effort to live on self-will and run the show ourselves (p. 76).

In discussing the approach to others and the reason for making amends even to those we dislike, A.A.'s sources emphasized the following verses:

Agree with thine adversary quickly, whiles thou art in the way with him; lest at any time the adversary deliver thee to the judge,

---

[109] Dick B., *That Amazing Grace*, p. 74.

and the judge deliver thee to the officer, and thou be cast into prison (Matthew 5:25).[110]

If a man say, I love God, and hateth his brother, he is a liar: for he that loveth not his brother whom he hath seen, how can he love God whom he hath not seen? (1 John 4:20).[111]

Step Nine, Restitution

[Step Nine: Made direct amends to such people wherever possible, except when to do so would injure them or others.]

Four sets of verses captured the attention of A.A.'s root sources in connection with straightening out the wreckage of the past and making restitution for harms done to others. The first set of verses—from the Sermon on the Mount—was apparently considered so important by Dr. Bob that, when he was quite ill, he used the verses in connection with amends and was immediately healed.[112] The four sets of verses are:

Therefore if thou bring thy gift to the altar, and there rememberest that thy brother hath ought against thee; leave there thy gift before the altar, and go thy way; first be reconciled to thy brother, and then come and offer thy gift (Matthew 5:23-24).[113]

---

[110] Holm, *The Runner's Bible*, p. 67; Chambers, *My Utmost for His Highest*, p. 182; Benson, *The Eight Points*, p. 32; Weatherhead, *Discipleship*, p. 112. See also *The Upper Room* for 1/12/36 or 1/12/39.

[111] Clark, *I Will Lift Up Mine Eyes*, p. 32; Benson, *The Eight Points*, pp. 36-37; Macmillan, *Seeking and Finding*, p. 99; Tileston, *Daily Strength for Daily Needs*, p. 103; Dick B., *The Akron Genesis*, p. 92, n. 10; *New Light on Alcoholism*, p. 272.

[112] *DR. BOB*, p. 308.

[113] Benson, *The Eight Points*, p. 30; MacMillan, *Seeking and Finding*, p. 176; Russell, *For Sinner's Only*, p. 120; Weatherhead, *Discipleship*, p. 113; Shoemaker, *The Conversion of the Church*, pp. 47-48; *The Gospel According to You*, p. 149; Holm, *The Runner's Bible*, p. 82; Chambers, *My Utmost for His Highest*, p. 268; *DR. BOB*, p. 308; *RHS* (the dedication page); E. Stanley Jones, *The Christ of the Mount*, p. 140.

Speak unto the Children of Israel, when a man or a woman shall commit any sin that men commit, to do a trespass against the Lord, and that soul shall be guilty; Then they shall confess their sin which they have done: and he shall make restitution for his guilt in full, and add unto it the fifth part thereof, and give it unto him in respect of whom he hath been guilty (Numbers 5:6-7, as the translation is rendered in Russell, *For Sinners Only*, p. 119).

For Sinners Only also referred to the Prodigal Son story in Luke, chapter 15. Russell said, "Sending prodigal sons back to their earthly as well as their Heavenly Father is a specialty of the Oxford Group."[114]

For Sinners Only also cited the conversation between Jesus and Zacchaeus recorded in Luke 19:1-10. Zacchaeus had told Jesus that if he had taken anything from any man by false accusation, he had restored the man fourfold. Jesus responded approvingly, "This day is salvation come to thy house."[115]

Step Ten and Daily Corrective Action

[Step Ten: Continued to take personal inventory and when we were wrong promptly admitted it.]

The elements of the Tenth Step can be found on page 84 of the Big Book. The Tenth Step instructions call primarily for a daily application of the spiritual principles learned in the previous nine steps; and the instructions add that AAs should strive to be helpful, loving, and tolerant toward others.

Thus the Big Book's Tenth Step directions state the alcoholic is to *continue* to watch for resentment, selfishness, dishonesty, and fear (tests derived from Step Four). If the "defects of character"

---

[114] Russell, *For Sinners Only*, p. 129. See also *What is the Oxford Group?*, pp. 63-64.

[115] Russell, *For Sinners Only*, p. 135; Lean, *Cast out Your Nets*, pp. 87-88; Macmillan, *Seeking and Finding*, p. 111; Weatherhead, *Discipleship*, pp. 115-16; Almond, *Foundations for Faith*, p. 13.

are encountered, he or she is to confess the problem to another (derived from Step Five). Then God is to be asked for help in eliminating the shortcoming (derived from Steps Six and Seven). If harm has been caused, amends are to be made promptly (derived from Steps Eight and Nine). The alcoholic is then to think of, and help others (derived from Steps Nine and Twelve). And a code of love and tolerance is proclaimed. In short, continuing surrender, continuing recourse to God for help, and continuing corrective behavior are specified as the elements for taking this step.

Clarence S. believed that alcoholics are forgiven by God for everything they have done—by reason of their surrender to the Lord. But, Clarence said, they still get "fouled up." And they may ask God's forgiveness when they do. Clarence pointed to the temptations the Devil presented to Jesus in the wilderness and to how—in response—Jesus utilized the power of God and told the Devil to take a hike:

> Then saith Jesus unto him, Get thee hence, Satan: for it is written, thou shalt worship the Lord thy God, and him only shalt thou serve. Then the Devil leaveth him, and, behold, angels came and ministered unto him (Matthew 4:10-11).[116]

These ideas involving daily inventory and housecleaning can be found in the Oxford Group concept of "Conservation."[117] Later, Oxford Group writers began speaking of "Continuance" as their Fifth "C," rather than "Conservation."[118] They called for

---

[116] Dick B., *That Amazing Grace*, pp. 75-76.

[117] Dick B., *Design for Living*, pp. 221-24; *New Light on Alcoholism*, p. 66; *Anne Smith's Journal*, pp. 49-53, 107, 143; Walter, *Soul Surgery*, 89-100.

[118] The Five C's have alternately been said to include either Conservation or Continuance. But Oxford Group historian and writer K. D. Belden of Great Britain recently wrote the author and explained that the later and preferred usage had become "Continuance." "Continuance" had supplanted "conservation" in usage; and this change may explain A.A.'s emphasis on the word "continued" in connection with the Tenth Step.

continuing repentance, "dying of self," as A.A.'s religious sources might have put it.[119] The significant Bible verses were:

> I am crucified with Christ: nevertheless I live; yet not I, but Christ liveth in me: and the life which I now live in the flesh I live by the faith of the Son of God, who loved me, and gave himself for me (Galatians 2:20).[120]

> Watch and pray, that ye enter not into temptation: the spirit indeed *is* willing, but the flesh *is* weak (Matthew 26:41).[121]

> Howbeit when he, the Spirit of truth, is come, he will guide you into all truth: for he shall not speak of himself; but whatsoever he shall hear, *that* shall he speak: and he will shew you things to come. He shall glorify me: for he shall receive of mine, and shall shew *it* unto you. All things that the Father hath are mine: therefore said I, that he shall take of mine, and shall shew *it* unto you (John 16:13-15).[122]

> If ye continue in the faith grounded and settled, and *be* not moved away from the hope of the gospel, which ye have heard, *and* which was preached to every creature which is under heaven; whereof I Paul am made a minister (Colossians 1:23).[123]

> Being confident of this very thing, that he which hath begun a good work in you will perform *it* until the day of Jesus Christ (Philippians 1:6).[124]

---

[119] Clark, *I Will Lift Up Mine Eyes*, p. 77.

[120] Howard J. Rose, *The Quiet Time* (Sussex, England, n.d.), p. 3; Streeter, *The God Who Speaks*, p. 92; Fosdick, *The Meaning of Faith*, p. 269; *The Upper Room* for 3/27/36 or 3/27/39 and 5/30/36 or 5/30/39.

[121] Rose, *The Quiet Time*, p. 3; Tileston, *Daily Strength for Daily Needs*, p. 100. See also Luke 21:36 and Holm, *The Runner's Bible*, p. 61; *The Upper Room* for 6/13/35.

[122] Rose, *The Quiet Time*, p. 3; Holm, *The Runner's Bible*, pp. 16, 129; Clark, *I Will Lift Up Mine Eyes*, p. 134; Streeter, *The God Who Speaks*, p. 113; Dick B., *The Akron Genesis*, p. 93; *New Light on Alcoholism*, p. 271.

[123] Dick B., *Anne Smith's Journal*, p. 52.

[124] Benson, *The Eight Points*, pp. 162-63.

Step Eleven, Prayer, Guidance, Growth, Power

[Step Eleven: Sought through prayer and meditation to improve our conscious contact with God *as we understood Him*, praying only for knowledge of His will for us and the power to carry that out.]

The Effectiveness of Prayer

The Big Book states:

> *Step Eleven* suggests prayer and meditation. We shouldn't be shy on this matter of prayer. Better men than we are using it constantly. It works, if we have the proper attitude and work at it.[125]

And many A.A. sources quoted the verse in the Book of James which confirmed the effectiveness of prayer:

> The effectual fervent prayer of a righteous man availeth much (James 5:16).[126]

A.A. sources also quoted from 1 John:

> And this is the confidence that we have in him, that, if we ask any thing according to his will, he heareth us: And if we know that he hear us, whatsoever we ask, we know that we have the petitions that we desired of him (1 John 5:14-15).[127]

---

[125] Big Book, pp. 85-86.

[126] Holm, *The Runner's Bible*, p. 62; *The Upper Room* for 8/19/35; Fosdick, *The Meaning of Faith*, p. 190; *The Meaning of Prayer*, pp. 157-58; Walter, *Soul Surgery*, p. 29; Macmillan, *Seeking and Finding*, p. 128; Roger Hicks, *How to Read the Bible* (London: Moral Re-Armament, n.d.), p. 35; Dick B., *Anne Smith's Journal*, pp 36-37.

[127] Holm, *The Runner's Bible*, p. 64; Clark, *I Will Lift Up Mine Eyes*, p. 24; Dick B., *Design for Living*, p. 162.

Eleventh Step Guidance Elements

In one sense, the Eleventh Step (as the Big Book presents the instructions for taking it) contains four elements: (1) *In the evening, before retiring* the alcoholic is to review his or her day, essentially to see how well the Tenth Step was practiced. Then ask forgiveness where there were mistakes or failures. And see what can be done to improve the situation for the future. (2) *In the morning, on awakening*, he or she is to ask for the guidance of God at that time *and* for the rest of the day. (3) *For spiritual growth*, there is to be prayer, meditation, study of "helpful books," and religious observances if the latter are part of one's belief system. (d) *In times of stress throughout the day*, he or she is to deal with agitation and doubt by turning to God for direction and strength.[128]

1. *The End of Day Review.*

In its Eleventh Step instructions, the Big Book states: "After making our review we ask God's forgiveness and inquire what corrective measures should be taken."[129] On this subject of forgiveness, the Good Book states:

> And the prayer of faith shall save the sick, and the Lord shall raise him up; and if he have committed sins, they shall be forgiven him (James 5:15).[130]

---

[128] For a thorough study of the origins and practices concerning guidance and quiet time, see Dick B., *Good Morning!: Quiet Time, Morning Watch, Meditation, and Early A.A.*

[129] Big Book, p. 86. See also the Big Book discussion on page 70 concerning sex conduct which falls "short of the chosen ideal." The text adds: "If we are sorry for what we have done, and have the honest desire to let God take us to better things, we believe we will be forgiven and will have learned our lesson."

[130] Holm, *The Runner's Bible*, p. 114; Fosdick, *The Meaning of Faith*, p. 190.

But if we walk in the light, as he is in the light, we have fellowship one with another, and the blood of Jesus Christ his Son cleanseth us from all sin (1 John 1:7).[131]

If we confess our sins, he is faithful and just to forgive us *our* sins, and to cleanse us from all unrighteousness (1 John 1:9).[132]

2. *Morning Quiet Time and Guidance.*

The "Morning Watch," or "Quiet Time," as the Oxford Group called it, had ancient origins in the Book of Psalms. Psalm 5:3 was often said to be the origin of the "morning watch" idea:

My voice shalt thou hear in the morning, O Lord; in the morning will I direct *my prayer* unto thee, and will look up.[133]

James 1:5 was another verse from the Book of James that A.A. sources frequently quoted concerning the importance of going to God for wisdom and guidance:

If any of you lack wisdom, let him ask of God, that giveth to all *men* liberally, and upbraideth not; and it shall be given him.[134]

And there were many Bible verses and concepts that supported the belief that God does guide and provide when He is sought.[135]

---

[131] Chambers, *My Utmost for His Highest*, p. 361; Howard, *Frank Buchman's Secret*, p. 109; Miles Phillimore, *Just for Today*, (Privately published pamphlet, 1940) p. 7; Almond, *Foundations for Faith*, p. 15.

[132] Almond, *Foundations for Faith*, p. 13.

[133] Holm, *The Runner's Bible*, p. 158; *The Upper Room* for 5/9/35, 7/1/35, 7/22/37; Fosdick, *The Meaning of Prayer*, p. 75; Dick B., *Good Morning!*.

[134] Holm, *The Runner's Bible*, p. 51; Fosdick, *The Meaning of Prayer*, p. 118; *The Meaning of Faith*, p. 239; Clark, *I Will Lift Up Mine Eyes*, p. 137.

[135] Oxford Group Founder Frank Buchman's biographer said, for example: "To Sam Shoemaker in 1920, Buchman wrote a seven-page foolscap letter, citing a formidable array of Biblical and theological authority for the practice" [listening to God]. Garth Lean, *On the Tail of a Comet: The Life of Frank Buchman* (Colorado Springs, CO: (continued...)

The following Bible verses refer to revelation from God:

For I [the Apostle Paul] neither received it [my gospel] of man,
neither was I taught *it*, but by revelation of Jesus Christ (Gal.
1:12).[136]

All scripture *is* given by inspiration of God . . . (2 Tim.
3:16).[137]

For to one is given by the Spirit the word of wisdom; to another
the word of knowledge by the same Spirit . . . (1 Cor. 12:8).[138]

For the prophecy came not in old time by the will of man: but
holy men of God spake *as they were* moved by the Holy Ghost (2
Peter 1:21).[139]

The Comforter, which is the Holy Ghost, whom the Father will
send in my name, he shall teach you all things.[140]

Other verses quoted as to "where God guides, He provides" were:

Trust in the Lord with all thine heart; and lean not unto thine own
understanding. In all thy ways acknowledge him, and he shall
direct thy paths (Proverbs 3:5-6).[141]

---

[135] (...continued)
Helmers & Howard, 1988), p. 75. See Dick B., *Good Morning!*, pp. 6, 8, 10-19, 32-33, 35-37, 40, 42-43.

[136] Streeter, *The God Who Speaks*, p. 91; Macmillan, *Seeking and Finding*, p. 140.

[137] See Dick B., *Design for Living*, p. 44, as to D. L. Moody, the evangelist.

[138] Streeter, *The God Who Speaks*, p. 123; compare Holm, *The Runner's Bible*, p. 138

[139] Holm, *The Runner's Bible*, p. 18.

[140] For discussion of "inspiration" and "revelation" as used in the Bible, see *The Abingdon Bible Commentary*, pp. 26-31; and Almond, *Foundations for Faith*, p. 13.

[141] *The Upper Room* for 5/15/35, 10/17/35; Holm, *The Runner's Bible*, pp. 39, 41, 61, 126; Tileston, *Daily Strength for Daily Needs*, p. 31; Clark, *The Soul's Sincere Desire*, p. 10; *I Will Lift Up Mine Eyes*, pp. 9, 28, 89, 151; Brown, *The Venture of Belief*, p. 40; Streeter, *The God Who Speaks*, p. 135; Benson, *The Eight Points*, p. 81.

I will instruct thee and teach thee in the way which thou shalt go: I will guide thee with mine eye (Psalm 32:8).[142]

Commit thy way unto the Lord; Trust also in him; and he shall bring *it* to pass (Psalm 37:5).[143]

For as many as are led by the Spirit of God, they are the sons of God (Romans 8:14).[144]

But as it is written, Eye hath not seen, nor ear heard, neither have entered into the heart of man, the things which God hath prepared for them that love him (1 Corinthians 2:9).[145]

For we walk by faith, not by sight (2 Corinthians 5:7).[146]

But the wisdom that is from above is first pure, then peaceable, gentle, *and* easy to be intreated, full of mercy and good fruits, without partiality, and without hypocrisy (James 3:17).[147]

A.A. sources suggested listening, and expecting to *receive* the wisdom from God: i.e., "Speak, Lord, thy servant heareth." Not "Hear Lord, thy servant speaketh!"[148]

---

[142] Drummond, *The Ideal Life*, p. 282; Wright, *The Will of God*, p. 9; Streeter, *The God Who Speaks*, p. 115; Benson, *The Eight Points*, p. 80; Holm, *The Runner's Bible*, p. 128; Tileston, *Daily Strength for Daily Needs*, p. 184; *The Upper Room* for 4/22/35.

[143] Holm, *The Runner's Bible*, pp. 127, 136; Clark, *I Will Lift Up Mine Eyes*, p. 28; Benson, *The Eight Points*, p. 81; Samuel M. Shoemaker, Jr., *The Experiment of Faith* (New York: Harper & Brothers, 1957), pp. 28-29; *How You Can Find Happiness* (New York: E. P. Dutton, 1947), p. 149; *The Upper Room* for 11/9/35, 9/25/38, 11/3/38.

[144] *What is the Oxford Group?*, p. 65; Jack C. Winslow, *Why I Believe in the Oxford Group* (London: Hodder & Stoughton, 1934), p. 39.

[145] *What is the Oxford Group?*, p. 65; Lean, *Cast Out Your Nets*, p. 30; Dick B., *The Akron Genesis*, p. 100; Holm, *The Runner's Bible*, p. 142.

[146] *What is the Oxford Group?*, p. 67.

[147] Holm, *The Runner's Bible*, p. 46; Wright, *The Will of God*, p. 167; Clark, *I Will Lift Up Mine Eyes*, p. 63; *The Upper Room* for 9/25/35.

[148] See Shoemaker, *National Awakening*, p. 86; Benson, *The Eight Points*, p. 66.

Adopting these biblical ideas, the Big Book said: "We relax and take it easy. We don't struggle. We are often surprised how the right answers come . . ." (p. 86). Probable sources were:

Be still, and know that I *am* God (Psalm 46:10).[149]

Speak, Lord; for thy servant heareth (1 Samuel 3:9).[150]

Lord, what wilt thou have me to do? (Acts 9:6).[151]

What shall I do, Lord? (Acts 22:10).[152]

3. *Further Work for Spiritual Growth.*

Big Book "spirituality" did not end with surrender, prayer, or listening. It suggested spiritual *growth*—through work with one's priest, minister, or rabbi; and through study of "helpful books" (p. 87). Anne Smith made similar suggestions in her Journal.[153] For

---

[149] Chambers, *My Utmost for His Highest*, p. 53; Holm, *The Runner's Bible*, p. 112; Rose, *The Quiet Time*; Brown, *The Venture of Belief*, p. 37; Benson, *The Eight Points*, pp. 63, 68, 72, 87; *The Upper Room* for 6/23/35, 9/7/35, 1/16/36 or 1/16/39, 3/20/36 or 3/20/39, 4/10/37, 7/3/37, 12/13/38; Dick B., *That Amazing Grace*, pp. 56, 88.

[150] Tileston, *Daily Strength for Daily Needs*, p. 157; Fosdick, *The Meaning of Prayer*, p. 66; Shoemaker, *Children of the Second Birth*, p. 16; *The Church Can Save the World*, p. 30; *National Awakening*, pp. 78, 83, 86, 88; *God's Control*, pp. 115-16; 121; Cecil Rose, *When Man Listens* (New York: Oxford University Press, 1937), p. 30; Foot, *Life Began Yesterday*, p. 4; Jack C. Winslow, *When I Awake* (London: Hodder & Stoughton, 1938), p. 48; Bremer Hofmeyr, *How to Listen* (New York: Moral Re-Armament, n.d.), p. 1; K. D. Belden, *Reflections on Moral Re-Armament* (London: Grosvenor, 1983), p. 35; Benson, *The Eight Points*, p. 66; *The Upper Room* for 4/2/37; Dick B., *The Akron Genesis*, pp. 95-96.

[151] Drummond, *The Ideal Life*, p. 306; Shoemaker, *A Young Man's View of the Ministry*, p. 80; *Religion That Works*, p. 65; Dick B., *Anne Smith's Journal*, p 124; *The Upper Room* for 6/5/36 or 6/5/39.

[152] Shoemaker, *Confident Faith*, pp. 107, 110, 115; *How to Find God*, p. 10; *Extraordinary Living for Ordinary Men* (Michigan: Zondervan, 1965), pp. 40-44, 46, 48.

[153] Dick B., *Anne Smith's Journal*, p. 83.

her, the Bible was "the main Source Book of all."[154] Thus the Good Book said:

> Study to shew thyself approved unto God, a workman that needeth not to be ashamed, rightly dividing the word of truth (2 Tim. 2:15).[155]

> Search the scriptures . . . (John 5:39).[156]

> And ye shall know the truth, and the truth shall make you free (John 8:32).[157]

4. *When Agitated and Doubtful.*

The major spiritual battles occur *all through the day*.[158] As to these situations, the Big Book suggested *continued* reliance on the guidance of God:

> As we go through the day we pause, when agitated or doubtful, and ask for the right thought or action. We constantly remind ourselves we are no longer running the show, humbly saying to ourselves many times each day "Thy will be done." We are then in much less danger of excitement, fear, anger, worry, self-pity, or foolish decisions. We become much more efficient. We do not tire so easily, for we are not burning up energy foolishly as we did when we were trying to arrange life to suit ourselves (pp. 87-88).

---

[154] Dick B., *Anne Smith's Journal*, p. 60.

[155] Tileston, *Daily Strength*, p. 68; *The Upper Room* for 4/27/38, 9/20/38. Clarence S. taught: "Read the Bible . . . know the Word of God so that you will understand it when you meditate." Clarence S., *Going Through the Steps*, 2d ed.(Altamonte Springs, FL: Stephen Foreman, 1985), p. 7.

[156] Holm, *The Runner's Bible*, p. 51; *The Upper Room* for 8/12/38; Dick B., *New Light on Alcoholism*, p. 270.

[157] Holm, *The Runner's Bible*, pp. 46, 107; Clark, *I Will Lift Up Mine Eyes*, p. 58; *The Upper Room* for 5/20/36, 6/28/36.

[158] See Ephesians 6:10-18; and discussion of the spiritual battle by Shoemaker, *God's Control*, pp. 27-32; and Clark, *I Will Lift Up Mine Eyes*, p. 38.

The Good Book precedents were:

> Be careful [anxious] for nothing; but in everything by prayer and supplication with thanksgiving let your requests be made known unto God. And the peace of God, which passeth all understanding, shall keep your hearts and minds through Christ Jesus (Philippians 4:6-7).[159]

> Take no thought for [be not anxious about] your life, what ye shall eat, or what ye shall drink; nor yet for your body, what ye shall put on. . . . for your heavenly Father knoweth that ye have need of all these things. But seek ye first the kingdom of God, and his righteousness; and all these things shall be added unto you (Matthew 6:25, 32-33).[160]

> Thou wilt keep *him* in perfect peace, *whose* mind *is* stayed on *thee*: because he trusteth in thee (Isaiah 26:3).[161]

Step Twelve, Awakening, Witness, Practice of Principles

[Step Twelve: Having had a spiritual awakening as the result of these steps, we tried to carry this message to alcoholics, and to practice these principles in all our affairs.]

---

[159] Holm, *The Runner's Bible*, pp. 61, 115, 147, 155; Tileston, *Daily Strength for Daily Needs*, pp. 53, 361; *The Upper Room* for 10/7/35, 10/20/35, 11/24/35; Fosdick, *The Meaning of Prayer*, p. 72; Clark, *I Will Lift Up Mine Eyes*, p. 93.

[160] Tileston, *Daily Strength for Daily Needs*, p. 61; Chambers, *My Utmost for His Highest*, p. 144; *Studies in the Sermon on the Mount*, pp. 54-57; Fosdick, *The Meaning of Faith*, pp. 192-93; Holm, *The Runner's Bible*, p. 144; *The Upper Room* for 5/10/37; Glover, *The Jesus of History*, p. 91; Streeter, *The God Who Speaks*, p. 81; E. Stanley Jones, *The Christ of the Mount*, p. 200; Dick B., *The Akron Genesis*, pp. 91-92.

[161] Holm, *The Runner's Bible*, pp. 112, 145; Tileston, *Daily Strength for Daily Needs*, p. 321; *The Upper Room* for 6/30/35, 7/13/35; 9/15/35; 10/22/35; 10/20/37; Clark, *The Soul's Sincere Desire*, pp. 10, 83; *I Will Lift Up Mine Eyes*, p. 93; Dick B., *The Akron Genesis*, pp. 91-92; *Good Morning!*, pp. 17, 40, 55, 64.

In one sense, the Twelfth Step has three elements: (1) The spiritual awakening which occurs when the alcoholic has taken the previous eleven Steps; (2) The message of hope to be carried to another alcoholic; (3) The practice of the principles learned from the Steps and to be applied in all of life's affairs.

The Spiritual Awakening. There have been many definitions of A.A.'s "spiritual awakening." It was described as a spiritual "experience" in the First Edition of the Big Book.[162] And the terms "spiritual experience" and "spiritual awakening" are both Oxford Group expressions.[163] For the author, at least, based on his own experience and much language in the Big Book, a spiritual experience has meant to him consciousness and *knowledge* of the power and presence of God in his life.[164] Another less easily understood expression was "God Consciousness."[165]

Early AAs and their spiritual sources referred to the following as to the change in attitude and receipt of power in their lives resulting from their conversion experiences:

> But ye shall receive power, after that the Holy Ghost is come upon you: and ye shall be witnesses unto me both in Jerusalem, and in all Judaea, and in Samaria, and unto the uttermost part of the earth (Acts 1:8).[166]

---

[162] See discussion in Appendix II of the Third Edition, pp. 569-70.

[163] Dick B., *Design for Living*, pp. 276-77.

[164] Big Book, pp. 25, 47, 51, 56, 63, 130, 162, 164; Kitchen, *I Was a Pagan*, pp. 157, 68; Brown, *The Venture of Belief*, pp. 24-26; S. M. Shoemaker, Jr., *With the Holy Spirit and with Fire* (New York: Harper & Brothers, 1960), p. 27. For other Oxford Group expressions for the experience, see Dick B., *Design for Living*, pp. 276-77.

[165] Big Book, p. 570; Begbie, *Life Changers*, pp. 41, 20; Philip Leon, *The Philosophy of Courage or the Oxford Group Way* (New York: Oxford University Press, 1939), pp. 110-11; Kitchen, *I Was a Pagan*, pp. 41, 75; Robert H. Murray, *Group Movements Throughout the Ages* (New York: Harper & Brothers, 1935), p. 349; Shoemaker, *Twice-Born Ministers*, p. 123; *How to Become a Christian*, p. 52; Clark, *The Soul's Sincere Desire*, p. 47.

[166] Holm, *The Runner's Bible*, p. 16; *The Upper Room* for 6/9/35, 11/12/35, 4/23/37, 10/29/37, 6/6/38, 12/31/38; Benson, *The Eight Points*, p. 101; Streeter, *The God Who Speaks*, p. 111; compare Dick B., *Anne Smith's Journal*, p. 22.

And when they had prayed, the place was shaken where they were assembled together; and they were all filled with the Holy Ghost, and they spake the word of God with boldness. . . . And with great power gave the apostles witness of the resurrection of the Lord Jesus: and great grace was upon them all (Acts 4:31, 33).[167]

I beseech you therefore, brethren, by the mercies of God, that ye present your bodies a living sacrifice, holy, acceptable unto God, *which is* your reasonable service. And be not conformed to this world: but be ye transformed by the renewing of your mind, that ye may prove what *is* that good, and acceptable, and perfect, will of God (Romans 12:1-2).[168]

Therefore if any man *be* in Christ, he *is* a new creature: old things are passed away; behold, all things are become new (2 Corinthians 5:17).[169]

Now unto him that is able to do exceeding abundantly above all that we ask or think, according to the power that worketh in us (Ephesians 3:20).[170]

---

[167] Shoemaker, *Religion That Works*, pp. 66-76; Macmillan, *Seeking and Finding*, pp. 162-63.

[168] *The Upper Room* for 12/17/35, 4/18/36, 4/3/38; Tileston, *Daily Strength for Daily Needs*, pp. 98, 196; Holm, *The Runner's Bible*, p. 106; Fosdick, *The Meaning of Faith*, p. 219; Phillimore, *Just for Today* (portion containing a study of Romans, chapter 12); Hicks, *How to Read the Bible*, p. 32; Chambers, *Studies in the Sermon on the Mount*, pp. 23, 60; Dick B., *Anne Smith's Journal*, pp. 46, 77-78, 102, 132.

[169] *The Upper Room* for 7/16/35, 5/1/38, 7/29/38; Holm, *The Runner's Bible*, p. 93; Chambers, *My Utmost for His Highest*, pp. 297, 317; Hicks, *How to Read the Bible*, p. 32; Streeter, *The God Who Speaks*, p. 111; E. Stanley Jones, *The Christ of the Mount*, p. 107. See also Dick B., *That Amazing Grace*, pp. 33-34; Dick B., *The Akron Genesis*, p. 205, containing a discussion of the verse by A.A. pioneer, William V. H. In *Going through the Steps*, Clarence S. quoted this verse—saying, "You are Reborn" (Altamonte Springs, FL: Stephen Foreman, 1985, n.d.).

[170] Oxford Group founder Frank Buchman frequently referred to this verse. See Dick B., *Design for Living*, pp. 369-70; Phillimore, *Just for Today*, pp. 12-13.

Carrying the Message. Witnessing was a critical part the AA's Twelfth Step—carrying to another alcoholic the message of hope and deliverance. "You have to give it away to keep it," said the early AAs and their sources.[171] Action was called for; and the following often-cited Bible verses spelled out the duty to get into action and witness:

And he [Jesus] saith unto them, Follow me, and I will make you fishers of men (Matthew 4:19).[172]

But wilt thou know, O vain man, that faith without works is dead (James 2:20)?[173]

Having therefore obtained help of God, I continue unto this day, witnessing both to small and great, saying none other things than those which the prophets and Moses did say should come: That Christ should suffer, *and* that he should be the first that should rise from the dead, and should shew light unto the people, and to the Gentiles (Acts 26:22-23).[174]

Now then we are ambassadors for Christ, as though God did beseech *you* by us: we pray *you* in Christ's stead, be ye reconciled to God (2 Corinthians 5:20).[175]

Practicing the Principles. Finally, there were spiritual principles to be practiced in daily living. Principles from the Sermon on the Mount, from 1 Corinthians 13, from the Book of

---

[171] See Dick B., *Design for Living*, p. 294; Dick B., *Anne Smith's Journal*, pp. 69, 65, 72-73, 85, 121, 138; Dick B., *New Light on Alcoholism*, pp. 272-74.

[172] Shoemaker, *Realizing Religion*, p. 82; *Twice-Born Ministers*, p. 16; Almond, *Foundations for Faith*, 2d ed., p. 25; Glenn Clark, *Fishers of Men* (Boston: Little, Brown, 1928); Dick B., *New Light on Alcoholism*, p. 272.

[173] Big Book, pp. 14-15, 76, 88, 93; *What Is The Oxford Group?*, p. 36; *DR. BOB*, p. 71; *Pass It On*, p. 147; Wing, *Grateful to Have Been There*, pp. 70-71.

[174] *What Is The Oxford Group?*, p. 25; Dick B., *Anne Smith's Journal*, p. 131.

[175] *What Is The Oxford Group?*, p. 35; *The Upper Room* for 8/28/38; Dick B., *Anne Smith's Journal*, p. 131.

James, from the Oxford Group's Four Absolutes, and from a number of other biblical sources as well.

The Big Book really does not specifically list the "principles" or describe the "works" that are to follow the obtaining of "faith." But we believe the following are *among* the principles the Big Book suggests should be practiced:

1. *Relying upon God* (Big Book, pp. 46, 50, 51-53, 68, 80, 98, 100, 120);
2. *Being rigorously honest* (pp. 58, 64, 67, 69, 73, 84, 86);
3. *Eliminating selfishness and self-centeredness* (pp. 62, 63, 69, 84, 86);
4. *Eliminating resentment, jealousy, and envy* (pp. 64-67, 84, 86, 145);
5. *Eliminating fear* (pp. 67-68, 84, 86, 145);
6. *Practicing patience, tolerance, kindliness, understanding, love, forgiveness, and helpfulness to others* (pp. 20, 77, 83, 84, 97, 118, 153);
7. *Being humble and serving* (pp. 73, 77);
8. *Overcoming the bondage of self, sharing by confession, making restitution, reconciling, and seeking guidance* (pp. 63, 73, 76, 77, 85-88).

There were many Good Book sources for the principles. And the Oxford Group's Rev. Harry Almond said: "A good place to start is with the Ten Commandments." In modern words, Almond summarized the Commandments as follows:

1. You shall have no other gods before me. 2. You shall not make for yourself a graven image . . . or . . . likeness. . . . You shall not bow down to them or serve them. 3. You shall not take the name of the Lord your God in vain. 4. Remember the sabbath day to keep it holy. 5. Honor your father and mother. 6. You shall not kill. 7. You shall not commit adultery. 8. You shall not

steal. 9. You shall not bear false witness against your neighbor. 10. You shall not covet.[176]

Then there were the Oxford Group's Four Absolutes. Then 1 Corinthians 13, as to which Professor Henry Drummond summarized the "love ingredients" as:

1. Patience. 2. Kindness. 3. Generosity. 4. Humility. 5. Courtesy. 6. Unselfishness. 7. Good temper. 8. Guilelessness. 9. Sincerity.[177]

These nine ingredients, said Drummond *and* Dr. Bob, were vital elements in living principles which Dr. Bob said could be simmered down to "love and service."[178]

The "essential" Book of James contained these A.A. principles, which were detailed earlier:

1. Patience. 2. Seeking the wisdom of God. 3. Avoiding temptation. 4. Telling the truth. 5. Avoiding anger. 6. Studying the word of God and "doing" it. 7. Helping the unfortunate. 8. Loving your neighbor. 9. Avoiding adultery and killing. 10. Backing up faith with works. 11. Bridling the tongue. 12. Avoiding envy and strife. 13. Avoiding lying. 14. Avoiding selfish lusts. 15. Avoiding pride. 16. Submitting to God. 17. Purifying hearts. 18. Being humble. 19. Avoiding speaking evil of another. 20. Doing good. 21. Avoiding riches for the sake of riches. 22. Avoiding grudges. 23. Avoiding swearing and false

---

[176] Almond, *Foundations for Faith*, 2d ed., p. 10. For the Ten Commandments themselves, see Exodus 20:3-17; Deuteronomy 5:6-21.

[177] Drummond, *The Greatest Thing in the World*, pp. 26-27; 1 Corinthians 13:4-6. See Benson, *The Eight Points*, p. 47: "The perfect life is simply a life of perfect love. Love is all in all. Jesus said that the whole law is summed up in the one word *love*. It embraces everything as St. Paul teaches in his glorious hymn to love" (1 Corinthians 13). See also Clark, *I Will Lift Up Mine Eyes*, pp. 65-66; Holm, *The Runner's Bible*, pp. 31-32; Dick B., *Anne Smith's Journal*, p. 131.

[178] *DR. BOB*, p. 338.

oaths. 24. Relying on prayer. 25. Confessing faults. 26. Converting sinners from the error of their ways.

The following A.A. principles seem to have come from the Sermon on the Mount:

1. Humility. 2. Compassion. 3. Meekness. 4. Spotless conduct. 5. Making peace with enemies. 6. Harmonizing actions with God's will. 7. Overcoming resentments. 8. Making restitution. 9. Avoiding retaliation. 10. Conducting prayers and good works anonymously. 11. Forgiving. 12. Seeking God and His righteousness first. 13. Engaging in self examination. 14. Doing the will of God. 15. Being rigorously honest. 16. Avoiding evil. 17. Being unselfish. 18. Loving.[179]

---

[179] See also Almond, *Foundations for Faith*, 2d ed., pp. 10-11, setting forth additional Oxford Group views of "sin—the disease" and urging avoidance of such conduct as murder, adultery, deceit, envy, slander, pride, theft, and greed.

Part 3

The Oxford Group's Contribution

"There was the Oxford Group with its dynamic course of action all mapped out. They [Bill and Dr. Bob] tried to base everything they did, every step they took toward formulating their program, on Oxford Group principles."[1]

---

[1] Robert Thomsen, *Bill W.* (New York: Harper & Row, 1975), p. 249.

8

Twenty-eight Oxford Group Principles That Influenced A.A.

The Oxford Group people were concerned with finding or rediscovering God, and then aligning their lives with His will. They studied the Bible to learn about God and His Universal Will; and they listened for His voice, acted in obedience to His Universal Will, and thereby learned His Particular Will for them.[1]

---

[1] See Horace Bushnell, *The New Life* (London: Strahan & Co., 1868), pp. 1-15; J. C. Pollock, *Moody: A Biographical Portrait of the Pacesetter in Modern Mass Evangelism* (New York: Macmillan, 1963), pp. 267-271; William R. Moody, *The Life of D. L. Moody* (New York: Fleming H. Revell, 1900), p. 496; Henry Drummond, *The Ideal Life* (New York: Hodder & Stoughton, 1897), pp. 268, 302—Drummond stating, "The Bible is God's will in words, in formal thoughts, in grace;" and then citing John 7:17 and stating "There is a will of God for me which is willed for no one else besides . . . a particular will;" F. B. Meyer, *The Secret of Guidance* (New York: Fleming H. Revell, 1896), p. 11; Robert E. Speer, *The Principles of Jesus* (New York: Fleming H. Revell, 1902), pp. 21-22; C. H. Hopkins, *John R. Mott: A Biography* (Grand Rapids: William B. Erdmans, 1979), pp. 223, 214; Henry B. Wright, *The Will of God and a Man's Lifework* (New York: Young Men's Christian Association Press, 1909), pp. 135, 146-47, 149; Garth Lean, *On the Tail of a Comet* (Colorado Springs: Helmers & Howard, 1988), p. 157; A. J. Russell, *For Sinners Only* (London: Hodder & Stoughton, 1932), pp. 23, 27-29; 35-36, 94, 211; Irving Harris, *The Breeze of the Spirit* (New York: The Seabury Press, 1978), p. 18; Samuel H. Shoemaker, *A Young Man's View of the Ministry* (New York: Association Press, 1923), pp. 78, 41; *Confident Faith* (New York:

(continued...)

Stress was laid on John 7:17 as the means for learning God's particular will and knowing about Him. Our review of the thoughts of Frank Buchman's *mentors* points up a steady and consistent stream of Bible authority for every concept—from the writings of the earliest identified writer, Horace Bushnell, to the many books by the Oxford Group's most articulate and prolific expositor, Sam Shoemaker.[2]

The Oxford Group did not have six steps, nor did it have twelve. But its life-changing program and principles provided the foundation of, and the structure for the A.A. Fellowship, Big Book, and Twelve Steps. In the beginning, A.A. was an integral part of the Oxford Group. Its founders developed their program from the Bible and from Oxford Group ideas. Before their Big Book was published, the AAs had developed six steps they took to recover. There was no particular agreement as to their form; and the six ideas have been edited and rephrased several times.[3] At least five of the ideas were Oxford Group ideas: (1) Honesty with self—conducting a moral self-examination; (2) Honesty with another person in confidence—sharing; (3) Making amends for harms done to others—restitution; (4) Working with other alcoholics without demand for prestige or money—witnessing; and (5) Praying to God to help them to do these things as best they could—two-way prayer. The first idea of powerlessness over alcohol has a more dubious Oxford Group root.[4]

---

[1] (...continued)
Fleming H. Revell, 1932), p. 106; *Religion That Works* (New York: Fleming H. Revell, 1928), pp. 55, 58, 64; and *Living Your Life Today* (New York: Fleming H. Revell, 1947), pp. 101-09.

[2] See our previous quotation from Sherwood Sunderland Day, *The Principles of the Group* (The Oxford Group, Printed at the Oxford University Press, n.d.), p. 3: "The principles of 'The Oxford Group' are the principles of the Bible."

[3] See Dick B., *The Akron Genesis of Alcoholics Anonymous* (Corte Madera, CA: Good Book Publishing Company, 1994), pp. 256-60. Here the author sets forth the various ways in which the six steps or ideas have been expressed.

[4] For the six step language as Bill there expressed it, see *The Language of the Heart: Bill W.'s Grapevine Writings* (New York: The AA Grapevine, Inc., 1988), p. 200.

In Appendix 2, we have presented almost 200 specific Oxford Group expressions that can be traced into the Big Book and other A.A. literature and language. We will also cover in a later chapter the role that Sam Shoemaker played in these similarities; and we will examine the Oxford Group concepts in light of their direct impact on the Twelve Steps. But the A.A. recovery program does not rest merely on step language or words and phrases. The Big Book is A.A.'s basic text. It provides the "instructions," the "directions," and the "suggestions" for actually taking and completing each step. So one cannot take or understand the steps without learning how the Big Book explains them and details the taking of them. And it is in this context that we here review the twenty-eight Oxford Group ideas that impacted on the Big Book, the Twelve Steps, the recovery program, and the fellowship of Alcoholics Anonymous.

Two basic points offer the backdrop for our study. The first is the Bible-as-the-source emphasis in Oxford Group writings. The second is the finding-of-God-and-His-will objectives of the Oxford Group life-changing program. And it is in that light that we will review twenty-eight Oxford Group principles which we believe influenced the spiritual program of Alcoholics Anonymous.[5]

Too many writers have tried to condense Oxford Group principles into sets of four-to-eight ideas. We believe that, in doing so, they have omitted a number of ideas that parallel, found their way to, or influenced A.A.'s basic spiritual ideas.[6]

---

[5] Before his death, Garth D. Lean (Frank Buchman's biographer) reviewed the twenty-eight principles we constructed. He wrote the author that, while he felt they were overlapping, they were and are valid as Oxford Group concepts. The Reverend T. Willard Hunter (Oxford Group field worker, writer, and speaker in America for many years) also validated the twenty-eight concepts in a personal interview with the author at Claremont, California. Hunter later suggested that the concepts be regrouped and consolidated for more easy flow. And this we have sought to do.

[6] See, for example, The Layman with a Notebook, *What Is The Oxford Group?* (London: Oxford University Press, 1933), pp. 7-9, speaking of "four points" and "four practical spiritual activities;" *DR. BOB and the Good Oldtimers* (New York: Alcoholics Anonymous World Services, Inc., 1980), pp. 54-55, speaking of the "five C's" and the

(continued...)

When we interviewed former Congressman John F. Seiberling in his office at the University of Akron in Ohio, we asked about his familiarity with our twenty-eight Oxford Group concepts. Seiberling stated he would "have had to be deaf not to have heard them." Seiberling attended the early A.A.-Oxford Group meetings in Ohio. He personally knew Dr. Bob, Anne Smith, T. Henry and Clarace Williams, and Bill Wilson, who also attended the meetings. He remarked that his mother, Henrietta Seiberling, the leader at many early A.A. meetings, very frequently spoke of *all* the concepts. We therefore believe Dr. Bob, Anne, and Bill would likewise "have had to be deaf not to have heard them." In other words, the ideas were coin of the realm when early AAs were the "alcoholic squad of the Oxford Group."

The "squib" or introductory description we have used at the beginning of our discussion of each concept does not represent Oxford Group language, but rather our own summary of the concept as we believe the Oxford Group saw it.[7]

In the Beginning, God

1. *God—Biblical Descriptions of Him*

    There is an Almighty, Loving God who has a personal interest in the well-being of every person.

---

[6] (...continued)
"five procedures;" Ernest Kurtz, *Not-God: A History of Alcoholics Anonymous*, exp. ed. (Minnesota: Hazelden, 1991), p. 49, speaking of the "five C's," the "Five Procedures," and "six basic assumptions;" Day, *The Principles of The Oxford Group*, pp. 5-11, speaking of "some" seven of the Bible principles; and Clarence Benson, *The Eight Points of the Oxford Group* (London: Oxford University Press, 1936)—which "Eight Points" were made the subject of examination in the recent book by Dennis C. Morreim, *Changed Lives. The Story of Alcoholics Anonymous* (Minneapolis: Augsburg, 1991), pp. 25-31.

[7] Before the reader begins, we suggest a comparison of the Oxford Group's focus on the will of God with the Big Book's focus on "Thy will be done," which, of course, is from the Lord's Prayer, taught by Jesus in his sermon on the mount. See Big Book pages 67, 85, 88. Compare pages 63, 76, 100, 164. Then see Matthew 6:10—"Thy will be done."

When the Oxford Group spoke of God, they were speaking of God as He is described in the Bible. The Bible calls God *Elohim*—Creator; *El Shaddai*—Almighty God; *Jehovah*—Lord; Father; Maker, Love; Spirit; and the Living God.[8] As *The Companion Bible* points out, God's names for Himself as Jehovah, in company with other words, reveal Him as Jehovah who will see, or provide; heals; is a banner or cover; sends peace; sanctifies; is Lord of hosts; is righteousness; is there; is most high; and is "my Shepherd."[9] In the New Testament, God reveals Himself as, the God of peace, God of grace, God of patience and consolation, God of hope, God of all comfort, Father of mercies, and God of love.[10] Jesus Christ, God's only begotten son, called Him "your Father" and "Our Father" when speaking to the Judeans in the sermon on the mount.[11] The Bible often speaks of God as "the living God."[12]

Oxford Group speaker and writer, Philip M. Brown, professor of international relations at Princeton, had this to say:

> The utter inadequacy of human speech to describe God leaves me almost inarticulate. I can fall back on the many *attributes* such as Omnipotent, Omniscient, All-Loving, King of Kings, Lord of Lords, Creator, Judge, Father of Mankind, to suggest in finite terms something of the Infinite. . . . So whether one prefers to

---

[8] See Andrew Jukes, *The Names of GOD in Holy Scripture* (Grand Rapids, Michigan: Kregel Publications, 1967); *The Companion Bible* (Grand Rapids, Michigan: Kregel Publications, 1990), Appendix 4; *New Bible Dictionary Second Edition* (Wheaton, Illinois: Tyndale House Publishers, 1987), pp. 427-31; and W. E. Vine, *Old and New Testament Words* (New York: Fleming H. Revell, 1981), pp. 160-61; Psalm 95:6.

[9] *The Companion Bible*, Appendix 4, p. 6. See Genesis 22:14; Exodus 15:26; Exodus 17:15; Exodus 31:13; Judges 6:24; 1 Samuel 1:3; Jeremiah 23:6; Ezekiel 48:35; Psalm 7:17; Psalm 23:1.

[10] Romans 16:20, 1 Peter 5:10, Romans 15:5, Romans 15:13, 2 Corinthians 1:3, 1 John 4:8.

[11] Matthew 6:8-9.

[12] See Acts 14:15 which speaks of "the living God, which made heaven and earth;" Isaiah 37:17, which calls God "the living God;" and *The Companion Bible* which discussed, at page 1614, the frequent use of the phrase "the living God" in both the Old and New Testaments.

speak of God, Jehovah, Father, Supreme Wisdom, Infinite, Power, Divine Providence, or any other designations, I do not much care. What does matter is the central fact of an identical experience.[13]

To this statement might be added those of William James and Horace Bushnell. James was highly thought of by both Bill W. and Dr. Bob.[14] And James, a self-described Christian, said this about God:

God is the natural appellation, for us Christians at least, for the supreme reality, so I will call this higher part of the universe by the name of God. We and God have business with each other; and in opening ourselves to his influence our deepest destiny is fulfilled. The universe, at those parts of it which our personal being constitutes, takes a turn genuinely for the worse or for the better in proportion as each one of us fulfills or evades God's demands. As far as this goes I probably have you with me, for I only translate into schematic language what I may call the instinctive belief of mankind: God is real since he produces real effects.[15]

Benson's *The Eight Points of the Oxford Group* quoted the following from a sermon by Dr. Horace Bushnell:

What do the Scriptures shew us, but that God has a particular care for every man, a personal interest in him, and a sympathy with him and his trials, watching for the uses of his one talent as attentively and kindly, and approving of him as heartily, in the right employment of it, as if He had given him ten. . . . How inspiring and magnificent to live, by holy consent. A life all

---

[13] Philip M. Brown, *The Venture of Belief* (New York: Fleming H. Revell, 1935), pp. 24-25.

[14] *Pass It On* (New York: Alcoholics Anonymous World Services, Inc., 1984), pp. 124; *DR. BOB*, p. 306.

[15] William James, *The Varieties of Religious Experience* (New York: First Vintage Books/The Library of America Edition, 1990), p. 461.

discovery, to see it unfolding, moment by moment, a plan of God, our own life-plan conceived in His paternal love.[16]

The Oxford Group variously described God, saying God is: God, Almighty God, Creator, Maker, Father, Spirit, Omnipotent, Love—a loving God, a personal God, the living God, Sovereign over all, Infinite, and Reality.[17]

When Bill Wilson had his religious experience in Towns Hospital, he observed that he had been in touch with "the Great reality. The God of the preachers."[18] In an early draft of the Big Book, Bill wrote that each of the early AAs told "the way in which he happened to find the living God."[19]

To this author, it is clear that Bill Wilson's "God of the preachers" and "living God" was God as Bill had heard Him taught and described at the Oxford Group meetings he had attended in New York and later in Akron and as Anne Smith had read about God to Bill and Dr. Bob at the Smith home in Akron.

---

[16] Benson, *The Eight Points*, pp. 3-4.

[17] See, for example, *What Is The Oxford Group?*, pp. 48, 110, 116; Geoffrey Allen, *He That Cometh* (New York: Macmillan, 1933), pp. 219-23; Benson, *The Eight Points*, pp. 46-47, 65, 73; Frank N. D. Buchman, *Remaking the World* (London: Blandford Press, 1961), pp. 13, 42, 67; Burnett Hillman Streeter, *The God Who Speaks* (London: Macmillan, 1943), pp. 11, 12, 13, 38, 84, 99, 101, 102, 104, 108, 109, 110; Philip Leon, *The Philosophy of Courage or the Oxford Group Way* (New York: Oxford University Press, 1939), pp. 26, 28, 30, 32-34, 48; Samuel Moor Shoemaker, *The Conversion of the Church* (New York: Fleming H. Revell, 1932), pp. 33, 49, 50, 51, 124; *National Awakening* (New York: Harper & Brothers, 1936), pp. 48, 55, 97, 107, 108; *Confident Faith*, pp. 17-18, 38, 54, 59, 74, 83, 96, 106, 107, 152, 183; *Realizing Religion*, p. 35; *Children of the Second Birth*, p. 42; *Christ's Words from the Cross* (New York: Fleming H. Revell, 1933), p. 43; *Living Your Life Today*, pp. 18-19; *How to Become a Christian* (New York: Harper & Brothers, 1953), p. 39; and *The Experiment of Faith* (New York: Harper & Brothers, 1957), p. 53.

[18] *Pass It On*, p. 121.

[19] The author inspected this draft during his visit to Stepping Stones in October of 1991. It contains the statement, "In these accounts each person will describe in his own language and from his own point of view the way in which he happened to find the living God." The material, as changed, wound up on page 29 of the Big Book, speaking of establishing a "relationship with God."

The Oxford Group often mentioned the Ten Commandments, among which, in Exodus 20:3, was the commandment: "Thou shalt have no other gods before Me." We therefore think it fair to say that, at the time Big Book ideas were being drawn from the Bible, the Oxford Group, and Shoemaker—as Dr. Bob and Bill W. said they were—God, as He is described in the Good Book, found His way into the Big Book and the Twelve Steps. This is true, however much ideas about Him and choosing a conception of Him may have been modified to "as we understood Him," "power greater than ourselves," and later "Higher Power," as A.A. evolved.

2. *God Has a Plan—His Will for Man*

God has a specific life-plan for every individual, with definite, accurate information for that individual if he or she wishes to see God's plan fulfilled.

Dr. Frank Buchman, the Oxford Group Founder, frequently spoke about "God's Plan."[20] So did the Reverend Sam Shoemaker.[21] Early AA's picked up on this concept.[22] And a host of other Oxford Group writings spoke of God's Plan.[23]

---

[20] Buchman, *Remaking the World*, pp. 48, 53, 63, 77, 78, 101, 144.

[21] Shoemaker, *Children of the Second Birth*, p. 27; *Religion That Works*, p. 19; *National Awakening*, pp. 41, 83, 89-98; and Dick B., *New Light on Alcoholism*, p. xiii.

[22] *DR. BOB*, p. 145; *Lois Remembers* (New York: Al-Anon Family Group Headquarters, 1987), p. 100. See also Dick B., *Anne Smith's Journal*, pp. 43, 58, 88-90, 94, 103, 123, 140. Compare Big Book stories at pp. 208-09; 302-03.

[23] Wright, *The Will of God*, pp. 3-12; Eleanor Napier Forde, *The Guidance of God* (Oxford: The Oxford Group, 1930), pp. 18-19; Alan Thornhill, *One Fight More* (London: Frederick Muller Ltd, 1943), p. 20; R. C. Mowat, *Modern Prophetic Voices: From Kierkegaard to Buchman* (Oxford: New Cherwell Press, 1994), pp. 8-9; Peter Howard, *Frank Buchman's Secret* (New York: Doubleday & Co., 1961), p. 17; Russell, *For Sinners Only*, p. 23; Benson, *The Eight Points*, pp. 1-17; Cecil Rose, *When Man Listens* (New York: Oxford University Press, 1937), pp. 25-38; Brown, *The Venture of Belief*, pp. 39-41; The Layman with a Notebook, *What Is The Oxford Group?* (New

(continued...)

In fact, one cannot really understand the Oxford Group program without understanding this biblical point. God has a plan. Its is beneficial. It can be learned—in its universal aspects—from the Bible and—in its particular aspects—through two-way prayer—praying and listening for guidance and obeying. A successful life-change involves complete surrender to, and conformity with, God's plan or will. When experienced through conversion, rebirth, being born again, surrender, or whatever it is called, there is "God-consciousness" and peace for the individual.

Three major Bible sources were quoted in the Oxford Group for the foregoing proposition.[24] In one of his British broadcasts, Frank Buchman said, "Why not try God's Plan?"[25] At another point, he said, "The Holy Spirit is the most intelligent source of information in the world today. He [the Holy Spirit] has the answer to every problem. Everywhere, when men will let Him, He is teaching them how to live."[26] Buchman cited Jeremiah 7:23 to substantiate his points:

> Obey my voice, and I will be your God, and ye shall be my people; and walk ye in all the ways that I have commanded you, that it may be well unto you.[27]

Buchman declared that God has a plan, and the combined moral and spiritual forces of the nation can find that plan.[28]

---

[23] (...continued)
York: Oxford University Press, 1933), p. 6; Howard Walter, *Soul Surgery: Some Thoughts on Incisive Personal Work*, 6th ed (Oxford at the University Press by John Johnson, 1940), pp. 26-27; Streeter, *The God Who Speaks*, pp. 7-17; Kitchen, *I Was a Pagan*, p. 122; and Stephen Foot, *Life Began Yesterday* (New York: Harper & Brothers, 1935), p. 173.

[24] Jeremiah 7:23; Isaiah 14:5; and Proverbs 3:5-6.

[25] Buchman, *Remaking the World*, p. 77.

[26] Buchman, *Remaking the World*, p. 12.

[27] Buchman, *Remaking the World*, p. 8.

[28] Buchman, *Remaking the World*, p. 48.

Buchman's spiritual mentor, Horace Bushnell, cited Isaiah 14:5—"I girded thee, though thou has not known me."[29] And Sam Shoemaker's friend Professor Philip Marshall Brown quoted from Proverbs 3:5-6 which reads:

> Trust in the Lord with all thine heart; and lean not unto thine own understanding. In all thy ways acknowledge him, and he shall direct thy paths.

Brown wrote:

> Each day should be a day of high adventure. I must keep spiritually fit in order to be responsive, sensitive, alert, and aware of the significance of every act. . . . I cannot do this unless I "wait on God" and seek humbly and confidently to ascertain His will in my life. He does speak to those who listen. "In all thy ways acknowledge Him, and He shall direct thy paths." This is the "abundant life" which Christ revealed.[30]

3. *Man's Chief End—To Do God's Will*

> Man's chief end is and ought to be to do the Will of God and thereby receive the blessings God promises to those whose lives are in alignment with His will.

Thy will be done! That's what A.A.'s Big Book says repeatedly. That's what the Lord's Prayer—which concludes almost every A.A. meeting—says. And that is the guide in much Christian prayer. From the Oxford Group viewpoint, this concept follows logically from God's plan. If God has a plan—a universal and general will that He spells out in His Word (the Bible) and a particular will that He will tell man if man listens—then man should certainly do his best to learn and obey the plan.

---

[29] Bushnell, *The New Life*, pp. iii, 1. See also, Wright, *The Will of God*, p. 3.

[30] Brown, *The Venture of Belief*. p. 40; see also Howard Rose, *The Quiet Time*, p. 2; and John 10:10.

Professor Henry Drummond quoted from Acts 13:22 to show that God desires "a man after Mine own heart, which shall fulfill all My will."[31] Drummond then cited eight ideas from the Bible which demonstrate the rewards for the man who has the will of God as his chief end:

First, man asks, "What am I here for?" Hebrews 10:9 answers, "Lo, I am come to do Thy Will, O God." Second, man needs sustenance. Jesus responds, saying, in John 4:34, "My *meat* is to do the will of Him that sent me" (emphasis added). Third, man needs society; and Jesus offers him a family, saying in Matthew 12:50, "For whosoever shall do the will of My Father which is in heaven, the same is My brother, and sister, and mother." Fourth, man needs to communicate. Jesus gives him the ideal prayer in Matthew 6:10: "Thy will be done." Fifth, man does not always need to pray, but sometimes to praise. The Psalms show that the ideal praise is of the Will of God. Drummond quoted Psalm 119:54, "Thy statutes have been my songs in the house of my pilgrimage." Psalm 119:97, "O how I love Thy law. It is my meditation all the day." Psalm 40:8, "I delight to do Thy Will, O my God." Sixth, man needs education and thus prays in Psalm 143:10, "Teach me to do Thy Will; for Thou art my God." Seventh, man is promised results when he asks God in accordance with His Will. 1 John 5:14-15 states, "If we ask anything according to His Will, He heareth us . . . and we know that we have the petitions that we desired from Him." Finally, there are the eternal rewards. 1 John 2:17 says, "He that doeth the will of God abideth for ever." Jesus said, "Not every one that saith unto Me, 'Lord, Lord' shall enter into the kingdom of heaven, but he that doeth the will of My Father Which is in heaven" (Matthew 7:21).[32]

---

[31] Acts 13:22 says in part: "He raised up unto them David to be their king; to whom also He gave testimony, and said, 'I have found David the son of Jesse, a man after Mine own heart, which shall fulfil all My will'."

[32] Drummond, *The Ideal Life*, pp. 232-43.

Oxford Group writers absorbed and elaborated upon Drummond's ideas.[33] Canon Streeter wrote:

> The only sensible course for the individual is to ask what is God's Plan for him, and then to endeavor to carry out that plan. For if we can discern anything of God's Plan for us, common sense demands that we give ourselves entirely to it.[34]

Shoemaker taught, "If we look after God's plan, He takes care of our needs." He cited Matthew 6:32-33:

> Your heavenly Father knoweth that ye have need of all these things. But seek ye first the kingdom of God, and his righteousness; and all these things shall be added unto you.[35]

Shoemaker also wrote the following on this subject:

> All life's wisdom, all its power, all its grace lies in the will which cooperates with the Will of God; in the mind that thinks God's thoughts after Him; in the heart that loves Him and loves His Will.[36]

> Give in, admit that God is, and that He has the great Answer to your life, and that your life never is nor will be complete without Him.[37]

---

[33] See, for example, Wright, *The Will of God*, p. 9; Forde, *The Guidance of God*, p. 27; K. D. Belden, *Reflections on Moral Re-Armament* (London: Grosvenor Books, 1983), pp. 54-55; and Benson, *The Eight Points*, pp. 12-13.

[34] Streeter, *The God Who Speaks*, p. 11; Forde, *The Guidance of God*, p. 18; Thornhill, *One Fight More*, p. 50; and Mowat, *Modern Prophetic Voices*, pp. 8-9.

[35] Shoemaker, *National Awakening*, p. 42.

[36] Shoemaker, *Christ's Words From The Cross*, p. 50

[37] Shoemaker, *National Awakening*, p. 47.

Put your situation into the hands of God and take your hands off it. . . . And now just a word to carry with you all day: "Let go, and let God. . . . Let go, and let God."[38]

Note the Big Book text on page 164, "Abandon yourself to God as you understand God." Similar language can be found in Anne Smith's Journal.[39] And compare the last words in Dr. Bob's story in the Big Book, "Your Heavenly Father will never let you down" (p. 181).

4. Belief—We Start with the Belief That He IS

Man must start his journey in doing God's Will by believing that God IS.

Regardless of where they started theologically, Oxford Group people *did not become* atheists or agnostics. They changed their lives through belief in God.[40] Frank Buchman did not preach the necessity for belief in God. He simply used such strong language about God that there could be no doubt about his belief. He talked about: (1) the "miracle-working power of the living God," (2) "God-control," (3) the fact that "God spoke to the prophets of old

---

[38] Shoemaker, *Living Your Life Today*, pp. 12-13.

[39] Dick B., *Anne Smith's Journal*, pp. 90-91.

[40] See our discussion in Chapter Seven under Step Two. *DR. BOB* stated at page 239, "As we have seen, early A.A. members were predominantly white, middle-class, and male. There were membership requirements—belief in God, making a surrender, and conforming to the precepts of the Oxford Group—in addition to having a desire (honest, sincere, or otherwise) to stop drinking. The requirements might be summed up by saying you had to believe before you began." From the Oxford Group and Bible requirements of "belief" as a condition of coming to God, acquiring Faith, and receiving deliverance, the author finds a very clear basis for the early A.A. attitude of "belief" described in the foregoing quote from *DR. BOB*. See Big Book, p. xvi, which (speaking of Bill Wilson) said: "Though he could not accept all the tenets of the Oxford Groups, he was convinced of the . . . necessity of belief in and dependence upon God." See also the last portion of Dr. Bob's story in the Big Book, where Dr. Bob states: "If you think you are an atheist, an agnostic, a skeptic, or have any other form of intellectual pride which keeps you from accepting what is in this book, I feel sorry for you" (p. 181).

[and] may speak to you," and (4) "When man listens, God speaks. When man obeys, God acts. "[41]

Many in the Oxford Group *began* their journey to "find God" through "Faith by Experiment." Garth Lean wrote of this in his book, *Good God, It Works*.[42] You give God control of your life (the Oxford Group way), find that the experiment works, and wind up with belief in God resulting from the success of the experience. Essentials are praying and listening, a decision to obey God's will, and obedience to it. We will see, at a later point, how the Oxford Group emphasis on John 7:17 fits into this picture.

Anne Smith gave a very simple statement of her belief:

> It is not enough to surrender sin, but we must also claim the victory of the resurrection life. It is God that does it.[43]

Professor Philip M. Brown made *his* case for knowing God through a religious experience. He said religious experiences throughout the ages have *established contact* with God and *hence proved His existence*:

> *The Presence of God.* I find throughout the diverse testimonies of religious experiences a striking unity and identity. Whether it be Socrates heeding his "Daimon," Mohammed listening to his "Voice," or Saint Francis and Marshal Foch in prayer, or Gandhi retiring into "the Silence," or simple Brother Lawrence at his ceaseless devotions in the kitchen: all testify to the irreducible minimum of religious experience, namely, the certainty of the "presence of God" in this universe. Men and women of all races, of different mental capacities, social and cultural backgrounds, unite throughout history in their common witness to the reality of God. They tell of the strength of heart and of mind, of the depth

---

[41] Buchman, *Remaking the World*, pp. 41, 42, 13, 24. See also, Cecil Rose, *When Man Listens*, p. 77; and Almond, *Foundations for Faith*. p. 23.

[42] Garth Lean, *Good God, It Works! An Experiment of Faith* (London: Blandford Press, 1974).

[43] Dick B., *Anne Smith's Journal*, p. 91.

of knowledge of life, of the charity and love that are poured into human beings whenever they establish contact with God.[44]

But the underlying premise comes from Hebrews 11:6:

But without faith it is impossible to please Him [God]; for He that cometh to God must believe that He is, and that He is a rewarder of them that diligently seek Him.

The Oxford Group cited this verse to establish that one must start the experiment of faith by believing that God is.[45] Professor Philip Leon wrote, "The facts with which I propose to start here as *undeniable* are God and myself."[46] Canon Grensted, the Oxford theologian, wrote in his foreword to *What Is The Oxford Group?* that the book is "for those who can understand a piece of direct and first-hand evidence for the ways of God's working in a human life."[47] Dr. Shoemaker wrote:

Security lies in a faith in God which includes an experiment. It lies in believing that God is. . . . There are three basic elements in the experiment. The first is a belief in God.[48]

When we come to believe in God at all, we come to believe in Him as having something definite to say about our lives. To believe in the fact of the will of God is only to believe in God in the concrete. As you cannot pray without words, so you cannot imagine God apart from His desires which touch us.[49]

---

[44] Brown, *The Venture of Belief*, p. 24.

[45] Leslie D. Weatherhead, *How Can I Find God?* (London: Hodder and Stoughton, 1933), p. 72; Shoemaker, *The Gospel According to You* (New York: Fleming H. Revell, 1934), p. 47; *National Awakening*, p. 40; *Religion That Works*, p. 55; and *Confident Faith*, p. 187.

[46] Leon, *The Philosophy of Courage*, p. 19 (italics added).

[47] *What Is The Oxford Group?* Foreword.

[48] Shoemaker, *National Awakening*, pp. 40-41.

[49] Shoemaker, *Religion That Works*, p. 55.

Sin—Estrangement from God—The Barrier of Self

5. *Sin As a Reality*

Sin is a reality—the selfishness and self-centeredness that
blocks man from God and from others.

The Oxford Group had lots to say about sin. They believed in
its reality. They defined it. They described it. They categorized it.
And they asserted its power and deadliness in blocking man from
God, from doing God's Will, and from bringing man's life into
harmony with God's plan. Frank Buchman said of sin:

I don't know if you believe in it or not, but it is here. Don't
spend the rest of the day arguing if it exists or not.[50]

What is the disease? Isn't it fear, dishonesty, resentment and
selfishness? We talk about freedom and liberty, but we are slaves
to ourselves.[51]

The root problems in the world today are dishonesty, selfishness
and fear.[52]

It isn't any intellectual difficulty which is keeping you from God.
It is sin.[53]

---

[50] Buchman, *Remaking the World*, p. 54.

[51] Buchman, *Remaking the World*, p. 38. Cecil Rose said in *When Man Listens* that
the word "barriers" expresses half the trouble of the world. He added, "Selfishness, fear,
resentment, pride do not live in the air. They live in men . . . If we are to go on being
honest with others we must go on being honest with ourselves" (pp. 41, 50). Compare
the Big Book's Tenth and Eleventh Step discussions concerning "selfishness, dishonesty,
resentment, and fear" (pp. 84, 86).

[52] Buchman, *Remaking the World*, p. 28.

[53] Begbie, *Life Changers*, quoting Buchman at page 14.

Sin is a word which denotes a choosing. The will chooses the bad. . . . This act of choosing constitutes the sin.[54]

Consciousness of God is the natural state of things. Sin is unnatural, and prevents the natural state of things from obtaining. Sin is unnatural in the sense that it is the will of the creature opposing itself to the will of the Creator. Always it is sin, and only it is sin, which blinds the eyes and hardens the heart of mankind.[55]

Frank Buchman thus made clear his belief that Sin is a reality. So did a host of Oxford Group writers, including Sam Shoemaker.[56] And they provided some very simple *definitions* of sin:

Sin was anything done contrary to the Will of God, as shown in the New Testament or by direct guidance.[57]

The best definition of sin that we have is that sin is anything in my life which keeps me from God and from other people.[58]

All selfishness is sin and all sin is a form of selfishness.[59]

The self is a self-defending system of habits over against other such systems. It is essentially separatist in relation to these other systems. Indeed, the defense is constituted by the separation, and

---

[54] Begbie, *Life Changers*, quoting Buchman at page 15.

[55] Begbie, *Life Changers*, quoting Buchman at page. 16.

[56] Brown, *The Venture of Belief*, pp. 30-33; Day, *The Principles of the Group*, pp. 5-6; Russell, *For Sinners Only*, pp. 317-29; *What Is The Oxford Group?*, pp. 17-24; Begbie, *Life Changers*, pp. 14-17; Benson, *The Eight Points*, pp. 20-21; Walter, *Soul Surgery*, pp. 64-78; Shoemaker, *The Conversion of the Church*, p. 29; *If I Be Lifted Up* (New York: Fleming H. Revell, 1931), p. 131; *God's Control*, pp. 30, 57; *Twice-Born Ministers*, p. 30; and *They're on the Way* (New York: E. P. Dutton, 1951), p. 154.

[57] Russell, *For Sinners Only*, quoting Buchman at page 61.

[58] Russell, *For Sinners Only*, p. 319; *What Is The Oxford Group?*, p. 19; and Foot, *Life Began Yesterday*, p. 67.

[59] Benson, *The Eight Points*, pp. 20-21.

this separation is itself the effect of the primal separation from God or unifying love.[60]

Sin is the thing that keeps us from being channels of God's power. Whatever keeps us from a living, loving relation with other people—or from a vital and open relationship with God—is sin.[61]

But if sin be looked upon as anything that puts a barrier between us and Christ, or between us and other people, then there are many things which we must call by the name of sin.[62]

One cannot open many pages of the New Testament without reading of sin; so we need not document the Bible's references to it. However, *What Is The Oxford Group?* does point to Paul's statement in Romans 3:23 to demonstrate sin's commonality: "For all have sinned, and fall short of the glory of God" (p. 19). A.A.'s original steps referred to "sin."[63] A.A.'s Big Book certainly speaks of self, self-will, selfishness, ego-centricity, and self-centeredness (pp. 60-64, 76). These, it says, are the roots of the "spiritual malady" which "blocks" or "shuts us off" from God (pp. 64, 66, 71).[64]

In his very first book, Shoemaker commented on the spiritual malady he called spiritual *misery*:

It is the unhappiness of *spiritual* people very often—souls who are too fine-grained to get along without religion, yet who have never come to terms with it. . . . Rest cures and exercise and motor drives will not help. The only thing that will help is religion. For

---

[60] Leon, *The Philosophy of Courage*, p. 129.

[61] Shoemaker, *How to Become a Christian*, p. 56.

[62] Shoemaker, *They're on the Way*, p. 154.

[63] *Pass It On*, p. 197. AA of Akron pamphlets also speak of eliminating sin from our lives.

[64] See Dick B., *Anne Smith's Journal*, pp. 92-93.

the root of the malady is estrangement from God—estrangement from Him in people that were made to be His companions.[65]

The Reverend Leslie D. Weatherhead added this insight to the Oxford Group view:

If God is seeking us and we are not found of him, the stop is on our side. . . . Let me indicate briefly some of the things which get in the way: 1. We can be quite sure that very often it is a disguised selfishness. Self is too much in the picture. . . . 2. The second thing that gets in our way is a love of sin. . . . 3. Another door that we shut against God is the fear of what people will say and think.[66]

Finding or Rediscovering God

6. *Surrender—The Turning Point*

Man can only do God's will and bring himself into alignment and harmony with God's plan when he has surrendered his will, his ego, and his sins to God. This is called self-surrender.

DR. BOB and the Good Oldtimers described "surrender" many times.[67] Obviously, early AAs were familiar with and practiced *surrender*. The discussions in *DR. BOB* suggest A.A.'s early "steps" began with a surrender (pp. 101-02). A surrender was made on the knees, accompanied by prayer (pp. 101, 118). *DR. BOB* used these words: "Surrender his will to God" (p. 110), "Surrender themselves to God" (p. 89), "surrender himself absolutely to God" (p. 131), and surrender of the life to God (p.

---

[65] Shoemaker, *Realizing Religion*, pp. 4-5.

[66] Leslie D. Weatherhead, *Discipleship* (New York: The Abingdon Press, 1934), pp. 23-24.

[67] See *DR. BOB*, pp. 77, 88, 89, 92, 93, 101, 102, 104, 110, 118, 131, 139, 141, 142.

139). Bill W. said, as to his surrender at Calvary Mission, that he was told [I had] "given my life to God."[68] Remnants of the practice could be found in Bill's early draft of the Twelve Steps which spoke of "on our knees."[69] Lois Wilson said the Oxford Group practice was "surrender your life to God."[70] Traces can be found in A.A.'s Big Book today where it says, "we could at last abandon ourselves utterly to him" (p. 63).[71] Also, "we decided to turn our will and our life over to God as we understood Him" (p. 60). Also, in the language of Step Three, "Made a decision to turn our will and our lives over to the care of God *as we understood Him*" (p. 59).

The idea of *self*-surrender was identified by Oxford Group mentors. Bushnell and Drummond spoke of "regeneration" through being "born again."[72] Speer and Meyer spoke of the new birth and receiving "*Christ in you.*"[73] There was also talk about "surrender of the will." Drummond discussed doing God's will and then said:

Do you think God wants your body when He asks you to present it to Him? Do you think it is for *His* sake that He asks it, that He might be enriched by it. God could make a thousand better with a breath. He wants your gift to give you His gift—your gift which was just *in the way* of His gift. He wants your will out of the way, to make room for His will. You give everything to God. God gives it all back again, and more. You present your body a living sacrifice that you may prove God's will. You shall prove it by getting back your body—a glorified body.[74]

---

[68] *Pass It On*, p. 118.

[69] *Pass It On*, p. 198.

[70] *Lois Remembers*, p. 92.

[71] And see Big Book, pp. 59, 164.

[72] Bushnell, *The New Life*, pp. 59-73; and Drummond, *The Ideal Life*, pp. 212-26.

[73] Speer, *The Principles of Jesus*, pp. 204-08; and Meyer, *The Secret of Guidance*, pp. 31-32, 110-16. See John 3:1-9; Colossians 1:23. To the same effect are Weatherhead, *Discipleship*, pp. 146-47; and Streeter, *The God Who Speaks*, pp. 109-11.

[74] Drummond, *The Ideal Life*, p. 286. See 1 Thessalonians 4:3, 1 Peter 1:15-16, Hebrews 10:9, 10; Romans 12:1-2.

Meyer said, "Our will must be surrendered;" and he cited these two Bible verses:

My judgment is just because I seek not mine own will, but the will of the Father which hath sent me (John 5:30).

If any man will do his will, he shall know (See John 7:17).[75]

But it was William James who captured the attention of the Oxford Group with his talk of "surrender" and the "turning point." Dr. Shoemaker quoted from James:

William James speaks with great emphasis upon this crisis of self-surrender. He says that it is "the throwing of our conscious selves on the mercy of powers which, whatever they may be, are more ideal than we are actually, and make for our redemption. . . . *Self-surrender* has always been and always must be regarded as *the vital turning-point of the religious life*, so far as the religious life is spiritual and no affair of outer works and ritual and sacraments. One may say that the whole development of Christianity in inwardness has consisted in little more than the greater and greater emphasis attached to this crisis of self-surrender (italics added)."[76]

Henry Wright nailed down the James concept by writing an entire chapter on the self-surrender involved in *doing God's Will*.[77] Wright cited Romans 6:16 for the principle of self-surrender:

Know ye not, that to whom ye present yourselves as servants unto obedience, his servants ye are to whom ye obey; whether of sin unto death, or of obedience unto righteousness.[78]

---

[75] Meyer, *The Secret of Guidance*, p. 11. Compare Streeter, *The God Who Speaks*, p. 126.

[76] Shoemaker, *Realizing Religion*, p. 30; James, *The Varieties of Religious Experience*, pp. 195-96.

[77] Wright, *The Will of God*, pp. 31-42.

[78] Wright, *The Will of God*, p. 31.

The Oxford Group followed the lead of the Buchman mentors on the matter of surrender.[79] So did Anne Smith.[80] Benson's *The Eight Points* said:

> The initial step and the indispensable step in the quest is *absolute surrender of our lives to God.* Surrender is "life under new management." . . . All that is in self, good, bad, and indifferent must be handed over to God. He will then give back whatever is fit for us to use. . . . Surrender is made possible by the operation of the Holy Spirit within us so that while we ourselves play our part in it, we can in no case suppose we are saving ourselves. . . . Repentance is the very breath of surrender (italics in original).[81]

What Is The Oxford Group? quoted several Bible verses in connection with surrender.[82] It then said:

> Surrender to God is our actual passing from a life of Sin to a life God-Guided and Christ-conscious. It is the giving up of our old ineffective spiritual lives and taking on a life of spiritual activity in everything we do or say. . . . Surrender is our complete severance from our old self and an endeavoring to live by God's Guidance as one with Christ. . . . Surrendering our lives to God means a complete giving back to God of the will-power He gave us at Creation which, with the Ages, has separated itself by Sin from the Giver, and our taking, in its place, His will as He intended our will should be when He first made man in His own image (p. 41).

---

[79] See Russell, *For Sinners Only*, pp. 31, 143; Brown, *The Venture of Belief*, pp. 28-30; Olive Jones, *Inspired Children* (New York: Harper & Brothers, 1933), pp. 136, 142-44; Winslow, *Why I Believe in the Oxford Group* (London: Hodder & Stoughton, 1934), pp. 28-29; Weatherhead, *Discipleship*, pp. 15-30; and C. Rose, *When Man Listens*, p. 26.

[80] Dick B., *Anne Smith's Journal*, pp. 93-95.

[81] Benson, *The Eight Points*, p. 5.

[82] See Chapter 7 of our title, and its discussion of Step Three.

Dr. Shoemaker wrote:

Surrender is a handle by which an ordinary person may lay hold
of the experience of conversion. It is the first step of the will. In
order to make surrender the decision of the whole life . . . we
must help people to see just what they are surrendering to God,
their fears, their sins, most of all their *wills*, putting God's Will
once and for all ahead of every other thing.[83]

William James said long ago that "self surrender has been and
always must be regarded as the vital turning-point of the religious
life." We need to help people see what goes into a decision of
surrender: a complete break with sin . . . so that it is quite
specific what they give to God—temper, fear, sex, inferiority,
pride, etc; the readiness from now on to listen to God . . . the
complete giving to God of the great trend of our lives.[84]

In the beginning was God.[85] The Oxford Group insisted on
belief that God *is*. Also that God has a plan to which man must
conform if he is to do well. Then, biblically speaking, came
sin—disobedience to God and separation from God.[86] Not
surprisingly, the disobedience and estrangement from God
occurred after man had been tempted by, and succumbed to the
lure that, in the act of disobedience, "ye shall be as gods."[87] We
might add that people have been in a peck of trouble ever
since—"playing God." And even A.A.'s Big Book addresses the
first move in a return to God: "First of all, we had to quit playing
God. It didn't work" (p. 62).

---

[83] Shoemaker, *The Conversion of the Church*, p. 78.

[84] Samuel M. Shoemaker, *The Church Can Save the World* (New York: Harper &
Brothers, 1938), pp. 113-14.

[85] Genesis 1:1. See Streeter, *The God Who Speaks*, pp. 100, 48.

[86] Genesis 2:17; 3:15; 3:23-24.

[87] Genesis 3:5.

William James called self-surrender the *turning point.*[88] This phrase commanded repeated attention in Oxford Group writings, particularly those of Sam Shoemaker.[89] And the phrase was apparently not lost in A.A. when the Big Book was written. For the Big Book's Twelve Step summary is preceded by these words:

> Half measures availed us nothing. We stood at the turning point. We asked His protection and care with complete abandon (p. 59).

7. *Soul-surgery—The "Art" or Way*

> Man's sin of self-centeredness is a spiritual disease requiring cure of his "sick soul" by Frank Buchman's "soul-surgery" art, called, for short, *Confidence, Confession, Conviction, Conversion, Conservation.*

In *The Varieties of Religious Experience*, Professor William James wrote a chapter titled, "The Sick Soul."[90] James said evil is a disease; and *worry* over the disease is itself *an additional form* of disease which only adds to the original complaint. Evil facts, he said, are as genuine a part of nature as good ones. Christianity's answer is deliverance: man must die to an unreal life before he can be born into the real life. Sick souls must be "twice-born" to be happy. There are two lives, the natural and the spiritual. We must lose one before we can participate in the other. Man has a divided self. To be at peace, he must be rid of the evil one. The sick soul must be rid of the evil will and must be unified with the good will. This can be accomplished by a new birth through the process of conversion.

---

[88] See Shoemaker, *Children of the Second Birth*, p. 16—setting forth one of Shoemaker's many quotations of this William James expression.

[89] Weatherhead, *Discipleship*, p. 16; Kitchen, *I Was a Pagan*, p. 67; Shoemaker, *Realizing Religion*, p. 30; *A Young Man's View of the Ministry*, p. 55; *Children of the Second Birth*, p. 30; *Religion That Works*, p. 48; *The Church Can Save the World*, p. 113; *God's Control*, p. 138; and *The Experiment of Faith*, p. 25.

[90] James, *The Varieties of Religious Experience*, pp. 121-54.

Frank Buchman accepted this "sick soul" concept. Harold Begbie explained Buchman's thinking in *Life Changers*.[91] Buchman believed sin keeps man from God. The soul must be freed from the tyranny of sin and gain the liberty of a will in harmony with God's will. The will of the soul must be converted to the divine will. Jesus's prescription for healing was: "According to your faith, be it done unto you" [Matthew 8:29]. Sin robs a man's soul of its natural health. As Buchman put it, there can be no living and transforming unity with the divine will—no "God Consciousness," as he called it—so long as the heart is clogged by selfishness. There must be confession and restitution. Man's sin is "walling him in from God;" man's will is raised against the consciousness of God. But "God comes to us when we ask Him"—with the whole will.

Begbie called Buchman a "soul surgeon." Buchman got sin into the open and then eradicated the disease by cutting it out at the roots. Buchman led man to hate his sin, long to be rid of it, long for freedom and health, and passionately crave the consciousness of God in his soul. Then, when the surgeon had delivered from the disease; he became the physician—telling men how to *exercise* by helping others through becoming savers of souls. Become life changers, said Frank Buchman! Buchman's formula was: hate sin, forsake sin, confess sin, and make restitution. The heart was thus cleansed of iniquity. There would be a new sense of Jesus's declaration in the sermon on the mount, "Blessed are the pure in heart; for they shall see God" (Matthew 5:8).

Howard Walter wrote *Soul Surgery* to detail Buchman's life-changing art—"an art," as Professor Drummond had defined it—for healing the sick soul and cleansing the impure heart. Walter's book was about personal evangelism. The personal work was called "Cure of Souls."[92] Jesus was called the Great Physician because

---

[91] Begbie, *Life Changers*, pp. 31-41.
[92] Walter, *Soul Surgery*, p. 21.

He perfectly "knew what was in a man" [John 2:25].[93] The "New Evangelism" began by laying siege to a particular soul. First, came early morning prayer. The worker's spirit became attuned to the Divine Spirit. The aim was to receive "leadings" through Divine Guidance. Howard Walter called the method, "Woo, Win, Warn;" but he deferred to Frank Buchman's soul-physician nomenclature which came to be known as the five C's: *Confidence, Confession, Conviction, Conversion, Conservation.*

Walter believed "the method comes from God."[94] Also, the Guidance as to how a particular soul should be helped.[95] Oxford Group writers often referred to the five C's and soul-surgery.[96] So did Anne Smith.[97] And Oxford Group writer Jack Winslow said:

> A third reason why my ministry so seldom bore fruit in trans-formed lives was that I lacked experience in what has been called the art of "soul-surgery." . . . And I cannot but pay this tribute to the Oxford Group, that it has taught me much that ought to have been taught to me in my theological college days as to the right ways of bringing men and women to the new life that is in Christ.[98]

Dr. Shoemaker also approved of Buchman's soul-surgery "art" and the Five C's. In *The Conversion of the Church*, Shoemaker said:

> I think that the great practical apostasy of the Church in our time lies in her forsaking the great function of "the cure of souls" (p. 12).

---

[93] Walter, *Soul Surgery*, p. 24. See Chapter Three of our work where Bill said: "I remember saying to myself, 'I'll do anything, anything at all. If there be a Great Physician, I'll call on him."

[94] Walter, *Soul Surgery*, p. 29.

[95] Walter, *Soul Surgery*, p. 28.

[96] Lean, *On the Tail of a Comet*, pp. 78-79; Spoerri, *Dynamic out of Silence*, p. 56; and Austin, *Frank Buchman as I knew him*, p. 19.

[97] Dick B., *Anne Smith's Journal*, pp. 96-97.

[98] Winslow, *Why I Believe in the Oxford Group*, pp. 60-61.

In his first book, Shoemaker explained the method of cure in the following way:

> And how do you do it? It may help to keep our object in view if we choose five words which will cover the usual stages of development: "Confidence; Confession; Conviction; Conversion; Conservation." You may feel this is a bit formidable and ready-made, but it is good to have the main points fixed. For these words I am indebted to Frank N. D. Buchman.[99]

We believe the five C's became the framework for A.A.'s Steps. "Confidence" became submerged in the method for working with others as well as the method for eliciting "Confession." "Confession" seems clearly to have wound up in A.A.'s Fifth Step.[100] "Conviction" may have become embodied in its Sixth Step. "Conversion" was certainly the process Bill Wilson discussed with Dr. Carl Jung as being the foundation of A.A.'s early success.[101] And "Conversion" was very possibly a part of the Third and Seventh Step ideas. Finally, "Conservation" seems to have comprehended the whole "maintenance," "growth," and "daily practice" ideas in Steps 10, 11, and 12.[102]

There is a good deal of scattered evidence in A.A. history that shows the Five C's and "soul surgery" were words used in early A.A. before the Steps were written—and even after. Early AAs spoke of "no pay for soul surgery."[103] This idea may have been incorporated in the language of A.A.'s original six steps, where its *fifth* step said, "We tried to help other alcoholics, with no thought of reward in money or prestige."[104] There is negative evidence that "soul surgery" was a term bandied about in early A.A. Dr.

---

[99] Shoemaker, *Realizing Religion*, pp. 79-80.

[100] Compare, *Pass It On*, pp. 128, 197.

[101] *Pass It On.* pp. 381-86. See also Nell Wing, *Grateful to Have Been There* (Illinois: Parkside Publishing, 1992), pp. 20-21.

[102] Compare Wing, *Grateful to Have Been There*, pp. 20-21.

[103] *DR. BOB*, p. 54.

[104] See Dick B., *The Akron Genesis*, pp. 256-58; and *Lois Remembers*, p. 92.

Kurtz reported in *Not-God* that both Lois Wilson (Bill's wife) and Henrietta Seiberling had an aversion to the term.[105]

The "five C's" are mentioned in *DR. BOB and the Good Oldtimers* (p. 54). Anne Smith wrote at length on each of the five in the pages of her Journal.[106] Richmond Walker, an early A.A. who wrote *Twenty-Four Hours A Day*, also referred to them.[107]

8. *Life-change—The Result*

> The Oxford Group was about Life-Changing. Man surrenders his life—past, present and future—into God's care and direction as part of a spiritual experience in which man's focus is then on changing others.

One can certainly read Harold Begbie's *Life Changers* and find Frank Buchman's concept of life-changing. The idea of "change," "life change," and "life changing" crops up again and again *in* Oxford Group writings and in writings *about* the Oxford Group.[108]

Benson's *The Eight Points of the Oxford Group* said:

1. Absolute surrender to which the Group witnesses includes all that the New Testament means by converting. It is conversion with a definite programme of world changing through life

---

[105] Kurtz, *Not-God*, p. 324, note 36.

[106] See Dick B., *Anne Smith's Journal*, pp. 41, 42, 49, 96, 97, 100, 107, 141.

[107] Richmond Walker, *For Drunks Only* (Hazelden, reprint), pp. 45-46; *The 7 Points of Alcoholics Anonymous*, rev. ed. (Seattle, WA: Glen Abbey Books, 1989), pp. 91-93.

[108] Winslow, *Why I Believe in the Oxford Group*, pp. 33, 57-61; *What Is The Oxford Group?*, p. 37; Leon, *The Philosophy of Courage*, p. 93; Russell, *For Sinners Only*, pp. 53-69; Walter, *Soul Surgery*, pp. 25, 30; Austin, *Frank Buchman As I Knew Him*, p. 26; Weatherhead, *Discipleship*, pp. 125-38; Foot, *Life Began Yesterday* p. 174; Kitchen, *I Was a Pagan*, p. 145; Lean, *On the Tail of a Comet*, p. 79; Almond, *Foundations for Faith*, p. 25; and Bremer Hofmeyr, *How to Change* (New York: Moral Re-Armament, n.d.). Note the title of Reverend T. Willard Hunter's thesis on the life of Frank Buchman—"World Changing Through Life Changing." See also, Shoemaker, *God's Control*, pp. 21-22; and *The Church Can Save the World*, pp. 93, 118, 124, 153.

changing. The Group is insistent that every Christian must be a life changer. The New Testament knows nothing of a self-contained conversion (p. 158).

2. The Oxford Group is only a means of bringing men and women into vital relationship with Jesus Christ. He is the only Savior. No one in the Group ever changed anybody (pp. 158-59).

3. Conversion, or what the Group calls "life changing," is the crisis when a man turns to Christ. That deep, initial experience cannot be skipped or slurred (pp. 162-63).

What Is The Oxford Group? said:

Those of us who have seen the wonders of the results of the life changing of the Oxford Group can only describe them as modern miracles. Men and women, who have never before realized that Sin can kill not only the soul but the mind, talents, and happiness as surely as the malignant physical disease, have found that the surrender to God, in actuality as well as in theory, means a new lease of life which brings with it a fuller joy of living than they have realized was possible for them. They have been reborn to the world as well as reborn to God. . . . Sinners who are obsessed by their sins find that they can be set free and reborn into spiritual liberty (p. 6).

Anne Smith wrote in her Journal: "The axis of this group [the Oxford Group] is the changed life."[109]

---

[109] Dick B., *Anne Smith's Journal*, p. 96.

The Path They Followed to Establish
a Relationship with God

9. *Decision*

The first essential in the Oxford Group life-changing path is a decision—a voluntary act in which man—on his knees— verbalizes his surrender, usually with another, and gives in to God, essentially saying "Thy Will be done."

In *The Will of God and a Man's Lifework*, Wright included a chapter on "The Decision to Do God's Will" (pp. 41-114). Wright said self-surrender requires a definite, conscious, personal compact between man and God. Man voluntarily gives God absolute possession of his life, and God comes in. There is an energizing, life-giving, impetus (within) of a "decision" to do God's will—often exemplified by the prayer, "Thy Will be done."[110] Absolute surrender was the "beginning" of "life under new management."[111] *What Is The Oxford Group?* said of the decision:

> The Oxford Group recommend our making the initial act of Surrender to God in the presence of another person who is already a Changed Life, or in the presence of a person who has for some time been an active Christian . . . to make our Surrender complete in the sight of God and Man; . . . [I]t is a simple decision put into simple language, spoken aloud to God, in front of a witness, at any time and in any place, that we have decided to forget the past in God and to give our future into His keeping. . . . The Lord's Prayer is a perfect example of Surrender to God. . . . The essential point in studying the Lord's Prayer as Surrender in its complete form is to ask ourselves if we really are convinced that

---

[110] Wright, *The Will of God*, pp. 50-51. See also Ebenezer Macmillan, *Seeking and Finding* (New York: Harper & Brothers, 1933), p. 273; Shoemaker, *Children of the Second Birth*, pp. 58, 175-87 (the latter pages containing an entire chapter on "Thy Will be done"); *If I Be Lifted Up*, p. 93; and *How to Find God*, p. 10.

[111] Benson, *The Eight Points*, p. 5; Dick B., *That Amazing Grace*, p. 67.

we believe in and act on every phrase in our daily lives. . . . "Thy will be done" are the four little words that give us the crux to the surrender of our will-power which is usually the last thing we wish to surrender to God (pp. 46-48).

The Oxford Group people often surrendered with these prayers:

O God, if there be a God, take command of my life; I cannot manage it myself.[112]

O Lord, manage me, for I cannot manage myself.[113]

O God, if there is a God, take charge of my life.[114]

O God, if there be a God, send me help now because I need it.[115]

Compare Bill Wilson's cry of surrender at Towns Hospital just before he had his dramatic religious experience in 1934:

If there be a God, let Him show himself.[116]

Also this part of the Big Book's Third Step Prayer:

---

[112] Brown, *The Venture of Belief*, pp. 26, 29-30.

[113] Russell, *For Sinners Only*, p. 80; Howard, *Frank Buchman's Secret*, p. 43; and Spoerri, *Dynamic out of silence*, pp. 36-37. Anne Smith suggested a similar prayer. See Dick B., *Anne Smith's Journal*, pp. 20-22. Frank Buchman told the story in the 1920's about a student, George Moissides, who uttered the prayer, "O God, manage me because I cannot manage myself." This, said Buchman, occurred for Moissides "when God came into his life." And Buchman apparently invited an entire student body at Robert College in Constantinople to repeat the boy's prayer. See Lean, *On the Tail of a Comet*, p. 113. Perhaps unaware of the "Victor story" as the probable origin of the "manage me" prayer, Rev. W. Irving Harris said a very similar prayer became known at Calvary Church as "Charlie's prayer." An "east-sider" named Charlie said "God, manage me, 'cause I can't manage myself." Harris, *The Breeze of the Spirit*, p. 10.

[114] Cecil Rose, *When Man Listens*, p. 22.

[115] Samuel M. Shoemaker, *How You Can Help Other People* (New York: E. P. Dutton, 1946), p. 60; and *How to Find God*, p. 6. See also Belden, *Reflections on Moral Re-Armament*, p. 16.

[116] *Pass It On*, p. 121.

God, I offer myself to Thee—to build with me and to do with me
as Thou wilt. . . . May I do Thy will always (p. 63).

Shoemaker wrote much on the decision process:

> [T]hese difficulties. . . must be gathered up in a new decision of
> the will and handed over to God in a new surrender . . . this step
> of decision. . . . It is true that only the Spirit of God converts any
> man: it is His direct action on the soul that alone converts. But we
> may draw near and put ourselves in a position to be converted by
> the simple act of self-surrender. . . . There must be a decision
> which the mind has collected, and the aspiration of the heart has
> felt, and pacts them into a moral choice. This is the act of self-
> surrender.[117]

> You are all familiar with the words of the Forty-sixth Psalm, "Be
> still, and know that I am God: I will be exalted among the
> heathen." . . . Here is the meaning which Dr. Moffatt finds in
> these familiar words, "Give in, admit that I am God." . . . I
> believe they are the gateway to a true faith, and show us the way
> to find God. Now the place where our wills pass out of our own
> hands and into God's is the place of surrender, and surrender is
> our answer to this command from God, "Give in." . . . I began
> understanding it when I "gave in" to God in an act of the will
> called self surrender. . . . We need to know little about His
> nature, the completeness of His self-revelation in Christ to make
> this initial step towards Him. Understanding will come later: what
> is wanted first is relationship. That begins, as thousands will tell
> you from experience, at the point where we "give in" to God.[118]

> God is God, and self is not God—that is the heart of it.[119]

---

[117] Shoemaker, *The Conversion of the Church*, pp. 39-40, 77.

[118] Shoemaker, *National Awakening*, pp. 45, 46, 51.

[119] Shoemaker, *National Awakening*, p. 48. Compare Big Book, p. 62: "This is the
how and why of it. First of all, we had to quit playing God. It didn't work."

He said he wanted to make a decision, and give himself completely to Christ, so we got down on our knees and he did it.[120]

I could give you a hundred instances of men and women whom, I have known, who have, at a critical place in their lives, made this momentous turning and have never retraced their steps or gone back on their decision.

. . . There are two elements in the complete experience of which I speak, if surrender grows into conversion: man's turn, and God's search. For some of us the critical element is the dedication of our own wills. For others it is the moment of God's invasion. Surrender is, then, not so much effort as is required in throwing ourselves over upon the mercy of God, but only so much as is needed to open the door of our life to Him.[121]

10. *Self-examination—A Moral Inventory*

The surrender process requires that man make a moral inventory of himself—taking stock of his sins and their consequences.

The Oxford Group believed in self-examination. Man cannot effectively implement his decision until he is ready to flee from his own sins. To do this, he needs to examine himself and see the results of his own focus on self and his own will-power. Oxford Group writers were fond of quoting (from Jesus's sermon on the mount) the proposition that one should "look for the log in his own eye before trying to cast out the speck in his brother's eye" (See Matthew 7:3-5).[122] Henry Drummond urged what the Oxford

---

[120] Shoemaker, *The Church Can Save the World*, p. 120. See also, Dick B., *Anne Smith's Journal*, pp. 27-19.

[121] Shoemaker, *Religion That Works*, pp. 46-47.

[122] For a discussion of this principle in the Sermon on the Mount, see Allen, *He That Cometh*, pp. 81, 140; Kitchen, *I Was a Pagan*, pp. 110-11; Shoemaker, *The Church Can Save the World*, pp. 88-121; *God's Control*, pp. 62-72; and Dick B., *Anne Smith's Journal*, p. 141; Compare Russell, *For Sinners Only*, pp. 309-16.

Group called the "moral test."[123] In *The Ideal Life*, Drummond declared that "willingness" to do God's Will is essential to "knowing" God's Will; but he said willingness had to commence with man's "in-look."[124] Man needs to "devote his soul to self-examination, to self examination of the most solemn and searching kind," said Drummond.[125]

Frank Buchman elaborated on the things to look *for*. He said:

1. International problems are based on personal problems of selfishness and fear.[126]

2. If you want an answer for the world today, the best place to start is with yourself.[127]

3. You will find selfishness and fear everywhere.[128]

4. The root problems in the world today are dishonesty, selfishness and fear—in men, and consequently in nations.[129]

5. Moral recovery starts when everyone admits his own faults instead of spot-lighting the other fellow's.[130]

As stated, Walter's *Soul Surgery* likened Buchman's life-changing art to the work of the "soul physician" endeavoring to "cure" diseases of the soul through surgery that cuts them out and eradicates them. Walter said the soul surgeon must familiarize himself with the particular person, hear from the lips of the patient

---

[123] See Walter, *Soul Surgery*, p. 43-44; and see discussion of this in Dick B., *Anne Smith's Journal*, pp. 31-36.

[124] Drummond, *The Ideal Life*, pp. 313, 319, 316.

[125] Drummond, *The Ideal Life*, p. 316.

[126] Buchman, *Remaking the World*, p. 3.

[127] Buchman, *Remaking the World*, p. 24.

[128] Buchman, *Remaking the World*, p. 24.

[129] Buchman, *Remaking the World*, p. 28.

[130] Buchman, *Remaking the World*, p. 46.

himself, and probe "to the root of the trouble."[131] To win the soul, the "physician" must "make the moral test." This requires the lost soul to make "entire self disclosure," so that the spiritual surgeon may possess all the data for an accurate diagnosis. Walter cited the example of a leading Canadian pastor who conducted what he called his "Moral Clinic."[132]

To this imagery, *The Eight Points of the Oxford Group* added the idea of a businessman's taking an inventory—checking his financial position by having "taken stock."[133] Cecil Rose used a similar illustration, talking about "this business of looking into the books" with a pencil and paper and notes.[134]

The foregoing ideas—a *moral test*, a *business inventory*, and *self-examination*, with *pencil and paper*—probably influenced the following A.A. Fourth Step instructions:

1. "Made a searching and fearless moral inventory of ourselves" (Big Book, p. 59).[135]

2. "A business which takes no regular inventory goes broke. Taking a commercial inventory is a fact-finding and fact-facing process. . . . We did exactly the same thing with our lives. We took stock honestly" (Big Book, p. 64).

3. "In dealing with resentments, we set them on paper. . . . We reviewed our fears thoroughly. We put them on paper. . . . Now about sex. . . . We reviewed our own conduct over the years past. . . . We got this all down on paper and looked at it" (Big Book, pp. 68-69).

---

[131] Walter, *Soul Surgery*, p. 69.

[132] Walter, *Soul Surgery*, pp. 41-48.

[133] Benson, *The Eight Points*, pp. 44, 162, 18, 7.

[134] Cecil Rose, *When Man Listens*, pp. 17-19.

[135] See in Anne Smith's journal, the "moral test." Dick B., *Anne Smith's Journal*, pp. 30-32, 72, 98, 99.

Sam Shoemaker spoke of a *written* check of one's conduct against the Four Standards:

> It would be a very good thing if you took a piece of foolscap paper and wrote down the sins you feel guilty of. Don't make them up—there will be plenty without that. . . . One of the simplest and best rules for self-examination that I know is to use the Four Standards which Dr. Robert E. Speer said represented the summary of the Sermon on the Mount—Absolute Honesty, Absolute Purity, Absolute Unselfishness, and Absolute Love. Review your life in their light. Put down everything that doesn't measure up. Be ruthlessly, realistically honest. . . . You will be amazed at what a lift it gives you just to face up to these things honestly.[136]

Anne Smith made many comments of a similar nature in her spiritual journal.[137] Her remarks should be compared with the following statements by Shoemaker:

> We thought we would take off the glasses, and begin to think about the fellow who was looking through them. As we talked, conviction developed that he was up against certain clearly defined sins in his own life. The first one was pride. . . . Finally, there was the sin of fear.[138]

> I never learned more about religious work than I learned from Frank Buchman when he said, "The first and fundamental need is ourselves." It is so much easier to skip this first requirement and go on and to ask what comes next. The whole process has got to begin with us. For a good many it must begin with a fresh sense of sin, and we might question ourselves about professional

---

[136] Shoemaker, *How to Become a Christian* (New York: Harper & Brothers, 1953), pp. 56-57. See also Cecil Rose, *When Man Listens*, pp. 18-19; Russell, *For Sinners Only*, pp. 20, 36; Olive Jones, *Inspired Children*, pp. 47-68; *Inspired Youth* (New York: Harper & Brothers, 1938), p. 41; Hofmeyr, *How to Change*, pp. 1-2; and Hallen Viney, *How Do I Begin?* (Copyright 1937 by The Oxford Group), pp. 2-4.

[137] Dick B., *Anne Smith's Journal*, pp. 30-36.

[138] Shoemaker, *The Conversion of the Church*, pp. 30-34.

ambition, discouragement and self-pity, grudges . . . intemperance, sins of the flesh and of the mind.[139]

Let us think of this also in connection with facing ourselves. . . . It is a real cross to face ourselves as we really are. How much better to take up that inescapable cross of having to find out about ourselves in the end—the whole, bitter, naked truth about our pride, our self-will, our duplicity—how much better to take up that cross of our own volition, and let God, and the people who are close to God, help us face ourselves as we are, with a view to being different.[140]

11. *Confession—Sharing with God and Another*

Sharing in confidence the results of our own self-examination with another whose life has been changed is vital to the surrender process.

It is well documented that the Oxford Group confession idea rested largely on the confess-your-faults language in James 5:16.[141] Oxford Group writers also cited Acts 19:18:

And many that believed came, and confessed, and shewed their deeds.[142]

---

[139] Shoemaker, *Twice-Born Ministers*, p. 182. As to "grudges" and the concept of a "grudge" list, see Big Book, p. 65; James 5:9 ("Grudge not, one against another, brethren, lest ye be condemned . . ."); Begbie, *Life Changers*, p. 38; and Shoemaker, *How to Become a Christian*, pp. 56-67. Oxford Group writer, Ebenezer Macmillan wrote at length on the importance of eliminating resentments, hatred, or the "grudge" that "blocks God out effectively" (See Macmillan, *Seeking and Finding*, pp. 98, 96-97).

[140] Shoemaker, *God's Control*, pp. 104-05.

[141] J. P. Thornton-Duesbury, *Sharing* (Pamphlet of The Oxford Group, published at Oxford University Press, no date), p. 5; Day, *The Principles of The Group*, p. 6; *What Is The Oxford Group?*, pp. 29, 31; Almond, *Foundations for Faith*, p. 13; Benson, *The Eight Points*, p. 18; Garth Lean, *Cast Out Your Nets* (London: Grosvenor, 1990), p. 48; and Shoemaker, *The Conversion of the Church*, p. 35. See also *Pass It On*, p. 128; and Dick B., *Anne Smith's Journal*, pp. 36, 38, 40, 99, 129, 131-32, 142, 144.

[142] Thornton-Duesbury, *Sharing*, p. 5; and *What Is The Oxford Group?*, p. 27.

Almost every Oxford Group book abounds with discussion of
"Sharing" by confession.[143]

The emphasis was on Sharing with God and with another.
There was to be absolute honesty, thoroughness, elimination of
secrecy in a life, confessing one's own part in sin, and putting the
past behind.[144] The following are some of Sam Shoemaker's
contributions on this important aspect of life-changing:

> I have found a way to draw confession from others. It is to
> confess first myself. And this is the surest way for those who
> have not so wonderfully attuned themselves to others that they get
> the heart's secrets which have never been told to anyone else—the
> kind of secrets that are cleansed by being aired a bit. To draw
> souls one by one, to buttonhole them and steal from them the
> secret of their lives, to talk them clean out of themselves, to read
> them off like a page of print, to pervade them with your spiritual
> essence and make them transparent, this is the spiritual science
> which is so difficult to acquire, so hard to practice.[145]

> If any man will to do His will, he shall know of the doctrine
> (John 7:17). We must get to the point of whether a man is willing
> to do His will in all areas. Take the four standards of
> Christ—absolute honesty, absolute purity, absolute unselfishness,
> and absolute love. When people's lives are wrong, they are
> usually wrong on one or more of these standards. Many quite
> respectable people have hidden things in their past and their
> present that need to come out in confidence with some one. A sin

---

[143] Walter, *Soul Surgery*, pp. 41-64; Begbie, *Life Changers*, pp. 37, 102-04, 169;
Benson, *The Eight Points*, pp. 18-29; *What Is The Oxford Group?*, pp. 25-35;
Weatherhead, *Discipleship*, pp. 31-44; Winslow, *Why I Believe in the Oxford Group*, pp.
27-31; Leon, *The Philosophy of Courage*, pp. 151-59; Thornton-Duesbury, *Sharing*, pp.
4-6; Day, *The Principles of the Group*, pp 6-7; Russell, *For Sinners Only*, pp. 41-42, 63-
64, 284; Cecil Rose, *When Man Listens*, pp. 48-50; Brown, *The Venture of Belief*, pp.
33-36; Olive Jones, *Inspired Children*, p. 136; Shoemaker, *Realizing Religion*, pp. 80-81;
The Church Can Save the World, pp. 110-12; and *The Conversion of the Church*, pp. 36-
39.

[144] See for example, Benson, *The Eight Points*, pp. 18-29.

[145] Shoemaker, *Realizing Religion*, pp. 80-81.

does not appear in all its exceeding sinfulness, until it is brought into light with another; and it almost always seems more hopelessly unforgivable and the person who committed it more utterly irredeemable, when it remains unshared. The only release and hope for many bound and imprisoned and defeated people lies in frank sharing. It is not costly to share our problems, or even our comfortable sins, but it is costly to share the worst thing we ever did, the deepest sin of our life, the besetting temptation that dogs us. . . . By our frank honesty about ourselves, and our willingness, under God as He guides us to share anything in our own experience that will help another person, . . . we shall get deep enough to know the real problem. At this point one of two things will probably happen. If the person is *honest with himself and with God*, he will be *honest also with us* and be ready to take the next step, which is a decision to surrender these sins, with himself wholly to God (italics added).[146]

We must find out how to go the rest of the way with our conversion. Personally, I am quite clear how this must start. It must start . . . by the sharing of these sins with another Christian who has found his way a bit farther than we have. . . . Of course, confession, in the absolute sense, is to God alone; but where there is a human listener, confession is found to be both more difficult and more efficacious. It is, as a matter of fact and experience, a relatively uncostly thing to fall on our knees and confess our sins to God . . . but it is a very costly thing to say these things out in the presence of a human being we can trust; and, as a matter of fact, this is extraordinarily effective in making the first break to get away from sins. . . . Some of us prefer the word "Sharing" to the formal word confession; it has not quite such still and formal connotations. . . . It is my conviction, and that of the Oxford Group with which I am associated, that the detailed sharing should be made with one person only. . . . We have known also the peculiar relief, having it something closely akin to the grace of God, which comes when "the worst" is known to at least one other human soul, when someone else carries with us in

---

[146] Shoemaker, *The Church Can Save the World*, pp. 110-12.

sympathetic understanding the secret which lay like lead in our hearts. . . . He may have reason to think he knows what your difficulty is, and he may share something parallel in his own life. . . . In any case, he will create the sort of atmosphere in which you can talk without fear, reserve or hurry.[147]

Note that A.A.'s Big Book says at page 73—after the person has examined himself by means of a written inventory:

They only thought they had lost their egoism and fear; they only thought they had humbled themselves. But they had not learned enough of humility, fearlessness and honesty, in the sense that we find it necessary until they had told someone else all their story.

12. *Conviction—Readiness to Change*

Man needs to be convinced—as part of the surrender process—that: (1) He has sinned against God. (2) Sin has Binding Power, Blinding Power, Deadening Power, and Propagating Power. (3) Christ can meet man's need to be rid of sin and to be aligned with God.

Terms like "sin" and "conviction of sin" are foreign to today's A.A. Such words will not be found in the Big Book text. But they certainly were in common usage in the biblically oriented meetings the early AAs attended and also in the Oxford Group-Shoemaker teaching and thinking to which they were exposed.[148] Shoemaker and other Oxford Group sources were teaching that man would not change, would not renounce his old self-willed, self-centered behavior until he was "convicted of sin."[149] And one of Frank

---

[147] Shoemaker, *The Conversion of the Church*, pp. 35-39.

[148] See Lois Wilson's Oxford Group notes which are set forth in full in Dick B., *New Light on Alcoholism*, pp. 337-39. Lois spoke much of "sin."

[149] See Shoemaker, *Realizing Religion*, p. 81; Walter, *Soul Surgery*, pp. 64-78; and Olive Jones, *Inspired Children*, where Miss Jones defined the Oxford Group idea of
(continued...)

Buchman's five C's was "Conviction." Dwight Moody, one of Buchman's mentors, said being "convicted of sin" meant becoming conscious of wrongdoing—finding out that you are lost.[150] Shoemaker and Buchman both taught there must be a desire to "hate and forsake" the sin or wrongdoing.[151] Begbie discussed the five C's in *Life Changers* and, as to the third "C," said:

> Conviction of sin, is the normal result of the impact upon a man of a quality of life which he instinctively knows to be superior to his own, the lack of which he recognizes as an offense against God, and as his fault and only his (p. 169).

We have discussed Frank Buchman's "Keswick Experience."[152] *The Eight Points of the Oxford Group* commented (as to Buchman): "He had been convicted of sin in his life." The Cross, it said, shows us to ourselves, exposes our excuses, unmasks our motives. The Cross makes us see the desperate nature of sin. The tragedy of Calvary, it said, was that ordinary people to whom little sins seemed harmless actually tried to murder "God." When the sight of what we are distresses us, we are then ready for the Gospel that there is forgiveness in Christ. For every "once" we look into our own hearts, said the author, let us look up twice to Christ.[153]

Soul Surgery had a chapter on Conviction.[154] Its author, Howard Walter, said Conviction is as closely related to Confession as Confession is to Confidence. It may come simultaneously with, or it may precede Confession. But confession of sin is *not*

---

[149] (...continued)
Conviction as follows: "*Conviction*, by which we come to the conscious realization of our sins which shut God away from us" (p. 135).

[150] William R. Moody, *The Life of D. L. Moody*, p. 239.

[151] Begbie, *Life Changers*, p. 38; and Shoemaker, *National Awakening*, p. 58. See also Hofmeyr, *How to Change*, p. 2.

[152] See, for example, Buchman, *Remaking the World*, pp. 312-15.

[153] Benson, *The Eight Points*, pp. 17, 28.

[154] Walter, *Soul Surgery*, pp. 64-78.

conviction of sin. "Conviction of sins means . . . a vision of his own personal guilt in the light of the revelation of God's holy love in Christ. It is the point where a man cries out to God, 'Against Thee only, have I sinned and done that which is evil in Thy sight.' Man is saying 'Father, I have sinned against heaven and in Thy sight, and am no more worthy to be called Thy son.'"[155]

Soul Surgery said the sinner should realize:

1. Sin's Binding Power: My sins are mightier than I. Psalm 63:3 says, "Iniquities prevail against me."
2. Sin's Blinding Power: Man suffers from moral myopia. He seems to say, "Evil, be thou my good." There is a gradual, tragic perversion of the moral vision.
3. Sin's Deadening Power: Man lacks the capacity for true moral indignation in the presence of the sin and wrong about him.
4. Sin's Propagating Power: Sin has the deadly power of passing on its taint to others in the family, the community, and even the next generation.[156]

Oxford Group writer Cecil Rose said:

Somewhere at the base of their life God is speaking to them, convicting them about the past and insistently pointing the new way. It is tremendously important that they should discover this themselves. . . . Christian revolution begins when a man is really willing for God to displace everything but Himself from a share in the control of life.[157]

Philip Brown wrote:

Surrender, as I see it, demands the expulsion of all conscious sin: the abject capitulation of pride, wilfulness, selfishness, the

---

[155] Walter, *Soul Surgery*, pp. 64-65. See Luke 15:21.

[156] Walter, *Soul Surgery*, pp. 67-75; and Hofmeyr, *How to Change*, p. 2. See also Lois Wilson's own review of these qualities of sin. Dick B., *New Light on Alcoholism*, p. 338.

[157] Rose, *When Man Listens*, pp. 62, 74-78.

abandonment of all deceptions, and of all that is unclean. It is quite clear that the impure in heart cannot either see or hear God.[158]

Shoemaker wrote:

It was consciousness of personal sin which drew from my friend those pathetic and tremendously healthy words: Oh! to be made over in the Spirit! I want a rebirth, but it comes not in one agony. Oh! how I want freedom from these deadening doubts, from this horrible, haunting sense, no "knowledge," of sin—this hopeless self-hatred and suffering. . . . By "conviction" two things are meant: conviction first of sin, and then a growing assurance that Christ can meet the need.[159]

We need to know how people behave under conviction of sin. We need to know what goes into a spiritual decision, and how to bring men to it. . . . We need the Cross, not as a theory, but as an experience of personal deliverance. We cannot evade some kind of pain: we can only choose between the pain of a divided mind and the pain of a crucified self. . . . We must let that Cross break us as it broke Him, cleanse and route the sin in us, bringing to us at last a united mind of forgiveness and peace.[160]

The heart of that problem is that many of us are wrong with God and wrong with each other: and what we need is to be right with God and right with each other. . . . The first step is not resurrection, it is crucifixion. . . . It is the crucifixion of pride, narrowness, stupidity, ignorant prejudice, intolerance. . . . There is no resurrection without crucifixion . . . either God's will is crucified on it [the Cross]; or our will is crucified on it so that God's will may prevail. Christ died to show us the everlasting

---

[158] Brown, *The Venture of Belief,* pp. 32-33. [See Matthew 5:8: "Blessed are the pure in heart; for they shall see God"]. And see Begbie, *Life Changers,* pp. 36-37, which discussed that verse.

[159] Shoemaker, *Realizing Religion,* pp. 21, 81-82.

[160] Shoemaker, *The Church Can Save the World,* pp. 153, 93-94.

victory and effectiveness of dying to self, that God might make His will prevail.[161]

Compare these two segments in A.A.'s Big Book:

Dr. Bob led me through all of these [six] steps. At the moral inventory, he brought up some of my bad personality traits or character defects, such as selfishness, conceit, jealously, carelessness, intolerance, ill-temper, sarcasm and resentments. We went over these at great length and then he finally asked me if I wanted these defects of character removed. When I said yes, we both knelt at his desk and prayed, each of us asking to have these defects taken away. The picture is still vivid. If I live to be a hundred, it will always stand out in my mind. It was very impressive and I wish every A.A. could have the benefit of this type of sponsorship today. Dr. Bob always emphasized the religious angle very strongly, and I think it helped. I know it helped me.[162]

Are we now ready to let God remove from us all the things we have admitted are objectionable? . . . If we still cling to something we will not let go, we ask God to help us be willing (p. 76).

Mel B. made this observation about "Conviction" as it reached A.A.:

In describing his spiritual change, Buchman always used references to the problem of sin and acceptance of Christ that were widely employed in the Oxford Group but never took root in AA. What did take root in AA, however, was the focus on the dangers of resentment and self-pity, and the urgency of releasing these in order to find sobriety, happiness, and well-being.

---

[161] Shoemaker, *National Awakening*, p. 5.

[162] This is from the story of A.A. pioneer Earl T. It is titled *He Sold Himself Short* (Big Book, pp. 287-96). Earl was one of Dr. Bob's proteges and went on to help organize A.A. in Chicago. The author believes some of the language in the story is not actually that of Earl T. The words are not typical of Dr. Bob or of his sponsees.

Learning from firsthand experience how resentment had blocked his own spiritual powers, Buchman developed an ability to target the same problem, and additional shortcomings in the lives of others. With modifications only in style and language, this became the essential method of AA when it began to form as part of the Oxford Group twenty-seven years later.[163]

13. *Conversion—The New Birth—Change*

Conversion occurs in the crisis of self-surrender in which man gives himself to God, is regenerated or reborn through the atoning and transforming power of Christ, and has part of God's nature imparted to him. God is inwardly experienced, and the barrier of sin is gone.

Everyone even remotely connected with the Oxford Group—including Bill Wilson—had something to say about conversion.[164] And the writers did not always approach the word in the same way. Some spoke of conversion as Surrender.[165] Some spoke of it as becoming born again.[166] Some spoke of it in terms of a spiritual or religious experience or awakening.[167] It was often called an "experience of Christ" or an "experience of God."[168] Some talked in terms of salvation.[169] But there was

---

[163] Mel B., *New Wine*, pp. 34-35.

[164] We do not include Dr. Bob, because Akron AAs are usually quoted as speaking of making surrenders. However, Anne Smith certainly discussed conversion in her Journal; and Anne quoted the William James definition of it. See Dick B., *Anne Smith's Journal*, pp. 37-38.

[165] Rose, *When Man Listens*, pp. 20-21; and *What Is The Oxford Group?*, pp. 43-44.

[166] Allen, *He That Cometh*, pp. 19, 32, 48-49; Jones, *Inspired Children*, p. 136; Shoemaker, *National Awakening*, p. 58; *How to Find God*, p. 7; and *How to Become a Christian*, 65-82.

[167] Brown, *The Venture of Belief*, pp. 21-22; Shoemaker, *Realizing Religion*, pp. 4-9; and Buchman, *Remaking the World*, pp. 19, 24, 35, 54.

[168] Buchman, *Remaking the World*, p. x; Benson, *The Eight Points*, p. 151; and Leon, *The Philosophy of Courage*, pp. 89, 112-13.

[169] Winslow, *Why I Believe In the Oxford Group*, p. 17.

general agreement in the Oxford Group that conversion involved a basic change in man—a change from self-centeredness to God-centeredness, from sin "control" to "God-Control."[170]

As we have mentioned, Oxford Group writers frequently quoted William James's definition of conversion:

> The process, gradual or sudden, by which a self, hitherto divided and consciously wrong, inferior and unhappy, becomes unified, consciously right, superior and happy.[171]

---

[170] Buchman, *Remaking the World*, pp. 3, 18, 24-25, 28-29, 30, 39, 42, 50, 63, 64, 69, 70, 95; Lean, *On the Tail of a Comet*, p. 83; Russell, *For Sinners Only*, pp. 324-29; Leon, *The Philosophy of Courage*, pp. 129-49; Shoemaker, *God's Control*, pp. 9-10; Foot, *Life Began Yesterday*, pp. 174-175; and Kitchen, *I Was a Pagan*, pp. 43-48; 89-90.

[171] James, *The Varieties of Religious Experience*, p. 177; Shoemaker, *Realizing Religion*, p. 22; Walter, *Soul Surgery*, p. 80; and Kitchen, *I Was a Pagan*, p. 69. Compare Brown, *The Venture of Belief*, p. 23; and Weatherhead, *Discipleship*, p. 16. There has been a good deal of fuzzy thinking when the word "conversion" has been used. William James was talking, from a psychological standpoint, about change—the unifying of a divided self through a religious experience. In the Bible, the term "conversion" means "a turning or returning to God" through God's work in man; and in the New Testament, the securing, through faith in Christ, of the salvation which Christ brought [See *New Bible Dictionary*: Second Edition (Illinois: Tyndale House Publishers, Inc., 1982), pp. 228-29]. Hence there is no "process." There is a miracle by grace. Ephesians 2:8-9 states clearly, "For by grace are ye saved through faith; and that not of yourselves: *it is* the gift of God: Not of works, lest any man should boast." Bill Wilson used the term "conversion" in his correspondence with Dr. Carl Jung. See *Pass It On*, pp. 381-86. The Oxford Group preferred the word "surrender." *What Is The Oxford Group?* said, "The word 'converted' is much despised amongst us moderns. It savours of religious hysteria, dramatic penitent-form scenes—which serve a very useful purpose for those whom only such scenes can awaken to a living Christ—old-fashioned British revivalism or the latest American religious fervour. But the word conversion itself, although not in habitual use by the Oxford Group, is a good one and there is no reason why, if it is our idea of surrender, any of us who want to use it should refrain from doing so. But Absolute Surrender to God, as seen by the Oxford Group, is conversion with a definite constructive spiritual policy added which ensures it being of positive use and fertility for us and for others" (p. 43). In his dissertation, Charles Knippel pointed out that Shoemaker alternated between talking of conversion as a one-time act [See Romans 10:9] and conversion as a process—not unlike that of A.A.'s Twelve Steps—where there is an initial act or decision [a new birth] followed by some procedures such as self-examination, confession, restitution, and then conservation involving growth through Bible study, prayer, listening, Guidance, and so on. Early

(continued...)

Harold Begbie added to this definition the statement, "Conversion is the only means by which a radically bad person can be changed into a radically good person."[172]

Henry Wright referred to two Bible verses in speaking of the crisis of self-surrender involved in conversion:

---

[171] (...continued)

Akron AAs simply spoke of "surrender" and used the word frequently in speaking of their "surrender to God" on their knees. See *DR. BOB*, pp. 88-89, 92, 101, 110.

We suggest, for simplicity of understanding, that a distinction be drawn between two things: (1) The new birth—being "born again of the Spirit." The Bible teaches that in the new birth, when man is born again of the spirit, he is then and there—by the grace of God—changed. He becomes at once a son of God—not by his works but by his faith. The change is wrought by God (Romans 10:9; 2 Corinthians 5:17; 1 John 3:1-2; e.g., Kitchen, *I Was a Pagan*, p. 43). Frank Buchman put the matter in simplest terms: Only three essential factors were involved in conversion—*Sin, Jesus Christ,* and (the result) *a Miracle*. See Walter, *Soul Surgery,* p. 86. (2) Fellowship with God through renewal of the mind. The Bible teaches that there is the additional problem of fellowship—the renewed mind walk to stay in fellowship with God. This *does* involve works—the task of walking in love, behaving as God would have us behave, obeying His commandments in order to manifest the fruits of the power received in the new birth (James, Chapter 2; 1 John 4:7-5:5; Ephesians 4:22-5:21). "Faith without works is dead" [barren, useless] (James 2:17, 20). In other words, there is a distinction between the *receipt* of power through new birth and the *utilization* or operation of that power and walking in fellowship. Both involve "change." In Vine's *Expository Dictionary of Old and New Testament Words*, the author says of the Greek noun, *anakainōsis*, "a renewal, is used in Rom. 12:2, 'the renewing (of your mind),' i.e., the adjustment of the moral and spiritual vision and thinking to the mind of God, which is designed to have a transforming effect upon the life; in Tit. 3:5, where 'the renewing of the Holy Spirit' is not a fresh bestowment of the Spirit, but a revival of His power, developing the Christian life; this passage stresses the continual operation of the indwelling Spirit of God; the Romans passage stresses the willing response on the part of the believer" (pp. 278-79). Garth Lean wrote the author, "When Michael and I met Buchman in 1931 and 1932, respectively, he much more used the word 'change.' The word 'conversion' had been cheapened and lost its content. Buchman was aware that 'change' happened in many different ways."

[172] Shoemaker, *Realizing Religion*, p.22, quoting Begbie. Harold Begbie, *Twice Born Men* (New York: Fleming H. Revell, 1909), p. 17.

The gospel of the kingdom of God is preached, and every man entereth violently into it.[173]

I beseech you therefore brethren, by the mercies of God that you present your bodies a living sacrifice holy, acceptable unto God, which is your reasonable service. And be not conformed to this world; but be ye transformed by the renewing of your mind, that you may prove what is that good, and acceptable, and perfect will of God.[174]

Canon Streeter wrote at great length on the power of God that works through Christ. Streeter said the power is made effective primarily by the Cross in two quite different ways: (1) Christ died on the Cross to pay the price for man's disobedience. Christ's death effected the liberation of man from his sins. When man

---

[173] Luke 16:16b. Wright said there has to be a break from positive sin, plus a definite, conscious act of ethical decision between God and man personally, without reservation . . . "You give everything to God." See Wright, *The Will of God*, pp. 69, 74, 63-65, 50.

[174] Romans 12:1-2. See Wright, *The Will of God*, at pages 64 and 74, where he said, "You present your body a living sacrifice that you may prove God's Will. You shall prove it by getting back your body—a glorified body." Note: It is the author's view that this is a "renewed mind" verse referring to "fellowship" and not to "sonship." See, for example, *The Revised English Bible* (Oxford: Oxford University Press, 1989), p. 143, "Therefore, my friends, I implore you by God's mercy to offer your very selves to him: a living sacrifice, dedicated and fit for his acceptance, the worship offered by mind and heart. Conform no longer to the pattern of this present world, but be transformed by the renewal of your minds. Then you will be able to discern the will of God, and to know what is good, acceptable, and perfect." The *New Bible Dictionary* says, "The initiative in regeneration is ascribed to God (John 1:13); it is from above (John 3:3, 7); and of the Spirit (John 3:5, 8) . . . The divine act is decisive and once and for all . . . The abiding results given in these passages are doing righteousness, not committing sin, loving one another, believing that Jesus is the Christ, and overcoming the world. These results indicate that in spiritual matters man is not altogether passive. He is passive in the new birth; God acts on him. But the result of such an act is far-reaching activity; he actively repents, believes in Christ, and henceforth walks in the newness of life. . . . There is no change in the personality itself; the person is the same. But now he is differently controlled. . . . We may define regeneration as a drastic act on fallen human nature by the Holy Spirit, leading to a change in the person's whole outlook. He can now be described as a new man who seeks, finds and follows God in Christ" (pp. 1015-1016). See also *The Abingdon Bible Commentary* (Nashville: Abingdon Press, 1929), p. 1160.

accepts Christ, he receives the spirit—Christ—and he is liberated from sin through the religion of faith in Christ. Streeter spoke of receipt of the spirit; and with that spirit, power; and with power, liberty; and the evidence of all this—the fruit of the Spirit—love, joy, peace.[175] (2) The Cross of Christ is the supreme example of surrender to the will of God, however great the humiliation or pain involved, with the result that we have the love of Christ when we have his faith and are more than conquerors through Christ who loved us.[176]

Walter made the following points in *Soul Surgery*:

1. Conversion can be viewed from two sides: On man's side, it is an act of faith in which the sinner deliberately and finally turns from all known sin and identifies himself with Christ, for the future, in a saving, victorious moral unity and fellowship. On God's side, it is an act of God's free grace by which God is able, through bearing human sin—in suffering redemptive love—to forgive the sinner and so to effect in Christ a new relationship in which the barrier of sin no longer remains.[177]

2. The basis of conversion is the awakening of a new self, and the vital element in this new birth is the dawning of a new affection which henceforth dominates the heart.[178]

3. God outside of us is a theory. God inside of us becomes a fact. God outside of us is an hypothesis; God inside of us is an experience. God the Father is the possibility of salvation. God

---

[175] Streeter, *The God Who Speaks*, pp. 108-11. See Galatians 3:2; Acts 1:8; 2 Corinthians 3:17; and Galatians 5:22. And see Colossians 1:27—"Christ in you, the hope of glory;" and Weatherhead, *Discipleship*, pp. 146-47.

[176] Streeter, *The God Who Speaks*, pp. 97-98. Streeter is clearly referring to Romans 8, particularly 35-37: "Who shall separate us from the love of Christ? shall tribulation, or distress, or persecution, or famine, or nakedness, or peril, or sword? . . . Nay, in all these things we are more than conquerors through him that loved us."

[177] Walter, *Soul Surgery*, p. 79.

[178] Walter, *Soul Surgery*, p. 82.

the Spirit is actuality of life, joy, peace, and saving power.[179]

Benson expressed the results of conversion in this way:

1. We become witness to the renewing power of Christ. Of Christ it says: I have overcome the world and I will come and put my overcoming Spirit in your weakness and fill you with my own victorious life and be in you the overcoming and conquering power. Christ's victory is ours, and we are victorious in it.[180]

2. He [Christ] has overcome sin; therefore the very sin—the personal sin of ours has been overcome. The soul is charged with a strength not its own.[181]

3. Man breathes a new atmosphere and is vitalized with a Divine Energy. What the law could not do, is now fulfilled by the impulse and inspiration of the Spirit of Christ.[182]

4. He breaks the power of canceled sin. He sets the prisoner free.[183]

Weatherhead described the riches of the glory of the mystery in the new birth, speaking of "Christ in me the hope of glory . . . Christ in him the hope of glory."[184]

---

[179] Walter, *Soul Surgery*, p. 82.

[180] Benson, *The Eight Points*, p. 119. See John 16:33.

[181] Benson, *The Eight Points*, p. 119.

[182] Benson, *The Eight Points*, p. 121-22.

[183] Benson, *The Eight Points*, p. 127. Benson seemed to refer to these Bible verses: Galatians 5:1; John 16:33; and 1 John 5:4-5.

[184] Weatherhead, *Discipleship*, pp. 146-147. Weatherhead was referring to Colossians 1:26-27, "Even the mystery which hath been hid from ages and from generations, but now is made manifest to his saints: To whom God would make known what is the riches of the glory of this mystery among the Gentiles; which is Christ in you, the hope of glory."

Shoemaker wrote a good deal on the "how" of conversion. He said:

> But can one have a conversion at will? And what must we do to have it? Well, we must want it with all our hearts and put ourselves in the way of it. God on His part has longed to win us for years. It has been we who have been unwilling. We must open ourselves to Him, and be prepared to accept all it will mean to be a child of God. First, we have got to be willing to break finally with sin; it is accepting evils and wrongs in themselves as inevitable, and giving up the fight. In this there can be no possible reservation or interpretation: we must embark on the business of cleansing ourselves through the grace of God, from top to bottom. And what the sum total of this means together with the absolutely yielded will, is best expressed in the old idea of self-surrender to God. . . . And this is primarily the business of the will—taking the Kingdom of Heaven by force. It takes will power to thrust out sin with one heave, even for a moment, and let God have place. . . . Given this readiness to yield, the open mind, the hungering soul, the penitent heart, the surrendered will, the attitude of expectation, and the sense of abysmal need, the whole life given in earnest prayer—what then? . . . You and God are reconciled the moment you surrender. . . . Self recedes. God looms up. Self-will seems the blackest sin of all, rebellion against God the only hell. The peace that passes understanding steals over you. . . . This impartation of Himself to us is God's part in the conversion. Our part is to ask, to seek, to knock. His part is to answer, to come, to open. . . . The real witness of the Spirit to the second birth is to be found only in the disposition of the genuine child of God, the permanently patient heart, the love of self eradicated.[185]

But I would also like to say that something happens the first time the soul says "Yes" to God with its whole force, that never wholly disappears. As terrible sin does something to the human

---

[185] Shoemaker, *Realizing Religion*, pp. 22-35.

heart which may be forgiven, but leaves its trace, so, thank God, does tremendous surrender leave such an ineradicable mark.[186]

Except a man be born again, he cannot see the Kingdom of God. Nicodemus saith unto him [Jesus Christ], How . . . ? (John 3:3-4). . . . If the Christian Church is to be effective again in the affairs of men, it must begin by once more illuminating this great truth of rebirth. . . . A man is born again when the control of his life, its center and its direction pass from himself to God. . . . The how of getting rid of sin, if you are in earnest about doing it at all: face it, share it, surrender it. Hate it, forsake it, confess it, and restore for it.[187]

When A.A. began in Akron, Ohio, on June 10, 1935, there were no Twelve Steps. Bill and Dr. Bob had the Bible and the principles of the Oxford Group to which both belonged.[188] There was no Third Step prayer of "decision." There was no Seventh Step prayer of "humility"—where the AA humbly asks removal of his shortcomings.[189] The "alcoholic squad of the Oxford Group" in Akron got down on their knees and surrendered their lives to God.[190] Prior to the Akron founding, Bill had simply gone to Calvary Church's rescue mission, knelt, and—as Mrs. Helen Shoemaker herself witnessed—"made a decision for Christ." In other words, the Oxford Group conversions in early A.A. usually involved a short prayer of surrender. Sometimes the surrender emphasized "Thy will be done" from the Lord's Prayer.[191] Sometimes there were words asking God to take charge of an

---

[186] Shoemaker, *The Conversion of the Church*, p. 79.

[187] Shoemaker, *National Awakening*, p. 55, 57, 58; and Allen, *He That Cometh*, pp. 19-43.

[188] *DR. BOB*, p. 96.

[189] See Dick B., *The Akron Genesis*, pp. 256-60, for the various forms the original "six" steps took.

[190] As we've shown, this was probably a confession that Jesus is Lord involving a belief in the heart that God raised Jesus from the dead. Romans 10:9.

[191] See *What Is The Oxford Group?*, pp. 47-48.

unmanageable life.[192] At least two Oxford Group writers (as well as Anne Smith) indicated their belief that God can "remove" the symptoms of sin.[193]

The author believes the following Big Book conversion language applies to both Steps Three and Seven:

> As we felt new power flow in, as we enjoyed peace of mind, as we discovered we could face life successfully, as we became conscious of His presence, we began to lose our fear of today, tomorrow, or the hereafter. We were reborn (p. 63).

> Many of us said to our Maker, *as we understood Him*: "God, I offer myself to Thee. . . . May I do Thy will always!" (p. 63).[194]

> When ready, we say something like this: "My Creator, I am now willing that you should have all of me, good and bad. I pray that you now remove from me every single defect of character which stands in the way of my usefulness to you and my fellows. Grant me strength, as I go out from here, to do your bidding, Amen." (p. 76).[195]

14. *Restitution—Righting the Wrong*

> The cord of sin which binds the convert to the past can only be cut by an amend—his act of restitution by which he acknowledges his faults to the people concerned and pays them back by apology or in kind for that which was taken from them.

---

[192] See Dick B., *The Akron Genesis*, p. 263; *Anne Smith's Journal*, pp. 20-21; *That Amazing Grace*, p. 90; C. Rose, *When Man Listens*, pp. 22, 74-75; Brown, *The Venture of Belief*, p. 30; and Winslow, *Why I Believe in the Oxford Group*, pp. 36, 38.

[193] See Allen, *He That Cometh*, p. 147; Kitchen, *I Was a Pagan*, p. 73; and Dick B., *Anne Smith's Journal*, pp. 46-47; *That Amazing Grace*, pp. 72-74; Psalm 103:10-12.

[194] This is a portion of what is commonly called the "Third Step Prayer."

[195] This is commonly called the Seventh Step Prayer.

Restitution was vital to Oxford Group life changing. Stories of Frank Buchman's life invariably mention two of his experiences. The first concerned "Keswick" which we have already discussed. In that situation, Buchman was "released" when he wrote letters of apology to the six ministers against whom he had a grudge.[196] The second account concerned "Bill Pickle at Penn State."[197]

Pickle was an alcoholic bootlegger on the college campus where Buchman was sent to teach the Bible and convert students to Christianity. Pickle was supplying the booze to potential converts. Buchman therefore went to work on Pickle first. The long and the short of the story is that Pickle decided to, and did become, a Christian. He was able to give up liquor and lead a model life. With Buchman's assistance, Pickle wrote apologies to his family for the way he had lived and had treated them. Pickle's behavior-change much influenced the later successful course of Buchman's witnessing at Penn State and in the Eastern college system.

The Keswick and Pickle stories illustrate Buchman's belief that restitution is a vital part of the surrender process. Oxford Group adherents felt likewise. Getting right with other people to get right with God was critical. Weatherhead wrote:

Nothing is clearer in the gospels than the direct teaching that our relation to God cannot be right unless our relations with men are as right as we can make them.[198]

Garth Lean wrote:

If you will put right what you can put right, God will put right what you can't put right. Restitution. That was the action I had to

---

[196] Buchman, *Remaking the World*, pp. 312-15; Begbie, *Life Changers*, pp. 166-67; Benson, *The Eight Points*, pp. x-xii; Walter, *Soul Surgery*, p. 61; Russell, *For Sinners Only*, pp. 56-60; Lean, *On the Tail of a Comet*, pp. 21-32; *What Is The Oxford Group?*, p. 60; and Howard, *Frank Buchman's Secret*, pp. 22-26.

[197] Buchman, *Remaking the World*, pp. 330-45; Russell, *For Sinners Only*, pp. 189-204; Howard, *Frank Buchman's Secret*, pp. 26-30; and Lean, *On the Tail of a Comet*, pp. 33-44.

[198] Weatherhead, *Discipleship*, p. 113.

take. Wherever I could do anything to right the wrongs I had
done I must do it. It has been said that you should do four things
with sin—hate it, forsake it, confess it, restore for it. I had to
restore for mine. . . . One footnote about restitution. No on has
the right to make restitution that implicates a third party.[199] The
Christian confesses his own sins, not those of other people.[200]

The Oxford Group writings had much to say about restitution.
Russell's *For Sinners Only*, *What Is The Oxford Group?*, and
Benson's *The Eight Points* all contained excellent summaries. One
of the most useful, related to A.A.'s Ninth Step process, is this:

> We cannot make effective contact with God, we cannot truly
> worship while our hearts are choked with resentments. . . . True
> worship enables us to test our conduct by God's Will for us and
> others. It redeems from blindness, listlessness and self concern
> and gives us new insight into our obligations to God's other
> children. . . . Our task today is to look at the Sermon on the
> Mount not as the wild dream of a Galilean visionary, but as a
> piece of realism—the only plan upon which men can live together
> in peace and security.[201]

We have mentioned a number of Bible verses Oxford Group
adherents cited for the restitution concept. *For Sinners Only* quoted
Numbers 5:6-7.[202] One of the most commonly cited verses is
from the Sermon on the Mount in Matthew 5:23-24.[203] *For*

---

[199] Compare the Big Book language of Step Nine, which suggests making direct
amends "except when to do so would injure them or others" (p.59); and see discussion
of this point at Big Book pages 79-82.

[200] Lean, *Cast Out Your Nets*, pp. 86, 90.

[201] Benson, *The Eight Points*, p. 31. Compare the Big Book's statement at page 77,
"Our real purpose is to fit ourselves to be of maximum service to God and the people
about us."

[202] Russell, *For Sinners Only*, pp. 119. See also, Thornton-Duesbury, *Sharing*, p. 6.

[203] Benson, *The Eight Points*, p. 30; Russell, *For Sinners Only*, p. 120; Weatherhead,
Discipleship, 113; Shoemaker, *The Conversion of the Church*, pp. 47-48; *The Gospel
According to You*, pp. 146-51; Macmillan, *Seeking and Finding*, p. 176; and *DR. BOB*,
(continued...)

Sinners Only also referred to the Prodigal Son story in Luke, Chapter 15, saying: "Sending prodigal sons back to their earthly as well as their Heavenly Father is a specialty of the Oxford Group."[204] Russell's book also discussded the conversation between Jesus and Zacchaeus recorded in Luke 19:1-10. Zacchaeus had told Jesus that if he had taken anything from any man by false accusation, he had restored the man fourfold. Jesus responded approvingly, "This day is salvation come to thy house."[205] In its discussion of restitution, *What Is The Oxford Group?* cited Acts 3:19: "Repent ye therefore, and turn again, that your sins may be blotted out" (p. 55).

In *The Eight Points of the Oxford Group*, the author made a number of other important points:

1. Christians must take the initiative in reconciling and mending a quarrel with an enemy—"agree with thine adversary quickly" [Matthew 5:25].[206]

2. The evil or fault of another must be overcome with good, with forgiveness, or it ends in futile, mental poisoning from anger and revenge.[207]

3. Christ died for us sinners, forgiving the very men who drove the nails through his hands and feet—the just for the unjust.[208]

---

[203] (...continued)
p. 308. Speaking from his personal experience in the Oxford Group, Willard Hunter wrote the author that this verse was "big"—referring to its importance to the Group.

[204] Russell, *For Sinners Only*, p. 129. See also *What Is The Oxford Group?*, pp. 63-64; and Almond, *Foundations for Faith*, p. 30.

[205] Russell, *For Sinners Only*, pp. 135. See also, Lean, *Cast Out Your Nets*, pp. 87-88; Macmillan, *Seeking and Finding*, p. 111; Almond, *Foundations for Faith*, p. 13; and Weatherhead, *Discipleship*, pp. 115-16.

[206] Benson, *The Eight Points*, p. 32. See also, Weatherhead, *Discipleship*, p. 110.

[207] Benson, *The Eight Points*, p. 33. See Romans 12:17-21.

[208] Benson, *The Eight Points*, p. 34. See also Macmillan, *Seeking and Finding*, pp. 109-20. Romans 5:7-8.

4. Resentment and revenge are cheap and conventional, but forgiveness is constructive and God-like.[209]

5. Before we can get right with God, we must leave no stone unturned to get right with men.[210]

6. He that loveth not his brother whom he hath seen, cannot love God whom he hath not seen.[211]

7. Restitution is openly cutting the cord of sin which has bound us to the life of wrong we have lived in the past. It is righting to the best of our ability wrongs we have committed in the past.[212]

8. Good must be accomplished, and not just a personal release from the burden of sin at the expense of the one wronged.[213]

Sam Shoemaker said:

I want to remind you that our experience of God is all bound up inextricably with our human relationships. "If a man love not his brother whom he hath seen, how can he love God whom he hath not seen" [1 John 4:20]. "If thou bring thy gift to the altar, and there rememberest that thy brother hath ought against thee, first go and be reconciled unto thy brother, and then come and offer thy gift" [Matthew 5:23-24]. It is idle for us to try to be in touch with God, or keep in touch with Him, so long as there are human relationships which must be righted at the same time.[214]

---

[209] Benson, *The Eight Points*, pp. 34-35. See also, Allen, *He That Cometh*, p. 115; Colossians 3:13.

[210] Benson, *The Eight Points*, pp. 36-37; See also, Russell, *For Sinners Only*, p. 128; Macmillan, *Seeking and Finding*, pp. 98-99; and Hofmeyr, *How to Change*, p. 3. Matthew 5:40-41; 6:14-15.

[211] 1 John 4:20. See Benson, *The Eight Points*, pp. 36-37; Macmillan, *Seeking and Finding*, p. 99; and Dick B., *The Akron Genesis*, p. 92.

[212] Benson, *The Eight Points*, p. 39; and *What Is The Oxford Group?*, pp. 55-56.

[213] Benson, *The Eight Points*, p. 41.

[214] Shoemaker, *The Conversion of the Church*, pp. 47-48.

But I am certain that the most important factor in continuance, second only to prayer, is in a series of new relationships. First with the family. . . . He may need to make a blanket-apology to the entire family for impatience, for temper, for wanting his own way, for wanting to play Providence to them all. There may be specific wrongs to be shared with individuals. Probably heretofore he has been confessing their sins to them; now he confesses his own. . . . A confessing Christian is a propagating Christian.[215]

By obedience, God gets us to where we begin fulfilling His plan. . . . Here is a man guided to make restitution for his resentment against some of his own family. If he does it fully, he reestablished relationships with them. . . . Christ . . . said, "Thou hypocrite, cast out first the beam out of thine own eye, then shalt thou see clearly to put out the mote that is in thy brother's eye" [Matthew 7:5].[216]

Compare this statement in A.A.'s Big Book:

We go to him [an enemy] in a helpful and forgiving spirit, confessing our former ill feeling and expressing our regret. Under no condition do we criticize such a person or argue (p. 77).

Jesus Christ

15.   *Jesus Christ—The Source of Power*

The Oxford Group believed in Jesus Christ as the Divine Redeemer and Way-Shower by whose transforming power man can be changed through surrender to Christ and an experience of Christ.

---

[215] Shoemaker, *The Conversion of the Church*, pp. 41-43.

[216] Shoemaker, *God's Control*, pp. 63-64. See also Allen, *He That Cometh*, p. 140; Kitchen, *I Was a Pagan*, pp. 110-11; and Dick B., *Anne Smith's Journal*, p. 30.

John 14:6 quoted Jesus Christ as follows:

Jesus saith unto him, I am the way, the truth, and the life: no man cometh unto the Father, but by me.

And Oxford Group people certainly spoke of, and believed in, Jesus Christ as the Way, the Truth, and the Life.[217] In addition, as Savior, Lord, and God's only begotten Son.[218]

Having written *For Sinners Only*, A. J. Russell wrote *One Thing I Know*.[219] Russell said that some, who did not read *For Sinners Only* with care or sympathy, felt there was not enough in it about Atonement. Russell said he was astonished. He said of himself:

Through faith in His loving sacrificial achievement on the Cross, and through the sincere endeavor attended by many failures to follow the commands of that Divine Redeemer and Way-Shower, our incomparable Lord, I know I am a new man in Christ Jesus; a new man who is still being saved from sin.[220] My theory, then, if I dare to have a theory of so mighty an event in history—Christ crucified from the foundation of the world—is no more and certainly no less than that expressed by the old hymn which is acceptable to Protestants and Catholics, High Church and Lower Church, Modernists and Fundamentalists:

There is a green hill far away,
Without a city wall,

---

[217] See Brown, *The Venture of Belief*, p. 49; Foot, *Life Began Yesterday*, p. 87; Benson, *The Eight Points*, p. 125; Shoemaker, *Religion That Works*, p. 28; *Christ and This Crisis*, p. 39; *They're on the Way*, p. 153; and Olive Jones, *Inspired Children*, p. 150. Compare Foot, *Life Began Yesterday*, p. 87.

[218] Shoemaker, *Religion That Works*, pp. 27-29; *Christ's Words from the Cross*, p. 11; Walter, *Soul Surgery*, p. 126; Benson, *The Eight Points*, pp. 158-59, 116, 126; and Almond, *Foundations for Faith*, pp. 14-21, 44, 56.

[219] A. J. Russell, *One Thing I Know* (New York: Harper & Brothers, 1933).

[220] Compare Ephesians 4:24; 2 Corinthians 5:17; Dick B., *That Amazing Grace*, p. 34.

> Where the dear Lord was crucified,
>   Who died to save us all.
> We may not know, we cannot tell
>   What pains He had to bear;
> But we believe it was for us
>   He hung and suffered there.[221]

Dr. L. W. Grensted, wrote an entire book in 1933 on *The Person of Christ*.[222] Grensted was a convinced spokesman for, and supporter of, the Oxford Group. *The Person of Christ* was on *The Calvary Evangel's* Oxford Group literature list. Grensted wrote the Foreword to *What Is The Oxford Group?* (at least two copies of which were owned and loaned to others by Dr. Bob).[223] Grensted concluded his Foreword with:

> Characteristically individual as this book is, it yet covers so much of the ground of the experience upon which the fellowship of the Group is based, and in a form at once so systematic and so readable, that I believe it may, under God, be used very widely to help others to bring home to them that challenge of the living Christ for which and for which alone the fellowship stands.[224]

Shoemaker's books were laced with references to, and teachings about, Jesus Christ. Shoemaker's *Confident Faith* had a chapter titled, "What Christ Means To Me." He commenced with John 13:13, "Ye call me Master and Lord: and ye say well; for so I am."[225] In his *The Conversion of the Church*, as well as in other books, Shoemaker spoke frequently of a "vital experience of Jesus

---

[221] Russell, *One Thing I Know*, pp. ix-xiii. In a telephone interview on February 9, 1992, A.A. oldtimer Earl H. (who has provided the author with much research assistance) informed the author that he had in his possession a copy of *One Thing I Know* with the signature in it of Anne Smith (Dr. Bob's wife).

[222] L. W. Grensted, *The Person of Christ* (New York: Harper & Brothers, 1933).

[223] Interview of the author with Sue Smith Windows, Dr. Bob's daughter, in Akron in June, 1991.

[224] *What Is The Oxford Group?*, Foreword by L. W. Grensted.

[225] Shoemaker, *Confident Faith*, p. 35.

Christ."[226] Shoemaker's *Religion That Works* had a chapter titled "The Necessity of Christ."[227] In *Realizing Religion,* Shoemaker wrote: "You need to find God. You need Jesus Christ."[228]

Thus far, we have been speaking of Oxford Group ideas about Jesus Christ as the means of man's gaining God's forgiveness, and Jesus Christ as the source of the power that regenerates and renews man. Also about Jesus Christ as the way to guidance by the Holy Spirit, Jesus Christ as a means of witness, and Jesus Christ as a central basis for unity and the fellowship of the Holy Spirit which he made available.

There is another side of the picture—Jesus Christ as the teacher and as the exemplar of doing God's Will. Henry Drummond's *The Ideal Life* had a chapter on "How To Know The Will of God." Drummond quoted Jesus from John 7:16, "My doctrine is not Mine, but His that sent Me." Also, John 5:30, "My judgment is just; because I seek not Mine own will, but the will of the Father Which hath sent me." Finally, John 7:17, "If any man will do His Will, he shall know of the doctrine, whether it be of God, or whether I speak of myself."[229]

These latter concepts are particularly important for their bearing on the A.A.-Oxford Group connection. For the teachings of Jesus Christ were central in the Four Absolutes, of which we shall write in a moment. Dr. Robert Speer's *The Principles of Jesus* contained a chapter titled, "Jesus and the Will of God." Speer wrote:

> The ruling principle in the life of Jesus, both in its prayer and in its service, was the will of God. Jesus conditioned His prayers on God's Will: "not My will, but Thine be done."[230] . . . Doing God's will was his "meat." "My meat is to do the will of Him that sent me, to finish His work."[231] . . . Also, portions of John

---

[226] Shoemaker, *The Conversion of the Church,* p. 109.

[227] Shoemaker, *Religion That Works,* pp. 21-30.

[228] Shoemaker, *Realizing Religion,* p. 9.

[229] Drummond, *The Ideal Life,* pp. 303-20.

[230] Luke 22:42.

[231] John 4:34.

6:38-40, particularly verse 38: "For I came down from heaven, not to do Mine own will, but the will of Him that sent me."[232]

Henry Wright pointed to Jesus's statement in John 8:29, "for I do always those things that please Him [God]."[233] Wright then discussed the "four touchstones" of Jesus's principles as Dr. Speer had reconstructed them in *The Principles of Jesus*. Wright said Speer's four touchstones or four standards were the "Four Absolutes" taught by Jesus and also by the Apostles concerning the will of God.[234]

The foregoing, then, are just short-hand views of the Oxford Group's total emphasis on Christ as Savior, Way-Shower, Exemplar of doing, and Teacher of, God's Will. But what has all that to do with Alcoholics Anonymous?

One can search the *text* of A.A.'s Big Book in vain for any affirmative reference to Jesus Christ as Son or God. And our reader will have to judge for himself—after reviewing the contents of this book—just how much the Oxford Group literature on Jesus Christ probably did influence the Big Book and the Steps.[235]

---

[232] Speer, *The Principles of Jesus*, pp. 21-24.

[233] Wright, *The Will of God*, p. 169.

[234] Wright, *The Will of God*, p. 165-69.

[235] As we pointed out in *Dr. Bob's Library*, and in *Anne Smith's Journal*, and will point out in other books to come, there were many Christian and biblical sources of A.A. ideas—and *not* just those derived from the Oxford Group.

Here are a few historical markers:

1. Dr. Bob and Bill said Jesus Christ's Sermon on the Mount contained the underlying spiritual philosophy of A.A.[236]

2. The Lord's Prayer—taught by Jesus—has always figured in A.A. literature and survives at the close of most A.A. meetings today.[237]

3. The Four Absolutes—culled from Jesus's teachings, including teachings in the Sermon on the Mount—were much utilized by early AAs. They were practiced by Dr. Bob throughout his

---

[236] *DR. BOB*, p. 228. Dr. Bob's own library contained a number of studies of the Sermon on the Mount. See Dick B., *Dr. Bob's Library*, pp. 38-40. It appears to be a common thought in A.A. that Emmet Fox's *The Sermon on the Mount* was the only book on that topic that was studied in early A.A. And it *was* much read and recommended by Dr. Bob and early AAs. See, Dick B., *Dr. Bob's Library*, pp. 35-36, 38-40; *DR. BOB*, p. 310; and the lengthy discussion in Mel B., *New Wine*, pp. 105-06, 111-14. Many thought and today think that Emmet Fox was affiliated with the Oxford Group. But he was not. In any event, Dr. Bob stressed reading the portion of the Bible *itself* that *contains* the Sermon; and he also read, studied, and loaned to others the following: Oswald Chambers, *Studies in the Sermon on the Mount* (London: Simpkin, Marshall, Ltd., n.d.); E. Stanley Jones, *The Christ of the Mount* (New York: The Abingdon Press, 1931); Glenn Clark, *The Soul's Sincere Desire* (Boston: Little, Brown & Co., 1925); and *I Will Lift Up Mine Eyes* (New York: Harper & Brothers, 1937). These, along with a good many other books that Dr. Bob, his wife, and the early AAs read, contained a great deal of study of Jesus's Sermon. See Dick B., *Dr. Bob's Library*, pp. 25-80; *Anne Smith's Journal*, pp. 79-86; and *The Akron Genesis*, pp. 84-96.

[237] *DR. BOB*, pp. 141, 148, 183; Pittman, *AA The Way It Began*, p. 197; Dick B., *Dr. Bob's Library*, pp. 12, 33-35, 39-40, 56-57, 59, 82, 87; and Mel B., *New Wine*, p. 157. As previously mentioned, "Thy will be done" (from the Lord's Prayer) is still present in the Big Book. See pp. 67, 85, 88. See also Cleveland Central Bulletin, Vol. 46, No. 11, August, 1988, page 2: "How Closing Meetings with the Lord's Prayer Became a Custom."

life; and they were—according to Bill Wilson—incorporated into Steps Six and Seven. They are still used in many parts of the United States by AAs.[238]

4. Not only was the Oxford Group known as "A First Century Christian Fellowship," but Dr. Bob and other Akron, Ohio members continued to refer to it in that way in the late 1930's and referred to themselves as a "Christian Fellowship."[239]

5. Anne Smith spoke frequently about Jesus Christ in her writings and in the Bible segments she taught the alcoholics and their families with whom she and Dr. Bob worked.[240]

6. While Bill Wilson was careful to eliminate Oxford Group language about Jesus Christ from the Big Book, Bill's own language in early drafts of the Big Book shows how much Jesus Christ probably figured in pre-Big Book thinking. Bill's

---

[238] *DR. BOB*, pp. 54, 163; *Pass It On*, pp. 127, 172; *AA Comes of Age*, pp. 75, 161; *The Language of the Heart*, pp. 196-00; and *Co-Founders*, pp. 12-14. See, as examples, *The Four Absolutes* published by Cleveland Central Committee of A.A.. See also *The New Way of Life*, p. 21; *Handles and Hodge Podge*, p. 25; and the *Central Bulletin*, all published by the Cleveland District Office of Alcoholics Anonymous. For a discussion of Bill's comments that the Four Absolutes are incorporated in Steps Six and Seven, see Dick B., *Anne Smith's Journal*, pp. 118-19; and Kurtz, *Not-God*, pp. 242-43. In a letter to Clarence S. from Bill Wilson, dated March 20, 1957, Bill Wilson said: "You folks who started the Cleveland group had been under the Oxford Group influence at T. Henry's. When you shifted to Cleveland, you merely changed your address and then had a meeting composed of alcoholics only. In fact, you carried the Oxford Group Absolutes with you and have used them ever since."

[239] We covered this point before. Here, for the reader's convenience, we suggest reference to *DR. BOB*, pp. 53-54; *Pass It On*, p. 130; our interview with Sue Windows in Akron, June 1991; and the Memo from Bob E. to Lois Wilson.

[240] See Dick B., *Anne Smith's Journal*. Anne not only recommended reading a number of books on the life of Jesus Christ, but spoke of Christ as the regenerating power that changes men. She quoted a number of Bible verses about Jesus Christ. Like the Oxford Group, she spoke of a maximum experience of Jesus Christ. Anne's references to Christ are so numerous we simply refer to the entire *Journal*.

manuscripts spoke of his being "born again" and of the "living God;" and they used other distinctly Christian words.[241]

The one reference to Jesus Christ in the Big Book text simply contains Bill Wilson's musings that he conceded to Christ the certainty of a great man, not too closely followed by those who claimed him.[242] As to Jesus Christ, Dr. Ernest Kurtz observed:

> Yet A.A.'s total omission of "Jesus," its toning down of even "God" to a "Higher Power" which could be the group itself, and its changing of the "verbal" first message into hopeless helplessness rather than salvation: these ideas and practices, adopted to avoid any "religious" association, were profound changes. Since these ideas and practices were consciously embraced to deny any Oxford Group implication. . . .[243]

If Jesus Christ had actually been omitted from A.A., we might not need to discuss him at all. However, the Big Book contains *direct quotes* from Jesus—as one from the Lord's Prayer,[244] and an additional one from the Sermon on the Mount.[245] Also, there are words in the Big Book—considering Dr. Bob's emphasis on the Sermon on the Mount and 1 Corinthians 13—that came directly from Christian teachings in the Bible—words such as patience, tolerance, kindness, love, forgiveness.[246]

---

[241] The author personally inspected draft manuscripts of the Big Book at Bill's home in Stepping Stones during the author's research visit there in October, 1991. In one manuscript, Bill said of his religious experience that he had been "born again." In another, he spoke of the "living God." As we have shown, both of these expressions were fundamental and common Bible, Christian, Oxford Group, and Shoemaker phrases. In *Lois Remembers*, Bill's wife spoke of her "joy and faith in his [Bill's] rebirth" (p. 98).

[242] Big Book, Third Edition, p. 11.

[243] Kurtz, *Not-God*, p. 50.

[244] "Thy will be done." See Matthew 6:10; Big Book, pp. 67, 88.

[245] "Love thy neighbor as thyself." See Matthew 5:43; compare James 2:8; and examine Big Book, p. 153.

[246] Patience [James 1:4; Big Book, p. 83]; Tolerance [1 Corinthians 13:4; Big Book, pp. 83, 127]; Kindness [1 Corinthians 13:4; Big Book, 83]; Love [1 Corinthians 13; Big Book, pp. 83, 127]; Forgiveness [Matthew 6:14; Big Book, p. 77].

Even today, A.A.'s "omission of Jesus" occurs primarily its "World Services" publication level.

The *Chicago* Area Alcoholics Anonymous Service Office publishes a talk delivered by John T., on October 5, 1943, to mark the fourth anniversary of the Chicago AA group.[247] The address mentioned: (1) the talk between "doubting Thomas" and Jesus.[248] (2) Jesus's response to the temptation of the devil: "It is written, Man shall not live by bread alone, but by every word that proceedeth out of the mouth of God."[249] It also publishes a talk first delivered in August of 1948, titled "The Devil and A.A." There it quotes, on page 4, Jesus's statement in John 8:44: "Ye are of *your* father the devil. . . . He was a murderer from the beginning, and abode not in the truth . . . for he is a liar, and the father of it."

As stated, "AA of Akron" publishes four pamphlets written and edited by members of Alcoholics Anonymous of *Akron*, Ohio. These urge sponsors to supply their "babies" with the Big Book, the pamphlet, and the Bible.[250] They point out, as Dr. Bob did, that: "The Bible tells us to put 'first things first.'"[251] They urge the reading of the Sermon on the Mount.[252] They speak of reading the *Upper Room*—the Methodist periodical that is filled with the teachings of Jesus.[253] They quote Jesus's statement in Matthew 6:34.[254] They quote Paul: "I can do all things through Christ which strengtheneth me."[255] They quote "Our Lord's two commandments: 'Thou shalt love the Lord they God with all thy heart, and with all thy soul and with all thy mind. And . . . thou

---

[247] *AA God's Instrument.*

[248] See John 20:24-29.

[249] Matthew 4:4; Luke 4:4.

[250] *A Manual for Alcoholics Anonymous*, pp. 3-4.

[251] *A Manual for Alcoholics Anonymous*, p. 7; Dick B., *That Amazing Grace*, p. 30.

[252] *A Manual for Alcoholics Anonymous*, p. 8.

[253] *A Manual for Alcoholics Anonymous*, p. 8.

[254] *A Manual for Alcoholics Anonymous*, p. 13.

[255] *Spiritual Milestones in Alcoholics Anonymous*, p. 3; Philippians 4:13.

shalt love thy neighbor as thyself.'"[256] They quote Paul: "But put ye on the Lord Jesus Christ . . ."[257] They say: "As a matter of fact, the good active member [of AA] is practicing Christianity at all times whether or not he knows it."[258] They teach: "Remember this simple thing: The entire structure of the Christian religion is built on Love. . . . Christ taught that there are two great commandments: to love God; and to love your neighbor as yourself."[259]

We have already referred to pamphlets published by the *Cleveland* District Office of A.A. And one by Roy L. Smith is titled *Emergency Rations*. It refers to a number of Jesus's teachings including: (1) Matthew 24:35: "Heaven and earth shall pass away, but my words shall not pass away." (2) Matthew 5:44: ". . . pray for them which despitefully use you, and persecute you." (3) Matthew 6:34 ". . . Sufficient unto the day *is* the evil thereof." [260]

At Founders Day in Akron, Ohio, the author found—when he attended two years in a row—that there were, on sale in the convention's bookstore, many copies of a title by Roman Catholic priest "Father John Doe." That book said much about Jesus and Christianity.[261] Later, the author was to learn that substantial Roman Catholic thinking about Christianity directly impacted on Bill Wilson's writing of the Conference Approved: (1) *Twelve Steps and Twelve Traditions* and (2) *Alcoholics Anonymous Comes of Age.*[262] In fact, Bill was quite explicit as to the input of Father

---

[256] *Spiritual Milestones in Alcoholics Anonymous*, p. 3; Matthew 22:36-40.

[257] *Spiritual Milestones in Alcoholics Anonymous*, p. 11; Romans 13:14.

[258] *Second Reader for Alcoholics Anonymous*, p. 12.

[259] *A Guide to the Twelve Steps of Alcoholics Anonymous*, p. 14.

[260] Roy L. Smith, *Emergency Rations*, rev. ed. (Cleveland: The Cleveland District Office of Alcoholics Anonymous, 1949), Rations 10, 25, 28.

[261] Father John Doe, *Sobriety and Beyond* (Indianapolis, The S.M.T. Guild, 1955).

[262] See the Foreword by John Cuthbert Fortd, S.J. in Mary C. Darrah, *Sister Ignatia: Angel of Alcoholics Anonymous* (Chicago: Loyola University Press, 1992), pp. ix-x; Robert Fitzgerald, S.J., *The Soul of Sponsorship: The Friendship of Father Ed Dowling*,

(continued...)

John Ford, S.J.; and Bill so stated in several letters he sent Sam Shoemaker.[263]

Lastly, there are the spiritual retreats for A.A.'s and their families that are currently conducted in many parts of the United States and England—retreats having been started initially by A.A. pioneer Clarence S. These retreats definitely emphasize the importance of the Bible and Jesus Christ in early A.A. and in taking the Twelve Steps today.[264]

---

[262] (...continued)
S.J. and Bill Wilson in Letters (Center City, MN: Hazelden, 1995), pp. 55-72. In a letter to Sam Shoemaker, dated May 2, 1958, Wilson wrote: "The Catholic Church also provides several retreat facilities for members of A.A. A great many Protestants go to them, find great benefit, and happily discover they are never proselytized. Although under Catholic auspices, they are pretty much A.A. affairs. Very often the retreat leader is a priest member of A.A."

[263] On June 14, 1957, Bill sent Sam Shoemaker a copy of a lengthy letter he had sent to Father John Ford. Bill said: "Entre nous, Father Ford is an AA member — one of great devotion and long standing. . . . He also went over Twelve Steps and Twelve Traditions with a fine-tooth comb and is most solicitous that we never get into a jam with the Church. He is one of our very best under-cover agents." In his May 14, 1957 letter to Ford at Weston College in Massachusetts, Bill said: "Please have my deepest appreciation for the careful pre-publication survey you have made of our book, 'A.A. Comes of Age', from the theological point of view. No one could agree more fully than I on the principle that we should avoid every possibility of theological dispute which might result in a justification for declaring Alcoholics Anonymous a heresy. What you have done might well make much difference in later time. Needless to say I have transferred nearly all your suggestions to the new book, hedging on a few points only." Shortly thereafter, Bill sent Sam Shoemaker another lengthy letter he [Bill] had written Father Ford on July 15, 1957. This letter indicates the publication details on anonymity that Bill discussed with Ford—Bill responding to Ford's questions about the treatment of Lillian Roth and of Father Ralph [Father John Doe].

[264] See Dick B., *That Amazing Grace*, pp. 3-7, 64-67, 83-114.

Spiritual Growth—Continuance

16. *Conservation—Continuance As an Idea*

> The changed, surrendered, converted person must maintain
> and grow in his life of grace through Bible study, prayer,
> waiting upon God for guidance, public worship, and
> witness.

The Oxford Group indicated a person's life-change was not
complete with that person's *conversion*. The Group called for daily
growth in the life of grace. They were speaking of the fifth of their
5 C's. Sometimes they called this "Conservation" and sometimes
"Continuance."[265] We will not go into much detail here on the
various aspects of "Conservation" since the individual topics it
comprehends are separately discussed in the balance of this
chapter.

Shoemaker made the following comments which explain the
essence of Conservation:

> Conversion is the beginning, not the ending of an experience of
> God. That experience continues when we use all the means Jesus
> put at our disposal for continuation—prayer, the Scriptures, the
> Church and Sacraments, Christian fellowship and worship. . . .
> Many situations in my life are not covered by the Sermon on the
> Mount. I need special guidance and illumination. . . . What
> infinite possibilities of learning the will of God, through
> communion with Him, may lie ahead of us, who can dare to
> imagine?[266]
>
> [Man needs] to live this life of grace. Too much stress cannot be
> laid on private prayer and Bible study, and public uniting with the

---

[265] See Walter, *Soul Surgery*, pp. 89-100; Shoemaker, *Realizing Religion*, p. 80;
Begbie, *Life Changers*, p. 169-70; Lean, *On the Tail of a Comet*, p. 79; *DR. BOB*, p.
54; and Dick B., *Anne Smith's Journal*, pp. 102-06.

[266] Shoemaker, *Religion That Works*, p. 14, 15.

Church. And there is no more empowering habit in the lives of those who seek to live the Christ-life than this "fishing for men," as Jesus called it.[267]

Reconstructing Conservation from the various Oxford Group writings, there were five aspects: (1) Prayer,[268] (2) Bible study,[269] (3) Guidance,[270] (4) Group worship,[271] and (5) Witness.[272] Cecil Rose wrote, "Surrender goes on. It is not

---

[267] Shoemaker, *Realizing Religion*, p. 82. See Matthew 4:19.

[268] Walter, *Soul Surgery*, p. 91, "First of all, then, we must guide the convert into a real and continuous and developing prayer life;" and p. 90, "Hence the importance of prayer as a daily exercise and a life-long study. In prayer we breath the tonic air of faith that defies every temptation to doubt and fear. In prayer our souls become assured that while *we* may fail God, He never fails us."

[269] Walter, *Soul Surgery*, p. 91, "In the second place, the new convert must learn to feed his soul, day by day, on God's living Word revealed in the Scriptures; and here, too, he cannot be left to himself, but needs and will usually welcome friendly guidance."

[270] Benson, *The Eight Points*, pp. 74-75, "Divine guidance must become the normal experience of ordinary men and women, says Dr. Buchman. Any man can pick up divine messages if he will put his receiving set in order. Definite, accurate, adequate information can come from the Mind of God to the mind of men . . . The crux of the Oxford Group Movement is its insistence upon the possibility and necessity of the guided life . . . No one can read the Bible without being impressed by the constant references to Divine Guidance." Compare Dick B., *Anne Smith's Journal*, p. 114; and *New Light on Alcoholism*, pp. 337-38 (for Lois Wilson's own notes on Guidance).

[271] This was the particular stress of Dr. Shoemaker. See *Realizing Religion*, p. 82. As to a possible effect of Shoemaker's emphasis on "uniting with the church," Dr. Bob's daughter, Sue Smith Windows, informed the author that Dr. Bob and his wife, Anne, joined a Presbyterian Church in Akron because of the Oxford Group's encouraging church affiliation [Personal interview with the author by Sue Windows in Akron, Ohio, June, 1991]. The author also verified that Dr. Bob and Anne were charter members of a Presbyterian church in Akron during A.A.'s formative years. Later, Dr. Bob became a communicant at St. Paul's Episcopal Church in Akron, Ohio. See Dick B., *New Light on Alcoholism*, p. 20-21; and *Dr. Bob's Library*, pp. 2-3.

[272] Walter, *Soul Surgery*, p. 92, "In the third place—and here most of all we are prone to fail in this work of individual conservation—following conversion the new convert must be set to work to win others." Shoemaker and Buchman often spoke of the necessity of "giving it away to keep it." In *Realizing Religion*, Shoemaker referred to the account in Acts 3:6, "Such as I have give I thee," and Paul's statement in 1 Thessalonians 2:8, that we should give "not the gospel of God only, but also our own

(continued...)

simply an initial act. It is a process carried deeper every day. We find out more of ourselves to give to God."[273]

Shoemaker wrote:

> We believe entirely that conversion is the experience which initiates the new life. But we are not fools enough to think that the beginning is the end. All subsequent life is a development of the relationship with God which conversion opened. For us its daily focal point is in what we call the "Quiet Time." As in all other private devotions, we pray and read the Bible. But the distinguishing element of a Quiet Time is listening for the guidance of God. "Speak Lord, for Thy servant heareth," is the expectant mood of a Quiet Time. The validity of what we believe to be God's guidance must show itself, in the long run, by more acute moral perception, more genuine human relationships, and increasing assurance of what one ought to do every hour of the day.[274]

> We talked of the daily Quiet Time, of Bible study, prayer and listening, and of the power of God to lead and guide those who are obedient enough to be led. We also talked of the need for early sharing of the experience through which he had passed and bringing others to the same place.[275]

Compare the following two statements in A.A.'s Big Book:

1. The spiritual life is not a theory. We have to live it (p. 83).

2. Every day is a day when we must carry the vision of God's will into all our activities (p. 85).[276]

---

[272] (...continued)
souls" (pp. 82-83). Shoemaker called this "fishing for men." See also, Lean, *Cast Out Your Nets*, p. 97.

[273] Rose, *When Man Listens*, p. 21.

[274] Shoemaker, *Children of the Second Birth*, p. 16. See 1 Samuel 3:9.

[275] Shoemaker, *Children of the Second Birth*, pp. 148-149.

[276] The significance and practices of early A.A. Quiet Time are thoroughly discussed in Dick B., *Good Morning! Quiet Time, Morning Watch, Meditation and Early A.A.* (San Rafael, CA: Paradise Research Publications, 1996).

17. *Daily surrender as a process*

"General" surrender to God must be accompanied by daily
self-examination and surrender to get rid of newly
accumulated sin and selfishness.

What Is The Oxford Group? said:

Our initial Surrender to God does not mean that henceforth we
shall be asleep to the world around us; that temptations will never
assail nor sins conquer us again, and that, if they do, God is not
living up to His part of the compact. . . . It means that after
Surrender we have to work and eat and sleep and laugh and play
as before, and that in the round of daily life come situations which
cause reactions against our spiritual good resolutions. . . . Sin
remains sin, but even if we only surrendered to God yesterday our
sin of to-day does not cancel that surrender. God knows and waits.
He waits to see if we will Surrender that sin of to-day to Him with
as much sincerity as we surrendered our lives yesterday; to see if
we will acknowledge it was lack of trust that made us fail to ask
Him to take that sin away from us while it was still temptation; to
see if we will confess that it was want of faith in His Guidance that
made us vulnerable to spiritual weakness. . . . Our lives will be
one continuous surrender: surrender to God of every difficulty that
confronts us, each temptation, each spiritual struggle; laying before
Him either to take away or to show to us in their proper spiritual
proportions (pp. 45-46).

The Eight Points of the Oxford Group had a chapter on "Daily
Checking," which said:

"Shine out O Light divine and show how far we stray." That is
the prayer of a man who is not satisfied to go on living a
haphazard, unverified life. When we speak of self-examination,
it suggests tests. It implies the selection of standards of judgment
by which we measure ourselves. . . . The saints are not people
who are better than the rest, but those who are trying to be better
than they are. The Group takes the four absolute standards of the

life of Christ—Absolute Love, Absolute Purity, Absolute Honesty and Absolute Unselfishness. These are applied as daily tests of life in all its issues. This practice of regular self-examination in the light of Christ has proved to be of genuine practical value in our Christian development.[277]

When I came to make a daily surrender I learned what a different experience this is from a general surrender. Daily checking on the four absolutes revealed to me things I had never questioned in myself. . . . The Quiet Time was no new method of prayer to me but it became increasingly searching. I came to a daily willingness to do anything for God. I made amends where He gave me light.[278]

Shoemaker had these things to say:

The daily and hourly renewal of the crucifixion of our selves, and the implantation of the will of God where our wills used to be, comes by seeking the mind of God through listening. . . . How many of us are grown up enough to remember that the important thing in prayer is not to change the will and mind of God, but to find them.[279]

There is need for rededication day by day, hour by hour, by which progressively, in every Quiet Time, the contaminations of sin and self-will are further sloughed off (for they do have a way of collecting) and we are kept in fresh touch with the living Spirit of God. A further surrender is needed when and whenever there is found to be something in us which offends Christ, or walls us from another. We shall need, in this sense, to keep surrendering so long as we live. . . . I believe that with a God of love, there is no limit to the number of times we may come back to Him in

---

[277] Benson, *The Eight Points*, pp. 44-45.

[278] Benson, *The Eight Points*, p. 149.

[279] Shoemaker, *The Church Can Save the World*, pp. 96-97.

surrender, provided only we mean it and are penitent for the past.[280]

The progress of the Christian life . . . consists of development and motion, with the direction of a clear path that is punctuated by critical periods or decisions, upon the conquest of which depends all the rest of the course. . . . And first we must say that the initial hurdle is deciding to run the Christian course at all. . . . The next hurdle for most of us arises when we begin to face ourselves honestly. . . . Next there comes a hurdle familiar . . . to us all as an experience, the hurdle of surrender to God. . . . For most people there is wrapped up in the decision to surrender to God the necessity to right all wrongs with men. . . . This is the hurdle of restitution. . . . Again: we all move forward in our Christian course by the help of other Christians. . . . [There] is a decision to keep on just when the full force of the meaning of a decision for Christ sweeps over us, and scares us with its bigness. . . . And then . . . the hurdles of fresh, vivid battle with returning, characteristic temptation.[281]

Compare these portions from A.A.'s Big Book:

Continue to watch for selfishness, dishonesty, resentment, and fear. When these crop up, we ask God at once to remove them. . . . When we retire at night, we constructively review our day. Were we resentful, selfish, dishonest or afraid? . . . After making our review we ask God's forgiveness and inquire what corrective measures should be taken. . . . As we go through the day. . . . We constantly remind ourselves we are no longer running the show, humbly saying to ourselves many times each day "Thy Will be done." . . . So we let God discipline us in the simple way we have just outlined (pp. 84-88).

---

[280] Shoemaker, *The Conversion of the Church*, p. 79.

[281] Shoemaker, *The Gospel According to You*, pp. 81-91.

18. *Guidance—The Walk by Faith*

The Holy Spirit gives Divine Guidance to a life that is changed from sin to God. It takes normal intelligence and guides it to the fullest harmony with God's Will, both for the good of the individual and for that of his neighbor.

Frank Buchman said:

Leaders everywhere now say that the world needs a moral and spiritual awakening. . . . The problem is how. . . . Now I find when we don't know how, God will show us if we are willing. When man listens, God speaks. When man obeys, God acts. We are not out to tell God. We are out to let God tell us. And He will tell us. The lesson the world most needs is the art of listening to God. . . . It is thoughts from God which have inspired the prophets through history.[282]

God spoke to the prophets of old. He may speak to you.[283]

By a miracle of the Spirit, God can speak to every man.[284]

Direct messages from the Mind of God to the mind of man—definite, direct, decisive. God speaks.[285]

Oxford Group writers often mentioned the God who speaks. And they couched their discussion in biblical terms. Theologian B. H. Streeter wrote an entire book titled, *The God Who Speaks*. Oxford Group author, Cecil Rose wrote:

---

[282] Buchman, *Remaking the World*, p. 35-36.

[283] Buchman, *Remaking the World*, p. 41.

[284] Buchman, *Remaking the World*, p. 42.

[285] Buchman, *Remaking the World*, p. 72. Compare Lois Wilson's comments in her Oxford Group notes which echo Buchman's comments, almost verbatim. Dick B., *New Light on Alcoholism*, p. 337. For similar remarks by Anne Smith, see Dick B., *Anne Smith's Journal*, pp. 57-62.

God speaks. That is the tremendous fact around which both the Old and New Testament are built—not that man can and may speak to God, but that God can and does speak to man. . . . We can only hope to live a life fully effective, and possessing a real sense of security and peace, if this truth that "God speaks" can be tested and found true by us. . . . *God has a plan. God speaks.* But if He is to be heard and His plan is to be known and carried out, *man must listen.* . . . The promise that our petitions will be answered is only to those who have first placed themselves in line with His Will. If God is to become for us the living, active God, at work directing our life and the world's, it is vital that we should learn how to listen. There is one condition to be fulfilled before we begin. We must be willing to hear anything God says to us.[286]

Eleanor Napier Forde cited Romans 8:26, explaining, "It is God's Spirit Who must pray through us, bringing to our minds the people and the needs for which to intercede." Miss Forde wrote of a little girl, saying "God could talk to her." And Forde suggested tests as to possible Divine origin of thoughts, including "intuitive conviction."[287]

Oxford Group people cited solid Biblical authority for their guidance concept. They stated:

To Sam Shoemaker in 1920, Buchman wrote a seven-page foolscap letter, citing a formidable array of Biblical and theological authority for the practice [listening to God—listening for Guidance—receiving "luminous thoughts" from God].[288]

No one can read the Bible without being impressed by the constant references to Divine Guidance. Abraham was guided.

---

[286] Cecil Rose, *When Man Listens*, pp. 27, 30-31.

[287] Eleanor Napier Forde, *The Guidance of God* (The Oxford Group, Printed at the University Press at Oxford by John Johnson, n.d.), pp. 25, 21.

[288] Lean, *On the Tail of a Comet*, p. 75. In a footnote, Lean added, "The thoughts which arose in such times of seeking God's guidance in later years became known in the verbal shorthand of Buchman and his friends, as 'guidance,' although neither he nor they considered that all such thoughts came from God."

. . . We find the same sense of guidance in Isaac, Jacob, Joseph, Moses . . . the life of David or of any of the other Old Testament heroes. . . . So also with the prophets. There are numerous passages in the Psalms. . . . We find the same evidence in the New Testament.[289]

In the New Testament a full relationship to God is described by saying that "we receive the Holy Spirit." If that phrase is vague to us, it is not vague to the writers of the New Testament. To those first Christians that gift clearly meant, not only the purifying and strengthening power of God within them, but His directing voice as well. He is the One who dictates their decisions in council. As their Master promised, they are given the words to say when called on to witness. Peter on the roof-top is told to go down and follow the messengers of Cornelius.[290] Philip to "get up and go south along the road from Jerusalem to Gaza;"[291] and Paul is directed not to enter Bithynia.[292] Here is a picture of men and women moving obediently under the effective guidance of God. Is God less able to guide us today?[293]

Revelation: This is the keystone in the Buchman theological arch. As far as he personally was concerned, revelation was probably in second place behind the redemption at the Cross of Christ. In later years the latter faded as an up-front public concern. The guidance of God, however, was top coinage to the end. . . . A recent book about Tournier carries this explanation that might have come out of Buchman himself: "God has a unique, detailed purpose for every man. He has prepared for this by giving specific gifts or temperaments, and it is our duty to

---

[289] Benson, *The Eight Points*, p. 75. See, for illustrations of Benson's points: Genesis 17; 26:2-6; 28; 35; Exodus 6; 2 Samuel 6; Psalm 105; Isaiah 7; Jeremiah 34; Ezekiel 38; Hosea 1; Malachi 3; Acts 7; 8:26; 10:4-43. See further discussion of biblical illustrations by Almond, *Foundations for Faith*, p. 22.

[290] Acts 10:1-21.

[291] Acts 8:26-30.

[292] Acts 16:6-9.

[293] Rose, *When Man Listens*, p. 28.

discover as best we can what God desires for every moment of our lives. The Bible gives broad outlines of this purpose, but God also speaks through the advice of friends, circumstances of life, or the ideas that come to mind during periods of meditation."[294]

As previously discussed, there are precise Bible references to *revelation*.[295] And much theological support for their significance.[296]

When Frank Buchman used words such as "God speaks," "inspiration," and "revelation," his language rested on specific Bible verses we have previously discussed. These supported his ideas that God can and does guide.[297] *What Is The Oxford Group?* said of Guidance:

1. One of the Oxford Group's "four practical spiritual activities" is "Listening to, accepting, relying on God's Guidance and carrying it out in everything we do or say, great or small" (pp. 8-9).

2. Divine guidance to a life changed from Sin to God is the Holy Spirit taking a normal intelligence and directing it in the fullest harmony with His will for the good of the individual and his neighbors (p. 67).

3. Suggestions as to conduct, solutions to material and spiritual difficulties are given by daily guidance. It is God using for our

---

[294] Hunter, *World Changing Through Life Changing*, pp. 135, 139.

[295] John 14:26; 1 Corinthians 12:8; Galatians 1:12; 2 Timothy 3:16; 2 Peter 1:21.

[296] For discussion of "inspiration" and "revelation" as used in the Bible, see *The Abingdon Bible Commentary*, pp. 26-31; *Divino Afflante Spiritu*: Encyclical Letter of Pope Pius XII, pp. 316-17; Vatican II *Dei Verbum*: Dogmatic Constitution on Divine Revelation, pp. 401-10, James J. Megivern, *Official Catholic Teachings: Bible Interpretation* (Wilmington, NC: McGrath Publishing Company, 1978); and Almond, *Foundations for Faith*, p. 13.

[297] Psalm 32:8; Psalm 37:5; Proverbs 3:6; Romans 8:14; 1 Corinthians 2:9; 2 Corinthians 5:7; James 3:17.

best, in partnership with us, the lives we have surrendered to His care (p. 67).

4. "Every good gift and every perfect boon is from above."[298] Life under guidance . . . is all-wise and all-embracing, building up our right God-appointed kind of ego (p. 67).

5. Divine guidance takes us away from that fear of tomorrow. . . . Not only is our to-day in God's keeping but our to-morrow; we have surrendered that to Him, too, so why fear whatever we think tomorrow must bring us as a logical sequence of to-day's events (pp. 67-68).

Benson's *The Eight Points of the Oxford Group* said:

God has a plan for every life. He will make known to us His plan day by day if we give Him a chance.[299]

God cannot do very much for us so long as we insist on playing the part of Providence to ourselves. Things begin to happen when we "let go" and "let God." . . . wait again in passive silence. . . . It is surprising how, while apparently thinking our own thoughts, difficulties are cleared away, problems solved, how doubt and uncertainty, trouble and despondence and mental disquiet give place to a sense of peace and joy. . . . There is scarcely a page of the Scriptures which does not witness to the fact of guidance. The plain promise of the Bible is that in all perplexities and anxieties we may expect illumination and direction. . . . God has a plan for every life and He will reveal it to us day by day when we fulfill the conditions. . . . So the Group insists upon absolute surrender to God—our selves, our

---

[298] See James 1:17, "Every good gift and every perfect gift is from above and cometh down from the Father of lights, with Whom is no variableness, neither shadow of turning." See Big Book, p. 14, "I must turn in all things to the Father of Light who presides over us all." See also Smith, *Emergency Rations*, Ration No. 4.

[299] Benson, *The Eight Points*, pp. 65.

sins, our will, time, possessions, ambitions, everything. He will guide us into His Will for us.[300]

Shoemaker said:

We are quite clear in our theology of the Holy Spirit. But we have forgotten that the ordinary man lays hold of God through experience, and not through definition. . . . For the Holy Spirit sounds very vague until we know that He brings with Him definite light. . . . God speaks in six great ways: (1) In nature and creation; (2) In the moral law; (3) In the Scriptures; (4) In Jesus Christ; (5) In human conscience; and (6) In history. . . . We cannot carry on a conversation with God through nature or moral law. We find God's general will in the Scriptures. We find God still more directly in Jesus Christ. But human conscience is no perfect reflector of God, and history only points to His existence and His general will. We want to know that God can and does speak directly to the human heart. The reason why some of us believe in guidance, at least in theory, is that the Old and New Testaments are full of instances of it, as specific as you please. Men said clearly that they were guided of God in this and that act and decision. . . . I prefer to see whether this sort of thing is not now possible to those who put their trust in God entirely.[301]

You can be in touch with God. We need to come to Him with a child's openness and simplicity. God always meets such an approach more than halfway, and takes the initiative with an open life. We need the help of others for whom being in touch with God is more familiar than it is for us. We need the constant recreation of the atmosphere of "Speak, Lord, for thy servant heareth,"[302] instead of the usual approach to God which is "Hear Lord, for thy servant speaketh." And we need to know that guidance is not for our private comfort or even illumination, but

---

[300] Benson, *The Eight Points*, pp. 68, 69, 70, 76, 78.

[301] Shoemaker, *The Conversion of the Church*, pp. 49-50.

[302] See 1 Samuel 3:9. Shoemaker frequently cited this verse. See Dick B., *New Light on Alcoholism*, pp. 44, 103, 202, 205, 228, 270, 316.

that by it God means to touch some actual human situation that needs to be touched and cured.[303]

Let it be said often, that there is no short-cut to truth which we are supposed to dig out with our minds: it is God's crystallization of truth from the facts we have and also from some facts which we cannot possibly know, but can only guess by what humanly we call a "flash of intuition." The guidance of religion is "intuition" *plus* [italics added]. It is not a substitute for, but a tremendous supplement to, the common processes of thought. The sustenance of the new spiritual life lies in the material which is in the Bible which is everlasting and universal; and then in God's direct messages to us, which are temporal and personal; but sometimes have widespread effects. Let man cultivate that time alone with the living God, day by day.[304]

A.A.'s Big Book contains many statements calling for guidance and direction from God. The following are two:

For we are now on a different basis; the basis of trusting and relying upon God. . . . We are in the world to play the role He assigns. Just to the extent that we do as we think he would have us, and humbly rely on Him, does He enable us to match calamity with serenity (p. 68).

We ask that we be given strength and direction to do the right thing (p. 79).[305]

---

[303] Shoemaker, *National Awakening*, p. 86.

[304] Shoemaker, *Twice-Born Ministers*, pp. 184-85. As to the "intuitive thought" and A.A., see Big Book, p. 84 ("We will intuitively know how to handle situations which used to baffle us"); p. 86 ("Here we ask God for inspiration, an intuitive thought or decision").

[305] Compare Rose, *When Man Listens*, pp. 38, 19; and see just a few of the endless examples in the Big Book of Oxford Group-Shoemaker Guidance concepts and language at Big Book, pp. 14, 49, 50, 57, 68, 69, 70, 79, 83, 85, 86, 87, 98, 100.

19.   *The Four Absolutes—Christ's Standards*

Absolute Honesty, Absolute Purity, Absolute Unselfishness, and Absolute Love are the essence of Jesus's teachings about the Will of God, the ideals for man's life, and the moral standards by which man's thoughts and actions may be tested for harmony with God's will.

As previously shown, the Oxford Group's Four Absolutes can be found in Frank Buchman's speeches;[306] in books about Buchman;[307] in descriptions of Oxford Group principles;[308] in Sam Shoemaker's writings;[309] in A.A. conference-approved books discussing the Oxford Group;[310] in Anne Smith's writings;[311] and in some A.A. Groups today.[312]

Almost every Oxford Group writer, including the Reverend Samuel M. Shoemaker, Jr., accepted the fact that the "Four

---

[306] Buchman, *Remaking the World*, pp. 36, 40, 96, 131.

[307] Russell, *For Sinners Only*, pp. 319-29; Howard, *Frank Buchman's Secret*, p. 29; Lean, *On the Tail of a Comet*, pp. 76-77; Spoerri, *Dynamic out of Silence*, p. 39; and Frank H. Sherry and Mahlon H. Hellerich, *The Formative Years of Frank N. D. Buchman* (Portion of book located at Frank Buchman's home at Allentown, Pennsylvania, and provided to the author by A.A. Oldtimer, Earl H.), pp. 237, 251.

[308] *What Is The Oxford Group?*, pp. 7-8; 73-118; Almond, *Foundations for Faith*, pp. 11-13; Benson, *The Eight Points*, pp. 44-57; Winslow, *Why I Believe in the Oxford Group*, pp. 24-32; Foot, *Life Began Yesterday*, p. 57; Kitchen, *I Was a Pagan*, p. 130; Hofmeyr, *How to Change*, p. 1; Viney, *How Do I Begin?*, pp. 2,3; and Howard Rose, *The Quiet Time*.

[309] Samuel M. Shoemaker, *Twice-Born Ministers*, p. 150; *The Church Can Save the World*, p. 110; *How to Become a Christian*, p. 57; *How You Can Help Other People* (New York: E. P. Dutton, 1946), p. 59; and see Helen Shoemaker, *I Stand by the Door*, pp. 24-26; and Dick B., *New Light on Alcoholism*, pp. 41, 67, 73, 130-31, 209, 211, 270-72, 315.

[310] *DR. BOB*, pp. 54, 163; *Pass It On*, pp. 114, 172; *AA Comes of Age*, pp. 68, 75, 161; *The Language of the Heart*, pp. 196-200; and *Co-Founders*, pp. 13-14.

[311] Dick B., *Anne Smith's Journal*, pp. 31-34, 59, 59-60, 64, 72, 75, 87-88, 98, 104-06, 108, 115, 116-20, 143.

[312] Mel B., *New Wine*, pp. 76, 138; Dick B., *That Amazing Grace*, pp. 29, 34, 50-55; and see the publications by the Cleveland District Office of A.A. and AA of Akron.

Absolutes," or "Four Standards," as they were also called, emerged directly from the research by Dr. Robert E. Speer into the heart of Jesus's teachings.[313] Speer set out to prove that Jesus taught some absolute moral standards, and he said that Jesus was the teacher of *absolute* principles.[314] Perfection was Jesus's standard.[315]

What Is The Oxford Group? defined the four absolutes:

1. Absolute purity demands a clean mind in a clean body and embraces clean conduct in business, in work and play, interest in world affairs, our use of our possessions, our attitudes toward relations, friends and acquaintances (p. 87).

2. Absolute unselfishness means unselfish according to the love we bear toward the object of our unselfishness. It is the sacrifice of ourselves and our interests to other people's interests without thought of reward (p. 97).

3. Absolute honesty means to ourselves the absolute truth, to others as truthful as we are to ourselves, tempered with common sense and kindliness (pp. 75-76).

4. Absolute love is best lived by the principles of 1 Corinthians 13 (p. 108).[316]

The Eight Points dealt with the issue of "perfection" called for in the Absolutes. The word "absolute" in the Oxford Group is used to speak of perfection. But the perfection is like the perfection of a father. God is perfect as a Father. A father is perfect when he loves his children with perfect love. And love in

---

[313] Lean, *On the Tail of a Comet*, p. 76; Spoerri, *Dynamic out of Silence*, p. 49; Samuel M. Shoemaker, *How You Can Help Other People*, p. 59; and Helen Smith Shoemaker, *I Stand by the Door*, p. 24.

[314] Speer, *The Principles of Jesus*, pp. 33-34.

[315] Speer, *The Principles of Jesus*, p. 34, citing Matthew 5:48.

[316] In Almond, *Foundations for Faith*, the author said at page 12: "1 Corinthians 13 is a full exposition of this standard. See also Ephesians 4:15-16, 25, and 31-32."

our Heavenly Father is no more an abstract, distant thing than is love in an earthly father. Christian perfection does not imply an exemption either from ignorance or mistake or infirmities or temptations. There is no absolute perfection on earth. There is no perfection which does not admit of a continual increase.[317] Humility is essential to perfection. Nine-tenths of our misery is due to self-centeredness. To get ourselves off our hands is the essence of happiness. We do not find ourselves until we are thrown outside of ourselves into something greater than ourselves and set free. The point is that we learn to love, by receiving Christ in our hearts by faith. The love which we then have is not our love. It is the love of Christ, expressing itself in us and through us. I love; yet not I, but Christ loveth in me. It is not merely that we are trying to approximate a standard without and separate from us, but God begins to dwell in us.

To understand Benson better, see 1 John 4:10-16:

Herein is love, not that we loved God, but that He loved us, and sent His Son to be the propitiation for our sins. Beloved, if God so loved us, we ought also to love one another. No man hath seen God at any time. If we love one another, God dwelleth in us, and His love is perfected in us. Hereby we know that we dwell in Him, and He in us, because He hath given us of His Spirit. And we have seen and do testify that the Father sent the Son to be the Savior of the world. Whosoever shall confess that Jesus is the Son of God, God dwelleth in him, and he in God. And we have

---

[317] Webster's Dictionary speaks of "perfect" and "perfection" as "being entirely without fault or defect." By this definition, there could be no "continual increase." However, Webster adds a usage: "the act or process of perfecting." This seems to be what *The Eight Points* spoke of. Further, unless one believes in the regenerating power of Christ within, which must, by the renewing of the mind, be brought into manifestation through "putting on" the mind of Christ, the *Eight Points* statement is most difficult to understand. See, therefore, Romans 12:1-2; Ephesians 3:17-19; 4:21-32; Philippians 2:5; 3:15; Colossians 3:1-16. Garth Lean wrote the author about the "perfection" issue, stating, "On perfection, the Scofield Bible may shed more light than Webster. Its note on Matthew 5, 'Be ye therefore perfect,' says: 'The word implies full development, growth into maturity or godliness, not sinless perfection'."

known and believed the love that God hath to us. God is love; and he that dwelleth in love dwelleth in God, and God in him.

God assimilates us to Himself. We are not saved by the love we exercise, but by the Love we trust.[318]

Shoemaker said this about the Four Absolutes:

> I asked him whether he had had a Quiet Time about the four standards: absolute honesty, purity, unselfishness, and love. He said he had, and produced a piece of yellow fool'scap from his pocket, neatly divided into four quarters, one for each standard, on which he had written down all the places where he felt he had fallen down on them. The paper was quite full. I shared honestly with him about my own sins. He said he wanted to make a decision, and give himself completely to Christ, so we got on our knees and he did it.[319]

> [There are] Four Standards which Dr. Robert E. Speer said represented the summary of the Sermon on the Mount—Absolute Honesty, Absolute Purity, Absolute Unselfishness, and Absolute Love.[320]

> Dr. Robert E. Speer, in one of his books, had said the essence of the ethics of the Sermon on the Mount was the Four Absolutes: Honesty, Purity, Unselfishness, and Love. . . . For thousands of young and not so young folk, fumbling and groping for a way of life, they [the Four Absolutes] became a sharp challenge—clear, demanding, giving a plain starting place. The Law came before Grace. Few could feel anything but guilt before any one of the Four Absolutes. . . . Absolute purity means to find some all-consuming and high faith and purpose which takes

---

[318] Benson, *The Eight Points*, pp. 44-57.

[319] Shoemaker, *The Church Can Save the World*, p. 119-20.

[320] Shoemaker, *How to Become a Christian*, p. 57. The Rev. Harry Almond said the following verses from the Sermon on the Mount explained the Four Absolutes: (1) Honesty, Matthew 5:33-37; (2) Purity, Matthew 5:27-28; (3) Unselfishness, Matthew 5:38-42; (4) Love, Matthew 5:43 and following. Almond, *Foundations for Faith*, pp. 11-13.

up and uses one's energies. . . . Absolute unselfishness—that
catches us all in a hundred places. . . . And then Absolute Love.
There were many minor irritations, but the cleavage between my
father and me . . . was a deep one. . . . I just knew that basic
dishonesty, impurity, selfishness, want of love, and withal a kind
of pervasive inferiority were holding me down.[321]

Some think the Four Absolutes of early A.A. vanished into
history. But even after Wilson and his few New York AAs had left
the Oxford Group in 1937 and after the Akron AAs had reluctantly
parted company in 1940, the *Central Bulletin*, which was the
official A.A. publication in Cleveland, Ohio, carried the Four
Absolutes on its masthead; and we have already shown they are
very much discussed and used in A.A. literature distributed in
Ohio, Illinois, and some other A.A. areas.

Bill Wilson demonstrated the frequency of their mention in the
Oxford Group, saying: "Little was heard of theology, but we
heard plenty of absolute honesty, absolute purity, absolute
unselfishness, and absolute love—the four principles of the Oxford
Group."[322] As we previously pointed out, Bill said the Four
Absolutes had been incorporated into A.A.'s Sixth and Seventh
Steps. Dr. Bob emphasized *Love* and Service [unselfishness],
exemplified by his special interest in 1 Corinthians 13 and Henry
Drummond's book about it. In any event, one can hardly pick up
the Big Book without finding, in many places, the strong emphasis
placed on unselfishness, love, and honesty. And possibly even
"purity," in the sense that Buchman used the phrase "pure in
heart" from Matthew 5:6. Buchman was talking about removing
the "blocks" to God. And so was the Big Book.[323]

---

[321] Helen Shoemaker, quoting Sam Shoemaker, in *I Stand by the Door*, p. 24.

[322] *Pass It On*, p. 127.

[323] Big Book, pp. 64, 71, 72.

20. *Quiet Time*

The Oxford Group observed some time in early morning for quietness, creating an atmosphere where one can be susceptible to Divine Guidance and sensitive to the sway of the Spirit.

For Sinners Only said of Quiet Time: The Group said the individual was guided by God both during the Quiet Time and throughout the day in the following ways:

Through the Holy Spirit in attentive prayer by means of:
    The Scriptures.
    The Conscience.
    Luminous Thoughts.
    Cultivating The Mind of Christ.
Through reading the Bible and prayer.
Through circumstances.
Through reason.
Through Church, Group, or Fellowship.[324]

Benson said in *The Eight Points of the Oxford Group* that one of the most valuable features of Oxford Group practices is "The Quiet Time."[325] Each member is urged to devote some time in the early morning to quietness. At that time, said Benson, it is possible to have the mind illumined by unhurried reading of the Bible, by prayer, and by waiting upon God for guidance. Oxford Group people not only *spoke* to God. In the stillness, they gave God a chance to speak to them. They said prayer is "colloquy with God." They learned to be still and wait for God.[326] The process involved: (1) Learning stillness. (2) Eliminating "overstrain." (3)

---

[324] Russell, *For Sinners Only*, p. 94. See also, Howard Rose, *The Quiet Time*.

[325] Garth Lean wrote the author stating that it should be called "God's Art, expressed through individuals and teams."

[326] See Psalm 46:10, "Be still and know that I am God" — often quoted in Oxford Group literature.

Eliminating the crowded program. "Be still and know that I am God," said Benson, meant that to know God we must be still. To be still we must know God. There must be silence in order to know God. The hurried mind and the distracted heart make a vital knowledge of God impossible. When we are ruffled, troubled about many things, in a state of agitation and flutter, we are not conscious of God; there is no receptive quietness.[327]

Compare these statements in A.A.'s Big Book:

> On awakening let us think about the twenty-four hours ahead. . . .
> Here we ask God for inspiration, an intuitive thought or a decision.
> We relax and take it easy. We don't struggle. We are often sur-
> prised how the right answers come after we have tried this for a
> while (p. 86).

Oxford Group author Jack Winslow wrote a good deal on Quiet Time, stating, among other things:

> The morning quiet time has come to mean to me a time when I
> seek to know God's plan for my day—when I come to Him for
> orders. After a time of quiet adoration and thanksgiving and the
> renewal of my self-surrender for His service, I ask Him for His
> directions, and listen receptive for them.[328]

Shoemaker said:

> I plead again for the keeping of the "Morning Watch"—coming
> fresh to God with the day's plans unmade, submitting first our
> spirits and then our duties to Him for the shedding of His white
> light on both. To steam full-speed through icebergs is irreligious.
> To start the day without one thought of our Maker is to invite
> catastrophe.[329]

---

[327] Benson, *The Eight Points*, pp. 58-73.

[328] Winslow, *Why I Believe in the Oxford Group*, p. 43

[329] Shoemaker, *Realizing Religion*, pp. 65-66.

Something happened to the quality of my time of prayer when I moved out of the old conception of a "Morning Watch" (which had a way of slipping round till evening), to the conception of a "Quiet Time." The emphasis was in a different place. Formerly, I had sought to find my way up to God. Now I let Him find His way down to me. Listening became the dominant note.[330]

We can only find the possible ways out in a Quiet Time with God. The way to find out what can happen in a Quiet Time is not to discuss all the metaphysical pros and cons of divine guidance, but to sit down and have a Quiet Time! Listen to God. . . . OBEY. The essence of the giving of ourselves to God is the willingness to do what He says, and the heart of the Quiet Time is asking Him what He wants.[331]

Quiet Times do not need to be confined to morning and evening. One of the most profitable Quiet Times I ever had was one Saturday afternoon on the top of a Fifth Avenue bus. . . . I often stop in at Trinity Church, downtown, for a Quiet Time at noon, when things have gotten a bit on my nerves at the office. The early morning is the best time for Quiet Time, but not the only time.[332]

21. *Bible Study*

God has revealed His Will for man through the Scriptures; and man must daily feed his soul on God's written Word. This is part of the Quiet Time and also Oxford Group life.

Henry Drummond said God gave us two helps in learning how to do His Will: (1) Christ, the Living Word; and (2) the Bible, the Written Word. He said that without Christ's Model Life, the ideal life would be incredible; but without the analysis of that life in the Word of God (the Bible), Christ's Model Life would be unintelligi-

---

[330] Shoemaker, *The Conversion of the Church*, p. 60.

[331] Shoemaker, *The Church Can Save the World*, p. 126.

[332] Shoemaker, *Children of the Second Birth*, p. 97.

ble.[333] Christ did the Will of God, and God's written Word—the Bible—makes the nature of his obedience intelligible.

Canon Streeter's title, *The God Who Speaks*, was almost wholly devoted to study of how God revealed His Will in the Old Testament and in the New Testament. Streeter pointed to the Bible's own testimony as to the divine guidance that God provided throughout history. Hence the Word reveals God's "general" or "universal" will; and it contains endless accounts of God's making specific facts, solutions, and directions known to those who listened.

For Sinners Only discussed prayerful study of the Bible as a means of receiving divine Guidance (p. 94).

Benson's *The Eight Points* detailed just how and what its author studied in the Bible in his Quiet Time. Benson said he preferred the life of Christ, the book of Acts or the Psalms (p. 68). He believed the mind can be illumined at the beginning of the day by unhurried reading of the Bible, by prayer, and by waiting upon God for guidance (p. 58). He cited a number of Psalms and Proverbs, which we discussed under the subject of Guidance, and which show that God will guide. He also pointed out that luminous thoughts can be checked with the mind of Christ as revealed in the New Testament (pp. 78-84).

There is scarcely a one of Shoemaker's thirty major books that does not study a portion of the Bible, quote a portion of it, illustrate a point with a Bible reference, or advocate regular study of the Bible—particularly in conjunction with Quiet Time. And sometimes all of these. Shoemaker wrote:

> Let us consider together these three great primary means which God gives for sustaining the experience when the sharp lines of conversion seem to grow dim, and we wonder whether it was real or not. First, the Bible. . . . The chief thing I want to emphasize about our use of the Bible is not so much the way each of us shall pursue our study of it, as the setting apart of a definite time each

---

[333] Drummond, *The Ideal Life*, p. 231.

morning for this, together with prayer . . . the results will justify
the effort; and granted the desire and determination to use this
time daily, with the Bible open before you, you will soon make
a method of study for yourself that will suit you better than
anything which this book might recommend.

. . . I want to give a few practical suggestions which one might
follow. One should have the best, that is the most accurate
translation obtainable, and it is well, to have some new
translation, like Moffatt's; we are in danger of learning phrases
rather than assimilating ideas, and the veneration of some for the
King James Version is near to bibliolatry. It is good to have a
marker where you make plenty of entries, and for this you want
a wide margin, and also a fresh copy. D. L. Moody, who was
noted especially for his familiarity with the Bible, "was always
wearing out Bibles, covering the margins with references and
notes, and allowing them to pass freely among his friends." Study
one book at a time, mastering the thought of it, the plan and
dominant ideas. Read what is there, not your own ideas into it.
Do not read hit or miss unsystematically; do not read
superstitiously, opening anywhere and expecting to find a fruitful
lesson for the day; and do not dwell too much on favorite
passages. . . . Read, as President Wilson urged the soldiers, long
passages that will really be the road to the heart of it. One may
read topically, using the concordance to seek out ideas on sin,
faith, prayer, the use of money, consecration or other subjects; or
biographically, as in the fascinating development of Peter from the
old faults and sins found in the gospel stories of him to the might
and influence of the Acts and Epistles. Read and know the Bible,
and all else, including public worship, will fall in its place.[334]

We find God's general will in the Scriptures. . . . [In Quiet
Time,] there was Bible study first, taking a book and studying it
straight through. . . . They will need constant help, suggestions
about how to study the Bible, where and what to read in it. For
most, the Gospels will come first.[335]

---

[334] Shoemaker, *Realizing Religion*, pp. 58-62.
[335] Shoemaker, *The Conversion of the Church*, pp. 49, 60, 79.

I find that reading Moffatt's Translation in the New Testament, after I have read the passage in the King James Version, is a great help to understanding it, especially in the Epistles. I recall my extreme prejudice against any translation except my beloved King James, not considering that the desire of God must be that I know the sense of the passage as well as enjoying the vehicle of it.[336]

Now guidance has got to become concrete and, in the best sense, habitual for ministers. This cannot come true without setting apart a definite time in the morning, the very first part of it, for sufficient prayer, Bible study, and listening for the Holy Spirit's direction.[337]

What about A.A. and the Bible? Without lamenting the obliteration of the Bible from mention in the text of the Big Book, one can still perceive the very obvious omission. Almost every Oxford Group concept survived in A.A. in one form or another. But mention and discussion of the Bible as the source of the concept did not. There are only two short Big Book sentences that even hint of former use of the Bible in early A.A.:

There are many helpful books also. Suggestions about these may be obtained from one's priest, minister, or rabbi (p. 87).

A.A.'s progressive move away from the Bible is also evident by the Bible's treatment in A.A.'s conference-approved histories. The Index to *DR. BOB and the Good Oldtimers*, which is often thought of as Dr. Bob's biography, contains 37 references to "The Holy Bible." Preparation and publication of the book was approved by the April, 1977 A.A. General Conference. The Index to *Pass It On*, which is considered to be Bill W.'s biography, refers to the Bible only five times. This book was published in 1984. Bill's own history of A.A., *Alcoholics Anonymous Comes of Age*, was published in 1957, just a few years after Dr. Bob died;

---

[336] Shoemaker, *Children of the Second Birth*, p. 97.

[337] Shoemaker, *Twice-Born Ministers*, p. 184.

and the Index makes no mention of the Bible. It seems that, under Bill's lead, and after Dr. Bob was gone, A.A. chose to eliminate the Bible as an official topic of discussion. But A.A.'s genesis in Bible ideas can hardly be ignored in view of the paramount position of the Bible in Oxford Group and Shoemaker writings as the source of information on the will and power of God. Nor can its dominant presence in early A.A. meetings be ignored. Nor can its significance in the following statement in *Anne Smith's Journal*:

> Of course the Bible ought to be the main Source Book of all. No day ought to pass without reading it.[338]

We believe that, as the "mother" of A.A.'s "first group, Akron Number One," as Bill phrased these words,[339] Anne Smith must have passed on to the first group the foregoing Bible emphasis.

22. *Prayer*

> Prayer is the natural complement of God-Direction. We cannot expect God to talk to us if we do not talk to Him. Prayer is an integral part of Quiet Time.

Canon Streeter wrote on the function of prayer, saying there a necessary interrelation between the idea of God's Plan and the view we entertain as to the nature and function of prayer.[340] He said of the Lord's Prayer that it should not be interpreted as a fixed form of words, but rather as an outline indicating a series of mental attitudes in which God should be approached by man. These are: (1) Lifting up the heart and mind to God in adoration; (2) The desire that God's Plan should be realized on earth; and (3) A trustful mention to our Heavenly Father of the individual's

---

[338] Dick B., *Anne Smith's Journal*, pp. 79-80.

[339] *The Language of the Heart*, p. 353.

[340] Streeter, *The God Who Speaks*, p. 17. Compare also Roger Hicks, *The Lord's Prayer and Modern Man* (London: Blandford Press, 1967).

material and spiritual needs. And Christ added the injunction that we "use not vain repetitions."[341] Because God knows what we have need of before we ask Him![342]

Benson's *The Eight Points* considered as a single process Quiet Time, reading the Bible slowly, praying, lingering, and waiting on God.[343] All these make us "receptive and sensitive to Divine leading. Petition is not the whole of prayer. We must practice the other great form of prayer, the openness of the soul to God so that the light and power and grace which 'cometh down from above'[344] may enter."[345] No Christian can be vital without the Bible, prayer and Guidance.[346]

What Is The Oxford Group? said:

> Prayer is the natural complement of God Direction. We cannot expect God to talk to us if we do not talk to Him. But it is not always essential continually to ask God for help in every move we make or in every problem of our lives. When we listen for His guidance during our Quiet Times, all requests asked or unasked are answered. However, real prayer receives a real answer in any place at any time. No supplication to God from the heart is ever lost (p. 69).

Walter stressed in *Soul Surgery* the importance of early morning prayer, saying "our own spirits are brought into tune with the infinite and made spiritually sensitive and strong and resourceful" (p. 41). He pointed to the number of great men who give an important place to believing, persistent sacrificial prayer

---

[341] Matthew 6:7-8.

[342] Streeter, *The God Who Speaks*, p. 18.

[343] Benson, *The Eight Points*, pp. 58-69, 79.

[344] This is a partial quotation from James 1:17, which reads, "Every good gift and every perfect gift is from above, and cometh down from the Father of lights, with whom is no variableness, neither shadow of turning." Note the reference to this verse in the Big Book at page 14.

[345] Benson, *The Eight Points*, p. 79.

[346] Benson, *The Eight Points*, p. 153.

which enables spiritual apprehension and power. He also said early morning prayer enables man to learn each day's program of procedure since God would never have us act in a haphazard manner. Such prayer transfers to our minds as much of God's perfect plan as we need to know (pp. 43-44).

Compare these comments in A.A.'s Big Book:

> We shouldn't be shy on this matter of prayer. Better men than we are using it constantly. It works if we have the proper attitude and work at it (pp. 85-86).

Shoemaker said of prayer:

> Whatever be one's theories about prayer, two things stand: man will pray as long as God and he exist, and the spiritual life cannot be lived without it. . . . People need to pray, and they pray. But it is an art—the art of discerning God's will—and one must learn it. For prayer is more than primitive awareness of the supernatural; for us Christians it is the communing of children with Father. . . . Obedience to the Voice which speaks in prayer must ever be the condition of hearing that Voice again. We ask for what we need, remembering that oftentimes we pray for a thing and He gives us a chance; and also that the essence of prayer is not childish asking for gifts, but the eternal questing for the disposition of God toward the ways of our life. And we are praying best when we come, quite empty of request, to bathe ourselves in His presence, and to "wait upon Him" with an open mind, concerned far more with His message to us than anything we can say to Him. . . . The prayer of confession and for forgiveness is perhaps the deepest, best prayer of all, and the one which we shall need most often if God gives us an acute sense of sin. However necessary it may be, prayer is seldom easy. . . . I have followed my own will so prayerfully and intensely that I do not know how to find another will. Sometimes the impression is vague and we are not sure it is from God. . . . Trusting Him, then, we must pray on, for we can do no other. And if we be faithful, we shall soon find that the reality of the experience of

prayer far outweighs the reality of the questionings which make us doubt it.[347]

Each morning, there should be continued relation with God in prayer, and daily waiting on God in Quiet. We give in afresh to God, admitting that He has the order and answer for the day.[348]

We talked for a little on the way to keep the New Life. We talked of the daily Quiet Time, of Bible study, prayer and listening, and of the power of God to lead and guide those who are obedient enough to be led.[349]

23.   *Listening to God for Leading Thoughts and Writing Down Guidance Received*

Frank Buchman said:

Anyone can hear the words of the Lord. It is only necessary to obey the rules. The first rule is that we listen honestly for everything that may come—and if we are wise, we write it down.[350]

The Reverend Howard Rose echoed those remarks and cited Jeremiah 30:1-2:

The word that came to Jeremiah from the Lord, saying, Thus speaketh the LORD God of Israel, saying, Write down all the words that I have spoken unto thee in a book.[351]

For Sinners Only described a Quiet Time experience its author, A. J. Russell, had:

---

[347] Shoemaker, *Realizing Religion*, pp. 63-65.

[348] Shoemaker, *National Awakening*, p. 53.

[349] Shoemaker, *Children of the Second Birth*, p. 53.

[350] Buchman, *Remaking the World*, p. 36. See also, Cecil Rose, *When Man Listens*, p. 37; and Bremer Hofmeyr, *How to Listen* (New York: Moral Re-Armament, n.d.).

[351] Rev. Howard Rose, *The Quiet Time*, p. 3.

As Ken Twitchell announced the Quiet Time, the undergraduates fumbled for pencils and guidance books and began to "listen to God." This was not simple meditation, which may be concentration on some aspect of Christ or the Gospel, but something more: a listening for definite messages applicable to present needs. As they were committed to doing God's will, that will could be known for them at any moment of necessity. . . . Yet in the afternoon of that same day at Oxford I had my first results from the Quiet Time. . . . Ken said, "Let's try the Quiet Time." We drew out slips of paper, relaxed, listened.

. . . Then, just as we were about to put our papers away, there suddenly crossed my ordinary, tumbled, human thoughts one of another order which seemed to possess luminous glow, differing sharply from the rest. . . . The new luminous thought had come so unexpectedly and with such a peculiar glow of rightness that I went to London and tried it. Within a few moments of the thought being transferred to the person in great authority whom it concerned, he rang me up on the telephone thanking me profusely. . . . So there *was* something in organized prayer for guidance, after all.[352]

What Is The Oxford Group? said:

The Oxford Group advocates our use of a pencil and note-book so that we may record every God-given thought and idea that comes to us during our time alone with Him, that no detail, however small, may be lost to us and that we may not shirk the truth about ourselves or any problem when it comes to us (p. 68).

Shoemaker wrote:

Listening became the dominant note of Quiet Time. Not the exclusive note. . . . But the bulk of the time is listening. Most of us find it indispensable to have a loose-leaf notebook, in which to write down the things which come to us. We find that in trying to remember what has come before, we block what is coming now;

---

[352] Russell, *For Sinners Only*, pp. 93-96.

we find it impossible to remember sometimes the things which
come even in a brief Quiet Time. The Chinese have a saying that
the strongest memory is weaker than the weakest ink. We do not
want to forget the slightest thing that God tells us to do; and I
have sometimes had a rush of detailed guidance which came
almost as fast as I could write it. . . . He may give us the
conviction of sin . . . and sends us to someone with restoration
and apology. He may send us a verse of encouragement like,
"Fear Not." "Go in thy might, have I not sent thee?" "All is
well." He may warn us against a wrong course, or a tedious and
time-killing person, or a tendency in ourselves. He may send us
to telephone or to call someone, or tell us to write a letter, or pay
a visit, or take some exercise, or read a book. Nothing which
concerns our lives is alien to His interest, or to the doing of His
Will. He may give us guidance about how to help someone, or
tell us what is the matter with them or us.[353]

P. G. suggested a Quiet Time together. So they prayed together,
opening their minds to as much of God as he understood,
removing first the hindrance of self-will, allowing the Spirit to
focus an impression upon the mind, like light upon a camera
exposed. There and then he lifted his own life to God, giving Him
entrance and sway.[354]

The man who knows God's will is the man who loves it. The man
who finds out what God wants is the man who cares what God
wants, who feels upon him the same kind of burdens God feels
and carries. If God can count on you, He can commit His secrets
to you. We have got to get on God's side before it's any use to
ask what is God's plan. Drummond . . . said, "Above all things,
do not touch Christianity unless you are willing to seek the
Kingdom of God first."[355] "Not every one that saith unto me,
'Lord, Lord, shall enter the kingdom of heaven; but he that doeth

---

[353] Shoemaker, *The Conversion of the Church*, pp. 60-66.

[354] Shoemaker, *Children of the Second Birth*, p. 47.

[355] Matthew 6:33.

the will of my Father who is in heaven."[356] God give us the grace to ask, "Lord, what wilt thou have me to do."[357]

Dr. Bob's wife, Anne, followed the Oxford Group practice of *writing down* "leading" thoughts. She did so before, during, and after Quiet Time periods of Bible study, prayer, and "meditation" that she and Dr. Bob and Bill observed together during Bill's stay with the Smiths in the summer of 1935.[358] Dr. Bob's daughter, Sue Windows, so informed the author during a personal interview in Akron in June of 1991. Sue also recalled that other early AAs followed this procedure. But the Oxford Group practice of writing down thoughts in a Guidance book never made it into the Big Book itself. Although the author has never heard this practice discussed in the many A.A. meetings he attends, he has certainly encountered in recovery center talk, and even in A.A., the idea of "keeping, and writing in, a daily journal."[359] Whether this concept springs from Oxford Group origins, we do not know.

24. *Checking*

> Luminous thoughts received in Quiet Time may not actually be Divine Guidance or from God. They may involve self-deception. They should be checked for harmony with God's Will by testing them with: 1) The Four Absolutes; 2) The Bible; 3) Teachings of the Church; 4) Circumstances; 5) Willingness to obey; 6) Advice of other surrendered Christians.

---

[356] Matthew 7:21.

[357] Acts 9:6. See Shoemaker, *Religion That Works*, pp. 64-65. Shoemaker frequently referred to this "what-wilt-thou-have-me-to-do" concept. See Shoemaker, *A Young Man's View of the Ministry*, p. 80. Compare *Confident Faith*, p. 107

[358] See Dick B., *Anne Smith's Journal*, pp. 53-62.

[359] Recently the author was speaking to the leaders of a Twelve-Step oriented, Christian recovery program in Okeechobee, Florida. The director, Mickey E., stated the entire program was based on Quiet Time; and then the leaders were invited to "journal" the thoughts they received from God on the subjects being discussed throughout the day.

Frank Buchman said of luminous or "guided" thoughts: The second rule [the first being honestly listening and writing down the thoughts] is that we test the thoughts that come, to see which are from God. Buchman's first suggested test is the Bible. He stated the Bible is steeped in the experience through the centuries of men who dared, under Divine revelation, to live experimentally with God. He pointed out that in the Bible, culminating in the life of Jesus Christ, we find the highest moral and spiritual challenge—complete honesty, purity, unselfishness and love. He pointed to another test: "What do others say who also listen to God?" He said that seeking is an unwritten law of fellowship and an acid test of one's commitment to God's plan. He said that no one can be wholly God-controlled who works alone.[360]

Henry Wright wrote a chapter entitled, "How to Find Out the Particular Will of God."[361] Wright asked how Jesus found out the particular will of God for himself. He said Jesus "did always those things that please Him [God]."[362] Wright said Jesus was therefore sure of God's presence and guidance.[363] Consequently, Wright asked what those things *were* that were pleasing to God. And he proposed going back to the teachings of Jesus and the Apostles to reconstruct the touchstones that applied to every question.[364]

Wright began with the work of Dr. Robert E. Speer who reconstructed from the teachings of Jesus the four standards in regard to which, said Wright, Jesus never allowed himself an exception and with reference to which his teaching is absolute and unyielding. These were the Four Absolutes—honesty, purity, unselfishness, and love—of which we have already written. Wright said these were the tests to be applied by a Christian to determine the particular will of God for each step of his career. The

---

[360] Buchman, *Remaking the World*, p. 36.

[361] Wright, *The Will of God*, pp. 153-176.

[362] John 8:29.

[363] John 8:29 (first half).

[364] Wright, *The Will of God*, pp. 165-66.

Christian was to ask, "Is the step which I planned to take an absolutely pure one, honest one, most unselfish one, the fullest possible expression of my love?"[365] Thus emerged the most basic form of Oxford Group "checking" or "tests," not only of luminous thoughts but also of the conduct of a person's life.

For Sinners Only said, "The conditions for effective guidance were the whole-hearted giving of one's self to Jesus Christ." The tests as to whether this was being done were:

1. Does it [the proposed conduct] go counter to the highest standards of belief that we already possess?
2. Does it contradict the revelations which Christ has already made in or through the Bible?
3. Is it absolutely honest, pure, unselfish, loving?
4. Does it conflict with our real duties and responsibilities to others?
5. If still uncertain, wait and continue in prayer, and consult a trustworthy friend who believes in the guidance of the Holy Spirit?[366]

What Is The Oxford Group? said, "In cases of difficulty, our guidance can be 'checked up' with the teachings of the Bible or by conference with others who are also receiving guidance in Quiet Time" (p. 69).

The Eight Points of the Oxford Group said:

The Group recognizes that guidance needs to be checked in various ways. If it is God's guidance, it will be in accord with the mind of Christ revealed in the New Testament[367] and in harmony with the four standards. . . . And because the individual may be swayed by personal facts such as lack of knowledge, the Group further emphasizes

---

[365] Wright, *The Will of God*, p. 173.

[366] Russell, *For Sinners Only*, p. 94. See also, Cecil Rose, *When Man Listens*, pp. 34-35; and Hofmeyr, *How to Listen*, p. 2.

[367] See Philippians 2:5, Romans 13:14; and Galatians 3:27.

the need for checking with other surrendered Christians. With these safeguards, we may expect guidance as to what letters to write, visits to pay, restitution to make and so forth. We have to guard against thrusting our own will upon God when we pray to Him to guide us. We need also to be warned against too readily taking for granted any idea that jumps into our head as Divine inspiration. A strong impulse is not necessarily a Divine Guidance. It may arise from a strong desire or a disordered imagination. One of the commonest fears felt about simple faith in Divine guidance is that it will lead to unchecked individualism. . . . the follower of the light will be continually correcting the first perception of it by a fuller experience, and by that of others who have followed it more faithfully. When a man keeps every avenue of his being open to Divine guidance, he acquires a firm conviction that he is being led, not always because of remarkable events but through daily hourly gifts of grace to meet every human need.[368]

Benson asked and answered this question:

When the Group speak of God's direct guidance, how do they know that what they hear is really a message from God and not only a prompting of the subconscious mind? May not this guidance be misleading and dangerous? It is possible to mistake the source of these impulses. But mistakes and dangers can be checked by applying a simple test to the guidance which we believe comes from God. He has given us the power to reason and compare. We are able to discern spiritual values, the higher from the lower, the Divine from human. God makes Himself known to the surrendered life in light of His Will for the world and His plan for our lives. Guidance is tested by the Divine scale and standard of values.[369]

Shoemaker made these comments about checking:

How then, do we know what is guidance? . . . Is not guidance simply conscience at work? "No Mummy," [said a little girl].

---

[368] Benson, *The Eight Points*, pp. 84-87.
[369] Benson, *The Eight Points*, pp. 151-52.

"Conscience tells you the difference between right and wrong; but guidance tells you which of several right things you ought to do." Then it must be tested by the Spirit of Christ. A man steeped in the New Testament will by so much, get better guidance than a man who is not. Guidance, if true, will never be found contrary to the New Testament. But Jesus . . . . also promised His Holy Spirit to "guide us into all truth."[370] Knowing the life of Jesus, His teachings, His principles and parables, His Spirit that was manifested all through all his words and acts, constitutes part of the discipline and preparation which are necessary if the Holy Spirit is to find us ready to hear and understand His will; but in themselves they are not sufficient direct inspiration for our practical decisions. We meet many cases not covered by the New Testament. . . . The Holy Spirit's guidance will never be contrary to the New Testament; it will really show us what the New Testament means for us in any given case. God's Will is sometimes made clear, also by circumstances. He guides us by open and closed doors. There is always a danger here of being overwhelmed by moral obstacles, which need to be ignored and crashed through: but there are unmistakable signs sometimes in circumstances. But chiefly guidance is to be tested by the concurrence of other guided people. . . . Individualistic guidance can, and sometimes does, run off the rails into undesirable courses. And, on the other hand, if we check guidance with those who believe in guidance, they simply quench the Spirit. . . . Find a man that believes in God's guidance. Better yet, find a group that is God-guided, and check it with them. This brings in the relation between reason and guidance. Guidance is no short-cut to knowledge. . . . Every bit of human knowledge one can have about people or things will help them, provided that knowledge can be surrendered to God and He be allowed to guide it in its application. There is no room for prejudiced thought: and much so-called thought is thought with a bias, defending a point of view, rationalizing a desire. But real, honest, dispassionate thinking should precede guidance. It must come in and do all that it can. Then it must retire, and leave the final disposition to God.

---

[370] John 16:13.

. . . *Guidance far exceeds intuition.*[371] Reason, then, goes as far
as it can. God is greater than reason, and makes the final decision
and reveals it to us through guidance. Some of you will find
yourselves hung up on the problem of guidance in small things.
. . . Personally, I am now content to obey my guidance and let
God decide what is big and what is little. Whatever He tells me
is "big" to me (italics added).[372]

At another [house-party], I learned still more about the pain which
is involved in merging one's life into a spiritual fellowship, of
thoroughly working with a group, sharing with them, being
"checked" by them when it was necessary, and at times having to
obey one's spiritual teacher.[373]

What about "Checking" and A.A.? Bill Wilson said:

Until the middle of 1937 *we in New York* had been working alongside the Oxford Groups. But in the latter part of that year *we* [in
New York] most reluctantly parted company with these great
friends. . . . For example, drinkers would not take pressure in any
form, excepting from John Barleycorn himself. They always had
to be led, not pushed. They would not stand for the rather
aggressive evangelism of the Oxford Groups. And they would not
accept the principle of "team guidance" for their own personal
lives. It was too authoritarian for them (italics added).[374]

Bill's discussion failed to point out, however, that the Oxford
Group not only practiced "checking" by *team*, but also with other
individuals. And there certainly were the other checks they used,
such as measuring proposed conduct by "yardsticks" in the Bible
and the teachings of Jesus Christ. But Bill added:

---

[371] Compare Big Book, pp. 84 and 86, which suggest that intuition alone is all that
is involved.

[372] Shoemaker, *The Conversion of the Church*, pp. 51-57.

[373] Shoemaker, *Twice-Born Ministers*, p. 125.

[374] *AA Comes of Age*, p. 74.

It was discovered that all forms of coercion, both direct and indirect, had to be dropped. We found that "checking" in the hands of amateurs too often resulted in criticism, and that resulted in resentment, which is probably the most serious problem the average alcoholic is troubled with.[375]

While most of us believe profoundly in the principle of "guidance," it was soon apparent that to receive it accurately, considerable spiritual preparation was necessary.[376]

This second explanation by Bill is sad. For the early Akron AAs did engage in just such "considerable" spiritual preparation. They read the Bible. They studied the teachings of Jesus. They adopted the Four Absolutes as guides. And, as previously shown, these Absolutes are still applied in some A.A. areas. The early AAs prayed and had Quiet Time. These things gave them considerable spiritual preparation. Dr. Bob and many other AAs studied the Bible and other Christian literature for the rest of their lives.[377] Dr. Bob continued to pray and try to live by the principles of the Four Absolutes.[378] In fact, Dr. Bob stated, in his remarks at Detroit, Michigan, in 1948, that he often "checked" his views on a problem against the Four Absolutes and with others—just as the Oxford Group had taught him. Anne Smith wrote frequently and favorably about the necessity for checking.[379]

"Checking" never made it to the Big Book or the Steps. Yet remnants of "guidance" *do* exist in the Big Book and particularly in its Eleventh Step discussion. The Big Book speaks, as the

---

[375] *Pass It On*, p. 172.

[376] *Pass It On*, p. 172.

[377] See Dick B., *Dr. Bob's Library*; and *The Books Early AAs Read for Spiritual Growth*.

[378] His daughter, Sue Smith Windows, so informed the author in a personal interview in Akron, Ohio in June, 1991.

[379] Dick B., *Anne Smith's Journal*, pp. 32, 50, 63, 108, 113, 115-16, 122, 144.

Oxford Group did, about "intuitive" thinking.[380] But both the
Oxford Group and Shoemaker (as one of their spokesmen) made
it very clear that they believed Guidance was a good deal *more*
than "intuitive" thinking.[381] It was revelation *received from God!*
That is why Buchman, Shoemaker, and others of the Oxford
Group spoke so much about the examples of Guidance in both the
Old and New Testament.[382]

Recent A.A. emphasis on a "Higher Power," which has often
become a "door knob," a "tree," or even the "group" has hardly
left the newcomer with a "Divine" source against which to check
the validity of his or her "intuitive" thought as far as God's will
is concerned. Moreover, the newcomer is often told: "Don't think.
Don't drink. Go to meetings." Such instructions might have value
for the confused, detoxing member in the earliest days of sobriety.
But they certainly move that newcomer far from the Oxford
Group's suggestions for "checking" thoughts and guidance ideas
for their conformity to the Bible, the teachings of Jesus Christ, the
Four Absolutes, the Church, and the informed help of like-minded
Christian believers.

The Bible, significant mention of Jesus Christ, the Four
Absolutes, Church as a favored observance, and checking with
"guided" believers are words and ideas that certainly are not a part

---

[380] See Big Book, p. 86: "an intuitive thought or decision;" and p. 84: "we will
intuitively know how to handle situations which used to baffle us." Bill Wilson's
secretary, Nell Wing, stated that early AAs read Thomas Troward, *The Edinburgh
Lectures on Mental Science* (New York: Dodd, Mead and Company, 1909). And
Troward's "new thought" ideas on "intuition" may have contributed to Wilson's
abandonment of "revelation" in favor of "intuition" (See, Troward, pp. 71-73.

[381] Shoemaker, *Twice-Born Ministers*, p. 184: "Let it be said often, this is no short-
cut to truth which we are supposed to dig out with our minds; it is God's crystallization
of truth from the facts we have and also from some facts which we cannot possibly *know*,
but can only guess by what humanly we call a 'flash of intuition.' The 'guidance' of
religion is 'intuition' *plus*. It is not a substitute for, but a tremendous supplement to, the
common processes of thought" (italics added).

[382] See, for example, James 1:5, 17; John 16:13, and the many verses from Psalms
and Proverbs quoted in our Oxford Group portions on Guidance, Quiet Time, and
Listening.

of either the Big Book or much of today's A.A. But note the price that has been paid. The Big Book presents this apparent quandary: "It is not probable that we are going to be inspired at all times" (p. 87). As to which we would ask, just how an AA is to determine what is and what is *not* "inspired" by God without the kind of checks provided in the Bible itself and in the teachings of religion, including the Oxford Group. How can the AA know if the "inspired" thought is guidance from God?

In fairness, we repeat these few lines—discussed all too little in today's A.A.—in which the Big Book does make *several* helpful (in fact, vital) suggestions:

> There are many helpful books also. Suggestions about these may be obtained from one's priest, minister, or rabbi. Be quick to see where religious people are right. Make use of what they offer (p. 87).

The Spiritual Experience or Awakening

25. *Knowledge of God's Will*

> Knowledge of God's Will comes to us from a study of His "universal" or "general" will as revealed in the Bible and in nature and from willingness to bend every effort in doing the general will and have God's "private" or "particular" will revealed to us by experiencing His guidance.

The Oxford Group wrote much on the importance of knowing God's will. They said God had a plan and that a person's life would go well if he or she learned the plan—God's will—and harmonized his or her life with the plan. But how to know it?

There were two basic rules: (1) Study the Bible which contains God's general or universal will for man. (2) Learn how to listen for God's "Voice" by which He reveals his particular or private will for man. In the sections on Guidance, Prayer, Bible Study, Quiet Time, Listening, and Checking, we have covered most of the Oxford Group material on *how* to know God's will. Here we simply review the biblical principles on *where* to find it.

Oxford Group sources and adherents believed the Bible contains God's Universal Will. Professor Henry Drummond expounded this idea in *The Ideal Life*.[383] Frank Buchman's most significant mentor, Henry B. Wright, reiterated the details in his *The Will of God and a Man's Lifework*, saying, for example:

> There is a part of God's will which every one may know. It is written in divine characters in two sacred books, which every man may read. The one of them is the Bible, the other is Nature. The Bible is God's will in words, in formal thoughts, in grace. Nature is God's will in matter and tissue and force. Nature is not often considered a part of God's will, but it is a part, and a great part, and the first part. . . . The laws of nature are the will of God for our bodies. As there is a will of God for our higher nature—the moral laws—as emphatically is there a will of God for the lower—the natural laws. If you would know God's will in the higher, therefore, you must begin with God's will in the lower, which simply means this—that if you want to live the ideal life you must begin with the ideal body. The law of moderation, the law of sleep, the law of regularity, the law of exercise, the law of cleanliness—this is the law or will of God for you.
>
> From the moral side there are three different departments of God's will. Foremost, and apparently most rigid of all, are the Ten Commandments. Now the Ten Commandments contain in a few sentences one of the largest . . . portions of God's will . . . the most venerable and universal expression of God's will for man. Following upon this there come the Beatitudes of Christ. This is another large portion of God's will. . . . But there is a third set of laws and rules which are not to be found exactly expressed in either of these. . . . Hence we must add to all this mass of law and beatitude many more laws and many more beatitudes which lie enclosed in other texts, and in other words of

---

[383] See, for example, Drummond, *The Ideal Life*, pp. 268-71.

Christ which have their place, like the rest, as portions of God's will.[384]

As we have already noted, Sam Shoemaker frequently wrote to the same effect, saying:

We find God's general will in the Scriptures.[385]

The sustenance of the new spiritual life lies in the material in the Bible, which is everlasting and universal; and then in God's direct messages to us, which are temporal and personal, but sometimes have widespread effects.[386]

There is a general will of God, and there is a particular will of God. All men everywhere who have lined up for the right, have been true and square and clean, have done the general will of God. One is grateful for them. But a man may do the general will of God and yet miss the particular will of God for him.[387]

The Bible from one end to the other tells us about Him [God], about His will for man and the world. Christ has proclaimed His Voice as no one else before or since. You may have trouble with the inspiration of the Scripture; I have trouble conceiving of it as possible that those words were concocted by man alone. But are you listening to them? Before there is any private revelation, we must accept and dig into and learn from this public revelation made before all men in the life and death of Jesus according to the immortal words in which that story has been enshrined for all time. But when we have done this, we may seek and expect and have personal and private revelation from Him. There are places in our lives not covered exactly by any law given in the Bible: if

---

[384] Wright, *The Will of God*, p. 137.
[385] Shoemaker, *The Conversion of the Church*, pp. 49-50.
[386] Shoemaker, *Twice-Born Ministers*, pp. 184-85.
[387] Shoemaker, *A Young Man's View of the Ministry*, p. 78.

we seek to obey the laws already written, God will give us His special will and command for us now if we ask Him.[388]

At this point, therefore, we need to focus on where the Oxford Group people found God's *particular* or *private* will for men and women. And the Oxford Group answer was: by *revelation*. They said that God may choose to reveal His particular will for man when man listens and obeys. The thrust of the obedience idea was said to lie in John 7:17:

> If any man will do his will, he shall know of the doctrine whether
> it be of God, or whether I speak of myself.

This difficult-to-understand verse was uttered by Jesus. And Oxford Group writers, from the earliest Buchman mentors to Shoemaker, interpreted the verse to mean that man would receive guidance from God as to God's particular will when man was *sincerely bending his efforts* to live by what he believed to be God's general will as revealed in Scripture.

A. J. Russell said John 7:17 was Sam Shoemaker's favorite verse.[389] And we have already noted the frequency of its appearance in Shoemaker writings. Shoemaker explained as follows:

> Jesus said, "If any man willeth to do his will, he shall know."
> That is to say, "If any man will begin by living up to as much as
> he understands of the moral requisites of God, he will later, in the
> light of his experience, come to see straight intellectually." . . .
> A moral experiment is worth ten times an intellectual investigation

---

[388] Shoemaker, *Christ and This Crisis*, p. 106. See also, Shoemaker, *Realizing Religion*, pp. 58-62; *The Church Alive*, pp. 75-77; and *How to Become a Christian*, pp. 108-10.

[389] Russell, *For Sinners Only*, p. 211.

in apprehending spiritual truth. Obedience is as much the organ of spiritual understanding as reason.[390]

There is a truth which we need to learn well and to get down deep in our bones if we are to help people: and that is the truth contained in the verse St. John 7:17: "If any man willeth to do His will, he shall know of the doctrine." So often we think that if we knew God, we should live a good life. This says, Live a good life, and you will know God! The attempt really to be rid of our sins seems to open us to God Who hovers over us with love all the time, and the readiness to stay in our sins seems to blind us to His Presence and make it impossible to believe that He exists.[391]

The soundest approach I know to religious discovery is found in St. John's Gospel, chapter 7, verse 17; "If any man willeth to do his will, he shall know of the doctrine." We are busy getting "willing to do His will," and that means changing many of our ways. The verse says clearly that this is the order: moral change, then intellectual perception. "Blessed are the pure in heart, for they shall see God."[392] A certain amount of "law" always precedes "grace."[393]

There is an intriguing verse in St. John's gospel (chapter 7, verse 17, based on ASV): "If any man wills to do his (God's) will, he shall know of the teaching, whether it is of God, or whether I speak from myself." We might boil this down to say that Jesus

---

[390] Shoemaker, *Religion That Works*, p. 36. Shoemaker is here referring to writings found in Bushnell, Robertson, and particularly Henry B. Wright, who said, in *The Will of God*, "It is here that the universal will of God is connected with the particular. Transgression of the universal will of God—the laws of nature and morality so far as they have been revealed—is sin and sin blocks the channel of communication. In other words, obedience to the universal will of God is the first step toward knowing the particular will of God . . . There must be a complete renunciation of self-will" (pp. 148-149).

[391] Shoemaker, *How You Can Help Other People*, p. 61.

[392] Matthew 5:8.

[393] Shoemaker, *The Experiment of Faith*, p. 36.

implied, "Don't begin at the theological end; begin at the moral end."[394]

We believe the foregoing Shoemaker quotes came from, and conformed to, the views of Henry Drummond, Henry B. Wright, and other Oxford Group writers. All believed in the condition for knowing God's particular will—*obedience to God's general will*.[395] And this is where the Four Absolutes were believed to be of such importance. The absolute standards represented vital statements about moral law that were reconstructed from the teachings of Jesus. And Oxford Group people believed that endeavoring to live by these Four Absolutes was essential to receiving knowledge of God's particular will in a situation.[396]

The order of A.A.'s Steps seems to follow the Oxford Group's obedience progression. And we have seen in an earlier chapter how Bill Wilson recounted Ebby Thacher's step-by-step instructions for an Oxford Group life-change. Step Three meant a *decision* to follow God's will. Steps Four through Nine represented *obedience* through acting in accordance with that perceived will. That seems to be why Bill Wilson felt the Four Absolutes were incorporated into Steps Six and Seven. Step Ten required a *daily effort* to *apply* the moral principles proposed in Steps Four through Nine. *Then* Step Eleven placed the alcoholic in a position, "through prayer and meditation," to *improve* the relationship with God by seeking further knowledge of God's will and the power to carry it out. The Bible was, by Oxford Group precepts, already the

---

[394] Shoemaker, *Under New Management*, p. 46.

[395] See Henry B. Wright, *The Will of God*, p. 117, citing John 7:17, and then discussing Robertson and Drummond (pp. 117-29). See also Drummond, *The Ideal Life*, 302; Brown, *The Venture of Belief*, pp. 28, 48; Cecil Rose, *When Man Listens*, p. 17; Russell, *For Sinners Only*, p. 211; and Benson, *The Eight Points*, p. 129.

[396] Reviewing the author's manuscript on April 2, 1992, Oxford Group authority T. Willard Hunter made the following comments: "The Oxford Group never claimed that any one could achieve any of the absolutes. As in target practice, you aim for the center of the bull's eye. They used to say, 'If you aim at nothing, you are likely to hit it.' In addition, it was clear that human struggle was of no avail. God supplied compliance with the standards in a life surrendered to God."

repository of knowledge of God's general will. Hence the focus, through Eleventh Step prayer and meditation, was upon receiving guidance in *understanding* the general will *and*, because of previous *obedience to the general will*, receiving *revelation as to God's particular will if God chose to reveal it.* Step Twelve represented the faith payoff that resulted from taking the foregoing steps.

Shoemaker explained:

> Surrender to God's will, which is the heart of faith, is summed up in the question, "Lord, what wilt thou have me to do?"[397] If a man says that and means it, he has settled the most momentous question of his career. It means that hypothetically and for the time being, at least, he gives up every preconceived notion of what he wants to do, every plan he ever had; lest the plan be outside the plan of his Father. So long as an "if" or a "but" remain in his mind, it cannot be surrender. We have got to wipe the slate clean, and then ask Him to write His will upon it.[398]

26. *The God consciousness Experience*

> The end of surrendering life completely to God through the power of Christ is a total change. There is an experience—the discovery and knowledge of God and His Power, the carrying of this message to others, and a difference in the way life is lived. There is rebirth—consciousness of being in harmony with God.

One could write volumes on what it means to have a life in harmony with God, to have estrangement removed, to be conscious of God's power and presence in daily life, to be helping others achieve a similar experience, and to be living life according to God's principles. Much of this is comprehended in the Oxford Group "Conservation" and "Continuance" ideas. But there are a

---

[397] See Acts 9:6; Referring to this verse, see Drummond, *The Ideal Life*, p. 306; and Shoemaker, *Confident Faith*, p. 107.

[398] Shoemaker, *A Young Man's View of the Ministry*, p. 80.

number of expressions used to explain the *end result* of the Oxford
Group life-change process. The following are some:

1.   An "experience of God."[399]
2.   A "vital experience of Jesus Christ."[400]
3.   A "religious experience."[401]
4.   A "spiritual experience."[402]
5.   A "spiritual awakening."[403]
6.   A "relationship with God."[404]
7.   A sense of the "power and presence of God."[405]
8.   Finding God.[406]
9.   Being "in touch with God."[407]
10. "Contact" with God.[408]

---

[399] Leon, *The Philosophy of Courage or the Oxford Group Way*, p. 110; Brown, *The Venture of Belief*, pp. 24-25; Weatherhead, *How Can I Find God?*, p. 66; Shoemaker, *The Conversion of the Church*, p. 113; and *How to Become a Christian*, p. 156.

[400] Shoemaker, *The Conversion of the Church*, p. 109; *Twice-Born Ministers*, p. 10—"a complete experience of Jesus Christ;" See Benson, *The Eight Points*—"a maximum experience of Jesus Christ" (p. xviii); and Buchman, *Remaking the World*, p. x.

[401] Shoemaker, *Realizing Religion*, p. 9; *Twice-Born Ministers*, p. 156; Brown, *The Venture of Belief*, pp. 21-24; and William James, *The Varieties of Religious Experience*.

[402] Shoemaker, *Twice-Born Ministers*, pp. 10, 61.

[403] Buchman, *Remaking the World*, pp. 19, 24, 35, 54; Shoemaker, *The Conversion of the Church*, p. 124; and Walter, *Soul Surgery*, p. 82.

[404] Shoemaker, *Children of the Second Birth*, p. 16; *Christ's Words from the Cross*, p. 50; Weatherhead, *Discipleship*, p 18; Benson, *The Eight Points*, pp. 48, 92; Macmillan, *Seeking and Finding*, p. 99; and Brown, *The Venture of Belief*, p. 11.

[405] Kitchen, *I Was a Pagan*, p. 157, 68; Brown, *The Venture of Belief*, pp. 24-26, 44; and Shoemaker, *With the Holy Spirit and with Fire*, p. 27.

[406] Shoemaker, *Realizing Religion*, p. 9; *God's Control*, p. 137; *How to Find God*; Kitchen, *I Was a Pagan*, p. 94; and Weatherhead, *How Can I Find God?*.

[407] Buchman, *Remaking the World*, p. 80; Foot, *Life Began Yesterday*, p. 132; Shoemaker, *The Conversion of the Church*, pp. 47-65; *National Awakening*, pp. 78-88; *How to Become a Christian*, p. 55; and *Under New Management*, p. 66.

[408] Benson, *The Eight Points*, p. 31; and Brown, *The Venture of Belief*, p. 24, 31.

11. "Conversion"[409]
12. "Surrender."[410]
13. "Change."[411]
14. Being "Born again."[412]
15. "God Consciousness."[413]

William James wrote an entire book *describing* religious experiences; and the foregoing words and phrases are really shorthand expressions for the following James ideas:

---

[409] Olive Jones, *Inspired Children*, p. 136; Shoemaker, *Children of the Second Birth*, p. 16; *Realizing Religion*, pp. 22-35; *Twice-Born Ministers*, p. 10; and Benson, *The Eight Points*, p. 62. We have already covered Shoemaker's frequent references to William James and "conversion." But we recently found two items in the Shoemaker files at the Archives of the Episcopal Church: (1) S. M. Shoemaker, *The Twelve Steps of AA: What They Can Mean to the Rest of Us* (New York: The Evangel, n.d.), where Shoemaker wrote at page 2, "Self-surrender is man's part in his own conversion. We cannot and do not convert ourselves; we offer ourselves to God in surrender, and He does the converting by His Holy Spirit, bringing us forgiveness and new life." (2) E. Stanley Jones, *Conversion* (Nashville, TN: Abingdon Press, 1959), where Shoemaker's friend Jones quotes William James; cites Clarence S.'s favorite verse (2 Corinthians 5:17); quotes the God-as-we-understand-Him idea of the Oxford Group; and then says that the "moment of surrender" is a growing conviction that Jesus is Lord—citing Romans 10:9 as "probably the earliest Christian creed."

[410] *What Is The Oxford Group?*, p. 40-57: Shoemaker, *Children of the Second Birth*, p. 16; Brown, *The Venture of Belief*, p. 28; and Weatherhead, *Discipleship*, pp. 15-30.

[411] Olive Jones, *Inspired Children*, p. 136; Shoemaker, *God's Control*, pp. 9, 11; *The Church Can Save the World*, pp. 124-125; *By the Power of God*, pp. 56, 10; Foot, *Life Began Yesterday*, p. 27; Begbie, *Life Changers*; See Mel B., *New Wine*, p. 23; and Dennis C. Morreim, *Changed Lives* (Minneapolis: Augsburg, 1991), p. 24.

[412] Shoemaker, *Twice-Born Ministers*, pp. 56, 10; *National Awakening*, p. 55-66; *By the Power of God*, pp. 28-33; *They're on the Way*, p. 157; *How to Find God*, p. 7; Allen, *He That Cometh*, pp. 19, 32, 48; Buchman, *Remaking the World*, p. 23; Drummond, *The Ideal Life*, p. 211; Begbie, *Life Changers*, p. 104; Allen, *He That Cometh*, pp. 19, 32, 48; and Olive Jones, *Inspired Children*, p. 136. Bill Wilson himself twice wrote in early manuscripts of the Big Book that he had "been born again" in the process of his conversion experience. See Dick B., *New Light on Alcoholism*, p. 55, n. 10.

[413] Begbie, *Life Changers*, pp. 16, 39; Leon, *The Philosophy of Courage*, pp. 110-111; Kitchen, *I Was a Pagan*, pp. 43, 75; Murray, *Group Movements Throughout the Ages*, p. 349; Shoemaker, *Twice-Born Ministers*, p. 123; and *How to Become a Christian*, p. 52.

[The four features of "saintliness" present in all religions are:] (1) The feeling of being part of a wider life—the conviction of the existence of an Ideal Power; (2) The person's feeling of the friendly continuity of this Power with his own life—the self having willingly surrendered its control; (3) The experience of elation and freedom which the changed life has when the confining self ceases to dominate the personality; (4) The shift of the emotional center towards love and compassion.[414]

If we practice by acting *as if* there were a God, feel *as if* we were free, consider Nature *as if* she were full of special designs, lay plans *as if* we were to be immortal, then we find those words do make a genuine difference in our moral life. Our faith that these objects actually exist proves to be a full equivalent in hindsight for a knowledge of what they might be if we were permitted positively to conceive them.[415]

To be converted, to be regenerated, to receive grace, to experience religion, to gain an assurance, are so many phrases which denote the process, gradual or sudden, by which a self, hitherto divided and consciously wrong, inferior and unhappy,

---

[414] James, *The Varieties of Religious Experience*, pp. 249-50.

[415] James, *The Varieties of Religious Experience*, p. 56. Sam Shoemaker once wrote an article titled "'Act As If—'The First Step Toward Faith." It appeared in the *Christian Herald* (October, 1954). The article was condensed and, in that form, appeared in the May, 1962 issue of *The Reader's Digest*. Shoemaker frequently quoted James's *Varieties*; and Dr. Charles Knippel stated that Shoemaker first read William James's book after his own conversion experience (in China, in 1918) under the pastoral care of Frank Buchman. Knippel believed that James's "act as if" thesis influenced Shoemaker and Shoemaker's "Act As If" article, and that Shoemaker's act-as-if approach left its broad mark on Wilson. See Knippel, *Samuel M. Shoemaker's Theological Influence*, pp. 132-33, 177-78. In both recovery center meetings and A.A. meetings, the author has often heard the expression "Act as if," and also the more confusing "Fake it until you make it." Whether either or both of these ideas have their genesis in Wilson, Shoemaker, or William James himself, we do not know.

becomes unified and consciously right, superior and happy, in consequence of its firmer hold upon religious realities.[416]

Oxford Group people said:

Now, how can we find this new quality of living? How can we capture that spirit that can change the world? It can only come from a genuine religious experience—that is valid for a change of heart, for changed social conditions, for true national security, for international understanding. It is valid because is originates in God, and issues in actual changes in human nature.[417]

The basis of conversion is the awakening of a new self, and the vital element in this new birth is the dawning of a new affection which henceforth dominates the heart. . . . It is this passion for the Unseen and the Eternal which above all else can change the heart, and strengthen the will, and illuminate the mind. Conversion is the birth of Love. . . . God outside of us is a theory; God inside of us becomes a fact. God outside of us is an hypothesis; God inside of us is an experience. . . . God the Spirit is actuality of life, joy, peace and saving power . . . and the consciousness that Another had grasped the hand, and that thereafter freedom and strength and peace had come.[418]

Peace, direction, power—the fullness of life—await the complete surrender of ourselves to God for His purposes.[419]

The testimony of those who have been changed by conversion and themselves have become changers of human life, whatever their various theological inheritance, is, that any form of wilfulness in the mind is a vital bar to the vital consciousness of God; that as

---

[416] James, *The Varieties of Religious Experience*, p. 177. This conception of a conversion or religious experience was very much accepted by Oxford Group writers, particularly Shoemaker. See Shoemaker, *Realizing Religion*, p. 22; *A Young Man's View of the Ministry*, pp. 11-12; Walter, *Soul Surgery*, p. 80; Jones, *Conversion*, p. 47

[417] Buchman, *Remaking the World*, p. 75.

[418] Walter, *Soul Surgery*, pp. 82-83.

[419] Cecil Rose, *When Man Listens*, p. 17.

soon as the mind, with real honesty and a consuming desire for
that divine consciousness, hates its sin, and turns to God, the will
is new born; and, finally, that henceforth life for them becomes
transfigured by a joy which seems to consist of, first, a poignant
conviction of the reality of God's response to their craving;
second, an entire sense of freedom from a division in personality;
and third, a sense of creative power in the lives of other men,
making for a like happiness with their own.[420]

The Presence of God. I find throughout the diverse testimonies of
religious experiences a striking unity and identity . . . all testify
to the irreducible minimum of religious experience, namely, the
certainty of the "presence of God" in this universe. Men and
women of all races, of different mental capacities, social and
cultural backgrounds, unite throughout history in their common
witness to the reality of God. They tell of the strength of heart
and of mind, of the depth of knowledge of life, of the charity and
love that are poured into human beings whenever they establish
contact with God. . . . Let me remind you again that the essence
of religious experience is the sense of the presence of God and of
His power to regenerate and guide men.[421]

Sam Shoemaker's writings are filled with similar descriptions
of the reality of sensing the presence of God and what He has
done; and also of the sense of peace and power and joy that come
from surrender. For example, he said:

Let go! Abandon yourself to Him. Say to Him, "Not my will but
Thine be done." Live it. Pray for it. Put yourself at His disposal
for time and for eternity. And if your experience is anything like
mine has been, you will find that Jesus gives to life a zest and a
glory, a peace and a purpose, which He only can give.[422]

---

[420] Begbie, *Life Changers*, p. 21.

[421] Brown, *The Venture of Belief*, pp. 24, 47.

[422] Shoemaker, *Religion That Works*, pp. 19-20. Abandon! How often that word and
emphasis appear in the Big Book! At page 59, "We asked His protection and care with
(continued...)

This experience, which I consider was my conversion, brought to me a kind of life which was entirely new to me. The fears were proved foolish. There was an integration of scattered impulses. I had victory where I never expected to have it.[423]

The Oxford Group experiment of faith—involving belief, decision, self-examination, confession, conviction, conversion, restitution, and continuance—*produced* change. A change brought about by God's power and not by the individual's own power. Shoemaker explained:

There may be much misgiving and great spiritual struggle: somewhere there must always be a great "giving in" that abandons self-generated power for God's power.[424]

The following comparative words from A.A.'s Big Book should be enough to indicate the influence of Oxford Group language (about the spiritual experience) on the language of A.A.:

In the face of collapse and despair, in the face of the total failure of their human resources, they found that a new power, peace, happiness, and sense of direction flowed into them (p. 50).

When many hundreds of people are able to say that consciousness of the Presence of God is today the most important fact of their lives, they present a powerful reason why one should have faith (p. 51).

---

[422] (...continued)
complete abandon." At page 63, "we could at last abandon ourselves utterly to Him." At page 164, "Abandon yourself to God as you understand God." We see Shoemaker, the Oxford Group, and Anne Smith in these phrases. See Dick B., *Anne Smith's Journal*, pp. 124-25. All emphasized surrendering as much of yourself as you understand to as much of God as you understand. The result of the experiment was an experience in which the power and presence of God were sensed.

[423] Shoemaker, *Twice-Born Ministers*, p. 55.

[424] Shoemaker, *By the Power of God*, p. 134.

In a few seconds he was overwhelmed by a conviction of the Presence of God. . . . He stood in the Presence of Infinite Power and Love. He had stepped from bridge to shore. For the first time, he lived in conscious companionship with his Creator (p. 56).

The great fact is just this, and nothing less: That we have had deep and effective spiritual experiences which have revolutionized our whole attitude toward life, toward our fellows and toward God's universe. The central fact of our lives today is the absolute certainty that our Creator has entered into our hearts and lives in a way which is indeed miraculous. He has commenced to accomplish those things for us which we could never do by ourselves (p. 25).

Next, we decided that hereafter in this drama of life, God was going to be our Director. . . . When we sincerely took such a position, all sorts of remarkable things followed. . . . As we felt new power flow in, as we enjoyed peace of mind, as we discovered we could face life successfully, as we became conscious of His presence, we began to lose our fear of today, tomorrow or the hereafter. We were reborn (pp. 62-63).

See to it that your relationship with Him is right, and great events will come to pass for you and countless others. This is the Great Fact for us (p. 164).

We conclude this review of the first twenty-six Oxford Group concepts—including the concept that a "spiritual awakening" occurs when the other steps are followed—with several points from Shoemaker and from the Bible.

First, in *Twice-Born Ministers*, Shoemaker said:

Such sayings as, "Ye must be born again,"[425] and "He that loseth his life for my sake . . . shall find it,"[426] and "Seek ye first the kingdom . . . and all these things shall be added,"[427]

---

[425] John 3:7.

[426] Matthew 10:39.

[427] Matthew 6:33.

became living to me as part of my own experience. Previously I had gone just far enough into Christianity to feel the burden of the law, and not far enough to reap the joy of the Spirit. Now things were different.[428]

Second, Oxford Group people quoted the following related Bible verses:

Verily, verily, I say unto thee, Except a man be born again, he cannot see the kingdom of God. . . . Except a man be born of water and *of* the Spirit, he cannot enter into the kingdom of God. Marvel not that I said unto thee, Ye must be born again.[429]

But seek ye first the kingdom of God, and his righteousness; and all these things shall be added unto you.[430]

Not every one that saith unto me, Lord, Lord, shall enter into the kingdom of heaven; but he that doeth the will of my Father which is in heaven.[431]

Then Peter said unto them, "Repent, and be baptized every one of you in the name of Jesus Christ for the remission of sins, and that ye shall receive the gift of the Holy Ghost. . . ." And when they had prayed, the place was shaken where they were assembled together; and they were all filled with the Holy Ghost, and they spake the word of God with boldness. . . . And with great power gave the apostles witness of the resurrection of the Lord Jesus: and great grace was upon them all.[432]

---

[428] Shoemaker, *Twice-Born Ministers*, p. 56.

[429] John 3:3, 5, 7. See Shoemaker, *National Awakening*, pp. 55-66; *Confident Faith*, pp. 137, 140; *God's Control*, p. 137; *Realizing Religion*, p. 35, 21; and Allen, *He That Cometh*, p. 19.

[430] Matthew 6:33. See Shoemaker, *National Awakening*, pp. 41-42; *God's Control*, p. 35; and Macmillan, *Seeking and Finding*, p. 226.

[431] Matthew 7:21. See Allen, *He That Cometh*, p. 139.

[432] Acts 2:1, 4, 38; 4:31, 33. See Shoemaker, *Religion That Works*, pp. 66-76; and Macmillan, *Seeking and Finding*, pp. 162-63.

But the fruit of the Spirit is love, joy, peace, longsuffering, gentleness, goodness, faith, meekness, temperance: against such there is no law.[433]

Now the Lord is that Spirit; and where the Spirit of the Lord is, there is liberty. But we all, with open face, beholding as in a glass the glory of the Lord are changed into the same image from glory to glory, even as by the Spirit of the Lord.[434]

Fellowship with God and Believers, and Witness by Life and Word

27. *Fellowship*

The Oxford Group was first called "A First Century Christian Fellowship." They endeavored to maintain the fellowship of the Holy Spirit—one of mutual sacrifice to win all men to the fellowship of the love of God revealed by Jesus Christ.

We have already discussed Frank Buchman's formation of what he and his friends called "A First Century Christian Fellowship."[435] Buchman had said, "It is . . . an attempt to get back to

---

[433] Galatians 5:22-23. See Walter, *Soul Surgery*, p. 54; and Streeter, *The God Who Speaks*, p. 111.

[434] 2 Corinthians 3:17-18. Streeter, *The God Who Speaks*, pp. 109-11. Compare the "Third Step Prayer" in the Big Book, p. 63: "God, I offer myself to Thee . . . Relieve me of the bondage of self, that I may better do Thy will. Take away my difficulties, that victory over them may bear witness to those I would help of Thy Power, Thy Love, and Thy Way of Life. May I do Thy will always!" The foregoing presents A.A.'s Third Step hope, and we suggest that the Twelfth Step "awakening" is a recognition of the truth of Buchman's statement "God comes to us when we ask Him." See Begbie, *Life Changers*, p. 37, and the statement at page 57 of the Big Book: "But He [God] has come to all who have honestly sought Him."

[435] Though the name became "Oxford Group," the name "A First Century Christian Fellowship" was much used at first. Clark, *The Oxford Group*, p. 35; Begbie, *Life Changers*, pp. 107,122; Olive Jones, *Inspired Children*, p. ix; Shoemaker, *Twice-Born*
(continued...)

the beliefs and methods of the Apostles."⁴³⁶ He said, "We not only accept their beliefs, but are also decided to practice their methods."⁴³⁷ Then Buchman described in detail the "elemental beliefs of a First Century Christianity":

1. The possibility of immediate and continued fellowship with the Holy Spirit—*guidance*.
2. The proclamation of a redemptive gospel—*personal, social, and national salvation*.
3. The possession of fullness of life—rebirth, and *an ever-increasing power and wisdom*.
4. The propagation of their life by individuals to individuals—*personal religion*.

Buchman said the foregoing beliefs produce an effective method of propagation

Love for the sinners.
Hatred of the sin.
Fearless dealing with sin.
The presentation of Christ as the cure for sin.
The sharing and giving of self, with and for others.⁴³⁸

Pointing to the following, powerful *fellowship* concepts, Begbie said Oxford Group people were more concerned with testifying to real experiences (brought about by God's power through Christ), than with teaching an abstract ethical doctrine:

---

⁴³⁵ (...continued)
Ministers, pp. 23, 46, 90; *Calvary Church Yesterday and Today*, p. 270; Hunter, *World Changing Through Life Changing*, p. 40; Lean, *On the Tail of a Comet*, p. 97; and *Pass It On*, p. 130. See S. M. Shoemaker, Jr., *A First Century Christian Fellowship: A Defense of So-Called Buchmanism by One of Its leaders*, a paper delivered in New York, December 10, 1928 (Reprinted from The Churchman, n. d.).

⁴³⁶ Lean, *On the Tail of a Comet*, p. 97.

⁴³⁷ Begbie, *Life Changers*, p. 122.

⁴³⁸ Begbie, *Life Changers*, p. 122.

1. Guidance.[439]
2. Salvation.[440]
3. Rebirth and the availability of God's power and wisdom through it.[441]
4. Individual, personal witness to others.[442]

Except for the word "salvation," these concepts pop up over and over in A.A. words, practices, and history. The Big Book talks about the guidance of God; so did Dr. Bob and Bill.[443] The Big Book uses the word "reborn," talks of "transformation," and speaks in one way or another about God's wisdom as contrasted to

---

[439] Rose said, in *When Man Listens*, "We shall, then, need to keep in close touch with those spiritual children of ours, helping them to see the fuller implications of their surrender, and particularly planning with them daring action; for fellowship is found most of all when we step into God-guided action together" (p. 53). A.A.'s "Tradition Two" states: "For our group purpose there is but one ultimate authority—a loving God as He may express Himself in our group conscience. Our leaders are but trusted servants; they do not govern." We believe this Tradition contains a very strong residual of the Oxford Group's Guidance idea that the Holy Spirit can and does operate in a fellowship of like-minded Christian believers. Tradition Two assumes that God actually expresses himself to and through the group in the way that Shoemaker and other writers mentioned when they were speaking of the concept of "koinonia."

[440] Winslow's *Why I Believe in the Oxford Group* said (quoting from Romans 1:16-17): "The Oxford Group has no new Gospel to proclaim. . . . that which the Apostles taught in the first Christian age, and which the Christian Church has taught from their days until ours. The Gospel is 'the power of God unto salvation to all who believe;' and no new Gospel can take its place" (p. 17). See also Macmillan, *Seeking and Finding*, pp. 139-51. We believe the Oxford Group was speaking of "spiritual wholeness"—the whole package of "God in Christ in you" made available to believers on the day of Pentecost. See John 3:16; John 10:10; Luke 24:47-49; Acts 1:5, 8; 2:1-4; 4:8-32; Romans 10:9-10; Ephesians 1:19; 2:8; Colossians 1:27, 2:9-10. After Pentecost, Peter boldly preached in Acts 4:12, "Neither is there salvation in any other [than Jesus Christ]: for there is none other name under heaven given among men, whereby we must be saved."

[441] Brown, *The Venture of Belief*, "[T]he essence of religious experience is the sense of the presence of God and of His power to regenerate and guide men" (p. 47).

[442] Winslow said the Oxford Group was "held together by the spiritual bond of a common self-surrender to Christ and a common determination to win the world to His allegiance, and . . . [exhibited] a quality of fellowship which . . . [gave] a new vision for what the Church of Christ might be." Winslow, *Why I Believe in the Oxford Group*, p. 19.

[443] See, for example, Big Book, page 86; *DR. BOB*, p. 314; and *Pass It On*, p. 172,

man's.[444] And A.A.'s Twelfth Step idea of "carrying the message" certainly bespeaks Witness.

The Oxford Group fellowship generated witness. Fresh from his recovery through the Oxford Group, Ebby Thacher felt compelled to seek out his friend, Bill. And Bill, fresh from his Oxford Group indoctrination in New York, felt compelled to search out another alcoholic (Dr. Bob as it turned out) when things were going badly and a drink was in prospect. And Bill and Dr. Bob, both having compared notes on Oxford Group service ideas, immediately went about Akron "oxidizing," after their long discussion on Mother's Day, 1935.[445]

What Is The Oxford Group? had this to say about fellowship: The Oxford Group offers Fellowship in Christ to the world, reborn souls to Churches, a sane, practical Christianity to put right the spiritual and material problems which confront us (p. 129).

In his chapter, "Lo! Here is Fellowship," Benson wrote:

"One man is not man." We need each other to realize ourselves. The story of human life on this planet is the record of man's slow learning of life's law of fellowship. . . . Living to himself, man is weak, poor, joyless, limited. In fellowship he becomes strong, rich, happy and expansive. It brings him to a greater fullness of life and a comradeship of spirit which mean personal enrichment to all. . . . Loneliness is the most terrible tragedy of the human spirit. . . . One of the greatest things the Oxford Group Movement is doing is to make fellowship possible. . . . Fellowship is one of the great words of the New Testament as it is also one of the great facts of Christian history. Now the New Testament makes it quite clear that fellowship is in the Holy Spirit. . . . It refers to fellowship with the Holy Spirit.[446] But even more, it means fellowship with one another in and through the Holy Spirit. It refers to a certain quality, intensity and power of fellowship which

---

[444] See Big Book, pp. 63, 569-70, 100.

[445] *DR. BOB* suggests at page 78 that "Oxidizing" was probably short for "Oxfordizing."

[446] See, for example, 2 Corinthians 13:14: "The grace of the Lord Jesus Christ, and the love of God, and the communion of the Holy Ghost, be with you all, Amen."

is created by the presence of the Holy Spirit in a group of people and by His action upon them. . . . Jesus . . . gathered . . . a fellowship of mutual service through sacrifice, and their task was to win all men to the fellowship of the love of God revealed by Jesus Christ. . . . This close, intimate communion with Christ drew them to each other in mutual affection and mutual helpfulness, each seeking to share with the other his own resources in Christ Jesus.[447]

Benson also said there are heartfelt needs the pulpit cannot meet. Sermons and books without fellowship are dead letters. The mind is haunted by fears, doubts, and failures. He said:

Suppose you could talk heart to heart with sympathetic souls who have had those very experiences and found a remedy, what strength and hope would come into your life. Well, that is exactly the spiritual climate which the Groups provide. . . . Through the power of fellowship separate personalities blend in a society of friends that has a characteristic quality and a power of concerned action which increase the potentialities of individuals.[448]

Benson pointed to the following verses on fellowship:

1 John 1:3:
That which we have seen and heard declare we unto you, that ye also may have fellowship with us; and truly our fellowship is with the Father, and with His Son, Jesus Christ.[449]

Philippians 1:3-5, 12:
I thank my God upon every remembrance of you, Always in every prayer of mine for you all making request with joy, For your fellowship in the gospel from the first day until now.

---

[447] Benson, *The Eight Points*, pp. 102-06.

[448] Benson, *The Eight Points*, pp. 108-09.

[449] Benson, *The Eight Points*, p. 112; See Dick B., *Anne Smith's Journal*, pp. 71, 120, 130), and Thornton-Duesbury, *Sharing*, p. 3.

But I would ye should understand, brethren, that the things which happened unto me have fallen out rather unto the furtherance of the gospel.[450]

Mark 10:45:
For even the Son of man came not to be ministered unto, but to minister, and to give His life a ransom for many.[451]

Galatians 3:28:
There is neither Jew nor Greek, there is neither bond nor free, there is neither male nor female: for ye are all one in Christ Jesus.[452]

Leslie Weatherhead cited:

Matthew 18:15-19:
Moreover if thy brother shall trespass against thee, go and tell him his fault between thee and him alone . . . But if he will not hear thee, then take with thee one or two more, that in the mouth of two or three witnesses every word may be established. And if he shall neglect to hear them, tell it unto the church. Verily I say unto you, Whosoever ye shall bind on earth shall be bound in heaven: and whatsoever ye shall loose on earth shall be loosed in heaven. Again I say unto you, That if two of you shall agree on earth as touching anything that they shall ask, it shall be done for them of my Father Which is in heaven.[453]

---

[450] Benson, *The Eight Points*, p. 112.

[451] Benson, *The Eight Points*, p. 112. Benson said this verse was "the national anthem of the Kingdom of fellowship."

[452] Benson, *The Eight Points*, p. 106;

[453] Weatherhead, *Discipleship*, p. 73, "I think we ought to feel that a unanimous finding of such a group is the mind of God concerning the situation. I believe that is implied in the New Testament."

Benson cited:

> Matthew 18:20:
> For where two or three are gathered together in My name, there
> am I in the midst of them.[454]

Shoemaker cited:

> Ephesians 2:19-22:
> Now therefore ye are no more strangers and foreigners, but fellow
> citizens with the saints and of the household of God; and are built
> upon the foundation of the apostles and prophets, Jesus Christ
> himself being the chief corner stone; In Whom all the building
> fitly framed together groweth into an holy temple in the Lord: In
> whom ye also are builded together for an habitation of God
> through the Spirit.[455]

There are several important ideas that found favor in the
Oxford Group concerning "Fellowship" and which derived from
the foregoing and other Bible verses: (1) There was Fellowship
with God and with His son, Jesus Christ.[456] (2) There was a
fellowship of believing people which was empowered by the Holy
Ghost.[457] (3) There was a communion with the Holy Spirit.[458]
(4) All believers had the common bond of being members of a
living body whose head was Jesus Christ himself.[459] (5) There
was no discrimination once all had the common bond.[460] (6)
There was a "corporate" experience where the Holy Spirit is found

---

[454] Benson, *The Eight Points*, p. 109.

[455] These are verses speaking of the body of Christ about which Shoemaker taught
when he was speaking of the Fellowship of the Holy Spirit. See Shoemaker, *Religion
That Works*, pp. 66-76.

[456] Thornton-Duesbury, *Sharing*, p. 3.

[457] Shoemaker, *Religion That Works*, p. 67.

[458] Shoemaker, *How to Find God*, p. 21.

[459] Day, *The Principles of the Group*, p. 9.

[460] Winslow, *Why I Believe in the Oxford Group*, p. 53.

through the group-experience of like-minded believers.[461] (7) God had a unique presence in the Group itself both by the fellowship tie of the spirit and by the Holy Spirit's ability to guide the group itself whose individuals received the spirit of God through their new birth.[462] (8) There was a unity in the fellowship that ended loneliness and encouraged commonality in purpose, in sharing with others, and in distribution of necessities.[463] (9) There was a focus on teamwork.[464] (10) There was a common mission of changing lives to change the world to Christ.[465] (11) There was an emphasis on service.[466]

Shoemaker wrote:

> Somewhere the new church will have a group for the sharing of experience, a working "koinonia." As those who are won increase, there will be need for a meeting where they see and hear one another, where those who are discouraged are lifted up again, where those who have had victories can share them with others, where new people can declare themselves. At first, this will be small. It grows out of changed lives. Convert people, and the group will develop as you relate them.[467]

> There would be plenty of diversity of experience, opinion and background amongst them to divide them hopelessly, unless they had a major unifying principle. That principle is the guidance of God, the Voice of Christ made new to them each day. Because they have Him, and put and keep Him first, they do not have disagreement, division, disunity.[468]

---

[461] Shoemaker, *Religion That Works*, p. 67.

[462] Benson, *The Eight Points*, p. 105, 113.

[463] Benson, *The Eight Points*, pp. 106-07.

[464] Day, *The Principles of the Group*, pp. 9-10.

[465] *What Is The Oxford Group?*, p. 12.

[466] Benson, *The Eight Points*, p. 110.

[467] Shoemaker, *The Conversion of the Church*, pp. 114-15.

[468] Shoemaker, *The Gospel According to You*, p. 190.

It has been my belief for several years that the surest sign of
spiritual awakening in our time is the emergence of the small
spiritual group. It is as if, in a day of widespread loneliness and
fear, the Holy Spirit were saying to us that the characteristic
manifestation of His life and power would not be just in changed
individuals, but in individuals found in relation to other
individuals from the first. . . . In that sense, we may be on the
brink of a real, permanent Christian revival; but it will work
slowly and surely in small groups. These are nothing new in the
life of the Church. Even in the ancient Jewish church, there were
small societies of friends who met weekly for devotion and
charity. . . . You can't organize them . . . they come about
through the impact of life upon life. The group cannot and will
not do everything. Its strength will be in fairly direct proportion
to what is happening to its members outside as well as inside the
meetings. . . . Dr. Elton Trueblood . . . says there are five
elements in common that are found in these informal groups: A
primary emphasis on commitment; an unequivocal belief in the
"priesthood of all believers;" . . . an emphasis on the reality in
fellowship; an emphasis on work—daily work—at the job level;
an unapologetic acceptance of spiritual discipline.[469]

The Spirit can communicate His truth to a spiritual fellowship of
believers in ways He cannot communicate to individuals: it is
another phase of Christ's meaning when He said that "where two
or three are gathered together in my name, there am I in the midst
of them."[470] He is wherever a believer is; but He is present in
heightened reality in the fellowship.[471]

28.   *Witness by Life and Word*

Sharing with others by personal evangelism (the fruits of a
life changed) *and* changing lives is essential. The Oxford
Group is witness for Christ—having a conviction of the

---

[469] Shoemaker, *With the Holy Spirit and with Fire*, pp. 109-18.

[470] Matthew 18:20.

[471] Shoemaker, *Religion That Works*, pp. 72-73.

existence of a living Christ and proof of God's forgiveness and the power of the Holy Spirit.

Frank Buchman said that personal knowledge of Christ is not a thing to be folded away and secretly treasured; it is to be put to work for others. He coined a phrase, part of which became well known to AAs: "The best way to keep an experience of Christ is to *pass it on.*"[472] Shoemaker turned the "pass it on" idea into a different expression, part of which also became well known to AAs: "You have to give it away to keep it." Anne Smith often taught this concept.[473]

Shoemaker wrote:

The only way to keep religion is to give it away. Give what you can right away; it will increase as you give it.[474]

The best way to keep what you have is to give it away, and no substitute has ever been found for personal Christian witness.[475]

We must begin giving away what we have, or we shall lose it. One of the first impulses after we hear a good story is to find someone to tell it to. And one of the first impulses after we have had a real Christian experience is to want to impart it to others.[476]

Get them into the stream of God's will and God's grace, till they ask Him to use them to help reconcile others. They will not keep this unless they give it away. That is a spiritual law—for them and for us.[477]

---

[472] Buchman, *Remaking the World*, p. x (emphasis added).

[473] Dick B., *Anne Smith's Journal*, pp. 65, 69, 72-73, 85, 121, 138.

[474] Shoemaker, *One Boy's Influence*, p. 15.

[475] Shoemaker, *They're On The Way*, p. 159.

[476] Shoemaker, *How to Become a Christian*, p. 80.

[477] Shoemaker, *The Church Alive*, p. 139. See also Shoemaker's interesting comment about Alcoholics Anonymous and "Twelfth Step Work" in Shoemaker, *By the Power of God*, p. 102.

Oxford Group people cited a number of Bible verses for Christian witness:

And we are His witnesses of these things; and so is also the Holy Ghost, Whom God hath given to them that obey Him.[478]

Having therefore obtained help of God, I continue unto this day, witnessing both to small and great, saying none other things than those which the prophets and Moses did say should come; That Christ should suffer, and that He should be the first that should rise from the dead, and should shew light unto the people, and to the Gentiles.[479]

Now then we are ambassadors for Christ, as though God did beseech you by us: we pray you in Christ's stead, be ye reconciled to God.[480]

In the mouth of two or three witnesses shall every word be established.[481]

For the life was manifested, and we have seen it, and bear witness, and shew unto you that eternal life, which was with the Father, and was manifested unto us.[482]

Oxford Group people said, about witnessing to deliverance:

For we must remember that the love of Christ, which we are called to share, is an active love. He was not content to live a life of "silent witness" and hope for the best. He went out seeking men. When we are filled with the same kind of love we shall do as He did. Life-changing is not a matter of special commission

---

[478] Acts 5:32. *What Is The Oxford Group?*, p. 36.

[479] Acts 26:22-23. *What Is The Oxford Group?*, p. 26.

[480] 2 Corinthians 5:20. *What Is The Oxford Group?*, p. 35. See Sangster, *God Does Guide Us*, p. 23.

[481] 2 Corinthians 13:1. *What Is The Oxford Group?*, p. 26.

[482] 1 John 1:2. *What Is The Oxford Group?*, p. 38.

nor of special gifts. It is a matter of how much real love for people we have, how much we want them to find the one complete answer to their need, and how much of God we have ourselves to share with them. . . . Life-changing is simply normal Christian living. It is doing Christ's work. If our aim falls below that level we are failing Him.[483]

God has liberated me from the tyranny of fear and from these particular sins which before I could not conquer, and life is so full of the joy of freedom, that if you would permit, I long to tell you by what methods God's healing came. It is this type of evangelism which sent St. Paul coursing through Asia Minor.[484]

Let the new convert understand at the outset, what many of us had to learn after many years, at painful cost, that the only way to live a normal buoyant, developing Christian life is to be constantly a missionary of Christ to others.[485]

Moreover, it meant a relentless crusade to induce other men and women not only to believe in the possibility of living the victorious life, but to live it.[486]

We can all be witnesses for Christ, all of us who are aware of what the power of Christ has done for us. . . . This message must be one not only of hope but of concrete proof of the Christ who was manifested unto us. It means telling others of our own experiences in Sin, of our Surrender, and after; of the power of God guidance in our lives and the spiritual strength given us to overcome our present difficulties, in accordance with the needs of those to whom we witness.[487]

---

[483] Cecil Rose, *When Man Listens*, pp. 54-55.
[484] Allen, *He That Cometh*, pp. 202-03.
[485] Walter, *Soul Surgery*, p. 93.
[486] Russell, *For Sinners Only*, p. 62.
[487] *What Is The Oxford Group?*, p. 37.

And now compare these words in A.A.'s Big Book:

Life will take on new meaning. To watch people recover, to see them help others, to watch loneliness vanish, to see a fellowship grow about you, to have a host of friends—this is an experience you will not want to miss.[488]

Outline the program of action, explaining how you made a self-appraisal, how you straightened out your past and why you are endeavoring to be helpful to him. . . . Make it plain he is under no obligation to you, that you hope only that he will try to help other alcoholics when he escapes his own difficulties.[489]

Never talk down to an alcoholic from any moral or spiritual hilltop; simply lay out the kit of spiritual tools for his inspection. Show him how they worked with you. Offer him friendship and fellowship. Tell him if he wants to get well you will do anything to help.[490]

Helping others is the foundation stone of your recovery. A kindly act once in a while isn't enough. You have to act the Good Samaritan every day, if need be.[491]

Your job now is to be at the place where you may be of maximum helpfulness to others.[492]

---

[488] Big Book, p. 89.

[489] Big Book, p. 94.

[490] Big Book, p. 95.

[491] Big Book, p. 97. Oxford Group writers often spoke of the "Good Samaritan." For the Biblical account of the "Good Samaritan," see Luke 10:25-37.

[492] Big Book, p. 102.

9

Sam Shoemaker—"Co-Founder" of A.A.

Shoemaker—An American Leader Revisited

Sam Shoemaker wrote in his personal journal for November, 1934:

A significant thing today . . . met Bill Wilson."[1]

This event occurred even before Bill got sober. Then, at A.A.'s Twentieth Anniversary Convention in St. Louis, Missouri, in 1955, Bill introduced Shoemaker to AAs, saying:

How well I remember that first day I caught sight of him [Shoemaker]. It was at a Sunday service in his church. I was still rather gun-shy and diffident about churches. I can still see him standing there before the lectern. His utter honesty, his tremendous forthrightness struck me deep. I shall never forget it.[2]

---

[1] Foreword by Sally Shoemaker Robinson (Sam's older daughter) in Terry Webb, *Tree of Renewed Life: Spiritual Renewal of the Church through the Twelve-Step Program* (New York: Crossroad, 1992), p. 7.

[2] *Alcoholics Anonymous Comes of Age* (New York: Alcoholics Anonymous World Services, Inc., 1957), p. 261.

So it was that the Reverend Sam Shoemaker and Bill Wilson met—even before Bill got sober in Towns Hospital, in December of 1934. And well before the A.A. fellowship was born in 1935.

Sam was no stranger to alcoholism. He had an uncle who was an alcoholic. Also, about nine years before he met Bill, Sam had, as rector of Calvary Church, taken over responsibility for Calvary Mission at 346 East Twenty-third Street,—"down in the Gas-House District." A famous cartoon depicted the shabby figure of a man, lurking at a dark street-corner. In the background shone a lighted cross and the words, "Calvary Mission." The caption said: "There is a place near-by, where a Carpenter still mends broken men."[3] In 1932-33, just a year before Bill made his decision for Christ, 48,168 men passed through the Mission doors to attend the services held there every night in the year. Of this number, 35,023 received a night's lodging, and tens of thousands had free meals. No matter what the motive for their coming, there was not a man among them who was not exposed to the influence of Jesus Christ—through the changed lives of those who spoke at the services and (informally) in the reading-room about what Jesus Christ had done for them.

Sam Shoemaker was a church man. He wrote hundreds of books, pamphlets, and articles—some of which can be found in our bibliography. He conducted regular worship services, delivered sermons, did pastoral counseling, participated in Vestry meetings, and wrote articles for *The Calvary Evangel* (the parish publication) on a regular basis. Sam was responsible for the church school (under the supervision of Olive Jones), a well-stocked book room (under management of Mrs. W. Irving Harris), a women's

---

[3] See John Potter Cuyler, Jr., *Calvary Church in Action: Being the Record of the Years 1932-3 in a Down-Town New York Parish* (New York: Fleming H. Revell, 1934), pp. 61-70. Much of the material in this segment can be found in the foregoing title and in Samuel M. Shoemaker, Jr., *Calvary Church Yesterday and Today* (New York: Fleming II. Revell, 1936). It has also been expanded by the recollections of Shoemaker's friends and associates, Mrs. W. Irving Harris, James W. Houck, Sr., James D. and Eleanor Newton, George Vondermuhll, Jr., T. Willard Hunter, and L. Parks Shipley, Sr.—all of whom spoke and corresponded with the author at length.

auxiliary, a women's benevolent society, a businessmen's group, and outdoor services in Madison Square. In the latter case, Shoemaker himself—backed by a vested choir and clergy—would often lead a march to Madison Square (in which A.A.'s founder-to-be, Bill Wilson, and other businessmen were involved). The group carried a sign: "Jesus Christ Changes Lives." At the outdoor services, participants would climb on a soap-box and give witness, accompanied by the singing of familiar Gospel hymns. In the midst of it all, Shoemaker was fully participating in the Oxford Group.

As to Shoemaker's church, Shoemaker's Assistant Minister, the Reverend W. Irving Harris (who became a good friend of Bill Wilson's), wrote:

> The Scriptures formed the basis of Sam Shoemaker's preaching. He was a "Bible Christian.". . . [A]s Calvary's program developed, two interesting points became ever more apparent: (1) Here was a place to learn the how of faith, both in sermons and in groups—How to find God. How to pray. How to read the Bible. How to pass faith on. And (2) much of the *how* flowed straight from the fellowship itself and a quality of life which is centered, not in individual hopes or even in personal vocations but in the supernatural Other, and is seen and understood—one might almost say absorbed—in the very process of participating in God's work and worship.[4]

For our purposes, it is vital to note how closely Shoemaker worked with several recovered Oxford Group alcoholics—Rowland Hazard, F. Shepard Cornell, Victor Kitchen, and later Charles Clapp, Jr. Shoemaker had even experimented with housing a group of drunks. And, according to his younger daughter Nickie, it was common for "wet" drunks to present themselves at Shoemaker's apartment in Calvary House where Shoemaker would then send them to Calvary Mission or to the Salvation Army to dry

---

[4] W. Irving Harris, *The Breeze of the Spirit: Sam Shoemaker and the Story of Faith at Work* (New York: The Seabury Press, 1978) pp. 18, 25.

out—asking them to return to him later for spiritual counseling and help.

Shoemaker assembled a large "metropolitan team."[5] The author was told by many Oxford Group people he interviewed that this team (or groups within the team) was called the businessmen's team.[6] And we have been able, through interviews and journals, to document most of the men who were involved.[7] The group was heavy with clergy, businessmen, and ex-alcoholics, with whom Bill Wilson became acquainted at Oxford Group house-parties, Oxford Group meetings, his work in the team, and elsewhere.[8] Lois Wilson confirmed Bill's membership in a team. Parks Shipley specifically recalls Bill's membership in the businessmen's team; and the Reverend Harris added: "Out of one businessmen's group came Ebby Thatcher [Thacher] who . . . heard the good news that a spiritual answer to alcoholism existed, and promptly relayed this to Bill Wilson."[9]

As we searched the Episcopal Church Archives in Austin, Texas, we soon learned how much regular written communication Shoemaker had with Bill's business and professional friends—Rowland Hazard, Professor Philip Marshall Brown, Victor C. Kitchen, F. Shepard Cornell, Hanford Twitchell, Parks Shipley, and others. We have concluded that a similar situation *must* have existed as to Shoemaker and Wilson, in the form of letters; but that correspondence is now missing from the Episcopal Archives. Nonetheless, the close association Shoemaker had with Wilson and all the above-listed Oxford Group activists is amply

---

[5] At the Episcopal Archives in Austin, Texas, the author found a list of the members that included many of Wilson's businessmen friends.

[6] James D. Newton commonly spoke of the team in this verbiage in the many interviews he gave the author.

[7] See Appendix 6, Dick B., *New Light on Alcoholism: The A.A. Legacy from Sam Shoemaker* (Corte Madera, CA: Good Book Publishing Company, 1994), pp. 333-36.

[8] See Appendices 5 and 7, Dick B., *New Light on Alcoholism*, pp. 329-32 and 337-41, containing portions of Sam Shoemaker's personal journal entries and Lois Wilson's Oxford Group notes, where the names are given explicitly.

[9] Harris, *The Breeze of the Spirit*, p. 41.

confirmed by the frequency of their mention in the extant Shoemaker personal journals for the period 1934-1936.

The Irving Harris Memorandum supplied to the author by Harris's widow further confirms the frequency of Shoemaker's confidential discussions with Wilson before the Twelve Steps were written and the Big Book was published (the latter, in 1939). Also, though it comes from hearsay evidence, there is the fact of the twice-stated and positive declaration by Shoemaker's long-time and close associate, the Reverend Garrett Stearly, to James D. Newton that Bill Wilson asked Shoemaker to write the Twelve Steps and that Shoemaker declined. Stearly said Shoemaker told Wilson the Steps should be written by Bill from the viewpoint of the alcoholic. Bill apparently, then, soon gave Shoemaker a copy of the proposed Big Book to review; for Shoemaker wrote:

> I never forgot that I was one of those who read the first mimeographed copy of the first book—I am afraid with considerable skepticism, for I was then under the shadow of the old group feeling that unless a thing were done directly under the auspices of the group, it was as good as not done at all.[10]

We have pointed out that Shoemaker said very specifically how closely he had worked with Bill from the very beginning (i.e., 1934). Shoemaker wrote, in a letter to H. H. Brown:

> Bill Wilson found his spiritual change in this House [Calvary House] when the Oxford Group was at work here many years ago. I have had the closest touch with Bill from that day to this.[11]

When Bill was newly out of Towns Hospital and less than sixty days sober, he had been working to help a chemistry professor

---

[10] Charles Taylor Knippel, *Samuel M. Shoemaker's Theological Influence on William G. Wilson's Twelve Step Spiritual Program of Recovery (Alcoholics Anonymous)*, Dissertation. St. Louis University, 1987, p. 70.

[11] Dick B., *New Light on Alcoholism*, pp. 251-52.

(Fred B.) with the professor's persistent drinking problem. Apparently Bill had had some short-lived success with the man. Shoemaker wrote Bill a letter on January 22, 1935, commending Bill for his work with the professor and suggesting that Bill might help yet another man who had a severe drinking problem.[12] Later, in the first months of 1935, Bill sponsored the chemistry professor as godfather at the man's baptism at Calvary Church on March 14, 1935. And, on March 24, 1935, Wilson was present when Fred B. and Bill's sponsor (Ebby Thacher) were confirmed as communicants at Calvary Episcopal Church—with Shoemaker present and officiating on both occasions.[13]

Bill generously acknowledged the Shoemaker link:

'Way back in 1934 he [Sam Shoemaker] began to teach us the principles and attitudes that afterward came to full flower in AA's Twelve Steps for recovery.[14]

We close this review of the earliest Shoemaker-Wilson moments by referring the reader to convincing evidence of the close, personal Shoemaker-Wilson link. First, there were the Shoemaker writings before A.A.'s basic text was published in the Spring of 1939. We have reviewed Shoemaker's major works, title by title, from 1921 through 1939; and we believe those who are familiar with A.A.'s Steps, Big Book, and language will be amazed at how many Shoemaker ideas poured forth into the A.A. repository.[15] Another more selective study was done of Step ideas and Shoemaker phrases.[16] Finally, in Appendix 2 to this particular work, we have listed almost 200 Shoemaker-Oxford Group words

---

[12] Dick B., *New Light on Alcoholism*, p. 246.

[13] See Dick B., *New Light on Alcoholism*, p. 246, and Appendix 10 thereof.

[14] Dick B., *New Light on Alcoholism*, p. 3.

[15] Dick B., *New Light on Alcoholism*, pp. 81-216.

[16] Samuel M. Shoemaker, *Courage to Change: The Christian Roots of the 12-Step Movement*, Compiled and Edited by Bill Pittman and Dick B. (Grand Rapids, MI: Fleming H. Revell, 1994).

and phrases which find an exact counter-part, or at least a parallel, in A.A. language.

Shoemaker's Major A.A. Input

On the practical side, Dr. Bob said (in his farewell address to A.A.): "Our Twelve Steps, when simmered down to the last, resolve themselves into the words 'love' and 'service.'"[17] Dr. Bob was often quoted as saying, of A.A.'s program, "Keep it simple."[18] And one distinguished historian concluded that this "keep it simple" advice exemplified a wariness of argument, analysis, and explanation. He believed this remark and idea constituted Dr. Bob's chief contribution to A.A.[19] We prefer to say, however, that—after an immense amount of Bible study, prayer, spiritual reading, and experience in working successfully with drunks—Dr. Bob's program *evolved* into a simple one.

Further, Dr. Bob's remarks about simplicity often had to do with toning down Bill Wilson's seemingly grandiose ideas and also with a concern that A.A. might "louse it [A.A.] up with Freudian complexes and things that are interesting to the scientific mind, but have very little to do with our actual A.A. work."[20] In contrast to his disdain for the program's becoming involved in *scientific* matters, Dr. Bob never shirked investigation and growth in *spiritual* subjects. He studied the Bible every day.[21] He

---

[17] *DR. BOB and the Good Oldtimers* (New York: Alcoholics Anonymous World Services, Inc., 1980), p. 338. Hereinafter, unless otherwise indicated, this title will be referred to as *DR. BOB*.

[18] See the comments about this in *The Co-Founders of Alcoholics Anonymous*, at pages 4-5, with a partial quote from Dr. Bob's final remarks about keeping it simple.

[19] See Ernest Kurtz, *Not-God*, Expanded ed. (Minnesota: Hazelden, 1991), p. 103.

[20] Dr. Bob put the "simplicity" idea in precisely the foregoing language in his farewell address to A.A. See *DR. BOB*, p. 338.

[21] Dick B., *Dr. Bob's Library: Books for Twelve Step Growth* (San Rafael, CA: Paradise Research Publications, 1994), pp. 2-18.

continually read spiritual literature.[22] He urged, without pushing, that others do likewise.[23] And Dr. Bob's simple *program*, coupled with his intense interest in spiritual growth—through Bible study, prayer, and reading—is what brings us back to Sam Shoemaker in this Oxford Group Part of our title.

One might ask why—if early AAs had the Bible in front of them, were praying, and were listening to God for their guidance—they would need the Oxford Group *or* Shoemaker at all. One answer is that they had a lot to learn, concerning what Shoemaker later called "the spiritual angle."[24] Bill Wilson, for example, had scarcely seen a Bible or been inside a church until he encountered the Shoemaker circle in New York and then—later—A.A.'s pioneer Bible students in Akron.[25] Dr. Bob was a Christian and had received excellent training in the Bible in his younger years. Much later, he began (or resumed) intense spiritual reading when he became affiliated with the Oxford Group in 1933. But the author has not yet discovered any significant evidence that Dr. Bob was either a great Bible student or an avid churchgoer during his long drinking career prior to 1933.

In short, the two founders needed help with medical facts and with what Dr. Silkworth called the "moral psychology" necessary to bring about an essential "psychic change."[26] Far more

---

[22] See Dick B., *Dr. Bob's Library*, in its entirety, and particularly the Foreword by Dr. Ernest Kurtz, pp. ix-x.

[23] *DR. BOB*, pp. 310, 150-51.

[24] See Samuel Shoemaker, Jr., "The Spiritual Angle," *The A.A. Grapevine* (New York: The AA Grapevine, Inc, November, 1992), pp. 21-27—reprinted from the October, 1955, issue of the *A.A. Grapevine*.

[25] See Dick B., *The Akron Genesis of Alcoholics Anonymous*, p. 64. Bill said in a tape, "I hadn't looked in the Bible, up to this time [the time he arrived in Akron] at all." See also Nell Wing, *Grateful to Have Been There* (Illinois: Parkside Publishing Corporation, 1992), where his former secretary said at page 48: "Bill was not a churchgoer and avoided joining any particular denomination." Kurtz's *Not-God* states at page 16: "Of Bill's earlier exposure to religion, little is known—probably because there is little to know. . . . [T]he young Bill Wilson had 'left the church' at about age twelve—on 'a matter of principle.'"

[26] See Silkworth's "Doctor's Opinion" at pages xxv, xxvii, and xxix.

important, however, for their life-changing program, they needed help with religious ideas, with Biblical interpretation, and with tools for spiritual growth. The two founders were novices when it came to theological ideas, religious practices, evangelism, the structure of a religious fellowship, and personal work.[27] And they certainly had no particular skills or experience when it came to bringing atheists and agnostics to a faith in God.

All these were realms in which both the Oxford Group and Shoemaker had developed specific ideas and practices. And, for Bill Wilson on the East Coast, Sam Shoemaker was the man of the hour. In Akron, Sam's writings were available to, read, and recommended by, Dr. Bob and Anne Smith, Henrietta Seiberling, T. Henry and Clarace Williams, and A.A. pioneers. As we have also shown, Shoemaker had a direct influence on the Akron beginnings through his continuing work with the Firestones and with the Reverend J. Carroll Wright, pastor of Dr. Bob's church.

---

[27] While the *following* remarks certainly do not seem applicable to Dr. Bob, Anne Smith, Henrietta Seiberling, T. Henry and Clarace Williams, and a good many of the early *Akron* AAs, they do represent Bill Wilson's appraisal of at least his own shortcomings in the religious area. An Episcopal priest, John F. Woolverton, came across a letter from Bill Wilson to Sam Shoemaker, dated February 15, 1945; and Woolverton made the following observations: "Yet the 'initial spiritual answer' to Wilson's problem of alcoholism did not stick. Exposure to the First Century Christian Fellowship [the Oxford Group] was, by Shoemaker's own candid admission, a matter of 'temporary inspiration' with Wilson. . . . What went wrong? What made Wilson declare in 1945 that aside from Catholic members of AA 'and a few others, we are as a group pretty deficient on the prayer and meditation side'?" See John F. Woolverton, "Evangelical Protestantism and Alcoholism 1933-1962: Episcopalian Samuel Shoemaker, The Oxford Group and Alcoholics Anonymous." Historical Magazine of the *Protestant Episcopal Church* 52:1, March, 1983, pp. 60-61. It is the author's view that Woolverton was urging a look back at what Shoemaker had, in the beginning, given Wilson and perhaps indirectly Dr. Bob, Anne, Henrietta, and the other Akron AAs in the realm of prayer, Bible study, and meditation practices. For these items of emphasis in Shoemaker's teachings and in those of the Oxford Group were very definitely heeded at A.A.'s birthplace and can most appropriately be deemed keys to early A.A.'s success. One need only listen to the tapes, examine the transcripts, and review the reading of Akron oldtimers for proof. See Dick B., *Dr. Bob's Library*, *Anne Smith's Spiritual Workbook*, *The Oxford Group & Alcoholics Anonymous*, *The Akron Genesis of Alcoholics Anonymous*, and *The Books Early AAs Read for Spiritual Growth*.

At this point, we need not again recount or even summarize what Shoemaker gave to A.A., its Big Book, and Twelve Steps. But we do want to review four major contributions.

Shoemaker's suggested experiment of faith

As stated, *Dr. Bob and Bill had no specific program for bringing atheists and agnostics to a faith in God.* Yet Bill seemed surrounded by such a group of unbelievers in New York. Others have seemingly overlooked the fact, or underplayed it—as even Bill did—that Bill was an atheist before he began recovery in the Oxford Group.[28] More important, Bill's friend and partner in the Big Book publication scheme was Hank P.; and Hank had been, or was, an atheist, as was Hank's vociferous newcomer friend, Jim B. In fact, Jim B. appeared at very early East Coast A.A. meetings *denouncing God!*[29] And we note that Wilson's success rate in New York was very low in those early days.[30]

Fortunately for Bill, Shoemaker had several important ideas which, we believe, made it possible for Wilson to put together A.A.'s approach to faith, and particularly to write the Big Book's chapter to the agnostics.[31] Shoemaker's concepts can be summarized by his own words for them—"the experiment of faith." This process enabled Shoemaker to move people from a condition of

---

[28] Bill said in the Big Book at page 10, "I was not an atheist." Nonetheless, Bill's wife, Lois, informed Reverend T. Willard Hunter, in a taped interview she gave Hunter toward the end of her life, that Bill had been an atheist "at the beginning." The author has a copy of this tape in his possession. See also our previous discussion where Bill characterized himself as a "conservative atheist" and reiterated this thought in *As Bill Sees It* (New York: Alcoholics Anonymous World Services, Inc., 1967), p. 276.

[29] *Alcoholics Anonymous Comes of Age* (New York: Alcoholics Anonymous World Services, 1957) contains Bill's discussion and characterization of these two men at page 163.

[30] *Pass It On* (New York: Alcoholics Anonymous World Services, Inc., 1984), p. 166. See also Kurtz, *Not-God*, pp. 41, 56, 62-63.

[31] See Big Book, pp. 44-57, Chapter 4: "We Agnostics."

estrangement from God (and little or no contact with Him) into a *relationship with Him.*[32]

Shoemaker used elements which came from some simple biblical tools as he saw them: To find or come to God, you start by believing God *IS*.[33] If you don't believe, you take the steps taken by others who do believe; but you must become *willing to obey* what is known of God's will.[34] You *seek* God by utter preoccupation with His plan, acting *as if* God *will* guide and provide.[35] You *ask* Him to tell you His plan.[36] You *surrender*, or give in, to as much of God as you understand.[37] You then "clean house" by getting rid of your sins through the process of self-examination, confession of faults, becoming willing to change, undergoing conversion (letting God change you), and making restitution. Then you find—or know, or are conscious of, or are awakened to—God, His power, His plan, and His presence, through your own *experience*. And we believe Shoemaker's suggested experiment became a major part of A.A. thinking. It was one of Shoemaker's major contributions.

Writing on A.A.'s Second Step, Shoemaker said:

How do we come to believe that a Power greater than ourselves can restore us to sanity? By looking at some people who have had the experience. Faith is better caught by contagion than taught by instruction. It is an amazing thing to come into a company of Alcoholics Anonymous and hear testimony to the difference that has been wrought in their lives . . . every church should also have informal gatherings where people seeking faith can hear

---

[32] See, for example, Samuel Shoemaker, Jr., *The Experiment of Faith* (New York: Harper & Brothers, 1957), particularly at page 10; *National Awakening* (New York: Harper & Brothers, 1936), pp. 40-41; and Big Book, p. 29.

[33] Hebrews 11:6.

[34] John 7:17.

[35] Matthew 6:33: "Seek ye first the kingdom of God . . . ;" and compare the Big Book's "God could and would if he were sought" (p. 60).

[36] 1 Samuel 3:9: "Speak, Lord; for thy servant heareth."

[37] Psalm 46:10 (Moffatt): "Give in, admit that I am God."

personal witness from believers, and where they can ask questions and have them answered.[38]

Shoemaker's suggestions on prayer

Shoemaker probably made a very substantial contribution to A.A.'s thinking about prayer. The approach hardly originated with Shoemaker. Nor was it unique *with* Shoemaker. Nonetheless, Bill's biographer said of Shoemaker's influence in this area:

> Perhaps the most important contribution Shoemaker made in Bill's life was in giving him a new interpretation of prayer. Prayer, Bill came to see, could be more than a listing of personal needs and desires, more than an attempt to influence the will of God. It could also be a method of discovering that will, and for this reason he [Bill] began to believe that it was as important to listen as to speak in prayer.[39]

Shoemaker's emphasis on "Thy will be done" may have become the touchstone for A.A. in its technique of praying "only" for a knowledge of God's will, and then surrendering to it.[40] And to this day, the Lord's Prayer—with its "Thy will be done"—is still the dominant way the world round for closing an A.A. meeting, just as it was for closing Oxford Group meetings.

Shoemaker's suggestions on morning devotions

Though one could hardly belong to the Oxford Group without hearing ideas about a "Morning Watch" and "Quiet Time," and though the Quiet Time was standard fare in Akron A.A., it seems that Shoemaker's own repeated teachings on the subject had much to do with the fact and form of its inclusion in the Big Book by

---

[38] Shoemaker, *12 Steps to Power*, p. 1.

[39] Recall that Shoemaker often quoted 1 Samuel 3:9 ("Speak, Lord"); Isaiah 6:8 ("Here *am* I"); and Acts 9:6: "Lord, what wilt thou have me to do?"

[40] For "Thy will be done," see Matthew 6:10; and Big Book, pp. 67, 85, 88, 63, 76.

Bill Wilson. Wilson omitted all specific references to the Bible in the basic text of the Big Book and hence eliminated mention of it as part of morning devotions. But the Big Book's discussion of morning devotions still reads much like the suggestion and remarks Shoemaker made about his own way of starting the day. Consider the very first radio talk Shoemaker gave on the subject on October 4, 1945:

> Good morning! . . . The morning sets the tone of the day. . . . how the day starts in the morning is not only an indication of what kind of life you are living, but what direction you are going in. . . . I'll tell you a secret: meet God first in the day, before you meet anybody else; and then you'll meet them in a different spirit. May I tell you what we do in our home? When my wife and I get up, the first thing we reach for is our Bibles—not a cigarette, nor a drink, nor the morning paper—but our Bibles, We read a chapter or two. Then we get quiet and spend some time in prayer. Our older daughter usually comes in for this time of devotion with us. In quietness we pray for the people, the causes, the immediate responsibilities of the day, and ask God to direct us and to use us to do His work and His will. We ask Him for direction. We work out our plans together, we get clear if anything has gotten between us, we include our daughter in our plans and talk about any decisions she may have to make. The family prayer-time ought to be a kind of crucible in which human tensions are washed out and human problems solved by the advice and help of one another, as we all wait upon God. Bring the family and business problems before Him, ask Him about them, and trust Him to tell you. Begin the day that way, and I think you really will have a "good morning", and a good afternoon, and a good evening—and a good life.[41]

---

[41] "Gems for Thought," A presentation of the American Broadcasting Co., No. 1, Thursday, October 4, 1945, from the first "Morning Radio Talk by the Rev. Samuel M. Shoemaker." See also, Dick B., *Good Morning! Quiet Time, Morning Watch, Meditation and Early A.A.* (San Rafael, CA: Paradise Research Publications, 1996), p. 2.

Now note the Big Book's suggestions for starting the day:

> On awakening let us think about the twenty-four hours ahead. We
> consider our plans for the day. Before we begin, we ask God to
> direct our thinking. . . . In thinking about our day we may face
> indecision. We may not be able to determine which course to
> take. Here we ask God for inspiration, an intuitive thought or a
> decision. . . . We usually conclude the period of meditation with
> a prayer that we be shown all through the day what our next step
> is to be, that we be given whatever we need to take care of such
> problems. . . . If the circumstances warrant, we ask our wives or
> friends to join us in morning meditation. . . . There are many
> helpful books also. Suggestions about these may be obtained from
> one's priest, minister, or rabbi (pp. 86-87).

Is there a correlation between Shoemaker's radio suggestions and
those found in the Big Book's suggestions as to morning meditation? We think so; for one can find similar suggestions by
Shoemaker dating from his earliest books and pamphlets down
through 1938 and after. Whether the Big Book adopted the
teachings of Shoemaker, or simply the many similar suggestions
and practices from other Oxford Group sources, the basic theme
seems remarkably similar in both the Oxford Group Quiet Time
practice and the Big Book's morning meditation suggestions. This
was a major contribution to A.A. practice and probably persists to
this day in the widespread use of Hazelden's *Twenty-Four Hours
a Day* and A.A.'s own and newly-published *Daily Reflections*. The
point here is that recovering people have reached, and still are
reaching, *outside* the Big Book for daily spiritual inspiration and
growth.

Shoemaker's Suggestions and Today's A.A.

All this by way of history. But what is the importance of
Shoemaker in relation to A.A. today? Just this. Bill Wilson
claimed that Shoemaker inspired *both* Dr. Bob and himself with
respect to the spiritual ideas that were essential to recovery. And

early A.A. in Akron, Ohio, was phenomenally successful. No one before had achieved much long-range success with the "seemingly hopeless," and "incurable" real alcoholic prior to the work which came to fruition in Akron's alcoholic squad of the Oxford Group, led by Dr. Bob. Consequently, what Shoemaker taught must have relevance to what can be expected to succeed if one hopes to see a change in the plummeting success rate that exists in today's A.A.[42]

There was nothing wrong with the Shoemaker ideas, nor with Dr. Bob's implementation of them. What, if anything, is wrong today, we believe, is the lack of a cadre in A.A. that is knowledgeable about, and can explain, the successful ideas Shoemaker taught. Shoemaker had a message that could reach people in all the early stages of recovery. It was a message of openness, compassion, and strong principles—coupled with a demand that there be honesty and a willingness to try.[43]

Suggestions for believers. For people with strong religious beliefs, Shoemaker taught: "Stand fast!" Shoemaker never stopped talking to A.A. in terms that Bible students, Christians, or people of any belief could understand. He spoke with conviction of God, of Jesus Christ, of the Holy Spirit, and of the Bible. He declared, in a major speech to A.A., that any person with a belief in God and with particular religious convictions could feel comfortable in A.A. because "God as we understood Him" could definitely be the God of their understanding. If we accept Shoemaker's lead, there is plenty of room in today's A.A. for people with an understanding of God as He is described in the Bible, in the Christian faith, and in other religions.

Writing on the Steps, Shoemaker said:

---

[42] For a discussion of this drop in success rate, see Dick B., *The Good Book and The Big Book: A.A.'s Roots in the Bible* (San Rafael, CA: Paradise Research Publications, 1996), pp. 7-10.

[43] See John 7:17.

AA often calls God or Christ a "Power greater than ourselves" because many people have formed unhappy associations with organized religions, and they do not want to stir up needless antagonisms. . . . Perhaps we all ought to be drawn to God by the fact that He is God, by the beauty of His perfection and the power of His love. . . . Self-surrender is man's part in his own conversion. We cannot and do not convert ourselves; we offer ourselves to God in surrender, and He does the converting by His Holy Spirit, bringing us forgiveness and new life. How many persons have I seen make that decision, take that step, and as a result find God and His power in their lives![44]

Suggestions for unbelievers. For those of little or no faith, Shoemaker suggested "acting as if" and seeing the God, or Power, "in other people." Such language might disturb those who believe in the God of the Bible.[45] But Shoemaker essentially was pointing out that many who enter A.A. have no religion, no faith, or no tolerance of religion as they knew it. He felt they could and should be helped to faith *at the start* by choosing, for a beginning, their own conception of God. But he often added that AAs needed church to help them understand God, conversion, prayer, and witness.

Suggestions for those considered hostile. What of a group in today's A.A. that may be increasing in numbers? Members who do not favor church attendance. Or members who are not tolerant of the mention of religion in A.A. Or members who do not like to hear that the A.A. program is directed toward a belief in God Almighty—the One with all power—however one understands Him.

---

[44] Shoemaker, *12 Steps to Power*, p. 1.

[45] Biblically, people who have not come to the Father through Jesus Christ are dead in trespasses and sins, and are without God and without hope. See, for example, John 14:6: "Jesus saith unto him, I am the way, the truth, and the life: no man cometh unto the Father, but by me;" John 3:16; Romans 10:9; and Ephesians 2:1-12.

It would seem from the little story below that Shoemaker's views may have had, and could still have, some impact on these people as well. Bill Wilson said, at a major A.A. gathering:

> A fellow came to Dr. Bob and said, "I'm an alcoholic; here is my history. But I also have this other 'complication.' Can I join A.A.?" Bob threw it out to all the other deacons, while the poor guy waited. Finally, there was some kind of hearing on it among the self-appointed elders. I remember how perfectly Bob put it to them. He reminded us that most of us were practicing Christians. Then he asked, "What would the Master have thought? Would He have kept this man away?" He had them cold! The man came in, was a prodigious worker, and was one of our most respected people.[46]

Shoemaker never wavered in his belief that AAs should know where they came from. And he never avoided mentioning God or Jesus Christ to AAs. He simply felt that A.A. should not attempt to spell out theological doctrine; and that theology should be left to the churches where it belonged and where, he also felt, AAs *individually* should belong. Also, the author found nothing in Shoemaker's approach to, or later comments about, A.A. to suggest Shoemaker accepted the idea that just "any god" would do, or that an A.A. could survive on the idea that all he or she had to do was "just not pick up that first drink" or "not drink and go to meetings."

The author believes A.A.'s Big Book teaches, and that Shoemaker would confirm, that if a real alcoholic in A.A. could, by himself or herself, just "not drink and go to meetings," he or she would not need God *or* A.A.

The Big Book makes clear that the first step in recovery requires AAs to concede to their innermost selves that they are alcoholics; that they have lost the ability to control their drinking;

---

[46] From Bill W.'s last major A.A. talk in 1969 at a dinner at the New York Hilton sponsored by the New York Intergroup Association, with more than 3,000 AAs and their families and friends in attendance to honor Bill. See *The Co-Founders of Alcoholics Anonymous*, p. 23.

and that neither self-knowledge nor fear nor willpower, nor any
other human power, can overcome their problem. Real alcoholics
suffer from *powerlessness* and *unmanageability*, says the A.A.
Fellowship. And Shoemaker's and the Oxford Group's "O God
manage me, for I cannot manage myself" prayer covers just that
point. The "manage me" prayer suggests to unbelievers that if they
have reached the point where alcohol has become their master,
their lives have become a wreck, and they believe or are even
willing to believe that God can change that situation, they are
ready for the experiment of faith that Shoemaker taught about. We
believe Shoemaker, and the A.A. program that followed him, were
suggesting that the newcomer throw himself or herself into the
experiment with utter dedication and expect to emerge "happy,
joyous, and free."[47]

In A.A. today, there seems to the author to be a widening
circle of those who have no religious convictions, want no
religious convictions, and apparently believe they need no religious
convictions to recover from alcoholism.[48] In fact, some AAs
believe that either mention or study in A.A. of its earlier Christian
roots is personally offensive, violative of A.A. Traditions, or just
plain irrelevant. But that was not the position Shoemaker took
when he taught, spoke to, and spoke of, A.A.[49] Nor is it the
view, in the author's experience, of a great many in today's A.A.
who—with A.A.'s current archivist—share the belief that whenever
a civilization or society perishes, there is always one condition
present—they forgot where they came from. We would add that if

---

[47] See Big Book, p. 133.

[48] Kurtz and Ketcham, *The Spirituality of Imperfection*: "The 'hidden God' is a
challenge, for if there is a God—and just about everybody at one time or another doubts
even this part—He, She, or It seems to be *hiding* [p. 107]. . . . Within Alcoholics
Anonymous, they learn that they can reclaim 'God,' calling that 'higher power' anything
they want, as long as they are willing to admit that they cannot control everything in
life" (pp. 108-09). While this author does not agree with the statements, they probably
represent a substantial body of opinion among AAs today. But the premise ignores the
fact that "Higher Power" in the *Big Book* definitely refers to God!

[49] See Dick B., *New Light on Alcoholism*, pp. 217-38.

AAs forget their roots, they may well lose sight, in the future, of where they are going in spiritual matters.

Specific Teachings

Now, what did Sam Shoemaker teach?

First, in effect, he asked: (1) Are you powerless?[50] (2) Has your life become unmanageable?[51] (3) Are you, or have you become, estranged from God?[52]

Second, where the reply was "yes," he suggested as a solution: (1) You need a power or force outside of, or greater than, yourself.[53] (2) You need a vital religious experience.[54] (3) You need to find God.[55] (4) You need a relationship with God.[56]

Finally, he taught—as to the means for meeting the needs: (1) Believe that God IS.[57] (2) Seek Him first.[58] (3) Surrender yourself to God.[59] (4) Make a decision to cast your will and your life on God.[60] (5) To as much of God as you understand.[61] (6) Examine yourself.[62] (7) Get honest with yourself, with God, and with another.[63] (8) Repent and desire change.[64] (9) Throw

---

[50] Shoemaker, *If I Be Lifted Up*, p. 131. Publishing data on this book and the others in this portion can be found in our bibliographical material on Shoemaker.

[51] Harris, *The Breeze of the Spirit*, p. 10.

[52] Shoemaker, *Realizing Religion*, p. 5.

[53] Shoemaker, *A Young Man's View of the Ministry*, p. 42; *If I Be Lifted Up*, p. 176.

[54] Shoemaker, *Realizing Religion*, p. 9.

[55] Shoemaker, *Realizing Religion*, p. 9.

[56] Shoemaker, *Children of the Second Birth*, p. 16.

[57] Shoemaker, *National Awakening*, p. 40.

[58] Shoemaker, *National Awakening*, p. 41.

[59] Shoemaker, *Realizing Religion*, p. 30.

[60] Shoemaker, *Twice-Born Ministers*, p. 134.

[61] Shoemaker, *Children of the Second Birth*, p. 47.

[62] Shoemaker, *God's Control*, pp. 104-05.

[63] Shoemaker, *The Church Can Save the World*, p. 112.

[64] Shoemaker, *Realizing Religion*, p. 19.

yourself on God's mercy and, by his grace, be transformed.[65] (10) Set things right with those you have harmed.[66] (11) Learn to pray effectively by seeking God's will, not just seeking answers for your own self-made designs.[67] (12) Study the Bible for this information, and all else will fall in its place.[68] (13) Live the spiritual principles of the Sermon on the Mount.[69] (14) Awaken to what God has done for you.[70] (15) Fish for men.[71] (16) Pass your discovery on and help others through sharing your successful experience.[72]

Did it work? It surely did. Even before there was an A.A.!

Bill Wilson's friends, Rowland Hazard, Shep Cornell, Vic Kitchen, and Charles Clapp, Jr., got sober and helped other alcoholics get sober by these principles before A.A. was born. All were close associates of Sam Shoemaker's. The point is not that A.A. was unnecessary, but rather that it was based on verities—on the light of the power of God—that had already been shed by the Bible, Jung, the Oxford Group, Shoemaker, other Christian writers of that day, and the experience of A.A.'s own co-founders.

Bill and Bob applied biblical truths. Anne Smith had written them down in her spiritual workbook and shared them with the many, including Bill Wilson, who visited and sometimes lived in the Smith home in Akron where A.A. was born. And the ideas worked. They worked for at least seventy-five percent (75%) of the drunks who really tried; and that record stands unequaled, except for the ninety-three percent (93%) success rate in the burgeoning Cleveland A.A. groups in their earliest days.[73]

---

[65] Shoemaker, *Realizing Religion*, pp. 30-31.

[66] Shoemaker, *Twice-Born Ministers*, p. 32.

[67] Shoemaker, *Religion That Works*, pp. 64-65.

[68] Shoemaker, *Realizing Religion*, pp. 58-62.

[69] Helen Shoemaker, *I Stand by the Door*, p. 24.

[70] Shoemaker, *If I Be Lifted Up*, p. 34.

[71] Shoemaker, *Realizing Religion*, p. 82.

[72] Shoemaker, *Twice-Born Ministers*, p. 56.

[73] *DR. BOB*, p. 261.

Those basic ideas can work today without fail if the light is not hid under a bushel.

A Dozen Shoemaker Ideas That "Took" in A.A.

One could reach any number of conclusions as to where the real impact from Shoemaker can be found in A.A. Also conclude that Shoemaker had no corner on the market. Many A.A. ideas which can be identified in Shoemaker writings can also be found in the Bible early AAs studied. They can be found in the Oxford Group literature (other than Shoemaker's) AAs read. They can be found in many other Christian books that were making the rounds in early A.A. They can be found in the writings of Dr. Bob's wife, Anne; and, to a *very* limited extent, in the writings of Emmet Fox, which some early AAs read.

But we have been looking at Bill's personal involvement with Shoemaker and the Shoemaker circle. We have reviewed and listed in Appendix 2 almost 200 specific Shoemaker-Oxford Group words and phrases, with parallels in A.A.; and we have quoted Bill's and Shoemaker's own remarks about their relationship. All these items have led the author to believe that about a dozen Shoemaker concepts hit Bill Wilson hard. We phrase the Shoemaker ideas in our own words and refer the reader to other chapters in this title for specific supporting references. Here, we believe, among others, are a dozen Shoemaker ideas that "took" in A.A.:

1. **Start from necessity**. People seek to find and know God and His power because of necessity—a necessity arising from their estrangement from God, the spiritual misery coming from that, their need for relief, and the unmanageable circumstances in their lives. Shoemaker often spoke of estrangement from a loving God—an estrangement that exists in people whom He meant to be His companions. And the Big Book, particularly its earliest drafts, spoke much about seeking, finding, and "rediscovering" God, and also of the necessity for doing it. Shoemaker defined people's spiritual misery in terms of their self-made religion or lack of it,

and their making or wanting to make "self" God or like God—a problem that Adam and Eve encountered. And the Big Book not only defined man's spiritual misery in terms of focus on self, self-will, and self-centeredness, but also suggested that the suffering person needs to make a decision to *quit* playing God. Playing God didn't work, said the Big Book. Shoemaker believed people turn to God out of their own necessity for help. And the Big Book specifically mentioned the alcoholic's need for divine help—God's help—with the alcohol problem and with ego problems such as anger, fear, and dishonesty that arise from self-centeredness.

Whence came the idea that AAs needed to admit that their lives had become unmanageable? In answer, we would point to the "unmanageability prayer" that appeared at Dr. Frank Buchman's Oxford Group meetings, in Oxford Group writings, in Anne Smith's spiritual Journal, and in Shoemaker's own writings and teachings. The *necessity and longing* for God, plus an unmanageable life, brings man *to* God, taught Sam Shoemaker. He said there was a gap that man was himself *powerless* to bridge.

A.A.'s First Step is founded upon the *powerless* and *unmanageable* ideas.

2. **Utilize an experiment of faith**. In their quest for God's help and power, people can either turn to the God in which they believe and about whom they have some understanding; or they can start with an experiment of faith. They *must* start with the belief that God IS, said Shoemaker. God either is or He isn't, he taught. So said Bill Wilson in the Big Book. On the other hand, if people have no belief or are unbelievers, they may start with an experiment. They can "surrender as much of themselves as they understand to as much of God as they understand." Not much understanding may exist or be possible for many, said Shoemaker; but start they must. And Shoemaker and many AAs have said such people can *begin to believe* when they "see God or Power" in the life of someone else. They can then "act as if," to use the William James and Shoemaker expression. They can commence by choosing their own conception of that Power (God) *for a*

beginning, take the action that successful believers took, and find God through their own experience—an experience sure to produce consciousness of the power and presence of God. Either believe and pray; or be *willing to believe, act, pray, and then experience* the knowledge and presence of God. Shoemaker and A.A. seemed agreed on that.

3. **Make self-surrender the turning point**. The experiment of faith begins with a crisis of self-surrender. William James made that point. Shoemaker espoused it over and over. Both Shoemaker and the Big Book characterized the surrender to God as an act in which the declarant humbly "gives in," admits that God is God, and says: *Thy* will, not mine, be done. This is the turning point.

4. **Use the Bible as the source for God's universal will**. Where do you find the will of God? There was no question in Shoemaker's mind. You look first in the Bible. Then, as we mention in the next point (Five), you pray, and you "listen" for revelation from God of His particular will. Dr. Bob and Anne Smith did all three. So did Bill Wilson at the beginning. There was *daily* Quiet Time, Bible study, prayer, and listening, during Bill Wilson's three month stay with Dr. Bob and Anne Smith in Akron in the summer of 1935. Some very important spiritual principles, acknowledged by early AAs to constitute the will of God, were found in the Four Absolute Standards of Jesus Christ (culled from Dr. Robert E. Speer's views of the teachings of Jesus Christ in the Bible). "Essential" principles, to use Dr. Bob's expression, were also found in the Sermon on the Mount, 1 Corinthians 13, and the Book of James. Shoemaker emphasized these. And these principles became lodged, early in A.A., in its concepts of honesty, purity, unselfishness, love, forgiveness, patience, tolerance, kindness, and the need for making restitution.

5. **Focus on prayer and listening**. What was the place of prayer? Shoemaker taught that man's big job was to ask God what *He* wants and expect to hear from *Him*, instead of telling Him

what man wants and then asserting God doesn't exist or won't help
when that person doesn't get what he or she asked for. A.A.
embodied this idea in its "prayer and meditation" language and in
the concept of "praying only" for a knowledge of God's will and
the power to carry it out. "Speak, Lord, thy servant heareth," was
the stance Shoemaker urged. "Lord, what wilt thou have me to
do?" was the approach Shoemaker taught. Then, said he, tell God:
"Thy will be done." This latter language, of course, came directly
from the Bible, and it often appears in the Big Book.

6. **Eliminate the blocks to God.** People must eliminate the
blockage from, and barriers to, God. "*Sins*," Shoemaker called
them. And so did early A.A. Sin, said both, involved those defects
or weaknesses in human character—primarily centered in
self—which kept man from seeing, knowing, and experiencing
God. Spiritual misery, Shoemaker called it. A spiritual malady, the
Big Book called it. All the same, *blockage*. The blocks were the
common manifestations of self, the unsuccessful manager. And the
most objectionable blocks were resentments or grudges, fears,
dishonesty, self-will or self-seeking, and *pride*. The last (and
deadliest), said Shoemaker, simply meant that man was standing
in the place of God instead of standing aside for Him.

7. **Follow a surrender path.** How did you eliminate the sin,
the barriers, the blocks? In his very first book, *Realizing Religion*,
Shoemaker talked about employing the Oxford Group's Five
C's—"confidence, confession, conviction, conversion, and
continuance." Did these concepts involve "works" instead of
God's "grace?" We leave an analysis of that theological question
to others, but we did discuss it in a previous title on the Oxford
Group and A.A. However, *action* was considered, both by Shoemaker and the instructions in the Big Book, to be necessary for
bringing a person into a relationship with God and moving his or
her life from sin into harmony with God's will. In the Oxford
Group and in Shoemaker's view, you accomplished this through a
life-changing process which involved the help of another. A

changed person gained the *confidence* of the initiate in need. Then led that person to share or *confess*; then brought the person to a *conviction* that he or she had fallen short of God's plan and must change; then assisted in a *conversion* (occurring through surrender to God of the initiate's will, sins, and ego); and then helped that person *continue* the experience. This continuance meant drawing on God's power and guidance. Then making things right with others, continuing to eliminate sins, trying to live by spiritual principles, and passing the experience *and* the principles on to others. There are clear parallels in A.A.

8. **Have a conversion experience or spiritual awakening**. What was the end result? A conversion experience, a religious experience, a spiritual experience, a maximum experience of Jesus Christ, God-consciousness, a spiritual awakening—all basically synonymous terms used by Shoemaker and, with the exception of the "Christ" experience, by the Big Book.

9. **Acknowledge that it was God's doing, not yours**. Realize that the life-change resulted from a miracle wrought by God, not simply from man's work. Marvel at what God has done for you, said Shoemaker, not at what you have done for yourself. Realize that a miracle has occurred and that God has done for you what you could not do for yourself, said the Big Book.

10. **Belong to a fellowship**. Recognize the importance of Fellowship. AAs often point to the fact that the Twelve Steps begin with the word "we." Whether one is talking about the Fellowship of the Holy Spirit, as Shoemaker did; or a "koinonia," like that in the First Century Church, to which Shoemaker often referred; or simply a "Fellowship of the Spirit," of which the Big Book speaks on page 164, Shoemaker and A.A. were both talking about fellowship as a vital medium for sharing experience, strength, and hope—*and* experiencing God's presence.

11. **Focus on a group**. Accept the importance of a "group." One might question whether the idea of a small group's importance was transmitted by Shoemaker to A.A. We can only say that Shoemaker came down hard on the importance of a "group" or "cell" within the church as being the place for dynamic life-changing to occur. And one need only read A.A. traditions and examine A.A. structure to see that AAs focus on the "group" as the means by which members of their fellowship can maintain their own awakening and help others to achieve that experience.

12. **Witness—pass it on**. Focus on witness, helping others, passing the life-change experience on. In one sense, the largest "Step" chapter in the Big Book is entitled, "Working With Others." The major focus of A.A. is on the "group's" having but one primary purpose—carrying the message; and on the individual's being responsible for reaching out with that message to, and helping, the alcoholic who still suffers.

10

Oxford Group Traces in A.A.'s Twelve Steps

Powerless, the Unmanageable Life and Step One

[Step One: We admitted we were powerless over alcohol—that our lives had become unmanageable.][74]

There is little to say about the Oxford Group's use of the expression "powerless" in relation to alcohol. A number of Bill Wilson's Oxford Group friends—Hazard, Cornell, Kitchen, and Clapp—were relieved of their alcoholism. All sought help from God and often called Him a "Power." Sam Shoemaker (who had helped each of these men) wrote: "It [sin] makes a gap between myself and the Ideal which I am *powerless* to bridge. . . . Only God, therefore, can deal with sin. He must contrive to do for us what *we have lost the power to do ourselves*" (emphasis added).[75] And Oxford Group people wrote much about the need for *finding*

---

[74] In this chapter and elsewhere in the book, *The Twelve Steps of Alcoholics Anonymous* are reprinted with permission of Alcoholics Anonymous World Services, Inc.

[75] Samuel M. Shoemaker, *If I Be Lifted Up* (New York: Fleming H. Revell, 1931), pp. 131, 133. Big Book, p. 50: "This Power has in each case accomplished the miraculous, the humanly impossible."

"Power" which, to them, referred to their separation from God and *powerlessness* over sin, resentment, fear, and so on.[76]

The *unmanageable life* was an entirely different matter. The acknowledgement that life had become unmanageable *often* marked the beginning of an Oxford Group (and early A.A.) surrender prayer. In our section on Oxford Group principle #9—the Decision—we have already discussed the "manage me" prayer. Variations of the "Victor's Story"—which set the stage for the Oxford Group prayer—were told again and again in Oxford Group writings.[77] As we have shown, there was a similar surrender story and prayer involving Shoemaker. And Sam's "unmanageable" prayer came to be called "Charlie's Prayer."[78]

Dr. Bob's wife, Anne Smith, several times suggested use of a virtually identical prayer.[79] And recall: The Big Book's First Step language reads as follows:

> . . . that *our lives had become unmanageable* (p. 59, italics added).

---

[76] See Theophil Spoerri, *Dynamic out of Silence: Frank Buchman's Relevance Today* (London: Grosvenor Books, 1976), p. 25; Stephen Foot, *Life Began Yesterday* (New York: Harper & Brothers, 1935); pp. 5-6, 8-9, 22, 29-35, 47, 62, 67, 80; and Harold Begbie, *Life Changers* (London: Mills & Boon, 1932), p. 22. See Anne Smith's comment on the subject in Dick B., *Anne Smith's Journal, 1933-1939: A.A.'s Principles of Success* (San Rafael, CA: Paradise Research Publications, 1994), p. 22. Also see some comparative thoughts from Shoemaker in Samuel M. Shoemaker, *Courage to Change: The Christian Roots of the 12-Step Movement*. Compiled and edited by Bill Pittman and Dick B. (Michigan: Fleming H. Revell, 1994), pp. 25-30.

[77] See A. J. Russell, *For Sinners Only* (London: Hodder & Stoughton, 1932), p. 79; Peter Howard, *Frank Buchman's Secret* (New York: Doubleday & Co., 1961), pp. 41-44; Spoerri, *Dynamic out of Silence*, pp. 34-37; Garth Lean, *On the Tail of a Comet: The Life of Frank Buchman* (Colorado Springs; Helmers & Howard, 1988), pp. 112-13; and Cecil Rose, *When Man Listens* (New York: Oxford University Press, 1937), pp. 19-22.

[78] See Irving Harris, *The Breeze of the Spirit: Sam Shoemaker and the Story of Faith-at-Work* (New York: The Seabury Press, 1978), p. 10. See also Samuel M. Shoemaker, *How to Find God*. Reprint from *Faith at Work* Magazine, n.d., p. 6; and *How You Can Help Other People* (New York: E. P. Dutton & Co., 1946), p. 60.

[79] Dick B., *Anne Smith's Journal*, pp. 19-21.

The foregoing step language is followed by A.A.'s well-known "a,b,c's," which are:

> Our description of the alcoholic, the chapter to the agnostic, and our personal adventures before and after make clear three pertinent ideas: (a) That we were alcoholic *and could not manage our own lives.* (b) That probably no human power could have relieved our alcoholism. (c) That God could and would if He were sought (p. 60, italics added).

A Power Greater Than Ourselves and Step Two

[Step Two: Came to believe that a Power greater than ourselves could restore us to sanity.]

In a chapter in *Life Began Yesterday*, which he titled "The Solution," Oxford Group writer, Stephen Foot, devoted a page to that solution, stating:

> There is at work in the world to-day a *Power* that has for many generations been neglected by masses of mankind, a *Power* that can change human nature—*that is the message of this book.* It is like the great power of the Niagara Falls, which existed for millenniums before man inhabited the earth. Then for thousands of years man lacked the knowledge to use the power and so it ran to waste. To-day, harnessed, it is bringing light into thousands of homes. So with this *Power* by which human nature can be changed. I have felt it in my own life and seen it at work in the lives of others; it is at work all over the world to-day, and through this *Power* problems are being solved (italics added).[80]

In one of the earliest, popular Oxford Group books, Harold Begbie wrote:

---

[80] Foot, *Life Began Yesterday*, p. 22.

The future of civilization, rising at this moment from the ruins of materialism, would seem to lie in an intelligent use by man of this ultimate source of spiritual *Power* (italics added).[81]

In the Big Book chapter, "There is a Solution," Bill Wilson concluded that will-power alone would not solve problems (pp. 22, 44). He made it clear that the solution lay in a relationship with God.[82] For those who doubted the existence of God, Bill wrote his chapter, "We Agnostics." He wrote it to enable agnostics to find and establish a relationship with what Bill and some Oxford Group people had described as a "Power." And they *all*, including Bill Wilson, called this Power "God."[83] Thus Bill wrote:

Lack of power, that was our dilemma. We had to find a power by which we could live, and it had to be a *Power greater than ourselves*. Obviously. But where and how were we to find this Power? Well, that's exactly what this book is about. Its main object is to enable you to find a Power greater than yourself which will solve your problem. . . . And it means, of course, that we are *going to talk about God* (p. 45).

We found that as soon as we were able to lay aside prejudice and express even a willingness to believe in a *Power greater than ourselves*, we commenced to get results, even though it was impossible for any of us to fully define or comprehend that *Power, which is God* (p. 46, italics added).

---

[81] Begbie, *Life Changers*, p. 22.

[82] See Big Book, pp. 29, 13, 28, 100, 164.

[83] For example, one long-time Oxford Group writer said: "Only the Power which raised Jesus Christ from the dead can, and will, raise us from our old nature and begin to form in us the new." K. D. Belden, *Reflections on Moral Re-Armament* (London: Grosvenor Books, 1983), p. 42.

As can be seen, Wilson used and emphasized the idea of "willing-ness to believe" as one means for finding a power greater than ourselves. And so did the Oxford Group.[84]

Anne Smith spoke much about the need for a power stronger than ourselves.[85] Sam Shoemaker wrote about "a Force outside himself, greater than himself" and "a vast Power outside themselves."[86]

Shoemaker often pointed to the need for a *relationship* with this Power (God).[87] In *Children of the Second Birth*, he wrote:

> We believe entirely that conversion is the experience which initiates the new life. But we are not fools enough to think that the beginning is the end! All subsequent life is a development of the relationship with God which conversion opened (p. 16).

The Decision to Surrender to God As You Understand Him and Step Three

[Step Three: Made a decision to turn our will and our lives over to the care of God, *as we understood Him.*]

Alcoholics Anonymous, the Oxford Group, and Rev. Sam Shoe-maker all emphasized, in their writings, that the *path* to a relationship with God involved a spiritual experience. But the path *began* with a *decision* to entrust the care of one's life to God. There had to be surrender to God.

---

[84] See, for example, K. D. Belden, *Meeting Moral Re-Armament* (London: Grosvenor, 1979), p. 28

[85] Dick B., *Anne Smith's Journal*, pp. 22, 23, 68.

[86] Dick B., *New Light on Alcoholism: The A.A. Legacy from Sam Shoemaker* (Corte Madera, CA: Good Book Publishing Company, 1994), pp. 179-80.

[87] Samuel M. Shoemaker, *Realizing Religion* (New York: Association Press, 1923), p. 42; *Confident Faith* (New York: Fleming H. Revell, 1932), p. 110; *Christ's Words from the Cross* (New York: Fleming H. Revell, 1933), p. 49; and *National Awakening* (New York: Harper & Brothers, 1936), p. 13.

Our own discussion of that surrender will be divided into three parts: (1) The decision. (2) God *as you understand Him.* (3) The surrender itself.

1. *The decision. What Is The Oxford Group?* said:

The Oxford Group initial act of Surrender is not, in any way, an outward and visible ceremony we feel we must shrink from; it is a simple *decision* put into simple language, spoken aloud to God, in front of a witness, at any time in any place, that we have *decided* to forget the past in God and to give our future into His keeping. Nothing more need be added; . . . (italics added).[88]

Anne Smith also spoke of beginning with a decision.[89] And, embodying this *decision* in Step Three, the Big Book said:

Made a decision to turn our will and our lives over to the care of God *as we understood Him* (p. 59, italics in original).

Being convinced, *we were at Step Three*, which is that we decided to turn our will and our life over to God as we understood Him (p. 60, italics in original).

This is the how and why of it. First of all, we had to quit playing God. It didn't work. Next, we *decided* that hereafter in this drama of life, God was going to be our Director (p. 62, italics added).

---

[88] The Layman with a Notebook, *What Is The Oxford Group?* (London: Oxford University Press, 1933), p. 47. See also Henry B. Wright, *The Will of God and a Man's Lifework* (New York: Young Men's Christian Association Press, 1909), pp. 43-114; Ebenezer Macmillan, *Seeking and Finding* (New York: Harper & Brothers, 1933), p. 273; Samuel M. Shoemaker, *Children of the Second Birth* (New York: Fleming H. Revell, 1927), pp. 175-87; *Religion That Works* (New York: Fleming H. Revell, 1928), pp. 46-47); *If I Be Lifted Up*, p. 93; *The Conversion of the Church* (New York: Fleming H. Revell, 1932), pp. 39-40, 77; and *The Church Can Save the World* (New York: Harper & Brothers, 1938), p. 120.

[89] Dick B., *Anne Smith's Journal*, p. 25.

Though our *decision* was a vital and crucial step, it could have little permanent effect unless at once followed by a strenuous effort to face, and to be rid of, the things in ourselves which had been blocking us (p. 64, italics added).

2. *God as you understand Him.* In Chapter Four of this title, we discussed the Oxford Group origins of "God as you understand Him." In two different accounts of Bill's first visits with his friend and sponsor Ebby Thacher, Bill indicated that Ebby had suggested to Bill, in 1934, that Bill should surrender himself to God *as Bill understood Him.*[90] The Oxford Group and Sam Shoemaker had frequently spoken of "surrendering as much of yourself as you understand to as much of God as you understand."[91] Hence Ebby's suggestion to Bill was quite consistent with what Ebby must have heard in the Oxford Group prior to the existence of A.A. Further, there was a similar Oxford Group surrender idea in vogue at this time; and Stephen Foot wrote:

Life began for me with a surrender of all that I know of self, to all that I knew of God.[92]

---

[90] See Bill Wilson, *Original Story*, a thirty-four page document located at the archives at Bill's Home at Stepping Stones. Each line of the document is numbered; and the author was permitted to copy and retain a copy of the document. On page 30, Bill stated: "This is what my friend [Ebby Thacher] suggested I do: Turn my face to God as I understand Him and say to Him with earnestness—complete honesty and abandon—that I henceforth place my life at His disposal and Direction forever" (lines 989-92). See also W. W., "The Fellowship of Alcoholics Anonymous," *Quarterly Journal of Studies on Alcohol* (Yale University, 1945): pp. 461-73, in which Bill is quoted on page 463 as saying that Ebby Thacher told him, "So, call on God as you understand God. Try prayer."

[91] See Shoemaker, *Children of the Second Birth*, pp. 27, 47; *How to Become a Christian* (New York: Harper & Brothers, 1953), p. 72; *How to Find God*, p. 6; "In Memoriam" (Princeton, The Graduate Council, June 10, 1956), pp. 2-3; and Dick B., *New Light on Alcoholism*, pp. 45, 350.

[92] Foot, *Life Began Yesterday*, pp. 12-13, 175. See also James D. Newton, *Uncommon Friends* (New York: Harcourt Brace, 1987), p. 154.

Anne Smith twice used this surrender-to-all-one-knows-of-God language in her Journal.[93]

3. *Surrender of the will to God's direction.* Sam Shoemaker wrote:

[Of a parishioner:] She surrendered to God her groundless fears, and with them turned over to Him her life for His direction.[94]

[Quoting a minister Shoemaker described as "The Militant Mystic":] That night I decided to "launch out into the deep:" and with the decision to cast my will and my life on God, there came an indescribable sense of relief, of burdens dropping away.[95]

Note the similarity of this Shoemaker language to the language of the Third Step itself and also to the language of the Big Book's so-called "Third Step Prayer" on page 63.

Self-examination, the Moral Inventory and Step Four

[Step Four: Made a searching and fearless moral inventory of ourselves.]

1. *Looking for your own fault or part.* In her Journal, Anne Smith quoted parts of the following verses from the Sermon on the Mount, which had been quoted in the Oxford Group and apparently followed in A.A.[96] The verses emphasized looking for your own fault, your own part in a bad relationship with another human being. Matthew 7:1-5 said:

---

[93] Dick B., *Anne Smith's Journal*, pp. 25, 95.

[94] Shoemaker, *Children of the Second Birth*, p. 82.

[95] Samuel M. Shoemaker, *Twice-Born Ministers* (New York: Fleming H. Revell, 1929), p. 184.

[96] Dick B., *Anne Smith's Journal*, p. 31.

Judge not, that ye be not judged. For with what judgment ye judge, ye shall be judged: and with what measure ye mete, it shall be measured to you again. And why beholdest thou the mote [speck] that is in thy brother's eye, but considerest not the beam [log] that is in thine own eye? Or how wilt thou say to thy brother, Let me pull out the mote out of thine eye; and, behold, a beam *is* in thine own eye? Thou hypocrite, first cast out the beam out of thine own eye; and then shalt thou see clearly to cast out the mote out of thy brother's eye.[97]

As we've covered before, the Oxford Group was big on identifying your own fault in a situation.[98]

A.A.'s Big Book said:

First, we searched out the flaws in our make-up which caused our failure (p. 64).

Putting out of our minds the wrongs others had done, we resolutely looked for our own mistakes. Where had we been selfish, dishonest, self-seeking and frightened? Though a situation had not been entirely our fault, we tried to disregard the other person involved entirely. Where were we to blame? The inventory was ours, not the other man's (p. 67).

Where had we been selfish, dishonest, or inconsiderate? Whom had we hurt? Did we unjustifiably arouse jealousy, suspicion or bitterness? Where were we at fault . . . (p. 69)?

---

[97] For Oxford Group writings citing these verses, see Geoffrey Allen, *He That Cometh* (New York: The Macmillan Company, 1932), pp. 81, 140; Victor Kitchen, *I Was a Pagan* (New York: Harper & Brothers, 1934), pp. 110-11; Shoemaker, *The Church Can Save the World*, pp. 81-121; and *God's Control* (New York: Fleming H. Revell, 1939), pp. 62-72. The verses were also cited in Oswald Chambers, *My Utmost for His Highest* ((London: Simpkin Marshall, 1927), pp. 169-74, a devotional used by Oxford Group people. Compare Russell, *For Sinners Only*, pp. 309-16.

[98] Spoerri, *Dynamic out of Silence*, pp. 25-26; Frank Buchman, *Remaking the World* (London: Blandford, 1961), p. 46; and Benson, *The Eight Points*, p. 28.

2. *Applying a moral test in your self-examination*. An Oxford Group examination meant "making the moral test." H. A. Walter's *Soul Surgery* was one of the earliest Oxford Group "texts." Dr. Bob used Walter's book a great deal.[99] Walter said the concept, "make the moral test," came from Frank Buchman's and Sherwood Eddy's "Ten Suggestions for Personal Work."[100] Anne Smith specifically mentioned Sherwood Eddy's ten suggestions in her Journal.[101] And this moral test required an examination of one's life to see how it measured up to the Oxford Group's Four Absolutes—honesty, purity, unselfishness, and love.[102]

3. *Making a written inventory*. An Oxford Group self-examination involved *writing* on a piece of paper the items in a person's life which showed where that person had fallen short of the moral standards set by Jesus Christ in the Sermon on the Mount and elsewhere. The standards could also be found in other New Testament writings. As we have previously shown, Sam Shoemaker summarized the self-examination technique as follows:

> It would be a very good thing if you took a piece of foolscap paper and wrote down the sins you feel guilty of. Don't make them up—there will be plenty without that. . . . One of the simplest and best rules for self-examination that I know is to use the Four Standards which Dr. Robert E. Speer said represented the summary of the Sermon on the Mount—Absolute Honesty, Absolute Purity, Absolute Unselfishness, and Absolute Love.

---

[99] Dick B., *Dr. Bob's Library* (San Rafael, CA: Paradise Research Publications, 1994), pp. 25, 78. In his 1992 visit to Stepping Stones (the Bill Wilson home at Bedford Hills in New York), the author found a copy of *Soul Surgery* in the copy of Anne Smith's Journal of which the Stepping Stones archives has custody.

[100] H. A. Walter, *Soul Surgery*, 6th ed (Oxford at the University Press, 1940—the earliest edition being published in 1919), pp. 43-44.

[101] Dick B., *Anne Smith's Journal*, pp. 30-32, 72, 98, 99.

[102] See C. Rose, *When Man Listens*, pp. 18-19; Olive Jones, *Inspired Children* (New York: Harper & Brothers, 1933), pp. 47-68; *Inspired Youth* (New York: Harper & Brothers, 1938), p. 41; and Hallen Viney, *How Do I Begin?* (Copyright, 1937 by The Oxford Group), pp. 2-4.

Review your life in their light. Put down everything that doesn't measure up. Be ruthlessly, realistically honest.[103]

The Four Absolutes as a test for moral behavior had much vitality in early A.A.:

At the core of the program were the "four absolutes": absolute honesty, absolute unselfishness, absolute purity, and absolute love. (In 1948, Dr. Bob recalled the absolutes as "the only yardsticks" Alcoholics Anonymous had in the early days, before the Twelve Steps. He said he still felt they held good and could be extremely helpful when he wanted to do the right thing and the answer was not obvious. "Almost always, if I measure my decision carefully by the yardsticks of absolute honesty, absolute unselfishness, absolute purity, and absolute love, and it checks up pretty well with those four, then my answer can't be very far out of the way," he said. The absolutes are still published and widely quoted at A.A. meetings in the Akron-Cleveland area).[104]

A.A.'s Big Book followed the Oxford Group lead on the subject of an inventory. It spoke of a *moral* inventory (p. 59). It spoke of the necessity for a *written* inventory—getting the facts about grudges, fears, sex conduct, and harms "on paper" (pp. 64, 68,

---

[103] Shoemaker, *How to Become a Christian*, pp. 56-57. See also Shoemaker, *The Conversion of the Church*, pp. 30-34; *Twice-Born Ministers*, p. 182; *God's Control*, pp. 104-05; and see Belden, *Meeting Moral Re-Armament*, p. 17.

[104] *DR. BOB and the Good Oldtimers* (New York: Alcoholics Anonymous World Services, Inc., 1980), p. 54, 163. See also *Alcoholics Anonymous Comes of Age*, pp. 68, 75, 161; *Pass It On*, p. 127, 171-73; *The Language of the Heart* (New York: The A.A. Grapevine, Inc., 1988), pp. 196-200; Richmond Walker, *For Drunks Only* (MN: Hazelden, n.d.), Preface, p. 3; p. 6; and Mel B., *New Wine: The Spiritual Roots of the Twelve Step Miracle* (MN: Hazelden, 1991), pp. 21, 41, 64, 76, 95, 98, 138, 139.

69, 70, 75). And it was insistent that the examination look for "our own mistakes . . . our faults . . . our wrongs" (pp. 67-69).

Confession, Sharing with Another and Step Five

[Step Five: Admitted to God, to ourselves, and to another human being the exact nature of our wrongs.]

1. *Confession of Faults.* A.A.'s Fifth Step requires the confidential sharing of faults; and it originated with the Bible verse in James 5:16 which reads:

Confess *your* faults one to another, and pray one for another, that ye may be healed. The effectual fervent prayer of a righteous man availeth much.[105]

A.A. literature indicates James 5:16 was the foundation for its Fifth Step.[106] That the James verse was in fact the root of A.A.'s confession Step is borne out by the fact that the Oxford Group often cited James 5:16 in connection with its "sharing for confession."[107] So did Sam Shoemaker.[108] And Anne Smith three times mentioned this verse in connection with admitting one's faults or sins.[109]

2. *Honesty with self, with God, and with another.* The Fifth Step concept of being honest with God, with another, and with

---

[105] See Dick B., *The Akron Genesis of Alcoholics Anonymous* (CA: Good Book Publishing Co., 1994), pp. 192-97, for a discussion of the impact of James 5:13-16 on the procedures early Akron AAs followed for prayer, healing, confession, and surrender.

[106] *Pass It On*, p. 128.

[107] J. P. Thornton-Duesbury, *Sharing* (Pamphlet of The Oxford Group, published at Oxford University Press, n.d.), p. 5; Sherwood Sunderland Day, *The Principles of The Group* (Oxford: Oxford University Press, n.d.), p. 6; and *What Is The Oxford Group?*, pp. 29, 31.

[108] Shoemaker, *The Conversion of the Church*, p. 35.

[109] Dick B., *Anne Smith's Journal*, pp. 36-40.

yourself, in your admission of shortcomings, was also a well established Oxford Group principle.[110]

Conviction, Readiness to Be Changed and Step Six

[Step Six: Were entirely ready to have God remove all these defects of character.]

The Oxford Group's "Five C's" were mentioned in *DR. BOB and the Good Oldtimers* and other books about early A.A.[111] They—Confidence, Confession, Conviction, Conversion, and Continuance—were the heart of the Oxford Group's life-changing art. And A.A.'s own steps parallel these concepts.[112]

A.A.'s Sixth Step concerned "repentance," or "willingness to be changed." Some, including this author, believe that the Oxford Group's "Conviction" idea was codified in A.A.'s Sixth Step.[113]

The Big Book treats *conviction* in two installments: First, it suggests a *review* of Steps One through Five after the Fifth Step confession has been completed. It asks if anything has been omitted. It uses the metaphor of building a foundation—using a

---

[110] Shoemaker, *The Church Can Save the World*, pp. 110-12; and Dick B., *Anne Smith's Journal*, p. 39.

[111] As to the Five C's, see Walter, *Soul Surgery*, pp. 21, 24, 28-29; and Shoemaker, *Realizing Religion*, pp. 79-80. As to A.A.'s mention of them, see *DR. BOB*, p. 54; Richmond Walker, *For Drunks Only: One Man's Reactions to Alcoholics Anonymous* (Center City, MN: Hazelden, n.d.), pp. 45-46; and *The 7 Points of Alcoholics Anonymous*, rev. ed. (Seattle: Glen Abbey, 1989), pp. 91-93.

[112] See Chapter Eight, *supra*. Confidence had to do with Fifth Step sharing, and the Twelfth Step concept of working with others. Confession with the Fifth Step. Conviction with the Sixth Step. Conversion with the Third and Seventh Steps. And Continuance with A.A.'s so-called "maintenance" steps—Ten, Eleven, and Twelve—which are dedicated to maintaining and growing in the spiritual condition that has been experienced through taking A.A.'s first nine Steps.

[113] See Mel B., *New Wine*, pp. 34-35.

figure of speech similar to that Anne Smith used.[114] Second, the Big Book sets forth the actual Sixth Step process:

> We have emphasized willingness as being indispensable. Are we now ready to let God remove from us all the things which we have admitted are objectionable? Can He now take them all—every one? If we still cling to something we will not let go, we ask God to help us to be willing (p. 76).

As we have shown, "willingness" was rooted in the Oxford Group's adaptation of John 7:17.

Surrender of Sins, God's Removal and Step Seven

[Step Seven: Humbly asked Him to remove our shortcomings.]

Both Anne Smith and the Oxford Group suggested God can *remove* sins or shortcomings.[115] So does the Bible.[116] And the idea of *humility*—humbly asking God's help in such a problem—was a common one in the Bible and in Sam Shoemaker's thinking.[117]

The life-change, transformation, or conversion that took place when one "surrendered" and "gave his life to God" was much discussed and probably little understood in early A.A. But Oxford

---

[114] For this figurative material, see Big Book, page 75; and Dick B., *Anne Smith's Journal*, p. 42.

[115] Allen, *He That Cometh*, p. 147; Kitchen, *I Was a Pagan*, p. 73; and Dick B., *Anne Smith's Journal*, pp. 46-47.

[116] See Psalm 103:11-12.

[117] James 4:10 states: "Humble yourselves in the sight of the Lord, and he shall lift you up." Writing in A.A.'s *Grapevine* about the Seventh Step, many years after the Twelve Steps were written, Shoemaker said: "We need help, grace, the lift of a kind of divine derrick." *Best of the Grapevine, Volume II* (New York: The AA Grapevine, Inc., 1986), p. 130.

Group founder, Frank Buchman, made it simple for his followers. He spoke of "Sin, Jesus Christ, and the result, a miracle."[118]

The miracle of the conversion seemingly could not, and did not need to, be explained. Sam Shoemaker wrote in his first book:

> What you want is simply a vital religious experience. You need to find God. You need Jesus Christ.[119]

As we have said, Dr. Carl Jung wrote Bill Wilson that the highest religious experience could be described as "the union with God." Jung quoted Psalm 42:1: "As the hart panteth after the water brooks, so panteth my soul after thee, O God."[120]

For those Oxford Group people who chose to speak in New Testament terms, surrender and conversion were rooted in John 3:3-8—being born again of the spirit.[121] In early A.A., there was simply a "surrender," which involved conversion, rebirth, and the removal of sin nature. Thus, in its "Seventh Step Prayer," the Big Book stated:

> My Creator, I am now willing that you should have all of me, good and bad. I pray that you now *remove* from me every single defect of character which stands in the way of my usefulness to you and my fellows. Grant me strength, as I go out from here, to do your bidding. Amen (p. 76, italics added).

---

[118] Frank Buchman often said, "Sin is the disease. Jesus Christ is the cure. The result is a miracle." See H. W. Bunny Austin, *Frank Buchman As I Knew Him* (London: Grosvenor Books, 1975), p. 10; Peter Howard, *Frank Buchman's Secret* (Garden City, NY: Doubleday & Co., 1961), p. 130; and Walter, *Soul Surgery*, p 86.

[119] Shoemaker, *Realizing Religion*, p. 9.

[120] *Pass It On*, pp. 384-85.

[121] See Henry Drummond, *The Ideal Life* (New York: Hodder & Stoughton, 1897), p. 211; Buchman, *Remaking the World*, p. 23; Begbie, *Life Changers*, p. 104; Allen, *He That Cometh*, pp. 19-43; Jones, *Inspired Children*, p. 136; Samuel M. Shoemaker, *National Awakening*, pp. 55, 57, 58; *Twice-Born Ministers*, pp. 56, 10; and *By the Power of God* (New York: Harper & Brothers, 1954), pp. 28-33.

But the Third Step (actually phrased only in terms of a *decision*) itself involved a surrender, rebirth, and conversion. The Big Book, in effect, created *two* surrenders in the Twelve Steps (in Three and Seven) where there had only been one in the Oxford Group and in early A.A. For, in Step Three, the Big Book spoke of conformity with God's will, utilization of His power, and the resultant rebirth:

> As we felt new power flow in, as we enjoyed peace of mind, as we discovered we could face life successfully, as we became conscious of His presence, we began to lose our fear of today, tomorrow or the hereafter. We were *reborn* (p. 63, italics added).[122]

Restitution, Amends and Steps Eight and Nine

[Step Eight: Made a list of all persons we had harmed, and became willing to make amends to them all.]

Anne Smith's Journal spoke of making a list.[123] Oxford Group people frequently spoke of "restitution," but at least one writer specifically used the word "amends."[124] A number of verses from the Bible were quoted in connection with restitution. Many came from the Sermon on the Mount. But the starting point seemed to be Jesus's statement: "Agree with thine adversary

---

[122] See Dick B., *The Akron Genesis*, pp. 328-30, for a discussion of the language Bill Wilson actually used in earlier Big Book drafts. Bill said, "For sure, I'd been born again." Bill also wrote that Ebby had been reborn. Lois Wilson spoke of Bill's being reborn. And Shoemaker wrote of the Calvary Mission—where both Ebby and Bill *were* reborn—that the Mission was a place were men, who wanted to, were reborn. Compare the remarks of Bill's friend, Victor Kitchen, in *I Was a Pagan*. Kitchen spoke of the sensation of release and freedom for all who face and confess their sins and then said a surrender prayer similar to that in the Big Book, concluding, "We were reborn into life. . . ." (pp. 66-68).

[123] Dick B., *Anne Smith's Journal*, p. 48.

[124] Benson, *The Eight Points*, p. 35.

quickly, whiles thou art in the way with him. . . ."[125] Again, the concept of "willingness" was involved; and we have already discussed the importance in the Oxford Group and to Shoemaker of John 7:17 as far as "willingness" to obey God's will was concerned.[126]

[Step Nine: Made direct amends to such people wherever possible, except when to do so would injure them or others.]

The Big Book specifically acknowledges the Oxford Group origins of "restitution to those harmed."[127] The Oxford Group felt that God's guidance was necessary in determining what atonement constitutes, the right time to make it, the form it should take, and to whom it should be made.[128] As we have previously mentioned, the Group cited a number of Bible verses for the importance of making amends.[129] Doing this, *and with forgiveness*, was vital in the Oxford Group and in A.A.[130]

The Big Book said, as to amends (Steps Eight and Nine):

We have a list of all persons we have harmed and to whom we are willing to make amends. . . . We subjected ourselves to a drastic self-appraisal. Now we go out to our fellows and repair the damage done in the past. If we haven't the will to do this, we ask until it comes. . . . At the moment we are trying to put our lives in order. But this is not an end in itself. Our real purpose is to fit ourselves to be of maximum service to God and the people about us (pp. 76-77).

---

[125] Matthew 5:25. See Weatherhead, *Discipleship*, p. 112; and Benson, *The Eight Points*, p. 32.

[126] And see, for example, Brown, *The Venture of Belief*, pp. 27-29.

[127] Big Book, p. xvi.

[128] *What Is The Oxford Group?*, p. 62. See Big Book, pp. 79, 80, 82, 83.

[129] (1) Numbers 5:6-7. See *Russell, For Sinners Only*, p. 119. (2) Matthew 5:23-24. See Benson, *The Eight Points*, p. 30. (3) Luke 19:1-9. See Almond, *Foundations for Faith*, p. 13. (4) Luke 15:10-32. See *What Is The Oxford Group?*, pp. 62-64.

[130] Benson, *The Eight Points*, pp. 34-36. Big Book, p. 77.

Although these reparations take innumerable forms, there are
some general principles which we find guiding. Reminding
ourselves that we have decided to go to any lengths to find a
spiritual experience, we ask that we be given strength and
direction to do the right thing, no matter what the personal
consequences may be. We may lose our position or reputation or
face jail, but we are willing. We have to be (p. 79).

Continued Inventory, Daily Surrender and Step Ten

[Step Ten: Continued to take personal inventory and when we
were wrong promptly admitted it.]

A.A.'s Tenth Step speaks to the critical importance of *maintaining*
one's spiritual condition achieved through taking the previous nine
steps. It urges helpfulness to others.[131] It also challenges
alcoholics "to *grow* in understanding and effectiveness." It says,
"This is not an overnight matter. It should continue for our
lifetime" (italics added).[132]

Step Ten seems rooted in Oxford Group "Conservation,"
"Continuance," and "Daily Surrender" ideas, as contrasted to the
basic and General Surrender of self that, in their A.A.
counterparts, can be found in Steps Three, Seven, or both.[133]

For the Oxford Group and Sam Shoemaker, this involved the
concept of "continuance" or "conservation"—the so-called fifth of
the "5 C's." In the Oxford Group/Shoemaker circles, in which
early AAs were traveling, there were five aspects of "continuance": (1) Prayer; (2) Bible study; (3) Guidance; (4) Group

---

[131] At the close of the Tenth Step instructions on page 84, the Big Book says: "Then
we resolutely turn our thoughts to someone we can help."

[132] See Big Book, pp. 84-85.

[133] See Nell Wing, *Grateful to Have Been There: My 42 Years with Bill and Lois, and
the Evolution of Alcoholics Anonymous* (Illinois: Parkside Publishing, 1992), p.
21—"Daily Practice." See also Dick B., *Anne Smith's Journal*, pp. 49-53.

worship; and (5) Witness. They were part of the continuing process of "Daily surrender."

We repeat these Oxford Group statements about *daily* surrender, daily inventory and amends, and daily spiritual contact:

> Our lives will be one continuous surrender: surrender to God of every difficulty that confronts us, each temptation, each spiritual struggle, laying before Him either to take away or to show to us in their proper spiritual proportions.[134]

> When I came to make a daily surrender I learned what a different experience this is from a general surrender. Daily checking on the four absolutes revealed to me things I had never questioned in myself. . . . I came to a daily willingness to do anything for God. I made amends where He gave me light.[135]

> There is need for rededication day by day, hour by hour, by which progressively, in every Quiet Time, the contaminations of sin and self-will are further sloughed off (for they do have a way of collecting) and we are kept in fresh touch with the living Spirit of God. A further surrender is needed when and whenever there is found to be something in us which offends Christ, or walls us from another. We shall need, in this sense, to keep surrendering as long as we live.[136]

The Big Book instructs, as to Step Ten:

> Continue to watch for selfishness, dishonesty, resentment, and fear.[137] When these crop up, we ask God at once to remove them.[138] We discuss them with someone immediately and make

---

[134] *What Is The Oxford Group?*, p. 46.

[135] Benson, *The Eight Points*, p. 149.

[136] Shoemaker, *The Conversion of the Church*, p. 79.

[137] Frank Buchman asked: "What is the disease? Isn't it fear, dishonesty, resentment, selfishness?" Buchman, *Remaking the World*, p. 38. A Step Four process.

[138] The Steps Six and Seven process.

amends quickly if we have harmed anyone.[139] Then we resolutely turn our thoughts to someone we can help.[140] Love and tolerance of others is our code (p. 84).[141]

Every day is a day when we must carry the vision of God's will into all of our activities. "How can I best serve Thee—Thy will (not mine) be done." These are thoughts which must go with us constantly. We can exercise our will power along this line all we wish. It is the proper use of the will (p. 85).

Quiet Time, Prayer, Bible Study, Listening, God's Will, Guidance and Step Eleven

[Step Eleven: Sought through prayer and meditation to improve our conscious contact with God *as we understood Him,* praying only for knowledge of His will for us and the power to carry that out.]

Prayer, Bible study, spiritual reading, listening for guidance, and Quiet Time were musts in early A.A.[142] In our review of the twenty-eight Oxford Group principles, we documented the role of these practices in the Oxford Group itself. We have shown from Bill Wilson's comments in *The Language of the Heart*, that Bill specifically acknowledged that A.A. got its ideas for Quiet Time, prayer, meditation, and guidance from the Oxford Group.[143] The Oxford Group frequently mentioned the necessity for establishing "contact with God."[144] And Oxford Group writer, Stephen Foot,

---

[139] The Steps Five, Eight, and Nine process.

[140] The Step Twelve process.

[141] The practice of principles Dr. Bob and other early AAs stressed as coming from the Sermon on the Mount, 1 Corinthians 13, and the Book of James.

[142] See our review from the perspective of Anne Smith's teachings and what went on in early Akron A.A. Dick B., *Anne Smith's Journal*, pp. 53-64; *That Amazing Grace*, pp. 31, 35, 44, 54, 56-57 76; and *Good Morning!*, pp. 58-64.

[143] *The Language of the Heart*, pp. 298, 196-97. See *DR. BOB*, pp. 131, 135-36.

[144] See, for example, Foot, *Life Began Yesterday*, p. 13.

used language about that contact, which seems to have been incorporated into Step Eleven almost verbatim. Foot said:

I will ask God to show me His purpose for my life and claim from Him *the power to carry that purpose out* (italics added).[145]

As we discussed in connection with A.A.'s Good Book roots, the Big Book's Eleventh Step instructions can be divided into four parts.[146]

First, those things the AA is to do each evening as he or she constructively reviews the day (p. 86). Then, as the Big Book says: "After making our review we ask God's forgiveness and inquire what corrective measures should be taken." While these remarks may not seem to qualify as "prayer and meditation," they are part of A.A.'s Eleventh Step instructions. And we have seen from *all* the twenty-eight Oxford Group principles how frequently the Group posed tests for determining how well a person was conducting daily surrender and quiet time activities.

Second, the Eleventh Step places great focus on how one commences the day (pp. 86-87). Recall that Anne Smith spoke of living "one day at a time."[147] The Big Book suggests, "On awakening, let us think about the twenty-four hours ahead. We consider our plans for the day." It then suggests three different approaches: (1) That we ask God to direct our thinking and keep the thought-life clear of wrong motives. [This certainly coincides with Oxford Group emphasis on, and discussion of guidance, quiet time, prayer, listening for leading thoughts, and checking.] (2) That we ask God for inspiration, an intuitive thought or a decision when facing "indecision." [Compare our Oxford Group discussion of Guidance.] (3) That we be shown all through the day what the next step is to be, that our needs be supplied in that regard, and

---

[145] Foot, *Life Began Yesterday*, p. 11.

[146] See Step Eleven discussion in Chapter 7 of this title.

[147] Dick B., *Anne Smith's Journal*, p. 51.

that our actions be free from selfish ends. [Again, Oxford Group teachings comprehend this subject matter.]

Third, the Eleventh Step includes what the author has often described as the Big Book's "lost paragraph;" and, more optimistically, its "growth paragraph." We call this the *growth* paragraph because Bill Wilson frequently spoke of A.A. as a "spiritual kindergarten."[148] In the Big Book's "spiritual growth" paragraph, Bill wrote as follows:

> If circumstances warrant, we ask our wives or friends to join us in morning meditation. If we belong to a religious denomination which requires a definite morning devotion, we attend to that also. If not members of religious bodies, we sometimes select and memorize a few set prayers which emphasize the principles we have been discussing. There are many helpful books also. Suggestions about these may be obtained from one's priest, minister, or rabbi. Be quick to see where religious people are right. Make use of what they offer (p. 87).

We believe many portions of our book demonstrate the Oxford Group and Anne Smith's influence on the foregoing paragraph.

Anne's whole family, and those—including Bill Wilson—who visited her home, were involved in a great deal of morning meditation. Anne and Dr. Bob were members of a religious denomination during most of the period from 1935 to the end of their lives.[149] Anne suggested specific prayers in her Journal. She recommended and used the Bible, many spiritual books, and daily Bible devotionals as part of the daily inspirational reading. And she suggested seeking help from others as to the materials which should be read. Sam Shoemaker's whole ministry involved

---

[148] See, for example, *As Bill Sees It*, p. 95; and Ernest Kurtz, *Shame and Guilt. Characteristics of the Dependency Cycle* (Minnesota: Hazelden, 1981), p. 12. Bill used similar language in letters to Sam Shoemaker and Clarence S. which the author has in his possession.

[149] See Dick B., *Dr. Bob's Library: Books for Twelve Step Growth* (San Rafael, CA: Paradise Research Publications, 1994), p. 3.

suggestions for reading, prayers, and meditation. And, on the occasion of Calvary Church's break with Frank Buchman, Shoemaker said he felt the *early* Oxford Group emphasis had been on work within *the churches*—a principle for spiritual growth Shoemaker often mentioned to AAs directly.

Finally, the Big Book speaks of the action to be taken throughout the day when agitated or in doubt. Essentially, it recommends seeking the guidance of God and surrendering to Him many times throughout the day, saying, "Thy will be done" (pp. 87-88). As we have shown, the Oxford Group teachings paralleled all aspects of these latter suggestions.

The Spiritual Awakening, Witness, Practice of Principles and Step Twelve

[Step Twelve: Having had a spiritual awakening as the result of these steps, we tried to carry this message to alcoholics, and to practice these principles in all our affairs.]

We believe A.A.'s Twelfth Step can and should be viewed as having three "parts." They are: (1) The spiritual awakening achieved through taking the preceding eleven steps. (2) The obligation to witness to others by "passing on" the message of how one received this deliverance through what God has done for that person. (3) The actual living of a changed life by "practicing the principles"—the principles learned from taking the Twelve Steps of recovery. And we will discuss the Oxford Group's contribution to these Twelve Step ideas by separately discussing each of the Twelfth Step's three "parts."

1. *The spiritual awakening*[150]

Professor William James, the Oxford Group, and Reverend Sam Shoemaker had many expressions for the "vital religious experience" or "conversion" which took place when a person surrendered his or her life to God, took the steps of confession, conviction, conversion, restitution, and continuance, and then experienced the fruits of the changed life. The religious experience was variously described as: (1) An experience of God. (2) A vital experience of Jesus Christ. (3) A religious experience. (4) A spiritual experience. (5) A spiritual awakening. (6) A relationship with God. (7) A sense of the power and presence of God. (8) Finding God. (9) Being in touch with God. (10) Contact with God. (11) Conversion. (12) Surrender. (13) Change. (14) Being born again. (15) God Consciousness.

Compare the following ideas in A.A.'s Big Book:

> There was a sense of victory, followed by such a peace and serenity as I had never known. There was utter confidence. I felt lifted up, as though the great clean wind of a mountain top blew through and through. God comes to most men gradually, but His impact on me was sudden and profound (Bill's Story, p. 14).

> The great fact is just this, and nothing less: That we have had deep and effective spiritual experiences which have revolutionized our whole attitude toward life, toward our fellows and toward God's universe (p. 25).

> With few exceptions our members find they have tapped an unsuspected inner resource which they presently identify with their own conception of a Power greater than themselves. Most of us think this awareness of a Power greater than ourselves is the essence of a spiritual experience.

---

[150] "Spiritual awakening" is an Oxford Group phrase. Buchman frequently spoke of a "spiritual awakening." See Buchman, *Remaking the World*, pp. 5, 24, 28. Shoemaker's title *National Awakening* bespeaks the idea; and he devoted a chapter of another book to the elements of awakening. Shoemaker, *By the Power of God*, chapter IX—"What Awakening Takes" (pp. 133-54).

Our more religious members call it "God-consciousness" (pp. 571-72).[151]

In the face of collapse and despair, in the face of the total failure of their human resources, they found that a new power, peace, happiness, and sense of direction flowed into them. . . . When many hundreds of people are able to say that the consciousness of the Presence of God is today the most important fact of their lives, they present a powerful reason why one should have faith (pp. 50-51).[152]

In a few seconds he was overwhelmed by a conviction of the Presence of God. . . . He stood in the Presence of Infinite Power and Love. He had stepped from bridge to shore. For the first time, he lived in conscious companionship with his Creator (p. 56).

Much has already been said about receiving strength, inspiration, and direction from Him who has all knowledge and power. If we have carefully followed directions, we have begun to sense the flow of His Spirit into us. To some extent we have become God-conscious (p. 85).

See to it that your relationship with Him is right, and great events will come to pass for you and countless others. This is the Great Fact for us (p. 164).

---

[151] See Chapter Six for our discussion of the twenty-eight Oxford Group principles, the discussion of "God Consciousness," and the frequency with which Oxford Group people used that phrase.

[152] See the latter part of this chapter containing quotes from the Oxford Group writings and from the Big Book which show the frequency with which Oxford Group people referred to consciousness of the power and presence of God in their lives.

2. *Witness—giving it away to keep it*

The second Twelfth Step idea comprehends *service*. Service through carrying the message—passing it on—giving it away to keep it—witnessing. We covered these points in our discussion of fellowship, witnessing, and service.

A large part of Anne Smith's Journal was devoted to service to others, life-changing, and "witnessing." Anne said:

Giving Christianity away is the best way to keep it.[153]

We can't give away what we haven't got.[154]

In one of his earliest pamphlets—one which Anne quoted in her spiritual journal—Sam Shoemaker spoke of "giving it away to keep it."[155] The following, from a much later Shoemaker book, exemplified this concept of "passing it on." Shoemaker wrote:

The best way to keep what you have is to give it away, and no substitute has ever been found for personal Christian witness.[156]

Compare the following thoughts from A.A.'s Big Book:

He [Bill Wilson] suddenly realized that in order to save himself he must carry his message to another alcoholic (p. xvi).

My friend [Bill Wilson's sponsor, Ebby Thacher] had emphasized . . . [that it was] imperative to work with others as he had worked with me. Faith without works was dead, he said. And how

---

[153] Dick B., *Anne Smith's Journal*, p. 69.

[154] Dick B., *Anne Smith's Journal*, p. 69.

[155] Samuel M. Shoemaker, *One Boy's Influence* (New York: Association Press, 1925), p. 15. See Dick B., *Anne Smith's Journal*, pp. 69, 85.

[156] Samuel M. Shoemaker, Jr., *They're on The Way* (New York: E. P. Dutton, 1951), p. 159. See also Dick B., *New Light on Alcoholism: The A.A. Legacy from Sam Shoemaker* (CA: Good Book Publishing, 1994), p. 274.

appallingly true for the alcoholic! For if an alcoholic failed to perfect and enlarge his spiritual life through work and self-sacrifice for others, he could not survive the certain trials and low spots ahead (p. 15).

Practical experience shows that nothing will so much insure immunity from drinking as intensive work with other alcoholics. It works when other activities fail. This is our *twelfth suggestion*: Carry this message to other alcoholics! (p. 89).

And be careful not to brand him as an alcoholic (p. 92).[157]

Keep his attention focussed mainly on your personal experience. . . . Tell him exactly what happened to you. Stress the spiritual feature freely (pp. 92-93).

It is important for him to realize that your attempt to pass this on to him plays a vital part in your own recovery (p. 94).

You will be most successful with alcoholics if you do not exhibit any passion for crusade or reform. Never talk down to an alcoholic from any moral or spiritual hilltop; simply lay out the spiritual tools for his inspection. Show him how they worked with you. Offer him friendship and fellowship. Tell him if he wants to get well you will do anything to help (p. 95).[158]

Helping others is the foundation stone of your recovery (p. 97).

Give freely of what you find and join us (p. 164).

---

[157] See Dick B., *Anne Smith's Journal*, p. 69, where we quote Anne as follows: "Share with people—don't preach, don't argue. Don't talk up nor down to people. Talk to them, and share in terms of their own experience, speak on their level."

[158] See Dick B., *Anne Smith's Journal*, p. 69, for her similar remarks.

3. *Living the changed life; practicing the spiritual principles*

Many claim Anne Smith's "favorite" Bible verse was "Faith without works is dead."[159] The verse certainly wound up in A.A.'s Big Book (pp. 14, 76, 88). And Anne wrote much about *living* by spiritual principles.

The Big Book really does not define the "principles" or describe the "works" in any orderly fashion. But we believe the following are *among* the principles it insists should be practiced: (1) Relying upon God (pp. 46, 50, 51-53, 68, 80, 98, 100, 120, 292); (2) Being rigorously honest (pp. 58, 64, 67, 69, 73, 84, 86); (3) Eliminating selfishness and self-centeredness (pp. 62, 63, 69, 84. 86); (4) Eliminating resentment, jealousy, and envy (pp. 64-67, 84, 86, 145); (5) Eliminating fear (pp. 67-68, 84, 86, 145); (6) Practicing patience, tolerance, kindliness, understanding, love, forgiveness, and helpfulness to others (pp. 20, 77, 83, 84, 97, 118, 153, 292). Other Twelfth Step principles embody the ideas of humility, forgiveness, and service—plus such other Oxford Group concepts as overcoming the bondage of self, confession, restitution, reconciliation, guidance, and so on.[160]

---

[159] See Nell Wing, *Grateful to Have Been There*, pp. 70-71; *DR. BOB*, p. 71; and *Pass It On*, p. 147. See Dick B., *Anne Smith's Journal*, pp. v, 54, 74.

[160] See, for example, *What Is The Oxford Group?*, which spoke of the four absolute ideals in the Sermon on the Mount and four practical activities—sharing of sins and as witness, surrendering your life to God's direction, making restitution, and relying on God for guidance. These, it said, were the means of living the "simple tenets of Christianity" (pp. 8-9). Of equal importance were the principles of 1 Corinthians 13, which were the subject of Drummond's *The Greatest Thing in the World*, and arrested the attention of Dr. Bob and many Oxford Group writers such as Benson (*The Eight Points*, p. 47). Shoemaker's *Confident Faith* spoke of the kind of relationship which comes to pass between those who find themselves cooperating with God. Those whose lives are integrated into the same great plan of God, who work together with complete honesty and accord, knowing all there is to be known about one another, dealing in the truth with love, and sharing in the work of making God and His holy spirit a reality to other people (p. 184). Bill's secretary, Nell Wing, said very simply that Bill took "Daily Practice" from the Oxford Group. Wing, *Grateful to have been there*, pp. 20-21.

The Oxford Group's "Four Absolutes"—honesty, purity, unselfishness, and love—are not mentioned as "absolutes" in the Big Book. But they were "yardstick" principles by which early AAs measured their conduct.[161] And the concepts of honesty, unselfishness, and love are still very much a part of A.A. thinking.

The Oxford Group neither could, nor tried to, lay special claim to God, the Bible, Jesus Christ, or the Holy Spirit; nor did they see themselves as a sect or religion. In fact, they proclaimed— whether warranted or not—a universality and compatibility with all Christian churches and religions. And as we take this brief look at Oxford Group traces in A.A.'s Big Book and Twelve Steps, we do not say that Oxford Group spiritual principles could not and cannot be found elsewhere. Bill Wilson himself said:

> The basic principles which the Oxford Groupers had taught were ancient and universal ones, the common property of mankind.[162]

And, of course, they *were*! Many of the Oxford Group principles came from the Old Testament—certainly not just the province of Christianity. And most Oxford Group principles came from the New Testament—certainly the province of all Christianity—Roman Catholic, Protestant, and other.

In making the foregoing statement about "ancient and universal" principles, Bill seemed desirous of broadening A.A.'s base. And he was safe—though the Oxford Group was the specific tutor—in pointing to Judeo-Christian origins. But when we point to Oxford Group traces in the Big Book and the Twelve Steps, we are pointing to the same source that A.A.'s co-founders did.

Oxford Group people often spoke of the beatitude, "Blessed are the pure in heart, for they shall see God."[163] And the Big Book, along with the Oxford Group, was concerned with removing the

---

[161] *DR. BOB*, p. 54.

[162] *AA Comes of Age*, p. 39. Compare *Twelve Steps and Twelve Traditions*, p. 16.

[163] Matthew 5:8.

"blocks" to God, which "shut ourselves off from the sunlight of
the Spirit."[164]

This picturesque language counsels a necessity for "cleansing"
to remove "blocks" in order to let God *in*. And 1 John 1:7 was a
verse that Frank Buchman often mentioned in this context. The
verse reads:

> But if we walk in the light, as he is in the light, we have
> fellowship one with another, and the blood of Jesus Christ his Son
> cleanseth us from all sin.[165]

We close by mentioning Bill's coverage of the "cleansing" idea
when he said, on page 98 of the Big Book, that the only condition
for getting well "is that he [the alcoholic] trust in God and clean
house." And we believe that the *practice* of spiritual principles
was—in Oxford Group and in A.A. parlance—intended to begin
with a "clean house"—a cleansing possible only by taking the life-
changing steps (guided and strengthened by the power of God).

---

[164] Big Book, pp. 64, 66, 71; and Dick B., *Anne Smith's Journal*, p. 93.

[165] Howard, *Frank Buchman's Secret*, p. 109; Belden, *Reflections on Moral Re-
Armament*, p. 51; Almond, *Foundations for Faith*, p. 15; and Phillimore, *Just for Today*,
p. 7. See also, 1 Corinthians 6:9-11, containing similar verses that meant a great deal
to Frank Buchman: "And such were some of you: but ye are washed, but ye are
sanctified, . . ." Howard, *Frank Buchman's Secret*, p. 40; Almond, *Foundations for
Faith*, pp. 10-11; and Spoerri, *Dynamic out of Silence*, p. 46.

Part 4

Other Spiritual Sources

"For the next three months, I [Bill Wilson] lived with these two wonderful people [Dr. Bob and Anne Smith]. I shall always believe they gave me more than I ever brought them."[1]

"The A.A. members of that time did not consider meetings necessary to maintain sobriety. They were simply 'desirable.' Morning devotion and 'quiet time,' were musts."[2]

---

[1] *DR. BOB and the Good Oldtimers*, p. 71.
[2] *DR. BOB*, p. 136.

11

Anne Smith—"Mother of A.A."

A Word about Anne

In our revised version of *Anne Smith's Journal, 1933-1939*, we devoted several pages to what Bill and Lois Wilson, early AAs, and others had to say about the contributions of Anne Ripley Smith (Dr. Bob's wife) to Alcoholics Anonymous.[1] Bill Wilson often called her the "Mother of A. A." He also said she was "one of the founders of Alcoholics Anonymous." We will now see why!

The following two additional comments about her bear repeating here:

> Anne's concern for the newcomer was both legendary and phenomenal--a greater concern, perhaps, than that of most A.A. members.[2]

> [She was] evangelist, nurse, salesman, employment bureau, all in one. . . . Anne's personal religion was simple and workable. She never sought to rewrite the Bible nor to explain it. She just accepted it.[3]

---

[1] Dick B., *Anne Smith's Journal, 1933-1939: A.A.'s Principles of Success* (San Rafael, CA: Paradise Research Publications, 1994), pp. 11-17.

[2] *DR. BOB and the Good Oldtimers* (New York: Alcoholics Anonymous World Services, Inc., 1980), p. 233.

[3] Dick B., *Anne Smith's Journal*, pp. 16-17.

The Elements of the Twelve Steps

Anne Smith began a spiritual quest, and also began keeping her spiritual Journal, in 1933. Her daughter, Sue, recalls that year as the starting point. And Anne frequently referred in her Journal to an Oxford Group Houseparty of 1933. We cannot be sure that Anne was referring specifically to the famous visit of Oxford Group Founder, Dr. Frank Buchman, and his team of thirty, to Akron, Ohio, in January, 1933. However, she must at least have been referring to Oxford Group activities which began to grow in Akron at that time. The Akron newspaper articles in January, 1933, told of Oxford Group events that centered around the Firestone family, the deliverance of Russell ("Bud") Firestone from alcoholism, and team witnessing in churches and at the Mayflower Hotel. But the papers also spoke of plans for subsequent houseparties and continuance of the Oxford Group team's work. History records that Anne Smith, T. Henry and Clarace Williams, Delphine Weber, and Henrietta Seiberling began attending Oxford Group events almost at once; and they were soon followed by Dr. Bob.

What is striking about Anne's spiritual Journal is its very specific language pertaining to, and its precise formulation of, each of twelve concepts Bill Wilson later codified into A.A.'s Twelve Steps for recovery from alcoholism. We have quoted her specific teachings throughout our title. Anne scarcely mentions liquor, but she certainly begins at the beginning—with the unmanageable life and the need for turning to God for help.

Here are her ideas as they seem to have found their way into the Twelve Steps, as AAs later put them together in 1939.

The Unmanageable Life and Step One

At three different places in her Journal, Anne prescribed a prayer for beginning one's search for a relationship with God. She wrote:

What do you do when you pray? O Lord manage me, for I cannot manage myself. That we are so in touch with the Holy Spirit that he can give us at that moment a message that is accurate and adequate. That is the release you want with people. Your prayers should always be different and straight to the point (pp. 26, 51, italics added).

Surrender is a simple act of will. What do we surrender? Our life. When? At a certain definite moment. How? *Oh God, manage me because I cannot manage myself* (p. 42, italics added).

Anne did not specify her source for this prayer. But the prayer was common in Oxford Group and Sam Shoemaker circles.[4] And Anne's "manage me" prayer was virtually identical to that in the "Victor story" and "Charlie's prayer" in the Oxford Group.

The Big Book's First Step language reads as follows:

We admitted we were powerless over alcohol—that *our lives had become unmanageable* (p. 59, italics added).

A Power Greater Than Ourselves and Step Two

Anne's language about "a power stronger than ourselves" closely resembles Big Book language. In a portion of her Journal which is titled, "Introduction," she spoke of this power. Her discussion had to do with "the beginning of the discovery that we can be set free from sin." Anne mentioned Romans 8, and the Apostle Paul, and said:

Paul speaks of a wish toward good, but power to carry it out is lacking. *A stronger power than his was needed.* God provided the power through Christ, so that we could find a new kind of relationship with God. Christ gives the power, we appropriate it. It is not anything that we do ourselves; but it is the appropriation

---

[4] See our discussion of the "manage me" prayer in Chapter 10 of this title.

of a power that comes from God that saves us from sin and sets us free (p. 37, italics added).

Anne repeated this language at page 56 of her Journal. The concept of a Power greater than one's own self, as a solution, was much discussed in Oxford Group literature that was mentioned by Anne and read by others in the Akron area. See the many parallels quoted in Appendix 2 to this title.[5]

In the Big Book chapter, "There is a Solution," Bill Wilson clarifies that will-power alone will not solve problems (pp. 22, 44). He points to the solution: establishing a relationship with God (p. 29). Then in his chapter, "We Agnostics," Bill wrote:

Lack of power, that was our dilemma. We had to find a power by which we could live, and it had to be a *Power greater than ourselves*. And it means, of course, that we are going to talk about God, . . . even though it was impossible for any of us to fully define or comprehend that Power, which is God (pp. 45-46 italics added).

A.A.'s Big Book not only states specifically, but also emphasizes, by the frequency of its mention, that the aim of its recovery program is the establishment of a relationship with God.[6] Shoemaker spoke of this relationship with similar frequency.[7] In *Children of the Second Birth*, he wrote:

We believe entirely that conversion is the experience which initiates the new life. But we are not fools enough to think that the beginning is the end! All subsequent life is a development of the relationship with God which conversion opened (p. 16).

---

[5] See also Stephen Foot, Life Began Yesterday (New York: Harper & Brothers, 1935), p. 22; Harold Begbie, *Life Changers* (London: Mills & Boon, 1932), p. 22.

[6] See Big Book, pp. 29, 13, 28, 100, 164.

[7] Samuel M. Shoemaker, *Realizing Religion* (New York: Association Press, 1923), p. 42; *Confident Faith* (New York: Fleming H. Revell, 1932), p. 110; *Christ's Words from the Cross* (New York: Fleming H. Revell, 1933), p. 49; *National Awakening* (New York: Harper & Brothers, 1936), p. 13.

Anne wrote:

> We must be in such relationship with God that He *can* guide us
> (p. 8, italics in original).

> God provided the power through Christ, so that we could find a
> new kind of relationship with God (p. 37).

> 2nd step. To get in right relationship with God (p. 62).

> Takes whole power of Christ to help us do the smallest thing.
> Step that puts man in position to receive the grace of God who
> alone commands. Surrender sins and wills putting God's will
> ahead. Whole thing begins to work (p. 57).

The Decision to Surrender to God
As You Understand Him and Step Three

A.A., Oxford Group, and Shoemaker language all emphasize that
the path to a relationship with God via a spiritual experience
begins with a *decision* to surrender to God. Anne's treatment of
the subject was no less precise. Our own discussion of the
surrender topic is divided into three parts.

1. *The decision.*

Speaking of a *decision* and "God *as you understand Him*,"
Anne wrote:

> Try to bring a person to a *decision* to "surrender as much of himself
> as he knows to as much of God as he knows." Stay with him until
> he makes a *decision* and says it aloud (p. 4, italics added).

Embodying this *decision* in A.A.'s Step Three, the Big Book said:

> Made a decision to turn our will and our lives over to the care of
> God *as we understood Him* (p. 59, italics in original).

2. *God as you understand Him.*

Bill indicated that Ebby (his friend and sponsor) had himself suggested to Bill *in 1934* that Bill surrender himself to God *as Bill understood Him.* Furthermore, both prior to 1934 and thereafter, Sam Shoemaker often spoken of "surrendering as much of yourself as you understand to as much of God as you understand."[8] Hence Ebby's suggestion to Bill was quite consistent with what Ebby had heard in the Oxford Group prior to the existence of A.A. Some Oxford Group writers used language quite similar to that which Anne used and *which we quoted above* as to surrendering all that one knows of self to all one knows of God.[9]

3. *The surrender.*

Anne defined surrender by referring to the language Professor William James used in *The Varieties of Religious Experience.*[10]:

> To be converted, to be regenerated, to receive grace, to experience religion, to gain an assurance, are so many phrases which denote the process, gradual or sudden, by which a self hitherto divided, and consciously wrong, inferior, and unhappy, becomes unified and consciously right, superior, and happy, in consequence of its firmer hold upon religious realities (p. 177).

Prefacing her use of the foregoing definition, Anne suggested that one surrender as much of himself as he knows to as much of God as he knows. Then, using James's language, she wrote:

---

[8] See Samuel M. Shoemaker, *Children of the Second Birth* (New York: Fleming H. Revell, 1927), pp. 27, 47; *How to Become a Christian* (New York: Harper & Brothers, 1953), p. 72; *How to Find God*, p. 6; "In Memoriam" (Princeton, The Graduate Council, June 10, 1956), pp. 2-3. See Dick B., *New Light on Alcoholism: The A.A. Legacy from Sam Shoemaker* (CA: Good Book Publishing Company, 1994), pp. 45, 350.

[9] Foot, *Life Began Yesterday*, pp. 12-13; Newton, *Uncommon Friends*, p. 154.

[10] William James, *The Varieties of Religious Experience* (New York: Vintage Books, 1990).

Release—surrender—conversion. William James defines it as "that process, gradual or sudden, by which a self divided, inferior, unhappy, and consciously wrong, becomes united, superior, happy, and consciously right." We usually have both sudden and gradual elements in our surrender (pp. 28, 56).

Sam Shoemaker frequently quoted the William James conversion definition.[11] And other Oxford Group writers referred to it.[12]

Writing of surrender, Anne said, "a real 100% surrender" meant surrender of a wide variety of things: (1) Will. (2) Thought of life. (3) Imagination. (4) Sub-conscious mind. (5) Time. (6) Possessions. (7) Possessive relationships. (8) Emotion. (9) Pride. (10) Fears. (11) Self Indulgence. (12) Laziness. (13) Tongue. (14) Plans "and all my rights." (15) Memory (p. 45). Anne used surrender language very similar to that in the Big Book's Third Step discussion, and to that used by Sam Shoemaker. She wrote:

Surrender is a complete handing over of our wills to God, a reckless abandon of ourselves, all that we have, all that we think, that we are, everything we hold dear, to God to do what he likes with . . . (p. 42).

Surrender . . . 1st step the life & will. Surrender--fears--sins-- most of all their wills--putting God's will ahead of everything (p. 61).[13]

---

[11] Shoemaker, *Realizing Religion*, p. 30; and see Dick B., *New Light on Alcoholism: The A.A. Legacy from Sam Shoemaker* (CA: Good Book Publishing Co., 1994), p. 41, n. 2.

[12] Compare Harold Begbie, *Twice-Born Men* (New York: Fleming H. Revell, 1909), pp. 16-18; *Life Changers*, p. 126; H. A. Walter, *Soul Surgery*, 6th ed. (Oxford: Printed at the University Press, 1940), p. 80. Recall too that Wilson referred to the James book by name in the Big Book (p. 28) and later called James a "founder" of A.A." (*Pass It On*, p. 124).

[13] Compare Shoemaker, *Children of the Second Birth*, p. 82; *Twice-Born Ministers* (New York: Fleming H. Revell, 1929), p. 134.

The Big Book's "Third Step Prayer" and discussion read:

> God, I offer myself to Thee—to build with me and to do with me as Thou wilt. Relieve me of the bondage of self, that I may better do Thy will. Take away my difficulties, that victory over them may bear witness to those I would help of Thy Power, Thy Love, and Thy Way of life. May I do Thy will always! We thought well before taking this step making sure we were ready; that we could at last abandon ourselves utterly to Him (p. 63).

Self-examination, the Moral Inventory and Step Four

Anne framed self-examination in terms of moral values, writing:

> Why are people so afraid to face their deepest problems? Because they think there is no answer. When they learn there is one, they will believe it can work out for them, and they will be really honest about themselves. . . . It is absolutely necessary to face people with the moral test. Fundamentally, sin is independence toward God, living without God. Seeing one's self as God sees one, brings hatred out of sin (p. 4).

> It's not self-examination but God's examination (p. 44).

> Much criticism is second-hand gossip. . . . When people persistently criticize, ask them, "What's wrong with *you*?" Years of clinical experience are back of this principle (p. 3).

Anne cited several Bible verses from the Sermon on the Mount, which were quoted in the Oxford Group and followed in A.A.[14] Anne wrote:

---

[14] Matthew 7:1-5. For Oxford Group writings citing these verses, see Allen, *He That Cometh*, pp. 81, 140; Victor Kitchen, *I Was a Pagan* (New York: Harper & Brothers, 1934), pp. 110-11; Shoemaker, *The Church Can Save the World*, pp. 81-121; *God's Control* (New York: Fleming H. Revell, 1939), pp. 62-72. The verses were also cited in the popular devotional, Oswald Chambers, *My Utmost for His Highest* ((London: Simpkin Marshall, 1927), pp. 169-74; Compare Russell, *For Sinners Only*, pp. 309-16.

Who checks another checks himself. If I have an urge to check because of personal feelings, I am not seeing in light of Christ's love. Criticism born of my own projection. Something wrong in me. Unless I can crystalize the criticism, *I had better look for mote in my eye* (p. 7, italics added).

We have previously quoted the Big Book's self-examination instructions, which suggested that one look first for one's *own* faults (Big Book, pp. 64, 67, 69).

As we have explained, the Oxford Group suggested "making the moral test."[15] H. A. Walter's *Soul Surgery* said that the concept, "make the moral test," came from Frank Buchman's and Sherwood Eddy's "Ten Suggestions for Personal Work."[16] Anne specifically mentioned Eddy's ten suggestions in her Journal (p. 14).

The moral test meant examining one's life to see how it measured up to the Oxford Group's Four Absolutes—honesty, purity, unselfishness, and love.[17] It meant writing down on a piece of paper the items in a person's life which showed where that person had fallen short of the standards set by Jesus in the Sermon on the Mount and elsewhere.

Anne frequently advocated testing or checking conduct against the four standards of Jesus. She wrote:

Test your thoughts. It is possible to receive suggestions from your subconscious mind. Check your thoughts by the four standards of Christ (p. 9).

[Quoting from Frank Buchman's ten suggestions for personal work, Anne wrote:] Make the moral test. 4 Standards (p. 14).

---

[15] See Dick B., *Design for Living: The Oxford Group's Contribution to Alcoholics Anonymous* (San Rafael, CA: Paradise Research Publications, 1995), pp. 184-88.

[16] Walter, *Soul Surgery*, pp. 43-44.

[17] See C. Rose, *When Man Listens*, pp. 18-19; Oliver Jones, *Inspired Children* (New York: Harper & Brothers, 1933), pp. 47-68; *Inspired Youth* (New York: Harper & Brothers, 1938), p. 41; Hallen Viney, *How Do I Begin?* (The Oxford Group, 1937), pp. 2-4.

Basis of an Interview. Is a challenge on the four standards (p. 29).

What to do with a person who is muddle-headed? Make a list. Help them to make a list of things (pp. 25, 29).

What thoughts do I expect? Am I ready to write them down and willing? It is not making my mind a blank but trusting God to use my mind, my thought life and my imagination. First of all come uncomfortable thoughts of wrong relationships with family, friends and people I work with. Resentments to be faced and set right. Restitution to be made, bills, letters, untidy desks, or house to be set straight (p. 43).

Behind every general need is a particular moral need, so that a general surrender will focus into one point (p. 51).

Surrender on one's moral issue. Destroy the thing that [?] nearest. Then next step becomes plain (p. 57).

Anne also made other references to the four absolutes and stated:

Why I [?]—had been absolutely honest but not living (p. 7).

[Referring to love:] Follow Christ's absolute commandment (p. 22).

Absolute honesty demands that we no longer wear a mask (p. 32).

Sharing . . . It is being honest even after it hurts (p. 34).

Every time we register aloud the new attitude and change of heart with absolute honesty another bridge is burned behind us and another stake is driven in to anchor and mark our progress (p. 46).

Check your life constantly by the four absolutes (p. 49).[18]

---

[18] *DR. BOB and the Good Oldtimers* (pp. 54, 163) shows the vitality of the Four Absolutes in early A.A. See also *Alcoholics Anonymous Comes of Age*, pp. 68, 75, 161; *Pass It On*, p. 127, 171-73; *The Language of the Heart* (New York: The A.A.
(continued...)

Dr. Bob went to great length in his last major talk to A.A. at Detroit, Michigan, in December, 1948, to elaborate on the importance of the four absolutes and how he applied them.[19] But the language of A.A.'s Big Book shifted from "absolute" to less stringent "standards." The self-examination of the *Big Book's* "moral inventory" required looking for "resentments" and "grudges;" "selfishness" and "self-seeking;" "dishonesty;" "fears;" and the harms to others that accompanied them.[20] These, said the Big Book, were the common manifestations of ego-centricity, self-centeredness, and self-will run riot that blocked the alcoholic from God and left that person spiritually sick.[21] These were the subjects which were—in A.A.'s Fourth Step, Tenth Step, and Eleventh Step inventories—to be listed on paper or in a daily review so they could be eliminated.[22]

Anne Smith was very practical in her treatment of the four absolute "yardsticks." And, long before the Twelve Steps were written, she wrote and taught about the manifestations of self that blocked people from God. The following were some of her comments:

---

[18] (...continued)
Grapevine, Inc., 1988), pp. 196-200; Richmond Walker, *For Drunks Only* (MN: Hazelden, n.d.), Preface, p. 3; p. 6; Mel B., *New Wine: The Spiritual Roots of the Twelve Step Miracle* (MN: Hazelden, 1991), pp. 21, 41, 64, 76, 95, 98, 138, 139.

[19] *The Co-Founders of Alcoholics Anonymous: Biographical sketches. Their last major talks* (New York: Alcoholics Anonymous World Services, 1972, 1975), pp. 12-14.

[20] Big Book: (1) Resentments and grudges, pp. 13, 64-67, 84, 86; (2) Selfishness and self-seeking, pp. 14, 61, 62, 67, 69, 84, 86; (3) Dishonesty, pp. 13, 28, 58, 65, 69, 70, 73, 84, 86; (4) Fear, pp. 62, 67, 68, 78, 84, 86; and (5) Harms to others, pp. 13, 67, 69, 70, 76, 77-84, 86.

[21] Big Book, pp. 64, 71, 72. See as to the Oxford Group definition of sin—"those sins which block us from God and from other people": Dick B., *The Oxford Group*, pp. 130-34.

[22] Big Book, pp. 64, 68-70, 84, 86.

Emotion—anger, irritability, envy, jealousy, hurt feelings, self pity, sentimentality, which is enjoyment without responsibility, wasting emotions (pp. 17, 45).[23]

Resentments to be faced and set right (p. 18).

What makes us ineffective . . . resentments (p. 31).

Fears—of inefficiency, incompetence, failing powers of application and success, about our body and its functions. Our minds, the way they work and the way they refuse to work; of infection, of serious illness, of a helpless and hopeless old age; of the loss of your husband's love, interpreting and misinterpreting his every movement, dreading every slight variation from the habitual routine of domestic life as a possible bringer of ill; afraid of what your children may do or be, or say, surrounding your whole family with an attitude of discomfort and nagging distrust of facing death; and of your secret self, of discouragement; and public speaking (pp. 17, 45).

Our pride and fear . . . (p. 32).

Fear and worry are atheism. And we have not left that behind when we take up this way of life. To be willing to be a fool for Christ's sake is something different from being foolish.[24] Fear of poverty, illness, death, fear of people, fear of opinions (p. 37).

List of my sharing. Not costly—fear—worry—small conviction. Fear of what people would think of me. Hadn't faced myself honestly (p. 32).

---

[23] Compare the following in the Big Book: (1) We are then in much less danger of excitement, fear, anger, worry, self-pity, or foolish decisions, p. 88; (2) The greatest enemies of us alcoholics are resentments, jealousy, envy, frustration, and fear, p. 145.

[24] See 1 Corinthians 4:10: "We *are* fools for Christ's sake, but ye *are* wise in Christ; we *are* weak, but ye *are* strong; ye *are* honorable, but we *are* despised." See Shoemaker, *Children of the Second Birth*, pp. 65-80. Shoemaker devoted an entire chapter to "A Fool for Christ;" and this was one of the books Anne Smith highly recommended.

How much place do fear and apprehension hold in my life (p. 50)?

I must let Christ run my life—always self before. Release from fear, timidity, inferiority. . . . Just a glimpse of a self-centered life. Fears as a child. Of trouble. Of what others thought. Of people (p. 53).

Telling a lie (pp. 18, 44).

Share dishonesty (p. 29).

Confession, Sharing with Another and Step Five

A.A.'s Fifth Step has a very clear origin in James 5:16:

Confess *your* faults one to another, and pray one for another, that ye may be healed. The effectual fervent prayer of a righteous man availeth much.[25]

The Fifth Step also suggests the confidential sharing of wrongs, shortcomings, and faults with another human being and with God. Anne Smith laid out these ideas in her Journal, saying:

Confess your faults one to another. Sharing is having your life at God's disposal (p. 55).

Sharing in Team Work. 1. Sharing the only basis of Scriptural team work. 3. Sharing builds a fellowship. 4. Sharing builds a team. 8. Honest sharing issues in action. 10. The only reason we don't share is because we cannot see the victory (p. 35).

Positive reasons why we should share. 1. As we live a spiritual life, sharing becomes natural. 2. There is no adequate presentation

---

[25] See Dick B., *The Akron Genesis of Alcoholics Anonymous* (CA: Good Book Publishing Co., 1994), pp. 192-97, for a discussion of the impact of James 5:13-16 on the procedures early Akron AAs followed for prayer, healing, confession, and surrender.

of Christ without sharing our own sins. 3. We share because
common honesty demands it. 4. Maximum usefulness demands it.
Begin with known, and go on with the unknown. 5. It's the
answer to loneliness. As we take down walls, we begin to give
ourselves to others. 6. Because it's the basis of spiritual
teamwork. The only answer to jealousy is to own up to it. Keep
free of mental reservation and you begin to trust each other and
become a spiritual power house for the community (p. 33).

Kinds of Sharing. 1. Sharing for cure. 2. Sharing for release
(confession). 3. Sharing for action. 4. Sharing for witness. 5.
Sharing to build up fellowship in a team. 6. As restitution and a
basis for honest living (p. 33).

Principles of Sharing. 1. All sharing must be under guidance. 2.
You do not tell everybody everything every time but you are
ready to tell anybody anything at any time under guidance. 3.
There is nothing in our lives that we are not willing to share. It
is the quality of willingness. 4. Never betray a confidence. 5.
Never share anybody else's sin. 6. Never involve another against
his wishes. 7. No detailed confessions in public. 8. The extent of
sharing in public should be co-extensive with the wrong done. If
you have wronged a community, you must share in a community.
9. It is not enough to share the truth, but share truth in love.
Ephesians 4:5. 10. Share specifically, uncomfortably so. 11.
Sharing in love without truth, sentimentality. Sharing truth
without love, brutality. 12. Pray before you share, quietly. 13.
We can make sharing with God alone a loophole, it may be too
general. It is more definite with a person. 14. Sharing is a matter
of being free from our own problems in order to be used by God.
15. Share your life completely with one person at a time, so that
there is nothing that you have not shared with someone at some
time (pp. 33-34).

Dangers of sharing: 1. Is it uncomfortable? 2. Is it dangerous to
me, or my reputation, or to Christ? 3. The world is full of
witness as to the dangers of not sharing, i.e., psychiatrists, ill
health, nervous breakdowns, hospitals, bad theology, unbelief,
spiritual impotency, divorce, asylums, broken homes, and lonely

lives. The only danger really is when people live a half truth and begin to compromise (p. 34).

Sharing in relationship to the Gospel: 1. Matthew 3:6 Sins Confessed.[26] 2. Mark 1:5 Sins Confessed.[27] 3. Matthew 4:1-11 Christ shares his temptations.[28] 4. James 5:16 Share "My Life". Not confess ye one another's sins.[29] 5. Acts 26 Paul's defence before Agrippa.[30] 6. 2nd. Cor 5:21 The inevitable sequence. Are

---

[26] Matthew 3:6 [Speaking of John the Baptist] "And were baptized of him in Jordan, confessing their sins."

[27] Mark 1:5 [Speaking of John the Baptist] "And there went out unto him all the land of Judaea, and they of Jerusalem, and were all baptized of him in the river of Jordan, confessing their sins."

[28] The account in Matthew 4:1-11 is of Jesus's being led up of the Spirit into the wilderness to be tempted of the devil. The devil came to Jesus, stating that if he (Jesus) were the Son of God, he could command stones to be made bread. But Jesus replied, quoting Scripture, and stated: "It is written, Man shall not live by bread alone, but by every word that proceedeth out of the mouth of God." Then the devil challenged Jesus to cast himself down from the pinnacle of the temple since it was written that God would give Jesus his angels to protect him. Again, Jesus quoted Scripture, stating, "It is written again, Thou shalt not tempt the Lord thy God." Finally, the devil offered Jesus all the kingdoms of the world and the glory of them if Jesus would fall down and worship him. Again Jesus quoted Scripture, telling the devil to "get thee hence," again stating, "for it is written, Thou shalt worship the Lord thy God, and him only shalt thou serve."

[29] James 5:16: "Confess *your* faults one to another, and pray for one another, that ye may be healed."

[30] Acts 26 tells of Paul's answers to King Agrippa concerning charges against him. Paul said he would answer "all the things whereof I am accused of the Jews." He told of his youth, his life as a Pharisee, and of his standing, judged "for the hope of the promise made of God unto our fathers." He asked Agrippa "Why should it be thought a thing incredible with you, that God should raise the dead?" Paul said he had shut many saints up in prison, and gave voice against them so they would be put to death. He said he had persecuted them. Then he told of his conversion on the road to Damascus. He said Jesus had appeared to make him (Paul) a minister and a witness and sending him to the Gentiles to open their eyes, turn them from darkness to light, and from the power of Satan to God so they could receive forgiveness of their sins. He said he had told all they should repent and turn to God and that he was saying nothing that Moses and the prophets had not said concerning things to come. He then said his message was "That Christ should suffer, *and* that he should be first that should rise from the dead, and should shew light unto the people, and to the Gentiles." Paul asked Agrippa if he believed the prophets. Agrippa replied to Paul, "Almost thou persuadest me to be a Christian." Agrippa then declared Paul had done nothing worthy of death or of bonds.

we willing to become sinners in the eyes of our friends that they become righteous, putting the atonement into practice in life. "Greater love hath no man than this, that a man lay down his life for his friends," so that your friends may see how to live.[31]

Sharing . . . 2. All sharing must be redemptive. 3. Being honest to God, self and other people . . . 9. We share to prove that no one's problem is unique . . . 11. It is being honest even after it hurts. 12. It is giving your real self to another person. 13. How unnatural it is not to live a sharing life. 14. I start by rebelling against sharing, so talk it over with one other person. 15. Sins appear different under four eyes. 16. Sharing burns out the pride of self.

James—Confess your faults one to another 5:16 & pray one for another that ye may be healed (p. 32).

I must share to be honest with God, myself & others (p. 32).

Each confession a fresh humiliation breaks down another barrier. You can get to the place where you have nothing left to defend—that is release. You can go naked to God (p. 18).

Inadequate sharing. We have not fully shared with some one else. Egoism or pride is one of the greatest of our enemies. Sharing with another under guidance roots it out (p. 16).

Confession. Don't be shocked at any confession. It is hypocritical for you yourself have at least thought of doing something similar. A man may share many problems, but not his deepest one. You must share deeply with him, *under guidance* [italics in original]; You may be guided to share your deepest sin, and this will clear the way for him to share his. The time will come when he will

---

[31] 2 Corinthians 5:21: "For he [God] hath made him [Christ] *to be* sin for us, who knew no sin; that we might be made the righteousness of God in him." Anne's quote about "Greater love hath no man" is from John 15:13: "Greater love hath no man than this, that a man lay down his life for his friends."

begin to tell you things about himself that he doesn't tell to others
(p. 4).

As shown above, Anne quoted James 5:16 twice in her Journal in
connection with admitting one's faults or sins. The Oxford Group
quoted James 5:16 in the confession context.[32] And so did Sam
Shoemaker.[33]

The concept of being honest with God, with another, and with
yourself was also a well established Oxford Group concept.[34] And
what is noteworthy here is the remarkable similarity between the
Big Book's Fifth Step language and that used by Anne Smith a
number of years before the Big Book was written. We suggest the
reader compare Anne's language above with the following in the
Big Book:

> This [casting out the weak items in the moral inventory] requires
> action on our part, which, when completed, will mean that we
> have admitted to God, to ourselves, and to another human being,
> the exact nature of our defects. . . . This is perhaps
> difficult—especially discussing our defects with another person.
> We think we have done well enough in admitting these things to
> ourselves. There is doubt about that. In actual practice, we usually
> find a solitary self-appraisal insufficient. . . . Time after time
> newcomers have tried to keep to themselves certain facts about
> their lives.
> . . . Almost invariably they got drunk. . . . They took inventory
> all right, but hung on to some of the worst items in stock. They
> only *thought* they had lost their egoism and fear; they only
> *thought* they had humbled themselves. But they had not learned
> enough of humility, fearlessness and honesty, in the sense we find
> it necessary, until they told someone else *all* their life story. . . .
> Psychologists are inclined to agree with us. . . . We have seldom

---

[32] J. P. Thornton-Duesbury, *Sharing* (Pamphlet of The Oxford Group, published at
Oxford University Press, n.d.), p. 5; Sherwood Sunderland Day, *The Principles of The
Group* (Oxford: University Press, n.d.), p. 6; *What Is The Oxford Group?*, p. 29, 31.

[33] Shoemaker, *The Conversion of the Church*, p. 35.

[34] Shoemaker, *The Church Can Save the World*, pp. 110-12.

told them the whole truth nor have we followed their advice.
Unwilling to be honest with these sympathetic men, we were
honest with no one else. . . . We must be entirely honest with
somebody if we expect to live long or happily in this world.
Rightly and naturally, we think well before we choose the person
or persons with whom to take this intimate and confidential step.
. . . we search our acquaintance for a close-mouthed, understanding friend. . . . We pocket our pride and go to it, illuminating every twist of character, every dark cranny of the past (pp.
72-75, italics in original).

Conviction, Readiness to Be Changed and Step Six

The third "C" in the Oxford Group's Five C's was Conviction;
and A.A.'s Sixth Step is deals with "repentance," or "willingness
to be changed." As we have said, some, including this author,
believe that the Oxford Group's "Conviction" idea was codified in
A.A.'s Sixth Step.[35]

Anne had the following things to say about willingness to
change and having God "remove" the defects of character
uncovered in the moral inventory and confession (Fourth and Fifth
Step) process:

[Specifically discussing "The Five C's"] 3. Conviction. . . . Stay
with him until he makes a decision and says it aloud (p. 4).

In the early stages, win confidence. Think of meeting the other
person's real needs. If you have a sense that something in him is
not shared, it will block progress in meeting his real needs. It is
like building a house and leaving huge boulders under it; you
can't build a spiritual life for another without clearing the
foundations. Many people go into tirades about sin in the national
life, but refuse to deal with it in their own life. Challenge them as
to how much they really care about such situations (p. 5).

---

[35] See Mel B., *New Wine*, pp. 34-35. AA of Akron's *Spiritual Milestones* specifically
urged to AAs: "Eliminate sin from our lives" (pp. 1-2).

Lives depend on our openness to do God's will, a channel not a source. God more concerned than we. Need not fuss and stew if they don't yield if you are not right with God's will (p. 6).

Obedience is one of the key-words of the Christian life. Refusal to obey blocks the channel, and prevents further word from God (p. 16).

Barriers to a full surrender. 1. Is there anything I won't give up? 2. Is there any apology I won't make. . . . 13. Ideas about self—holding on to my own judgment of things, people, common sense and reason (p. 18).

Be willing to ask God where I am failing and to admit sin (p. 18).

Look out for denials, protests, self-justification, evasions, undue emotions (p. 25).

The next step is the Cross. Get them to the place where they appropriate it. Get them to face up to the thing that is their cross in life. Pray aloud with them. We cannot pray anyone else into the Kingdom. . . . It is not enough to surrender sin, but we must also claim the victory of the resurrection life. It is God that does it. Nothing you can do is of any use (pp. 25, 30).

Have you a Christ that can rid you of your sins and send you on your way rejoicing (p. 26)?

What is it that gives you the ability to make a right diagnosis? The fact that you have had a deep conviction yourself. . . . Do not be diverted from your main purpose of conquering sins. . . . If this is to happen, men have to have free minds, and to smash old modes of thought and points of view which have been built up on a rigid interpretation of the Bible. The Holy Spirit is ready to dictate a perfect plan (p. 19).

What makes us ineffective? 1. Trying to keep up appearances. 2. Pride in station of life. 3. Self pity—the most unnerving atmosphere in which one can live. 4. Memory of unshared sins:

undone restitutions; possessions; unfulfilled guidance; self consciousness; unwillingness to surrender something; unwillingness to check plans with someone else; resentments; sentimental relationships; undue solicitude to find God's will (p. 31).

There are some definite barriers which we must recognize. There is also growth, and each day we see more and more things that need to be surrendered. A small sense of sin means a small sense of Christ. The closer you get to Christ, the more sensitive you become to sin. The whiter the cloth, the more easily it is stained (pp. 37, 56).

If there is anything in us which blocks God's work, it matters to God. Sin isn't merely an inconvenience to us, it is serious business. Keep your marginal areas free from sin in your life. Marginal areas of discipline must be so clear that you don't come within a mile of temptation. What are your marginal areas?—tongue, imagination. Be watchful always. John Wesley said, "Give me a hundred men who fear nothing but God and hate nothing but sin, and I will sweep the world" (p. 38).

It is because we have ignored sin in our presentation of the Gospel that the message of the Gospel has lost its sting and blasting power. Our first need is an emetic, not a narcotic. This emetic is facing the barrier, that is, our specific sins which are keeping us from Christ and from this complete and utter giving of ourselves to Christ. The real test of a surrendered life is that we are nice to live with. Surrender takes away the shams and gives us real life. Complete surrender brings us to the point where the most trivial of incidents will witness to the love of God. . . . You can't surrender sin if you won't admit it. . . . Be willing to admit a tendency to see ourselves as passions and instincts. The issue is to run away or surrender. Surrender to Christ or criticize the group. The welling up of criticism is the externalization of more sin (p. 42).

The Big Book describes the Sixth Step itself in just one paragraph:

> We have emphasized willingness as being indispensable. Are we
> now ready to let God remove from us all the things which we
> have admitted are objectionable? Can He now take them
> all—every one? If we still cling to something we will not let go,
> we ask God to help us to be willing (p. 76).

As shown, Anne spoke mainly about facing up to the things that
need to be changed, and then being willing to turn to God to be rid
of these "sins."

Surrender of Sins, God's Removal and Step Seven

For many Oxford Group people, surrender and conversion were
rooted in John 3:3-8—being born again of the spirit.[36] Anne
Smith used a number of expressions for surrender, conversion, and
this new birth; and many found their way into A.A. and its Big
Book. She wrote:

> Conversion. This is the turning to God, the decision, the
> surrender (p. 4).

> A maximum experience of Jesus Christ leads to a radical change
> in personal life, bringing about a selfless relationship to people
> about one, which is a challenge to those we come in contact with
> (p. 29).

> God is willing to take my past spiritual experience and weld it in
> a new spiritual experience, God has spoken. The moment I hear
> and obey His voice and come to the place of complete surrender

---

[36] See Henry Drummond, *The Ideal Life* (New York: Hodder & Stoughton, 1897),
p. 211; Frank Buchman, *Remaking the World* (London: Blandford Press, 1961), p. 23;
Begbie, *Life Changers*, p. 104; Geoffrey Allen, *He That Cometh* (New York: Macmillan,
1932), pp. 19-43; Jones, *Inspired Children*, p. 136; Samuel M. Shoemaker, *National
Awakening*, pp. 55, 57, 58; *Twice-Born Ministers*, pp. 56, 10; *By the Power of God*
(New York: Harper & Brothers, 1954), pp. 28-33.

on every area of my life, is the moment of *rebirth*, reunion with Christ and a start on great revival campaign. *Rebirth*, reunion, revival involves decision, discipline and dare. . . . Surrender involves the explosive experience of a Holy Ghost conversion, the expulsive power of a new affection (p. 42, italics added).

[Speaking of sins such as possessiveness, temper, selfishness, dishonesty, and pride:] Christ can only *remove* them and replace with a new quality of life. Read Romans 12 (p. 36, italics added).[37]

Paul's advice. Stop trying to be good. Sounds dangerous. Really honest person knows he cannot reach goal of Goodness God desires. Face the truth. Do not pretend you can go on lifting yourself by your own boot straps. In all humility to God, "What would thou have me to do?" . . . I'm wrong Father. You know better than I, you have more wisdom, show me the way (p. 61).

In its "Seventh Step Prayer," the Big Book states:

My Creator, I am now willing that you should have all of me, good and bad. I pray that you now *remove* from me every single defect of character which stands in the way of my usefulness to you and my fellows. Grant me strength, as I go out from here, to do your bidding. Amen (p. 76, italics added).

Restitution, Amends, and Steps Eight and Nine

As previously stated, Anne specified as one of the barriers to a full surrender, "Any restitution I won't make" (pp. 18, 43). She

---

[37] Oxford Group writer, Geoffrey Allen, said, in *He That Cometh*, that God can *remove* the things which fall short of the standard of fearless, spontaneous love, and which are symptoms of sin with which the devil may make us complacent (p. 147). Anne Smith recommended Allen's book in her Journal. Victor Kitchen, a popular Oxford Group writer in 1934 and a friend of Bill Wilson's, wrote, in *I Was a Pagan*, about God's *removing* selfish desire at the time of surrender. Kitchen said, "God simply lifted that desire entirely out of my life" (pp. 73-74).

repeated this reference to setting things right and making restitution, listing "Resentments to be faced and set right" and "Restitution to be made" (pp. 18, 43). Then, in describing how to help people change, she wrote: "Help them make a list of things" (pp. 25, 29). Returning to the subject of amends, she wrote: "Restitution. In the matter of restitution, international retraction should be made by a positive, public statement equal in scope to the amount of damage done" (pp. 26, 51). On the topic of "willingness," she wrote:

> God can make me willing in the day of His power. Joy comes in being committed right to the very end. Attempt great things of God, and see the daily victories of the living God. This involves and enterprises discipleship under the guidance of the Holy Spirit, running up our colors, and helping others to run up theirs (p. 42).

As we point out in our discussion of Oxford Group principles, Anne did not devote nearly as much space in her Journal to the restitution topic as she did to many other concepts which influenced A.A.

Continued Inventory, Daily Surrender and Step Ten

A.A.'s Tenth Step speaks to maintenance of the spiritual condition achieved through taking the previous nine Steps. It also challenges alcoholics "to grow in understanding and effectiveness." It says, "This is not an overnight matter. It should continue for our lifetime."[38]

For the Oxford Group and Sam Shoemaker, this involved the concept of "continuance" or "conservation"—the so-called fifth of the "Five C's."[39] In the Oxford Group/Shoemaker circles, in which early AAs were traveling, there were five aspects of

---

[38] See Big Book, pp. 84-85.

[39] See Begbie, *Life Changers*, p. 169 [calling the process "Continuance"]; Walter, *Soul Surgery*, pp. 89-100 [calling it "Conservation"]; and Shoemaker, *Realizing Religion*, pp. 79-80 [calling it "Conservation"].

"continuance": (1) Prayer; (2) Bible study; (3) Guidance; (4) Group worship; and (5) Witness.[40] They were part of the continuing process of "Daily surrender."[41]

Anne was right on target with these ideas for maintaining the spiritual glow and growing in the application of spiritual principles. She wrote:

> Continuance. Stay with the newly surrendered person until he grows up and becomes a life-changer. Laugh him out of his growing pains. When he becomes a life-changer, we need not fear for him, because other people's needs will drive him back to God (p. 4).

> Be willing to live a day at a time, an hour at a time (p. 9).[42]

> 3. What are the symptoms of let down or compromise in myself? . . . 5. Are quiet times increasingly real?. . . 7. Is there some relationship I am content to leave where it is? 8. Am I giving the right nurture to those changed? . . . 13. How much better do I know my Bible this year than last? . . . 14. Is my reading guided? (p. 10).

> Be willing to ask God where I am failing and to admit sin. 1. Am I nicer to live with? 2. Better to work with? 3. More efficient with my job? (p. 18).

> Paderewski [the famous concert pianist]: If I go one day without practicing the piano, I notice it in my playing; if I go two days my friends notice it; if I go three days the audience notices it (p. 31).

> Am I so living with God that Christ is being breathed around? You cannot sublimate an instinct that you don't recognize. You

---

[40] Dick B., *Design for Living*, pp. 221-24.

[41] Dick B., *Design for Living*, pp. 224-27.

[42] See our subsequent Eleventh Step discussion of *guidance* and Bill's uses of the "one day at a time" slogan.

can't surrender sin if you don't admit it. A personal relationship with Jesus Christ depends on doing difficult things (p.42).

Willingness to maintain an antiseptic attitude with regard to personal situations while in the process of redemption. To be willing to face up that I alone am responsible for my attitude. Claim from God humility, patience, courage, faith, and love. These are gifts. We cannot qualify for them (p. 43).

Let your waking thought be surrender, a 100% *daily* surrender (p. 43, italics added).

After surrender [italics in original]: The difference is that when you discover sin and problems in your life, you know the answer, and you have the cure. There must be a focus of the issue when the mind is made up: then follows development. As we grow closer to Christ we keep seeing more sin, but we know the cure (p. 44).

"Continue in the faith . . . and be not moved away from the hope of the Gospel." Colossians 1:23.[43]

One of the weaknesses of what may be termed the "Old Evangelism" of the mass type was the lack of continuance. It seemed to be taken for granted that a surrendered person would naturally be able to continue what he had begun and would henceforth know of himself what the steps of strengthening should be. The truth is that many many people reached by the mass method did discover and take these steps, but it is safe to say that the majority fell by the wayside. The Oxford Group Movement believes strongly in Continuance. It further believes that every person (surrendered) needs careful nurture and help in life changing.

---

[43] Colossians 1:23: "If ye continue in the faith grounded and settled, and *be* not moved away from the hope of the gospel, which ye have heard, *and* which was preached to every creature which is under heaven; whereof I Paul am made a minister."

Anne devoted three pages to suggested steps for continuance (pp. 46-49). Here are the subject headings for items Anne covered as to continuance—subjects treated in more detail in Chapter Eight:

1. Face the past for what it really was.
2. Burn all bridges behind you.
3. Witness to some friend who has come to you.
4. Practice daily surrender.
5. Daily Quiet Time.
6. Be alert for symptoms of let-down.
7. Blocks to Guidance.
8. Let all your reading be guided.
9. Let friends and relationships with others be guided.
10. Unite with a fellowship of kindred souls.
11. Don't try, but trust.
12. This quality of life is an adventure not an arrival.
13. Worth remembering.

The Big Book summarizes the Tenth Step process as follows: "Continued to take personal inventory and when we were wrong promptly admitted it" (p. 59). It suggests details:

Continue to watch for selfishness, dishonesty, resentment, and fear. When these crop up, we ask God at once to remove them. We discuss them with someone immediately and make amends quickly if we have harmed anyone. Then we resolutely turn our thoughts to someone we can help. Love and tolerance of others is our code (p. 84).

Quiet Time, Prayer, Bible Study, Listening, God's Will, Guidance and Step Eleven

Prayer, Bible study, spiritual reading, listening for guidance, and the Quiet Time were supremely important in early A.A. Anne Smith was in the thick of sharing and teaching about them.

And here are some of the specifics Anne wrote in her Journal and shared with others in the morning meetings, on the telephone, and in the "spiritual pablum" visits by early AAs and their families to her home:

1. **Prayer**.

Why not answered. Until we are ready to fulfil the conditions, the deepest wishes of our heart cannot be realized. . . . Intercessory prayer—pray that Spirit may tell you what to pray for. . . . A way to find God's will not to change it. Right orientation of soul toward God. Conceive God as Father and it is not unnatural to lay before Him our hopes and needs—interest—fears (p. 58).

Petitionary prayers. Expressions of sound instinct as long as we do not use to set right something for a grudging God. Means expression of our wants which we deeply feel and which it would be hypocrisy to pretend we didn't. These we submit not because we distrust His goodness or desire to bend His Will but because He is our Friend. Similarly it would be unnatural not to submit to God the needs of others and our hopes and fears for them. If then we didn't find ourselves desiring to pray for them as we pray for ourselves we are not traveling in right direction (p. 58).

Intercessory prayer. If successful, weighty testimony. (p. 59).

Prayer for others to hold them before God, to Him to give the thing they need but in spiritual concentration putting our personality, known or unknown, explained or unexplained, at His service. God's prayer—a trust in God—fellow man and myself. Correct me—direct—praise—adoration and thanksgiving. Romans II. God can guide thru other people (p. 59).

Difference [?] would make in attitude of prayer. Quiet approach of a child ready to receive. Not about our needs but taking matters to God and having communion with Him (Your Heavenly Father knows ye have needs of all these things).[44] More ready

---

[44] From Matthew 6:33 in the Sermon on the Mount, "for your Father knoweth what things ye have need of, before ye ask him."

to hear than we to pray. Would to be shown spirit of prayer—gladness and faith (p. 6).

2. **Guidance.**

Guidance. Guidance is the principle of the Bible, its very structure. "God spoke" to Moses, to the prophets, to the Apostles. Paul was constantly guided by the Holy Spirit. Jesus was in constant touch with the Father. The Acts of the Apostles is called the Book of the Holy Spirit. The Bible is *guidance written down.* Modern theologians rule these things out of the Bible, because they don't realize that they still happen (Psalms 73 and 139). These things are in the background of the human race. The Constitution was written under Guidance. Hymn writers throughout the ages have realized guidance. The Holy Spirit is the teacher. "He will guide you into all truth" (p. 8, italics in original).[45]

What are the conditions of receiving God's guidance? We must be in such relationship with God that He *can* guide us; He will not force Himself on us.[46] The Sons of God are those who are guided by the Spirit of God. If we are wholly surrendered, we can absolutely count on guidance. Constant renewal of consecration is necessary. *Surrender is not an attitude attained; it is an attitude maintained.* The major condition is being absolutely willing and looking for God's direction in *all* things. We cannot receive guidance if we hold back an area, an habit, a plan. We must be alert to His direction in *Everything*; little things, as well as big ones such as career and marriage (p. 8, italics in original).

How does guidance come? Granted we are living so we can receive guidance, it comes to us in all the ways of human understanding. It could come in no other way. If God spoke in any other way we wouldn't understand it at all. Don't expect guidance

---

[45] From John 16:13, "Howbeit when he, the Spirit of truth, is come, he will guide you into all truth . . ."

[46] Compare Big Book, p. 164.

in abnormal ways. Guidance is normal. Specifically, guidance comes through intelligent knowledge of the Bible, through *conscience* [italics in original], through *circumstance* [italics in original]. But some of us must surrender our conscience, because we are over conscientious. We always feel we must do the difficult or uncomfortable thing. God speaks through circumstance, but He may guide us to overcome circumstance. Guidance comes through reason and through common sense. Guidance is not a substitute for what you should do yourself. *guidance is thinking plus God* [italics in original].[47] God will guide us in many ways; through church; through Fellowship. The clearest guidance comes through a group, although we are not always willing to have another help us decide.[48] Guidance comes through direct intuitive thought.[49] Just as we learn sometimes to know what a close friend is thinking, so we can really learn to think Christ's thoughts. Normal thoughts. The important thing is that they come with a sense of urgency enough for action. Guidance is not all black and white. But the more you give out to others, the more you will seek it (p. 8).

How can we proceed on guidance? A. Get the facts. B. *Expect* to be guided. When there are no barriers between you and God, you do expect guidance, and you act on the highest thought you have. God covers our mistakes in a marvelous way. We must not feel that there must be an overwhelming emotion. The basis of guidance is faith, not feeling, not analysis.[50] Act on simple thoughts, and more will come.[51] So long as you keep on moving on the

---

[47] Recall that Sam Shoemaker made this same point about intuition *plus*.

[48] See A.A.'s Tradition Two, which reads: "For our group purpose there is but one ultimate authority—a loving God as He may express Himself in our group conscience. Our leaders are but trusted servants; they do not govern." Big Book, p. 564.

[49] See Big Book, p. 86, which states: "Here we ask God for inspiration, an intuitive thought or a decision."

[50] 2 Corinthians 5:7: "For we walk by faith, not by sight." See *What is The Oxford Group?*, p. 67.

[51] See Big Book, p. 87, which states, "What used to be the hunch or the occasional inspiration gradually becomes a working part of the mind. Being still inexperienced and having just made conscious contact with God, it is not probable that we are going to be
(continued...)

guidance you do get, you will get more. (Example of natives in a forest walking with lights on their feet; as long as they move forward, the lights shine on ahead; when they stop the light stops). Be willing to live a day at a time, an hour at a time.[52] C. Test your thoughts. It is possible to receive suggestions from your subconscious mind. Check your thoughts by the four standards of Christ; and by other guided persons. Each will have a part of the truth and thus make up the whole. Move forward as a phalanx. Act on the highest conviction that you have. It is well that we do not know what will happen a year ahead. Christ told his disciples He had many things to tell them—"But you cannot hear it now." Our course is guided by lighthouses. You may think you have been sent to a place for one reason, but when you are there you may find it is for another reason. D. Trust God fully for results. Walk by faith, not by sight. The Cross looks like a failure. Your guidance may look like a failure . . . (p. 9—italics in original).

We believe in television. Are you prepared to graduate in prayer? "I will lead you and guide you in all truth, and bring all thoughts to your remembrance" (John).[53] You will do three hours work in two hours if you live under guidance. Is your family worshipping on that basis? Have a wireless, out on which the whole family can tune in? "A spiritual aerial for every working home in England and the world." (Frank's [Frank Buchman's] message). [See p. 26 of Anne's Journal].

---

[51] (...continued)
inspired at all times. . . . Nevertheless, we find that our thinking will, as time passes, be more and more on the plain of inspiration. We come to rely upon it."

[52] For Bill's use of this expression, see *As Bill Sees It: The A.A. Way of Life . . . selected writings of A.A.'s co-founder* (New York: Alcoholics Anonymous World Services, 1967): (1) "Above all, take it one day at a time" (p. 11). (2) "One day at a time" (p. 317). (3) "The idea of 'twenty-four-hour living' applies primarily to the emotional life of the individual. Emotionally speaking, we must not live in yesterday, nor in tomorrow" (p. 284).

[53] Compare what Jesus promised the "Comforter"—God's gift of holy spirit which would be given on the Day of Pentecost (Acts 2:1ff)—would do: see John 14:26 and John 16:13.

3. Listening.

Watch your thoughts. Your thoughts can come from three sources. 1. Subconscious. 2. The devil. 3. God.[54] Your job to be a good signal man and know the difference between red and green lights. God's thoughts are—1. Not in conflict with the Bible. 2. Will stand the test of all four standards. 3. The test of circumstances. 4. The test of other guided people. 5. The test of action.[55] If you have foolish thoughts, it is because you are foolish (unwise not ignorant). God is never capricious. Persevere till God's thought becomes your thought (p. 14, italics in original).

4. Bible study and reading.

Let all your reading be guided. [See our section on the books Anne read and recommended]. . . . Of course the Bible ought to be the main Source Book of all. No day ought to pass without reading it. . . . *Let friendships and relationships with others be guided.* . . . When occasions arise which lead one into temptation, evasion is not the right way to meet them. Rather have a "Quiet Time" if possible before meeting them and go with a prayer in your heart. Lean on God and not on yourself (p. 16, italics in original).

5. Quiet Time.

Effective Quiet Time: 1. Objective, God and obedience. 2. Attentive prayer and being willing to act immediately. 3. Stillness and surrender of all known sins. *Results of an effective Quiet Time*: 1. Overflowing life. 2. Attitude made clear. 3. Strength for everything. No guidance in the world leaves you out of power and the presence of God (p. 44, italics in original).

---

[54] Compare 2 Peter 5:8-9; *The Devil and A.A.* (Chicago: Chicago Area Alcoholics Anonymous Service Office, n.d.), pp. 1-18; Dick B., *That Amazing Grace: The Role of Clarence and Grace S. in Alcoholics Anonymous* (San Rafael, CA: Paradise Research Publications, 1996), pp. 74-76, 90.

[55] As we discussed in connection with "checking," these were O.G. ideas.

Daily Quiet Time: This cannot be emphasized too much. Not a day should be missed. The early morning hours are best. It may be that more than one quiet time will be needed during the day. Whenever need arises one should stop and pray and listen. The method of holding quiet time varies some with each individual. All include prayer and Bible reading and study and patient listening to God. If you have difficulty in getting help in quiet time, go to some surrendered person and share the difficulty. Those who have progressed farther than you feel the same need of that quiet time and from it find strength and power to do God's will. How much more then a beginner needs it. In quiet we close the switch between us and God from which Power and Guidance come. If that switch is not closed by you, that Power and Guidance cannot come (p. 47, italics in original).

Be alert for symptoms of let-down. . . . One of the first of these symptoms is a sudden disgust with "the whole business" and feeling that it is the "bunk." It is your own soul that is in a funk. Other symptoms of let-down are: No guidance seems to come in Quiet Time, or what guidance does come is too vague; or the guidance received does not seem to work out rightly. Note the blocks to guidance below. Share with a more mature surrendered person. Never give up. A child does not learn to walk in a day. The feeling "What's the use" that comes when you failed or slipped in the face of a challenge or did not follow the guidance you received. You may be too confident in your own strength. Remember that you do not change your inner life. God changes it. He must be kept constantly in the center of life as He is seen in Christ. The answer to this feeling is prayer and new surrender. Lean on Christ, not on yourself. The feeling of revulsion after you have really shared in a meeting or with an individual your change. Sometimes people feel that they have "made a fool of themselves." This feeling of revulsion must be given up. Self is in the center of it and not Christ. This feeling is the grip of the old life seeking to hold you, or if you prefer, The Devil fighting to keep you for his own (p. 47, italics in original).

What to do in these moments is rather simple. Get down on one's knees and give up completely to Christ and His will for you, remembering that anything that pulls you down is your enemy while God is your best friend in the world. Recall that the new life is infinitely better than the old. If release does not come anew, go to some surrendered person and share the "let down." Have a Quiet Time and prayer together, and you will find release again (p. 48).

We have said the Big Book's Eleventh Step instructions can be divided into four parts.

First, those things the AA is to do each evening as he or she constructively reviews the day (p. 86). And we have seen from Anne's Journal how frequently she posed tests for determining how well a person was conducting daily surrender and quiet time activities.

Second, the Eleventh Step places great focus on how one commences the day (pp. 86-87). Recall that Anne Smith spoke of living "one day at a time." The Big Book suggests, "On awakening, let us think about the twenty-four hours ahead. We consider our plans for the day." It then suggests three different approaches: (1) That we ask God to direct our thinking and keep the thought-life clear of wrong motives. [This certainly coincides with Anne's emphasis on, and discussion of guidance, quiet time, prayer, listening for leading thoughts, and checking.] (2) That we ask God for inspiration, an intuitive thought or a decision when facing "indecision." [The relevance of Anne's prayer and meditation comments seems clear to us.] (3) That we be shown all through the day what the next step is to be, that our needs be supplied in that regard, and that our actions be free from selfish ends. [Again, Anne's comments comprehend this subject matter.]

Third, the Eleventh Step process covers what the author has often described as the Big Book's "lost paragraph;" and, more optimistically, the "growth paragraph." We call this the *growth* paragraph because Bill Wilson frequently spoke of A.A. as a "spiritual kindergarten."[56] We believe many portions of our title

---

[56] See, for example, *As Bill Sees It*, p. 95.

demonstrate Anne's influence on the paragraph. Anne's whole family, and those—including Bill Wilson—who visited her home, were involved in a great deal of morning meditation. Anne and Dr. Bob maintained membership in a religious denomination for most of the period from 1935 to the end of their lives. Anne suggested specific prayers in her Journal. She recommended and used the Bible, many spiritual books, and daily Bible devotionals as part of the daily inspirational reading. And she suggested seeking help from others as to the materials which should be read.

Fourth, the Big Book speaks of the action to be taken throughout the day when agitated or in doubt. Essentially, it recommends seeking the guidance of God and surrendering to him many times throughout the day, saying, "Thy will be done" (pp. 87-88). Anne's words paralleled all aspects of these latter suggestions.

The Spiritual Awakening, Witness, Practice of Principles and Step Twelve

We have viewed A.A.'s Twelfth Step as having three "parts": (1) The spiritual awakening obtained as the result of taking the preceding eleven steps. (2) The obligation to witness to others by "passing on" the message of how one received deliverance through God. (3) The actual living of a changed life by "practicing the principles"—the principles learned from taking the twelve steps of recovery.

We will discuss Anne's writing concerning Twelfth Step ideas under the aforementioned three topics.

1. The Spiritual Awakening.

As we've shown, Anne adopted William James's definition of "conversion"—the one so often quoted by Reverend Sam Shoemaker. But the attributes of a spiritual awakening were covered by her in substantial detail:

A general experience of God is the first essential, the beginning. We can't give away what we haven't got. We must have a genuine contact with God in our present experience. Not an experience of the past, but an experience of the present—actual, genuine. When we have that, witnessing to it is a natural, just as we want to share a beautiful sunset. We must be in such close touch with God that the whole sharing is guided. The person with a genuine experience of God and with no technique will make fewer mistakes than one with lots of technique, and no sense of God. . . . We must clearly see and understand our own experience (p. 2).

Creation of spirit of man. Made that spirit part of himself. Own spirit in us. Made man incomplete in his soul, so that he never finds such peace and happiness apart from God as he finds in him. Prophets helped find God. His Son in the fullness of time when all else went awry. Herein is love, not that we loved God but that He loved us and sent His Son to be propitiation of our sins. 1 John 4:10. God tries to reach down to us, and we [?] to reach Him. Made us free to choose—represents our freedom. Projects us so much light as we can stand. Gives us as much as we can comprehend. Reveals all we can grasp. Let perfection down into world—lest it dazzle our sight and we go blind. Observance wrapped in the body of baby. Many of God's approaches are small, still, ourselves. Jesus human in all points belongs to natural order spiritual [?] God in His character. Humanity apparent—divinity evident in Him. Humanity approaches God through a perfect High Priest, in Him God visited man as through a perfect reminder (p. 6).

(Kagawa) Even the Christian church of today misunderstands Christ here. The purpose of our having mystical experience is not that we may achieve our own personal satisfaction, but that we may succor the poor, help those who are in trouble, and educate the masses (p. 20).

(Elinor Forde) [*sic*] A maximum experience of Jesus Christ leads to a radical change in personal life, bringing about a selfless relationship to people about one, which is a challenge to those we come in contact with (pp. 25, 29).

Crucifixion is open to the world so that anyone can see it was a public atonement. Sharing is a simple transparency. It is a sick world—the remedy rests on Christ himself, the healer of the world (p. 35).

Claim victory, power, purpose, to become free children of God; victory in the department of the mind, no slavery, no effort (self), no judging of guidance by results (p. 44).

Don't try, but trust. Any kind of goodness that you try to achieve with effort will be self-righteousness which has self in the center. That is why it is repellent. "Not having mine own righteousness" is Paul's phrase.[57] The only effort we need to put forth is that of daily surrender and daily contact with Christ. We find release not by our own efforts but by what Christ does for us and in us when we open every area of our lives to him (p. 49, italics in original).

The quality of life is an adventure not an arrival. We surrender to God from more and more and from more to maximum. As E. Stanley Jones says, "Christianity is an *obtainment* not an attainment and the more we obtain, the more we see there is to obtain." Maturity comes from fuller self renunciation and surrender and often it takes new experience to bring us farther along the way. The goal is "Be ye therefore perfect, even as your Father in Heaven is Perfect" (p. 49, italics in original).[58]

When Paul gave up trying to be good and surrendered his life fully to the Lord, then came peace, power and joy (p. 61).

---

[57] See Philippians 3:9, "And be found in him [Christ], not having mine own righteousness, which is of the law, but that which is through the faith of Christ, the righteousness which is of God by faith."

[58] Compare Matthew 5:48 in the Sermon on the Mount.

God's gift in Christ is gladness and humility. This goodness not my own will spring up in me in amazing strength and power. I will go through the world with a song in my heart because God so loved the world and me (p. 62).

Compare one of the ideas in the Big Book's final page of text:

Ask Him in your morning meditation what you can do each day for the man who is still sick. The answers will come, if your own house is in order. But obviously you cannot transmit something you haven't got. See to it that your relationship with Him is right, and great events will come to pass for you and countless others. This is the Great Fact for us (p. 164).

2. Witness—giving it away to keep it.

A large part of Anne's Journal was devoted to sharing with, and service to, others; life-changing; and "witnessing." She said:

Giving Christianity away is the best way to keep it (p. 64).

We can't give away what we haven't got (p. 2).

When we have that [a general experience of God], witnessing to it is natural, just as we want to share a beautiful sunset. . . . Share with people—don't preach, don't argue. Don't talk up nor down to people. Talk to them, and share in terms of their own experiences, speak on their level (p. 2).

People reveal themselves and their problems by: 1. *Silence*. A sudden silence indicates that you have touched some real problem. 2. *Talkativeness*. Sometimes they filibuster so that you know they would not talk so much unless there was something they didn't want to say. 3. *Nervousness*. That goes back to some unsurrendered, unshared thing in their lives. Nervousness generally comes from an inner conflict. Watch the hand. You will be able to see that this person is hopelessly divided inside; a divided personality. 4. *Criticism* [italics in original]. In order not only to answer criticism, but to meet the needs of others, we must acquire the knowledge, first, that what the Groups teach is Biblical; second, of what psychology teaches. It is sometimes difficult to answer criticism, because it has to do not only with our own mistakes, but with things beyond our control. Dr. Grensted says this is due to the principles of "projection."[59] People project upon a group or upon another person, some problem they themselves have. (Examples: two ladies had their first glass of champagne, and it was too much for them. One said indignantly to the other, "You are intoxicated; you've got two noses.") People will project upon you the things they hate in themselves. It is important to understand this principle of projection. Much criticism is second-hand gossip. The way to meet it is to say, "Come and see" (p. 3, italics in original).[60]

Confidence. We need to make friends with people first. Get a person to talk about his interests. Reverence what other people reverence; don't stifle the truth they have, but lead on from that. (Example: the atheist who finally said he believed in helping people;—an excellent beginning point.) Make points of contact through reading people, with outright sinners, and with intellectual leaders like Nicodemus.[61] Learn to feel at home with all sorts of people. Learn to intrigue people with stories of individual lives that have been changed. Tell a business man how a business man has been changed, and how he finds it works in his business (p. 4).

How to interview. Jesus's talk with the Samaritan woman at the well (John 4). Jesus was exhausted, but the woman's need challenged him. We may suddenly be confronted with someone's need when we are tired. "Give me to drink." The natural approach. Jesus guided the conversation naturally where He

---

[59] Dr. L. W. Grensted was a distinguished Oxford Group adherent and theologian who wrote several titles popular in the Oxford Group. See Dick B., *The Oxford Group*, p. 68; *New Light on Alcoholism*, p. 321. Grensted wrote the foreword to *What Is The Oxford Group?*

[60] See the account of witnessing among Jesus Christ's apostles in John 1:46.

[61] See John chapter three.

wanted it. After He had aroused her curiosity, she asks, "Where do you get this living water?" Don't be too serious with people; intrigue them, play with them if they want to play; learn how to talk about things they are interested in—fishes to fishermen, water to the woman drawing water. "Will become a spring of water"—a positive statement. We must be positive about what we know from our experience works. "How can I get it?"—the crux of the interview. "Go call your husband"—Jesus goes straight to her sin (p. 5, italics in original).

Winning others. In the early stages, win confidence. Think of meeting the other person's needs. If you have a sense that something in him is not shared, it will block progress in meeting his real needs (p. 5, italics in original).

For that which we have seen and heard declare we unto you that ye also may have fellowship with us—and truly our fellowship is with the Father and with His Son, Jesus Christ.[62] 1st fellowship came to me when others witnessed how Christ had changed their lives. That made me want first the joy and release they had. Then came 2nd Step—how rotten—resentful—picked flaws—hard for me to be honest about myself—the flaws I picked were ones I had in my own life. 3rd—fellowship with Christ means living His work—the human fellowship is as natural by [?] and its so very sweet and comes proportionately as I give. Read further in John III:2 [*sic*]—Beloved I wish above all things that thou mayest prosper and be in health, even as thy soul prospereth. . . . Imagine the President speaking over a nation-wide hookup saying: My fellow citizens, my best wish for you is that your material prosperity and your physical health may be just in proportion to your spiritual well-being (pp. 11-12).

What should come into a witness. Conciseness. Talking in pictures. Get to some apex—the one thing you want to get across. Humour—A light touch should come in. Concrete instances rather than vague statements. Paint pictures of the new life more forcibly

---

[62] See 1 John 1:3.

than the old. Relate your witness to one person in the crowd. Learn to chisel your witness to different people. Learn to hang it on any hook, and make it illustrate principle. *Ten suggestions for personal work*: 1. Get a point of contact. 2. Diagnose the person's real difficulty. 3. Make the moral test (4 standards). 4. Avoid argument. 5. Aim to conduct the interview yourself. 6. Adapt the truth to the hearer's need. 7. Bring the person face to face with Christ. 8. Show the way out of the special difficulty. 9. Bring the person finally to the point of decision and action. 10. Start the person on the new life with simple, concrete and definite suggestions, regarding Bible study, prayer, overcoming temptation and service to others (p. 14, italics in original).

(KAGAWA) Christ's basic principle, which he expressed in saying that we must love even the very least of them, did not arise from his teaching, neither did it come from his practice. It grew out of the fact that he had entered into the consciousness of God.[63] The consciousness of atonement, that is the conscious sharing of the atoning purposes of God.[64] Whoever would bear responsibility for others must have sympathies broad enough to include the failures, the human derelicts. He has not entered into the consciousness of God who looks at some mean fellow whom society counts worthless, and says, "Oh that fellow he's hopeless; he's just a good-for-nothing!" The nearer to God we come, the more conscious we grow of our responsibility towards those worthless folk who are regarded as the very dirt under one's feet. If we ask why it was that Christ always chose the worthless folk, it was because he possessed a one hundred per cent consciousness of God; he shared to perfection his own consciousness of the redemptive purpose of God (p. 19).

---

[63] Anne's notes use the word "conscienceness," but we believe this was an error which occurred in typing from her hand-written material. We believe, from the context of her writing, and from the sources upon which she relied, that she spoke of "consciousness."

[64] See previous footnote.

As we saw, in one of his earliest pamphlets—one which Anne quoted in her spiritual journal—Sam Shoemaker spoke of "giving it away to keep it."[65]

3. Living the changed life practicing the spiritual principles.

Many claim Anne Smith's "favorite" Bible verse was "Faith without works is dead."[66] We have already covered many of Anne's remarks about spiritual principles, but the following are additional specifics:

Faith [italics in original]. Go ahead on faith, not feelings. Emotion is the fruit and not the root of your faith. It may or it may not come. Jesus continually puts the emphasis on faith. . . . If you have given your life to God, trust Him and go ahead with that (p. 2).

Proceed with imagination and real faith—expect things to happen. If you *expect* things to happen, they *do* happen. This is based on *faith in God*, not on our own strength. A negative attitude toward ourselves or others cuts off God's power; it is evidence of lack of faith in His power. If you go into a situation admitting defeat, of course you lose (p. 2—italics in original).

We must keep before us the maximum perspective of our task as Christians. (John 15:13-17). . . . You must be willing to lay down alongside another's [life] perhaps for years (p. 2).[67]

---

[65] Samuel M. Shoemaker, *One Boy's Influence* (New York: Association Press, 1925), p. 15.

[66] See Nell Wing, *Grateful to Have Been There* (IL: Parkside Publishing, 1992), pp. 70-71; *DR. BOB*, p. 71; *Pass It On*, p. 147.

[67] John 15:13-17: "Greater love hath no man than this, that a man lay down his life for his friends. Ye are my friends, if ye do whatsoever I command you. Henceforth I call you not servants; for the servant knoweth not what his lord doeth: but I have called you friends; for all things that I have heard of my Father I have made known unto you. Ye have not chosen me, but I have chosen you, and ordained you, that ye should go and bring forth fruit; and *that* your fruit should remain: that whatsoever ye shall ask of the

(continued...)

You can count on people who stay with you in a movement like this, because they stay with you for God's sake, and not for popularity's sake (p. 3).

Stay with the newly surrendered person until he grows up and becomes a life-changer. Laugh him out of his growing pains. When he becomes a life-changer, we need not fear for him, because other people's needs will drive him back to God (p. 4).

How can we do the maximum job that God will have us do (p. 15)?[68]

Christ's basic principle, which he expressed in saying that we must love even the very least of them, did not arise from his teaching, neither did it come from his practice. It grew out of the fact that he had entered into the consciousness of God (p. 19).

(Elinor Forde) [*sic*] Foundation of this Philosophy. A maximum experience of Jesus Christ leads to a radical change in personal life, bringing about a selfless relationship to people about one, which is a challenge to those we come in contact with. . . . No one can do for me what Jesus Christ has done for me. . . . Fellowship of love must exceed fellowship of hate and be just as demanding. . . . No criticism. No slumping with tongue (pp. 25, 26).[69]

Being honest to God, self and other people. . . . It is being honest even after it hurts. It is giving your real self to another person (p. 34).

---

[67] (...continued)
Father in my name, he may give it you. These things I command you, that ye love one another."

[68] Compare Big Book, p. 77: "Our real purpose is to fit ourselves to be of maximum service to God and the people about us."

[69] Dr. Bob frequently spoke of guarding that erring member, the tongue. See *DR. BOB*, p. 338. Anne often spoke to the same effect in her Journal. Considering the popularity of the Book of James with Dr. Bob, Anne, and the Akron AAs, we have little doubt that the emphasis came from James 3:1-18. Thus James 3:8 states: "But the tongue can no man tame; *it is* an unruly evil, full of deadly poison."

Do we condemn, condone, or construct (p. 35)?

Little sins: 1. Possessiveness—holding on to what one has. A fear of not hating sin enough, self-justification, excusing oneself. 2. Moods and manners, giving way to feelings, temper, irritability, want of control. 3. Getting one's own back, evil for evil, self-opinionated. . . 5. Forcing one's own opinion—unkind tongue, cutting answers, scandal, exaggeration, enlarging when speaking, looking down others. 6. Self-pity. Listen to others' troubles, your own disappear.. . 9. Being selfish and scheming with friends. . . 11. Branding certain races of people (Ephesians 1:2, 3). 12. Self-consciousness—conceit. . . 15. Petty dishonesties. 16. Borrowing and not returning. 17. Pilfering. . . 18. Asserting rights. Show kindness. 19. Liking people who like you and not liking people who don't appeal to you. . . 21. Pride of race, face, place and grace. 22. Christ can only remove them and replace with a new quality of life. Read Romans 12. . . . 24. Idolatry—worship other things but God, other people, ourselves, such practices as we have found to work. . . 27. Timidities—Being shy, fear. 28. Self-pity—wasting time over self when we ought to be taking full responsibility. . . 30. Self-dependence--Indispensability, self-importance, letting sin come between us and the work God intends us to do (p. 36, italics in original).

Good People's Sins: . . . Impatience with people and circum-stances. . . Indiscipline of tongue (James 3). . . Fear and worry, are atheism. . . Fear of poverty, illness, death, fear of people, fear of opinions. Intolerance: We must be free of intolerance toward classes, races, and points of view. If you feel you have to defend something, it is something in yourself. We don't have to defend a point of view. This way of living is not a point of view to be defended. It is a life to be shown. Christ needs not defense, but proclamation (p. 37).

Worry about money leads into all sorts of terrible mistakes, and into fear. . . . Live more simply. Get rid of unnecessary things. . . . God's answer to materialism is a basis of Christian living that lifts above material things (p. 40).

Claim from God humility, patience, courage, faith and love (p. 43).

Egoism or pride is one of our greatest enemies (p. 48).

When you bury a sin, don't visit the grave too often (p. 49).

I must let Christ run my life—always self before. Release from fear, timidity, inferiority (p. 53).

Beatitudes: Poor in spirit—the separated; those who mourn (feel world's sorrow); the meek who inherit; hunger and thirst after righteousness (after surrender, not self-righteousness); are merciful (merciful to sins of others), Mercy and righteousness make pure in heart. Peacemakers (p. 60).

Start the person on a new life with simple, concrete and definite suggestions, regarding Bible study, prayer, overcoming temptation and service for others (p. 14).

The strength of a man's decision is his willingness to be held to it. Stretched as God wants me to be stretched—consistent living, discipline, no letting down, no retiring age, a life spent in action. The proportion—thinking and living for other people (p. 24).

Never let your zeal flag; maintain the spiritual glow: Romans 12:11, Moffat.[70]

The Books Anne Recommended

Anne recommended a large number of books for spiritual growth (pp. 16 and 48). She said she felt these should be part of a Christian's diet. She also devoted four entire pages to Toyohiko Kagawa and to Kagawa's *Love: The Law of Life*, which both she

---

[70] The King James Version of Romans 12:11 reads: "Not slothful in business; fervent in spirit; serving the Lord;"

and Dr. Bob had read (pp. 13, 18-20).[71] This book is still in the possession of Dr. Bob's family. As we mention in a moment, Anne discussed, at page 46 of her Journal, an early book by Sam Shoemaker; and she quoted E. Stanley Jones at page 48, having earlier recommended *all* of the Jones books for spiritual reading. And that is enough for our preliminaries. Except, we hasten to point out, that the Bible was, with Anne, as it was, with Dr. Bob, number one on her recommended reading list.

Anne wrote, pages 16 *and* 48:

> Of course the Bible ought to be the main Source Book of all. No day ought to pass without reading it. Read until some passage comes that "hits" you. Then pause and meditate over its meaning for your life. Begin reading the Bible with the Book of Acts and follow up with the Gospels and then the Epistles of Paul. Let "Revelation" alone for a while. The Psalms ought to be read and the Prophets.

Dr. Bob agreed with Anne about the Bible's importance; read it, cover to cover, three times; read it nightly; and studied a familiar verse every morning.[72] He said the early AA's "were convinced that the answer to their problems was in the Good Book."[73] The Bible was stressed as reading material in the early A.A. recovery program.[74] And Dr. Bob frequently quoted passages from it.[75]

Anne held the Oxford Group view that God could and would guide reading, and that He should be asked to do so. She felt other guided people could help with such guidance. She wrote:

---

[71] Toyohiko Kagawa, *Love: The Law of Life* (Philadelphia: The John C. Winston Company, 1929).

[72] See Dick B., *Dr. Bob's Library: Books for Twelve Step Growth* (CA: Paradise Research Publications, 1994), pp. 13-14.

[73] *DR. BOB and the Good Oldtimers* (New York: A.A. World Services, Inc., 1980), p. 96.

[74] *DR. BOB*, pp. 150-51.

[75] *DR. BOB*, pp. 314, 310; Dick B., *That Amazing Grace*, pp. 25-26, 30-31.

Let all your reading be guided. What does God want me to read? A newly surrendered person is like a convalescent after an operation. He needs a carefully balanced diet of nourishing and easily assimilated food. Reading is an essential part of the Christian's diet. It is important that he read that which can be assimilated and will be nourishing. If you do not know what books to read see some one who is surrendered and who is mature in the Groups (p. 16, italics in original).

Then she was specific. She suggested, "Biographies, or stories of changed lives are very helpful for the young Christian" (p. 16). And she listed the following Oxford Group titles in that category:

1. *Life Changers* by Begbie.[76]
2. *Children of the Second Birth* by Shoemaker.[77]
3. *New Lives for Old* by Reynolds.[78]
4. *For Sinners Only* by Russell.[79]
5. *Twice-Born Men* by Begbie.[80]
6. *Twice-Born Ministers* by Shoemaker.[81]

Dr. Bob's family still owns copies of most of these books, or has donated copies to Dr. Bob's Home in Akron, Ohio. Dr. Bob is known to have read them all.[82]

---

[76] Harold Begbie, *Life Changers* (London: Mills & Boon, Ltd., 1932).

[77] Samuel M. Shoemaker, Jr., *Children of the Second Birth* (New York: Fleming H. Revell, 1927).

[78] Amelia S. Reynolds, *New Lives for Old* (New York: Fleming H. Revell, 1929).

[79] A. J. Russell, *For Sinners Only* (London: Hodder & Stoughton, 1932).

[80] Harold Begbie, *Twice-Born Men* (New York: Fleming H. Revell, 1909).

[81] Samuel M. Shoemaker, *Twice-Born Ministers* (New York: Fleming H. Revell, 1929).

[82] See Dick B., *Dr. Bob's Library*, pp. 20-21.

Next, Anne recommended these popular titles:

1. *He That Cometh* by Oxford Group member Geoffrey Allen.[83]
2. *The Conversion of the Church* by Shoemaker.[84]
3. "All of E. Stanley Jones' books are very good."[85]
4. *The Meaning of Prayer* and *The Manhood of the Master* by Fosdick.[86]

Anne took special note of Dr. Shoemaker's *If I Be Lifted Up*.[87] She said, "An understanding of the Cross and its meaning for life is absolutely essential. The best popular interpretation I know is, 'If I be Lifted Up', Shoemaker. It is a group of lenten sermons. Christ ought to be as real to us as our nearest and best friend" (p. 16).

Finally, Anne recommended books on the life of Christ. She said, "One should by all means read at least one book on the life of Christ a year for a while. More would be better" (p. 16). She said the following "are all good":

---

[83] Geoffrey Allen, *He That Cometh* (New York: The Macmillan Company, 1933). This book was also on Sam Shoemaker's *Evangel* list of recommended Oxford Group literature.

[84] Samuel M. Shoemaker, *The Conversion of the Church* (New York: Fleming H. Revell, 1932). This book also was on *The Evangel* Oxford Group literature list.

[85] For some of the best known Jones books, see E. Stanley Jones, *Christ at the Round Table* (New York: The Abingdon Press, 1928); *The Christ of Every Road* (New York: The Abingdon Press, 1930); *The Christ of the Mount* (New York: The Abingdon Press, 1930)—Dr. Bob's family still owns a copy; *The Christ of the Indian Road* (New York: The Abingdon Press, 1925); *Christ and Human Suffering* (New York: The Abingdon Press, 1930); *Victorious Living* (New York: The Abingdon Press, 1936); *The Choice Before Us* (New York: The Abingdon Press, 1937); *Along the Indian Road* (New York: The Abingdon Press, 1939). See also Dick B., *Dr. Bob's Library*, pp. 36, 37, 64-66.

[86] Harry Emerson Fosdick, *The Meaning of Prayer* (New York: Association Press, 1926); *The Manhood of the Master* (London: Student Christian Movement, 1924). Dr. Bob read a good many Fosdick books.

[87] Samuel M. Shoemaker, *If I Be Lifted Up* (Mew York: Fleming H. Revell, 1931).

1. *The Life of Jesus Christ* by Stalker.[88]
2. *Jesus of Nazareth* by Barton.[89]
3. *The Jesus of History* by Glover.[90]
4. *The Man Christ Jesus* by Speer.[91]

She added emphatically, "See your ministers for others if you desire. But get those biographies of the Master which bring out his humanity" (p. 16).[92]

Anne said much about Toyohiko Kagawa's books. As to Kagawa's views on truth and the faults of others, Anne wrote:

> Though I myself do not have the memory of having told a lie, I think myself innocent, yet when anyone else commits robbery. . . . I must ask forgiveness of God for it. The Jesus who thought like that was truly the King of Truth. The Kingship of Truth becomes God-consciousness. One bears the fault of others on his shoulders and asks forgiveness of God for them, as if they were his own. . . . Students and learned men who have never undertaken to bear the consequences of the failures of others find it impossible to grasp this (p. 13).

Then, as to Kagawa on saving and serving others, she wrote:

> The moment we ourselves are saved, we must set ourselves to saving others. The way Christ became the Atoning Lamb was by his hanging on the Cross and dying there. And Christianity for me means to dedicate myself to serve others even unto death. That, I am convinced, is the true way of Jesus Christ. Christianity

---

[88] Rev. James Stalker, *The Life of Jesus Christ* (New York: Fleming H. Revell, 1891).

[89] George A. Barton, *Jesus of Nazareth: A Biography* (New York: The Macmillan Company, 1922).

[90] T. R. Glover, *The Jesus of History* (New York: Association Press, 1919).

[91] Robert E. Speer, *Studies of the Man Christ Jesus* (New York: Fleming H. Revell, 1896).

[92] Compare the remarks at Big Book, p. 87.

means to save others. That is the way of the Cross, and the true way of Christ (p. 13).

Finally, as to Kagawa's remarks on loving men to the uttermost:

> To love men to the uttermost—that is what Christ does. To that end, sin must be redeemed. . . . To turn blind eyes and deaf ears toward these [prostitutes, unemployed, slum conditions] this is sin! Christ was fully conscious of such conditions. . . . He thought as God does about them, he suffered profoundly in his soul about them, and so was put on the Cross and died (p. 13).

Anne was truly attempting to grasp the meaning of Christian love, forgiveness, witness, and service. Her remarks foreshadowed Dr. Bob's later observation that A.A.'s Twelve Steps—which he said were based on the philosophy of the Sermon on the Mount—could be simmered to their essence as Love and Service.[93]

Anne devoted three more pages to Kagawa's views on love. On page 19, she wrote:

> Christ's basic principle, which he expressed in saying that we must love even the very least of them . . . grew out of the fact that he had entered into the consciousness of God. The consciousness of atonement, that is, the conscious sharing of the atoning purposes of God.

On page 20:

> The purpose of our having mystical experience is not that we may achieve our own personal satisfaction, but that we may succor the poor, help those who are in trouble, and educate the masses.

---

[93] *DR. BOB*, pp. 338, 228.

And on page 21:

> It may be that from the standpoint of criminology, criminals are
> physiologically different from other men, and cannot become
> better men. But from Christ's standpoint, they can be saved. The
> reason that prayer meetings have grown musty is because we have
> ceased to believe in the power of God which can save. We do not
> sincerely believe in prayer.
> . . . Christ must enter more deeply into our experience, and we
> must pray with deep conviction. Is it not written that prayer is
> inevitably answered? Christ went through with his death upon the
> Cross courageously because he believed that salvation could be
> made complete. . . . We must pray with faith, though others may
> think us superstitious.

This is just a taste of the thoughts of the lady of faith, courage,
and love—rightly called the "Mother of A.A."

In 1923, Sam Shoemaker wrote a little book that was published
by the International Committee of the Young Men's Christian
Association. It was titled *One Boy's Influence*.[94] And it was the
story of Dr. Shoemaker's meeting a young man on a train from
Chicago. It told how Sam shared his experience with the young
man and brought him to a decision for Christ. The young man, in
turn, was interested in helping others to change to a better life; and
Shoemaker told of the methods the young man used, the influence
that he had, and the life-changes that occurred through his work.
Anne read this book and discussed part of it at pages 46 and 47 of
her Journal. She wrote:

> One thing you will not do, and that is, not to witness beyond your
> experience. Sam Shoemaker in his little book, "One Boy's
> Influence," says, "There are two directions in which a man's
> mind must be continually travelling if he was to be successful and
> useful as a Christian—one upwards toward God, the other is out
> towards men." Then he goes on to tell this young man who is but

---

[94] Shoemaker, Jr., *One Boy's Influence, supra.*

a recently surrendered lad that the only key to religion is to give it away; it will increase as you give it.

This appears to be one of the earliest recitals of the A.A. adage that "you have to give it away to keep it"—a principle which Sam Shoemaker often espoused.

Spiritual Principles

Oxford Group Principles

About 1926, Sam Shoemaker encouraged Sherry Day to outline the main New Testament principles which he and Day both accepted, and which formed a central part of Shoemaker's own credo.[95]

It is not our intention here to discuss Sherry Day's seven principles at any length; and most of Anne's treatment of these principles can be found in Chapter Two of this present title.[96] However, from our observation of Anne's language, we believe she had these very principles before her in some form as she was writing; for she dealt with each specifically. We therefore list Day's principles and document in our footnotes the places where Anne's specific discussion of them can be found.

Day said, "It is never possible to find Life—peace with God—victory—power by merely trying to follow out principle." He said, "That life comes to one as a possession through but one gateway—a personal experience of Jesus Christ and Him crucified."[97] Day said further that the Oxford Group was a life—that life which is hid in Christ with God; and that the following principles are revelations or pictures of what is bound to take place in any life that is surrendered to the Will of God:

---

[95] See Chapter Two of this title—"Reverend Sherry Days's Principles of the Group."

[96] See also, Dick B., *New Light on Alcoholism: The A.A. Legacy from Sam Shoemaker* (CA: Good Book Publishing Company, 1994), pp. 68-72.

[97] Day, *The Principles of the Group*, pp. 3-4.

1. **God-guidance.** [98]

2. **Fearless dealing with sin.** [99]

3. **Sharing.** Anne covered Day's points in the following pages of her Journal (2-3, 5, 11, 13, 25, 33, 46, 51, 55).

4. **The necessity for adequate, intelligent, expressional activity.** Anne also stressed, as Day put it, "using one's spiritual muscles to maintain spiritual health" (pp. 13-14, 25, 33, 46, 51, 55).

5. **Stewardship.** Anne emphasized such stewardship (pp. 16, 31, 39-40).

6. **Team-work.** Anne spoke much about "teams" and teamwork (pp. 12, 15, 26).

7. **Loyalty.** Anne also advocated this loyalty (pp. 12, 15, 25).

Biblical Principles

As previously stated, Reverend Day said the principles of the Oxford Group were the principles of the Bible; and Anne's sixty-four page Journal is liberally salted with Biblical principles and references. She emphasized the following:

---

[98] Anne discussed "God-guidance" and "two-way prayer" at pages 2, 8, 9, 10, 15, 16, 27, 31, 38, 47, 50, 51, 58, 59.

[99] Anne discussed these points at pages 4, 13, 16, 34, 38, 48. And it is interesting that the Big Book's Fourth Step self examination language stated, "Made a searching and fearless moral inventory of ourselves."

1. John 15:13-17.[100] Anne said these verses represent the "maximum perspective of our task as Christians" (p. 2).

2. John 4—"Jesus talk with the Samaritan woman at the well"—for the Oxford Group "Confidence" concept and "How to interview" (p. 5).

3. The Epistle of 1 John for the concept that we love God because He first loved us and sent His Son for the propitiation of our sins (p. 6).[101]

4. 1 John 1:3 for the concept of fellowship with believers and the Heavenly Father (pp. 11, 16).[102]

5. The Epistle of 3 John for God's Will that all should "prosper and be in health" (p. 12).[103]

6. 1 Corinthians 13 for the concept of Love (p. 15). Both Anne and Dr. Bob read Kagawa's *Love: The Law of Life*, and Anne devoted three full pages to a discussion of Kagawa's book (pp. 19-21).[104]

---

[100] Jesus said: "Greater love hath no man than this, that a man lay down his life for his friends. Ye are my friends, if ye do whatsoever I command you. Henceforth I call you not servants; for the servant knoweth not what his lord doeth: but I have called you friends; for all things that I have heard of my Father I have made known unto you. Ye have not chosen me, but I have chosen you, and ordained you, that ye should go and bring forth fruit, and *that* your fruit should remain: that whatsoever ye shall ask of the Father in my name, he may give it you. These things I command you, the ye love one another."

[101] 1 John 4:10, "Herein is love, not that we loved God, but that he loved us, and sent his Son *to be* the propitiation for our sins."

[102] 1 John 1:3, "That which we have seen and heard declare we unto you, that ye also may have fellowship with us: and truly our fellowship *is* with the Father, and with his Son Jesus Christ."

[103] 3 John 2, "Beloved, I wish above all things that thou mayest prosper and be in health, even as thy soul prospereth."

[104] Toyohiko Kagawa, *Love: The Law of Life* (Philadelphia: The John C. Winston Company, 1929).

7. Ephesians 4:8-11 for the proposition that divinely endowed leaders have been taken out of captivity to sin, brought into captivity for Christ, and given as a gift to men by the ascended Christ (p. 23).[105]

8. James 5:16 for confession (p. 32).[106]

9. Ephesians 4:15 for speaking the truth in love (p. 33).[107]

10. Sharing as a concept direct from the Gospel—citing Matthew 3:6; Mark 1:5; Matthew 4:1-11; James 5:16; Acts 26:22; 2 Corinthians 5:21 (p. 34). These verses all are foundational for Oxford Group practices of Sharing for Confession and Sharing for Witness.[108]

11. Romans 12 for the transformation and regeneration that occurs through the power of Christ (p. 36).[109]

---

[105] Ephesians 4:8, 11, "Wherefore he saith, When he ascended up on high, he led captivity captive, and gave gifts unto men . . . And he gave some, apostles; and some, prophets; and some, evangelists; and some, pastors and teachers."

[106] James 5:16, "Confess *your* faults one to another, and pray for one another, that ye may be healed. The effectual fervent prayer of a righteous man availeth much."

[107] Ephesians 4:15, "But speaking the truth in love, may grow up into him in all things, which is the head, *even* Christ."

[108] Matthew 3:6, "And were baptized of him in Jordan, confessing their sins;" Mark 1:5, "And there went out unto him all the land of Judaea, and they of Jerusalem, and were all baptized of him in the river of Jordan, confessing their sins;" Matthew 4:1-11, "Then was Jesus led up of the Spirit into the wilderness to be tempted of the devil . . . But he answered and said, It is written, Man shall not live by bread alone, but by every word that proceedeth out of the mouth of God. . . . Jesus said unto him, It is written again, Thou shalt not tempt the Lord thy God. . . . it is written, Thou shalt worship the Lord thy God, and him only shalt thou serve . . .;" James 5:16 (confess your faults); Acts 26:22 . . . "Having therefore obtained help of God, I continue unto this day, witnessing both to small and great . . .;" 2 Corinthians 5:20-21, "Now then we are ambassadors for Christ . . ."

[109] Romans 12:1-2, "I beseech you therefore, brethren, by the mercies of God, that ye present your bodies a living sacrifice, holy, acceptable unto God, *which is* your reasonable service. And be not conformed to this world: but be ye transformed by the renewing of your mind, that ye may prove what *is* that good, and acceptable, and perfect, will of God."

12. Romans 8 for the power of the Holy Spirit that brings about change (p. 39).[110]

13. Matthew 6:33 for seeking the Kingdom of God first (p. 39).[111]

14. Acts 5 for the truth of Gamaliel's warning that if teachings about Jesus Christ are of God, they cannot be overthrown (p. 41).[112]

15. Rebirth, reunion with Christ, revival which she said involve decision, discipline and dare—the doing of definite things—citing, in other parts of the Journal, verses in Matthew, Romans, and James (p. 42).

16. Romans 12:11 and Galatians 1:23 for "maintaining the spiritual glow" by continuing to serve God—"fervent in the spirit"—after surrender has been accomplished (p. 46).[113]

17. The Beatitudes in the Sermon on the Mount for the Christ-like virtues to be cultivated (p. 60).[114]

---

[110] Romans 8:11, "But if the Spirit of him that raised up Jesus from the dead dwell in you, he that raised up Christ from the dead shall also quicken your mortal bodies by his Spirit that dwelleth in you."

[111] Matthew 6:33, "But seek ye first the kingdom of God, and his righteousness; and all these things shall be added unto you."

[112] Acts 5:38-39, "And now I say unto you, Refrain from these men, and let them alone: for if this counsel or this work be of men, it will come to nought; But if it be of God, ye cannot overthrow it; lest haply ye be found even to fight against God."

[113] Romans 12:11, "Not slothful in business; fervent in spirit; serving the Lord." Galatians 1:23, "But they had heard only, That he [the Apostle Paul] which persecuted us in times past now preacheth the faith which once he destroyed."

[114] Matthew 5:3-11, "Blessed are 'the poor in spirit' . . . 'they that mourn' . . . 'the meek' . . . 'they which do hunger and thirst after righteousness' . . . 'the merciful' . . . 'the pure in heart' . . . 'the peacemakers' . . . 'they which are persecuted for righteousness sake' . . . 'ye, when men shall revile you, and persecute you, and shall say all manner of evil against you falsely, for my sake.'"

18.   1 Samuel 15:22: There is a sense of being saved only when
       preceded by moral destitution, being lost, bankrupt; and
       then God is not interested in sacrifices, but in obedience and
       listening (p. 63).[115]

Miscellaneous

Anne mentioned some other points that will sound familiar to AAs.
For example, she discussed the *Group* (pp. 3, 26, 52-53);[116] trust
in God (p. 9);[117] the forgiveness of God (p. 13);[118] being of
"maximum service to God" (p. 15);[119] patience, tolerance,
humility, and love (pp. 6, 17-18, 37, 43);[120] courage, faith,
peace, power, and joy (pp. 17, 24).[121] Yes—and a "day at a
time!" Anne suggested, at page 9, "Be willing to live a day at a
time, an hour at a time." Dr. Bob once commented that the A.A.
motto "Easy does it" meant you take it a day at a time.[122]

---

[115] 1 Samuel 15:22, "And Samuel said, Hath the Lord *as great* delight in burnt
offerings and sacrifices, as in obeying the voice of the Lord? Behold, to obey *is* better
than sacrifice, *and* to hearken than the fat of rams."

[116] See Big Book, p. 564, in which A.A. Traditions Two, Four, Five, Six, and Seven
deal with the A.A. *group.*

[117] See Big Book, pp. 68 and 98 for "trust in God."

[118] See Big Book, p. 86, "we ask God's forgiveness."

[119] See Big Book, p. 77, "to be of maximum service to God . . ."

[120] Compare Big Book, p. 83: "patience, tolerance, kindliness and love." And see,
as to humility, pp. 13, 73, 57, 63, 68.

[121] Compare Big Book, page 68, "All men of faith have courage;" page 63 as to
peace of mind and Power; page 133, "happy, joyous, and free."

[122] *DR. BOB*, p. 282.

12

Dr. Bob and the Literature

It is not our intention here to deal with Dr. Bob's importance to A.A.'s founding and fellowship; for that has been well-covered in our other titles and in A.A. histories. But what has been uniquely missing is an understanding of the enormous amount of spiritual literature that Dr. Bob read, the nature of that literature, and the degree to which Dr. Bob emphasized it to AAs in their recovery. Clarence S. tells the story, for example, that Dr. Bob kept a log of the spiritual literature he circulated. Then, when it was returned, he quizzed AAs on what they had read. You could not get a second book until you returned the first.[1]

Our first section will therefore deal with what we have called Dr. Bob's Library. This material has been the subject of one of our earlier titles.[2] And, to conserve space, we will focus in this title on those books which appeared to us to have had a direct impact on A.A.'s basic ideas, thinking, and language.

---

[1] Dick B., *That Amazing Grace: The Role of Clarence and Grace S. in Alcoholics Anonymous* (San Rafael, CA: Paradise Research Publications, 1996), p. 31.

[2] Dick B., *Dr. Bob's Library: Books for Twelve Step Growth* (San Rafael: CA: Paradise Research Publications, 1994). In the footnotes to this present title, we will indicate whether a particular book is still owned by Dr. Bob's family or still in existence. Occasionally, we will indicate the source of information as to how and where the books were used in early A.A. More details can be found in the foregoing title.

The Bible

We have already shown how much the Bible was read and used in early A.A. It certainly was Number One in Dr. Bob's library. He often led meetings by reading from it. And, for the most part, the King James Version was the Bible in use.

Books about the Bible

1. *God's Great Plan, a Guide to the Bible* by R. Llewelyn Williams.[3]

2. *The Fathers of the Church.*[4]

Christian Classics

1. *The Confessions of St. Augustine.*[5] Dr. Sam Shoemaker, Harry Emerson Fosdick, and a number of Oxford Group writers frequently quoted St. Augustine's *Confessions*—a 1,500 year old Christian classic. The best known quote, perhaps, is "for Thou madest us for Thyself, and our heart is restless, until it repose in Thee" (p. 1). The *Confessions* Introduction contained this exhortation, "Seek for yourself, O man; search for your true self. He who seeks shall find—but, marvel and joy, he will not find himself, he will find God, or, if he find himself, he will find himself in God" (p. x).

---

[3] R. Llewelyn Williams, *God's Great Plan, a Guide to the Bible* (Hoverhill Destiny Publishers, n.d.). Owned by family.

[4] *The Fathers of the Church* (New York: CIMA Publishing, 1947). Owned by family.

[5] *The Confessions of St. Augustine*, trans. by E. B. Pusey (New York: A Cardinal Edition, Pocket Books, 1952). Owned by family. See *DR. BOB and the Good Oldtimers* (New York: Alcoholics Anonymous World Services, Inc., 1980), p. 310. Hereafter, unless otherwise indicated, this volume will be referred to as *DR. BOB.*

2. *The Imitation of Christ* by Thomas à Kempis.[6] The translator said, "As we step back, the picture takes shape: a person stands before God, profoundly alone; God embraces him with a deep and unutterable love; and with great humility he strives to love God in return" (p. xlix). In a chapter entitled, "Counsels on the Spiritual Life," à Kempis said:

> As you meditate on the life of Jesus Christ, you should grieve that you have not tried more earnestly to conform yourself to Him, although you have been a long while in the way of God. A Religious who earnestly and devoutly contemplates the most holy Life and Passion of Our Lord will find it in an abundance of all things profitable and needful to him, nor need he seek any other model than Jesus (pp. 64-65).

3. *The Practice of the Presence of God* by Brother Lawrence.[7] Brother Lawrence said:

> I still believe that all spiritual life consists of practicing God's presence, and that anyone who practices it correctly will soon attain spiritual fulfillment. To accomplish this, it is necessary for the heart to be emptied of everything that would offend God. He wants to possess your heart completely. Before any work can be done in your soul, God must be totally in control (p. 29).

> If someone surrenders himself entirely to God, resolving to do anything for Him, the Lord will protect that person from deception. He will also not allow such a person to suffer through trials for very long, but will give him a way of escape that he might endure it [1 Corinthians 10:13] (p. 15).

---

[6] Thomas à Kempis, *The Imitation of Christ*, A New Reading of the 1441 Latin Autograph Manuscript by William C. Creasy (Georgia: Mercer University Press, 1989). Owned by family. Widely read in Oxford Group, according to K. D. Belden.

[7] Brother Lawrence, *The Practice of the Presence of God* (Pennsylvania: Whitaker House, 1982). Betty Smith recalls that Dr. Bob, her father-in-law, read this book. Henrietta Seiberling's family are clear that Henrietta read it. Brother Lawrence was often quoted by Glenn Clark, an author whose books were favorites of Dr. Bob.

The quotes, though written nearly 300 years ago, must sound familiar to AAs. Their Big Book speaks frequently of the power and presence of God (pp. 51, 56, 162). The Brother Lawrence book is filled with insights on how to remain in the presence of God daily.

The Life of Jesus Christ

Dr. Bob's wife, Anne, wrote in her Journal, "One should by all means read at least one book on the life of Christ a year for a while. More would be better."[8] She listed the following books, saying they "are all good." Dr. Bob and Anne's daughter, Sue Smith Windows, wrote the author that her father read them all:

1. *Jesus of Nazareth: A Biography* by George A. Barton.[9]

2. *The Life of Jesus Christ* by Rev. James Stalker.[10]

3. *Studies of the Man Christ Jesus* by Robert E. Speer.[11]

4. *The Jesus of History* by T. R. Glover.[12]

5. *The Manhood of the Master* by Harry Emerson Fosdick.[13]

---

[8] Dick B., *Anne Smith's Journal: A.A.'s Principles of Success* (San Rafael, CA: Paradise Research Publications, 1994), pp. 82-83.

[9] George A. Barton, *Jesus of Nazareth: A Biography* (New York: The Macmillan Company, 1922).

[10] James Stalker, *The Life of Jesus Christ*, new & revised ed. (New York: Fleming H. Revell, 1891).

[11] Robert E. Speer, *Studies of the Man Christ Jesus* (New York: Fleming H. Revell, 1896). The reader will recall that Speer formulated the "Four Absolutes" in his title *The Principles of Jesus*.

[12] T. R. Glover, *The Jesus of History* (New York: Association Press, 1930).

[13] Harry Emerson Fosdick, *The Manhood of the Master* (London: Student Christian Movement, 1924). Fosdick provided much support to early A.A. *Alcoholics Anonymous Comes of Age* (NY: Alcoholics Anonymous World Services, 1957), pp. 322-24.

6. *The Man from Nazareth* by Harry Emerson Fosdick.[14]

7. *Jesus and Our Generation* by Charles Whitney Silkey.[15]

Daily Bible Devotionals

Much is made today in recovery programs of daily meditation books. The little book, *Twenty-Four Hours a Day*, has sold in the millions and is distributed to patients in many recovery centers, the author having been one of those patients; and recently, Alcoholics Anonymous itself published a meditation book.[16] The Big Book's Eleventh Step discussion mentions "morning meditations" and "helpful books." The following are the devotionals Dr. Bob read and used:

1. *Daily Strength for Daily Needs* by Mary W. Tileston.[17] We included a sample page of this devotional in an earlier title.[18]

2. *My Utmost for His Highest* by Oswald Chambers.[19] Sue Windows informed the author that her mother and father frequently used this book as a daily Bible devotional. Lois Wilson said that she and Bill frequently read this devotional.[20] Frank Buchman's

---

[14] Harry Emerson Fosdick, *The Man from Nazareth* (New York: Harper & Brothers, 1949).

[15] Charles Whitney Silkey, *Jesus and Our Generation* (Chicago: University of Chicago Press, 1925).

[16] See *Twenty-Four Hours a Day* (Minnesota: Hazelden, 1975); *Daily Reflections* (New York: A.A. World Services, Inc., 1990).

[17] Mary W. Tileston, *Daily Strength for Daily Needs* (Boston: Roberts Brothers, 1893). Owned by family. One of Dr. Bob's favorite authors, Glenn Clark, recommended this title "For the Morning Watch." See Glenn Clark, *Fishers of Men* (Boston: Little, Brown, 1928), p. 98.

[18] Dick B., *The Akron Genesis of Alcoholics Anonymous* (Corte Madera, CA: Good Book Publishing Company, 1994), p. 355.

[19] Oswald Chambers, *My Utmost for His Highest* (London: Simpkin Marshall, Ltd. 1927). Owned by family.

[20] See Bill Pittman, *AA The Way It Began* (WA: Glen Abbey Books, 1988), p. 183.

biographer (Garth D. Lean) wrote the author that Chambers' devotional was widely read and recommended within the Oxford Group though Chambers was not an Oxford Group member. Mrs. W. Irving Harris also confirmed the wide Oxford Group usage of Chambers' book.[21] Each page contained a date; a topic such as "God First;" a Bible verse or verses on the topic; a comment; and Bible citations to study.[22]

3. *The Runner's Bible* by Nora Smith Holm.[23] This interesting book discussed groups of Bible verses under such topics as: "Walk in Love," "Rejoice Always," "In Everything Give Thanks," and "Fear Not, Only Believe." The Bible verses in each group give exhortation and comfort to the reader on the topics mentioned. The book is not necessarily a "daily" devotional, but is a guide to the study of familiar and "favorite" Bible verses. Dr. Bob did such a study each day as a part of his devotions.[24]

4. *The Upper Room: Daily Devotions for Family and Individual Use.*[25] *DR. BOB and the Good Oldtimers* mentions this periodical frequently; and hence confirms its wide use in early Akron A.A.[26] Dr. Bob's daughter told us that her mother-in-law, Lucy Galbraith, frequently brought copies to her son Ernie's home to be

---

[21] Telephone conversation with the author. This fact was also confirmed by Mark Guldseth, *Streams* (Fritz Creek, Alaska: Fritz Creek Studios, 1982), p. 160.

[22] For a sample page, see Dick B., *The Akron Genesis*, p. 351.

[23] Nora Smith Holm, *The Runner's Bible* (New York: Houghton Mifflin Company, 1915). Owned by family; The use of this book by early AAs, at the behest of Dr. Bob, is mentioned in the memorial issue A.A.'s *Grapevine* published at the time of Dr. Bob's death. See *RHS*, p. 34.

[24] See *DR. BOB*, p. 314.

[25] This booklet first began publication as a quarterly in April of 1935. It was edited by Grover Carlton Emmons, and was published by the General Committee on Evangelism through the Department of Home Missions, Evangelism, Hospitals, Board of Missions, Methodist Episcopal Church, South, 650 Doctors' Building, Nashville, Tennessee. The author has a copy of the first issue as well as most of the other issues which were published and circulated among early AAs between 1935 and 1939.

[26] See *DR. BOB*, pages 151, 139, 71, 178, 220, 311.

taken to Oxford Group meetings. Sue said Lucy sometimes actually brought the quarterlies to the early A.A. meetings herself.[27] Each devotional page began with a date and then quoted a Bible verse. Next, a comment on the verse. Next, several suggested Bible verses to be read on the topic. Next, a prayer; and finally, the "Thought for the Day."[28] Many of the topics (though not necessarily the source verse) would be very familiar to AAs today.[29]

5. *Victorious Living* by E. Stanley Jones.[30] The families of Dr. Bob and of Henrietta Seiberling all confirmed that the E. Stanley Jones books were favorites of the Akron founders. And the personal story of an of early AA mentioned *Victorious Living and the Bible* as two of the books to which she turned for help.[31]

6. *Abundant Living* by E. Stanley Jones.[32]

7. *Handles of Power* by Lewis L. Dunnington.[33]

8. *I Will Lift Up Mine Eyes* by Glenn Clark.[34]

---

[27] Interview by the author of Sue Smith Windows in Akron, Ohio, during Founders Day Conference in June, 1991.

[28] For a sample page, see Dick B., *The Akron Genesis*, p. 349.

[29] For example, "My voice shalt thou hear in the morning, O Lord; in the morning I will direct my prayer unto thee: (Psalm 5:3-Eleventh Step); "Be still, and know that I am God" (Psalm 46:1-Third Step); "In all thy ways acknowledge him and he shall direct thy paths" (Proverbs 3:6-Eleventh Step); "Confess your faults one to another" (James 5:16-Fifth Step).

[30] E. Stanley Jones, *Victorious Living* (New York: Abingdon Press, 1936). Owned by family. For a sample page of this daily Bible devotional, see Dick B., *The Akron Genesis*, pp. 353-354.

[31] *Alcoholics Anonymous* (New York: Works Publishing Company, 1939), p. 223.

[32] E. Stanley Jones, *Abundant Living* (New York: Abingdon-Cokesbury Press, 1942). Owned by family; and see John 10:10; Ephesians 3:20.

[33] Lewis L. Dunnington, *Handles of Power* (New York: Abingdon-Cokesbury Press, 1942). Owned by family.

[34] Glenn Clark, *I Will Lift Up Mine Eyes* (New York: Harper & Brothers, 1937). Owned by family.

9. *The Meaning of Prayer* by Harry Emerson Fosdick.[35] In his Preface, Fosdick put his task this way:

> In a study such as this, the Bible is the invaluable laboratory manual which records all phases of man's life with God and God's dealing with man. . . . Each chapter is divided into three sections: Daily Readings, Comment for the Week, and Suggestions for Thought and Discussion. This arrangement for daily devotional reading—"The Morning Watch," for intensive study, and for study group discussion—has met such wide acceptance in my previous book that it has been continued here.[36]

For each day, Fosdick presented a thought, Bible verses for study, and a commentary. He then concluded with a prayer for that day.

Prayer

There is probably no single category of books which Dr. Bob owned that evidenced more extensive study than the books he read on prayer. A.A.'s co-founder, Bill Wilson, was particularly respectful of Dr. Bob's primacy in that area. Bill said:

> He [Dr. Bob] prayed, not only for his own understanding, but for different groups of people who requested him to pray for them. . . . I was always glad to think that I was included in these prayers. . . . And I sort of depended on him to get me into heaven. Bob was far ahead of me in that sort of activity (*DR. BOB*, p. 315).

We list here the authors and books Dr. Bob read on the subject of prayer and, where the author was a favored one, leave discussion

---

[35] Harry Emerson Fosdick, *The Meaning of Prayer* (New York: Association Press, 1926). Owned by family. See the section below on "Prayer."

[36] Fosdick, *The Meaning of Prayer*, p. xi.

of details to that part of this chapter on "Authors of Special Interest to Dr. Bob."

1. **Glenn Clark**. Clark's books were powerhouses on prayer. His first, *The Soul's Sincere Desire*, was immensely popular in the 1930's; and Dr. Bob and other early Akron AAs used it widely.[37] Other Clark books on prayer were *The Lord's Prayer and Other Talks on Prayer from The Camps Farthest Out, I Will Lift Up Mine Eyes*, and *How to Find Health through Prayer*.[38]

2. **Starr Daily**. Daily's book, *Recovery*, records many extraordinary healings effected through the personal ministry of Rev. Roland J. Brown, who was a pastor of the Parkside Baptist Church in Chicago at the time of Daily's writing. Daily called his book "a book of miracles, a document of answered prayers."[39]

3. **Lewis L. Dunnington**. Dunnington was pastor of Endion Methodist Church in Duluth, Minnesota. In *Handles of Power*, he proposed, "a definite and simple technique of prayer for unlocking the illimitable resources of God's abundance."[40] He focused on "Silent Communion Cards," which he advocated repeating slowly at the beginning and end of each day, and as often through the day as possible. An example is a card based on the phrase, "God the Father dwells within me and fulfills every need" (p. 73).

---

[37] Glenn Clark, *The Soul's Sincere Desire* (Boston: Little, Brown, and Company, 1925). Sue Smith Windows informed the author in a personal interview at Akron in June, 1991, that the Clark books were favorites of Dr. Bob. Henrietta Seiberling's children particularly mentioned this Clark book as part of Henrietta's reading. Nell Wing, Bill Wilson's secretary, lists the book as among those early AAs read. See Pittman, *AA The Way It Began*, p. 192. Owned by family.

[38] Glenn Clark, *The Lord's Prayer and Other Talks on Prayer from The Camps Farthest Out* (MN: Macalester Park Publishing Co., 1932); *I Will Lift Up Mine Eyes*, supra; and *How to Find Health through Prayer* (Harper & Brothers, 1940). All owned by family.

[39] Starr Daily, *Recovery* (St. Paul, Minnesota: Macalester Park Publishing Company, 1948), p. 11. Owned by family.

[40] See Dunnington, *Handles of Power*, p. 10. Owned by family.

4. **Mary Baker Eddy**. Mrs. Eddy's *Christian Science Textbook with Key to the Scriptures* was the basic textbook used by Christian Scientists.[41] It set forth the Christian Science method for using the Christian Science textbook and the Bible for deliverance. Both Bill Wilson and Dr. Bob studied this work.[42]

5. **Charles and Cora Fillmore**. Their book, *Teach Us to Pray*, focused on the Unity approach.[43]

6. **Harry Emerson Fosdick**. Fosdick was very supportive of early A.A.; and Dr. Bob owned and read a large number of his books.[44] Fosdick's *The Meaning of Prayer* was recommended by Anne Smith in her Journal.[45] Fosdick frequently quoted Thomas à Kempis. Fosdick's little book is a compendium on Christian prayer and contains a number of expressions familiar to AAs. For example, Fosdick said:

> Prayer opens our lives to God so that his will can be done in and through us, because in true prayer we habitually put ourselves into the attitude of *willingness to do whatever God wills* (p. 59).

> Prayer . . . when it is at its best, never says, Thy will be *changed*, but it says tremendously, Thy will be *done!* (p. 66).[46]

7. **Emmet Fox**. We will discuss Fox's books in our sections on "The Sermon on the Mount" and "Authors of Special Interest to

---

[41] Mary Baker Eddy, *Science and Health with Key to the Scriptures* (Boston: Published by the Trustees under the Will of Mary Baker G. Eddy, 1916). Owned by family.

[42] See *Lois Remembers* (New York: Al-Anon Family Group Headquarters, 1979), p. 84; Ernest Kurtz, *Not-God* (MN, Hazelden, 1991), p. 54; and Pittman, *AA The Way It Began*, p. 150.

[43] Charles and Cora Fillmore, *Teach Us to Pray* (Lee's Summit, Missouri: Unity School of Christianity, 1950). *DR. BOB* mentions, p. 310.

[44] Mel B., *New Wine*, pp. 145-47.

[45] See Fosdick, *The Meaning of Prayer*; and Dick B., *Anne Smith's Journal*, p. 82.

[46] Compare Big Book, pp. 85, 88.

Dr. Bob." But most of Fox's works do belong, as well, in this section on Prayer. Dr. Bob owned a Fox pamphlet entitled, *Getting Results by Prayer*.[47] And Fox's *The Sermon on the Mount* studied the Sermon on the Mount per se and the Lord's Prayer, which is part of it.[48] In *The Sermon on the Mount*, Fox called the Lord's Prayer the "greatest of all prayers" (p. 162). He said it contained "the implied command that we are to pray not only for ourselves but for all mankind" (p. 166). He added:

> Our business is to bring our whole nature as fast as we can into conformity with the Will of God, by constant prayer and unceasing, though unanxious watching. "Our wills are ours to make them Thine" (p. 174).[49]

8. **Gerald Heard**. Dr. Bob owned and read Heard's *A Preface to Prayer*.[50] A number of Heard's books were recommended by Glenn Clark as "stimulating to prayer and thought."[51]

9. **E. Stanley Jones**. Dr. Bob owned and read a large number of Jones's books. We will discuss them further in our section on "The Sermon on the Mount" and elsewhere. Glenn Clark often recommended Jones's books in connection with prayer.[52] See Glenn Clark's interesting discussion of his work in the prayer realm with E. Stanley Jones, Toyohiko Kagawa, and others during World War II.[53] Jones's *Victorious Living*, contained Bible verses

---

[47] Owned by family.

[48] Emmet Fox, *The Sermon on the Mount* (New York: Harper & Row, 1934).

[49] In a taped address he made in 1948, Arch T. (credited with being the founder of A.A. in Detroit, Michigan) said he read Fox's *The Sermon on the Mount* while he was in Akron City Hospital after he got sober in September of 1938. Arch said the book changed his life. He lived with the Smiths in Akron for his first ten months.

[50] Gerald Heard, *A Preface to Prayer* (New York: Harper & Brothers, 1944). Owned by family.

[51] Glenn Clark, *Two or Three Gathered Together* (New York: Harper & Brothers. 1942), pp. 74-75.

[52] Clark, *Two or Three Gathered Together*, p. 74; *Fishers of Men*, p. 97.

[53] Glenn Clark, *A Man's Reach* (New York: Harper & Brothers, 1949), pp. 269-79.

for each day of the year under such titles as "How Can I Find God," "What Is Conversion," and "The Power That Gives Release."[54] This book contained much on prayer. Since Anne Smith recommended "all" the Jones books of the time; and Dr. Bob read all those books, we believe he read *Victorious Living*.[55]

10. **Frank Laubach**. Dr. Bob owned and read Laubach's *Prayer (Mightiest Force in the World)*.[56] Laubach was one of those who worked with Glenn Clark at The Camps Farthest Out, the retreat attended by Dr. Bob and Anne, and by Clarence S.[57]

11. **Charles M. Layman**, *A Primer of Prayer*.[58]

12. **Rufus Mosely**, *Perfect Everything*.[59]

13. **William R. Parker**. Parker's *Prayer Can Change Your Life* is mentioned in *DR. BOB* (p. 310). Parker said he had a Key, the discovery of "the Kingdom of Heaven exactly where Jesus of Nazareth had said it was, and is, within" (p. x). He said the purpose of his book was "to reveal the Key, detail our experiments, and show precisely how prayer was applied to

---

[54] E. Stanley Jones, *Victorious Living* (New York: The Abingdon Press, 1936), pp. 30, 52, 273.

[55] Glenn Clark recommended this book in *Two or Three Gathered Together*, p. 74.

[56] Frank C. Laubach, *Prayer (Mightiest Force in the World)* (New York: Fleming H. Revell, 1946). Owned by family.

[57] Betty Smith, Dr. Bob's daughter-in-law, informed the author in a telephone interview in December, 1991, that the Smiths attended The Camps Farthest Out and "loved it." See also, Dick B., *That Amazing Grace*, p. 16. For a discussion of Clark's camps, see Clark, *A Man's Reach*, pp. 250-51.

[58] Charles M. Layman, *A Primer of Prayer* (Nashville, Tidings, 1949). Owned by family.

[59] Rufus Mosely, *Perfect Everything* (MN: Macalester Park Publishing, 1949). Owned by family.

individual problems by following the directions of the successful prayers of the past" (p. xi).[60]

14. **F. L. Rawson**, *The Nature of True Prayer.*[61]

Healing

Dr. Bob also read the following books on healing:

1. *Christian Healing* by Charles Fillmore.[62]

2. *Healing in Jesus Name* by Ethel R. Willitts.[63]

3. *Heal the Sick* by James Moore Hickson.[64]

The Sermon on the Mount

We emphasize again that the primary focus of both Dr. Bob and his wife, Anne, was on the Bible itself—not on books about subjects *in* the Bible.[65] As previously covered, Dr. Bob and Bill cited the Sermon on the Mount [Matthew chapters 5-7] as containing the underlying philosophy of A.A. A good deal has been said in A.A. about Emmet Fox and his book on the Sermon, but Dr. Bob's reading on the Sermon was not confined to Fox's

---

[60] Dr. William R. Parker and Elaine St. Johns, *Prayer Can Change Your Life: A New Edition of a Modern Classic* (New York: Prentice Hall Press, 1957).

[61] F. L. Rawson, *The Nature of True Prayer* (Chicago: The Marlow Company, n.d.). Owned by family.

[62] Charles Fillmore, *Christian Healing* (Kansas City: Unity School of Christianity, 1936).

[63] Ethel R. Willitts, *Healing in Jesus Name* (Chicago: Ethel R. Willitts Evangelists, 1931).

[64] James Moore Hickson, *Heal the Sick* (London: Methuen & Co., 1925).

[65] See *DR. BOB* at page 96, where Dr. Bob mentions the specific portions of the Bible itself that were "absolutely essential," namely, the Sermon on the Mount, the 13th Chapter of 1 Corinthians, and the Book of James.

book. The following are the books Dr. Bob studied on the specific topic of Jesus's sermon:

1. *Studies in the Sermon on the Mount* by Oswald Chambers.[66] Chambers had a highly significant approach to the Sermon on the Mount. He said that Jesus's message can only produce despair unless one has received the Holy Spirit.[67] Chambers did a line-by-line study of the Sermon.

2. *The Christ of the Mount* by E. Stanley Jones.[68] Jones told of a group with which he met in a Himalayan retreat who "asked ourselves whether in Christ we had a message that was vital and inescapable if we were to find life and God." Jones said, "We were driven at once to the Sermon on the Mount" (p. 7). Jones contended the Sermon on the Mount is not in Christian Creeds, but should be. He suggested a creed that says, "I believe in the Sermon on the Mount and in its way of life, and I intend, God helping me, to embody it" (p. 12). He believed the history of Christendom would have been different had there been such a creed. He said, "The greatest need of modern Christianity is the rediscovery of the Sermon on the Mount as the only practical way to live" (p. 14). Speaking of the receipt of the Holy Spirit on Pentecost [in Acts 2], he added that Pentecost divorced from the Sermon on the Mount is spiritual pow-wow, not spiritual power (p. 18).

3. *The Sermon on the Mount* by Emmet Fox. Fox did a detailed study in this book of both the Sermon on the Mount and the Lord's Prayer. His book has been much mentioned in A.A., and we shall

---

[66] Oswald Chambers, *Studies in the Sermon on the Mount* (London: Simpkin, Marshall, Ltd., n.d.). Owned by family.

[67] See Chapter Five of this title—*The Sermon on the Mount*.

[68] E. Stanley Jones, *The Christ of the Mount: A Working Philosophy of Life* (New York: The Abingdon Press, 1931). Owned by family.

have more to say of it in the section discussing favored authors.[69] Dr. Bob often read and recommended this Emmet Fox book.

4. *The Soul's Sincere Desire, The Lord's Prayer and Other Talks on Prayer from The Camps Farthest Out,* and *I Will Lift Up Mine Eyes* by Glenn Clark. Each of the foregoing books included a study on prayer, with great emphasis on the Lord's Prayer which, of course, is part of the Sermon on the Mount (see Matthew 6:9-13). The resilience of the Lord's Prayer in the A.A. of today is evident from the fact that it is the prayer used at the conclusion of almost every A.A. meeting.[70]

Love

Dr. Bob simmered A.A.'s Twelve Steps to two principles—love and service.[71] And he certainly read some powerful Christian works on love:

---

[69] *DR. BOB* mentions, p. 310. Bob E.'s List. *AA The Way It Began* includes it in the ten books Nell Wing, Bill Wilson's secretary, said early AAs read; and see lengthy discussion in Mel B., *New Wine*, pp. 105-06, 111-14.

[70] The author personally attended A.A. meetings in Marin County, California, just about daily for five years. Almost every meeting ended with the Lord's Prayer. He found this to be true at A.A. meetings he has attended in the San Francisco Bay Area, and at A.A. Conferences and meetings throughout California, and in Arkansas, Hawaii, Kentucky, Maryland, Minnesota, New York, Vermont, Rhode Island, Florida, Wisconsin, Ohio, Washington, and West Virginia. But see Mel B.'s suggestion in *New Wine* that the days of the Lord's Prayer in A.A. meetings may be numbered. Mel opines, "The purpose of A.A. is to help alcoholics, not simply to promote use of a certain prayer" (Mel B., *New Wine*, p. 157). This opinion, possibly growing in strength, should be contrasted with the fact that early AAs in Akron considered themselves a "Christian Fellowship" and were endeavoring with great success to follow the precepts of Jesus Christ, among which was his direction to Judeans to pray the Lord's Prayer. See, for example, *DR. BOB*, pp. 118: "Dr. Bob was a prominent man in Akron. Everybody knew him. When he stopped drinking, people asked, 'What's this not-drinking-liquor club you've got over there?' 'A Christian fellowship,' he'd reply." See also *DR. BOB* and its discussion of the Frank Amos report, pp. 128-32, 134-36.

[71] *DR. BOB*, p. 338.

1. *Love: The Law of Life* by Toyohiko Kagawa.[72] Anne Smith devoted four of the sixty-four pages of her Journal to Kagawa's *Love*. Dr. Bob read and studied *Love*; and Glenn Clark spoke frequently of Kagawa in Clark's autobiography.[73] Kagawa was a Christian pastor in Japan. He is said to have lived out utterly the life of love, which he conceived to have been the essence of Christ's teaching. He wrote at least five books on the Christian religion, constituting his interpretation, from different aspects, of the significance of Jesus. In the first chapter of *Love*, Kagawa wrote, "Where Love is, there is God. Love is my all in all" (p. 47). Kagawa wrote on every aspect of Love: Love and Creation, Physical and Psychic Love, Love and Sexual Desire, Love and Romance, Love and Marriage, the Ethics of Love, Love and Law, Love and Violence, Love and Economics, Love and Society, and many others—the last being Love and God.

2. *The Greatest Thing in the World* by Henry Drummond.[74] This tiny booklet contained Henry Drummond's study of 1 Corinthians 13. Bob E., an early AA in Akron, wrote Bill W.'s wife, Lois, that Dr. Bob frequently gave this booklet out to the people with whom he worked.[75]

3. *The Soul's Sincere Desire* by Glenn Clark.[76] Clark had the following to say on love and prayer:

Now we come to the most essential of all the laws of Prayer: there must be Love in it (Clark then quotes 1 Corinthians 13). And he [Paul] might have added: And though there be prayers,

---

[72] Toyohiko Kagawa, *Love: The Law of Life* (Philadelphia: The John C. Winston Company, 1929). Owned by family.

[73] Clark, *A Man's Reach*, pp. 256, 258, 261-64, 276, 278.

[74] Henry Drummond, *The Greatest Thing in the World* (New Jersey: Spire Books, Fleming H. Revell, 1968). This essay was written about 1884 and has been re-printed over and over. Owned by family. Bob E.'s List. *DR. BOB* mentions, pp. 151, 310-11.

[75] See previous reference to Bob E.'s Memo to Lois Wilson.

[76] Owned by family.

they shall fail; but if love be in the prayer it shall not fail. Jesus wrought not a single miracle where He did not first love, and where the love was not returned unto Him. The greater the miracle the greater the love (pp. 69-70).

When congregations come together to pray, not merely to listen to a sermon or to go through a ritual, when love lives in the prayers and self is forgotten, then we may expect miracles again: for the blind to see, the lame to walk, and those possessed of fear and terror to be set free from demons (p. 73).

The Oxford Group

We have thus far located only eight Oxford Group books in possession of Dr. Bob's family—other than books by Dr. Sam Shoemaker, an East Coast leader in the Group. But these eight books did thoroughly cover Oxford Group principles and practices. All were on *The Calvary Evangel's* Oxford Group book lists:

1. *For Sinners Only* by A. J. Russell.[77] Russell was a British writer and journalist. His book told a good many stories about Oxford Group people including founder, Dr. Frank Buchman, and Dr. Samuel Shoemaker. Russell covered the nuts and bolts of Oxford Group principles and practices, with chapters on "Sin," "Restitution," and other Oxford Group concepts. He outlined Oxford Group ideas about God's having a plan and mankind's need to fit in with it; about God's guidance and God's power being available for all those who chose to work with the plan. Russell covered Sharing by Confession and by Witness, early morning listening to God in Quiet Time, Fellowship, Surrender, Life-Changing, the Four Absolutes, and the "miracle" at Reverend Sam Shoemaker's Calvary Church.

---

[77] A. J. Russell, *For Sinners Only* (London: Hodder & Stoughton, 1932). Owned by family. Anne Smith mentions. *DR. BOB* mentions, p. 310. Nell Wing said it was read by early AAs. See Pittman, *AA The Way It Began*, pp. 192, 197.

2. *He That Cometh* by Geoffrey Allen.[78] Allen laid out some important Oxford Group ideas about coming from lonely individualism "into a deep fellowship of common need and common obedience with other disciples of the Christ" (Preface). He pointed out that people must start their journey to God by coming as babes. He discussed being born again, sin, service, listening to God, and love.

3. *Soul Surgery* by Howard A. Walter.[79] This book on personal evangelism described in detail an "art" Dr. Frank Buchman developed for bringing people to Christ and changing their lives. Its five, major life-changing concepts seem readily identifiable in A.A. today. (1) *Confidence* comprehends not only A.A.'s technique of sharing by confession, but also its program of working with another through gaining that person's confidence. (2) *Confession* found its way directly to A.A.'s Fifth Step. (3) *Conviction* describes an individual's need for a deep conviction of sin—the person must recognize his own need to change, something covered by A.A.'s Sixth Step. (4) *Conversion* describes the Surrender process incorporated into A.A.'s Third and Seventh Steps. (5) *Conservation* (or "Continuation," as it was also called) corresponds to A.A.'s Tenth, Eleventh, and Twelfth Steps, which involve "maintaining" one's life-change and communicating to others the means by which one's life change was accomplished.

4. *What is The Oxford Group?* by the Layman with a Notebook.[80] Dr. Bob owned and loaned several copies of this book. It was a primer on the Oxford Group. It explained the

---

[78] Geoffrey Allen, *He That Cometh* (New York: The Macmillan Company, 1933). Anne Smith mentions.

[79] Howard A. Walter, *Soul Surgery: Some Thoughts on Incisive Personal Work* (Calcutta: Association Press, 1919). Owned by family. *DR. BOB* mentioned its concepts: soul surgery, and the five C's—Confidence, Conviction, Confession, Conversion, and Conservation (p. 54).

[80] The Layman with a Notebook, *What Is The Oxford Group?* (London: Oxford University Press, 1933). Owned by family.

Oxford Group. It covered the Four Absolutes—Honesty, Purity, Unselfishness, and Love—which it said were the keys to the kind of spiritual life God wishes us to lead. It detailed *four spiritual activities* which the Oxford Group advocated "to be spiritually reborn, and to live in the state in which these four points [the Four Absolutes] are the guides to our life in God" (p. 8): (1) Sharing of our sins and temptations with another Christian whose life was given to God, and using Sharing as Witness to help others, still unchanged, to recognize and acknowledge their sins. (2) Surrender of the life into God's keeping and direction. (3) Restitution. (4) Listening to, accepting, relying on God's Guidance, "and carrying it out in everything we do or say, great or small" (pp. 8-9). A student of A.A. can readily find the following A.A. Step concepts in the four "activities": (1) Acknowledgement of shortcomings and confession (Steps Four and Five), (2) Becoming willing to change, and asking God for help in that process (Steps Six and Seven), (3) Making decisions to surrender and change (Steps Three and Seven), (4) Making restitution (Steps Eight and Nine), (4) Relying on prayer and meditation for God's guidance and power (Step Eleven), and (6) Practicing spiritual principles in all one's affairs (Step Twelve).

5. *Life Changers* by Harold Begbie.[81] This was one of the earliest books written about Oxford Group Founder, Dr. Frank N. D. Buchman, and his life-changing program. It was widely read in the Oxford Group, in Shoemaker's church circle, and in early A.A.

6. *Twice-Born Men* by Harold Begbie.[82] Though this book was written by Begbie long before there was an Oxford Group, the book itself was very popular in the Oxford Group. And it set the

---

[81] Harold Begbie, *Life Changers: Narratives of a Recent Movement in the Spirit of Personal Religion* (London: Mills & Boon, Ltd., 1932). Owned by family.

[82] Harold Begbie, *Twice-Born Men* (New York: Fleming H. Revell, 1909). Owned by family.

stage for the many narrative stories in the Oxford Group about conversions, the new birth, and life change. The story telling was often called "sharing." The theme was adopted by Sam Shoemaker when he wrote his titles, *Twice-Born Ministers* and *Children of the Second Birth*. Anne Smith highly recommended the reading of these life-changing narratives. The practice of sharing life-changing experiences at meetings became the heart of story telling in today's A.A. meetings and literature.

7. *New Lives for Old* by Amelia S. Reynolds.[83] This account of life changes through Oxford Group practices was popular in Shoemaker's Calvary Church. The author found a copy in the archives at Calvary Church in New York during his 1993 visit there.

8. *One Thing I Know* by A. J. Russell.[84] After he had written the immensely popular Oxford Group book, *For Sinners Only*, Russell apparently found himself under fire for not having said enough about the Christian concepts of Atonement, the Virgin Birth, the Star of Bethlehem, and the "Sacraments of the Gospels." Russell said he wrote this second book to state, in language clear, simple, and emphatic, an unqualified belief in the divinity of Jesus Christ and his atonement on Calvary—and also to underline his sincere desire for Christian unity.[85]

---

[83] Amelia S. Reynolds, *New Lives for Old* (New York: Fleming H. Revell, 1929). Anne Smith recommended.

[84] A. J. Russell, *One Thing I Know* (New York: Harper & Brothers, 1933). Owned by family.

[85] For an extended discussion, see Dick B., *Design for Living*, pp. 212-13. One A.A. oldtimer, Earl H., informed the author several years ago that he [Earl] had a copy of *One Thing I Know*, which contains an inscription by Dr. Bob's wife, Anne Smith.

Dr. Samuel M. Shoemaker, Jr.

Though Bill Wilson attributed the Twelve Steps in large part to Dr. Samuel M. Shoemaker, the author found no evidence of any books by Shoemaker in Bill's possession at his home at Stepping Stones in Bedford Hills or elsewhere, other than a book written after 1939.[86] Dr. Bob's family owns virtually no Shoemaker books. However, Anne Smith did recommend the following in her Journal, and all are on *The Calvary Evangel's* Oxford Group book list. Sue Smith Windows confirmed to the author in writing that her father, Dr. Bob, read the following books:

1. *Children of the Second Birth.*[87] Shoemaker narrated the stories of people in New York who were born again through a Calvary Church conversion experience that initiated a new life for them. He pointed out that, although the conversion is the starting point, all subsequent life is a development of a relationship with God. He said the daily focal point of a reborn life is the Quiet Time, where "we pray and read the Bible. But the distinguishing element of a Quiet Time is listening for the guidance of God" (p. 16). Shoemaker's last words in this book were, "It will be a great day for the Christian cause when the world begins to realize that 'Thy will be done' does not belong on tombstones, but ought to be graven into the lives of eager men and women who have enlisted in God's warfare beyond return and beyond recall" (p. 187).

2. *Confident Faith.*[88] This was a collection of Shoemaker sermons on believing. Shoemaker stated "the supreme confidence

---

[86] For a thorough study of the Shoemaker influence on A.A. ideas and of Bill Wilson's relationship with Shoemaker, see Dick B., *New Light on Alcoholism: The A.A. Legacy from Sam Shoemaker* (Corte Madera, CA: Good Book Publishing Company, 1994).

[87] Samuel M. Shoemaker, *Children of the Second Birth* (New York: Fleming H. Revell, 1927).

[88] Samuel M. Shoemaker, *Confident Faith* (New York: Fleming H. Revell, 1932). Owned by family.

is faith in Almighty God" (p. 17). He said the secret of faith and the secret of confidence were: "Just keep looking at Jesus Christ with your will set His way. That will be enough" (p. 20). He explained what Christ meant to him: (1) An historical character, A mortal man. (2) The revelation, in time and finite life, of the character of Infinite God. (3) The Supreme Interpreter of Life, and (4) Rescuer from sin (pp. 35-47). Shoemaker spoke of the Communion of the Saints "who love and serve" the Lord (p. 93). And he dealt with Saul's conversion which, he believed, simply found Saul in "willing surrender of the self to God and His mercy and His plan, as represented in the words, 'What shall I do, Lord?'" (pp. 114-15). Shoemaker concluded with "the romance of real religion," as he called it: (1) The colossal romance in cooperating with the Spirit that controls this universe. (2) The romance of a relationship between God and those who honestly love and seek His will. (3) The romance of a relationship which comes to pass between those who find themselves thus cooperating with God. (4) The romance of a fight to free the souls of men from ignorance, selfishness, and sin. (5) The romance of a risk to bet everything you have on God.

3. *If I Be Lifted Up*.[89] This was Shoemaker's book about the Cross. The book's theme was from the words of Jesus in John 12:32, "And I, if I be lifted up from the earth, will draw all *men* unto me." Shoemaker said that, in these words, Jesus "sees the Prince of this world—the spirit of worldliness, I suppose we should say—expelled" (p. 11). Shoemaker believed the Cross would draw suffering people because "misery loves company." It would draw sinning people because they can see "His disapproval of sin, and His suffering for our sin." It would draw thinking people because "suffering love, bearing the burdens of others, remains life's last word" (pp. 12-15). In words familiar to AAs, Shoemaker said:

---

[89] Samuel M. Shoemaker, *If I Be Lifted Up* (New York: Fleming H. Revell, 1931).

[The Cross] restores us as the conscious children of God's love. Its final word is not concerned with how little we *can do* for ourselves, but with how much God *has done* for us (p. 115).[90]

Let us never forget to tell men that their redemption stands in the Cross of Christ: but let us never forget to tell them also that the appropriation of redemption stands in their own choice and design (p. 172).

4. *The Conversion of the Church.*[91] Shoemaker believed the primary work of the Church was the re-making of the inner lives of individuals, through the power of the living Christ (p. 11). He discussed sins "that hold us back from the fullness of spiritual power" (p. 30). He listed pride, exclusiveness, silence or hypocrisy in affectional life, "resting his case in a point of view," and fear. He described the Oxford Group life-changing process of confession, surrender, and continuance. Then living in touch with God through Bible study, prayer, guidance, and fellowship.

5. *Twice-Born Ministers.*[92] In this book, a dozen men in the ministry told of their experience of conversion, or rebirth. Shoemaker said that, for a Christian, conversion ultimately means a complete experience of Jesus Christ. The ministers spoke of honesty with self, seeking the kingdom of God first, surrender, confession, the break with particular sins, restitution and forgiveness, Quiet Time, and peace coming from life-change.

---

[90] Compare the following remark in A.A.'s "Big Book," where Bill Wilson said of his friend, Ebby Thacher, who carried the Oxford Group message to Bill: "But my friend [Ebby] sat before me, and he made the point blank declaration that God had done for him what he could not do for himself. His human will had failed" (p. 11). Bill then incorporated the same thought in the Big Book's "promises" when he wrote at page 84, "We will suddenly realize that God is doing for us what we could not do for ourselves."

[91] Samuel M. Shoemaker, *The Conversion of the Church* (New York: Fleming H. Revell, 1932).

[92] Samuel M. Shoemaker, *Twice-Born Ministers* (New York: Fleming H. Revell, 1929).

6. *One Boy's Influence.*[93] Anne Smith discussed this little booklet at some length in her Journal. Shoemaker told the story of how he led a young man to a conversion experience and then impressed upon the young man the vital importance of passing on to others the message about the experience. Shoemaker was teaching, "You have to give it away to keep it."

7. *Pamphlets.* Two Shoemaker pamphlets are still in possession of Dr. Bob's family. We also found them with the copy of Anne's Journal located at Stepping Stones. The first was titled, *Three Levels of Life*. It was later published in the 13th chapter of *Confident Faith*.[94] Shoemaker's three levels were: (1) Instinctive desire; (2) Conscientiousness; and (3) Grace. And he said:

God help us all to be buoyed above our carelessness, above our carefulness, into the region of His care for us, into the free upper ether of His grace! (*Confident Faith*, p. 166).

The second pamphlet was titled, *What If I Had But One Sermon to Preach?* It was subsequently published in the first chapter of Shoemaker's *Religion That Works*.[95] The topic was John 17:3:

And this is life eternal, that they might know thee the only true God, and Jesus Christ, whom thou hast sent.

Shoemaker said, if he had but one sermon to preach, its subject would be the homesickness of the human soul for God. He said we all thwart the spiritual nature by sin. The Cross is the medicine of the world. Human beings can be lifted up by conversion. Man

---

[93] Samuel Moor Shoemaker, Jr., *One Boy's Influence* (New York: Association Press, 1925).

[94] *Confident Faith* is owned by Dr. Bob's family.

[95] Samuel M. Shoemaker, *Religion That Works* (New York: Fleming H. Revell, 1928). This pamphlet is owned by Dr. Bob's family and was included in the copy of Anne Smith's Journal the author inspected at Bill's home at Stepping Stones.

must be born again by utter self-dedication to the will of God; and the way is acceptance of God in Christ Jesus.[96]

Two of A.A.'s Other "Founders"

Professor William James

In 1902, Professor William James wrote *The Varieties of Religious Experience*.[97] A.A.'s Big Book mentioned it at page 28. After Bill Wilson had his dramatic spiritual experience at Towns Hospital in New York, he read the James book in order to understand what had just happened to him. *Pass It On* related that Bill "now had his spiritual experience ratified by a Harvard professor, called by some *the* father of American psychology."[98] Bill later said William James "had been a founder of Alcoholics Anonymous."[99] As we have already covered, James's definition of "conversion" much influenced Shoemaker, Anne Smith, and other Oxford Group people.[100]

James might have been the source of the phrase "higher power," which AAs began to use in later years. For James wrote, "we are saved from the wrongness by making proper connection

---

[96] For many other Shoemaker books available in the 1930's, most of which were probably read by Dr. Bob, see Dick B., *New Light on Alcoholism: The A.A. Legacy from Sam Shoemaker* (Corte Madera, CA: Good Book Publishing Company, 1994), pp. 319, 347-51, 353-55. See also our discussion below of the Oxford Group Literature List in Shoemaker's parish publication, *The Calvary Evangel*.

[97] William James, *The Varieties of Religious Experience* (New York: New American Library, 1958). *DR. BOB* mentions the James book at page 306, stating, "The book, though not popular among Akron AAs, was a favorite of Dr. Bob's."

[98] *Pass It On* (Alcoholics Anonymous World Services, Inc., 1984), pp. 124-25.

[99] *Pass It On*, p. 124.

[100] James, *The Varieties of Religious Experience*, p. 157. Shoemaker quotes this definition in his first book, *Realizing Religion*, at page 22. So does Howard A. Walter in *Soul Surgery*, p. 119. See also Harold Begbie, *Twice-Born Men* (New York: Fleming H. Revell, 1909), pp. 16-17.

with the higher powers" (p. 383, *cf.* 99).[101] But James chose to call the supreme reality by the name of God—and AAs may have followed his lead in their Big Book. James wrote:

> God is the natural appellation, for us Christians at least, for the supreme reality, so I will call this higher part of the universe by the name of God (p. 389).

In any event, A.A.'s Big Book refers to James's book primarily to show there are "a multitude of ways in which men have discovered God" (Big Book, p. 28).

Dr. Carl Jung

A.A.'s Big Book also referred to Dr. Carl Jung and cited Jung as the source of A.A.'s "spiritual solution"—that the mind of a chronic alcoholic can only be healed by "vital spiritual experiences."[102] Years after the founding of A.A. in 1935, Bill Wilson wrote Dr. Carl Jung and said the concept of a spiritual or religious experience—in short, a genuine conversion—"proved to be the foundation of such success as Alcoholics Anonymous has since achieved."[103] And Dr. Bob seemed to have taken an interest in A.A.'s other "founder"—Dr. Carl Jung. For Dr. Bob owned and read Dr. Jung's book, *Modern Man in Search of a Soul.*[104] Jung wrote:

> Among all my patients in the second half of life—that is to say, over thirty-five—there has not been one whose problem in the last

---

[101] For a more likely Oxford Group source of the expression, "Higher Power," see the book by Bill Wilson's Oxford Group friend and writer, Victor C. Kitchen, *I Was a Pagan* (New York: Harper & Brothers, 1934), p. 85. For further discussion, see Dick B., *New Light on Alcoholism*, p. 87

[102] See Big Book, pp. 26-27.

[103] *Pass It On*, pp. 382-83.

[104] C. J. Jung, *Modern Man in Search of a Soul* (New York: Harcourt Brace Jovanovich, Publishers, 1933). Owned by family.

resort was not that of finding a religious outlook on life. It is safe
to say that every one of them fell ill because he had lost that
which the living religions of every age have given to their
followers, and none of them has really been healed who did not
regain his religious outlook (p. 264).

Authors of Special Interest to Dr. Bob

Various people have said that this or that author or book was a
favorite of Dr. Bob's.[105] But we cannot state with any certainly
which particular books were Dr. Bob's "favorites." We can and
shall list below the authors of books most frequently mentioned by
Dr. Bob, his wife (Anne), his family, and A.A.'s pioneers. We
also list those authors who, by the sheer number of their books
that Dr. Bob owned, seem to have been favored in his reading.

1. James Allen.

A. *As a Man Thinketh*.[106] The title of this popular
pamphlet was probably taken from the first part of Proverbs 23:7,
"For as he thinketh in his heart, so *is* he." James Allen said:

Man is manacled only by himself: thought and action are the
jailers of Fate—they imprison, being base; they are also the angels
of Freedom—they liberate, being noble (p. 18).

---

[105] For example, Sue Smith Windows told the author that the Glenn Clark books were
favorites. Dorothy S. M. said that Drummond's *The Greatest Thing in the World*, Emmet
Fox's *The Sermon on the Mount*, and *The Upper Room* were the "three main books at
that time" (*DR. BOB*, pp. 310-11). *DR. BOB* said William James' *The Varieties of
Religious Experience* "was a favorite of Dr. Bob's" (p. 306). Pittman's *AA The Way It
Began* said the Bible, Drummond's book, James's book, *The Upper Room*, and Russell's
For Sinners Only constituted Dr. Bob's "required reading" (p. 197). In his memo to Lois
Wilson, Bob E. mentioned Drummond, Fox, and James Allen's *As a Man Thinketh* as
particularly important to Dr. Bob.

[106] James Allen, *As a Man Thinketh* (New York: Peter Pauper Press, Inc., n.d.). *RHS*
mentions, p. 34. Bob E.'s List. Nell Wing's List in *AA The Way It Began*, p. 192.

Good thoughts and good actions can never produce bad results;
bad thoughts and actions can never produce good results (p. 24).

Keep your hand firmly upon the helm of thought (p. 64).

    B. *Heavenly Life.*[107]

    2. Harold Begbie. Anne Smith's Journal recommended two of
Harold Begbie's many books. Dr. Bob read them both.

    A. *Twice-Born Men.*[108] This earliest of Begbie's titles was
written in 1909. Begbie said he wrote his book as a footnote in
narrative to Professor James's *Varieties* "to bring home to men's
minds this fact concerning conversion, that, whatever it may be,
*conversion is the only means by which a radically bad person can
be changed into a radically good person*" (p. 17). Begbie covered
"new birth" and becoming "born again." And he gave examples.

    B. *Life Changers.*[109] In this book, Dr. Frank Buchman,
founder of the Oxford Group, was referred to throughout as "F.
B." Begbie discussed almost every aspect of Oxford Group ideas
which came into such prominence in the 1930's: (1) Sin (pp. 14-
15). (2) Soul Surgery (pp. 24-41). (3) God Consciousness (p. 39).
(4) Confession (p. 104). (5) The belief elements of Frank
Buchman's "A First Century Christian Fellowship"—forerunner of
the Oxford Group (p. 122). (6) The origin of Buchman's five
C's—Confidence, Confession, Conviction, Conversion, and
Continuance (pp. 169-70). (7) Quiet Time for prayer, Bible study,
and "listening for the direction of the Holy Spirit" (pp. 169-70).
(8) Sharing (p. 175).

---

    [107] James Allen, *Heavenly Life* (New York: Grosset & Dunlap, n.d.). Owned by
family.

    [108] Harold Begbie, *Twice-Born Men* (New York: Fleming H. Revell, 1909).

    [109] Harold Begbie, *Life Changers: Narratives of a Recent Movement in the Spirit of
Personal Religion* (London: Mills & Boon, Limited, 1932). Owned by family.

3. **Oswald Chambers**.

A. *My Utmost for His Highest*. This particular daily Bible devotional by Chambers was in use by Dr. Bob, Anne Smith, Bill Wilson, Lois Wilson, and Henrietta Seiberling. It was also widely read by members of the Oxford Group. Bill Wilson's wife, Lois, specifically mentioned in her Oxford Group Notebook that she was reading this book and "really saw myself."[110] For further information, see our discussion under "Daily Bible Devotionals."

B. *Studies in the Sermon on the Mount*. Dr. Bob studied the Sermon on the Mount in the Bible itself (Matthew 5-7). And he fleshed out his study with books about Jesus's sermon by such men as Glenn Clark, Oswald Chambers, Emmet Fox, and E. Stanley Jones—none of whom was a "member" of the Oxford Group or connected with Dr. Samuel Shoemaker's Calvary Church. For further information, see our discussion under "The Sermon on the Mount."

4. **Glenn Clark**. Clark was a professor of English and also an athletic director at Macalester College in Minnesota. He gained fame as a writer of prayer books and as the founder of "The Camps Farthest Out," where there were meditations, prayers, discussions, talks on Jesus and other biblical topics, Bible study, singing, and quiet time.[111] As covered, Dr. Bob's daughter said that Glenn Clark's books were favorites of Dr. Bob's; and his daughter-in-law said that Dr. Bob and Anne attended Clark's Camps Farthest Out. Clarence S., Bob's sponsee, followed suit.

A. *The Soul's Sincere Desire*.[112] Clark wrote this essay after what he termed God's blessing him over a period of three

---

[110] See discussion in Dick B., *The Akron Genesis*, p. 151.

[111] See Clark's autobiography, *A Man's Reach*.

[112] Glenn Clark, *The Soul's Sincere Desire*, (Boston: Little, Brown, 1925). Owned by family.

years "with an almost continuous stream of answered prayer." This, he said, resulted in a "peace and happiness and absolute liberation from the bondage of fear and anger and the life-destroying emotions that came to me and revealed to me the practicability of finding the Kingdom of Heaven in the practical world of men" (p. 3). His book was written to demonstrate "how you pray" (p. 4). He used the Lord's Prayer and the Twenty-third Psalm as a frame for prayer. Dr. Bob and Henrietta Seiberling favored this book; and so, apparently, did early AAs since it was one of the ten books A.A.'s first archivist said they read.[113]

B. *Fishers of Men.*[114] Clark wrote this book to answer the question, how to save men. Clark was not a "member" of the Oxford Group, but quoted many of its evangelical sources, such as Henry Drummond, John Mott, and H. A. Walter. Clark proposed an attitude described in the New Testament record of the Good Samaritan. He said, "I have faith that the man's need may be met, I have faith in God's power to meet it, I have faith that the love I have for the man may furnish a channel for the bringing of the need and the power together" (p. 4). Clark's Bibliography is of special interest because it recommended a good many of the books Dr. Bob read. Because of the early date of this Glenn Clark book, in relation to Dr. Bob's quest, and because of the popularity of all Glenn Clark's books with Dr. Bob, his wife, Henrietta Seiberling, and early AAs, we wonder—without knowing—whether Dr. Bob's library and reading list were in fact influenced by Clark's recommendations in the bibliography of *Fishers of Men*.

C. *I Will Lift Up Mine Eyes.*[115] Clark based this book on a story about "hind's feet"—taken from 2 Samuel 22:34—"He maketh my feet like hind's *feet*: and setteth me upon my high

---

[113] See Pittman, *AA The Way It Began*, p. 192.

[114] Glenn Clark, *Fishers of Men*. (Boston: Little, Brown, 1928). Owned by family.

[115] Glenn Clark, *I Will Lift Up Mine Eyes* (New York: Harper & Brothers, 1937). Owned by family.

places." This verse contains a figure of speech concerning the deftness and accuracy with which a mother deer tests the difficult spots on a mountain, finds the safe path, and then places both sets of her feet in precisely the same spot to enable a safe journey for herself and the baby deer. A friend said to Clark, "All you have to do is to make your feet like hind's feet and God will do the rest." The friend continued, "First, something happens inside one. Get that? Inside one—deep, deep down inside one." He then said, "[H]ere is the miraculous part that you will find hard to believe—after the change happens inside, everything begins to change *outside* too" (p. 2—italics in original). After that introduction to his topic, Clark discussed a number of key phrases which may also have arrested Dr. Bob's attention. The expressions included: (1) Jesus' statement, "Have Faith in God," (2) "As a man thinketh in his heart, so is he," and (3) "The tongue can no man tame."[116] Clark proposed some prayer studies which he called "leaders." The studies were based on the Lord's Prayer and on the following in Philippians 4:8:

> Finally, brethren, whatsoever things are true, whatsoever things *are* honest, whatsoever things *are* just, whatsoever things *are* pure, whatsoever things *are* lovely, whatsoever things *are* of good report; if *there be* any virtue, and if *there be* any praise, think on these things.

D. *Two or Three Gathered Together.*[117] Clark took this title from Matthew 18:20, where Jesus said, "For where two or

---

[116] Compare the parallel interests: (1) Faith: Clark ("Have faith in God," p. 11); Dr. Bob ("As long as people have faith and believe" - *RHS*, p. 28); (2) As a man thinketh: Clark ("As a man thinketh," p. 11); Dr. Bob ("As a man thinketh," *RHS*, p. 34); (3) The tongue: Clark ("the tongue can no man tame," p. 14); Dr. Bob ("guard that erring member the tongue," *DR. BOB*, p. 338). Of course, one cannot say Dr. Bob got these biblical ideas and phrases only from Glenn Clark; but there is a remarkable degree of similarity between the ideas Clark wrote about and those which attracted Dr. Bob's specific attention.

[117] Glenn Clark, *Two or Three Gathered Together* (New York: Harper & Brothers, 1942). Owned by family.

three are gathered together in my name, there am I in the midst of them." Clark mentioned the names of many of the Christian leaders of prayer who became important in Dr. Bob's reading—E. Stanley Jones, Harry Emerson Fosdick, Sherwood Eddy, and Rufus Jones. Clark had received a letter from Toyohiko Kagawa—another of Dr. Bob's favorites—proposing that prayer become the spearhead for a Kingdom of God Movement in America and the world. And Clark described that movement, which involved the men we mentioned and several others. According to Clark, all believed there is special power when two or more Christians are gathered together in prayer. Their starting point was Jesus's declaration in the Sermon on the Mount, "Seek ye first the kingdom of God." And the Movement was to give itself three definite, distinct forms of expression: (1) The Quiet Hour for cultivating the vital experience of God in each individual heart. (2) The Prayer Group for cultivating the expression of vital, cooperative prayer with others. (3) The opening of avenues for bringing the strength and inspiration of the Quiet Hour and of the Prayer Group into vital, constructive expression in the social movements of the day. Recommending something that may also be referred to in the Big Book's Eleventh Step discussion, Clark said:

> With people who are new to the discipline of deepening the prayer life, it is often well to use the first half or two-thirds of the time for study centered around some book. Merely reading aloud *The Practice of the Presence of God* by Brother Lawrence for the first half hour will do wonders in lifting a group into the attitude and spirit of true prayer (p. 73).[118]

Clark then listed many of the authors and books that Dr. Bob read and that we have covered in this book.[119]

---

[118] Compare Big Book, p. 87: "If circumstances warrant, we ask our wives or friends to join us in morning meditation."

[119] On pages 74-75, Clark specifically mentioned Drummond, Heard, Starr Daily, E. Stanley Jones, Fosdick, Weatherhead, *Tertium Organum*, and Frank Laubach. Of Emmet

(continued...)

E. *How to Find Health through Prayer.*[120] Clark believed healing necessitated removal of *particular* blockages to God—selfishness, anger, fear—followed by prayer for a healing (pp. 29-37). Clark said it was not the prayer that created the miracle, but the healing state of consciousness that prayer induces. He said: (1) "The best way to induce it is to live daily practicing the presence of God" (p. 79), and (2) "Turn off hate and fear and self and turn on Faith and Hope and Love," in so doing, you "step into the Secret Place of the Most High where all healing power abides" (p. 79). His meditations used Bible verses such as "underneath are the everlasting arms" [Deuteronomy 33:27].

F. *The Man Who Talks with Flowers.*[121]

G. *Clear Horizons.*[122]

H. *The Lord's Prayer and Other Talks on Prayer from The Camps Farthest Out.* See also our discussion under "Prayer."

I. *God's Reach.*[123]

J. *Touchdowns for the Lord: The Story of "Dad" A. J. Elliott.*[124]

---

[119] (...continued)
Fox, Clark says, "and *The Sermon on the Mount* by Emmet Fox to those who lean toward New Thought" (p. 74).

[120] Glenn Clark, *How to Find Health through Prayer* (New York: Harper & Brothers, 1940). Owned by family.

[121] Glenn Clark, *The Man Who Talks with Flowers* (Minnesota: Macalester Park Publishing Company, 1939). Owned by family.

[122] A bound quarterly, volume 2 (St. Paul: Macalester Park Publishing Company, 1941). Glenn Clark, editor. Owned by family.

[123] Glenn Clark, *God's Reach* (MN: Macalester Park Publishing, n.d.). Owned by family.

[124] Glenn Clark, *Touchdowns for the Lord: The Story of "Dad" A. J. Elliott.* (Minnesota: Macalester Park Publishing Co., 1947).

5. Lloyd Douglas. Dr. Bob owned a good many books by Lloyd Douglas, who was a Christian minister in an Akron Church in the 1930's. The books are all still owned by Dr. Bob's family. We will not detail them because most involve fiction, but we have listed them in the footnote.[125]

6. Henry Drummond.

A. *The Greatest Thing in the World*. See our discussion under "Love."

B. *Natural Law in the Spiritual World*.[126]

7. Harry Emerson Fosdick. Fosdick, the famous pastor of Riverside Church in New York, had more than a passing impact on A.A., both before and after the Big Book was completed.[127] His endorsement of A.A. is included in the Big Book at page 574. Dr. Bob owned and read a good many Fosdick books long before the publication of the Big Book, and even before A.A. So did Dr. Bob's wife, Anne. The following are some of their Fosdick books:

A. *The Meaning of Service*.[128] Fosdick said:

One of the most inveterate and ruinous ideas in the history of human thought is that neither service to man nor any moral righteousness whatsoever is essential to religion. In wide areas of

---

[125] Lloyd Douglas, *The Robe* (Mass: Houghton Mifflin, 1942); *The Big Fisherman* (Mass: Houghton Mifflin, 1948); *White Banners* (N.Y.: Grosset & Dunlop, 1936); *Green Light* (N. Y.: Houghton Mifflin, 1935); *Forgive Us Our Trespasses* (N. Y.: Grosset & Dunlop, 1932).

[126] Henry Drummond, *Natural Law in the Spiritual World* (New York: John B. Alden, 1887). Owned by family.

[127] See the discussion of Fosdick in Mel B., *New Wine*, pp. 143-47, 153.

[128] Harry Emerson Fosdick, *The Meaning of Service* (London: Student Christian Movement, 1921). Owned by family.

religious life, to satisfy God has been one thing, to live in righteous and helpful human relations has been another (p. 1).

. . . *[T]he inevitable expression of real Christianity is a life of sacrificial service* (p. 18, italics in original).

Fosdick commented on verse after verse in the New Testament to show the New Testament emphasis on service. After one series of Bible quotes, Fosdick said, "Read these verses and observe one thing: the Master's earnest desire to share with his disciples the best blessings he had. His peace, his love, his joy—he did not wish to keep them to himself. . . . *Before we can fully enjoy anything we must share it*" (pp. 56-57, italics in original). He concluded his book with a chapter, titled "The Motive of Gratitude," saying:

The distinguishing quality of the Christian motive for unselfishness lies here: *we are expected to live sacrificial lives, because we ourselves are the beneficiaries of sacrificial living beyond our power to equal or repay* (pp. 194-95, italics in original).

B. *The Meaning of Prayer.*[129] For further information, see our discussion in "Prayer."

C. *The Manhood of the Master.*[130] This book was arranged for daily and weekly Bible studies on topics pertaining to Jesus's ministry.

D. *As I See Religion.*[131] Fosdick viewed genuine religion as inward communion from which come peace and power.

---

[129] Harry Emerson Fosdick, *The Meaning of Prayer*. (New York: Association Press, 1926). Anne Smith mentions. Glenn Clark recommended this book for the "Morning Watch" in *Fishers of Men* (p. 98).

[130] Harry Emerson Fosdick, *The Manhood of the Master* (London: Student Christian Movement, 1924). Anne Smith mentions.

[131] Harry Emerson Fosdick, *As I See Religion* (New York: Grossett & Dunlap, 1932). Owned by family.

E. *On Being a Real Person.*[132] Fosdick wrote this book on personal counseling. Writing on the practical use of faith, Fosdick said:

> No man can really become an unbeliever; he is psychologically shut up to the necessity of believing—in God, for example, or else in no God, or else in the impossibility of deciding. One way or another, in every realm, man is inherently a believer in something or other, positive or negative, good or bad, or indifferent (pp. 240-41).

> A constructive faith is thus the supreme organizer of life, and, lacking it, like Humpty Dumpty we fall and break to pieces, and the wonder is whether all the king's horses and all the king's men can ever put us together again (p. 264).

F. *A Great Time to Be Alive.*[133]

G. *The Man from Nazareth.*[134] Fosdick wove the story of Jesus's ministry in terms of the way Jesus was seen by his contemporaries.

8. **Emmet Fox**. We leave to evaluation by others just how much influence Emmet Fox had on A.A. The matter has certainly been discussed in recent writings.[135] One author, Mel B., stated, "Bill Wilson freely acknowledged the importance of the book (Fox's *The Sermon on the Mount*) to A.A." (p. 111). But such acknowledgments do not appear in any of A.A.'s official histories such as *AA Comes of Age, Pass It On*, or *DR. BOB and the Good*

---

[132] Harry Emerson Fosdick, *On Being a Real Person* (New York: Harper & Brothers, 1943). Owned by family.

[133] Harry Emerson Fosdick, *A Great Time to Be Alive* (New York: Harper Brothers, 1944). Owned by family.

[134] Harry Emerson Fosdick, *The Man from Nazareth: As His Contemporaries Saw Him* (New York: Harper & Brothers, 1949). Owned by family.

[135] See, for example, Mel B., *New Wine*, pp. 5, 105-06, 111-14.

Oldtimers. Igor Sikorsky, Jr., asserted that Emmet Fox was one of "A.A.'s Godparents," but Sikorsky's book contains no documentation of the asserted close relationship between Fox and A.A.[136] Emmet Fox was not connected with the Oxford Group or Sam Shoemaker, to whom Bill Wilson attributed A.A.'s ideas; and Fox, in fact, wrote a good deal about what he claimed was the mythology of certain biblical concepts such as sin and atonement.[137]

However, sin and atonement concepts were very much a part of the belief system of the Oxford Group and of Shoemaker. Whatever conflict there may be between the views of Oxford Group writers and Fox (as to the Bible), the fact is that Dr. Bob did read and recommend Fox's *The Sermon on the Mount*. And Dr. Bob owned and read several other Fox books and pamphlets. Anne Smith did *not* mention Fox or his ideas in her Journal. But Nell Wing listed Fox's *The Sermon on the Mount* as among ten books she believed "Early AAs Read."[138] The following Fox books were a part of Dr. Bob's collection:

A. *The Sermon on the Mount.*[139] DR. BOB mentioned this title at pages 310-11, attributing to Dorothy S. M. the statement that Dr. Bob got her the book. Dorothy said there were three main books of her time, namely, *The Upper Room* (actually a periodical), Drummond's *The Greatest Thing in the World*, and Fox's *The Sermon on the Mount*. See also *DR. BOB* at page 151, which, again quoting Dorothy S. M., said: "Many remember that 'The Sermon on the Mount,' by Emmet Fox, was also very popular." In any event, Dr. Bob owned it and read it, and the book is still in his family's possession.

---

[136] See Igor I. Sikorsky, Jr., *AA's Godparents: Carl Jung, Emmet Fox, Jack Alexander* (Minnesota: CompCare Publishers, 1990).

[137] Emmet Fox, *The Sermon on the Mount* (New York: Harper & Row, 1934), pp. 4-5, 7-8.

[138] Pittman, *AA The Way It Began*, p. 192.

[139] Fox, *The Sermon on the Mount.* On Bob E.'s list.

B. *Find and Use Your Inner Power.*[140]

C. *Power through Constructive Thinking.*[141]

D. *Alter Your Life.*[142]

E. *Emmet Fox pamphlets.* The author found that the following Fox pamphlets were owned by Dr. Bob's family: *Getting Results by Prayer* (1933), *You Must Be Born Again* (1936), *The Great Adventure* (1937), and *Your Heart's Desire* (1937).

9. **E. Stanley Jones**. This leading American religious figure during A.A.'s founding years has been much overlooked in A.A. histories. Bill Wilson apparently never mentioned E. Stanley Jones. Yet, as of 1991, a copy of Jones's *Along the Indian Road* was among the very, very *few* A.A. spiritual source books at Bill Wilson's home at Stepping Stones.[143] Glenn Clark frequently mentioned Jones.[144] Former Congressman John Seiberling informed the author that his mother, Henrietta Seiberling, owned and read a number of E. Stanley Jones books.[145] In writing about guided reading, Anne Smith stated in her Journal, "all of E. Stanley Jones' books are very good."[146] Sue Smith Windows, Dr. Bob's daughter, told the author her father read a number of

---

[140] Emmet Fox, *Find and Use Your Inner Power* (New York: Harper & Brothers, 1937). Owned by family.

[141] Emmet Fox, *Power through Constructive Thinking* (New York: Harper & Brothers, 1932). Owned by family.

[142] Emmet Fox, *Alter Your Life* (New York: Harper, 1950). Owned by family.

[143] During his visit to Stepping Stones at Bedford Hills, New York, in October, 1991, the author located a copy of this book in the upstairs library of the Wilson home.

[144] See, for example, Clark, *One Man's Reach*, 276-78; *Two or Three Gathered Together*, p. 74; *Fishers of Men*, p. 97.

[145] Letter to the author from John F. Seiberling, dated August 14, 1991.

[146] See Dick B., *Anne Smith's Journal*, p. 82. (The statement quoted in the text will be found on pages 16 and 48 of the Journal itself—these page numbers being those which were assigned to the Journal copy in the possession of A.A.'s General Services Archives in New York).

the Jones books.[147] And several years ago, Dr. Bob's family still owned several of E. Stanley Jones' books. They were:

A. *The Christ of the Mount.*[148] See our discussion under "The Sermon on the Mount."

B. *Along the Indian Road.*[149]

C. *Abundant Living.*[150] Many of the book's topics—how to find God, self-centeredness, resentments, fear, and guidance—will be familiar to AAs.

D. *Victorious Living.* See our discussion under "Daily Bible Devotionals."

E. *Other E. Stanley Jones books.* There were several other E. Stanley Jones books of the era prior to the Big Book's publication of which Anne Smith spoke indirectly in her Journal when she lauded "all of E. Stanley Jones' books." Sue Smith Windows wrote the author that all the books Anne mentioned were read by Dr. Bob. We do not know if any of the Jones books mentioned in the following footnote was *not* read. But we set forth in our footnote some important Jones books of the time.[151]

---

[147] Interview with Sue Windows, Founders Day Conference, in June, 1991.

[148] E. Stanley Jones, *The Christ of the Mount* (New York: The Abingdon Press, 1931).

[149] E. Stanley Jones, *Along the Indian Road* (New York: Abingdon Press, 1939).

[150] E. Stanley Jones, *Abundant Living.* (New York: Abingdon-Cokesbury Press, 1942).

[151] E. Stanley Jones, *The Christ of the Indian Road (New York: Abingdon Press, 1925); Christ at the Round Table* (New York: The Abingdon Press, 1928); *The Christ of Every Road* (New York: The Abingdon Press, 1930); *Christ and Human Suffering* (New York: The Abingdon Pres, 1933); *The Choice Before Us* (New York: The Abingdon Press, 1937); *The Christ of the American Road* (New York: Abingdon-Cokesbury Press, 1944); *Way to Power & Poise* (New York: Abingdon Press, 1949).

10. **Toyohiko Kagawa**. Dr. Bob spoke frequently of God as a God of love.[152] So did his wife, Anne.[153] And though Dr. Bob owned and read Kagawa's book on love; and though the discussion of it occupied four pages of Anne Smith's Journal; and though Kagawa is frequently mentioned by the other writers, such as Clark and Jones; neither he nor his book, *Love: The Law of Life*, has surfaced in A.A. histories.[154] Kagawa, a Christian pastor, wrote no fewer than five books on the Christian religion. These books contained his interpretation, from different aspects, of the significance of Jesus. *Love* is a study of a great many ingredients of Christian love. Kagawa stated, "The love of Christ stands out as the greatest thing known to humanity" (p. 37).

11. **Charles M. Sheldon**. Sheldon, a young Christian minister in Topeka, Kansas, wrote *In His Steps* and read it to his congregation. The book has reportedly sold 30 million copies since its publication in 1897. The opening question in the book was, "What would Jesus do?" The theme verse was 1 Peter 2:21: "For even hereunto were ye called; because Christ also suffered for us, leaving us an example, that ye should follow his steps."[155]

Religion and the Mind

One could characterize the following books as having to do with the "mental" or "psychological" aspects of Dr. Bob's spiritual quest. But they also cover more general discussions of religion:

---

[152] *DR. BOB*, p. 110.

[153] *DR. BOB*, p. 117; Kurtz, *Not-God*, p. 55. In her signed statement for the author, dated June 8, 1991, Sue Windows stated on page 2, "Mother often used the expression, 'God is love.'"

[154] Toyohiko Kagawa, *Love: The Law of Life* (Philadelphia: The John C. Winston Company, 1929). Owned by family.

[155] Charles M. Sheldon, *In His Steps* (Pennsylvania: Whitaker House, 1979). See the recommendation of this book by Glenn Clark in *Fishers of Men*, p. 97. Henrietta Seiberling's daughter, Dorothy Seiberling, wrote the author on August 14, 1991, that Henrietta had read *In His Steps*. Owned by family.

1. *In Tune with the Infinite* by Ralph Waldo Trine.[156] Often quoting Scripture, Trine aimed at perfect peace. He wrote:

This is the Spirit of Infinite Peace, and the moment we come into harmony with it there comes to us an inflowing tide of peace, for peace is harmony. A deep interior meaning underlies the great truth, "To be spiritually minded is life and peace." To recognize the fact that we are spirit, and to live in this thought, is to be spiritually minded, and so to be in harmony and peace (p. 135).

We need more faith in every-day life—faith in the power that works for good, faith in the Infinite God, and hence faith in ourselves created in His image (p. 147).[157]

A knowledge of the Spiritual Power working in and through us as well as in and through all things, a power that works for righteousness, leads to optimism. . . . He it is who realizes the truth of the injunction, "Rest in the Lord, wait patiently for Him and He shall give thee thy heart's desire" (pp. 148-49).

In the degree, then, that we work in conjunction with the Supreme Power do we need the less to concern ourselves about results (p. 149).

William James discussed Trine's writing at some length in his *The Varieties of Religious Experience*.[158]

2. *The Man Who Knew* by Ralph Waldo Trine.[159]

---

[156] Ralph Waldo Trine, *In Tune with the Infinite* (New York: Thomas Y. Crowell, 1897). Owned by family,

[157] Compare the following language in the Big Book at page 68, "we are now on a different basis, the basis of trusting and relying upon God. We trust infinite God rather than our finite selves. . . . Just to the extent that we do as we think He would have us, and humbly rely on Him, does He enable us to match calamity with serenity."

[158] See James, *The Varieties of Religious Experience*, pp. 93, 302.

[159] Ralph Waldo Trine, *The Man Who Knew* (New York: Bobbs Merrill, 1936). Owned by family.

3. *Modern Man in Search of a Soul* by Dr. Carl G. Jung. See discussion under A.A.'s "Founders."[160]

4. *Peace of Mind* by Joshua Loth Liebman.[161] Dr. Bob proclaimed:

> We're all after the same thing, and that's happiness. We want peace of mind. The trouble with us alcoholics was this: We demanded that the world give us happiness and peace of mind in just the particular way we wanted to get it—by the alcohol route. And we weren't successful. But when we take time to find out some of the spiritual laws, and familiarize ourselves with them, and put them into practice, then we do get happiness and peace of mind (*DR. BOB*, p. 308).

Bill Wilson made a special gift of Liebman's book to Dr. Bob.[162]

5. *Psychology of a Christian Personality* by Ernest M. Ligon.[163] Ligon examined Christian personality from the standpoint of the Sermon on the Mount.

6. *Religion Says You Can* by Dilworth Lupton.[164] The Reverend Dr. Dilworth Lupton was the pastor of Cleveland's First Unitarian Church and played a role in the growth of A.A. in Cleveland, once the Cleveland AAs had severed their Oxford Group connection in Akron, Ohio.[165] Lupton wrote:

---

[160] Dr. Carl G. Jung, *Modern Man in Search of a Soul* (New York: Harcourt, Brace and Company, 1933). Owned by family. See Mel B., *New Wine*, page 15.

[161] Joshua Loth Liebman, *Peace of Mind* (New York: Simon & Schuster, 1946). Owned by family.

[162] Bill's inscription—which the author has inspected—reads, "To Smitty - my wonderful friend of AA. Bill, Xmas '46." Owned by family.

[163] Ernest M. Ligon, *Psychology of a Christian Personality* (New York: Macmillan, 1935). Owned by family.

[164] Dilworth Lupton, *Religion Says You Can* (Boston: The Beacon Press, 1938). Owned by family.

[165] For a discussion of Lupton's role, see Kurtz, *Not-God*, pp. 84-85.

At the heart of this book's message is my personal faith that religion, more than any other human experience, can help a man so re-create his character and personality that he can stand like a rock against adversity. By religion I do not mean church-going lip service to creeds—I mean rather that amazing awareness that men have felt through the ages that they were of "finer stuff than the stars" (p. ix).

The truly religious man, of whatever faith, possesses a third line of defense. He finds power not only in himself and in his friends and affections: he also draws on the power of God. . . . Christian religion is one of the most valuable and potent influences that we have for producing that harmony and peace of mind and that confidence of soul which is needed to bring health (pp. 80-81).

7. *The Rediscovery of Man* by Dr. Henry C. Link.[166] Link focused on psychology, which, he said, is a study of habits and their formation. He believed that psychology has rediscovered man and the powers of which he is capable when his mind has been freed from prevailing fallacies about himself. He believed that *personality* is an attribute and defines the extent to which the individual has developed habits and skills which interest and serve other people. He believed that the Christian concept of personality does not stop with the process of service, of loving one's neighbor, or being one's brother's keeper. All of these aspects of personality are rediscovered in the concept of obedience to moral law. He believed Christ is the great liberator in the world today and inspires man to achieve his highest personality under Christ's codes.

---

[166] Henry C. Link, *The Rediscovery of Man* (New York: Macmillan, 1939). Owned by family.

Quiet Time

Dr. Bob owned a book on Quiet Time titled *The Quiet Time*. Its author was S. D. Gordon.[167]

We will mention several other titles as part of this Quiet Time category. All were well known Oxford Group books of the 1920's and 1930's, and specifically addressed the topic of Quiet Time. It seems likely they were read by Dr. Bob, Anne, Henrietta, and T. Henry and Clarace Williams; for all made Quiet Time the focus of their prayer and meditation life. Their Quiet Time involved Bible study, two-way prayer (praying to God and listening for guidance from God), writing down the leading thoughts received, and utilizing devotionals and other Christian literature to aid their study and thinking process. The Oxford Group Quiet Time books are:

1. *The Guidance of God* by Eleanor Napier Forde.[168]
2. *When Man Listens* by Cecil Rose.[169]
3. *The Quiet Time* by Howard J. Rose.[170] This Oxford Group pamphlet outlined the Quiet Time procedure and contained the verses of Scripture that pertain to it.
4. *God Does Guide Us* by W. E. Sangster.[171]
5. *The God Who Speaks* by Burnett Hillman Streeter.[172]
6. *What Is The Oxford Group?* by The Layman with a Notebook.

---

[167] S. D. Gordon, *The Quiet Time* (London: Fleming, n.d.). Owned by family.

[168] Eleanor Napier Forde, *The Guidance of God* (Oxford: Printed at the University Press, 1930). Portions of Miss Forde's comments appear to have been quoted by Anne Smith in her Journal; and Anne mentions Eleanor Forde by name in the Journal.

[169] Cecil Rose, *When Man Listens* (New York: Oxford University Press, 1937).

[170] Howard J. Rose, *The Quiet Time* (New York: Oxford Group at 61 Gramercy Park North, 1937).

[171] W. E. Sangster, *God Does Guide Us* (New York: The Abingdon Press, 1934).

[172] Burnett Hillman Streeter, *The God Who Speaks* (New York: The Macmillan Co., 1936).

7. *How Do I Begin?* by Hallen Viney.[173] This little pamphlet is a primer on how to receive and write down leading thoughts from God.

8. *Vital Touch with God: How to Carry on Adequate Devotional Life* by Jack C. Winslow.[174]

9. *When I Awake* by Jack C. Winslow.[175]

10. *How to Find Reality in Your Morning Devotions* by Donald W. Carruthers.[176] Though Carruthers was apparently not a "member" of the Oxford Group, his pamphlet was much recommended by Dr. Samuel Moor Shoemaker and was frequently used by Oxford Group people.

The Weatherhead Puzzle

Where is Leslie D. Weatherhead? An important name that is missing from A.A. histories and from our list of Dr. Bob's books is that of Dr. Leslie D. Weatherhead. Weatherhead was mentioned in passing by Glenn Clark.[177] But we have included this discussion on Weatherhead because of his close connection with the Oxford Group in the 1930's, and the fact that two of his books—with Henrietta Seiberling's name written in them—are linked to Bill Wilson's scanty library of biblical materials.[178]

---

[173] Hallen Viney, *How Do I Begin?* (New York: The Oxford Group at 61 Gramercy Park, 1937).

[174] Jack C. Winslow, *Vital Touch with God: How to Carry on Adequate Devotional Life*, Reprint of an article in *The Calvary Evangel*, n.d.

[175] Jack C. Winslow, *When I Awake* (London: Hodder & Stoughton, 1938).

[176] Donald W. Carruthers, *How to Find Reality in Your Morning Devotions* (Pennsylvania State College, n.d.)

[177] See Clark, *Two or Three Gathered Together*, p. 74.

[178] Leslie D. Weatherhead, Ph,D., D.D., was Minister Emeritus of The City Temple, London, and formerly President of the Methodist Conference in Great Britain. He authored some twenty-five titles.

Weatherhead's *Discipleship* is located in the upstairs library at Bill Wilson's home at Stepping Stones in New York.[179] The book contains a virtual manual on Oxford Group principles and practices that found their way into A.A. Its chapters include: (1) Surrender, (2) Sharing, (3) The Quiet Time, (4) Fellowship, (5) Guidance, (6) The Will of God, (7) Restitution, and (8) Witness. Did Dr. Bob read it? We just don't know. Bill Wilson's former secretary, Nell Wing, owns another Weatherhead book, *Psychology and Life*.[180] This book is inscribed with Henrietta Seiberling's name and was a present from Bill to Nell. We also mention here Weatherhead's *How Can I Find God?*.[181]

Weatherhead's books dealt with a challenge, also tendered in the Big Book: Find God now![182] Henrietta Seiberling read Weatherhead, and Henrietta was much involved in the early spiritual education of Dr. Bob and Bill W. Weatherhead's books are on target as to the Oxford Group principles that influenced Bob and Bill. And we believe they might well have formed a part of Dr. Bob's reading, or, at least, the ideas from Weatherhead that Henrietta may have imparted to Dr. Bob.

The Calvary Evangel List of Oxford Group Literature

There are a great many books and pamphlets by Oxford Group people and about the Oxford Group that were published in the

---

[179] Leslie D. Weatherhead, *Discipleship* (New York: The Abingdon Press, 1934). The author inspected this book at Stepping Stones and found Henrietta's name written in it. Henrietta's daughter, Dorothy Seiberling, had told the author that many of Henrietta's books had been sent to A.A. This may have been one. In any event, it wound up at Bill's home at Bedford Hills, New York.

[180] Leslie D. Weatherhead, *Psychology and Life* (New York: Abingdon Press, 1935).

[181] Leslie D. Weatherhead, *How Can I Find God?* (New York: Fleming H. Revell, 1934). We did not find this among Bill Wilson's or Dr. Bob's books.

[182] The Big Book's actual language, on page 59, states: "But there is One who has all power—that One is God. May you find Him now!"

1920's and thereafter.[183] We believe our current bibliography (under Oxford Group, Oxford Group Mentors, and Shoemaker) lists all the titles of any significance in the United States and abroad that might have been read by, or have influenced AAs. For several reasons we have not previously listed them.

We have found no evidence to date that Bill Wilson had more than two or three Oxford Group books in his possession in the 1930's; and we have found none by Dr. Samuel Shoemaker—to whom Bill attributed most of the Steps. We have not yet tracked down more than six Oxford Group books that Henrietta Seiberling owned and read. And they are in our list of books that Dr. Bob read.[184] Similarly, we have not seen more than eight Oxford Group books and five Sam Shoemaker books that Dr. Bob owned and which are still owned by his family. And we have listed these. We have also listed other Oxford Group-Shoemaker books mentioned by Anne Smith and known to have been read by her husband.

But the previously listed books may not include a good many Oxford Group books of the 1930's which Henrietta Seiberling probably read. They also may not include all of what Dr. Bob described as the "immense" number of books recommended to him by the Oxford Group. For one thing, the furnace room at T. Henry's house always had Oxford Group materials available for the 1930's meetings there. Therefore, to be sure our readers know all the Oxford Group books which were probably read by Dr. Bob, we include here the entirety of the books listed as Oxford Group literature in *The Calvary Evangel* in the 1930's. And, since we

---

[183] See the bibliography at the end of this title, and also Dick B., *The Books Early AAs Read For Spiritual Growth*, 5th ed. (CA: Paradise Research Publications, 1996).

[184] The Oxford Group books known to have been read by Henrietta Seiberling, and our sources of information about that fact, are: (1) *Life Changers* by Harold Begbie (John Seiberling's letter to the author, dated August 14, 1991); (2) *For Sinners Only* by A. J. Russell (J. Seiberling letter, 8/14/91); (3) *Soul Surgery* by H. A. Walter (J. Seiberling letter, 8/14/91) (4) *Inspired Children* by Olive M. Jones (Dorothy Seiberling's letter to the author, dated July 19, 1991); (5) *If I Be Lifted Up* by Samuel M. Shoemaker (J. Seiberling letter, 8/14/91); (6) *Children of the Second Birth* by Samuel M. Shoemaker (Dorothy Seiberling's letter to the author, dated August 14, 1991).

first assembled this list, we have run across other early titles at the Shoemaker collection in the Episcopal Church Archives in Texas, along with some sent us by Oxford Group people. These additional titles can be found in our bibliography.

As they were listed in 1935-1939 issues of *The Calvary Evangel*, the following Oxford Group books were recommended:

1. *Inspired Youth* by Olive Jones.[185]
2. *For Sinners Only* by A. J. Russell.[186]
3. *I Was a Pagan* by V. C. Kitchen.[187]
4. *Life Began Yesterday* by Stephen Foot.[188]
5. *The Church Can Save the World* by S. M. Shoemaker.[189]
6. *The God Who Speaks* by B. H. Streeter.[190]
7. *Children of the Second Birth* by S. M. Shoemaker.[191]
8. *Twice-Born Ministers* by S. M. Shoemaker.[192]
9. *If I Be Lifted Up* by S. M. Shoemaker.[193]
10. *Confident Faith* by S. M. Shoemaker.[194]
11. *The Gospel According to You* by S. M. Shoemaker.[195]
12. *Inspired Children* by Olive Jones.[196]
13. *What Is The Oxford Group?* by The Layman with a Note

---

[185] Olive Jones, *Inspired Youth* (New York: Harper & Brothers, 1938).

[186] A. J. Russell, *For Sinners Only* (London: Hodder & Stoughton, 1932).

[187] V. C. Kitchen, *I Was a Pagan* (New York: Harper & Brothers, 1934).

[188] Stephen Foot, *Life Began Yesterday* (New York: Harper & Brothers, 1935).

[189] Samuel M. Shoemaker, *The Church Can Save the World* (New York: Harper & Brothers, 1938).

[190] Burnett Hillman Streeter, *The God Who Speaks* (New York: The Macmillan Company, 1936).

[191] Samuel M. Shoemaker, *Children of the Second Birth* (New York: Fleming H. Revell, 1927).

[192] Samuel M. Shoemaker, *Twice-Born Ministers* (New York: Fleming H. Revell, 1929).

[193] Samuel M. Shoemaker, *If I Be Lifted Up* (New York: Fleming H. Revell, 1931).

[194] Samuel M. Shoemaker, *Confident Faith* (New York: Fleming H. Revell, 1932).

[195] Samuel M. Shoemaker, *The Gospel According to You* (New York: Fleming H. Revell, 1934).

[196] Olive Jones, *Inspired Children* (New York: Harper & Brothers, 1933).

book.[197]

14. *Religion That Works* by S. M. Shoemaker.[198]
15. *The Conversion of the Church* by S. M. Shoemaker.[199]
16. *National Awakening* by S. M. Shoemaker.[200]
17. *The Venture of Belief* by Philip M. Brown.[201]
18. *Realizing Religion* by S. M. Shoemaker.[202]
19. *Church in Action* by Jack Winslow.[203]
20. *Why I Believe in the Oxford Group* by Jack Winslow.[204]
21. *Soul Surgery* by Howard Walter.[205]
22. *When Man Listens* by Cecil Rose.[206]
23. *The Guidance of God* by Eleanor Napier Forde.[207]
24. *New Leadership* by Garth Lean and Morris Martin.[208]
25. *The New Enlistment* by Wilfrid Holmes-Walker.[209]

---

[197] The Layman with a Notebook, *What Is The Oxford Group?* (London: Oxford University Press, 1933).

[198] Samuel M. Shoemaker, *Religion That Works* (New York: Fleming H. Revell, 1928).

[199] Samuel M. Shoemaker, *The Conversion of the Church* (New York: Fleming H. Revell, 1932).

[200] Samuel M. Shoemaker, *National Awakening* (New York: Harper & Brothers, 1936).

[201] Philip M. Brown, *The Venture of Belief* (New York: Fleming H. Revell, 1935).

[202] Samuel M. Shoemaker, *Realizing Religion* (New York: Association Press, 1923).

[203] Though we have made an extensive search for this book, and for information about it, we have not been able to obtain any information. We asked Oxford Group offices in the United States and in the United Kingdom. We have also made inquiry of long-time Oxford Group activists in the United States and abroad, and of Shoemaker associates, all to no avail.

[204] Jack C. Winslow, *Why I Believe in the Oxford Group* (London: Hodder & Stoughton, 1934).

[205] Howard A. Walter, *Soul Surgery: Some Thoughts on Incisive Personal Work*, 6th ed. (Oxford at the University Press by John Johnson, 1940). 1st ed. published, 1919.

[206] Cecil Rose, *When Man Listens* (New York: Oxford University Press, 1937).

[207] Eleanor Napier Forde, *The Guidance of God* (Oxford, The Oxford Group, printed at the University Press by John Johnson, 1930).

[208] Garth Lean and Morris Martin, *New Leadership* (London: Wm. Heinemann, Ltd., 1936).

[209] Wilfrid Holmes-Walker, *The New Enlistment* (London: The Oxford Group, n.d.).

26. *How Do I Begin* by Hallen Viney.[210]
27. *The Quiet Time* by Howard Rose.[211]
28. *How to Find Reality in Your Morning Devotions* by Donald Carruthers.[212]
29. *The Person of Christ* by L. W. Grensted.[213]
30. *Calvary Church in Action* by John Potter Cuyler, Jr.[214]
31. *Seeking and Finding* by Ebenezer Macmillan.[215] This is one of the very few Oxford Group books the author found in Bill Wilson's library at Stepping Stones, Bedford Hills, New York.
32. *Christ's Words from the Cross* by Samuel M. Shoemaker.[216]

Books Henrietta, Clarence S., and Pioneers Mentioned

Many spiritual books recommended to AAs were read by Henrietta Seiberling, Clarence S., and some of the other early pioneers. These are covered adequately in our titles, *The Books Early AAs Read for Spiritual Growth* and *That Amazing Grace: The Role of Clarence and Grace S. in Alcoholics Anonymous.*[217]

---

[210] Hallen Viney, *How Do I Begin?* (New York: Oxford Group at 61 Gramercy Park, North, 1937).

[211] Howard J. Rose, *The Quiet Time* (Sussex: Howard J. Rose, 6 The Green, Slaugham, Haywards Heath, n.d.).

[212] Donald W. Carruthers, *How to Find Reality in Your Morning Devotions* (Pennsylvania State College, n.d.).

[213] L. W. Grensted, *The Person of Christ* (New York: Harper & Brothers, 1933).

[214] John Potter Cuyler, Jr., *Calvary Church in Action* (New York: Fleming H. Revell, 1934).

[215] Ebenezer Macmillan, *Seeking and Finding* (New York: Harper & Brothers, 1933).

[216] Samuel M. Shoemaker, Jr., *Christ's Words from the Cross* (New York: Fleming H. Revell, 1933).

[217] Dick B., *The Books Early AAs Read for Spiritual Growth*, 5th ed. (San Rafael, CA: Paradise Research Publications, 1996); *That Amazing Grace*, p. 31.

13

Quiet Time and the Devotionals

It Began in the Bible

Early AAs unquestionably heard that the will of God can be found in the Good Book. Sam Shoemaker taught that God's *general will* is in the Scriptures.[1] Later, he wrote: "The Bible from one end to the other tells us about Him [God], about His will for man and the world."[2] Phrasing the idea slightly differently, Oxford Group progenitors said the Bible contains God's *universal will*.[3] Professor Henry Drummond (much quoted by Shoemaker and whose books were read by Dr. Bob) wrote: "The Bible is God's will in words, in formal thoughts, in grace."[4] Drummond gave the Ten Commandments and the Beatitudes of Christ as examples.[5] AAs themselves underlined knowing the will of God; and since

---

[1] Samuel M. Shoemaker, Jr., *The Conversion of the Church* (New York: Fleming H. Revell, 1932), pp. 49-50; *A Young Man's View of the Ministry* (New York: Association Press, 1923), p. 78.

[2] Samuel M. Shoemaker, *Christ and This Crisis* (New York: Fleming H. Revell, 1943), p. 106.

[3] Henry Drummond, *The Ideal Life: Addresses Hitherto Unpublished* (New York: Hodder & Stoughton, 1897), pp. 268-71; Henry B. Wright, *The Will of God and a Man's Lifework* (New York: The Young Men's Christian Association Press, 1909), p. 137.

[4] Drummond, *The Ideal Life*, p. 268.

[5] Drummond, *The Ideal Life*, pp. 270-71; see also, Wright, *The Will of God*, p. 137.

their spiritual sources all taught them that God's universal will is
found in the Bible, we think it vital to start with the Bible to find
what Scripture has to say about getting in touch with, and knowing
God, and His will, in the morning and throughout the day, by
prayer, meditation, and the study of His word.[6]

The Morning Watch and Prayer

Before the captivity, the Hebrews divided the night into three
"watches": (1) From sunset to ten p.m., (2) from ten p.m. to two
a.m., and (3) from two a.m. to sunrise. The first watch period was
called the "beginning of the watches;"[7] the second, the "middle
watch;"[8] and the third, the "morning watch."[9] Collectively, the
three were called the "night watches."[10]

When the Israelites became subject to Roman power, most
adopted the Roman method of dividing the watches—increasing the
number from three to four: (1) Evening watch—sunset to 9:00
p.m.;[11] (2) Midnight watch—9:00 p.m. to midnight;[12] (3) Cock-
crowing watch—midnight to 3:00 a.m.;[13] and (4) Morning
watch—3:00 a.m. to sunrise.[14]

The watches marked the time in only a general way. The
"watch," as a word, had special significance in Bible times

---

[6] For the many examples of A.A. concern over the will of God (particularly as
expressed in the language of its Eleventh Step), see *Alcoholics Anonymous*, 3rd ed. (New
York: Alcoholics Anonymous World Services, Inc., 1976), pp. 59, 63, 67, 85, 87;
Alcoholics Anonymous Comes of Age (New York: Alcoholics Anonymous World
Services, 1979), p. 105; Dick B., *The Good Book and The Big Book: A.A.'s Roots in the
Bible* (San Rafael, CA: Paradise Research Publications, 1995), p. 69.

[7] Lamentations 2:19.

[8] Judges 7:19.

[9] Exodus 14:24; 1 Samuel 11:11.

[10] Psalms 63:6; 119:148.

[11] Mark 13:35.

[12] Luke 12:38.

[13] Luke 12:38.

[14] Matthew 14:25; Mark 6:48.

primarily because of its relationship to the function of the "watchmen." The cities of old relied upon the watchmen for protection. Men were employed to watch day and night on the top of the city walls and especially by the gates.[15] Other watchmen had the duty of patrolling the streets of the city and preserving order.[16] We will examine primarily the "morning watch," which ended at sunrise. The Hebrew and Greek texts' references to "watch" speak of a "watch," a "guard," a "time during which guard was kept," a "guarding," and a "time of watch."[17]

In His Word, God ascribed special significance to the watches, as far as prayer and meditation were concerned. The morning—sunrise—the end of the morning watch—was often mentioned:

Thus will I bless thee while I live: I will lift up my hands in thy name. My soul shall be satisfied as *with* marrow and fatness; and my mouth shall praise *thee* with joyful lips. When I remember thee upon my bed, *and* meditate on thee in the *night* watches (Psalm 63:4-6).

Arise, cry out in the night: in the beginning of the watches pour out thine heart like water before the face of the Lord . . . (Lamentations 2:19).

But I will sing of thy power; yea I will sing aloud of thy mercy in the morning: for thou hast been my defence and refuge in the day of my trouble (Psalm 59:16).

---

[15] E.g., 2 Samuel 18:26; James M. Freeman, *Manners and Customs of the Bible* (Plainfield, New Jersey: Logos International, 1972), p. 147.

[16] E.g., Song of Solomon 3:3; Freeman, *Manners and Customs of the Bible*, p. 248.

[17] For discussions of the watches, see *New Bible Dictionary*, 2d ed. (Wheaton, IL: Tyndale House, 1982), pp. 1242-43; *Vine's Expository Dictionary of Old and New Testament Words* (New York: Fleming H. Revell, 1981), p. 200; *The Abingdon Bible Commentary* (New York: Abingdon Press, 1920), p. 77a; *Wilson's Old Testament Word Studies* (McLean, VA: Mac Donald Publishing Co., n.d.), p. 474.

It is a good *thing* to give thanks unto the Lord, and to sing praises unto thy name, O most High: To shew forth thy loving-kindness in the morning, and thy faithfulness every night (Psalm 92:1-2).

Cause me to hear thy loving-kindness in the morning; for in thee do I trust: cause me to know the way wherein I should walk; for I lift up my soul unto thee (Psalm 143:8).

The Lord God hath given me the tongue of the learned, that I should know how to speak a word in season to *him that is* weary: he wakeneth morning by morning, he wakeneth mine ear to hear as the learned. The Lord God hath opened mine ear, and I was not rebellious, neither turned away back (Isaiah 50:4-5).

God Speaks Through His Word

In the Old Testament, "the word (*dabar*) of God" is used 394 times of a divine communication which comes from God to men in the form of commandment, prophecy, warning or encourage-ment.[18] From beginning to end, the Bible speaks of communi-cations from God as the "word of God" or the "word of the Lord." The words of God collectively are spoken of as God's "Word." A.A. sources spoke often and authoritatively of the Bible as *the* Word of God.[19] And these sources were agreed that one

---

[18] *New Bible Dictionary*, p. 1259.

[19] See, for example, F. B. Meyer, *The Secret of Guidance* (New York: Fleming H. Revell, 1896), p. 120; Henry Drummond, *The Ideal Life*, pp. 227-320; William R. Moody, *The Life of D. L. Moody* (New York: Fleming H. Revell, 1920), pp. 497, 19; Wright, *The Will of God and a Man's Lifework*, p. 137; Donald W. Carruthers, *How to Find Reality in Your Morning Devotions* (Pennsylvania: State College, n.d.), p. 1; Jack C. Winslow, *When I Awake* (London: Hodder & Stoughton, 1938), p. 62; "Vital Touch with God" (Reprint from *The Calvary Evangel*, n.d.), p. 5. For a discussion of the primary A.A. sources, see Dick B., *Design for Living: The Oxford Group's Contribution to Early A.A.* (San Rafael, CA: Paradise Research Publications, 1995), pp. 1-67; *The Good Book and The Big Book*, pp. 12-38.

who wished to learn the "will of God" should start with the "word of God."[20]

The following verses from the Old Testament illustrate the language in the Bible itself which characterized the Bible and its words as the Word of God:

> After these things the word of the Lord came unto Abram in a vision, saying, Fear not, Abram: I *am* thy shield, *and* thy exceeding great reward (Genesis 15:1).

> And the child Samuel ministered unto the Lord before Eli. And the word of the Lord was precious in those days; *there was* no open vision (1 Samuel 3:1).

> Thy word have I hid in mine heart, that I might not sin against thee (Psalm 119:11).

> Thy word *is* true *from* the beginning: and every one of thy righteous judgments *endureth* forever (Psalm 119:160).

> I rejoice at thy word, as one that findeth great spoil (Psalm 119:162).

> The word of the Lord came expressly unto Ezekiel (Ezekiel 1:3).[21]

> And say unto the Ammonites, Hear the word of the Lord God; Thus saith the Lord God . . . (Ezekiel 25:3).

> The burden of the word of the Lord to Israel by Malachi (Malachi 1:1).

---

[20] See, for example, Samuel M. Shoemaker's usages in *Realizing Religion* (New York: Association Press, 1933), pp. 58-62; *A Young Man's View of the Ministry*, p. 78; *Twice-Born Ministers* (New York: Fleming H. Revell, 1929), pp. 184-185; *The Conversion of the Church*, pp. 49-50; *Christ and This Crisis*, p. 106.

[21] See discussion in Winslow, *When I Awake*, p. 49.

In the Gospels, Jesus Christ characterized God's Word as follows:

> I have given them thy word; and the world hath hated them, because they are not of the world, even as I am not of the world (John 17:14).

> Sanctify them through thy truth: thy word is truth (John 17:17).

> Now the parable is this: The seed is the word of God (Luke 8:11).

In 1 Thessalonians 2:13, the Apostle Paul said the following about the word of God:

> For this cause also thank we God without ceasing, because when ye received the word of God which ye heard of us, ye received it not *as* the word of men, but as it is in truth, the word of God, which effectually worketh also in you that believe.

In Hebrews 4:12, Paul said:

> For the word of God *is* quick and powerful, and sharper than any twoedged sword, piercing even to the dividing asunder of soul and spirit, and of the joints and marrow, and *is* a discerner of the thoughts and intents of the heart.

And Revelation, the final book of the Bible, states in chapter 1, verses 1-3:

> The Revelation of Jesus Christ, which God gave unto him, to shew unto his servants things which must shortly come to pass; and he sent and signified it by his angel unto his servant John:

> Who bare record of the word of God, and of the testimony of Jesus Christ, and of all things that he saw.

Blessed is he that readeth, and they that hear the words of this prophecy, and keep those things which are written therein: for the time is at hand.

The Bible and How God Revealed His Written Word

The Old Testament frequently indicated how the word of God was revealed to people, namely by vision (Isaiah 1:1-2; Habakkuk 2:2-3),[22] by word (Jeremiah 1:2-4), and by instruction of the spirit (Nehemiah 9:20; Psalm 143:10; Proverbs 1:3; Ezekiel 2:2).[23] The New Testament further explained that this word of God was revealed to the spirit of believers by God, who *is* spirit.[24] The following verses elaborated:

Knowing this first, that no prophecy of the scripture is of any private interpretation. For the prophecy came not in old time by the will of man: but holy men of God spake *as they were* moved by the Holy Ghost (2 Peter 1:20-21).[25]

All scripture *is* given by inspiration of God, and *is* profitable for doctrine, for reproof, for correction, for instruction in righteousness (2 Timothy 3:16).[26]

---

[22] See Winslow, *When I Awake*, p. 49.

[23] See Nora Smith Holm, *The Runner's Bible* (New York: Houghton Mifflin, 1915), p. 52.

[24] John 4:24: "God *is* a Spirit." The word "a" should be deleted as it is not used in Greek texts. The correct translation would be "God *is* [added by King James Version] Spirit." See also as to the Comforter or Holy Spirit or Spirit of truth which will teach: John 14:16, 26; 15:26; 16:7-15; Acts 1:4, 5, 8; and Holm, *The Runner's Bible*, pp. 16, 17, 104; Harry Almond, *Foundations for Faith*, 2d ed. (London: Grosvenor, 1980), p. 23.

[25] See Holm, *The Runner's Bible*, p. 18; Wright, *The Will of God*, p. 147.

[26] See E. Stanley Jones, *Victorious Living* (New York: Abingdon Press, 1936), p. 262. As to Dwight L. Moody, the evangelist, see Dick B., *Design for Living*, p. 44. For the Roman Catholic view of the Scripture, see the Encyclical Letter of Pope Pius XII, "Divino Afflante Spiritu," September 30, 1943, in James J. McGivern, *Official Catholic*

(continued...)

But I certify you, brethren, that the gospel which was preached of me is not after man. For I neither received it of man, neither was I taught it, but by the revelation of Jesus Christ (Galatians 1:11-12).[27]

The Good Book Says of Meditation, Study, and Prayer

Meditate in the Word of God!

A word about "meditation." Merriam Webster's Collegiate Dictionary, Tenth Edition, defines "meditate" in terms of engaging in contemplation or reflection and, when directed at an object, "to focus one's thoughts on: reflect on or ponder over."

Thus, when the Bible speaks of "meditating," as it often does, it is usually speaking of focusing thoughts on, pondering over, and studying *the word of God*.[28] That interpretation is usually clear from the verse itself and certainly from the context. The following are some of the many verses which speak of "meditating" on God, His work, and His word. Some of the verses were mentioned in the religious literature early AAs read for spiritual growth.[29] In the verses, the Word of God is variously referred to as His word, His commandments, His precepts, His teachings, His statutes, and His law:

---

[26] (...continued)
Teachings: Bible Interpretation (Wilmington, NC: McGrath Publishing Company, 1978), p. 316.

[27] See Wright, *The Will of God*, p. 145; Burnett Hillman Streeter, *The God Who Speaks* (London: MacMillan and Co., 1936), p. 91; Ebenezer Macmillan, *Seeking and Finding* (New York: Harper & Brothers, 1933), p. 140.

[28] See Spiros Zodhiates, *The Hebrew-Greek Key Study Bible*, rev. ed. (AMG Publishers, 1991); see page 32 of the Hebrew and Chaldee Dictionary portion, number 1897.

[29] For a list of these materials, see Dick B., *The Books Early AAs Read for Spiritual Growth*, 4th ed. (San Rafael, CA: Paradise Research Publications, 1996).

My meditation of him [God] shall be sweet: I will be glad in the Lord (Psalm 104:34).[30]

I will meditate also of all thy work, and talk of thy doings (Psalm 77:12).

But his delight is in the law of the Lord; and in his law doth he meditate day and night. And he shall be like a tree planted by the rivers of water, that bringeth forth his fruit in his season; his leaf also shall not wither; and whatsoever he doeth shall prosper (Psalm 1:2-3).[31]

O how love I thy law! it *is* my meditation all day (Psalm 119:97).

I have more understanding than all my teachers: for thy testimonies *are* my meditation (Psalm 119:99).

I will meditate in thy precepts, and have respect unto thy ways. I will delight myself in thy statutes: I will not forget thy word (Psalms 119:15-16).

Let the proud be ashamed; for they dealt perversely with me without a cause: but I will meditate in thy precepts (Psalm 119:78).

My hands also will lift up unto thy commandments, which I have loved; and I will meditate in thy statutes (Psalm 119:48).

Mine eyes prevent [precede] the *night* watches, that I might meditate in thy word (Psalm 119:148).

The Old Testament was describing a thinking process which focused thoughts on, pondered, and studied about God, His works, and His word. And in addressing his faithful helper Timothy, Paul

---

[30] See Holm, *The Runner's Bible*, p. 38.

[31] Mary Wilder Tileston, *Daily Strength for Daily Needs* (New York: Grosset & Dunlap, 1884), p. 258.

warned against seducing spirits and doctrines of devils with lies in hypocrisy. He urged the word of God and prayer and the rejection of profane and old wives fables. He spoke of reading, exhortation, and doctrine. And he concluded:

> Meditate upon these things; give thyself wholly to them; that thy profiting may appear to all. Take heed unto thyself, and unto the doctrine; continue in them; for in doing this thou shalt both save thyself, and them that hear thee (1 Timothy 4:15-16).

Study the Scriptures!

What did the Word of God have to say about the meditation *process*? Jesus said

> Search the scriptures. . . (John 5:39).[32]

> Ye do err, not knowing the scriptures, nor the power of God (Matthew 22:19).[33]

Believers in the first century Christian Church heeded what they were taught about the word of God, but then checked the teachings against the word itself to be sure the teachings conformed to the word of God. Speaking of the Bereans, the Book of Acts said:

> These [the believers from Berea] were more noble than those in Thessalonica, in that they received the word with all readiness of mind, and searched the scriptures daily, whether those things were so. Therefore many of them believed; also of honourable women which were Greeks, and of men, not a few (Acts: 17:11-12).

---

[32] See Holm, *The Runner's Bible*, p. 51; *The Upper Room* for 8/12/38; Dick B., *New Light on Alcoholism* (Corte Madera, CA: Good Book Publishing Company, 1994), p. 270.

[33] See Jones, *Victorious Living*, p. 262; Holm, *The Runner's Bible*, p. 51.

Finally, Paul wrote Timothy that the word of God was to be studied and "worked" carefully to assure that it was being correctly interpreted:

> Study to shew thyself approved unto God, a workman that needeth not to be ashamed, rightly dividing the word of truth. But shun profane *and* vain babblings: for they will increase unto more ungodliness (2 Timothy 2:15-16).[34]

The Book of James—a favorite in early A.A.—stated:

> Wherefore lay apart all filthiness and superfluity of naughtiness, and receive with meekness the engrafted word, which is able to save your souls. But be ye doers of the word, and not hearers only, deceiving your own selves (James 1:21-22).[35]

Meditate and Pray in the Morning!

The most recognized source in God's word pertaining to *morning* prayer and meditation can be found in Psalm 5:1-3:

> Give ear to my words, O Lord, consider my meditation. Hearken unto the voice of my cry, my King, and my God: for unto thee will I pray. My voice shalt thou hear in the morning, O Lord; in the morning will I direct *my prayer* unto thee, and will look up.

Several of the spiritual books and pamphlets giving rise to early A.A. ideas cited Psalm 5:1-3 in connection with morning prayers,

---

[34] See Tileston, *Daily Strength for Daily Needs*, p. 68; Jones, *Victorious Living*, p. 327; *The Upper Room* for 4/27/38, 9/20/38; Oswald Chambers, *My Utmost for His Highest* (New Jersey: Barbour & Company, 1963), p. 350.

[35] See Holm, *The Runner's Bible*, p. 47; Roger Hicks, *How to Read the Bible* (Moral Re-Armament, n.d.), p. 33.

devotions, and meditation.[36] And the following verses advocated starting afresh with God each morning:

> But unto thee have I cried, O Lord; and in the morning shall my prayer prevent [precede] thee (Psalm 88:13).[37]

> And in the morning, then ye shall see the glory of the Lord . . . (Exodus 16:7).[38]

> Cause me to hear thy lovingkindness in the morning; for in thee do I trust; cause me to know the way wherein I should walk; for I lift up my soul unto thee (Psalm 143:8).[39]

> It is a good thing to give thanks unto the Lord, and to sing praises unto thy name, O most High; To shew forth thy lovingkindness in the morning, and thy faithfulness every night (Psalm 92:1-2).

Relax, Be Patient, Be Still, Listen, Await Direction!

The stance of the believer was to be one of rest, patience, stillness, waiting upon God in silence, expecting God to do the directing:

> Rest in the Lord, and wait patiently for him: fret not thyself because of him who prospereth in his way, because of the man who bringeth wicked devices to pass (Psalm 36:7).[40]

---

[36] *The Upper Room* for 5/9/35; Holm, *The Runner's Bible*, p. 158 and dedication page; E. Stanley Jones, *Victorious Living*, p. 68; Harry Emerson Fosdick, *The Meaning of Prayer* (New York: Association Press, 1915), p. 75; Clarence I. Benson, *The Eight Points of the Oxford Group* (London: Humphrey Milford, Oxford University Press, 1936), p. 79.

[37] Winslow, *When I Awake*, p. 17; Fosdick, *The Meaning of Prayer*, p. 74.

[38] See Tileston, *Daily Strength for Daily Needs*, p. 183.

[39] Holm, *The Runner's Bible*, p. 158; Streeter, *The God Who Speaks*, p. 115; K. D. Belden, *The Hour of the Helicopter*, p. 21; *Meeting Moral Re-Armament*, p. 26.

[40] See Tileston, *Daily Strength for Daily Needs*, p. 140; Holm, *The Runner's Bible*, p. 95; Howard J. Rose, *The Quiet Time* (The Oxford Group, n.d.), p. 3.

Be still, and know that I *am* God: I will be exalted among the heathen, I will be exalted in the earth (Psalm 46:10).[41]

Trust in the Lord with all thine heart; and lean not unto thine own understanding. In all thy ways acknowledge him, and he shall direct thy paths (Proverbs 3:5-6).[42]

Let the words of my mouth and the meditation of my heart, be acceptable in thy sight, O Lord, my strength, and my redeemer (Psalm 19:14).

Order my steps in thy word: and let not any iniquity have dominion over me (Psalm 119:133).

My soul *waiteth* for the Lord more than they that watch for the morning: I *say, more than* they that watch for the morning (Psalm 130:6).

My soul, wait thou only upon God: for my expectation is from him. He *is* my rock and my salvation: *he is* my defence; I shall not be moved. In God *is* my salvation and my glory: the rock of my strength, *and* my refuge, *is* in God. Trust in him at all times: ye people, pour out your heart before him: God is a refuge for us. Selah (Psalm 62:5-8).[43]

---

[41] See Rose, *The Quiet Time*, pp. 1,2; *The Upper Room* for 6/23/35; Benson, *The Eight Points of the Oxford Group*, p. 63; Chambers, *My Utmost for His Highest*, p. 41.

[42] Meyer, *The Secret of Guidance*, p. 7; Rose, *The Quiet Time*, p. 2; Holm, *The Runner's Bible*, p. 126; *The Upper Room*, for 5/15/35; Tileston, *Daily Strength for Daily Needs*, p. 31; Glenn Clark, *I Will Lift Up Mine Eyes* (New York: Harper & Row, 1937), pp. 18, 28, 88, 151; Streeter, *The God Who Speaks*, p. 191; Dick B., *Dr. Bob's Library: Books for Twelve Step Growth* (San Rafael, CA: Paradise Research Publications, 1994), pp. 96-97.

[43] See Fosdick, *The Meaning of Prayer*, p. 46.

Speak, Lord; for thy servant heareth (1 Samuel 3:9).[44]

Lord, what wilt thou have me to do? (Acts 9:6).[45]

Search me, O God, and know my heart: try me, and know my thoughts (Psalm 139:23).[46]

Watch, Continue in Prayer, Give Thanks, Don't Be Anxious!

Watch and pray (Matthew 26:41; Mark 13:33; Luke 21:36).[47]

Offer unto God thanksgiving; and pay thy vows unto the Most High. And call upon me in the day of trouble; I will deliver thee, and thou shalt glorify me (Psalm 50:14-15).[48]

Continue in prayer, and watch in the same with thanksgiving (Colossians 4:2).[49]

Giving thanks always for all things unto God and the Father in the name of our Lord Jesus Christ (Ephesians 5:20).[50]

Be not therefore anxious for the morrow; for the morrow will be anxious for itself. Sufficient unto the day is the evil thereof [Matthew 6:34—part of the Sermon on the Mount. (Quoted from the Revised Version)].[51]

---

[44] See Rose, *The Quiet Time*, p. 3; Fosdick, *The Meaning of Prayer*, p. 66; Winslow, *When I Awake*, p. 48; Tileston, *Daily Strength for Daily Needs*, p. 157; E. Stanley Jones, *Victorious Living*, p. 258; Dick B., *New Light on Alcoholism*, p. 44.

[45] Dick B., *New Light on Alcoholism*, p. 44, n. 12.

[46] See Tileston, *Daily Strength for Daily Needs*, p. 34; Fosdick, *The Meaning of Prayer*, p. 114.

[47] See Rose, *The Quiet Time*, p. 3; Holm, *The Runner's Bible*, p. 61; *The Upper Room*, for 6/13/35.

[48] Holm, *The Runner's Bible*, p. 38.

[49] See Holm, *The Runner's Bible*, p. 37; Tileston, *Daily Strength for Daily Needs*, p. 252; E. Stanley Jones, *Victorious Living*, p. 68.

[50] See Tileston, *Daily Strength for Daily Needs*, p. 88.

[51] Holm, *The Runner's Bible*, p. 41.

Be careful [anxious] for nothing; but in every thing by prayer and supplication with thanksgiving let your requests be made known unto God. And the peace of God which passeth all understanding, shall keep your hearts and minds through Christ Jesus (Philippians 4:6-7).[52]

Write Down the Thoughts That Come!

Thus speaketh the Lord God of Israel, saying, Write thee all the words that I have spoken unto thee in a book (Jeremiah 30:2).[53]

And the Lord answered me, and said, Write the vision, and make *it* plain upon tables, that he may run that readeth it (Habakkuk 2:2).[54]

Believe!

And all things, whatsoever ye shall ask in prayer, believing, ye shall receive (Matthew 21:22).[55]

Therefore I say unto you, what things soever ye desire, when ye pray, believe that ye receive *them*, and ye shall have *them* (Mark 11:24).[56]

And this is the confidence that we have in him, that, if we ask any thing according to his will, he heareth us: And if we know

---

[52] See Tileston, *Daily Strength for Daily Needs*, p. 53; Holm, *The Runner's Bible*, p. 61; E. Stanley Jones, *Victorious Living*, p. 137; Clark, *I Will Lift Up Mine Eyes*, p. 93; Fosdick, *The Meaning of Prayer*, p. 72; Roger Hicks, *How to Read the Bible: Notes for Revolutionaries* (London: The Oxford Group, n.d.), p. 35.

[53] See Rose, *The Quiet Time*, p. 3; E. Stanley Jones, *Victorious Living*, p. 253; Hallen Viney, *How Do I Begin?* (The Oxford Group, 1937), p. 3.

[54] D. M. Prescott, *A New Day: Daily Readings for Our Time*, new ed. (London: Grosvenor Books, 1979), p. 31.

[55] Holm, *The Runner's Bible*, p. 42.

[56] Holm, *The Runner's Bible*, p. 42.

that he hear us, whatsoever we ask, we know that we have the petitions that we desired of him (1 John 5:14-15).[57]

It Works!

The effectual fervent prayer of a righteous man availeth much (James 5:16).[58]

Quiet Time Roots

The Oxford Group

As a young man of thirty, Frank Buchman met the famous evangelist F. B. Meyer who asked if Buchman was giving God enough uninterrupted time really to tell Buchman what to do.[59] And Meyer often expressed such views on "listening.":

It is not necessary to make long prayers, but it is essential to be much alone with God; waiting at His door; hearkening for His voice; lingering in the garden of Scripture for the coming of the Lord God in the dawn or cool of the day. No number of meetings, no fellowship with Christian friends, no amount of Christian activity can compensate for the neglect of the still hour.[60]

---

[57] Holm, *The Runner's Bible*, p. 64; Clark, *I Will Lift Up Mine Eyes*, p. 24; Dick B., *Design for Living*, p. 162.

[58] See Fosdick, *The Meaning of Prayer*, p. 158; Holm, *The Runner's Bible*, pp. 62, 114; *The Upper Room* for 8/19/35; Winslow, *When I Awake*, pp. 42-43; Hicks, *How to Read the Bible*, p. 35; Howard Walter, *Soul Surgery*, 6th ed. (Oxford at the University Press, John Johnson, 1940), p. 29; MacMillan, *Seeking and Finding*, p. 128; Dick B., *The Good Book and The Big Book*, pp. 102-03.

[59] From Garth Lean, *On the Tail of a Comet: The Life of Frank Buchman, a Small Town American Who Awakened the Conscience of the World* (Colorado Springs: Helmers & Howard, 1988), pp. 35-36.

[60] F. B. Meyer, *The Secret of Guidance* (New York: Fleming H. Revell, 1896), pp. 28-29.

Obey exactly and immediately the commands of the inner still small voice. It can be recognized by the fact that it never alters, never asks questions, but is always direct and explicit. Often it asks for an obedience which is against, or above, what we might naturally feel disposed to give. Listen to that still small voice—the voice of the Spirit of God. . . .[61]

As we pointed out in Chapter Two, Buchman gave at least an hour each day thereafter in the early morning to listening to God, a period which he came to refer to as a "quiet time."[62]

And Buchman's mentor, Henry B. Wright, had written a book which also impacted on Buchman's quiet time ideas:

The central theme of Wright's book (*The Will of God*) was that an individual could, through "two-way prayer"—listening for guidance as well as talking—find God's will for his life and for the ordinary events of the day. Wright himself set aside half an hour for such listening prayer first thing every morning. At such times—and indeed at any time in the day—he declared that what he called "luminous thoughts" came from God, provided only that the human receiver was clean enough to pick them up. These thoughts Wright wrote down in a notebook and always tried to carry out.[63]

Wright's two-way prayer practices certainly coincided with those Buchman espoused. And Buchman once wrote Wright from China saying, "Much of the best in my message is due to you."[64]

Buchman took the position that communing with God had been the practice of the saints down through the ages; and he believed anyone could have such contact. In 1920, he sent Sam Shoemaker

---

[61] F. B. Meyer, *Five Musts* (Chicago: Moody Press, 1927), p. 107.

[62] Lean, *On the Tail of a Comet*, p. 36.

[63] Lean, *On the Tail of a Comet*, p. 74.

[64] Theophil Spoerri, *Dynamic out of Silence: Frank Buchman's Relevance Today* (London: Grosvenor Books, 1976), p. 39.

a seven-page letter citing Scriptural and theological authority for his thesis. Buchman said:

> This listening to God is not the experience of a few men. It's the most sane, normal, healthful thing a person can do. . . . I am absolutely convinced from my clinical reactions both at Princeton and in other places that it is possible for babes in Christ to have this experience.[65]

B. H. Streeter, the distinguished Oxford University theologian, became one of Buchman's colleagues and supporters. And Streeter wrote the following in *The God Who Speaks*:

> There is an inner coherence between the conception of God's plan and the two convictions—that conscience is the "voice of God", and that certain intuitions, which come to the individual with an imperative quality, may be interpreted as "divine guidance." . . . I will only suggest that in the phenomenon of prophecy we find, in its highest and most intensified form, that conviction of direct communication between human and divine which appears also in the belief that conscience is the voice of God and that divine guidance is a possibility in normal experience (p. 15).

> Popular Christianity, however, has inclined to forget that Christ said: "But when ye pray, use not vain repetitions, as the heathen do: for they think that they shall be heard for their much speaking. Be not ye therefore like unto them: for your Father knoweth what things ye have need of, before ye ask him" (Mt. vi.7-8). It would seem, then, to accord well with Christ's teaching that, whenever possible, we should begin the day by attuning the soul to the contemplation of the Divine (by some act of aspiration, or by the reading of scripture or other noble words) and should then, before offering any petitions of personal needs, wait in silence—listening, if haply the inner voice should bring some guidance, some indication of the part in God's plan which the worshipper may be called upon to play that day. Often to those

---

[65] Lean, *On the Tail of a Comet*, p. 75.

who listen so there comes a thought or word, clear and definite, pointing to action (pp. 18-19).

Eleanor Napier Forde has been a tireless worker for the Oxford Group from the 1920's to the date of this writing. She married Oxford Group activist James Draper Newton; and she was a friend of, and co-worker with, Oxford Group founder, Dr. Frank Buchman, and Buchman's chief American lieutenant, the Reverend Samuel M. Shoemaker. In 1930, Eleanor Forde's Oxford Group pamphlet, *The Guidance of God*, was published. She wrote:

We turn to think of God's Presence in the quiet time. We take for granted the fact that He is always with us. One has but to read the inspiring memoirs of Brother Lawrence . . . or recall the Jongleur de Dieu, turning his somersaults to the glory of God, to realize this. That he can hearten us, walking along the street, or see that we are in a given place at the right moment goes without saying. The reason why the quiet time is of supreme importance is that there we can shut out the world with its clamour of duty, its conflicting appeals, and our own tangled thoughts, and realize the presence of God—"the ineffable something that holds the mind." . . . The quiet time is not to bring that world into touch with us, but to carry us out of ourselves, beyond its frontier, where our spirits may be swept by the Spirit of worship and wonder, which is the very climate of the Unseen. . . . The purpose of quiet time, then, is not primarily to obtain direction but to come into the stillness—"that greatest and most awful of all goods which we can fancy," where God can find and commune with us. We need time enough to forget time, and this often means the sacrifice of other interests and almost inevitably that last precious hour of morning sleep. It is not too much to say that for many people the power of the whole day completely depends on that first hour alone with God, and the man who would move mountains must have given God his ear before the rush of life is upon him.[66]

---

[66] Eleanor Napier Forde, *The Guidance of God* (Oxford: The Oxford Group, 1930), pp. 23-24.

Shortly after the Forde pamphlet was published, A. J. Russell's popular *For Sinners Only* appeared on the scene.[67] As to quiet time, Russell wrote:

> Here I had my first practical experience of the Quiet Time, a first principle of the Group and one of the biggest obstacles to the newcomer, but a principle on which the Group can make no compromise. Guidance must come to all those who surrender to God's will. As Ken Twitchell announced the Quiet Time the undergraduates fumbled for pencils and guidance-books and began to "listen in" to God. This was not simple meditation, which may be concentration on some aspect of Christ or the Gospel, but something more: a listening for definite messages applicable to present needs. As they were committed to doing God's will, that will could be known for them at any moment of necessity (p. 93).

Jack C. Winslow wrote a great deal on Oxford Group principles.[68] In his title, *When I Awake*, he wrote:

> I am constantly asked to give, or find myself needing to give, simple instruction about how to keep what some call a "quiet time" and others a "morning watch" with God. . . . I am dealing here solely with the time of private prayer which it is essential all Christians should keep, morning by morning, if they desire to go forward in the Christian life. . . , there is the great debt I owe to the Oxford Group, through which I have learnt much during the last few years, particularly with regard to what I have called "the prayer of attention," and the waiting upon God with confident expectation for definite and concrete guidance (pp. 5-6).

> If we want power in our own lives—victory over the things that get us down, and the invigorating sense of adequacy for any tasks or situations that await us through the day—we must let the Spirit of God re-charge us morning by morning (p. 12).

---

[67] A. J. Russell, *For Sinners Only* (London: Hodder & Stoughton, 1932).

[68] See, for example, Jack C. Winslow, *Why I Believe in the Oxford Group* (London: Hodder & Stoughton, 1934).

The morning watch with God is also the surest guarantee of progress. . . . If I appear to stand exactly where I did a year ago, it must mean that I have been missing all those things which God was waiting to teach and give me. In my own experience this kind of stagnation is most often due to the fact that my quiet times with God have become formal and uncreative. On the other hand, if I can really say with the prophet (Isaiah 1:4), "Morning by morning He wakeneth mine ear to hear as they that are taught," then I find that I begin at once to go forward. I grow in understanding of God as I meditate on the Bible. I get fresh glimpses of His character, His purposes, the ways of His working (p. 13).

Since I learnt morning by morning to commit the day to God, to try to see His plan for each day so far as He chose to show it, and to wait for whatever orders He might wish to give me, life has had for me a thrill and a purpose such as it never had before. . . . The quiet hour with God in the early morning is also a sure secret of inward peace. . . . I have risen from bed with a sense of anxiety or worry—perhaps troubled about definite problems for which I could see no solution; perhaps haunted by that vague sense of depression about nothing in particular which so many experience in the early morning. I have entered on my quiet tryst with God, and in the stillness, as I have committed myself with all my anxieties to God, peace has stolen back into my soul (pp. 14-15).

The stress on this watch with God as the *morning* watch is of vital importance. . . . It is the time when we are most free from distractions. . . . The early morning is also the time when our minds should be at their freshest. . . . There is something in our psychological make-up which makes us peculiarly susceptible to deeper intuitions in our first minutes of re-awakened consciousness (pp. 17-18).

In March, 1935, during a speech to 35,000 people at Hamlet's Castle in Denmark, Dr. Frank Buchman summed up what he believed to be the importance of his ideas on listening for the guidance of God. In graphic terms that were frequently repeated thereafter (even, in part, by Bill Wilson's wife Lois, in her Oxford Group Notes), Buchman said:

By a miracle of science millions can think and feel as one.
Barriers of time and space are swept away. A commonwealth of
many nations and languages becomes a family. Radio listeners
understand that miracle. And they will also understand the Oxford
Group, which is showing people how to listen in to God. "God
calling the world" is becoming a daily experience in the lives of
hundreds and thousands of people in the more than fifty countries
where the Oxford Group is at work. We accept as commonplace
a man's voice carried by radio to the uttermost parts of the earth.
Why not the voice of the living God as an active, creative force
in every home, every business, every parliament? Men listen to
a king when he speaks to people over the air. Why not to the
King of Kings? He is alive, and constantly broadcasting. . . . The
Holy Spirit is the most intelligent source of information in the
world today. He has the answer to every problem. Everywhere
when men will let Him, He is teaching them how to live. . . .
Divine guidance must become the normal experience of ordinary
men and women. Any man can pick up divine messages if he will
put his receiving set in order. Definite, accurate, adequate
information can come from the Mind of God to the minds of men.
This is normal prayer.[69]

Thoughts of Bill W.'s Teacher and Friend, Sam Shoemaker

Dr. Shoemaker began explaining and pleading for morning prayer
time in the very first of his published titles. Like so many religious
leaders of his day, Shoemaker first called morning prayer time the
"Morning Watch." In *Realizing Religion*, he wrote:

Frances R. Havergal said long ago that the reason the churches
lacked power was that so few Christians were spending the first
hour of the day alone with God. "Our sense of perceptions of all
kinds," says Dr. Henry Churchill King, "are far acuter in the
morning." One could name literally hundreds of great spiritual

---

[69] Frank N. D. Buchman, *Remaking the World* (London: Blandford Press, 1961), pp.
11-12.

leaders who have considered this the most luminous and precious and indispensable hour of the day, as the study of their lives will make plain to anyone. This practice of the "Morning Watch" is the most fruitful personal habit of religion for those who use it; and were you to draw a line between the strong and the weak Christians, you would find, I believe, the cultivation or neglect of this chief source of their difference in power. It takes dogged will to choose with unbroken regularity half an hour—less is almost too brief a time to "get into the spirit" of it—the first thing every day. But the results will justify the effort; and granted the desire and determination to use this time daily, with the Bible open before you, you will soon make a method of study for yourself that will suit you better than anything which this book might recommend (pp. 60-61).[70]

If the reader will pardon a personal testimony, the time when the writer began to have a hitherto unknown power in his own life, and some slight influence spiritually in the lives of others, coincides exactly with the time when he changed the chief time of prayer from the last thing at night to the first thing in the morning. I plead again for the keeping of the "Morning Watch"—coming fresh to God with the daily plans unmade, submitting first our spirits and then our duties to Him for the shedding of His white light upon both. "To start full-speed through icebergs is irreligious. To start the day without one thought of our Maker is to invite catastrophe" (pp. 65-66).

By the time he was writing *Religion That Works* just a few years later, Shoemaker was most eloquently championing the guided life. He said:

I believe enormously in the possibility of a guided life, influenced and led at every step by the Holy Spirit. Conversion is the beginning, not the ending of an experience of God. That experience continues when we use all the means Jesus put at our

---

[70] Samuel M. Shoemaker, Jr., *Realizing Religion* (New York: Association Press, 1923).

disposal for continuation—prayer, the Scriptures, the Church and the Sacraments, Christian fellowship and worship. . . . Many situations in my life are not covered by the Sermon on the Mount. I need special guidance and illumination. The prophets of Israel had it. The apostles had it. Where is it gone to in this age? We believe in the Holy Spirit as we believe in some dead human character: he was once, but he is gone. The deepest need of our age, the cure for most of our back-door attempts to establish communication with the other worlds, is a rediscovery of the Holy Spirit. What infinite possibilities of learning the will of God, through communion with Him, may lie ahead of us, who can dare to imagine? (pp. 14-15).[71]

Still later, Shoemaker expanded upon the availability of guidance and upon the time or times for obtaining it. At this point, however, Shoemaker preferred to call the period for communion with God his "Quiet Time." He stated:

We want to know that God can and does speak directly to the human heart. The reason why some of us believe in guidance, at least in theory, is that the Old and New Testaments are full of instances of it, specific as you please. Men said clearly that they were guided of God in this and that act and decision. You may try to psychologize all this away if you want; but I prefer to see whether this sort of thing is not now possible to those who put their trust in God entirely.[72]

As an aside, the author would point out that he was privileged to examine Shoemaker's personal journals for the period 1931 to 1936. Shoemaker's daughters made this possible. And the journals were just as described by Shoemaker in his books. They were voluminous in content. They were hand-written. They were contained in small loose-leafed ringed binders. And they were

---

[71] Samuel M. Shoemaker, Jr., *Religion That Works* (New York: Fleming H. Revell, 1928).

[72] Shoemaker, *The Conversion of the Church*, p. 50.

detailed in their references to Scripture, to Shoemaker's colleagues and family, to dates and plans and places, and to inspirational thoughts concerning each of these.

Ye Must Be Born Again!

Before we get to the *specifics* of quiet time practices among A.A.'s root sources, it is essential to review what those sources believed was the condition precedent to receiving *any guidance at all*.[73]

In his first major title (*Realizing Religion*), Sam Shoemaker carefully pointed out where people must start:

Now St. Augustine said truly: "We are not born Christians, but we become Christians (p. 5)."

What you want is simply a vital religious experience. You need to find God. You need Jesus Christ (p. 9).

God on His part has longed to win us for years. It has been we who have been unwilling. We must open ourselves to Him, and be prepared to accept all that it will mean to be a child of God (pp. 28-29).

In answer to objections, Shoemaker later wrote:

The world does not need an awakening any more than the Church does. It was to an educated religious gentleman [Nicodemus] that Jesus said, "Ye must be born again."[74] That imperative is a judgment against those who withstand conversion. But it is a hope

---

[73] For some preliminary thoughts on Oxford Group understanding of the importance of 1 Corinthians chapter 2, and of being born again of God's spirit in order to discern spiritual matters, see Streeter, *The God Who Speaks*, p. 110; Benson, *The Eight Points of the Oxford Group*, p. 79.

[74] See John 3:3, 5-8.

held out to those fearful and self-depreciating people who do not think themselves capable of conversion.[75]

The Book of Acts records this about Paul's trip to Ephesus:

> He [Paul] said unto them, Have ye received the Holy Ghost since ye believed? And they said unto him, We have not so much as heard whether there be any Holy Ghost. And he said unto them, Unto what then were ye baptized? And they said, Unto John's baptism. Then said Paul, John verily baptized with the baptism of repentance, saying unto the people, that they should believe on him which should come after him, that is, on Christ Jesus. When they heard *this*, they were baptized in the name of the Lord Jesus. And when Paul had laid *his* hands upon them, the Holy Ghost came on them; and they spake with tongues, and prophesied (Acts 19:1-6).

As she so often did in her sharing with early AAs and their families, Dr. Bob's wife Anne Ripley Smith stressed the need for a "receiving set," for "power," in order to be saved, made complete, receive revelation, and be set free.[76] Anne wrote:

> Paul speaks of a wish toward good, but power to carry it out is lacking. A stronger power than his was needed. God provided the power through Christ, so that we could find a new kind of relationship with God. Christ gives the power, we appropriate it. It is not anything that we do ourselves; but it is the appropriation of a power that comes from God that saves us from sin and sets us free.[77]

---

[75] Shoemaker, *Religion That Works*, p. 14; *Children of the Second Birth* (New York: Fleming H. Revell, 1927), p. 32.

[76] Cp. Romans 10:9; 1 Corinthians 12:7-11; John 8:31, 32; Matthew 22:29.

[77] See Dick B., *Anne Smith's Journal, 1933-1939: A.A.'s Principles of Success* (San Rafael, CA: Paradise Research Publications, 1995), pp. 22-24.

A.A. pioneer Clarence S. pointed out that William V. H. had given him a verse in his earliest A.A. days—a verse that changed his life.[78] The verse was 2 Corinthians 5:17:

> Therefore if any man *be* in Christ, *he is* a new creature: old things are passed away; behold, all things are become new.[79]

The Apostle Peter explained the change which Clarence S. experienced at the time of his rebirth:

> Being born again, not of corruptible seed, but of incorruptible, by the word of God, which liveth and abideth forever (1 Peter 1:23).[80]

Oxford Group writer K. D. Belden pointed out:

> That is why we need a Saviour: to save us from ourselves, not just our actions. Only the Power which raised Jesus Christ from the dead can, and will, raise us from our old nature and begin to form in us the new.[81]

The important thing, in examining the roots of "quiet time," "listening," "revelation," and "guidance," is to understand that the Oxford Group emphasized surrender to God, and the relationship with God, *as the first pre-requisite to receiving God's guidance.*

---

[78] Dick B., *That Amazing Grace: The Role of Clarence and Grace S. in Alcoholics Anonymous* (San Rafael, CA: Paradise Research Publications, 1996), pp. 33-34.

[79] See also Streeter, *The God Who Speaks*, p. 111; Howard C. Blake, *Way to Go: Adventures in Search of God's Will* (Merrifield, VA: Pooh Stix Press, 1992), p. 79.

[80] Clarence explained a number of times that he had been born again at the home of T. Henry Williams in Akron. See Dick B., *That Amazing Grace*, pp. 16, 27-28, 52, 68, 83-84, 92-93. The nature of the change is described in Clarence's all-important verse, 2 Corinthians 5:17—Clarence was a new man in Christ. The reason for the change is explained in 1 Peter 1:23—that he had been born again of incorruptible seed (the seed of Christ).

[81] K. D. Belden, *Reflections on Moral Re-Armament* (London: Grosvenor Books, 1983), p. 42.

First, one surrendered, became converted, and "gave his life to God." *Then* that person sought the guidance from the Heavenly Father. It was not the other way around. Shoemaker, for example, was famous for getting people on their knees *before* he helped them seek a life-change through God's help.[82] Frank Buchman was well-known for his declaration, "Sin, Jesus Christ, and (the result) a Miracle."[83] The approach was not the other way around.

For many early AAs, the prerequisite surrender apparently involved saying the "Sinners Prayer."[84] For some, the very clear salvation mandate of Romans 10:9-10 was not overlooked:

> That if thou shalt confess with thy mouth the Lord Jesus, and shalt believe in thine heart that God hath raised him from the dead, thou shalt be saved. For with the heart man believeth unto righteousness, and with the mouth confession is made unto salvation.[85]

---

[82] See how it all began in China as recounted by Sam Shoemaker in the chapter entitled "The Turning Point" in *Faith at Work: A Symposium Edited by Samuel Moor Shoemaker* (n.p.: Hawthorne Books, 1958), pp. 80-84. See also the accounts in Samuel M. Shoemaker, Jr., *Children of the Second Birth* (New York: Fleming H. Revell, 1927), pp. 122-23, 148, 171, 178. Years later, Shoemaker was still getting people on their knees surrendering their lives to God. See accounts in Duncan Norton-Taylor, "Businessmen on Their Knees," *Fortune*, October, 1953; "Pittsburgh Steels Itself for 2000," *For A Change*, August-September, 1994, pp. 8-9; and Michael J. Sider, *Taking the Gospel to the Point: Evangelicals in Pittsburgh and the Origins of the Pittsburgh Leadership Foundation* (Pittsburgh: Pittsburgh Leadership Foundation, n.d.), pp. 5-12.

[83] See Walter, *Soul Surgery*, p. 86; Almond, *Foundations for Faith*, pp. 10-29.

[84] Dick B., *That Amazing Grace*, p. 27.

[85] Discussing surrender in terms of the conversion it was meant to bring about, E. Stanley Jones wrote: "Incidentally this phrase 'Jesus is Lord' was probably the earliest Christian creed: 'If you confess with your lips that Jesus is Lord . . . you will be saved' (Romans 10:9). 'No one can say "Jesus is Lord" except by the Holy Spirit' (1 Corinthians 12:3)." Jones points to the well-known William James definition of conversion and says: "Surrender is a surrender of as much of myself as I know today, to as much of Christ as I know today. . . . At the center of that feeling will be a growing conviction that Jesus is Lord. He will be Lord of you, your possessions, your relationships, your future, and your all." E. Stanley Jones, *Conversion* (Nashville: Abingdon Press, 1959), pp. 46-47, 63-64.

Shoemaker and other A.A. sources referred to Romans 10:9, but with surprising *infrequency.*[86]

As we discuss the receipt of revelation from God (or "guidance," as the Oxford Group called it), it is important to note that, according to the Bible, an *unbeliever* does not receive revelation (or guidance) from God.[87] 1 Corinthians 2:9-12, 14 state:

> But as it is written, Eye hath not seen, nor ear heard, neither have entered into the heart of man, the things which God hath prepared for them that love him. But God hath revealed *them* unto us by his Spirit: . . . even so the things of God knoweth no man, but the Spirit of God. Now we have received, . . . the spirit which is of God; that we might know the things that are freely given to us of God. . . . But the natural man receiveth not the things of the Spirit of God: for they are foolishness unto him: neither can he know *them*, because they are spiritually discerned.[88]

In the Old Testament and in the Gospels, God was able to communicate with people who had the spirit *upon* them:

---

[86] Samuel M. Shoemaker, Jr., *If I Be Lifted Up* (New York: Fleming H. Revell, 1931), p. 83; Glenn Clark, *Touchdowns for the Lord: The Story of "Dad" A. J. Elliott* (Minnesota: Macalester Park Publishing Company, 1947), pp. 55-56.

[87] The term "guidance"—much used by the Oxford Group to describe information received from the true God—doesn't occur in the King James Version of the Bible. However, the term "guide" does occur several times in such verses as: (1) Psalm 73:24: "Thou shalt guide me with thy counsel . . ."; and (2) Isaiah 58:11: "And the Lord shall guide thee . . ." "Revelation" is the biblical term for the Oxford Group concept of guidance. See, for example, Galatians 2:2 and Ephesians 3:3. There are three revelation manifestations of the gift of holy spirit, and these are mentioned in 1 Corinthians 12:7-11. They are: (1) word of knowledge, (2) word of wisdom, and (3) discerning of spirits.

[88] The word "natural" in verse 14 is translated from the Greek word *psuchikos*. In Jude 19, this Greek word is translated "sensual" in the King James Version and is accompanied by the appositive phrase, "having not the spirit." Not surprisingly, therefore, the NIV translates the first phrase in 1 Corinthians 2:14: "the man without the spirit." Romans 8:9 also sheds light on this topic: ". . . Now if any man have not the Spirit of Christ, he is none of his."

And I will come down and talk with thee [Moses] there: and I will take of the spirit which *is* upon thee, and will put *it* upon them. . . . And the Lord came down in a cloud, and spake unto him, and took of the spirit that *was* upon him, and gave *it* unto the seventy elders: and it came to pass, *that*, when the spirit rested upon them, they prophesied, and did not cease (Numbers 11:17, 25).

The Book of Isaiah adds this:

As for me, this *is* my covenant with them, saith the Lord; my spirit that *is* upon thee, and my words which I have put in thy mouth, shall not depart out of thy mouth, nor out of the mouth of thy seed's seed, saith the Lord, from henceforth and forever (Isaiah 59:21).[89]

After Pentecost, it became possible for believers to receive the gift of holy spirit *in* them and hence themselves to receive and bring forth communications from God.[90] The following verses illustrate what was promised and what believers received:

And, behold, I [Jesus Christ] send the promise of my Father upon you; but tarry ye in the city of Jerusalem, until ye be endued with power from on high (Luke 24:49).[91]

And, [he, Jesus Christ] being assembled together with *them* [the apostles], commanded them that they should not depart from Jerusalem, but wait for the promise of the Father, which, *saith* he, ye have heard of me. For John truly baptized with water; but ye shall be baptized with the Holy Ghost not many days hence. . . . ye shall receive power, after that the Holy Ghost is come upon you: and ye shall be witnesses unto me both in Jerusalem, and in all

---

[89] See Streeter, *The God Who Speaks*, p. 114.

[90] See Streeter, *The God Who Speaks*, p. 109.

[91] See Streeter, *The God Who Speaks*, p. 125.

Judaea, and in Samaria, and unto the uttermost part of the earth (Acts 1:4-5, 8).[92]

Then Peter said unto them, Repent, and be baptized every one of you in the name of Jesus Christ for the remission of sins, and ye shall receive the gift of the Holy Ghost. For the promise is unto you, and to your children, and to all that are afar off, *even* as many as the Lord our God shall call (Acts 2:38-39).

While Peter yet spake these words, the Holy Ghost fell on all them which heard the word. And they of the circumcision which believed were astonished, as many as came with Peter, because that on the Gentiles also was poured out the gift of the Holy Ghost. For they heard them speak with tongues, and magnify God (Acts 10:43-44).

But when the fullness of time was come, God sent forth his Son, made of a woman, made under the law, to redeem them that were under the law, that we might receive the adoption of sons. And because ye are sons, God hath sent forth the Spirit of his Son into your hearts, crying Abba, Father. Wherefore thou art no more a servant, but a son; and if a son, then an heir of God through Christ (Galatians 4:4-7).[93]

Whereof I [Paul] am made a minister, according to the dispensation of God which is given to me for you, to fulfill the word of God; *Even* the mystery which hath been hid from ages and from generations, but now is made manifest to his saints: To whom God would make known what *is* the riches of the glory of this mystery among the Gentiles; which is Christ in you, the hope of glory (Colossians 1:25-27).[94]

---

[92] See Streeter, *The God Who Speaks*, p. 111. See also Shoemaker's discussion in Samuel M. Shoemaker, *With the Holy Spirit and with Fire* (New York: Harper and Brothers, 1960), pp. 25-26.

[93] See Streeter, *The God Who Speaks*, p. 94.

[94] See the explanation of Oxford Group commentator Leslie D. Weatherhead, *Discipleship* (London: Student Christian Movement Press, 1934), pp. 146-147.

Sam Shoemaker devoted an entire chapter of his title, *National Awakening*, to explaining the relevance of surrender (via the new birth) as a prerequisite to keeping alive—through Bible study, public worship, prayer, and *listening*—the life that is received through Christ in the new birth.[95]

Quiet Time Practices

By the time "prayer and meditation" reached A.A., its root sources had defined very specifically what "quiet time" involved. Yet today's Twelve Step meditation often involves only a three to five minute glance at a dated, one-page reflection.[96] Usually, there is no Bible verse involved. Often there is a quote from "Conference Approved" A.A. literature; and the quote is frequently accompanied by comments of a writer who makes no mention of God, the Bible, or prayer. One A.A. historian recently commented:

> There are not only many "meditation books" today; there are too many. Squibs for "daily meditation" are useful, for beginners. But perhaps some are being locked into beginnerhood—into spiritual infancy. . . . Meditation, like food, loses nutrients when it is canned.[97]

We would add that mediation *books* are scarcely the heart of the "morning watch" or "quiet time" or "prayer and meditation." Certainly not as morning and daily time with God were originally practiced. Sam Shoemaker acknowledged that help, via the reading

---

[95] Samuel M. Shoemaker, Jr., *National Awakening* (New York: Harper & Brothers, 1936), pp. 55-66.

[96] See, *Twenty-four Hours a Day*, rev. ed. (Center City, MN: Hazelden, 1975); *Daily Reflections* (New York: Alcoholics Anonymous World Services, 1991); Mel B., *Walk in Dry Places* (Center City, MN: Hazelden, 1996).

[97] From Ernest Kurtz's Foreword in *The Soul of Sponsorship*, by Robert Fitzgerald, S. J. (Center City, MN: Hazelden, 1995), p. xi.

of books and the receiving of instruction, was often needed in getting *started*; but he pointed out that more was required:

> Donald Carruthers' pamphlet on *How to Find Reality in Your Morning Devotions* has helped hundreds in this early stage: I was with him in China in the days when he was working out this pamphlet in the laboratory of experience, and I know it is born of experiment and not theory. There will be a constant tendency to drop back from the full faith that God's Holy Spirit can guide, and to say that the Bible is enough, or prayer is enough. . . . A full-orbed Quiet Time means Bible study, prayer, ample time to wait upon God in quiet, writing down what is given to us with those who are closest to us—certainly with husband or wife, or with one or more of the "spiritual family. . . ."[98]

Morning prayer time originally involved quality time devoted to practicing the presence of God. It involved substantial time. Quiet time. Peaceful time. Study of the Word of God. Sometimes with assistance in *that* study. Prayer. Listening. Writing down thoughts received. And checking with Scripture, often with other believers, to be sure that the thoughts received constituted genuine divine guidance and not just deception from some other spiritual source.

Before looking at what A.A. borrowed and where there is room for improvement in today's practices, we need to have before us a detailed picture of the precise practices that were developed by A.A.'s sources from the Bible, the Oxford Group, Sam Shoemaker's teachings, and the early Bible devotionals.

A Definite, Adequate, Early Time

F. B. Meyer's question of Frank Buchman was, essentially: "Do you give God *enough uninterrupted time* to tell you what to do?"

From that point on, Buchman and his First Century Christian Fellowship emphasized several things. They heeded the Biblical

---

[98] Shoemaker, *The Conversion of the Church*, p. 80.

statement that *morning* was the time to begin the walk with God.[99] They set aside half an hour to an hour in the morning for their meditation in the Bible, reading of helpful books, and two-way prayer (which involved speaking to God and listening to God). These practices took time. So did the writing down of thoughts to insure they were not lost and could be checked.

Time, then, was an important factor: a definite time, early time, morning time, fresh time, adequate time—adequate time to learn about God, to study about God's will, to petition God, and to hear from God. As a guide,, Carruthers wrote:

> *Have a definite time each morning.* The morning period before breakfast is most desirable. *Day telegrams* are delivered immediately. *Night letters* are delayed until the following morning. Give God the first moments of your day. It will remove the friction from the rest of the day's duties. The Psalmist wrote, "In the morning will I order my prayer unto thee, and wiil keep watch." It was a habit of Jesus, "a great while before it was day."[100]

Sam Shoemaker clarified, as to the "time" for Quiet Time, stating:

> Quiet Times do not need to be confined to morning and evening. One of the most profitable Quiet Times I have had was one Saturday afternoon on the top of a Fifth Avenue bus.[101]

Quiet, Peaceful, Relaxed Stance

"Time" was important in early meditation. But so was the *kind of time*. The essence of "quiet" time, of course, was that the time

---

[99] See discussion in Winslow, *When I Awake*, "The Morning Watch," pp. 9-21.

[100] See Carruthers, *How to Find Reality in Your Morning Devotions*, p. 3. Compare the cited verses with Psalm 5:3; Mark 1:35.

[101] Shoemaker, *Children of the Second Birth*, p. 97.

was to be "quiet."[102] Biblical instructions were: (a) "Be still, and know that I am God. . . ." (Psalm 46:10).[103] (b) "Thou [God] wilt keep *him* in perfect peace, *whose* mind *is* stayed on *thee*: because he trusteth in thee" (Isaiah 26:3).[104] (c) "Take no thought for [don't be anxious about] your life, what ye shall eat, or what ye shall drink; nor yet for your body, what ye shall put on. . . . for your heavenly Father knoweth that ye have need of these things" (Matthew 6:25, 32).[105] (d) "Be careful for [anxious about] nothing; but in everything by prayer and supplication with thanksgiving let your requests be made known unto God. And the peace of God, which passeth all understanding, shall keep your hearts and minds through Christ Jesus" (Philippians 4:6-7).[106]

Shoemaker, and the others who taught AAs, *often* talked about "shutting the door." The morning time for Bible study, reading, prayer, listening, and checking was to be done and was done in an unhurried, relaxed, quiet, peaceful setting. Carruthers wrote:

> *Have a definite place where you can be alone.* . . . Seek the out of doors frequently to feel the holy hush of nature newly born. Make your bedroom a gateway into His presence. Shut the door on the world and all that would distract. Closet yourself with the Lord Jesus. Let nothing on your part make such intimacy difficult.[107]

---

[102] See discussion in Winslow, *When I Awake*, in the chapter titled, "Entering Into Stillness," pp. 22-28.

[103] See Dick B., *The Good Book and The Big Book: A.A.'s Roots in the Bible* (San Rafael, CA: Paradise Research Publications, 1995), p. 156. This verse occurred often in the devotionals used by early AAs.

[104] See Dick B., *The Good Book and The Big Book*, p. 159. This verse also received much attention from the devotionals used by early AAs.

[105] See Dick B., *The Good Book and The Big Book*, p. 159. Dr. Bob firmly believed what he wrote in his personal story in the Big Book at page 181: "Your heavenly Father will never let you down!"

[106] See Dick B., *The Good Book and The Big Book*, p. 158, for the frequency with which this concept was quoted in A.A. devotional sources.

[107] Carruthers, *How to Find Reality in Your Morning Devotions*, p. 3.

As mentioned above, the Bible itself called for being "still" (Psalm 46:10)—the better, we would add, to hear the "still small voice."[108] The Bible called for meditating, focusing thoughts, and "staying the mind" on God and His Word if one wanted the perfect peace necessary to receiving divine guidance.[109] The Bible also called for controlling one's mind—for rejecting "anxiety."[110] Anxiety, a corollary of fear, simply defeated the believing necessary to receive God's help and guidance. In his pamphlet, *How Can God Guide Me?*, Howard J. Rose wrote:

> Get into a comfortable position—sit, recline or kneel, whichever gives greatest relaxation of mind and body. Cultivate stillness of mind by an act of will, thinking peaceful and restful thoughts. Have unhurried quiet and sense of leisure, avoiding all tenseness (Psalm 37:7).[111]

Reading the Bible

Oxford Group people, and certainly Sam Shoemaker, agreed with Dr. Bob's wife Anne Smith that "the Bible ought to be the main Source Book of all. No day ought to pass without reading it."[112] Dr. Bob certainly followed this practice—daily.[113]

Shoemaker wrote: "Read and know the Bible, and all else, including public worship, will fall in its place."[114] A.A.'s teachers believed the Bible contained the general or universal will

---

[108] See 1 Kings 19:12.

[109] See, for example, Isaiah 26:3.

[110] See, for example, 2 Corinthians 10:5; Philippians 4:6-7.

[111] Howard J. Rose, *How Can God Guide Me?* (private pamphlet, n.d.: formerly *The Quiet Time*, published by the Oxford Group, n.d.), p. 2. Psalm 37:7 states: "Rest in the Lord, and wait patiently for him; fret not thyself because of him who prospereth in his way, because of the man who bringeth wicked devices to pass."

[112] See Dick B., *Anne Smith's Journal, 1933-1939: A.A.'s Principles of Success* (San Rafael, CA: Paradise Research Publications, 1995), p. 80.

[113] Dick B., *Dr. Bob's Library: Books for Twelve Step Growth* (San Rafael, CA: Paradise Research Publication, 1994), pp. 13-14.

[114] Shoemaker, *Realizing Religion*, p. 62.

of God, and they hardly expected one to seek the will of God without studying and knowing the Word of God. Thus Shoemaker wrote:

> We find God's general will in the Scriptures. . . . [In] "Quiet Time". . . . Listening became the dominant note. Not the exclusive note: for there was Bible study first, taking a book and studying it straight through. . . . At the beginning it will be simple, perhaps. They will need constant help, suggestions about how to study the Bible, where and what to read in it.[115]

> Now, guidance has got to become concrete and, in the best sense, habitual for ministers. This cannot come true without the setting apart of a definite time in the morning, the very first part of it, for sufficient prayer, Bible study, and listening for the Holy Spirit's directions.[116]

The Bible itself makes clear the vital necessity for *studying* Scripture: (a) "Study to shew thyself approved unto God, a workman that needeth not to be ashamed, rightly dividing the word of truth," said Paul in 2 Timothy 2:15.[117] (b) "Search the scriptures," said Jesus as recorded in John 5:39.[118] And the Book of Acts commended believers in Berea, who received the word of God from Paul and Silas, but checked it out daily in Scripture itself. Acts 17:11 said: "These [the Bereans] were more noble than those in Thessalonica, in that they received the word with all readiness of mind, and searched the scriptures *daily*, whether those things were so" (italics added).

Several Oxford Group and Shoemaker adherents had some catch words for Bible study: (1) Read it through. (2) Pray it in ["Ask God

---

[115] Shoemaker, *The Conversion of the Church*, pp. 49, 60, 79.

[116] Samuel M. Shoemaker, Jr., *Twice-Born Ministers* (New York: Fleming H. Revell, 1929), p. 184.

[117] See Dick B., *The Good Book and The Big Book*, p. 157, for other references to this verse.

[118] See Dick B., *The Good Book and The Big Book*, p. 157.

to open the Word to you and bring the Truth to light so that you might behold wondrous things"]. (3) Write it down ["Mark your Bible. Blaze the trail where the Light found you in your hour of need"]. (4) Work it out ["His words and His example and His influence still fling down their challenge upon us to "Be Christlike"] (5) Pass it On ["Avoid being afraid to share crusts of bread even when you have not yet been given the entire loaf. . . . 'Quickly, Go Tell'"].[119]

We will see in a moment why Oxford Group people checked their "luminous thoughts" (their "guidance") against Scripture to make sure what they heard was in fact divine guidance and conformed to the will of God as expressed in the word of God. To check one's thoughts against Scripture, one had to read, study, and know Scripture! Moreover, guidance from God enabled one, through the power of the holy spirit, to understand the universal will of God as communicated to mankind in the Bible. The two were interrelated.

Using Devotionals

In the author's opinion, the A.A. Step area that has gotten most out of whack historically, and from a spiritual perspective, concerns the use of devotionals and meditation books.[120] Some Twelve Step people today seem to look at meditation books as their sole spiritual diet for the day. No Bible. No prayer. No listening. No assistance from clergy. Just reading what A.A. historian Ernest Kurtz called a "squib"—then dashing off into the maelstrom of life. But there is no evidence that this was the practice of the Oxford Group, of Sam Shoemaker, of those who

---

[119] See Carruthers, *How to Find Reality in Your Morning Devotions*, pp. 1-3; Almond, *Foundations for Faith*, pp. 30-31; Miles G. W. Phillimore, *Just for Today* (Privately published pamphlet, 1940), last page.

[120] Big Book, p. 87, states: "There are many helpful books also. Suggestions about these may be obtained from one's priest, minister, or rabbi. Be quick to see where religious people are right. Make use of what they offer."

regularly read the devotionals outside of A.A.'s environs, or even of the early AAs themselves.

A record from Acts 8 will illustrate the point. It concerns Philip, the revelation he received as to where to go to help a worshipper, and what was necessary for that searcher to know in order to understand the word of God. The chapter says, in part:

And the angel of the Lord spake unto Philip, saying, Arise, and go toward the south unto the way that goeth down from Jerusalem unto Gaza, which is desert. And he arose and went: and, behold, a man of Ethiopia, an eunuch of great authority under Candace queen of the Ethiopians, who had the charge of all her treasure, and had come to Jerusalem for to worship, was returning, and sitting in his chariot read Esaias the prophet. Then the Spirit said unto Philip, Go near, and join thyself to this chariot. And Philip ran thither to *him*, and heard him read the prophet Esaias, and said, **Understandest thou what thou readest?** And he said, How can I, except some man should guide me? And he desired that he would come up and sit with him. The place of the scripture which he read was this, He was led as a sheep to the slaughter; and like a lamb dumb before his shearer, so opened he not his mouth; In his humiliation his judgment was taken away: and who shall declare his generation? for his life is taken from the earth. And the eunuch answered Philip, and said, I pray thee, of whom speaketh the prophet this? Of himself, or of some other man? Then Philip opened his mouth, and began at the same scripture, and preached unto him Jesus (Acts 8:26-35—bold print added).[121]

Often, when they read it, students of the word of God simply cannot understand it without instruction and help.[122] Also, there are those—as in the foregoing case of Philip the evangelist—who have gift ministries to further the work of the church and aid

---

[121] See discussion in Samuel M. Shoemaker, *With the Holy Spirit and with Fire* (Harper and Brothers, 1960), pp. 32-33.

[122] Sometimes it is due to the fact that they do not have the spirit of God in them to enable them to discern spiritual truths. See 1 Corinthians 2:14.

students in understanding.[123] The suggestion in the Book of Acts is not that the eunuch did not need to read the Word, but rather that he needed assistance in understanding it.

Devotionals and meditation books are *not* the word of God. They are simply "helpful books." Sam Shoemaker pointed out:

> *Read before you pray*. Read the Bible systematically. You may find *helpful* the serial books of devotion called Forward Day by Day, or the Upper Room or E. Stanley Jones' "Abundant Living." Use any devotional book that helps you. This draws your mind towards God, and makes you ready to pray (italics added).[124]

> They [students seeking Christ] will need to form steady and adequate devotional habits. Prayer is a new experience. When shall they do it? How? With what help from books? Bible study must begin at once, but the most elementary instruction may be needed. A fine young churchman in my parish, who had started on a vital spiritual pilgrimage, said to me, "I have never read nor heard the Bible outside of church." That will go for tens of thousands of young people. Hand them a Bible, and they do not know where to turn. I suggested John 3, Romans 7 and 8, and Luke 12 and 15. But people need a plan—either a year-round lectionary, a plan to study a book at a time (which will require a commentary), or a topical study of, say, faith, or money, or prayer. We all ought to know, and have on hand, good books that help in this, books that initiate experience. I think a live church ought to have a book-stall, where vital books are on sale; and all of us ought to be good book salesmen, who make them known to others.[125]

---

[123] See Ephesians 4:11: "And he gave some, apostles; and some, prophets; and some, evangelists; and some, pastors and teachers."

[124] Samuel M. Shoemaker, Jr., *How to Find God* (New York: Faith at Work, n.d.), p. 15.

[125] *Sam Shoemaker at His Best: Extraordinary Living for the Ordinary Man* (New York: Faith at Work, 1964), pp. 62-63.

Note that Shoemaker practiced what he preached. In the 1930's he maintained a book-stall at Calvary Church which contained, recommended through *The Calvary Evangel*, and distributed, all the important Oxford Group books of the 1930's.[126]

However, in the Oxford Group, there was no substitute for the Word of God—an exacting study of it. Frank Buchman often said of the Bible: (1) Observe accurately. (2) Interpret honestly. (3) Apply drastically.[127] Devotionals were simply used to aid in the study.[128]

Praying to God

We will not write a discourse on prayer, for prayer was not the expert province of Oxford Group people or of early AAs. Both had some guidelines. And their root writings often did provide some basic ideas about kinds of prayer and how to pray. The emphasis, however, was on *listening*. Oxford Group people talked of "two-way" prayer. Prayer was talking to God; but the dominant aspect was listening.

Harry Emerson Fosdick was sometimes quoted by Oxford Group writers; and Anne Smith recommended Fosdick's book on *The Meaning of Prayer*.[129] In Fosdick's view, "Prayer is neither chiefly begging for things, nor is it merely self-communing; it is that loftiest experience within the reach of any soul, communion with God."[130] Fosdick pointed to the comment of Brother Lawrence about what praying meant to him (Brother Lawrence):

---

[126] See Dick B., *Design for Living: The Oxford Group's Contribution to Early A.A* (San Rafael, CA: Paradise Research Publications, 1995), pp. 114-19.

[127] Almond, *Foundations for Faith*, p. 31; Phillimore, *Just for Today*, last page.

[128] See, for example, K. D. Belden, *The Hour of the Helicopter* (Somerset, England: Linden Hall, 1992), pp. 21, 49; *Meeting Moral Re-Armament* (London: Grosvenor Books, 1979), p. 26.

[129] Dick B., *Anne Smith's Journal*, p. 82; Shoemaker, *Realizing Religion*, p. 64 (recommending Fosdick's book).

[130] Fosdick, *The Meaning of Prayer*, p. 32.

"That we should establish ourselves in a sense of God's presence, by continually conversing with Him."[131]

Anne Smith wrote specifically about the types of prayer. She spoke of: (1) intercessory prayer ("pray that Spirit may tell you what to pray for").[132] (2) petitionary prayers ("Means expression of our wants which we deeply feel and which it would be hypocrisy to pretend we didn't. These we submit . . . because He is our Friend. Similarly it would be unnatural not to submit to God the needs of others.").[133] (3) prayers of praise—"adoration and thanksgiving."[134] And (4) prayers for guidance. She herself cited Romans 2; but James 1:5 and Psalm 32:8 were two of the most commonly quoted verses (in A.A.'s root sources) which contained God's promises of guidance.[135]

Jack Winslow suggested, as to the Morning Watch:

> (a) Opening moments of silent adoration: "Our spirit bows in humble and thankful adoration before our Creator."[136] (b) Praise and thanksgiving: "We praise God for all that He is in Himself. We thank Him for all that He has done, is doing, and will do."[137] (c) The Daily Surrender: "a simple act of will, by which we once again yield ourselves completely to the Divine Will, that God may direct and use us all the day through. This it is—since

---

[131] Fosdick, *The Meaning of Prayer*, p. 33.

[132] Dick B., *Anne Smith's Journal*, p. 56; Winslow, *When I Awake*, p. 17; see Romans 8:26-27.

[133] Dick B., *Anne Smith's Journal*, p. 56; see Philippians 4:6-7; 1 John 5:14-15.

[134] Dick B., *Anne Smith's Journal*, p. 57; ·ee 1 Thessalonians 5:18: "In every thing give thanks: for this is the will of God in Christ Jesus concerning you."

[135] James 1:5: "If any of you lack wisdom, let him ask of God, that giveth to all *men* liberally, and upbraideth not; and it shall be given him." Psalm 32:8: "I will instruct thee and teach thee in the way which thou shalt go: I will guide thee with mine eye." For the many A.A. sources quoting these verses, see Dick B., *The Good Book and The Big Book: A.A.'s Roots in the Bible* (San Rafael, CA: Paradise Research Publications, 1995), pp. 154-55.

[136] Winslow, *When I Awake*, pp. 28-29.

[137] Winslow, *When I Awake*, pp. 29-34.

He will never force us—which makes us available to Him."[138]
(d) Intercession: "My own usual practice is to restrict my early
morning intercessions to *people* for whom I wish to pray, and it
is a part of the morning watch that I would not on any account let
go."[139] (e) The Prayer of Attention: "Speak, Lord, for thy
servant heareth."[140]

Shoemaker's focus was (and ours in this section is) on *listening*.
Thus, in *The Conversion of the Church*, Shoemaker wrote,
"Listening became the dominant note [in Quiet Time]. Not the
exclusive note: for there [was] . . . 'also ordinary prayer,
confession, petition, thanksgiving, intercession.'"[141]
He said:

Let great prayers help you to pray. Make frequent use of books
of prayer. Let us really know the treasure-houses of inspired
devotional utterance. There comes a time in private prayer when
we want to talk to God out of our hearts, and in our own words.
But the prayers of others will help us to do this. As we fill those
ancient and modern and universal prayers with our own needs,
they will live for us, and help us to lift up our hearts to God.[142]

Hearing *from* God

In *Children of the Second Birth*, Shoemaker wrote:

We believe entirely that conversion is the experience which
initiates the new life. But we are not fools enough to think that the
beginning is the end! All subsequent life is a development of the

---

[138] Winslow, *When I Awake*, pp. 35-40.

[139] Winslow, *When I Awake*, pp. 41-46; see James 5:15-16.

[140] Winslow, *When I Awake*, pp. 47-53; see 1 Samuel 3:9 and Dick B., *The Good
Book and The Big Book*, p. 156, for a discussion of the many root sources quoting this
verse.

[141] Shoemaker, *The Conversion of the Church*, p. 60.

[142] Samuel M. Shoemaker, Jr., *How to Find God* (New York: Faith at Work, n.d.),
p. 16.

relationship with God which conversion opened. For us its daily focal point is what we call the "Quiet Time." As in all other private devotions, we pray and read the Bible. But the distinguishing element of a Quiet Time is listening for the guidance of God. "Speak, Lord, for Thy servant heareth," is the expectant mood of a Quiet Time. The validity of what we believe to be God's guidance must show itself, in the long run, by more acute moral perception, more genuine human relationships, and increasing assurance of what one ought to do with each hour of the day.[143]

[Speaking of a Quiet Time with P.G.:] P.G. suggested a Quiet Time together. So they prayed together, opening their minds to as much of God as he understood, removing first the hindrance of self-will, allowing the Spirit to focus an impression upon the mind, like light upon a camera (p. 47).

Shoemaker often emphasized "letting go" to God:

There is a plan He has for us bigger than our own plan, and we are afraid of it. Somewhere we hold back. Somewhere we keep control of our own destiny. Let go! Abandon yourself to Him. Say to Him, "Not my will but Thine be done." Live it, Pray for it. Put yourself at His disposal for time and eternity.[144]

Several Oxford Group writers provided specifics as to "listening." One involved the Chinese Proverb we have already mentioned: "God gave a man two ears and one mouth. Why don't you listen twice as much as you talk?"[145]

Cecil Rose wrote:

---

[143] Samuel M. Shoemaker, Jr., *Children of the Second Birth* (New York: Fleming H. Revell, 1927), p. 16.

[144] Shoemaker, *Religion That Works*, p. 19.

[145] Garth Lean, *Cast out Your Nets: Sharing Your Faith with Others* (London: Grosvenor, 1990), p. 25.

God has a plan. God speaks. But if He is to be heard and His plan is to be known and carried out, *man must listen.* That means a new approach to God for many of us. Our attitude when we have prayed has been, "Listen, Lord, for Thy servant speaketh." Our prayer has been what Canon Streeter classifies as "pagan" prayer—the attempt to bend God to our desires and make Him the servant of our needs. . . . Prayer, when it consists of this one-sided address by us to God, becomes increasingly unreal and is eventually dropped or only formally retained. Christian prayer begins with the desire to know God's will for us. . . . The promise that our petitions will be answered is only to those who have first placed themselves in line with His Will. If God is to become for us the living, active God, at work directing our life and the world's, it is vital that we should learn how to listen. There is one condition to be fulfilled before we begin. We must be willing to hear anything God says to us. . . . The important thing is for us to make, each for himself, the thrilling discovery that God has spoken to us. Once we have made that discovery, God will shape our "quiet times" and develop them until they express a full personal relationship with Him, and include our thanksgiving, worship, petition, intercession, as part of our life with Him. . . . This does not mean that, when we have a "quiet time," we resign our reasoning powers. The idea that listening to God means making your mind a blank is a curious misconception which has hindered many people. It does mean that you leave room for God to lead you beyond your human thoughts, and tell you things you could never know yourself. The next thing we shall find is that we are able better to interpret God's other ways of speaking to us through circumstances, through other people, through the Bible. We are learning to know His voice in our "quiet time," and we recognize it better elsewhere.[146]

---

[146] Cecil Rose, *When Man Listens* (New York: Oxford University Press, 1937), pp. 30-34.

Addressing the question of how to begin, Hallen Viney wrote:

"For one thing it means getting up earlier to listen to God. An alarm clock may be a help. If you feel chained to your bed, put the clock out of reach across the room." "How long should I listen?" "As long as you feel you need. Most of us began with a few minutes and find we need an hour or so now. Some people sit up in bed with a pencil and note-book, others dress first." "What happens? Do I hear a voice or something?" "No, God normally talks to people through their thoughts. It's the natural way for Him to reach you. Let Him put questions to you about your business, and your home life, and the bit of the world you live in. Think over the problems of the day against the background question, 'What does God want?' rather than 'What do I want?' You will find convictions forming in your mind as to the right thing to do. Write these convictions down."[147]

Howard Rose had a host of specific comments about listening:

1. Get into a comfortable position, sit, recline or kneel, whichever gives greatest relaxation of mind and body. Cultivate stillness of mind by an act of will, thinking peaceful and restful thoughts. Have unhurried quiet and sense of leisure, avoiding all tenseness (Psalm 37:7).

2. Confess any known sin and seek forgiveness through Christ (1 John 1:5-9).

3. Seek the in-dwelling presence of Christ, claiming His promise "I am with you always." He is there. Realize Him. "Abide in me, and I in you." (Gal. 2:20).

4. Dedicate the body, soul and spirit to Him for the day. This act of committal entails the bringing to God the belief of the mind, the love of the heart and the service of the will. (Rom. 12:1-2).

---

[147] Hallen Viney, *How Do I Begin?* (New York: The Oxford Group, n.d.), p. 5.

5. Pray that the Holy Spirit may take complete charge of the thought life, that only God's thoughts may enter the mind. (Romans 8:26-27; John 16:15).

6. In the attitude of "Speak Lord for Thy Servant heareth," wait patiently and quietly, listening for what He has to say, what He has to reveal to us concerning ourselves, what He wants us to do in His service, what message He wants us to hear, what piece of work He wants us to do, or what new truth He wants us to learn about Himself. (John 16:13-14).

7. Thoughts are given by way of: 1. Warnings: (a) Personal. (Wrong motives, thoughts, actions, etc., are revealed which might become an occasion for sin). (b) Concerning others. (Insight is given into the difficulties of those one is trying to help). 2. Some action to be taken, instructions re plans, etc. 3. Letters to write. 4. Visits to pay. 5. Thoughts to share with others. 6. Instructions re prayer, praise, what to read, etc. 7. Miscellaneous thoughts and promises.[148]

In his pamphlet, *How to Listen to God*, Chaplain John E. Batterson added these thoughts:

1. God is alive. He always has been and He always will be. 2. God knows everything. 3. God can do anything. 4. God can be everywhere—all at the same time. (These three are the important differences between God and us human beings.). 5. God is invisible—we can't see Him or touch Him—But God is here. He is with you now. He is beside you. He surrounds you. He fills the room or the whole place where you are right now. He is in you now. He is in your heart. 6. God cares very much for you. He is interested in you. He has a plan for your life. He has an answer for every need and problem you face. 7. God will tell you all that you need to know. He will not always tell you all that you want to know. 8. God will help you do anything that He asks you to do. 9. Anyone can be in touch with God, anywhere and at any

---

[148] Howard J. Rose, *The Quiet Time.* Consult the entire four page pamphlet.

time, if the conditions are obeyed. These are the conditions: A. To be quiet and still. B. To listen. C. To be honest about every thought that comes. D. To test the thoughts to be sure that they come from God. E. To obey.[149]

TUNE IN. Open your heart to God. Either silently or aloud, just say to God in a natural way that you would like to find His plan for your life—you want His answer to the problem or situation that you are facing just now. Be definite and specific in your request (p. 2).

LISTEN. Just be still, quiet, relaxed and open. Let your mind go "loose." Let God do the talking! Thoughts, ideas and impressions will begin to come into your mind and heart. Be alert and aware and open to every one (p. 2).

Writing Down Thoughts

From a number of different Oxford Group activists, the author has heard the story of how Oxford Group founder Dr. Frank Buchman explained the difference between "Guidance" and "Quiet Time." Buchman simply held up a pencil. Explaining "Quiet Time," Sam Shoemaker wrote:

> Most of us find it indispensable to have a loose-leaf note-book, in which to write down the things which come to us. We find that in trying to remember what has come before, we block what is coming now: we find it impossible to remember sometimes the things which come even in a brief Quiet Time. The Chinese have a saying that "the strongest memory is weaker than the weakest ink." We do not want to forget the slightest thing that God tells us to do: and I have sometimes had a rush of detailed guidance which came almost as fast as I could write it.[150]

---

[149] Chaplain John E. Batterson, *How to Listen to God* (pamphlet, n.d.), p. 1.
[150] Shoemaker, *The Conversion of the Church*, p. 60.

Shoemaker also said:

Fix the results of your praying by writing down what comes to you. Many thoughts pass through your mind as you wait listening before God. Some are more important, some less; but writing them down will help you remember them, so that you can carry them out. Bishop Slattery, in some notes he made for an address, wrote, "Prayer—Note book—Wait—Listen—Write down what is given you." Take plenty of time for this, so as not to be hurried, or skimp your time with God. Twenty minutes at least every morning for *listening prayer*.[151]

Cecil Rose concurred with Shoemaker's view, stating:

One practical hint is well worth taking. Use a note-book and pencil. Put down the thoughts which come in "quiet time." A typist who appeared minus her note-book when her employer wanted to dictate letters, would not hold her post long. It would not help her to plead that she could remember everything without taking it down. There is no reason why we should be less efficient with God. The Chinese say that the strongest memory is weaker than the palest ink.[152]

Howard Rose said:

Many find it a real help to write down the ideas and thoughts which the Holy Spirit has caused to arise in the mind. The advantage of this is two-fold: it is an aid to concentration and acts as a reminder of duties to be performed. It is also of value in checking at the close of day the thoughts received each morning and through the day. (Jer. 30:2).[153]

---

[151] Shoemaker, *How to Find God*, p. 16.

[152] Cecil Rose, *When Man Listens* (New York: Oxford University Press, 1937), p. 37.

[153] Howard J. Rose, *How Can God Guide Me?* (formerly *The Quiet Time*) (London: privately published pamphlet, n.d.). p. 3. See also Viney, *How Do I Begin?*, pp. 3-4;

(continued...)

"Checking" the Guidance

There has been criticism of the Oxford Group idea of checking—criticism based either on lack of understanding of the purpose of checking or criticism based on the misapplication of the principle by Oxford Group people themselves. But the reason for "checking" is quite understandable; and—for Oxford Group people—essential if one is not to go awandering, telling himself and others that "God told me," when in fact the thoughts and guidance did not come from God.

Oxford Group adherents often quoted and relied upon James 1:17:

Every good gift and every perfect gift is from above, and cometh down from the Father of lights, with whom is no variableness, neither shadow of turning.[154]

In other words, the true God will never steer us into trouble; hence *thoughts from God will be good thoughts.*

For Sinners Only laid out in detail the Oxford Group suggestions for making sure that "guidance" *was* guidance from God, and not from some other source.[155] Oxford Group people commonly pointed out they did not believe that every thought received in Quiet Time was a thought or directive from God. Therefore, they checked thoughts to be sure the thoughts accorded with God's will as expressed in the Bible, with the teachings of Jesus Christ, and with other biblical principles of love. And the author has laid out in several other titles the principles of,

---

[153] (...continued)
Carruthers, *How to Find Reality in Your Morning Devotions*, pp. 9-10; Batterson, *How to Listen to God*, p. 2;

[154] See Dick B., *The Good Book and the Big Book*, pp. 40, 72, 89-90, 187; The Layman with a Notebook, *What is The Oxford Group?* (London: Oxford University Press, 1933), p. 67; C. Irving Benson, *The Eight Points of the Oxford Group* (London: Oxford University Press, 1936), p. 79.

[155] A. J. Russell, *For Sinners Only* (London: Hodder & Stoughton, 1932), p. 94.

objections to, and tests for, guidance as the Oxford Group saw the process.[156]

Cecil Rose wrote:

> Of course, every thought that comes to us in the "quiet time" is not God's guidance. We need to test the voices that come to us along a line that has been so long disused or blocked. We have immediate cause to reject promptings which conflict with what we already know of His will. Nothing which is unloving, impure, dishonest, or selfish comes from God. Other suggestions which come to us may have to be talked out with some experienced person who knows how to listen to God. In other cases we may have to wait for clearer conviction in our own minds. Sometimes the only test is to make the venture and act. We shall make mistakes. But an honest mistake is of far more use to God than the timid inaction which makes no venture.[157]

Note the following from the Book of James, a favorite with early AAs:

> But if ye have bitter envying and strife in your hearts, glory not, and lie not against the truth. This wisdom descendeth not from above, but *is* earthly, sensual, devilish. For where envying and strife *is*, there *is* confusion and every evil work. But the wisdom that is from above is first pure, then peaceable, gentle, *and* easy to be intreated, full of mercy and good fruits, without partiality, and without hypocrisy (James 3:14-17).[158]

Small wonder there was vital necessity for checking which wisdom was from which source!

---

[156] Dick B., *Design for Living*, pp. 260-69. See also Forde, *The Guidance of God*, pp. 19-22.

[157] Rose, *When Man Listens*, p. 35.

[158] For Oxford Group references to this verse, see Dick B., *Design for Living*, pp. 232, 242.

Clearing the Receiver

The Oxford Group concepts of "Sin," the "Five C's," and the "Four Absolutes" were critical to the life changing process.[159]

Sin, said the Oxford Group, was anything that blocked you from God and from other people. The Five C's were the principal elements in the life-changing program of "soul surgery" that cut the blocks of sin away through the power of God and enabled the adherent to have an experience of Christ and change his or her life. The tests for the "sins" or shortcomings that needed to be removed were the four "standards" or four "absolutes" as they were variously called—absolute honesty, absolute purity, absolute unselfishness, and absolute love. These four standards were the marks of the perfect life Jesus Christ lived and taught. They were the "yardsticks" (as Dr. Bob called them) or goals by which Oxford Group people tried to measure their lives and toward which they pointed their actions. The Oxford Group people were seeking to "put off the old man" and to "put on the new man" which they had received by grace in the course of their rebirth and resultant changed lives.[160]

For us, it is important to know that the "lens" had to be clear for the reborn people to receive messages from God. The "receiving set" had to be in good order. Even Bill's wife, Lois Wilson, touched on some of the points in the following extracts from notations in her "Oxford Group Notebook":

1.   "Definite adequate, accurate information from God."

3.   "Sat. A.M. Chas Haines—Bible . . . Home Quiet Time."

---

[159] For full discussion, see Dick B., *Design for Living*, pp. 29-33, 103-04, 166-70, 175-81, 184-211, 221-69.

[160] See Ephesians 4:22, 24. See how Clarence S. quoted these verses in connection with the Third Step of Alcoholics Anonymous. Dick B., *That Amazing Grace: The Role of Clarence and Grace S. in Alcoholics Anonymous* (San Rafael, CA: Paradise Research Publications, 1996), p. 68.

4. "I realized that I had not really put my reliance in God but have been trying under guidance as I thought to do it all myself."

6. "List of sins: Feeling of being special, self conscious, feeling of inferiority, self-indulgence in small things, dependency on human law."

7. "Sin blinds, binds, multiplies, deadens."

9. "Oxford Group is spiritual revolution whose concern is vital Christianity under dictatorship of spirit of God."

10. "A new spirit is abroad in the world, a new illumination can bring men & women of every social situation back to the basic principles of the Christian faith."

14. "Helen Shoemaker—Surrender to God."

In these limited remarks, Lois was expressing some of what she had heard and noted about the removal of "blocks to God" at the Oxford Group meetings and houseparties she and Bill had attended.[161]

The Oxford Group was concerned with removing sin. *Sin* that "blinds, binds, multiplies, and deadens." Sin that blocked an effective relationship with God and blocked guidance from God.[162]

Remember, there are one or two conditions attached to this listening. It's rather like telephoning; God can't talk through a dirty contact. If you want to hear what He has to say, you must first find out, as I had to, whether you've got a good connection. . . . if you really want to listen to God you have to be more definite. If something goes wrong with the telephone, the trouble shooter doesn't say, "I don't claim this telephone is working well, but it's as good as the next one." First of all he's got to find the

---

[161] See Dick B., *The Akron Genesis of Alcoholics Anonymous* (Corte Madera, CA: Good Book Publishing Company, 1994), pp. 150-55.

[162] See Dick B., *Design for Living*, pp. 192-97.

fault in the telephone and then put it right. . . . there are four
pretty good tests to help you to be definite in finding these faults.
They are absolute honesty, absolute purity, absolute unselfishness,
and absolute love. When I first met this Oxford Group crowd I
didn't know much about religion, but I did know what honesty
meant, and when I thought about absolute honesty some very
concrete faults came into my mind. It was uncomfortably definite.
. . . Well, like the trouble shooter with the faulty telephone, it's
not enough just to know what is wrong and leave it at that. The
thing is to put it right. . . . Don't worry about the theory now. A
lot of people can switch on the light without knowing much about
electricity. The main thing is to get the light. In the same way, a
lot of people get into first-hand touch with God without knowing
all the theory at first.[163]

We believe we have established that the Oxford Group life-
changing principles of *decision, moral inventory, confession,
conviction, conversion, restitution,* and *continuance* spilled over
into A.A.'s Twelve Steps. In fact, the steps are framed on those
ideas. And critically important to A.A.'s prayer and meditation
Step was the elimination of spiritual infirmities by which "we [the
AAs] shut ourselves off from sunlight of the Spirit."[164] The
Steps were about removing the blocks.[165] Clearing the receiving
set.

Chaplain Batterson wrote about "blocks" to receiving guidance,
saying:

BLOCKS? What if I don't seem to get any definite thoughts?
God's guidance is as freely available as the air we breathe. If I am
not receiving thoughts when I listen, the fault is not God's.
Usually it is because of something *I will not do*: A. Something
wrong in my life that I will not face and make right. B. A habit
or indulgence I will not give up. C. A person I will not forgive.

---

[163] Viney, *How Do I Begin?*, pp. 2-4.

[164] Big Book, p. 66.

[165] Big Book, p. 71: "We hope you are convinced now that God can remove
whatever self-will has blocked you off from Him."

D. A wrong relationship in my life I will not give up. E. A restitution I will not make. F. Something God has already told me to do that I will not obey. Check these points and be honest. Then try listening again.[166]

Obeying the "Voice"

We have frequently discussed the tremendous significance of the Oxford Group's "experiment of faith" based on John 7:17. A.A.'s own "program of action," and the Oxford Group's program for life-change, were based on the idea that one could hear from God and receive the benefits of God's guidance when one *obeyed* God's known directives, whether they were set out in the Bible itself or received through messages from God. The key to listening was starting the experiment by making a decision, finding and forsaking faults, righting wrongs, and then tuning in to God.

As we've said, Frank Buchman was famous for the statement:

> God alone can change human nature. The secret lies in that great forgotten truth that when man listens, God speaks; when man obeys, God acts.[167]

The Eleventh Step

The Text of the Eleventh Step

Let's begin with the precise wording of Step Eleven itself: "Sought through prayer and meditation to improve our conscious contact with God *as we understood Him*, praying only for knowledge of His Will for us and the power to carry that out."

---

[166] Batterson, *How to Listen to God*, p. 3. See similar language in Shoemaker, *Twice-Born Ministers*, p. 92.

[167] Buchman, *Remaking the World*, p. 46.

First, let's look at "contact with God." The language was Oxford Group language.[168] Second, at "conscious contact" with God or, as Oxford Group people called it, "God consciousness."[169] Third, at the phrase "God as we understood Him." This concept of surrendering as much of ourselves as we understand to as much of God as we understand was Oxford Group all the way.[170]

And what of prayer for "knowledge of His will for us and the power to carry that out"? A glance at the writings of Stephen Foot will bring to mind this compellingly similar language: "I will ask God to show me His purpose for my life and claim from Him the power to carry that purpose out."[171]

There are other similarities between the Big Book language, and Oxford Group and Shoemaker writings. But the important thing here is that both the *language* of Step Eleven and the *idea* of praying for knowledge of God's will and for the power to carry out that will were Oxford Group in thinking. So was the idea of "prayer and meditation." It came from the Bible, as our Bible citations have shown.

A. J. Russell's popular book also showed the Oxford Group linkage between God's guidance and God's power:

---

[168] Sam Shoemaker's friend and Oxford Group colleague Dr. Philip Marshall Brown wrote "of the charity and love that are poured into human beings whenever they establish contact with God." See Philip Marshall Brown, *The Venture of Belief* (New York: Fleming H. Revell, 1935), p. 24. Oxford Group writer Stephen Foot said: "Contact with God is the necessary fundamental condition, and that is made through prayer and listening . . ." See Stephen Foot, *Life Began Yesterday* (London: William Heinemann, Ltd., 1935), p. 16.

[169] See Harold Begbie, *Life Changers*, 12th ed. (London: Mills & Boon, Ltd, 1932), p. 39; Victor C. Kitchen, *I Was a Pagan* (New York: Harper & Brothers, 1934), pp. 41, 43, 75; Samuel M. Shoemaker, Jr., *Twice-Born Ministers* (New York: Fleming H. Revell, 1929), p. 123.

[170] See Shoemaker, *Children of the Second Birth*, pp. 47, 25; *How to Become a Christian* (New York: Harper & Brothers, 1953), p. 72; Dick B., *The Good Book and The Big Book*, pp. 53-62; *Design for Living*, p. 306.

[171] Foot, *Life Began Yesterday*, p. 13.

God had a plan. They were trying to fit in with it. Knowledge of that plan, God's guidance and God's power were available for all who chose to work in with that plan. This guidance and power transcended every form of self-determination. God-guidance in God's strength could be the normal experience of everybody at all times.[172]

Oxford Group people often said: "Where God guides, He provides." Listen for the will of God, they said; and the power to carry it out will be present.

Big Book Examples of Guidance Language

There is scarcely a part of the Big Book that does not involve requests for God's guidance and direction.[173] Following are several examples:

I placed myself unreservedly under His care and direction (p. 13).

I was to sit quietly when in doubt, asking only for direction and strength to meet my problems as He would have me (p. 13).

When we drew near to Him He disclosed Himself to us (p. 57)!

God will show us how to take a kindly and tolerant view of each and every one (p. 67).

We ask Him to remove our fear and direct our attention to what He would have us be (p. 68).

In meditation, we ask God what we should do about each specific matter. The right answer will come, if we want it (p. 69).

---

[172] A. J. Russell, *For Sinners Only* (London: Hodder & Stoughton, Ltd., 1932), p. 23.

[173] See Dick B., *New Light on Alcoholism: The A.A. Legacy from Sam Shoemaker* (Corte Madera, CA: Good Book Publishing Company), pp. 168-69 for illustrations.

We earnestly pray for the right ideal, for guidance in each questionable situation, for sanity, and for strength to do the right thing (p. 70).

We ask that we be given strength and direction to do the right thing, no matter what the personal consequences may be (p. 79).

So we clean house with the family, asking each morning in meditation that our Creator show us the way of patience, tolerance, kindliness and love (p. 83).

He will show you how to create the fellowship you crave (p. 164).

Ask Him in your morning meditation what you can do each day for the man who is still sick. The answers will come, if your own house is in order (p. 164).

Specific Guidance Ideas

The Big Book's specifics on practicing Step Eleven are all borrowed from the Oxford Group and from the Bible's prayer and meditation precepts:

On Retiring at Night: AAs are to conduct a constructive review of the day (p. 86). Their "meditation" concerns the success they had, during the day, in practicing the principles of the Tenth Step. For the Tenth Step required a continuing moral inventory—looking for resentments, selfishness, dishonesty, and fear that cropped up during the day (p. 84). All these were manifestations of the self-centeredness decried by the Oxford Group. And if one has fallen short, there is to be a request for God's forgiveness (p. 86). The request for forgiveness—involving *prayer for forgiveness*—rests on James 5:15 and 1 John 1:7-9, containing ideas well known to the Oxford Group:

And the prayer of faith shall save the sick, and the Lord shall raise him up; and if he have committed sins, they shall be forgiven him (James 5:15).

But if we walk in the light, as he [God] is in the light, we have fellowship one with another, and the blood of Jesus Christ his Son cleanseth us from all sin (1 John 1:7).

If we confess our sins, he [God] is faithful and just to forgive us *our* sins, and to cleanse us from all unrighteousness (1 John 1:9).[174]

Having asked forgiveness, AAs are then to inquire of God "what corrective measures should be taken" (p. 86). The Oxford Group's Garth Lean wrote:

God said I must apologise and restore as far as I was able. There was no escaping it. God's searchlight beam kept playing upon them [his mistakes]. This action was for me as definite a test as Christ's command to the blind man to bathe his eyes in the pool of Siloam or to the rich young ruler to sell all he had.[175]

On Awakening. Today's AAs seem, with respect to Step Eleven, to talk mostly about prayer and meditation *on arising* in the morning. And most of the *Big Book* suggestions as to what is to be done "on awakening" are very similar to the practices followed by Sam Shoemaker and other Oxford Group people.

The Big Book speaks of laying out plans for the day and asking God to direct one's thinking (p. 86). This approach mirrors the suggestions in Shoemaker's "Good Morning" radio broadcast quoted in Chapter Ten of this title. Next, the Big Book speaks of *indecision* and the need for asking *God* for inspiration, an *intuitive*

---

[174] See Dick B., *The Good Book and The Big Book*, pp. 101-02, 153.

[175] Garth Lean, *Cast out Your Nets: Sharing Your Faith with Others* (London: Grosvenor, 1990), p. 87.

thought or a decision (p. 86).[176] There was much Oxford Group talk about "intuitive" thinking.[177] And Anne Smith wrote: "Guidance comes through direct intuitive thought."[178]

Speaking of *how* to receive the "intuitive thought," the Big Book suggests relaxing, taking it easy, and not struggling (p. 86). These same ideas can be found in the biblical and Oxford Group materials we discussed above and that Anne Smith covers.[179]

The Big Book's "morning watch" segment ends: "We usually conclude the period of meditation with a prayer that we be shown all through the day what our next step is to be, that we be given whatever we need to take care of such problems" (p. 87). The Oxford Group's Victor Kitchen (one of Bill Wilson's friends and businessmen's team colleagues) wrote:

> Where I used to plan the day, making a list of all the jobs I thought I had to finish, all the people I thought I had to see, all 'phone calls I thought I had to make and all the letters I thought I had to write, I now simply ask God's guidance on the day.[180]

Pursuing Spiritual Growth. The author has often called this Eleventh Step segment the "lost paragraph" because it seems to have been forgotten and is seldom discussed in meetings. The paragraph suggests asking wives or friends "to join us in morning meditation" if circumstances warrant (p. 87). This brings to mind

---

[176] Bill Wilson's emphasis on "intuition" may have been influenced by the title *Thomas Troward, the Edinburgh Lectures on Mental Science* (New York: Dodd, Mead & Co., 1909). This is a book mentioned by Bill's secretary, Nell Wing, as having been read by early AAs, see particularly the chapter on "intuition," pp. 71-73.

[177] Eleanor Napier Forde, *The Guidance of God* (Oxford: The Oxford Group, 1930), p. 21: "The fourth signpost is an intuitive conviction that a course of action is inherently right, the certainty that, hard as it may be, there can be no other way." See also, Samuel M. Shoemaker, Jr., *Twice-Born Ministers* (New York: Fleming H. Revell, 1929), p. 184; *The Conversion of the Church*, pp. 53-55.

[178] Dick B., *Anne Smith's Journal, 1933-1939: A.A.'s Principles of Success* (San Rafael, CA: Paradise Research Publications, 1995), p. 58.

[179] Dick B., *Anne Smith's Journal*, pp. 60-63.

[180] Kitchen, *I Was a Pagan*, p. 122.

Shoemaker's own family convocation as described in his "Good Morning" radio broadcast. It also calls up memories of the Quiet Time Dr. Bob's daughter recounted—in which her mother gathered "the guys" in the Smith home each morning for Bible study, prayer, listening, and guidance.

The Big Book hints of membership in religious bodies—almost a taboo topic in many A.A. meetings today (p. 87). Yet A.A. pioneers were gently nudged toward attendance at a religious group, though not all of them did.[181] The Big Book also suggests, "There are many helpful books"—a topic we have previously discussed.[182]

Throughout the Day, When Agitated or Doubtful. The Big Book's final Eleventh Step segment deals with the need for guidance in the face of possible anxiety. It says: "As we go through the day we pause, when agitated or doubtful, and ask for the right thought or action" (p. 87). The pertinent source verses include:

1. "Be still, and know that I *am* God" (Psalm 46:10).
2. "Lord, what wilt thou have me to do?" (Acts 9:6).
3. "What shall I do, Lord?" (Acts 22:10).
4. "Speak, Lord; for thy servant heareth" (1 Samuel 3:9).
5. "Thou wilt keep *him* in perfect peace, *whose* mind *is* stayed *on thee*: because he trusteth in thee" (Isaiah 26:3).
6. "Take no thought for [be not anxious about] your life, what ye shall eat, or what ye shall drink; nor yet for your body, what ye shall put on. . . . for Your Heavenly Father knoweth that ye have need of all these things. But seek ye first the kingdom of God, and his righteousness; and all these things shall be added unto you" (Matthew 6:25, 32-33).

---

[181] See (1) Big Book: p. 28—"Not all of us join religious bodies, but most of us favor such memberships;" (2) *DR. BOB and the Good Oldtimers* (New York: Alcoholics Anonymous World Services, 1980), p. 131—"Important, but not vital, that he [the alcoholic] attend some religious service at least once weekly;" (3) Dick B., *That Amazing Grace*, p. 92.

[182] Big Book, p. 87.

7. "Be careful for [anxious about] nothing; but in everything by
   prayer and supplication with thanksgiving let your requests be
   made known unto God. And the peace of God, which passeth all
   understanding, shall keep your hearts and minds through Christ
   Jesus" (Philippians 4:6-7).

Ending its Eleventh Step "Quiet Time" suggestions, the Big
Book exhorts AAs in stress to say to themselves "many times each
day 'Thy will be done'" (p. 88)—from the Lord's Prayer in the
Sermon on the Mount.[183]

---

[183] See Matthew 6:10; Shoemaker, *Children of the Second Birth*, pp. 175-87. Note
that this entire chapter is devoted to "Thy will be done." See also The Layman with a
Notebook, *What is the Oxford Group?* (London: Oxford University Press, 1933), p. 48.

Part 5

History to the Rescue

"Whenever a civilization or society perishes, there is always one condition present. They forgot where they came from."[1]

---

[1] A.A.'s archivist, Frank M., quoting Carl Sandburg.

14

Putting It All Together

A history of early A.A.'s spiritual principles and successes will be of little value unless several conditions are present. It is important to:

1. know the sources for the principles and practices.
2. untangle the facts from the myths.
3. make sure that the history includes as many of the contributing segments as can be located.
4. know if the segments have direct relevance to recovery today.
5. be sure that the historical elements were those which produced success.
6. make sure that the history is useful for an individual AA's spiritual foundation and growth.
7. be sure that Twelve Step, religious, and recovery communities see accuracy and integrity in the reports about what early AAs believed and did.
8. see that the historical elements are put in sufficiently simple form that they will not be discarded as "too intellectual," "too complicated," "too religious," and "too remote in time" to be of real help in today's world of spiraling alcoholism and addiction.

651

Summary of Sources

The reader has seen the diversity of sources that actually
contributed to early A.A.'s spiritual program.

There can be little doubt of the *Bible's primary importance*.
Oxford Group principles were biblical principles; and Oxford
Group writings were grounded in the Bible. All the Akron A.A.
pioneers focused on the Bible. And the most *basic ideas* in A.A.'s
Four Absolutes, original six steps, and ultimate Twelve Steps can
be located in the Bible itself.

A First Century Christian Fellowship (later known as the
Oxford Group) provided the heart of A.A.'s *life-changing structure
and language*. It supplied it in the development of the A.A.
Fellowship, Steps, and Big Book. Thus, on July 14, 1949, Bill
Wilson wrote Sam Shoemaker:

> So far as I am concerned, and Dr. Smith too, the O.G. seeded
> AA. It was our spiritual wellspring at the beginning.

Bill wrote Shoemaker on July 27, 1953:

> You needn't look too hard for the virtues because if the book
> [*A.A. Comes of Age*] has them, they stem mostly from you and
> the old time O.G. in the first place. With every passing day, I'm
> more grateful for all of that which I hope will be suitably
> recorded in a short history of A.A. on which I've begun work.

On February 7, 1957, Bill wrote Sam:

> About three years ago I had a talk with Father Ed Dowling about
> this forthcoming history. I told him what you and the O.G. had
> done for us and how reluctant I had been all these years to
> publicly disclose it. Then I explained how prudence had suggested
> that this be deferred because the Pope at one time had written off
> the O.G. meetings for the attendance of Catholics.

Then, on April 23, 1963, Bill wrote Sam:

> It is also entirely true that the substance of A.A.'s Twelve Steps
> was derived from the O.G.'s emphasis on the essentials and your
> unforgettable presentation of this material time after time. After
> the alcoholics parted company with the O.G. here in New York,
> we developed a word-of-mouth program of six steps which was
> simply a paraphrase of what we had heard and felt at your
> meetings. The Twelve Steps of A.A. simply represented an
> attempt to state in more detail, breadth and depth, what we had
> been taught—primarily by you. Without this, there could have
> been nothing—nothing at all.

In other words, just as the Bible was the source of A.A.'s basic
ideas, the *Oxford Group* was the *source* of A.A.'s recovery
program language and structure; and Bill frequently said so. In
addition, however, there were innumerable ways in which *Sam
Shoemaker*, as a major Oxford Group leader, *passed the Oxford
Group message* forward to AAs. Shoemaker's books, pamphlets,
articles, and sermons were a source. Shoemaker's
colleagues—Irving and Julia Harris, Garrett Stearly, Ray Purdy,
J. Herbert Smith, Charles Haines, Rowland Hazard, Shepard
Cornell, Hanford Twitchell, Victor Kitchen, Charles Clapp, Jr.,
and many others in the businessmen's team—worked directly with
Bill. The Oxford Group example of a fellowship, teams, groups,
story-telling, and meetings directly shaped the practices of AAs in
their life-changing work with alcoholics.

And now for Dr. Bob's wife, Anne Ripley Smith. After reading
and re-reading Anne Smith's Journal, the author is convinced that
Anne was a major source for the ideas that found their way into
the Big Book and the Twelve Steps. And the author's views were
possibly shared by Lois Wilson, Henrietta Seiberling, and historian
Ernest Kurtz.[1]

---

[1] Kurtz wrote: "This writer was struck in his interviews of 6 and 7 April, 1977, that
both Lois [Wilson] and Henrietta Seiberling stressed that Anne Smith's role in the
(continued...)

Anne Smith's spiritual journal was begun in 1933 and continued until 1939. She wrote down and analyzed the ideas she heard and studied in the Bible, the Oxford Group, and the Christian literature early AAs were reading. She shared specifically the contents of her journal with AAs and their families in the Smith home. She conducted Quiet Time for more than an hour each day in the Smith home. She counseled AAs and their families; she provided room and board for AAs; she helped them find jobs; and she read Scripture, interpreted Oxford Group ideas, and taught early AAs and their families what she knew from her reading of Christian literature, listening, and attendance at meetings. She was always at the fore in A.A. meetings—spotting the newcomer, extending greetings, and making the people feel welcome. And Clarence S.— a pioneer and one of Dr. Bob's sponsees—said: "Anne was a mother to me." He said there were many things he would take to Anne that he did not feel free to take to Bob. Clarence's widow, Grace, said:

> I don't remember any specific thing Clarence said Anne had taught him from the Bible. I do know she was a much softer, gentler person. She had patience and love. She really loved those men. And she took time to explain and talk to them, and teach them the Word of God. Clarence made that clear to me. . . . Clarence was bowled over with Anne's compassion and love for a bunch of drunk men.[2]

We've also covered the literature that Dr. Bob and the other early AAs read, the specific capabilities and efforts of T. Henry and Clarace Williams, and the stalwart assistance of Henrietta Seiberling. But we should close with the importance of the daily devotionals such as *The Upper Room, My Utmost for His Highest,*

---

[1] (...continued)
beginning of A.A. has been much underrated." Ernest Kurtz, *Not-God: A History of Alcoholics Anonymous*, exp. ed. (Center City, MN: Hazelden, 1991), pp. 320-21, n.15.

[2] Dick B., *That Amazing Grace: The Role of Clarence and Grace S. in Alcoholics Anonymous* (San Rafael, CA: Paradise Research Publications, 1996), pp. 29-30.

The Runner's Bible, and *Daily Strength for Daily Needs*. Frank Amos reported to John D. Rockefeller, Jr., that Quiet Time was a *must* in early A.A. And we know that the devotionals were an important part of that Quiet Time, along with Bible study, prayer, and listening. Many many ideas that AAs took from the Bible, the Oxford Group, the literature they read, and Anne Smith were presented to them *daily* in simplified form through the devotionals. There was a Bible verse, a comment for meditation, a prayer, and a thought for the day. *A Manual for Alcoholics Anonymous* instructed:

> First off, your day will have a new pattern. You will open the day with a quiet period. This will be explained by your sponsor. You will read the "Upper Room," or whatever you think best for yourself.[3]

Many of the Bible verses we have covered were mentioned over and over in *The Upper Room* quarterlies for the mid-1930's:

1. **Psalm 46:10**: Be still, and know that I am God;
2. **Isaiah 26:3**: Thou wilt keep *him* in perfect peace, *whose* mind *is* stayed *on thee*: because he trusteth in thee.
3. **2 Corinthians 5:17**: Therefore if any man *be* in Christ, *he is* a new creature: old things are passed away; behold, all things are become new;
4. **John 3:3**: Verily, verily, I say unto thee, Except a man be born again, he cannot see the kingdom of God;
5. **John 7:17**: If any man will do his will, he shall know of the doctrine, whether it be of God, or *whether* I speak of myself;
6. **James 5:16**: Confess *your* faults one to another, and pray for one another, that ye may be healed. The effectual fervent prayer of a righteous man availeth much;

---

[3] *A Manual for Alcoholics Anonymous*, 6th rev. ed. (Akron, OH: AA of Akron, 1993), p. 8.

7. **Matthew 5:23**: Therefore if thou bring thy gift to the altar, and there rememberest that thy brother hath ought against thee; Leave there thy gift before the altar, and go thy way; first be reconciled to thy brother, and then come and offer thy gift;
8. **Matthew 6:10**: Thy will be done . . . ;
9. **Matthew 6:33**: But seek ye first the kingdom of God and his righteousness; and all these things shall be added unto you.
10. **Matthew 7:21**: Not every one that saith unto me, Lord, Lord, shall enter into the kingdom of heaven; but he that doeth the will of my Father which is in heaven.

The list could go on and on as to *The Upper Room* and also as to other devotionals we mentioned. The point is that AAs were not only exposed to the contents of the Bible, the structure of the Oxford Group life-changing steps, and the teachings of Anne Smith; they were frequently hearing the specific Bible verses upon which their principles rested. They saw and heard them in the Bible devotionals.

Correcting Some Errors

Errors have crept into A.A. spiritual history as the years have passed; and we need to summarize the facts this title assembled.

First, the "sermon on the mount" was not written by Emmet Fox. The sermon was delivered by Jesus, and is recorded in Matthew, chapters five through seven. Early AAs studied a number of commentaries on the sermon on the mount, including those by Oswald Chambers, Glenn Clark, Emmet Fox, and E. Stanley Jones. Fox was not a member of the Oxford Group; nor were Jones, Chambers, or Clark. "God as we understood Him" is an expression that, in one form or another, was used in the Oxford Group, by Sam Shoemaker, and by Anne Smith long before the Twelve Steps and Big Book were written. We have found no evidence that the Twelve Steps came from ten "Holiness" ideas of John Wesley. The Oxford Group did not, per se, have twelve steps, nor six steps. The expression "higher power" was seldom, if ever, used in the Oxford Group. The expression "power greater than ourselves" came from the Oxford Group and referred to God. When the Oxford Group spoke of a "Power," they were commonly speaking of God. "Thy will be done" came from Jesus's sermon on the mount. The Lord's Prayer came from Jesus's sermon on the mount. The "principles" that early AAs practiced, and through which they took their written moral inventories, were the principles (or *yardsticks*, as Dr. Bob called them) of the Oxford Group's Four Absolutes.

Founded upon a Rock

There have been many suppositions about the sources of the Twelve Steps. People have tried to find the principles in all kinds of religions; and they have given the steps a variety of interpretations when it came to such matters as "God," "sin," and "conversion." However commentators may have "sourced" the Steps, Bill and Dr. Bob *both* said A.A. and its Steps were inspired by, and based on the philosophy of, Jesus's sermon on the mount.

Here it is important to see what Jesus taught in that sermon:

Not every one that saith unto me, Lord, Lord, shall enter into the kingdom of heaven; but he that doeth the will of my Father which is in heaven. Many will say to me in that day, Lord, Lord, have we not prophesied in thy name? and in thy name have cast out devils? and in thy name done many wonderful works? And then will I profess unto them, I never knew you: depart from me, ye that work iniquity. Therefore whosoever heareth these sayings of mine, and doeth them, I will liken him unto a wise man, which *built his house upon a rock*: And the rain descended, and the floods came, and the winds blew, and beat upon that house; and it fell not: for it was *founded upon a rock*. And every one that heareth these sayings of mine, and doeth them not, shall be likened unto a foolish man, which built his house upon the sand. And the rain descended, and the floods came, and the winds blew, and beat upon that house; and it fell: and great was the fall of it (Matthew 7:21-27; italics added).

Most of the early AAs (who stayed sober) believed the Bible was a rock upon which their deliverance by God from the awful specter of alcoholism could be founded. They studied the Good Book. They looked for God's will in the Good Book. From the Bible, they learned about the power of God. They learned from the Good Book how to pray to God and listen for further revelation of His particular will for them. They learned how to be reborn so that they could receive the power of God and utilize it to serve and glorify Him and be of maximum service to others. And they found that what they had learned and applied actually produced recovery from the ravages of alcoholism as well as help in dealing with other problems in their lives.

The Spiritual Concepts in a Nutshell

When one approaches the roots of the Big Book material and the Twelve Steps it contains, certain underlying points become clear—particularly from the earlier manuscripts.

A.A.'s spiritual sources emphatically affirmed the existence of God—the Creator—the Almighty God described in the Bible. They presupposed that God is love, all-powerful, a healer, a deliverer, forgiving, and a communicator of His will for man. They saw God as having a plan, and mankind as having the end of conforming to that plan. They presumed the necessity for belief in God—a belief often called "faith." They posited that man had become estranged from God, needed to find Him, and needed to establish a relationship with Him and become His companions. They presumed that a surrender of the will to God marked the turning point in the path to the relationship with God. In the earlier days, the surrender involved coming to God through God's only begotten son, Jesus Christ.

There was an assumption that man is blocked from God by barriers that were originally—in the Steps themselves—called sin. The sources required a searching examination for the sin, a confession of it, a conviction that it needed to be forsaken, a transformation which eradicated the sin and which only God could effect, and a restorative process called restitution. The sources presumed that when a right relationship had been established with God, great things would come to pass. Then they pointed to the necessity for a daily self-appraisal and housecleaning; daily communion with, and reliance upon, God; daily efforts to witness to others as to the power of God; and daily efforts to align one's life with the will of God, and improve one's spiritual relationship with Him by practicing the principles of love He laid down in His word.

The Steps

1. A.A.'s First Step ideas derive in part from several solid, biblical ideas: Without God, people suffer from *spiritual misery*. Their lives become unmanageable because they have devised their own, ineffective human ways.[4] They have tried, without success, to be like God.[5] Alcohol has become an illusory solution for the problem. For the real alcoholic, life has become unmanageable; alcohol has accelerated the unmanageability; and the real alcoholic—on his or her own power—lacks the ability to escape either the deadly effects of alcohol or the destructive life situations it inevitably helps to cause. Dr. Jung later told Wilson that the power to be overcome was aptly called the Devil.[6]

2. The Second Step offers the alcoholic a solution—power![7] And the alcoholic has several tasks in order to access that power:

---

[4] Genesis 3:14-24; Proverbs 16:25; Samuel M. Shoemaker, Jr., *Realizing Religion* (New York: Association Press, 1923), pp. 4, 7.

[5] Genesis 3:4-5.

[6] 2 Corinthians 4:4; *The Devil and A.A.* (Chicago: Chicago Area Alcoholics Anonymous Service Office, 1948), p. 18; 1 Peter 5:8; Dick B., *That Amazing Grace: The Role of Clarence and Grace S. in Alcoholics Anonymous* (San Rafael: CA: Paradise Research Publications, 1996), p. 90; *Anne Smith's Journal, 1933-1939: A.A.'s Principles of Success* (San Rafael, CA: Paradise Research Publications, 1994), pp. 60, 61.

[7] Dick B., *Anne Smith's Journal*, pp. 24, 61.

There must be *belief*.[8] There must be *willingness* to surrender to, and obey, the power.[9] And there must be action—*seeking* the "One who has all Power"—God.[10] For the unbelievers and agnostics, Bill Wilson inserted Shoemaker's experiment of faith based on John 7:17.[11] Bill also deleted the word God and substituted an Oxford Group expression—"Power greater than ourselves."[12] The expression still meant "God," which Bill confirmed by retaining and mentioning "God," pronouns referring to Him, and other descriptions of Him at least 400 times in the Big Book. At any rate, the assumption was that if the atheist or agnostic followed God's known will—as the Oxford Group had laid it out, and as Bill had tried to codify it in the Steps—that person would "come to believe"—as the Oxford Group interpretation of John 7:17 suggested.

3. The Third Step marked the beginning of the action. A *decision* was required.[13] The decision was, and, to some extent, still is, made on the knees.[14] It was the turning point.[15] It was the surrender.[16] It required proclaiming that the alcoholic was casting his will and his life on Almighty God.[17] The Oxford Group had long spoken of surrender to God *as one understood Him*. And that

---

[8] Hebrews 11:6; Samuel M. Shoemaker, Jr., *National Awakening* (New York: Harper & Brothers, 1936), p. 40-41.

[9] John 7:17; Samuel M. Shoemaker, Jr., *Religion That Works* (New York: Fleming H. Revell, 1928), pp. 46, 58, 64; Philip Marshall Brown, *The Venture of Belief*, 2d ed. (New York: Fleming H. Revell, 1935), pp. 29, 36

[10] Matthew 6:33; Shoemaker, *National Awakening*, p. 41; Big Book, p. 59.

[11] John 7:17; Samuel M. Shoemaker, Jr., *How to Find God* (New York: Faith at Work, n.d.), pp. 4-6.

[12] Dick B., *Design for Living: The Oxford Group's Contribution to Alcoholics Anonymous* (San Rafael, CA: Paradise Research Publications, 1995), pp. 302-04, 341.

[13] Brown, *The Venture of Belief*, pp. 26-28; Big Book, p. 60.

[14] Samuel M. Shoemaker, Jr., *Twice Born Ministers* (New York: Fleming H. Revell, 1929), p. 30.

[15] Psalm 46:10; Shoemaker, *Religion That Works*, p. 48; *National Awakening*, pp. 45-54

[16] Dick B., *Anne Smith's Journal*, pp. 25-26, 97-98.

[17] Shoemaker, *Twice Born Ministers*, p. 134.

very Oxford Group "God as we understood Him" palliative seems to have been inserted into the Steps to satisfy Bill's handful of atheists and agnostics in New York. But the expression still meant "God."[18] So did the expression "Higher Power" which Bill used twice in the Big Book.[19] Though Bill later expanded this "higher power" idea to mean "the group," that idea was, to Dr. Bob's wife, one of several "funk holes."[20]

The decision to surrender was verbalized. It was sometimes phrased "O, God, manage me because I can't manage myself."[21] It was sometimes phrased: "O God, if there be a God, take command of my life; I cannot manage it myself."[22] For some, it was simply "Thy will be done"—from the Lord's Prayer.[23] In Akron, and sometimes in New York, it involved accepting Jesus Christ as one's Lord and Savior.[24] This with the result that one was born again.[25] It also involved a recognition that the individual is *not* God; a decision to *quit playing God*; and the symbolic prayer letting God be God by bowing to His will.[26]

4. The Fourth Step is loaded with biblical concepts which were the subject of comment by the Oxford Group, Shoemaker, Bill Wilson, Dr. Bob, and Anne Smith. The first has to do with self-examination—looking for sins (areas in one's life which fall short

---

[18] Samuel M. Shoemaker, Jr., *Children of the Second Birth* (New York: Fleming H. Revell, 1927), pp. 47, 25.

[19] Victor C. Kitchen, *I Was a Pagan* (New York: Harper & Brothers, 1934), p. 85; Norman Vincent Peale, *The Power of Positive Thinking*, Special Peale Center Edition (New York: Peale Center for Christian Living, 1978, 1952), pp. 262-75.

[20] Dick B., *Anne Smith's Journal*, pp. 89-90.

[21] Dick B., *Anne Smith's Journal*, pp. 20-22.

[22] Brown, *The Venture of Belief*, p. 30.

[23] Matthew 6:10; The Layman with a Notebook, *What is the Oxford Group?* (London: Oxford University Press, 1933), p. 48.

[24] Shoemaker, *Religion That Works*, p. 74; Dick B., *That Amazing Grace*, pp. 27, 52, 68.

[25] John 3:3-4; Shoemaker, *National Awakening*, pp. 55-66; *Twice Born Ministers*, pp. 10, 56.

[26] Shoemaker, *National Awakening*, p. 48.

of adherence to God's will).[27] The second idea is that there is to be a *moral* inventory; or, as the Oxford Group and Anne Smith put it, a "moral test."[28] As we've covered, the Oxford Group and the Big Book spoke in terms of making a business inventory to enable the discarding of damaging goods. The original inventory used the Four Absolutes as the yardsticks by which to take the inventory; and these, of course, were totally biblical in origin.[29] The final point, already covered at some length, involved the *writing down* of shortcomings.[30]

5. The Fifth Step involved several important concepts. First, James 5:16—the confession of faults. Second, confessing them to God and to another human being.[31] Finally, the Big Book's stated purposes of achieving honesty, humility, and loss of fear.[32]

6. The Sixth Step has its roots in "conviction" of sin.[33] In Oxford Group terms, this meant admitting failure to live up adequately to the challenge of the Four Absolutes. The Step is

---

[27] Matthew 7:1-5; Geoffrey Allen, *He That Cometh* (New York: The Macmillan Company, 1933), pp. 81, 140, 143; Samuel M. Shoemaker, Jr., *The Church Can Save the World* (New York: Harper & Brothers, 1938), pp. 88-121; Dick B., *Anne Smith's Journal*, pp. 30-31.

[28] H. A. Walter, *Soul Surgery: Some Thoughts on Incisive Personal Work*, 6th ed. (London: Blandford Press, n.d.), pp. 43-44; Dick B., *Anne Smith's Journal*, p. 32.

[29] Dick B., *Anne Smith's Journal*, p. 33.

[30] Dick B., *Anne Smith's Journal*, p. 32.

[31] Dick B., *Design for Living*, p. 191; *Anne Smith's Journal*, p. 39.

[32] Honesty, of course, relates to the Four Absolutes (Dick B., *Design for Living*, pp. pp. 190-91). Humility to the elimination of self as God (*Design for Living*, p. 184; Walter, *Soul Surgery*, p. 57). Fear to the fear which Buchman asserted as a dominant factor in people's lives. See Frank N. D. Buchman, *Remaking the World* (London: Blandford Press, 1961), pp. 24, 28, 38, 46.

[33] Psalms 51:4; 65:3; John 16:8; Luke 15:21; Romans 5:8; 7:14; 2 Corinthians 11:29; Walter, *Soul Surgery*, pp. 64-78; Dick B., *The Good Book and The Big Book: A.A.'s Roots in the Bible* (San Rafael, CA: Paradise Research Publications, 1996), pp. 144-45; *That Amazing Grace*, pp. 51-52.

founded on man's need to hate and forsake the sin.[34] And it deals with God capacity to *remove* the sin.[35]

7. Step Seven is a mixture of "conversion," "change" from a life filled with shortcomings, and the part God plays in the transformation.[36] It was rooted in a new birth, the regenerating power of Christ, and the humble request for God's help in the process.[37]

8. Many fail to realize the biblical ideas in the Eighth Step process. Step Eight calls for willingness to move out with the power and love of God and touch the lives of others with forgiveness and restoration for things gone wrong. John 7:17 was the foundation for willingness—the action consistent with God's will that establishes the fruitfulness of doing that will. And two other verses point to God's will: (1) "If a man say, I love God, and hateth his brother, he is a liar: for he that loveth not his brother whom he hath seen, how can he love God whom he hath not seen" (1 John 4:20)?[38] (2) "Agree with thine adversary quickly. . . ." (Matthew 5:25).[39]

9. The Ninth Step—making direct amends for harm done—is almost uniquely Oxford Group in origin.[40] Yet it is founded, from

---

[34] Shoemaker, *National Awakening*, p. 58; Dick B., *Design for Living*, p. 193.

[35] Psalm 103:12; Allen, *He That Cometh*, p. 147; Dick B., *Anne Smith's Journal*, p. 46.

[36] John 3:3-7; Romans 12:1-2; James 4:7, 10; Dick B., *Design for Living*, pp. 197-206; *Anne Smith's Journal*, pp. 45-47; *The Good Book and The Big Book*, pp. 145-47.

[37] Psalm 103:10-12; Matthew 7:7-11; 12:43-45; James 5:13-16; Dick B., *That Amazing Grace*, pp. 72-74.

[38] Shoemaker, *12 Steps to Power*, p. 2; Glenn Clark, *I Will Lift Up Mine Eyes* (New York: Harper & Brothers, 1937); Clarence I. Benson, *The Eight Points of the Oxford Group* (London: Humphrey Milford, Oxford University Press, 1934), pp. 36-37; Dick B., *The Akron Genesis of Alcoholics Anonymous* (Corte Madera, CA: Good Book Publishing Company, 1994), p. 92

[39] Benson, *The Eight Points*, p. 32; *The Upper Room* for 1/12/36.

[40] A. J. Russell, *For Sinners Only* (London: Hodder & Stoughton, 1932), p. 120.

the A.A. standpoint, on well-known verses and stories in the Sermon on the Mount and the Gospel of Luke.[41]

10. Step Ten involves primarily the daily application of the principles set forth in Steps Four through Nine. There are a number of pertinent verses.[42] The Oxford Group root was called "Continuance." And perhaps the most significant Bible verse is: "Watch and pray, that ye enter not into temptation: the spirit indeed *is* willing, but the flesh *is* weak" (Matthew 26:41).[43]

11. Step Eleven ideas constituted a major part of the Oxford Group program, were a "must" in early A.A., and can be found throughout the Bible. First, there was the efficacy of prayer.[44] Second, there was the end-of-the-day review, seeking God's forgiveness for mistakes made.[45] Third, the morning quiet time involved Bible study, Christian literature, devotionals, prayer to God, and listening for the "voice" of God. But the details are best left to our other titles on this all-important subject.[46] The fourth idea concerned further spiritual growth through study of Scripture and other books.[47] The final idea concerned the daily walk in

---

[41] Matthew 5:23-24; Luke, Chapter 15; Luke 19:1-10. See also Numbers 5:6-7 and the translation quoted in Russell, *For Sinners Only*, p. 119.

[42] Galatians 2:20; Matthew 26:41; John 16:13-15; Colossians 1:23; Philippians 1:6; James 4:7. See Dick B., *The Good Book and The Big Book*, pp. 149-51; *That Amazing Grace*, p. 76; *Anne Smith's Journal*, pp. 49-53; *Design for Living*, pp. 317-19.

[43] See Dick B., *The Good Book and The Big Book*, p. 151, n. 113.

[44] James 5:16; Walter, *Soul Surgery*, p. 29; Dick B., *Anne Smith's Journal*, pp. 36-37.

[45] James 5:15; 1 John 1:7; 1 John 1:9; Harry J. Almond, *Foundations for Faith*, 2d ed. (London: Grosvenor Books, 1980), pp. 13, 15; Dick B., *The Good Book and The Big Book*, p. 153.

[46] Psalm 5:3; 32:8; 37:5; 46:10; Proverbs 3:5-6; 1 Samuel 3:9; Acts 9:6; 22:10; Romans 8:14; 1 Corinthians 2:9; 2 Corinthians 5:7; James 1:5; 3:17; 4:8; Dick B., *Good Morning! Quiet Time, Morning Watch, Meditation, and Early A.A.* (San Rafael: CA: Paradise Research Publications, 1996); *That Amazing Grace*, p. 54; *The Good Book and The Big Book*, pp. 154-57.

[47] John 5:39; John 8:32; 2 Timothy 2:15; Dick B., *The Good Book and The Big Book*, pp. 157, n. 145; 185, n. 18.

communion with God.[48] And it meant doing so without anxiety, and with *trust* in God.[49]

12. The three major ideas in Step Twelve are not difficult to trace as to source. First, the concept of a spiritual experience or spiritual awakening seems to have come almost exclusively from the Oxford Group.[50] But the oft-cited idea that a "new man" emerged from the "new birth" rested largely on 2 Corinthians 5:17: "Therefore if any man *be* in Christ, *he is* a new creature; old things are passed away; behold, all things are become new."[51] Second, the necessity for witnessing, or sharing by witness, was both Oxford Group and biblical in origin.[52] AAs, the Oxford Group, and Shoemaker often said—in one form or another: "You have to give it away to keep it."[53] Third, the principles to be practiced had at least four major sources: (1) The Oxford Group's Four Absolutes; (2) 1 Corinthians 13; (3) The Sermon on the Mount; (4) the Book of James.

The Will of God

We cannot "put it all together" without a brief review of the subject of "God's Will." The Big Book and the Sermon on the

---

[48] *Spiritual Milestones in Alcoholics Anonymous* said: "We should always strive to make God a companion rather than someone from whom we constantly demand gifts" (p. 4).

[49] Isaiah 26:3; Matthew 6:10, 25, 32-33; Philippians 4:6-7; Dick B., *The Good Book and The Big Book*, pp. 158-59; *Anne Smith's Journal*, p. 64.

[50] Many times, Frank Buchman used language like this: "Our own country needs a moral and *spiritual awakening*;" Buchman, *Remaking the World*, p. 19 (italics added). Shoemaker frequently spoke of a spiritual awakening, but he also referred to "spiritual experience," using language like this: "The conspiracy of silence, about sin, about deliverance, about *spiritual experience*, has lasted long enough; Shoemaker, *Twice Born Ministers*, p. 61 (italics added).

[51] Dick B., *That Amazing Grace*, p. 34; *The Good Book and The Big Book*, p. 161.

[52] Matthew 4:19; Acts 16:22-23; 2 Corinthians 5:20; James 2:20; Dick B., *The Good Book and The Big Book*, pp. 161-62; *Design for Living*, pp. 325-26; *Anne Smith's Journal*, p. 315.

[53] Samuel M. Shoemaker, Jr., *One Boy's Influence* (New York: Association Press, 1925), p. 15.

Mount use the phrase, "Thy will be done." Jesus spoke of the importance of doing the will of his Father. The importance of the Ten Commandments and the Beatitudes often surfaced in A.A.'s roots. And one cannot reach A.A.'s Eleventh Step without dealing with the question of the will of God and how to find it. For it is readily apparent from a reading of the Twelve Steps and the Big Book, as well as other A.A. literature, that A.A. inherited a strong emphasis on the importance of aligning and harmonizing one's life with the will of God.

Sam Shoemaker, along with many other Oxford Group and religious writers, told people to look for the will of God in the Bible, and also to seek it through prayer and worship. Writing in *The Calvary Evangel* on the Twelve Steps, Shoemaker said:

> Religion is relationship with God, and we must give something to it if we would deepen and enrich a relationship. Prayer and study of the Bible, and the attendance on Christian worship, are the three classical ways of keeping in touch with God. . . . Time was when prayer was unreal to me, and the Bible dull; but then came the experience of finding Christ with power, and then both things began to be real. . . . We must set apart time each day for this; first thing in the morning. . . . And don't forget—God sometimes sends over His own direct Word to us for our encouragement and guidance.[54]

In more explicit terms, Shoemaker frequently wrote along the following lines:

> There is a general will of God, and there is a particular will of God. All men everywhere at all times who have lined up for the right, been true and square and clean, have done the general will of God. But a man may be doing the general will of God and yet miss the particular will of God for him. It is not enough to have done good: We want to do the highest, most good. We want to

---

[54] S. M. Shoemaker, Jr., *The Twelve Steps of AA* (New York: The Evangel, n.d.), pp. 5-6; *12 Steps to Power* (Faith At Work News, December, 1983).

know just the one thing that God wants with us, the one niche we can fill, and then live to the uttermost. . . . Surrender to the will of God is all summed up in the great question of Paul: "Lord, what wilt Thou have me to do?" . . . So long as there is an "if" or a "but" to it, it is not surrender. We have got to wipe the slate clean, and then ask Him to write His will upon it.[55]

Early AAs seemed convinced of the applicability of the Bible's two great commandments on love:

And thou shalt love the Lord thy God with all thy heart, and with all thy soul, and with all thy mind, and with all thy strength; this *is* the first commandment. And the second *is* like, *namely* this, thou shalt love thy neighbor as thyself. There is none other commandment great than these (Mark 12:30-31).[56]

Spiritual Milestones in Alcoholics Anonymous stated:

The unselfish helping of others is the practice of love, upon which Christian philosophy is based. Remember at all times our Lord's two commandments [quoting the above].[57]

Dr. Bob stated that A.A.'s Steps could be simmered down to "love and service."[58] So one of the foundations upon which A.A. philosophy was based was the commandment to practice the love of God. The Good Book said:

By this we know that we love the children of God, when we love God, and keep his commandments. For this is the love of God, that we keep his commandments: and his commandments are not grievous (1 John 5:2,3).

---

[55] Samuel M. Shoemaker, Jr., *My Life-Work and My Will*, pamphlet, n.d., pp. 3-5.

[56] See also Deuteronomy 6:5; Leviticus 19:18. Cp. Big Book, p. 153.

[57] *Spiritual Milestones in Alcoholics Anonymous* (Akron, OH: AA of Akron, 1974), p. 3.

[58] *DR. BOB and the Good Oldtimers* (New York: Alcoholics Anonymous World Services, 1980), p. 338.

Dr. Bob and the other early AAs seemed to find *service* very forcefully explained in the Book of James. The following were often cited:

> But wilt thou know, O vain man, that faith without works is dead? (James 2:20).

> Pure religion and undefiled before God and the Father is this, To visit the fatherless and widows in their affliction, and to keep himself unspotted from the world (James 1:27).

> If a brother or sister be naked and destitute of daily food, and one of you say unto them, Depart in peace, be *ye* warmed and filled; not withstanding ye give them not those things which are needful to the body; what doth *it* profit? Even so faith, if it hath not works, is dead, being alone (James 2:15-17).

The Big Book several times quoted James 2:17, 20, 26. To which, *Spiritual Milestones* added:

> All we need to do in the St. James passage is to substitute the word "alcoholic" for "fatherless and widows" and we have Step Twelve. As a matter of fact, before we gave up alcohol, we were very definitely fatherless and widows.[59]

A.A.'s Big Book and Steps are filled with commandments from the Good Book: The Ten Commandments, the Sermon on the Mount, 1 Corinthians 13, and other passages. Two AA of Akron pamphlets went so far as to say:

> But, asks the alcoholic, where can I find a simple, step-by-step religious guide? The Ten Commandments give us a set of Thou Shalts and Thou Shalt Nots; the Twelve Steps of AA give us a program of dynamic action; But what about a spiritual guide? Of course, the answer is, that by following the Ten Commandments

---

[59] *Spiritual Milestones*, p. 14.

and the Twelve Steps to the letter, we automatically lead a spiritual life, whether or not we recognize it.[60]

There IS NO MYSTERY in the Spiritual side of AA. As a matter of fact, the good, active member is practicing Christianity at all times whether or not he knows it.[61]

There is more to the will of God than God's commandments; and the early AAs seemed quite aware of this fact. We need not review all that has been said about God as love and about His healing power, forgiveness, redemption, and kindness.[62] But AAs were tapped in to the importance of the power of God in bringing God's blessings to the lives of those who align their lives with His will. *Spiritual Milestones* said:

The Power of God has been likened to the electric power line that runs by our homes. We can fill the home with the finest of appliances—kitchen range, washing machine, vacuum cleaner, television—but until we plug into the electric power line, they do not run. So are our lives unsatisfactory until we plug in on the Power of God.[63]

Early AAs knew the goodness of God's will for them. And they frequently studied, and often quoted the beneficent promises He makes to His children in His word.[64] These include: (1) answering prayers asked according to his will; (2) forgiving, healing, delivering, and crowning with lovingkindness and tender mercies; (3) wishing above all things that His children prosper and be in health; (4) directing the paths of those who acknowledge Him in their ways; (5) supplying all their needs; (6) bringing safety to those who put their trust in Him; and (7) providing them

---

[60] *Spiritual Milestones*, p. 1.

[61] *Second Reader for Alcoholics Anonymous* (Ohio: AA of Akron, 1980), p. 12.

[62] Psalm 103:3,4; Almond, *Foundations for Faith*, pp. 31, 38.

[63] *Spiritual Milestones*, p. 16.

[64] Dick B., *The Good Book and The Big Book*, pp. 195-98.

with spiritual power enabling Him to do exceeding abundantly above all that they could ask or think.[65]

---

[65] 1 John 5:14-15; Psalm 103:2-4; 3 John 2; Proverbs 3:6; Philippians 4:19; Psalm 23; Proverbs 29:25; Ephesians 3:20; Colossians 1:13; Clark, *I Will Lift Up Mine Eyes*, pp. 25, 28, 89, 143, 147; Phillimore, *Just for Today*, pp. 12-13; Dick B., *Anne Smith's Journal*, pp. 71, 131; *Dr. Bob's Library*, p. 97; *A Manual for Alcoholics Anonymous*, p. 8; *Spiritual Milestones*, p. 3.

15

Use It or Lose It!

Resources

If you examine our bibliography, read the ten titles we have previously published, or attempt to study the tens of thousands of pages of spiritual roots materials we have read, you may be overwhelmed by the sheer quantity of data. There presently exists—in the spiritual realm—a repository of early A.A. historical specifics that is not too difficult to find. In a moment, we will discuss the importance of these details. But the reader need not search for difficult-to-locate used books, attempt to acquire out-of-print titles, or pay for expensive reprints. Many of the materials here discussed can be found in archives, seminary libraries, and private AA collections. Some are floating around A.A. and Al-Anon offices. Some are still being distributed or sold. Some will soon be made available through the internet. And here they are.

The Bible and Bible References

Dr. Bob and Anne recommended regular *study of the Bible itself*. That resource is still the nation's best seller! They also read and recommended "helpful books." *The Upper Room* was a favorite; and that quarterly is still published regularly. Often the very verses that were studied in the 1930's are discussed in today's issues. *My*

Utmost for His Highest by Oswald Chambers can be found in most bookstores—particularly Christian bookstores. The same can be said for Henry Drummond's *The Greatest Thing in the World*. So too James Allen's *As a Man Thinketh* and Charles Sheldon's *In His Steps*. William James's *The Varieties of Religious Experience*, Carl Jung's *Modern Man in Search of a Soul*, and Emmet Fox's *The Sermon on the Mount* are available in many bookstores and libraries. So also the works of Augustine, à Kempis, and Brother Lawrence. All are inexpensive, even if not purchased at used book-stores. Moreover, if one wants a highly useful and brief Bible reference that Dr. Bob and others often used, he or she can search out Nora Smith Holm's *The Runners Bible*—this title with a little more effort. To get in touch with the spiritual tools early AAs used in the Bible, there is little point in reading meditation books or annotated Bible versions which seldom, if ever, contain the original *verses* early AAs *actually studied, or* those Bible commentaries early AAs *actually used.*[1]

Shoemaker's Teachings

Let's move on to the man Bill Wilson said was the *teacher* of A.A.'s principles and Steps. The man is the Reverend Sam Shoemaker, who wrote over thirty books, countless articles and pamphlets, and hundreds of sermons. Must you read all these? Why not try the three articles Shoemaker wrote on the Twelve

---

[1] Mel B., a distinguished A.A. historian, who interviewed Bill Wilson on the subject several times, said: "There is simply no doubt that the Twelve Steps and also the Twelve Traditions came out of the Bible; actually they came out of a small part of the New Testament. I don't think Bob or Bill ever denied this; in fact, Bill told me two or three times that the Sermon on the Mount was the main inspiration" (Letter to the author, 11/7/96). The reader should have learned from our title, however, that an enormous number of Bible verses and Bible ideas—many more than those in Matthew Chapters 5 to 7 (containing the Sermon), 1 Corinthians 13, and the Book of James—were studied.

Steps themselves?[2] Surely these can teach *you* the relevant ideas that Shoemaker really taught in *his* books, articles, sermons, Oxford Group sharing, and personal visits with Bill Wilson. Then there are the two addresses Shoemaker gave at A.A. International Conventions in 1955 and 1960.[3] Next, during a visit to the Wilson home at Stepping Stones, in Bedford Hills, New York, the author saw on the shelf above Bill Wilson's desk at Wit's End a title prepared by Shoemaker's daughter, Nickie Haggart: *Sam Shoemaker at His Best: Extraordinary Living for the Ordinary Man*. The volume does a splendid job of reporting some of Shoemaker's best writings. Finally, there are several reprints of an article Shoemaker published in *The Calvary Evangel* in 1935. That article is titled *How to Find God*—reprinted by Faith at Work. These few simple items can be of immense help in understanding the specifics of what Sam Shoemaker taught early AAs.

Oxford Group Primers

The author has set forth in this work, and in his title *Design for Living*, the specifics about Oxford Group roots, history, writings, principles, practices, and language that impacted on A.A. If one wishes to study for himself or herself, there are some key books (often difficult to buy) which have been or perhaps will be re-printed and made available either by individual AAs or Oxford Group centres in Great Britain and Washington, D.C.

---

[2] See Samuel M. Shoemaker, Jr., "12 Steps to Power" (*Faith at Work News*, December, 1983; "The Twelve Steps of AA: What They Can Mean to the Rest of Us" (New York: *The Calvary Evangel*, n.d.); "Those Twelve Steps as I Understand Them," *Volume II, Best of the Grapevine* (New York: The AA Grapevine, Inc., 1986), pp. 125-34.

[3] *Alcoholics Anonymous Comes of Age* (New York: Alcoholics Anonymous World Services, 1957), pp. 261-70—containing the full text of the 1955 address; Dick B., *New Light on Alcoholism: The A.A. Legacy from Sam Shoemaker* (Corte Madera, CA: Good Book Publishing Company, 1994), pp. 220-24—containing excerpts from the 1960 address. The following pages (224-37) contain comments on other Shoemaker writings about A.A.

These are Walter's *Soul Surgery* (covering the Five C's); Day's *The Principles of the Group* (discussing seven basic, biblical principles of the Oxford Group); Thornton-Duesbury's *Sharing* (a primer on confession and witnessing); Forde's *The Guidance of God* (the foundational pamphlet on "guidance"); Howard Rose's *The Quiet Time*, Cecil Rose's *When Man Listens*, and Viney's *How Do I Begin?* (all three showing how "Quiet Time" was practiced).

And, if one is interested in a fairly recent compilation of Oxford Group meditation thoughts, there is Prescott's *A New Day: Daily Readings for Our Time* (London: Grosvenor Books, 1979)—given to the author by a long-time Oxford Group activist (Jim H.) who went to meetings with Bill Wilson and is A.A.'s member with the longest sobriety today (over 62 years).

Anne Smith's Journal

Then there is Anne Smith's spiritual journal. For now, the author offers his own title, *Anne Smith's Journal: 1933-1939*. Unfortunately, the full contents may have been lost (so Dr. Bob's daughter believes). Copies are located at Stepping Stones and at A.A. General Services in New York. And, when the author introduced his books in Akron (at a time when they were available at Dr. Bob's Home), he turned over to Dr. Bob's Home a copy of Anne's Journal in bound form for display and study there. And Anne's Spiritual Journal certainly deserves far more than the attention it has received in the last sixty years!

Possibilities

While preparing his comprehensive history this last year, the author traveled a great deal, presented many historical talks and seminars, and reached some conclusions about how A.A.'s rich history of spiritual ideas and practices can profitably be revived, studied, and disseminated today. Some of the observations concern events in which the author has been involved. Some involve activities conducted by others. And some involve possibilities for which a good many of the author's correspondents seem to be hungering.

For starters, Clarence S. (during his lifetime) gave out free copies of *DR. BOB and the Good Oldtimers* to those who attended the retreats Clarence founded and which continue today. That book also marked the beginning of the author's historical quest. And here are some possibilities for making *spiritual* history details available to AAs and others today:

1. Displaying early historical archives, spiritual roots books, and publications about these at every A.A. Conference. This is something which was done on a *very* limited basis by an individual group at A.A.'s last International Convention; but the material was much circumscribed in content and scope. Similar material was formerly made available at the annual Founders Day in Akron.

2. Making the same material readily available for reading and study at A.A. General Services, Central offices, and Intergroup offices throughout the world. This situation exists today on a highly limited basis and is hampered by the notion that only "Conference Approved" literature should be stocked or available at A.A. offices.

3. Expanding collections at non-A.A. locations which AAs nonetheless frequent: sober clubs (such as Alano Clubs), half-way houses, treatment centers, veteran centers, correctional facility libraries, alcoholism councils, substance abuse libraries, and addiction study centers (for one, plans seem to be underway at Brown University).

4. Initiating historical seminars at A.A. Conferences. This was done by the author's own home AA group for two years in a row and was widely appreciated by audiences in excess of 600 AAs. It was attempted on a more limited scale at A.A. conferences in West Virginia and Minnesota; and one is planned for the Los Angeles area.

5. Making historical book collections, archival materials, and historical studies available at such popular unofficial A.A. historical sites as Dr. Bob's Home in Akron, Stepping

Stones in New York, Founders Hall in Vermont, and The Wilson House in Vermont. This has begun at Dr. Bob's Home, The Wilson House, and possibly at Stepping Stones, according to information the author has received.

6. Encouraging archivists to bring such materials to A.A. conventions and gatherings. This has been done by the archivist at Dr. Bob's Home and several other AAs with whom the author has communicated.

7. Encouraging individual AAs and individual A.A. groups to start spiritual/historical study groups. This is how the original Big Book Seminars began. And their widespread communication of Big Book and Step materials has blessed thousands, including the author.

8. Including information on the foregoing in A.A. publications, recovery center publications, therapy publications, alcoholism and addiction publications, religious publications, medical publications, correctional publications, and employee assistance publications.

9. Placing the materials on the Internet. This is already underway on "home pages" such as that found at the author's website; and on sites now publishing material in full—including the Big Book First Edition.

10. Including in A.A.'s in-house publication, *The Grapevine*, regular, specific, newly unearthed spiritual history items written by knowledgeable historians. Early issues *did* carry articles by Reverend Sam Shoemaker, for example.

Many more ideas can be propounded and hopefully will be. But the mentality which attempts to shield AAs from non "Conference Approved" literature needs to be changed, in terms of what early AAs did in the spiritual realm, what the Twelve Traditions really mean in terms of history, and why an index of forbidden reading should *never* be part of A.A. thinking. The author has several times witnessed attempts by individual AAs to "ban" the very presence of a Bible, religious, and historical literature from A.A. meetings—even to stifle their mention. But these AAs seem unaware of what A.A.'s General Service Office published in the August-September, 1978, issue of its publication, *Box 4-5-9*. The article was titled, "What 'Conference-Approved' Means." The article said in part:

> When you see . . . the words "This is A.A. General Service Conference-approved literature," they mean only one thing. Such a publication represents the broadest possible consensus of A.A. thinking. It is *not* just one small locality's interpretation, nor the ideas of only one member. "As far as humanly possible," the seal says, in effect, "this piece reflects the spectrum of opinion of our whole Fellowship." . . . It does *not* mean the Conference disapproves of any other publications. Many local A.A. central offices publish their own meeting lists. A.A. as a whole does *not* oppose these, any more than A.A. disapproves of the Bible or books on health or any other publications from any source AA's find helpful. What any A.A. member reads is no business of G.S.O., or of the Conference, naturally. . . . Many groups have found that the *place* where literature is displayed in the meeting room can be very important. . . . It may be even more important that all Conference-approved A.A. material is exhibited *clearly separate from any other publications*. If new members or visitors see religious or medical pamphlets or other material about alcoholism mixed up with A.A. literature, they can become terribly confused about A.A. . . . Tradition Six becomes blurred when people see church, health, and A.A. publications all stacked together.[4]

A.A. certainly did not "ban," "disapprove of," or separately "stack" such literature during its beginnings; and it should be most cautious about censorship thinking today. For example, though early AAs studied Emmet Fox—who is hardly a favorite of the author's—the author was astonished to learn that an A.A. group in the Southwestern United States was banned from a listing in an

---

[4] *Box 4-5-9: News and Notes from the General Service Office of A.A.*, Volume 23, No. 4, August-September, 1978, pp. 1, 6.

A.A. meeting schedule because the group studied Emmet Fox's Sermon on the Mount. What if they had studied the Bible? Or the life of Jesus Christ? Or the teachings of St. Paul? Or St. Augustine? Or Brother Lawrence? Or Harry Emerson Fosdick? Or Glenn Clark? Or E. Stanley Jones? Would this have endangered individual sobriety, the Twelve Step recovery program, or the unity of A.A. as a whole? Would members have been ostracized?

The Big Book itself says most AAs favor religious affiliations—an assertion of questionable accuracy in today's picture. The Big Book recommends "helpful books" (as part of Eleventh Step suggestions for growth)—books to be suggested possibly by one's rabbi, minister, or priest. And Bill Wilson himself wrote about the frequency of Roman Catholic Retreats for AAs—some of which have come to the author's attention in Central California and in Hawaii. On May 2, 1958, Wilson wrote Sam Shoemaker as follows:

> There is no reason why a group of A.A.'s shouldn't get together for Bible study; no reason at all why a group of A.A.'s in a church should not associate themselves into a sort of spiritual kindergarten fellowship, into which anyone might be invited. As a matter of fact, I am anxious to see this sort of thing tried. Have you ever thought of inaugurating something like this in your own congregation? Could you open up your church basement to a group operating on strictly A.A. principles? . . . You might find a lot of people coming upstairs for the complete treatment. Any number of individuals in A.A., especially the indifferent or agnostic sort, are doing the same thing, one by one. It is our experience that these separate undertakings should begin on a very small scale and quietly—no tub-thumping.

In a moment, we will have some challenges which suggest that A.A.—whose "only medicine is God"—as one *Grapevine* article commented, can still handle God, the Bible, and even Jesus Christ. These to show how early AAs met individual needs and began spiritual quests. Such material, handled from an historical perspective, could hardly endanger today's AAs or their meetings—where one now frequently hears that A.A. is *not* religious, that religion belongs in the church, and that the word "God" will scare away the newcomer. Here, five historical comments—some already quoted—are in order:

> When asked about using the word "God" in A.A., its venerable pioneer, Clarence S. said: "If the word 'God' will drive you out of A.A., booze will drive you back if you are fortunate enough to live that long."[5]

> When Dr. Bob and Bill suggested to Henrietta Seiberling that they should not talk too much about religion or God, Henrietta said: "Well, we're not out to please the alcoholics. They have been pleasing themselves all these years. We are out to please God. And if you don't talk about what God does, and your faith, and your guidance, then you might as well be the Rotary Club or something like that. Because God is your only source of power."[6]

> Commenting on the stubborn resistance to God that some newcomers have, Bill Wilson said: "Mine was exactly the kind of deep-seated block we so often see today in new people who say they are atheistic or agnostic. Their will to disbelieve is so powerful that apparently they prefer a date with the undertaker to an open-minded and experimental quest for God.[7]

> On November 9, 1954, at the Grand Ballroom of the Commodore Hotel in New York, Bill told the story of the founding of A.A. He concluded: "Who invented AA? It was God Almighty that invented AA."[8]

---

[5] Dick B., *That Amazing Grace: The Role of Clarence and Grace S. in Alcoholics Anonymous* (San Rafael, CA: Paradise Research Publications, 1996), p. 89.

[6] Dick B., *The Akron Genesis of Alcoholics Anonymous* (Corte Madera, CA: Good Book Publishing Company, 1994), p. 98.

[7] *The Language of the Heart: Bill W.'s Grapevine Writings* (New York: The A.A. Grapevine, 1988), pp. 245-46.

[8] Sam Shoemaker's notes on the Wilson address, p. 5, located at the Episcopal Archives in Austin, Texas. Copy in the author's possession.

Quoting Herbert Spencer, the Third Edition of the Big Book states: "There is a principle which is a bar against all information, which is proof against all arguments and which cannot fail to keep a man in everlasting ignorance—that principle is contempt prior to investigation" (p. 570).

Challenges

Hundreds of thousands of alcoholics and addicts pour into Twelve Step rooms today. They do not come from the sources of yesteryear. Many an early AA newcomer came to Dr. Bob for help at the behest of that alcoholic's wife. Hundreds, if not thousands, came to early Cleveland A.A. in response to newspaper ads and notices, carrying the full name and address of Clarence S. In Detroit, large numbers came as the result of radio broadcasts by Arch T. and a friend. Today their initial attendance is often forced by a court, a probation officer, a recovery center, a veterans' program, or an intervention. Counselors, therapists, employee assistance programs, and others often insist that A.A. be tried.

And the problem is: Where are the *sponsors* or oldtimers who know the spiritual roots? Who know how and why early A.A. succeeded? Who know who Dr. Bob and Anne and Sam Shoemaker are, and what they taught? Who know the basic precepts of the Oxford Group? Or who have any knowledge of the Good Book ideas in which A.A.'s roots were planted.

In other titles, we have covered why we believe the spiritual roots are important. These roots demonstrate what early AAs were doing when they achieved seventy-five percent (75%), eighty percent (80%), ninety-three percent (93%), and perhaps even one hundred percent (100%) success rates, *among alcoholics who really tried the A.A. recovery path.* They show very clearly the nature of God, upon whom early AAs relied for the power to recover. They show the principles of the Bible which early AAs studied and which spelled out God's love and will and power. They help readers to understand the Oxford Group/Shoemaker words and phrases and Bible ideas which abound in the Big Book. They help clergy and churches to understand the real religious foundations of A.A. They help others to learn and utilize those foundations. And they give comfort and direction to bewildered AAs who believe in God, studiy His word, are Christians, and perhaps were church members at an earlier time.

They can help bewildered people whose minds are fogged, and whose emotions are filled with guilt and fear and rage and frustration and despair. They can encourage understanding among those in churches, denominations, and unbelievers, who distrust A.A. *either for* its "erroneous" religious doctrines or for its "excessively" religious ideas. And they can help to show what the word "religious" meant in early A.A. before later publicists began coining unique, confusing, and supposedly distinct meanings phrased in terms of "spirituality."

In the preceding segment, we have listed some possibilities for utilizing the resources now available. And here are some ideas the author has seen at work *already*. This last year, in various parts of the United States, the author has attended and spoken at four spiritual retreats for AAs and their families. The retreats covered the Big Book, the Twelve Steps, A.A.'s spiritual history, and opportunities for prayer and healing. The author also attended and spoke at meetings where Scripture was discussed in relation to the Big Book and Twelve Steps.

In one meeting, the author felt like he was attending old-time A.A. The meeting opened with a prayer. The contents of an issue of *The Upper Room* (a current issue) were covered, along with a full reading of the Scripture referred to in the issue. And the group then read from a chapter of A.A.'s Conference Approved *DR. BOB and the Good Oldtimers* which told all present how A.A. had operated in its highly successful early days. The author was invited to speak on the spiritual history. There was a time for prayer and healing. And the meeting closed with the Lord's Prayer—just as most A.A. meetings do today. The entire time was three hours; and scarcely a soul stirred.

We think such a meeting puts Scripture, the devotionals, prayer, healing, and spiritual history in an appropriate context. All present at the meeting were ardent Twelve-Steppers; and there were a number of new people present. Several of these live in a half-way house supported by AAs in the group. We've seen love, structure, service, and success in that group.

Proverbs 1:1-7 begins as follows:

> The proverbs of Solomon, the son of David, king of Israel; To know wisdom and instruction; to perceive the words of understanding; To receive the instruction of wisdom, justice, and judgment, and equity; To give subtilty to the simple, to the young man knowledge and discretion. A wise *man* will hear, and will increase learning; and a man of understanding shall attain unto wise counsels; To understand a proverb, and the interpretation; the words of the wise, and their dark sayings. The fear [reverence or respect] of the Lord *is* the beginning of knowledge: *but* fools despise wisdom and instruction.

A.A. does not offer much to fools. It presents real hope to those who are desperately ill from alcoholism and are in despair over life's problems. It can—if presented in an accurate historical context—offer a tried, rock-solid spiritual solution to those who have failed—because of alcoholism—to manage their own lives. To those who know they are not God. And to those who hunger to understand the nature, love, forgiveness, and power of God. God—Who provided the essential "divine help" to the seemingly hopeless and helpless alcoholics of A.A.'s earliest days.

END

Appendix 1

THE TWELVE STEPS OF ALCOHOLICS ANONYMOUS

1. We admitted we were powerless over alcohol—that our lives had become unmanageable.

2. Came to believe that a Power greater than ourselves could restore us to sanity.

3. Made a decision to turn our will and our lives over to the care of God *as we understood Him*.

4. Made a searching and fearless moral inventory of ourselves.

5. Admitted to God, to ourselves, and to another human being the exact nature of our wrongs.

6. Were entirely ready to have God remove all these defects of character.

7. Humbly asked Him to remove our shortcomings.

8. Made a list of all persons we had harmed, and became willing to make amends to them all.

9. Made direct amends to such persons wherever possible, except when to do so would injure them or others.

10. Continued to take personal inventory and when we were wrong promptly admitted it.

11. Sought through prayer and meditation to improve our conscious contact with God *as we understood Him*, praying only for knowledge of His will for us and the power to carry that out.

12. Having had a spiritual awakening as the result of these Steps, we tried to carry this message to alcoholics, and to practice these principles in all our affairs.

The Twelve Steps are reprinted with permission of Alcoholics Anonymous World Services, Inc. Permission to reprint the Twelve Steps does not mean that A.A. has reviewed or approved the contents of this publication, nor that A.A. agrees with the views expressed herein. A.A. is a program of recovery from alcoholism only - use of the Twelve Steps in connection with programs and activities which are patterned after A.A., but which address other problems, or in any other non-A.A. context, does not imply otherwise.

Appendix 2

Parallel Oxford Group-Big Book Phrases

There are remarkable similarities between words and phrases in Oxford Group literature and those in A.A.'s Big Book. The similarities would be of less significance if Bill Wilson had not attributed almost every A.A. idea to the Oxford Group and if A.A. biographies and histories had not re-affirmed the link. We do not say that the following Oxford Group language directly found its way to the Big Book, but the reader will see striking parallels. We have gone through thousands of pages of Oxford Group language. We've also reviewed the Big Book page by page for similarities. And we have set out below quotes from Oxford Group books, largely in the chronological order that their parallels appear in the Big Book. The full titles for the Oxford Group books we cite can be found in our Bibliography.

1.   I've got religion.[1]
2.   A vast Power outside themselves.[2]
3.   A Force outside himself, greater than himself.[3]
4.   A power within yet coming from outside myself—a power far stronger than I was.[4]
5.   A Personal God.[5]
6.   New power and direction came to her when she started listening to God.[6]

---

[1] Shoemaker, *Children of the Second Birth*, pp. 118, 165. Big Book, p. 9.

[2] Shoemaker, *A Young Man's View of the Ministry*, p. 42. Big Book: "Power greater than ourselves," pp. 10, 46, 47, 59.

[3] Shoemaker, *If I Be Lifted Up*, p. 176. See also, Kitchen, *I Was a Pagan*, p. 78; Big Book, *supra*, pp. 10, 45, 46, 47, 59.

[4] Kitchen, *I Was a Pagan*, p. 63. See Big Book, pp. 10, 36, 47, 59.

[5] Shoemaker, *Children of the Second Birth*, p. 61. Big Book, pp. 10, 12: "a God personal to me."

[6] Foot, *Life Began Yesterday*, p. 112. Big Book, p. 10: "When they talked of a God . . . who was love, superhuman strength and direction. . . ."

7. Love of God.[7]
8. Marvel at what God has done for you.[8]
9. Surrender of all one knows of self to all one knows of God.[9]
10. God-consciousness.[10]
11. Relationship with God.[11]
12. Self was the centre of my life, not God.[12]
13. Willingness to believe.[13]
14. Willingness.[14]
15. God comes to us when we ask Him.[15]
16. They prayed together, opening their minds to *as much of God as he understood.*[16]
17. She surrendered to God . . . and . . . turned over to Him her life for His direction.[17]
18. To give up sin men must do four things: Hate, Forsake, Confess, Restore.[18]

---

[7] *What Is The Oxford Group?*, p. 112; Allen, *He That Cometh*, p. 219. Big Book, p. 10: "God. . . who was love."

[8] Shoemaker, *If I Be Lifted Up*, pp. 13, 84; Big Book, pp. 11, 84: "God is doing for us what we could not do for ourselves."

[9] Foot, *Life Began Yesterday*, pp. 175, 12-13; Big Book, p. 12: "Why don't you choose your own conception of God?"

[10] Kitchen, *I Was a Pagan*, pp. 28, 41, 75, 96, 28; Begbie, *Life Changers*, p. 39. Big Book, pp. 13, 85, 570.

[11] Shoemaker, *Children of the Second Birth*, p. 16; Kitchen, *I Was a Pagan*, p. 113; Benson, *The Eight Points of the Oxford Group*, pp. 48, 92. Big Book, pp. 13, 28, 29, 100, 164.

[12] Foot, *Life Began Yesterday*, p. 9; Begbie, *Life Changers*, p. 17. Big Book, p. 14: "It meant destruction of self-centeredness. I must turn in all things to the Father of Light." See James 1:17.

[13] Brown, *The Venture of Belief*, p. 26. Big Book, p. 12: "It was only a matter of being willing to believe."

[14] Brown, *The Venture of Belief*, p. 36. Big Book, p. 12.

[15] Begbie, *Life Changers*, p. 37. Big Book, p. 12: "I had needed and wanted God. There had been a humble willingness to have Him with me—and He came."

[16] Shoemaker, *Children of the Second Birth*, pp. 25, 47; *The Gospel According to You*, p. 128; Big Book, p. 67, 88, 13: "I humbly offered myself to God, as I then understood Him, to do with me as He would."

[17] Shoemaker, *Children of the Second Birth*, p. 82. Big Book, p. 13: "I placed myself unreservedly under His care and direction." The Shoemaker language is very similar to the language of A.A.'s Third Step as it was written in the multi-lith copy that preceded publication of the First Edition of the Big Book.

[18] Shoemaker, *Children of the Second Birth*, p. 94. Big Book, p. 13: "I ruthlessly faced my sins and became willing to have my new-found Friend take them away, root and branch."

19. Have you looked back into your life and carefully considered *every wrong* you have ever done to anyone and *endeavored to set it right?*[19]
20. *Listen to the guidance of the Holy Spirit*, said the Group, and you will hear Him saying, "Be ye reconciled one towards another." I began to listen.[20]
21. Witness is Sharing with others the main reasons and the concrete results of our surrender to God. . . . "*Faith apart from works,*" said St. James, "*is barren.*"[21]
22. Design for living.[22]
23. Coming so wholly into the *confidence* of the one we seek to help along the avenue of personal friendship that we know his verdict in his own case.[23]
24. Wretched man that I am! Who shall deliver me from the body of this death?[24]
25. By the grace of God.[25]
26. The Solution.[26]
27. Be ready to confess your own shortcomings honestly and humbly.[27]
28. Spiritual experience.[28]
29. In God's hands, and awaits His wise direction . . .[29]
30. Higher Power.[30]

---

[19] Russell, *For Sinners Only*, p. 128. Big Book, p. 13: "We made a list of people I had hurt. . . I expressed my entire willingness to approach these individuals admitting my wrong. . . I was to right all such matters to the utmost of my ability."

[20] Russell, *For Sinners Only*, p. 135. Big Book, p. 13: "I was to sit quietly when in doubt, asking only for direction and strength to meet my problems as He would have me."

[21] *What Is The Oxford Group?*, p. 36. Big Book, p. 14: "Particularly was it imperative to work with others as he had worked with me. Faith without works is dead, he said."

[22] Kitchen, *I Was a Pagan*, p. 167. Big Book, pp. 15, 28.

[23] Walter, *Soul Surgery*, p. 30. Big Book, p. 18: "But the ex-problem drinker who has found the solution . . . can generally win the entire confidence of another alcoholic. . . . Until such an understanding is reached, little or nothing can be accomplished."

[24] This quotation is from Romans 7:24. See Shoemaker, *Religion That Works*, p. 45. Big Book, p. 24: "unable, at certain times, to bring into our consciousness with sufficient force the memory of the suffering and humiliation of even a week or a month ago . . . beyond human aid."

[25] Begbie, *Life Changers*, p. 17. Big Book, p. 25: "But for the grace of God . . ."

[26] Foot, *Life Began Yesterday*, p. 21. Big Book, pp. 17, 25: "There is a solution."

[27] Walter, *Soul Surgery*, p. 57. Big Book, p. 25: "the self-searching, the leveling of our pride, the confession of shortcomings which the process requires for its successful consummation."

[28] Shoemaker, *Twice-Born Ministers*, pp. 61, 10. Big Book, pp. 17, 29: "spiritual experience."

[29] Kitchen, *I Was a Pagan*, p. 108. Big Book, pp. 28, 100, 120, 124.

[30] Kitchen, *I Was a Pagan*, p. 85. Big Book, pp. 43, 100.

31. This Power by which human nature can be changed . . . and through this Power problems are being solved.[31]

32. There is at work in the world today a Power that has for many generations been neglected by masses of mankind.[32]

33. I made the surrender of my will to the Divine purpose, as a calm, resolute, intelligent and reasonable act of submission to the Power controlling the world.[33]

34. He made a decision to surrender to God.[34]

35. Peace, direction, power—the fullness of life—await the complete surrender of ourselves to God for His purposes.[35]

36. I had, in other words, actually to *become* God-conscious.[36]

37. Refusal to believe is as much a decision as the willingness to believe.[37]

38. A man had simply to step out of his own light to become immediately and keenly conscious of the presence of God.[38]

39. "I was keen on self-management—a self-determinist—the captain of my own soul. . . . *And there is the real secret of all human difficulty.* . . . I—the *self-sufficient* V. C. Kitchen—would continue to live outside the law of fellowship."[39]

40. God-sufficiency.[40]

---

[31] Foot, *Life Began Yesterday*, p. 22. Big Book, p. 45: "But where and how were we to find this Power?"

[32] Foot, *Life Began Yesterday*, p. 22; "I could not quite make out just what this secret or power *was*" See Kitchen, *I Was a Pagan*, p. 28. Big Book, p. 45: "Well, that's exactly what this book is about. Its main object is to enable you to find a Power greater than yourself which will solve your problem."

[33] Foot, *Life Began Yesterday*, p. 30. Big Book, p. 45: "And it means, of course, that we are going to talk about God."

[34] Foot, *Life Began Yesterday*, p. 44; "I surrender Thee my entire life, O God," Kitchen, *I Was a Pagan*, p. 67. Big Book, p. 46: "It was impossible for any of us to fully define or comprehend that Power, which is God."

[35] Cecil Rose, *When Man Listens*, p. 17. Big Book, p. 50, 46: "We began to be possessed of a new sense of power and direction, provided we took other simple steps."

[36] Kitchen, *I Was a Pagan*, p. 41. Big Book, p. 47: "At the start, this was all we needed . . . to effect our first conscious relation with God as we understood Him."

[37] Cecil Rose, *When Man Listens*, p. 27. Big Book, p. 47: "Am I even willing to believe that there is a Power greater than myself."

[38] Kitchen, *I Was a Pagan*, p. 43. Big Book, p. 51: "Many hundreds of people are able to say that the consciousness of the Presence of God is today the most important fact of their lives."

[39] Kitchen, *I Was a Pagan*, pp. 39, 61. Big Book, pp. 52: "We agnostics and atheists were sticking to the idea that self-sufficiency would solve our problems."

[40] Shoemaker, *If I Be Lifted Up*, pp. 106-07. Big Book, p. 52-53: "Others showed us that 'God-sufficiency' worked with them. . . ."

41. God is, or He isn't.[41]
42. He is the all-pervading Reality.[42]
43. Conscious of the presence and the companionship of God.[43]
44. Creator.[44]
45. Maker.[45]
46. Director.[46]
47. Father.[47]
48. Infinite Power.[48]
49. Spirit.[49]
50. I then and there admitted my inability to quit [drinking] of my own will and asked God to take charge of the matter. . . . God simply lifted that desire entirely out of my life.[50]
51. God floods in when a man is honest.[51]
52. We must surrender our wills to a greater Will, and that will set us free.[52]
53. We must be absolutely honest with ourselves.[53]

---

[41] Shoemaker, *Confident Faith*, p. 187. Big Book, p. 53: "God either is, or He isn't."

[42] Streeter, *The God Who Speaks*, p. 12; Shoemaker, *The Gospel According to You*, p. 47: The great thing that all of us long for in religion is the reality of the Presence of God. See also, Begbie, *Life Changers*, p. 104. Big Book, p. 55: "He was there. He was as much a fact as we were. We found the Great Reality deep down within us."

[43] Begbie, *Life Changers*, p. 16. Big Book, p. 56: "He lived in conscious companionship with his Creator."

[44] Brown, *The Venture of Belief*, p. 25; Begbie, *Life Changers*, p. 16; and Streeter, *The God Who Speaks*, p. 109. Big Book, pp. 13, 25, 28, 56, 68, 72, 75, 76, 80, 83, 158, 161.

[45] Benson, *The Eight Points of the Oxford Group*, p. 73. Big Book, p. 57.

[46] Streeter, *The God Who Speaks*, p. 10; Big Book, p. 62: "God was going to be our Director."

[47] *What Is The Oxford Group?*, p. 48; Shoemaker, *The Conversion of the Church*, p. 49. Big Book, p. 62.

[48] Brown, *The Venture of Belief*, p. 25. Big Book, p. 68.

[49] Walter, *Soul Surgery*, p. 27. Big Book, p. 85.

[50] Kitchen, *I Was a Pagan*, p. 74. Big Book, p. 57: "Save for a few brief moments of temptation the thought of drink has never returned. . . . God had restored his sanity. . . . He humbly offered himself to his Maker—then he knew."

[51] Begbie, *Life Changers*, p. 103. Big Book, p. 57: "Even so has God restored us all to our right minds. . . . He has come to all who have honestly sought Him."

[52] Foot, *Life Began Yesterday*, p. 35. Big Book, p. 57: "When we drew near to Him, He disclosed Himself to us!"

[53] *What is the Oxford Group?*, p. 77. Big Book, p. 58: "Those who do not recover are people . . . who are constitutionally incapable of being honest with themselves."

54. How did I accomplish the self-deflation. . . ?[54]
55. Let go! Abandon yourself to Him. Say to Him, "Not my will but Thine be done."[55]
56. It was this power of the Spirit flowing into me that . . . gave me not only the courage [but also] the strength . . . I needed.[56]
57. You need to find God.[57]
58. My real education did not begin till the day I found God.[58]
59. The crisis of self-surrender has always been and must always be regarded as the vital *turning* point of the religious life.[59]
60. Abandon yourself to Him.[60]
61. O Lord, manage me, for I cannot manage myself.[61]
62. The first action is mental action, it is a decision of the will to make a *decision*—one decides that one has not controlled one's life particularly well hitherto, and therefore it had better be put under new management.[62]
63. He made his decision.[63]
64. The decision to cast my will and my life on God.[64]

---

[54] Kitchen, *I Was a Pagan*, p. 47. Big Book, p. 58: "Some of us have tried to hold on to our old ideas and the result was nil until we let go absolutely. Remember that we deal with alcohol—cunning, baffling, powerful. Without help it is too much for us."

[55] Shoemaker, *Religion That Works*, p. 19. Big Book, p. 58: "The result was nil until we let go absolutely."

[56] Kitchen, *I Was a Pagan*, pp. 78-79; Big Book, p. 59: "But there is One who has all power—that One is God."

[57] Shoemaker, *Realizing Religion*, p. 9; Big Book, p. 59: "But there is One who has all power—that One is God. May you find Him now!"

[58] Kitchen, *I Was a Pagan*, p. 94; Big Book, p. 59: "May you find Him now!"

[59] Shoemaker, *Realizing Religion*, p. 30; Begbie, *Life Changers*, p. 126; For the frequent references by Shoemaker to "the turning point," see Dick B., *New Light on Alcoholism*, p. 41; Big Book, p. 59: "We stood at the turning point."

[60] Shoemaker, *Religion that Works*, p. 19; Big Book, p. 59: "We asked His protection and care with complete abandon."

[61] Russell, *For Sinners Only*, p. 79; Howard, *Frank Buchman's Secret*, pp. 41-44; and Harris, *The Breeze of the Spirit*, p. 10. For the many usages of the "manage me" prayer, see Dick B., *Anne Smith's Journal*, pp. 20-22; Big Book, p. 59: "We admitted . . . that our lives had become unmanageable."

[62] Foot, *Life Began Yesterday*, p. 10; Big Book, p. 59: "Made a decision to turn our will and our lives over to the care of God *as we understood Him*."

[63] Shoemaker, *Children of the Second Birth*, p. 125; Big Book, p. 59: "Made a decision."

[64] Shoemaker, *Twice-Born Ministers*, p. 134. Big Book, p. 60: "Being convinced, we were at Step Three, which is that we decided to turn our will and our life over to God as we understood Him."

65. [Man needs to] devote his soul to self-examination, to self examination of the most solemn and searching kind.[65]
66. We are bidden by Frank Buchman to "make the moral test."[66]
67. The first step for me was to be honest with God, the next to be honest with men.[67]
68. If a person is honest with himself and with God, he will be honest also with us.[68]
69. God . . . satisfied unsound desire by *removing* the desire itself.[69]
70. He was wounded for our transgressions. He was bruised for our iniquities; the chastisement of our peace was upon Him, and with His stripes we are healed. . . . Be ready to confess your own shortcomings honestly and humbly.[70]
71. How can anyone who professes to love God and his neighbor as himself, as all Christians must do, allow a wrong he has done to anyone to go unrighted?[71]
72. I discovered four things which needed putting right in my life. . . . There was a restitution which I would not make.[72]
73. Every person I have wronged I have seen and made restitution to him, in so far as I was able.[73]
74. In order to leave nothing undone in the attempt to make things right with people I had wronged, I wrote fourteen letters of confession of specific wrong.[74]
75. Spiritual awakening.[75]

---

[65] Drummond, *The Ideal Life*, p. 316. Big Book, p. 59: "Made a fearless and searching moral inventory of ourselves."

[66] Walter, *Soul Surgery*, pp. 43-44. Big Book, p. 59: "moral inventory of ourselves."

[67] Foot, *Life Began Yesterday*, p. 11. Big Book, p. 59: "Admitted to God, to ourselves, and to another human being the exact nature of our wrongs."

[68] Shoemaker, *The Gospel According to You*, p. 38. Big Book, p. 59: "Admitted to God, to ourselves, and to another human being. . . ."

[69] Kitchen, *I Was a Pagan*, p. 73. Big Book, p. 59: "Were entirely ready to have God remove all these defects of character."

[70] Walter, *Soul Surgery*, p. 57 (citing Isaiah 53:4, 5). Big Book, p. 59: "Humbly asked Him to remove our shortcomings."

[71] Russell, *For Sinners Only*, p. 128. Big Book, p. 59: "and became willing to make amends to them all."

[72] Shoemaker, *Twice-Born Ministers*, p. 92. Big Book, p. 59: "Made a list of all persons we had harmed."

[73] Russell, *For Sinners Only*, p. 128. Big Book, p. 59: "Made direct amends to such people wherever possible, except when to do so would injure them or others."

[74] Shoemaker, *Twice-Born Ministers*, p. 166. Big Book, p. 59: "Made direct amends to such people wherever possible. . . ."

[75] Buchman, *Remaking the World*, pp. 19, 24, 35, 54; and Shoemaker, *The Conversion of the Church*, p. 124. Big Book, p. 60: "Having had a spiritual awakening . . ."

76.   Contact with God is the necessary fundamental condition, and that is made through prayer and listening. . . .[76]

77.   I will ask God to show me His purpose for my life and claim from Him the power to carry that purpose out.[77]

78.   God is and is a Rewarder of them that seek Him.[78]

79.   Opening their minds to as much of God as he understood, removing first the hindrance of *self-will*.[79]

80.   Selfish and self-centered.[80]

81.   That is what the Oxford Group is working for, changed lives, God-centered in place of self-centered.[81]

82.   Self-will seems the blackest sin of all.[82]

83.   For most men, the world is centered in self, which is misery.[83]

84.   Self was at the bottom of many of these actions.[84]

85.   There is a good deal of sorrow in our life of our own making.[85]

86.   A very large part of human misery is of our own making.[86]

---

[76] Foot, *Life Began Yesterday*, p. 13. Big Book, p. 59: "Sought through prayer and meditation to improve our conscious contact with God. . . . "

[77] Foot, *Life Began Yesterday*, p. 11. Big Book, p. 59: "Praying only for knowledge of His will for us and the power to carry that out."

[78] Shoemaker, *Religion That Works*, p. 68; *The Gospel According to You*, p. 47. Big Book, p. 60: "God could and would if He were sought."

[79] Shoemaker, *Children of the Second Birth*, p. 47. Big Book, p. 60: "Any life run on self-will can hardly be a success."

[80] Kitchen, *I Was a Pagan*, p. 103. Big Book, p. 61: "Our actor is self-centered—ego centric."

[81] Foot, *Life Began Yesterday*, p. 47. Big Book, p. 62: "Selfishness—self centeredness! That, we think, is the root of our troubles."

[82] Shoemaker, *Realizing Religion*, pp. 31-32. Big Book, p. 52: "Our troubles . . . arise out of ourselves, and the alcoholic is an extreme example of self-will run riot."

[83] Shoemaker, *Realizing Religion*, p. 11. Big Book, p. 62: "We alcoholics must be rid of this selfishness. We must, or it kills us! God makes that possible. And there often seems no way of entirely getting rid of self without His aid."

[84] Foot, *Life Began Yesterday*, p. 9. Big Book, p. 62: "We have made decisions based on self which later placed us in a position to be hurt."

[85] Shoemaker, *Confident Faith*, p. 149. Big Book, p. 62: "So our troubles, we think, are basically of our own making."

[86] Shoemaker, *The Gospel According to You*, p. 38. Big Book, p. 103: "After all, our problems were of our own making. Bottles were only a symbol."

87. When you blow away the clouds of your self-pity, self-will, self-centeredness, all that you will find left is a universe of opportunity, with God to help you, and a miserable, petty little self sitting down in the midst of it, refusing to play.[87]

88. God showed me, however, that it was not only possible to be honest in advertising, but to be unselfish, loving and pure.[88]

89. An experience of God means . . . a new charge of strength flowing into the will . . . a new direction and a new power to choose correctly and rightly . . . [and] a new affection—strengthened, invigorated, cleansed.[89]

90. Where He [God] guides, He provides.[90]

91. We were reborn into life. . . . I know what is meant by "The Peace that Passeth All Understanding."[91]

92. All anxiety and fear has flown out the window never to return. God has time and time again vindicated this faith in Him by taking care of our needs as each need has arisen.[92]

93. I surrender Thee my entire life, O God. I have made a mess of it, trying to run it myself. You take it—the whole thing—and run it for me, according to Your will and plan.[93]

94. When I gave my life to God, however, He freed me from this bondage.[94]

95. She saw how definite sin was blocking her from Christ.[95]

---

[87] Shoemaker, *God's Control*, p. 57. Big Book, p. 62: "Neither could we reduce our self-centeredness much by wishing or trying on our own Power. We had to have God's help."

[88] Kitchen, *I Was a Pagan*, p. 120. Big Book, p. 63: "Being all powerful, He provided what we needed, if we kept close to Him and performed His work well."

[89] Kitchen, *I Was a Pagan*, p. 104. Big Book, p. 63: "We felt new power flow in . . . we enjoyed peace of mind . . . we discovered we could face life successfully . . . we became conscious of His presence."

[90] Shoemaker, *Children of the Second Birth*, p. 160. Big Book, p. 63: "Being all powerful, He provided what we needed, if we kept close to Him and performed His work well."

[91] Foot, *Life Began Yesterday*, p. 68. Big Book, p. 63: "We were reborn."

[92] Kitchen, *I Was a Pagan*, p. 121. Big Book, p. 63: "As we became conscious of His presence, we began to lose our fear of today, tomorrow or the hereafter."

[93] Kitchen, *I Was a Pagan*, p. 67. Big Book, p. 63; "God, I offer myself to Thee—to build with me and to do with me as Thou wilt. . . . Take away my difficulties, that victory over them may bear witness to those I would help of Thy Power, Thy Love, and Thy Way of life. May I do Thy will always!"

[94] Kitchen, *I Was a Pagan*, p. 145. Big Book, p. 145: "Relieve me of the bondage of self, that I may better do Thy will."

[95] Shoemaker, *Twice-Born Ministers*, p. 32; and *They're On The Way*, p. 154. Big Book, p. 64: "Our decision . . . could have little permanent effect unless at once followed by a strenuous effort to face, and be rid of, the things in ourselves which had

(continued...)

96. If, then, I want God to take control of my life, the first thing I must do is produce the books. A good way to begin this examination of the books is to test my life beside the Sermon on the Mount.[96]

97. If when a trader finds his way into the bankruptcy court, it is revealed that for years he has not taken stock, he is very severely censured.[97]

98. I found that self crept into almost everything. . . . And . . . this selfishness has as surely shut me off from a true consciousness of God.[98]

99. The thing which is striking about much of the misery one sees is that it is *spiritual* misery. . . . The root of the malady is estrangement from God.[99]

100. What is our real problem? . . . Isn't it fear, dishonesty, resentment, selfishness?[100]

101. Selfishness, fear, resentment, pride, do not live in the air. They live in men.[101]

102. Any remnant of resentment, hatred or grudge blocks God out effectively.[102]

103. I ceased struggling to pull myself *up* and stepped out of the way so that His light could shine *down* to me.[103]

---

[95] (...continued)
been blocking us; p. 71: "God can remove whatever self-will has blocked you off from Him."

[96] Rose, *When Man Listens*, pp. 17-18. Big Book, p. 64: "Taking a commercial inventory is a fact-finding and a fact-facing process. . . We did exactly the same thing with our lives."

[97] Benson, *The Eight Points*, p. 44. Big Book, p. 64: "A business which takes no regular inventory usually goes broke. . . We took stock honestly. First, we searched out the flaws in our make-up which caused our failure."

[98] Kitchen, *I Was a Pagan*, p. 46; Foot, *Life Began Yesterday*, p. 9: "Self was at the bottom of many of these actions. . . . Self was the centre of my life, not God." Big Book, p. 64: "Being convinced that self, manifested in various ways, was what had defeated us, we considered its common manifestations."

[99] Shoemaker, *Realizing Religion*, pp. 4-5. Big Book, p. 64: "all forms of spiritual disease . . . we have been spiritually sick. . . . When the spiritual malady is overcome, we straighten out mentally and physically."

[100] Buchman, *Remaking the World*, p. 38. Big Book, p. 64: "Resentment is the 'number one' offender. . . . In dealing with resentments, we set them on paper."

[101] Rose, *When Man Listens*, p. 41. Big Book, p. 64: "We asked ourselves why we were angry."

[102] Macmillan, *Seeking and Finding*, p. 98; Shoemaker, *Twice-Born Ministers*, p. 182; Benson, *The Eight Points*, p. x (grudges). Big Book, p. 65: "On our grudge list we set opposite each name our injuries."

[103] Kitchen, *I Was a Pagan*, pp. 48; see also, pp. 42, 44, 46. Big Book, p. 66: "When harboring such feelings we shut ourselves off from the sunlight of the Spirit."

104. Thy will be done.[104]
105. It means confessing our part in the sinning. Blaming others and thereby making excuses for ourselves is not sharing, but is sheer selfishness.[105]
106. Moral recovery starts when everyone admits his own faults instead of spotlighting the other fellow's.[106]
107. Fear may be the great paralyser; its effect a negation of action and not a stimulus.[107]
108. The root problems in the word today are dishonesty, selfishness and fear—in men, and consequently in nations.[108]
109. Hundreds . . . have fallen ill, some . . . have committed suicide, because they had no faith to substitute for fear: and fear literally ate the heart out of them. And its antidote is faith in God. The emotion of worship, of trust, of faith, is strong enough to offset fear.[109]
110. God . . . is not only the answer to disharmony in sex relations; not only our Guide, Counsellor and Friend. . . . He is Judge, Provider and Stabilizer.[110]
111. It takes the power of God to *remove* these fears and mental conditions.[111]

[104] Wright, *The Will of God* pp., 50-51; Macmillan, *Seeking and Finding*, p. 273; *What Is The Oxford Group?*, pp. 46-48; Shoemaker, *Children of the Second Birth*, pp. 175-87; *If I Be Lifted Up*, p. 93; and *How to Find God*, p. 10. Big Book, p. 67, 88.

[105] Benson, *The Eight Points*, p. 28. Big Book, p. 67: "We resolutely looked for our own mistakes. . . . Where were we to blame? . . . When we saw our faults we listed them."

[106] Buchman, *Remaking the World*, p. 46. Big Book, p. 67: "Though a situation had not been entirely our fault, we tried to disregard the other person entirely. . . . We admitted our wrongs honestly."

[107] Foot, *Life Began Yesterday*, p. 31. Big Book, p. 67: "The word 'fear' is bracketed. . . . This short word somehow touches about every aspect of our lives. It was an evil and corroding thread; the fabric of our existence was shot through with it."

[108] Buchman, *Remaking the World*, p. 28. Big Book, pp. 67-68: "But did not we, ourselves set the ball rolling? Sometimes we think fear ought to be classed with stealing. It seems to cause more trouble."

[109] Shoemaker, *Confident Faith*, p. 172. Big Book, p. 68: "For we are now on a different basis; the basis of trusting and relying upon God. We trust infinite God rather than our finite selves."

[110] Kitchen, *I Was a Pagan*, p. 104. Big Book, p. 69: "In meditation, we ask God what we should do about each [sex] matter. The right answer will come, if we want it. God alone can judge our sex situation. . . . [W]e let God be the final judge. . . . We earnestly pray for the right idea, for guidance . . . for sanity . . . for the strength to do the right thing."

[111] Kitchen, *I Was a Pagan*, p. 143. Big Book, p. 71: "We hope you are convinced now that God can remove whatever self-will has blocked you off from Him."

112. Putting our sins and spiritual problems into words to another makes us absolutely honest with God.[112]

113. One of God's most effective ways of introducing us to ourselves is to send us another person, whom we can trust, to tell them the whole truth about our lives as far as we know it.[113]

114. We greatly need to come out into the open—to take off the mask and drop the pose, and to be our real selves, honest about our mistakes and sins, frank about our thoughts and intentions, willing to let other people know us.[114]

115. I have found that to deal drastically with sins it is necessary to share them completely with someone in whom we have confidence.[115]

116. They are prepared to pocket their pride, risk their reputation, hazard their material interests for the sake of living in the open with their fellows.[116]

117. One human soul going out to another in all humility . . .so completely and fearlessly that for once in his life a man can know the immense relief of being absolutely honest without reservation or concealment.[117]

118. I believe that there is no other sure way to a full "surrender" to God.[118]

119. To summarize the various stages of spiritual adventure: first, the will to believe; second, the honest facing and sharing of all conscious sin; third, the complete surrender of self to God; and, fourth, the willingness to obey His will.[119]

---

[112] *What Is The Oxford Group?*, p. 32. Big Book, p. 72: "We have admitted to God, to ourselves, and to another human being the exact nature of our defects."

[113] Rose, *When Man Listens*, p. 49. Big Book, p. 73: "But they had not learned enough of humility, fearlessness and honesty, in the sense we find it necessary, until they told someone else *all* their life story."

[114] Rose, *When Man Listens*, p. 43. Big Book, p. 73-74: "They took inventory all right, but hung on to some of the worst items in stock. They only *thought* they had lost their egoism and fear; they only *thought* they had humbled themselves. . . . We must be entirely honest with somebody if we expect to live long and happily in this world."

[115] Brown, *The Venture of Belief*, pp. 33-34. Big Book, p. 74: "We think well before we choose the person or persons with whom to take this intimate and confidential step. . . . We search our acquaintance for a close-mouthed, understanding friend."

[116] Rose, *When Man Listens*, p. 44. Big Book, p. 75: "We pocket our pride and go to it, illuminating every twist of character, every dark cranny of the past."

[117] Brown, *The Venture of Belief*, p. 35. Big Book, p. 75: "Once we have taken this step, withholding nothing, we are delighted. We can look the world in the eye. We can be alone at perfect peace and ease."

[118] Brown, *The Venture of Belief*, p. 35. Big Book, p. 75: "We feel we are on the Broad Highway, walking hand in hand with the Spirit of the Universe."

[119] Brown, *The Venture of Belief*, p. 36. Big Book, p. 76: "We have emphasized complete willingness as being indispensable. Are we now ready to let God remove from us all the things we have admitted are objectionable."

120. God cannot take over my life unless I am *willing*.[120]
121. I then and there admitted my inability to quit of my own will and asked God to take charge of the matter.[121]
122. It takes the power of God to *remove* the desire for these indulgences.[122]
123. My concern must be to try to be more worthy of this daily sacrament of being alive. I cannot do this unless I "wait on God" and seek humbly and confidently to ascertain His will in my life.[123]
124. A further point in the moral challenge which the Oxford Group presents is that known as restitution, viz. putting right, as far as in our power, wrongs committed in the past.[124]
125. If while we hesitate we realize that God is really with us and that an act of restitution . . . is necessary, our hand, God-guided, without hesitation creeps up to the post box and the letter goes beyond our recalling, to carry out one more act of atonement that will set us free from our past selves.[125]
126. Voluntary confession and restitution bring home the seriousness of wrong-doing more effectively than any other curative method.[126]
127. These first steps of restitution are absolutely necessary if I am to start the new life clear with God and other people. . . . [The] great task that is waiting: to cooperate with God and to ask God to make us fit for Him to use.[127]

---

[120] Rose, *When Man Listens*, p. 17. Big Book, p. 76: "If we still cling to something we will not let go, we ask God to help us be willing."

[121] Kitchen, *I Was a Pagan*, p. 74. Big Book, p. 75: "My Creator, I am now willing that you should have all of me, good and bad."

[122] Kitchen, *I Was a Pagan*, p. 143. Big Book, p. 76: "I pray that you now remove from me every single defect of character which stands in the way of my usefulness to you and my fellows."

[123] Brown, *The Venture of Belief*, p. 40. Big Book, p. 76: "Grant me strength, as I go out from here, to do your bidding."

[124] Winslow, *Why I Believe in the Oxford Group*, p. 31. Big Book, p. 76: "Now we go out to our fellows and repair the damage done in the past."

[125] *What Is The Oxford Group?*, p. 59. Big Book, p. 76: "If we haven't the will to do this, we ask until it comes."

[126] Russell, *For Sinners Only*, p. 124. Big Book, p. 76: "We subjected ourselves to a drastic self-appraisal. . . . We attempt to sweep away the debris which has accumulated out of our effort to live on self-will and run the show ourselves."

[127] Rose, *When Man Listens*, p. 20. Foot, *Life Began Yesterday*, p. 98. Big Book, p. 77: "At the moment we are trying to put our lives in order. But this is not an end in itself. Our real purpose is to fit ourselves to be of maximum service to God and the people about us."

128. [T]he same series of exceedingly simple steps. First, they said, that I would have to make clean contact. . . . To get my contact points clean, they said, I would have to face up to my sins. . . .[128]
129. There will be a great many things I can never put right now.[129]
130. Peace, direction, power—the fullness of life—await the complete surrender of ourselves to God for His purposes.[130]
131. We are giving a far more adequate picture of Christ's power by sharing the thing from which He has saved us than we should by making no mention of our own problems and their solution. . . . Frequently, for example, a father has won the confidence of his boy by telling him something of the conflicts of his own youth and what Christ has done for him.[131]
132. "I went to a theological student who seemed to me to be troubled, to be suffering, and confessed to him my own secret sin—impurity. The . . . student came to life, confessed his secret sin to me, and ended our talk by saying, 'Prayer is going to mean something now.'"[132]
133. There is a hunger for fellowship with God and man, and there are many who have found that hunger satisfied in themselves and in others, along this double road of confession and witness.[133]
134. The answer is a God-guided, released life with constant outgo into the lives of needy people. An experience that is not shared dies or becomes twisted and abnormal.[134]
135. The most remarkable result of all . . . all anxiety and fear has flown out of the window never to return.[135]
136. The fourth signpost is an intuitive conviction that a course of action is inherently right, the certainty that, hard as it may be, there can be no other way.[136]

---

[128] Kitchen, *I Was a Pagan*, p. 56. Big Book, p. 77: "We are there to sweep off our side of the street. . . ."

[129] Rose, *When Man Listens*, p. 20. Big Book, p. 83: "There may be some wrongs we can never fully right."

[130] Rose, *When Man Listens*, p. 17. Big Book, p. 83: "We are going to know a new freedom and a new happiness."

[131] Thornton-Duesbury, *Sharing*, pp. 7-8. Big Book, p. 83: "We will not regret the past nor wish to shut the door on it."

[132] Begbie, *Life Changers*, p. 103. Big Book, p. 84: "No matter how far down the scale we have gone, we will see how our experience can benefit others."

[133] Thornton-Duesbury, *Sharing*, p. 10. Big Book, p. 84: "That feeling of uselessness and self-pity will disappear."

[134] Day, *The Principles of the Oxford Group*, p. 8. Big Book, p. 84: "We will lose interest in selfish things and gain interest in our fellows. Self-seeking will slip away."

[135] Kitchen, *I Was a Pagan*, p. 121. Big Book, p. 84: "Fear of people and of economic insecurity will leave us."

[136] Forde, *The Guidance of God*, p. 21. Big Book, p. 84: "We will intuitively know how to handle situations which used to baffle us."

137. Expressional activity . . . does mean using one's spiritual muscles to maintain spiritual health.[137]
138. The deepest thing in the Christian religion is not anything we can do for God, it is what God has already done for us.[138]
139. There is need for rededication day by day, hour by hour, by which progressively, in every Quiet Time, the contaminations of sin and self-will are further sloughed off (for they do have a way of collecting).[139]
140. What is the disease? Isn't it fear, dishonesty, resentment, selfishness? We talk about freedom and liberty, but we are slaves to ourselves.[140]
141. That is what the Oxford Group is working for, changed lives, God-centered in place of self-centered, and the change continuing every day under the guidance of His Holy Spirit.[141]
142. Our job, whether it be in business or society, is to serve the world as God shall direct.[142]
143. Nevertheless, not my will, but Thy will be done.[143]
144. Those who have entered in . . . tell us that we may expect another prize—a new conviction that God exists and a new understanding of His will, as well as a new strength and happiness in His free service. If any man willeth to do his will, he shall know . . . [John 7:17].[144]
145. Christ does not merely teach men what to do, he gives them power to do it.[145]

---

[137] Day, *The Principles of the Oxford Group*, p. 8. Big Book, p. 84: "Our whole attitude and outlook upon life will change." See also Belden, *Meeting Moral Re-Armament*, p. 20.

[138] Shoemaker, *If I Be Lifted Up*, pp. 161-62. Big Book, p. 84: "We will suddenly realize that God is doing for us what we could not do for ourselves."

[139] Shoemaker, *The Conversion of the Church*, p. 79. Big Book, p. 84: "We continue to take personal inventory and continue to set right any new mistakes as we go along."

[140] Buchman, *Remaking the World*, p. 38. Big Book, p. 84: "Continue to watch for selfishness, dishonesty, resentment, and fear."

[141] Foot, *Life Began Yesterday*, p. 47. Big Book, p. 84: "We have entered the world of the Spirit. Our next function is to grow in understanding and effectiveness."

[142] Foot, *Life Began Yesterday*, p. 60. Big Book, p. 85: "Every day is a day when we must carry the vision of God's will into all of our activities. 'How can I best serve Thee—Thy will (not mine) be done.'"

[143] Shoemaker, *If I Be Lifted Up*, p. 93; *A Young Man's View of the Ministry*, p. 70. Big Book, p. 85: "Thy will (not mine) be done."

[144] Streeter, *The God Who Speaks*, p. 126. Big Book, p. 85: "Much has already been said about receiving strength, inspiration, and direction from Him who has all knowledge and power."

[145] Streeter, *The God Who Speaks*, p. 151. Big Book, p. 85: "If we have carefully followed directions, we have begun to sense the flow of His Spirit into us."

146. Paul has undergone a revolutionary internal change . . . the result of the indwelling of a living spirit—divine and identical with the risen Jesus.[146]
147. I "emerged" into God-consciousness.[147]
148. Experience shows that the individual is guided by God, both during the quiet time and throughout the day.[148]
149. We must be relaxed from all tension, of haste or unbelief, or too impatient seeking.[149]
150. "Be still and know that I am God." . . . The hurried mind and the distracted heart make a vital knowledge of God impossible.[150]
151. Where I used to plan the day . . . I now simply ask God's guidance on the day.[151]
152. They tell of the strength of heart and mind, of the depth of knowledge of life, of the charity and love that are poured into human beings whenever they establish contact with God.[152]
153. It meant letting go of your own plans and desires for your own life, and trusting that God could run it better than yourself.[153]
154. We talked of daily Quiet Time, of Bible study, prayer and listening, and of the power of God to lead and guide those who are obedient enough to be led.[154]
155. Spiritual growth, however, was . . . to enter into new forms of usefulness for man and God.[155]

---

[146] Streeter, *The God Who Speaks*, p. 92. Big Book, p. 85: "to sense the flow of His Spirit into us."

[147] Kitchen, *I Was a Pagan*, p. 43; Begbie, *Life Changers*, p. 39. Big Book, p. 85: "To some extent we have become God-conscious."

[148] Rose, *The Quiet Time*, p. 1. Big Book, p. 86: "We consider our plans for the day. Before we begin, we ask God to direct our thinking."

[149] Shoemaker, *The Conversion of the Church*, p. 50. Big Book, p. 86: "We relax and take it easy."

[150] Benson, *The Eight Points*, p. 63. Big Book, p. 86: "We don't struggle. We are often surprised how the right answers come after we have tried this for a while."

[151] Kitchen, *I Was a Pagan*, p. 123. Big Book, p. 86: "Here we ask God for inspiration, an intuitive thought or a decision."

[152] Brown, *The Venture of Belief*, p. 24. Big Book, p. 87: "having just made conscious contact with God."

[153] Shoemaker, *Children of the Second Birth*, pp. 74, 187. Big Book, pp. 87-88: "We constantly remind ourselves we are no longer running the show, humbly saying to ourselves many times each day 'Thy will be done.'"

[154] Shoemaker, *Children of the Second Birth*, pp. 148-49. Big Book, p. 87: "We usually conclude . . . with a prayer that we be shown all through the day what our next step is to be, that we be given whatever we need to take care of such problems."

[155] Kitchen, *I Was a Pagan*, p. 168. Big Book, p. 77: "Our real purpose is to fit ourselves to be of maximum service to God and the people about us."

156. Buchman . . . forbade his people to speak or write "one inch" beyond their experiences.[156]
157. Tell Queen Sophie how God changed your life.[157]
158. The best way to keep an experience of Christ is to pass it on.[158]
159. Having therefore obtained help of God, I continue unto this day, witnessing both to small and great.[159]
160. Recognize . . . the man in need who is longing to *find* God.[160]
161. The willingness to obey His will.[161]
162. They have "got something." That is an evasive phrase for saying they believe in and trust God.[162]
163. If you will throw the onus of decision off yourself and on to Him, giving Him only a ready and obedient will, you will be amazed at the way things work out for you.[163]
164. It works.[164]
165. If they listen to us instead of to God, they will depend on us instead of Him.[165]

---

[156] Hunter, *World Changing through Life Changing*, p. 111. Big Book, p. 92: "Keep his attention focussed mainly on your personal experience."

[157] From the story Ellie Newton told the author, when Ellie asked Frank Buchman what she should say to a queen. Big Book, p. 93: "Tell him exactly what happened to you."

[158] Buchman, *Remaking the World*, p. x. Big Book, p. 94: "It is important for him to realize that your attempt to pass this on to him plays a vital part in your own recovery."

[159] The Biblical reference is Acts 26:22. *What is the Oxford Group?*, p. 26. Big Book, p. 94: "Make it plain that he is under no obligation to you, that you hope only that he will try to help other alcoholics when he escapes his own difficulties."

[160] Kitchen, *I Was a Pagan*, p. 99. Big Book, p. 95: "If he is to find God, the desire must come from within."

[161] Brown, *The Venture of Belief*, p 36. Big Book, p. 93: "The main thing is that he be willing to believe in a Power greater than himself and that he live by spiritual principles."

[162] Shoemaker, *Religion That Works*, p. 34. Big Book, p. 98: "The only condition is that he trust in God and clean house."

[163] Shoemaker, *Religion That Works*, p. 62. Big Book, p. 100: "We realize that the things which came to us when we put ourselves in God's hands were better than anything we could have planned."

[164] Nichols, *The Fool Hath Said*, p. 171; Benson, *The Eight Points*, pp. 28-29, 118; and Big Book, p. 88: "It works—it really does."

[165] Rose, *When Man Listens*, p. 62. Big Book, p. 98: "We simply do not stop drinking so long as we place dependence upon other people ahead of dependence on God."

166. All testify to the irreducible minimum of religious experience, namely, the certainty of the "presence of God" in this universe.[166]
167. Here were students who were being brought . . . to a new and abiding consciousness of God's presence and His claims upon their lives.[167]
168. Misery of our own making.[168]
169. First Things First.[169]
170. Many did hesitate to call this force the "power of God."[170]
171. An experience that is not shared dies or becomes twisted and abnormal.[171]
172. The person with an experience of God and a poor technique will make fewer mistakes in the end than the person with a high technique and no God.[172]
173. New power and new direction came to her when she started listening to God.[173]
174. The conception of God . . . left on the mind by the Book of Genesis is that of the transcendent Creator who in the beginning made heaven and earth.[174]
175. Somewhere a great Reality is born, which brings a new discovery of God and new tides of life.[175]
176. A vital living Presence Who could actually be "felt."[176]

---

[166] Brown, *The Venture of Belief*, p. 24. Big Book, p. 25: "The central fact of our lives today is the absolute certainty that our Creator has entered into our hearts and lives in a way which is indeed miraculous."

[167] Shoemaker, *Twice Born Ministers*, p. 123. Big Book, p. 130: "This dream world has been replaced by a great sense of purpose, accompanied by a growing consciousness of the power of God in our lives."

[168] Shoemaker, *The Gospel According to You*, p. 103. Big Book, p. 133: "We made our own misery. God didn't do it."

[169] Macmillan, *Seeking and Finding*, p. 17. Big Book, p. 135: "First Things First."

[170] Kitchen, *I Was a Pagan*, p. 16. "consciousness of the power of God in our lives."

[171] Shoemaker, *God's Control*, p. 21. Big Book, p. 157: "The two friends spoke of their spiritual experience and told him about the course of action they carried out."

[172] Forde, *The Guidance of God*, p. 8. Big Book, p. 164: "Ask Him in your morning meditation what you can do each day for the man who is still sick. The answers will come, if your own house is in order. But obviously you cannot transmit something you haven't got."

[173] Foot, *Life Began Yesterday*, p. 112. Big Book, p. 158: "The lawyer gave his life to the care and direction of his Creator, and said he was perfectly willing to do anything necessary. . . . He had begun to have a spiritual experience."

[174] Streeter, *The God Who Speaks*, p. 71. Big Book, p. 161, "They had visioned the Great Reality—the loving and All Powerful Creator."

[175] Shoemaker, *National Awakening*, pp. 23, 46-47. Big Book, p. 161: "They had visioned the Great Reality."

[176] Kitchen, *I Was a Pagan*, p. 68: Big Book, p. 162: "Many of us have felt . . . the Presence and Power of God within its walls."

177. All subsequent life is a development of the relationship with God which conversion opened.[177]
178. Let go! Abandon yourself to Him.[178]
179. The New Testament makes it quite clear that fellowship is in the Holy Spirit. . . . It refers to a certain quality, intensity and power of fellowship . . . created by the presence of the Holy Spirit in a group of people.[179]
180. Fellowship is of the essence of the Group.[180]
181. Spirit of the universe.[181]
182. We are told that conversion is "gradual or sudden."[182]
183. Nine-tenths of our misery is due to self-centeredness. To get ourselves off our hands is the essence of happiness.[183]
184. They recognize that the [sex] instinct is at bottom a God- given one.[184]
185. It is the way of young-mindedness to treat one's spiritual defects as a problem, not a fate.[185]
186. And we must honestly ask ourselves where lies our final security; whether it lies in people and things or whether it lies in God.[186]
187. God in mercy strip us this day of the last vestiges of self reliance, and help us to begin anew trusting to nothing but His grace.[187]

---

[177] Shoemaker, *Children of the Second Birth*, p. 16. Big Book, p. 164: "See to it that your relationship with Him is right, and great events will come to pass for you and countless others."

[178] Shoemaker, Religion That Works, p. 19. Big Book, p. 164: "Abandon yourself to God as you understand God."

[179] Benson, *The Eight Points*, p. 105. Big Book, p. 164: "We shall be with you in the Fellowship of the Spirit."

[180] Murray, *Group Movements Throughout the Ages*, p. 349. Big Book, pp. 152, 153, 162: "It is a fellowship in Alcoholics Anonymous. . . . Thus we find the fellowship, and so will you. . . . Some day we hope that every alcoholic who journeys will find a Fellowship of Alcoholics Anonymous at his destination."

[181] Nichols, *A Fool Hath Said*, p. 28; Big Book, p. 46.

[182] Shoemaker, *Realizing Religion*, p. 27. Compare Big Book, p. 569.

[183] Benson, *The Eight Points*, p. 56. Big Book, p. 14: "It meant destruction of self-centeredness."

[184] Begbie, *Life Changers*, p. 176. Big Book, p. 69: "We remembered always that our sex powers were God-given and therefore good . . ."

[185] Shoemaker, *Twice Born Ministers*, p. 36. Big Book, p. 76: "I pray that you now remove from me every single defect of character which stands in the way of my usefulness to you and my fellows."

[186] Shoemaker, *National Awakening*, p. 35. Big Book, p. 68: "Wasn't it because that self-reliance failed us. . . . We are now on a different basis. . . . We trust infinite God rather than our finite selves."

[187] Shoemaker, *If I Be Lifted Up*, p. 166. Big Book, p. 68: ". . . Self-reliance failed us."

Bibliography

Alcoholics Anonymous

Publications About

A Guide to the Twelve Steps of Alcoholics Anonymous. Akron: A.A. of Akron, n.d.

A Program for You: A Guide to the Big Book's Design for Living. Minnesota: Hazelden, 1991.

Alcoholics Anonymous. (multilith volume). New Jersey: Works Publishing Co., 1939.

A Manual for Alcoholics Anonymous. Akron: A.A. of Akron, n.d.

B., Dick. *Anne Smith's Journal, 1933-1939: A.A.'s Principles of Success*. San Rafael, CA: Paradise Research Publications, 1994.

———. *Design for Living: The Oxford Group's Contribution to Early A.A.* San Rafael, CA: Paradise Research Publications, 1995.

———. *Dr. Bob's Library: Books for Twelve Step Growth*. San Rafael, CA: Paradise Research Publications, 1994.

———. *Good Morning! Quiet Time, Morning Watch, Meditation, and Early A.A.* San Rafael, CA: Paradise Research Publications, 1996.

———. *New Light on Alcoholism: The A.A. Legacy from Sam Shoemaker*. Corte Madera, CA: Good Book Publishing Company, 1994.

———. *That Amazing Grace: The Mission and Message of A.A.'s Clarence and Grace S.* San Rafael, CA: Paradise Research Publications, 1996.

———. *The Akron Genesis of Alcoholics Anonymous: An A.A.-Good Book Connection*. Corte Madera, CA: Good Book Publishing Company, 1994.

———. *The Books Early AAs Read for Spiritual Growth*. 4th ed., San Rafael, CA: Paradise Research Publications, 1996.

———. *The Good Book and The Big Book: A.A.'s Roots in the Bible*. San Rafael, CA: Paradise Research Publications, 1995.

———, and Bill Pittman. *Courage to Change: The Christian Roots of the 12-Step Movement*. Grand Rapids, MI: Fleming H. Revell, 1994.

B., Jim. *Evolution of Alcoholics Anonymous*. New York: A.A. Archives.

B. Mel. *New Wine: The Spiritual Roots of the Twelve Step Miracle*. Minnesota: Hazelden, 1991.

705

Bishop, Charles, Jr. *The Washingtonians & Alcoholics Anonymous*. WV: The Bishop of Books, 1992.

———, and Bill Pittman. *To Be Continued . . . . . The Alcoholics Anonymous World Bibliography: 1935-1994*. Wheeling W. VA: The Bishop of Books, 1994.

Central Bulletin, Volumes I-II. Cleveland: Central Committee, Oct. 1942-Sept. 1944.

Conrad, Barnaby. *Time Is All We Have*. New York: Dell Publishing, 1986.

E., Bob. *Handwritten note to Lois Wilson on pamphlet entitled "Four Absolutes."* (copy made available to the author at Founders Day Archives Room in Akron, Ohio, in June, 1991).

———. Letter from Bob E. to Nell Wing. Stepping Stones Archives.

Fitzgerald, Robert. *The Soul of Sponsorship: The Friendship of Fr. Ed Dowling, S.J., and Bill Wilson in Letters*. Center City, MN: Hazelden, 1995.

Hunter, Willard, with assistance from M. D. B. *A.A.'s Roots in the Oxford Group*. New York: A.A. Archives, 1988.

Knippel, Charles T. *Samuel M. Shoemaker's Theological Influence on William G. Wilson's Twelve Step Spiritual Program of Recovery*. Ph. D. dissertation. St. Louis University, 1987.

Kurtz, Ernest. *Not-God: A History of Alcoholics Anonymous*. Exp. ed. Minnesota: Hazelden, 1991.

———. *Shame and Guilt: Characteristics of the Dependency Cycle*. Minnesota: Hazelden, 1981.

———, and Katherine Ketcham. *The Spirituality of Imperfection: Modern Wisdom from Classic Stories*. New York: Bantam Books, 1992.

McQ, Joe. *The Steps We Took*. Arkansas: August House Publishing, 1990.

Morreim, Dennis C. *Changed Lives: The Story of Alcoholics Anonymous*. Minneapolis: Augsburg Fortress, 1991.

Morse, Robert M, M.D., and Daniel K. Flavin, M.D. "The Definition of Alcoholism." *The Journal of the American Medical Association*. August 26, 1992, pp. 1012-14.

P., Wally. *But, for the Grace of God . . . .: How Intergroups & Central Offices Carried the Message of Alcoholics Anonymous in the 1940s*. West Virginia: The Bishop of Books, 1995.

Poe, Stephen E. and Frances E. *A Concordance to Alcoholics Anonymous*. Nevada: Purple Salamander Press, 1990.

Playfair, William L., M.D. *The Useful Lie*. Illinois: Crossway Books, 1991.

Robertson, Nan. *Getting Better Inside Alcoholics Anonymous*. New York: William Morrow & Co., 1988.

S., Clarence. *Going through the Steps*. Winter Park, FL: Dick Stultz, 1981.

———. *Going through the Steps*. 2d ed. Altamonte Springs, FL: Stephen Foreman, 1985.

———. *My Higher Power—The Lightbulb*. Winter Park, FL: Dick Stultz, 1981.

———. *My Higher Power—The Lightbulb*. 2d ed. Altamonte Springs, FL: Stephen Foreman, 1985.

Second Reader for Alcoholics Anonymous. Akron: A.A. of Akron, n.d.

Seiberling, John F. *Origins of Alcoholics Anonymous*. (A transcript of remarks by Henrietta B. Seiberling: transcript prepared by Congressman John F. Seiberling of a telephone conversation with his mother, Henrietta in the spring of 1971): Employee Assistance Quarterly. 1985; (1); pp. 8-12.

Smith, Bob and Sue Smith Windows. *Children of the Healer*. Illinois: Parkside
Publishing Corporation, 1992.
Spiritual Milestones in Alcoholics Anonymous. Akron: A.A. of Akron, n.d.
T., John. *A.A.: God's Instrument*. Reprint of speech delivered at Fourth Anniversary
Meeting of the Chicago A.A. Group on October 5, 1943.
The Four Absolutes. Cleveland: Cleveland Central Committee of A.A., n. d.
Thomsen, Robert. *Bill W*. New York: Harper & Row, 1975.
Webb, Terry. *Tree of Renewed Life: Spiritual Renewal of the Church through the
Twelve-Step Program*. New York: The Crossroad Publishing Co., 1992.
Wilson, Bill. *How The Big Book Was Put Together*. New York: A.A. General Services
Archives, Transcript of Bill Wilson Speech delivered in Fort Worth, Texas, 1954.
——. *Bill Wilson's Original Story*. Bedford Hills, New York: Stepping Stones
Archives, n.d., a manuscript whose individual lines are numbered 1 to 1180.
——. "Main Events: Alcoholics Anonymous Fact Sheet by Bill." November 1, 1954.
Stepping Stones Archives. Bedford Hills, New York.
——. "The Fellowship of Alcoholics Anonymous." *Quarterly Journal of Studies on
Alcohol*. Yale University, 1945, pp. 461-73.
——. *W. G. Wilson Recollections*. Bedford Hills, New York: Stepping Stones
Archives, September 1, 1954 transcript of Bill's dictations to Ed B.
Wilson, Jan R., and Judith A. Wilson. *Addictionary: A Primer of Recovery Terms and
Concepts from Abstinence to Withdrawal*. New York: Simon and Schuster, 1992.
Wilson, Lois. *Lois Remembers*. New York: Al-Anon Family Group Headquarters, 1987.
Windows, Sue Smith. (daughter of A.A.'s Co-Founder, Dr. Bob). Typewritten
Memorandum entitled, *Henrietta and early Oxford Group Friends, by Sue Smith
Windows*. Delivered to the author of this book by Sue Smith Windows at Akron,
June, 1991.
Wing, Nell. *Grateful to Have Been There: My 42 Years with Bill and Lois, and the
Evolution of Alcoholics Anonymous*. Illinois: Parkside Publishing Corporation, 1992.

Publications Approved by Alcoholics Anonymous

Alcoholics Anonymous. 3rd ed. New York: Alcoholics Anonymous World Services, Inc.,
1976.
Alcoholics Anonymous. 1st ed. New Jersey: Works Publishing, 1939.
Alcoholics Anonymous Comes of Age. New York: Alcoholics Anonymous World
Services, Inc., 1957.
A Newcomer Asks . . . York, England: A.A. Sterling Area Services, n.d.
As Bill Sees It: The A.A. Way of Life . . . *selected writings of A.A.'s Co-Founder*. New
York: Alcoholics Anonymous World Services, Inc., 1967.
Daily Reflections. New York: Alcoholics Anonymous World Services, Inc., 1991.
DR. BOB and the Good Oldtimers. New York: Alcoholics Anonymous World Services,
Inc., 1980.
44 Questions. New York: Works Publishing, Inc., 1952.
Members of the Clergy Ask about Alcoholics Anonymous. New York: Alcoholics
Anonymous World Services, 1961, 1979-revised 1992, according to 1989 Conference
Advisory Action.

Pass It On. New York: Alcoholics Anonymous World Services, Inc., 1984.

Questions & Answers on Sponsorship. New York: Alcoholics Anonymous World Services, Inc., 1976.

The A.A. Grapevine: "RHS"—issue dedicated to the memory of the Co-Founder of Alcoholics Anonymous, DR. BOB. New York: A.A. Grapevine, Inc., 1951.

The Co-Founders of Alcoholics Anonymous. New York: Alcoholics Anonymous World Services, Inc., 1972.

The Language of the Heart. Bill W.'s Grapevine Writings. New York: The A.A. Grapevine, Inc., 1988.

This is A.A. . . . An Introduction to the AA Recovery Program. New York: Alcoholics Anonymous World Services, Inc., 1984.

Twelve Steps and Twelve Traditions. New York: Alcoholics Anonymous World Services, Inc., 1953.

The Bible—Versions of and Books About

Authorized King James Version. New York: Thomas Nelson, 1984.

Bullinger, Ethelbert W. *A Critical Lexicon and Concordance to the English and Greek New Testament.* Michigan: Zondervan, 1981.

Burns, Kenneth Charles. "The Rhetoric of Christology." Master's thesis, San Francisco State University, 1991.

Every Catholic's Guide to the Sacred Scriptures. Nashville: Thomas Nelson, 1990.

Harnack, Adolph. *The Expansion of Christianity in the First Three Centuries.* New York: G. P. Putnam's Sons, Volume I, 1904; Volume II, 1905.

Jukes, Andrew. *The Names of GOD in Holy Scripture.* Michigan: Kregel Publications, 1967.

Megivern, James J. *Official Catholic Teachings: Bible Interpretation.* North Carolina: McGrath Publishing Company, 1978.

Moffatt, James. *A New Translation of the Bible.* New York: Harper & Brothers, 1954.

New Bible Dictionary. 2d ed. Wheaton, Illinois: Tyndale House Publishers, 1987.

On, J. Edwin. *Full Surrender.* London: Marshall, Morgan & Scott, 1951.

Puskas, Charles B. *An Introduction to the New Testament.* Mass.: Hendrickson Publishers, 1989.

Revised Standard Version. New York: Thomas Nelson, 1952.

Serenity: A Companion for Twelve Step Recovery. Nashville: Thomas Nelson, 1990.

Strong, James. *The Exhaustive Concordance of the Bible.* Iowa: Riverside Book and Bible House, n.d.

The Abingdon Bible Commentary. New York: Abingdon Press, 1929.

The Companion Bible. Grand Rapids, MI: Kregel Publications, 1990.

The Revised English Bible. Oxford: Oxford University Press, 1989.

Vine, W. E. *Vine's Expository Dictionary of Old and New Testament Words.* New York: Fleming H. Revell, 1981.

Young's Analytical Concordance to the Bible. New York: Thomas Nelson, 1982.

Zodhiates, Spiros. *The Hebrew-Greek Key Study Bible.* 6th ed. AMG Publishers, 1991.

Bible Devotionals

Chambers, Oswald. *My Utmost for His Highest*. London: Simpkin Marshall, Ltd., 1927.
Clark, Glenn, *I Will Lift Up Mine Eyes*. New York: Harper & Brothers, 1937.
Fosdick, Harry Emerson. *The Meaning of Prayer*. New York: Association Press, 1915.
Holm, Nora Smith. *The Runner's Bible*. New York: Houghton Mifflin Company, 1915.
Jones, E. Stanley. *Abundant Living*. New York: Abingdon-Cokesbury Press, 1942.
————. *Victorious Living*. New York: Abingdon Press, 1936.
The Upper Room: Daily Devotions for Family and Individual Use. Quarterly. 1st
    issue: April, May, June, 1935. Edited by Grover Carlton Emmons. Nashville:
    General Committee on Evangelism through the Department of Home Missions,
    Evangelism, Hospitals, Board of Missions, Methodist Episcopal Church, South.
Tileston, Mary W. *Daily Strength for Daily Needs*. Boston: Roberts Brothers, 1893.

Publications by or about the Oxford Group & Oxford Group People

Allen, Geoffrey Francis. *He That Cometh*. New York: The Macmillan Company, 1933.
Almond, Harry J. *Foundations for Faith*. 2d ed. London: Grosvenor Books, 1980.
Begbie, Harold. *Life Changers*. New York: G. P. Putnam's Sons, 1927.
Belden, Kenneth D. *Beyond the Satellites: If God Is Speaking-Are We Listening?* London:
    Grosvenor Books, 1987.
————. *Meeting Moral Re-Armament*. London: Grosvenor Books, 1979.
————. *Reflections on Moral Re-Armament*. London: Grosvenor Books, 1983.
————. *The Hour of the Helicopter*. Somerset, England: Linden Hall, 1992.
Benson, Clarence Irving. *The Eight Points of the Oxford Group*. London: Humphrey
    Milford, Oxford University Press, 1936.
Blake, Howard C. *Way to Go: Adventures in Search of God's Will*. Burbank, CA: Pooh
    Stix Press, 1992.
Brown, Philip Marshall. *The Venture of Belief*. New York: Fleming H. Revell, 1935.
Buchman, Frank N. D. *Remaking the World*. London: Blandford Press, 1961.
————, and Sherwood Eddy. *Ten Suggestions for Personal Work* (not located).
————. *The Revolutionary Path: Moral Re-Armament in the Thinking of Frank Buchman*.
    London: Grosvenor, 1975.
Cook, Sydney and Garth Lean. *The Black and White Book: A Handbook of Revolution*.
    London: Blandford Press, 1972.
Day, Sherwood Sunderland. *The Principles of the Group*. Oxford: University Press, n.d.
Dorsey, Theodore H. *From a Far Country: The Conversion Story of a Campaigner for
    Christ*. Huntington, Indiana: Our Sunday Visitor Press, n.d.
Foot, Stephen. *Life Began Yesterday*. New York: Harper & Brothers, 1935.
Forde, Eleanor Napier. *Guidance: What It Is and How to Get It*. Paper presented by
    Eleanor Napier Forde at Minnewaska, New York, September, 1927.
————. *The Guidance of God*. Oxford: Oxford University, 1930.
Hadden, Richard M. "Christ's Program for World-Reconstruction: Studies in the Sermon
    on the Mount." *The Calvary Evangel*, 1934-35, pp. 11-14, 44-49, 73-77, 104-07,
    133-36.
Hamilton, A. S. Loudon. *MRA: How It All Began*. London: Moral Re-Armament, 1968.

——. *Some Basic Principles of Christian Work*. The Oxford Group, n.d.

Harris, Irving. *An Outline of the Life of Christ*. New York: The Oxford Group, 1935.

——. *Out in Front: Forerunners of Christ. A Study of the Lives of Eight Great Men*. New York: The Calvary Evangel, 1942.

——. *The Breeze of the Spirit*. New York: The Seabury Press, 1978.

Hicks, Roger. *How Augustine Found Faith: Told in His Own Words from F. J. Sheed's Translation of The Confessions of St. Augustine*. N.p., 1956.

——. *How to Read the Bible*. London: Moral Re-Armament, 1940.

——. *The Lord's Prayer and Modern Man*. London: Blandford Press, 1967.

Hofmeyr, Bremer. *How to Change*. New York: Moral Re-Armament, n.d.

——. *How to Listen*. London: The Oxford Group, 1941.

Holmes-Walker, Wilfrid. *The New Enlistment*. London: The Oxford Group, circa 1937.

Howard, Peter. *Frank Buchman's Secret*. Garden City: New York: Doubleday & Company, Inc., 1961.

——. *That Man Frank Buchman*. London: Blandford Press, 1946.

——. *The World Rebuilt*. New York. Duell, Sloan & Pearce, 1951.

Hunter, T. Willard, with assistance from M.D.B. *A.A.'s Roots in the Oxford Group*. New York: A.A. Archives, 1988.

——. *"It Started Right There" Behind the Twelve Steps and the Self-help Movement*. Oregon: Grosvenor Books, 1994.

——. *World Changing Through Life Changing*. Thesis, Newton Center, Mass: Andover-Newton Theological School, 1977.

Hutchinson, Michael. *A Christian Approach to Other Faiths*. London: Grosvenor Books, 1991.

——. *The Confessions*. (privately published study of St. Augustine's *Confessions*).

Jones, Olive M. *Inspired Children*. New York: Harper & Brothers, 1933.

——. *Inspired Youth*. New York: Harper & Brothers, 1938.

Kitchen, V. C. *I Was a Pagan*. New York: Harper & Brothers, 1934.

Lean, Garth. *Cast out Your Nets*. London: Grosvenor, 1990.

——. *Frank Buchman: A Life*. London: Constable, 1985.

——. *Good God, It Works*. London: Blandford Press, 1974.

——. *On the Tail of a Comet: The Life of Frank Buchman*. Colorado Springs: Helmers & Howard, 1988.

——, and Morris Martin. *New Leadership*. London: William Heinemann, 1936.

Leon, Philip. *The Philosophy of Courage or the Oxford Group Way*. New York: Oxford University Press, 1939.

Letter 7, The: The South African Adventure. A Miracle Working God Abroad. Oxford: the Groups, A First Century Christian Fellowship, 1930.

Macmillan, Ebenezer. *Seeking and Finding*. New York: Harper & Brothers, 1933.

Martin, Morris H. *The Thunder and the Sunshine*. Washington D.C.: MRA, n.d.

——. *Born to Live in the Future*. n.l.: Up With People, 1991.

Mowat, R. C. *Modern Prophetic Voices: From Kierkegaard to Buchman*. Oxford: New Cherwel Press, 1994.

——. *The Message of Frank Buchman*. London: Blandford Press, n.d.

——. *Decline and Renewal: Europe Ancient and Modern*. Oxford: New Cherwel Press, 1991.

Newton, Eleanor Forde. *I Always Wanted Adventure*. London: Grosvenor, 1992.

Newton, James Draper. *Uncommon Friends: Life with Thomas Edison, Henry Ford, Harvey Firestone, Alexis Carrel, & Charles Lindbergh*. New York: Harcourt Brace, 1987.

Nichols, Beverley. *The Fool Hath Said*. Garden City: Doubleday, Doran & Company, 1936.

Phillimore, Miles. *Just for Today*. Privately published pamphlet, 1940.

Prescott, D. M. *A New Day: Daily Readings for Our Time*. London: Grosvenor Books, 1979.

Reynolds, Amelia S. *New Lives for Old*. New York. Fleming H. Revell, 1929.

Roots, Logan Herbert. *The Two Options*. London: The Oxford Group, n.d.

Rose, Cecil. *When Man Listens*. New York: Oxford University Press, 1937.

Rose, Howard J. *The Quiet Time*. New York: Oxford Group at 61 Gramercy Park, North, 1937.

Russell, Arthur J. *For Sinners Only*. London: Hodder & Stoughton, 1932.

Sangster, W. E. *God Does Guide Us*. New York: The Abingdon Press, 1934.

Spoerri, Theophil. *Dynamic out of Silence: Frank Buchman's Relevance Today*. Translated by John Morrison. London: Grosvenor Books, 1976.

Streeter, Burnett Hillman. *The God Who Speaks*. London: Macmillan & Co., Ltd., 1936.

The Layman with a Notebook. *What Is the Oxford Group?* London: Oxford University Press, 1933.

Thornton-Duesbury, Julian P. *Sharing*. The Oxford Group. n.d.

Viney, Hallen. *How Do I Begin?* The Oxford Group, 61 Gramercy Park, New York., 1937.

Waddy, Charis. *The Skills of Discernment*. London: Grosvenor Books, 1977.

Walter, Howard A. *Soul Surgery: Some Thoughts on Incisive Personal Work*. Oxford: The Oxford Group, 1928.

Weatherhead, Leslie D. *Discipleship*. London: Student Christian Movement Press, 1934.

———. *How Can I Find God?* London: Fleming H. Revell, 1934.

———. *Psychology and Life*. New York: Abingdon Press, 1935.

Winslow, Jack C. *Church in Action* (no data available to author).

———. *Vital Touch with God: How to Carry on Adequate Devotional Life*. The Evangel, 8 East 40th St., New York, n.d.

———. *When I Awake*. London: Hodder & Stoughton, 1938.

———. *Why I Believe in the Oxford Group*. London: Hodder & Stoughton, 1934.

Books by or about Oxford Group Mentors

Bushnell, Horace. *The New Life*. London: Strahan & Co., 1868.

Chapman, J. Wilbur. *Life and Work of Dwight L. Moody*. Philadelphia, 1900.

Cheney, Mary B. *Life and Letters of Horace Bushnell*. New York: Harper & Brothers, 1890.

Drummond, Henry. *Essays and Addresses*. New York: James Potts & Company, 1904.

———. *Natural Law in the Spiritual World*. Potts Edition.

———. *The Changed Life*. New York: James Potts & Company, 1891.

———. *The Greatest Thing in the World and Other Addresses*. London: Collins, 1953.

————. *The Ideal Life*. London: Hodder & Stoughton, 1897.

————. *The New Evangelism and Other Papers*. London: Hodder & Stoughton, 1899.

Edwards, Robert L. *Of Singular Genius, of Singular Grace: A Biography of Horace Bushnell*. Cleveland: The Pilgrim Press, 1992.

Findlay, James F., Jr. *Dwight L. Moody American Evangelist*. Chicago, University of Chicago Press, 1969.

Fitt, Emma Moody, *Day by Day with D. L. Moody*. Chicago: Moody Press, n.d.

Goodspeed, Edgar J. *The Wonderful Career of Moody and Sankey in Great Britain and America*. New York: Henry S. Goodspeed & Co., 1876.

Guldseth, Mark O. *Streams*. Alaska: Fritz Creek Studios, 1982.

Hopkins, C. Howard. *John R. Mott, a Biography*. Grand Rapids: William B. Erdmans Publishing Company, 1979.

James, William. *The Varieties of Religious Experience*. New York: First Vintage Books/The Library of America, 1990.

Meyer, F. B. *Five Musts*. Chicago: Moody Press, 1927.

————.*The Secret of Guidance*. New York: Fleming H. Revell, 1896.

Moody, Paul D. *My Father: An Intimate Portrait of Dwight Moody*. Boston: Little Brown, 1938.

Moody, William R. *The Life of D. L. Moody*. New York: Fleming H. Revell, 1900.

Mott, John R. *The Evangelization of the World in This Generation*. London, 1901.

————. *Addresses and Papers* (no further data at this time).

————. *Five Decades and a Forward View*. 4th ed. New York: Harper & Brothers, 1939.

Pollock, J. C. *Moody: A Biographical Portrait of the Pacesetter in Modern Mass Evangelism*. New York: Macmillan, 1963.

Smith, George Adam. *The Life of Henry Drummond*. New York: McClure, Phillips & Co., 1901.

Speer, Robert E. *Studies of the Man Christ Jesus*. New York: Fleming H. Revell, 1896.

————. *The Marks of a Man*. New York: Hodder & Stoughton, 1907.

————. *The Principles of Jesus*. New York: Fleming H. Revell Company, 1902.

Stewart, George, Jr. *Life of Henry B. Wright*. New York: Association Press, 1925.

Wright, Henry B. *The Will of God and a Man's Lifework*. New York: The Young Men's Christian Association Press, 1909.

Publications by or about Samuel Moor Shoemaker, Jr.

Shoemaker, Samuel Moor, Jr. "Act As If." *Christian Herald*. October, 1954.

————. "A First Century Christian Fellowship: A Defense of So-Called Buchmanism by One of Its Leaders." Reprinted from *The Churchman*, circa 1928.

————. *A Young Man's View of the Ministry*. New York: Association Press, 1923.

————. *Calvary Church Yesterday and Today*. New York: Fleming H. Revell, 1936.

————. *Children of the Second Birth*. New York: Fleming H. Revell, 1927.

————. *Christ's Words from the Cross*. New York: Fleming H. Revell, 1933.

————. *Confident Faith*. New York: Fleming H. Revell, 1932.

————. *Faith at Work*. A symposium edited by Samuel Moor Shoemaker. Hawthorne Books, 1958.

————. *God's Control*. New York: Fleming H. Revell, 1939.

————. *How to Become a Christian*. New York: Harper & Brothers, 1953.

————. "How to Find God." *The Calvary Evangel*. July, 1957, pp. 1-24.

————. *If I Be Lifted Up*. New York: Fleming H. Revell, 1931.

————. *Morning Radio Talk No. 1, by Reverend Samuel M. Shoemaker*, American Broadcasting Co., 1 page transcript of program for October 4, 1945.

————. *My Life-Work and My Will*. Pamphlet, Christian Ministry Conference, Concord, NH, circa 1930.

————. *National Awakening*. New York: Harper & Brothers, 1936.

————. *One Boy's Influence*. New York: Association Press, 1925.

————. *Realizing Religion*. New York: Association Press, 1923.

————. *Religion That Works*. New York: Fleming H. Revell, 1928.

————. *Sam Shoemaker at His Best*. New York: Faith At Work, 1964.

————. *The Calvary Evangel, monthly articles in*. New York. Calvary Episcopal Church.

————. *The Church Can Save the World*. New York: Harper & Brothers, 1938.

————. *The Conversion of the Church*. New York: Fleming H. Revell, 1932.

————. *The Gospel According to You*. New York: Fleming H. Revell, 1934.

————. "The Spiritual Angle." *The A.A. Grapevine*. New York: The A.A. Grapevine, Inc., October, 1955.

————. "The Twelve Steps of AA: What They Can Mean to the Rest of Us." *The Calvary Evangel*. New York: The Evangel, 1953.

————. "Those Twelve Steps As I Understand Them." *Best of the Grapevine: Volume II*. New York: The A.A. Grapevine, Inc., 1986.

————. "12 Steps to Power." *Faith At Work News*. Reprint. 1983.

————. *Twice-Born Ministers*. New York: Fleming H. Revell, 1929.

————. *What the Church Has to Learn from Alcoholics Anonymous*. Reprint of 1956 sermon. Available at A.A. Archives, New York.

————. *With the Holy Spirit and with Fire*. New York: Harper & Brothers, 1960.

Calvary Mission. Pamphlet. New York: Calvary Episcopal Church, n.d.

Cuyler, John Potter, Jr. *Calvary Church in Action*. New York: Fleming H. Revell, 1934.

Harris, Irving. *The Breeze of the Spirit*. New York: The Seabury Press, 1978.

Norton-Taylor, Duncan. "Businessmen on Their Knees." *Fortune*. October, 1953.

Olsson, Karl A. "The History of Faith at Work" (five parts). *Faith at Work News*. 1982-1983.

"Pittsburgh Man of the Year." *Pittsburgh Post Gazette*. January 12, 1956.

"Sam Shoemaker and Faith at Work." Pamphlet on file at Faith At Work, Inc., 150 S. Washington St., Suite 204, Falls Church, VA 22046.

Sider, Michael J. *Taking the Gospel to the Point: Evangelicals in Pittsburgh and the Origins of the Pittsburgh Leadership Foundation*. Pittsburgh: Pittsburgh Leadership Foundation, n.d.

"Ten of the Greatest American Preachers." *Newsweek*. March 28, 1955.

The Pittsburgh Experiment's Groups. Pittsburgh: The Pittsburgh Experiment, n.d.

Tools for Christian Living. Pittsburgh: The Pittsburgh Experiment, n.d.

Spiritual Literature-Non-Oxford Group

[Almost all of these books were owned, studied, recommended, and loaned to others by Dr. Bob and his wife, Anne.]

Allen, James. *As a Man Thinketh*. New York: Peter Pauper Press, n.d.
Brother Lawrence. *The Practice of the Presence of God*. Pennsylvania: Whitaker House, 1982.
Carruthers, Donald W. *How to Find Reality in Your Morning Devotions*. Pennsylvania: State College, n.d.
Chambers, Oswald. *Studies in the Sermon on the Mount*. London: Simpkin, Marshall, Ltd., n.d.
Clark, Glenn. *Fishers of Men*. Boston: Little, Brown, 1928.
———. *I Will Lift Up Mine Eyes*. New York: Harper & Brothers, 1937.
———. *The Lord's Prayer and Other Talks on Prayer from The Camps Farthest Out*. Minnesota: Macalester Publishing Co., 1932.
———. *The Soul's Sincere Desire*. Boston: Little, Brown, 1925.
———. *Touchdowns for the Lord. The Story of "Dad" A. J. Elliott*. Minnesota: Macalester Park Publishing Co., 1947.
Fosdick, Harry Emerson. *As I See Religion*. New York: Grosset & Dunlap, 1932.
———. *The Man from Nazareth*. New York: Harper & Brothers, 1949.
———. *The Meaning of Faith*. New York: The Abingdon Press, 1917.
———. *The Meaning of Prayer*. New York: Association Press, 1915.
———. *The Meaning of Service*. London: Student Christian Movement, 1921.
Fox, Emmet.*The Sermon on the Mount*. New York: Harper & Row, 1934.
———. Pamphlets: *Getting Results by Prayer* (1933); *The Great Adventure* (1937); *You Must Be Born Again* (1936).
Glover, T. R. *The Jesus of History*. New York: Association Press, 1930.
Gordon, S. D. *The Quiet Time*. London: Fleming, n.d.
Heard, Gerald. *A Preface to Prayer*. New York: Harper & Brothers, 1944.
Hickson, James Moore. *Heal the Sick*. London: Methuen & Co., 1925.
James, William. *The Varieties of Religious Experience*. New York: First Vintage Press/The Library of America Edition, 1990.
Jones, E. Stanley. *Abundant Living*. New York: Cokesbury Press, 1942.
———. *Along the Indian Road*. New York: Abingdon Press, 1939.
———. *Christ and Human Suffering*. New York: Abingdon Press, 1930.
———. *Christ at the Round Table*. New York: Abingdon Press, 1928.
———. *The Choice Before Us*. New York: Abingdon Press, 1937.
———. *The Christ of Every Road*. New York: Abingdon Press, 1930.
———. *The Christ of the Indian Road*. New York: Abingdon Press, 1925.
———. *The Christ of the Mount*. New York: Abingdon Press, 1930.
———. *Victorious Living*. New York: Abingdon Press, 1936.
Jung, Dr. Carl G. *Modern Man in Search of a Soul*. New York: Harcourt Brace Jovanovich, 1933.
Kagawa, Toyohiko. *Love: The Law of Life*. Philadelphia: The John C. Winston Company, 1929.

Kempis, Thomas à. *The Imitation of Christ*. Georgia: Mercer University Press, 1989.

Laubach, Frank. *Prayer (Mightiest Force in the World)*. New York: Fleming H. Revell, 1946.

Layman, Charles M. *A Primer of Prayer*. Nashville: Tidings, 1949.

Parker, William R., and Elaine St. Johns. *Prayer Can Change Your Life*. New ed. New York: Prentice Hall, 1957.

Rawson, F. L. *The Nature of True Prayer*. Chicago: The Marlowe Company, n.d.

Sheldon, Charles M. *In His Steps*. Nashville, Broadman Press, 1935.

Silkey, Charles Whitney. *Jesus and Our Generation*. Chicago: University of Chicago Press, 1925.

Speer, Robert E.. *Studies of the Man Christ Jesus*. New York: Fleming H. Revell, 1896.

Stalker, James. *The Life of Jesus Christ*. New York: Fleming H. Revell, 1891.

The Confessions of St. Augustine. Translated by E. B. Pusey. A Cardinal Edition. New York: Pocket Books, 1952.

Williams, R. Llewelen, *God's Great Plan, a Guide to the Bible*. Hoverhill Destiny Publishers, n.d.

Willitts, Ethel R. *Healing in Jesus Name*. Chicago: Ethel R. Willitts Evangelists, 1931.

Subject Index

A

à Kempis, Thomas (*The Imitation of Christ*) 539, 546
AA of Akron
  A Manual for Alcoholics Anonymous 16, 218, 226, 227, 234, 354, 655, 670, 705
  Second Reader for Alcoholics Anonymous 355, 669, 706
  Spiritual Milestones in Alcoholics Anonymous 354, 355, 665, 667, 707
Abandon yourself 301, 406, 407, 629, 690, 703
Absolute honesty 44, 66-68, 90, 101, 231, 324, 326, 361, 370, 371, 373, 374, 458, 459, 490, 637, 639
Absolute love 45, 66, 68, 101, 226, 231, 324, 326, 361, 370, 371, 373, 374, 458, 459, 637, 639
Absolute purity 44, 66, 68, 101, 324, 326, 361, 370, 371, 373, 374, 458, 459, 637, 639
Absolute unselfishness 44, 66, 68, 101, 224, 231, 324, 326, 361, 370, 371, 373, 374, 458, 459, 637, 639
Act as if 10, 11, 404, 444, 712
Agnostics 9, 94, 151, 165, 169, 176, 177, 185, 301, 431, 432, 452, 484, 660, 661, 688
Agree with thine adversary quickly 213, 268, 344, 464, 663
Akron 430, 431, 434, 437, 442, 445
Akron Beacon Journal 125
Alcoholism
  100% hopeless, apart from divine help 3, 5, 115, 164
Alexander, Jack 148, 573
Allen, James (*As a Man Thinketh*) 139, 224, 563, 564, 672
Amends 12, 103-105, 213, 214, 232, 262, 268, 269, 271, 290, 343, 361, 464, 465, 467, 468, 502, 503, 506, 663, 683, 691
Amos, Frank B. 21, 144, 145, 551, 655
Anger 190, 193, 212, 215, 217, 279, 285, 344, 444, 492, 566, 569
Anonymity 214, 236-238, 356
Anxiety 607, 621, 646, 665, 693, 698
  take no thought for [be not anxious about]--Matt. 6:25-34 280, 620, 646
  thou wilt keep him in perfect peace (Isa. 26:3) 280, 646, 655
Apology 40, 341, 342, 346, 386, 499
Apostle Paul, The 552
Ask, seek, knock 219

D

D., Bill (A.A. oldtimer) 15, 19, 134, 150

Daily Bible devotionals. *See also* Devotionals, Meditation 240, 470, 514, 541, 565, 575

Daily meditation books 541

Daily Quiet Time 359, 384, 700

Daily Strength for Daily Needs (Mary Tileston) 166, 191, 193, 194, 195, 197, 201, 217, 218, 226, 230, 231, 233, 236, 252, 261, 262, 269, 272, 276-278, 280, 282, 541, 595, 597-601, 655, 709

Day at a time 234, 235, 469, 504, 510, 513, 536

Day, Sherwood S. (*The Principles of the Group*) 57, 157, 184, 262, 290, 305, 325, 326, 416, 417, 460, 497, 531, 674, 709

Decision 42, 43, 47, 48, 50, 67, 68, 91-93, 95, 97, 100, 118, 121-123, 180, 181, 187, 203, 208, 251-253, 302, 308, 311, 318, 320, 321, 327, 331, 334, 336, 340, 362, 368, 369, 373, 376, 392, 394, 400, 407, 424, 436, 438, 441, 444, 450, 453, 454-456, 459, 464, 469, 485, 498, 501, 502, 509, 513, 520, 524, 530, 535, 610, 639, 640, 645, 660, 661, 683, 688, 690, 693, 700, 701

Defects 12, 100-103, 200, 202, 260, 263, 267, 268, 270, 332, 446, 461, 497, 498, 683, 691, 696, 703

Deflation 75, 108, 115, 132, 241, 246, 690

Devotionals. *See also* Daily Bible devotionals 22, 23, 31, 37, 132, 137, 139, 142, 157, 172, 211, 240, 470, 514, 541, 565, 575, 580, 587, 619, 620, 623-626, 654-656, 664, 681, 709

Diet (for a Christian) 150, 524, 526, 623

Director (God) 387, 408, 454, 565, 689

Disease 42, 82, 112, 115, 148, 202, 245, 286, 304, 312, 313, 317, 463, 467, 694, 699

Dishonesty 101, 102, 198, 260, 262, 270, 304, 322, 362, 374, 444, 446, 467, 491, 493, 502, 506, 643, 694, 695, 699

Divine Guidance 73, 314, 358, 363, 364, 366, 367, 375, 377, 378, 387, 390, 604, 608, 619, 621, 623

Dowling, Father Edward 355, 652, 706

DR. BOB mentions 546, 549, 551, 552, 553, 561

Drummond, Henry 24, 70, 72-74, 78, 132, 222-226, 231, 232, 250, 261, 262, 265, 277, 278, 285, 289, 299, 300, 308, 313, 321, 322, 349, 374, 377, 378, 386, 396, 400, 401, 403, 463, 476, 501, 552, 563, 566, 568, 570, 573, 587, 590, 672, 691, 711, 712

Du Val, Billy 91, 92, 94, 95

E

E., Bob (A.A. oldtimer) 116,
138, 141, 143, 150, 223,
224, 352, 551, 552, 563,
573, 706
Early Akron A.A. 107, 468, 542
Easy Does It 234, 235, 536
El Shaddai ("God Almighty") 293
Eleventh Step. *See* Steps, Twelve;
Eleventh Step
Elohim (God, emphasizing his role
as the Creator) 293
Envy 197, 198, 224, 284-286,
476, 492
Epistles of Paul 525
Evangelist(s) 24, 56, 65, 69, 71,
276, 481, 534, 549, 593,
602, 625, 712, 715
Everlasting arms 569
Exclusiveness 559
Experience, strength, and hope
64, 116, 447
Eye, thy brother's (speck in) 219,
255, 346, 457

F

Face the past 506
Faith
act as if 10, 11, 404, 444,
712
But without, it is impossible to
please Him (God) 160,
251, 303
experiment of 71, 77, 93, 94,
160, 166, 172, 174, 176,
184, 186, 194, 277, 295,
302, 303, 312, 399, 407,
432, 433, 440, 444, 445,
640, 660
How to pass, on 425
without works is dead 7, 17,
107, 109, 190, 194,

195, 230, 283, 335,
476, 521, 668, 687
Father (God) 438
Fear 100, 102, 115, 144, 185,
198, 227, 261, 265, 267,
270, 279, 284, 304, 307,
311, 322, 324, 328, 341,
358, 362, 367, 386, 408,
418, 421, 440, 444, 450,
464, 467, 476, 491-493,
497, 500, 504, 506,
522-524, 542, 553, 559,
566, 569, 575, 591, 621,
642, 643, 662, 681, 682,
693, 694, 695, 696, 698,
699
Fellowship xvii, xviii, 2-4, 8, 17,
18, 32, 37, 38, 48, 49,
51, 52, 55-57, 61, 63, 64,
77, 121, 126, 137, 142,
143, 144, 151, 154, 168,
170, 174, 180, 204, 207,
216, 217, 231, 235, 275,
290, 291, 335-337, 348,
349, 352, 357, 375, 388,
392, 410, 411, 410, 411,
410, 411-418, 422, 424,
425, 431, 440, 447, 448,
455, 474, 475, 478, 493,
494, 506, 509, 519, 522,
533, 537, 551, 553, 554,
559, 564, 582, 602, 610,
619, 643, 644, 652, 653,
677, 678, 688, 698, 703,
707, 710, 712
Fifth Step. *See* Steps, Twelve;
Fifth Step
Firestone, Bud (son of Harvey)
482
First Century Christian
Fellowship, A 352, 410,
564
First Century Christianity, a 411
First things first 18, 217, 218,
234, 251, 354, 702

G

H

I

L

M

Q

T

U

Scripture Index

Dick B.'s Historical Titles on Early A.A.'s Spiritual Roots and Successes

Dr. Bob's Library: Books for Twelve Step Growth   (Revised Paradise Edition)
  Foreword by Ernest Kurtz, Ph.D., Author, *Not-God: A History of Alcoholics Anonymous*.
A study of the immense spiritual reading of the Bible, Christian literature, and Oxford Group books done and
recommended by A.A. co-founder, Dr. Robert H. Smith. Paradise Research Pub.; 104 pp.; 8 1/2 x 11; velo
bound; 1994; $13.00; ISBN 1-885803-00-1. (Previous title: *Dr. Bob's Library: An A.A-Good Book Connection*).

Anne Smith's Journal, 1933-1939: A.A.'s Principles of Success   (Rev. Paradise Ed.)
  Foreword by Robert R. Smith, son of Dr. Bob & Anne Smith; co-author, *Children of the Healer*.
Dr. Bob's wife, Anne, kept a journal in the 1930's from which shared with early AAs and their families ideas
from the Bible and the Oxford Group which impacted on A.A. Paradise Research Publications; 176 pp.; 6 x
9; perfect bound; 1994; $14.00; ISBN: 1-885803-01-X. (Previous title: *Anne Smith's Spiritual Workbook*).

Design for Living: The Oxford Group's Contribution to Early A.A.   (Rev. Paradise Ed.)
  Foreword by Rev. T. Willard Hunter; author, columnist, Oxford Group activist.
A comprehensive history of the origins, principles, practices, and contributions to A.A. of "A First Century
Christian Fellowship" (also known as the Oxford Group) of which A.A. was an integral part in the
developmental period between 1931 and 1939. Paradise Research Publications; 269 pp.; 8 1/2 x 11; velo bound;
1995; $18.95; ISBN: 1-885803-12-5. (Previous title: *The Oxford Group & Alcoholics Anonymous*).

The Akron Genesis of Alcoholics Anonymous
  Foreword by former U.S. Congressman John F. Seiberling, Director of the Peace Center, Akron University,
  whose mother, Henrietta Seiberling, was instrumental in A.A.'s founding.
The story of A.A.'s birth at Dr. Bob's Home in Akron on June 10, 1935. It tells what early AAs did in their
meetings, homes, and hospital visits; what they read; and how their ideas developed from the Bible, the Oxford
Group, and Christian literature. It depicts the roles of A.A. founders and their wives, and of Henrietta
Seiberling, and T. Henry and Clarace Williams. Good Book Publishing Co.; 290 pp., 8 1/2 x 11; velo bound;
1996; $17.95; ISBN: 1-885803-10-9.

The Books Early AAs Read for Spiritual Growth   (5th ed.)
An exhaustive bibliography and brief summary of all the books known to have been read and recommended for
spiritual growth by early AAs in Akron and on the East Coast. Paradise Research Publications; 50 pp.; 8 1/2
x 11; velo bound; 1995; $10.00; ISBN: 1-885803-04-4.

New Light on Alcoholism: The A.A. Legacy from Sam Shoemaker
  Forewords by Nickie Shoemaker Haggart, daughter of Rev. Sam Shoemaker; and Mrs. W. Irving Harris,
  friend of Sam Shoemaker and Bill Wilson; widow of Shoemaker's assistant minister, Rev. W. Irving Harris.
A comprehensive history and analysis of the all-but-forgotten specific contributions to A.A. spiritual principles
and practices by New York's famous Episcopal preacher, the Rev. Samuel M. Shoemaker, Jr.—dubbed by Bill
W. as a "co-founder" of A.A. and credited by Bill as the well-spring of A.A.'s spiritual recovery ideas. Good
Book Publishing Co.; 412 pp.; 6 x 9; perfect bound; 1994; $19.95; ISBN: 1-881212-06-8.

The Good Book and The Big Book: A.A.'s Roots in the Bible
  Foreword by Robert R. Smith, son of Dr. Bob & Anne Smith; co-author, *Children of the Healer*.
The author shows conclusively that A.A.'s program of recovery came primarily from the Bible. This is a
history of A.A.'s biblical roots as they can be seen in A.A.'s Big Book, Twelve Steps, and Fellowship.
Paradise Research Publications; 256 pp.; 6 x 9; perfect bound; 1995; $17.95; ISBN: 1-885803-05-2.

That Amazing Grace: The Role of Clarence and Grace S. in Alcoholics Anonymous
  Foreword by Harold E. Hughes, former U.S. Senator from, and Governor of, Iowa, and founder of SOAR
Precise historical details of early A.A.'s spiritual practices—from the recollections of Grace S., widow of
venerable A.A. pioneer, Clarence S. Paradise Research Pub.; 160 pp.; 6 x 9; perfect bound; 1996; $16.95;
ISBN: 1-885803-06-0.

Good Morning!: Quiet Time, Morning Watch, Meditation, and Early A.A.
A practical guide to Quiet Time—considered a "must" in early A.A. Discusses biblical roots, history, helpful
books, and how to. Paradise Research Pub.; 107 pp.; 8 1/2 x 11; velo bound; 1996; $15.50; ISBN: 1-885803-
09-5.

"When I first became curious about the history of A.A. and of its spiritual origins, I read all the standard A.A. histories as well as every pertinent periodical essay I could locate. I congratulated myself thinking I had a complete picture of A.A.'s beginnings.

"Then I had the good fortune to be introduced to the A.A. history books of Dick B. I was richly rewarded with a far greater knowledge of A.A.'s factual history and, more significantly, of the precise nature of the spiritual origins and perspectives of A.A.'s Twelve Steps and A.A.'s profound ethical insights. I was delighted with these volumes, opulent in information, having every assertion documented in scholarly fashion, and written in a compelling, page-turning style.

"*Turning Point* is Dick B.'s most ambitious work to date. In it, he supplies us with a mosaic of his first ten works, integrating a veritable wealth of new material and profiling the 'why and how' of the remarkable success of early A.A. He also indicates numerous practices and personages of early A.A. still awaiting investigation, thus titillating us with the implied promise of more to come. Godspeed, Dick!"

Father Paul Blaes, M.A., Ph.D.,
Roman Catholic Diocese of Kansas City, Missouri

Inquiries, orders, and requests for
catalogs and discount schedules
should be addressed to:

Dick B.
c/o Good Book Publishing Company
P.O. Box 959
Kihei, Maui, Hawaii 96753-0959
1-808-874-4876 (phone & fax)
email: dickb@dickb.com
Internet Home Page: "http://dickb.com"

About the Author

Dick B. writes books on the spiritual history of early A.A. They show how the basic and highly successful biblical ideas used by early AAs can be valuable tools for success in today's A.A. The religious and recovery communities are using his research and titles to work more effectively with alcoholics, addicts, and others involved in Twelve Step programs.

The author is an active, recovered member of Alcoholics Anonymous; a retired attorney; and a Bible student. He has sponsored more than sixty-five men in their recovery from alcoholism. Consistent with A.A.'s traditions of anonymity, he uses the pseudonym "Dick B."

He has had ten titles published: *Good Morning!: Quiet Time, Morning Watch, Meditation, and Early A.A.*; *That Amazing Grace: The Role of Clarence and Grace S. in Alcoholics Anonymous*; *The Good Book and The Big Book: A.A.'s Roots in the Bible*; *New Light on Alcoholism: The A.A. Legacy from Sam Shoemaker*; *The Books Early AAs Read for Spiritual Growth*; *Design for Living: The Oxford Group's Contribution to Early A.A.*; *The Akron Genesis of Alcoholics Anonymous*; *Anne Smith's Journal*; *Dr. Bob's Library*; and *Courage to Change* (with Bill Pittman). These have been discussed in news articles and reviewed in *Library Journal, Bookstore Journal, For A Change, The Living Church, Sober Times, NECAD Newsletter, Recovery News, Episcopal Life, MRA Newsletter*, and *Ohioana Quarterly*.

Dick is the father of two married sons (Ken and Don) and a grandfather. As a young man, he did a stint as a newspaper reporter. He attended the University of California, Berkeley, where he received his A.A. degree, majored in economics, and was elected to Phi Beta Kappa in his Junior year. In the United States Army, he was an Information-Education Specialist. He received his A.B. and J.D. degrees from Stanford University, and was Case Editor of the Stanford Law Review. Dick became interested in Bible study in his childhood Sunday School and was much inspired by his mother's almost daily study of Scripture. He joined, and later became president of, a Community Church affiliated with the United Church of Christ. By 1972, he was studying the origins of the Bible and began traveling abroad in pursuit of that subject. In 1979, he became much involved in a Biblical research, teaching, and fellowship ministry. In his community life, he was president of a merchants' council, Chamber of Commerce, church retirement center, and homeowners' association. He served on a public district board and was active in a service club.

In 1986, he was felled by alcoholism, gave up his law practice, and began recovery as a member of the Fellowship of Alcoholics Anonymous. In 1990, his interest in A.A.'s Biblical/Christian roots was sparked by his attendance at A.A.'s International Convention in Seattle. He has traveled widely; researched at archives, and at public and seminary libraries; interviewed scholars, historians, clergy, A.A. "old-timers" and survivors; and participated in programs, panels, and seminars on early A.A.'s spiritual history.

The author is the owner of Good Book Publishing Company, writes a newsletter, and has several works in progress. Much of his research and writing is done in collaboration with his older son, Ken, who holds B.A., B.Th., and M.A. degrees. Ken has been a lecturer in New Testament Greek at a Bible college and a lecturer in Fundamentals of Oral Communication at San Francisco State University. Ken is a computer specialist.

Dick is a member of the American Historical Association, the Maui Writers Guild, and The Authors' Guild. He is available for panels, seminars, talk shows, and interviews.

Catalog & Order Sheet

How to Order Dick B.'s Historical Titles on Early A.A.

Order Form

Qty.

Send: ____ Turning Point (comp. history of early A.A.) @ $29.95 ea. $_____

____ New Light on Alcoholism (Sam Shoemaker) @ $19.95 ea. $_____

____ Design for Living (Oxford Group & A.A.) @ $18.95 ea. $_____

____ The Good Book and The Big Book @ $17.95 ea. $_____

____ The Akron Genesis of Alcoholics Anonymous @ $17.95 ea. $_____

____ That Amazing Grace (Clarence & Grace S.) @ $16.95 ea. $_____

____ Good Morning! (Quiet Time) @ $15.50 ea. $_____

____ Anne Smith's Journal @ $14.00 ea. $_____

____ Dr. Bob's Library @ $13.00 ea. $_____

____ Books Early AAs Read (5th ed.) @ $10.00 ea. $_____

Shipping and Handling Shipping and Handling $_____
   Add 10% of retail price (minimum $3.00)

   Total Enclosed $_____

Name: _____ (as it appears on your credit card, if using one)

Address: _____

City: _____ State: ___ Zip: _____

Tel.: _____ **Credit card:** MC VISA Exp. _____

CC Account #: _____ Signature _____

Special Offer for You!

A set of the author's ten titles normally sells for $174.20, plus Shipping and Handling. Using this Order Form, you may purchase sets of **all ten titles** at a discount for **only $149.95 per set**, AND the author will pay the Shipping and Handling for you! (Please note: the offer of free Shipping & Handling **does not apply** outside the U.S.)

Please mail this Form, with your check, money order, or credit card authorization, to: Dick B., c/o Good Book Publishing Co., Box 959, Kihei, HI 96753-0959. Please make your check or money order payable to **"Dick B."** in U.S. dollars drawn on a U.S. bank. If you have any questions, please phone or fax: 1-808-874-4876.